Broadcast News Writing, Reporting, and Producing

Fourth Edition

Ted White

ELSEVIER

Amsterdam • Boston • Heidelberg • London
New York • Oxford • Paris • San Diego
San Francisco • Singapore • Sydney • Tokyo

Focal Press is an imprint of Elsevier

Focal
Press

Focal Press is an imprint of Elsevier
200 Wheeler Road, Burlington, MA 01803, USA
Linacre House, Jordan Hill, Oxford OX2 8DP, UK

Recognizing the importance of preserving what has been written, Elsevier prints its books on acid-free paper whenever possible.

Library of Congress Cataloging-in-Publication Data
APPLICATION SUBMITTED

British Library Cataloguing-in-Publication Data
A catalogue record for this book is available from the British Library.

ISBN: 0-240-80659-X

For information on all Focal Press publications
visit our website at www.books.elsevier.com

05 06 07 08 09   10 9 8 7 6 5 4 3 2 1

Printed in the United States of America

B

R

Fc

Contents

Foreword

They tell me that time has not speeded up, and that there are exactly as many minutes in an hour, hours in a day, days in a week, and weeks in a year as there were when the first edition of Ted White's fine how-to-do-it book on broadcast news was published. I don't believe it though. It seems to me that the world must be spinning faster and time must have accelerated for so many events to have unfolded and so much to have changed so much. News has been called the first draft of history, but the pace of change both in the wide world we cover and inside the smaller universe of broadcast news, has been such that the first draft of anything these days requires constant revision.

Few things are as they were before the attacks of 9/11. "The occasion," to quote Abraham Lincoln, "is piled high with difficulty, and we must rise to the occasion." And although the technological and structural changes in radio and television have not been as profound, they have been equally dramatic. They certainly have affected my own life and work at CBS where I've worked (if you can call it work) for nearly four decades now in radio where I still do *The Osgood File* and in television, where I've anchored *SUNDAY Morning* since 1984.

Some things do not change, however. The fundamentals don't. Reporting and writing are still at the heart of broadcast news, both in radio and television. You can have the greatest studio in the world, the latest equipment, the hottest signal, the catchiest news theme music, and the coolest news set ever designed, but if your reporting and writing aren't good, nothing is going to happen. You still have to find out what's going on, talk with the principals and witnesses, gather your information, assemble your facts into a coherent story, and then tell it. The writing part is easy. As Terence Smith's father, the great sportswriter, Red Smith, once said, "All a writer has to do is open a vein and bleed all over the page. Nothing to it."

That's true, but not very helpful, I'm afraid. Ted White's approach is easier, both on your health and on the carpet.

Ted and I worked together at CBS in New York. Our colleagues were wonderful people like Walter Cronkite, Douglas Edwards, Eric Severeid, Lowell Thomas, Hughes Rudd, Dallas Townsend, and Richard C. Hottelet. We had great editors like Hal Terkel and Marian Glick who had learned from the masters, Edward R. Murrow himself, and Murrow's own radio editor and writer, Ed Bliss. Our bosses were Joe Dembo and Emerson Stone, and their bosses were people like Richard Salent, Bill Leonard, and Fred W. Friendly.

So, when Mr. White tells students about radio and television news, he knows whereof he speaks. And when he writes in this book about the nuts and bolts of how to gather news and organize it so that it makes sense, he knows whereof he writes. You may decide after reading this book that broadcast news writing, reporting, and producing are not for you. This would be a sensible decision nobody could argue with. But if you do pursue this field anyway, you won't find anybody better to show you the ropes than Ted White.

Charles Osgood

Preface

Broadcast News Writing, Reporting, and Producing examines the skills, techniques, and challenges of working in broadcast news. Along with complete coverage of the fundamentals, the text presents up-to-date examples and issues through actual scripts and interviews with the people who bring us the news.

As you read the book, you may notice the extensive coverage of reporting. Eight of the book's 25 chapters focus on everything from basic skills and specialty reporting to research techniques and ethics. As in previous editions, the text is accompanied by scripts written by working journalists, including some in Iraq who often discuss the stories they are covering and the techniques they use. This edition covers in great detail the embedded journalist policy established by the Pentagon, and we have expanded the report on how broadcast journalists performed on 9/11. The earlier edition of this book had only a brief report on that terrorist attack because it took place only days before the scheduled printing of that book. The editors and I faced a similar dilemma with this new edition when, only a few weeks before the publication date, the world was shocked by what many are describing as the greatest catastrophe in history, an earthquake and Indian Ocean tsunami on December 26, 2004, that, as of this writing a month later, is estimated to have killed over 210,000 people. We will have more on the tsunami disaster later in the book.

The new edition takes hard looks at two major issues facing the profession—the disastrous incidents of plagiarism, deceit, and lying by journalists at two major national newspapers; and the growing debate over whether there is a liberal or conservative bias in the media. On the eve of another presidential election, we examine the nightmare media coverage of the last one in 2000 when everyone got the results wrong. We also examine, in more depth, the unfortunate increase in the amount of excessive reporting of high-profile stories such as the Washington, D.C.-area sniper killings, the Lacy Peterson and Chandra Levy murder cases, and the sexual assault case involving NBA star Kobe Bryant.

I believe this is the most complete assemblage of reporting techniques and scripts by outstanding correspondents available in a broadcast news text. Journalists such as Betsy Aaron, Bob Dotson, the late Charles Kuralt, Charles Osgood, Susan Stamberg, and Richard Threlkeld not only provided scripts for the book but also discussed how they write and report. The work of such distinguished reporters as the late Edward R. Murrow and the late Pauline Frederick is also examined and analyzed closely. I also spoke with numerous producers about their philosophies and techniques and what it takes to get good newscasts on the air every day and night.

Supplementing this is the emphasis throughout on real-life situations. The problems that reporters, writers, assignment editors, and producers face every day are discussed in detail. You'll find entire chapters devoted to interviewing, covering breaking stories, delivering the news, and finding a job. Two chapters are devoted to ethics. We also have expanded the chapter on technology, with a detailed report on the most dramatic change in news gathering equipment, the satellite phone, more commonly referred to as the "videophone."

Whenever possible, I've relied on the voices of the experts—through interviews and transcripts of professional seminars and conferences—to teach future professionals how it's done.

Instructors may want to assign the writing, review, and discussion exercises at the end of each chapter. These exercises ask students to apply what they've read, not just to summarize it. You'll find answers to the exercises in the Instructor's Manual, along with sample syllabi and my suggestions for organizing the course, whether it be a reporting, writing, or all-in-one course. The Instructor's Manual is available at www.focalpress.com.

One of the most important aspects of this new edition is that it literally **will not get old**. That's because between editions, we will update every subject in the book as it becomes necessary.

You will note as you go through the book that there will be author notes along the way, pointing out that certain subjects and stories are still developing and will be updated periodically on the publisher's homepage.

Among the reasons we are so proud of this book is that we had the assistance and input of so many professional journalists. It would have been impossible to write without the assistance of a great number of people. Much of this help came from colleagues in the broadcast news industry with whom I worked over the years. Significant contributions also came from journalism professors, research assistants, editors, and a variety of administrative assistants and public relations personnel throughout the country. I will try to thank by name all who have helped produce this book, but there have been so many of you that I am likely to miss a few. Please forgive me if one of them is you.

At the top of the "thank you" list is Ben Silver. Our relationship goes back more than 30 years to when we both worked for *CBS News*. Ben, now professor emeritus of the Walter Cronkite School of Journalism at Arizona State University, was a gold mine of information. I thank him for his research and for locating and interviewing knowledgeable practitioners whom we quote throughout the book. His examination of the vigorous news operations going on in Phoenix, where he lives, was particularly useful.

Charlie Osgood, too, has been a friend and colleague over the years, and the foreword he wrote for the book is greatly appreciated, as are the scripts that he has permitted me to reproduce, and the wisdom he has shared with us. We all miss Charles Kuralt who graciously allowed me to use two of his famous "On the Road" scripts and then described how he produced such gems. I also appreciate the help I received from Karen Beckers, Kuralt's wonderful secretary who has had the good fortune to end up with the same job in Charlie Osgood's office.

The list of other correspondents who assisted me is extensive. Betsy Aaron and Richard Threlkeld allowed me to share their scripts and insights with you. I thank them also for providing photos from their private collections.

My thanks to Roger Welsch for sending me one of his "Postcard from Nebraska" stories. And thanks also to Bob Faw and David Culhane for all their help over the years.

60 Minutes correspondent Ed Bradley gave me new insight into, among other things, the hopes and problems of African Americans in broadcast journalism. I thank *Dateline NBC* correspondent Robert McKeown (formerly of *CBS News*) for sharing with us, as so many others did, what it was like to report during the Gulf and Iraqi wars.

The *ABC News* team also provided me with many pages of copy. Special thanks to all who took time to speak with me, including Barry Serafin and former correspondent Morton Dean. News commentator Paul Harvey contributed a sample of his unique writing style; thanks also to his secretary, June Westgard.

Friend and former colleague Rob Sunde, who was among the veteran journalists who passed away in 2003, provided lots of useful information for young people trying to get started in broadcast news.

NBC News correspondent Bob Dotson was more than generous, giving me not only a sample of his splendid writing but very detailed notes on how he thinks and works when he's putting a story together. NBC's Roger O'Neil is not only an excellent journalist, but also refreshingly frank in describing the shortcomings of many of those working in broadcast news. Thanks to Chris Vanocur of KTVX-TV in Salt Lake City for sharing his Olympic scandal exposé with us.

The news staff at CNN was very cooperative. Former anchor Bernard Shaw, in particular, gave his views on a variety of subjects, including the Gulf War and the problems associated with reporting live and covering politics. We also thank CNN correspondent Walter Rodgers for his report from Iraq, along with Kawain McClarin who assisted us in obtaining scripts and photos. We appreciate the help of NBC, for providing a photo of David Bloom and one of his reports from Iraq before his tragic death. Thanks also to Brian Williams' assistant, Melanie Ludlum, Howard Kurtz of *The Washington Post*, and the gang at The Poynter Institute: Kelly McBride, Jill Geisler, Chip Scanlan, Jan Schaffer, Bob Steele, and Keith Woods for allowing us to use so much of their research and writings on a variety of ethical issues and other subjects.

CNN investigative reporter Jim Polk provided a lot of good advice about an investigative beat he has covered for many decades. Thanks also to friend and former CNN colleague Don Shoultz, an editor-producer for *Headline News;* and to my former CNN boss, Ed Turner.

Many thanks also to the people at NPR, where, as Susan Stamberg reminds us, women journalists have made tremendous progress. I thank Susan and Cokie Roberts for their scripts and input on a variety of subjects and issues in broadcast news. I also appreciate the time that Nina Totenberg spent with me discussing her involvement in the leak of sexual harassment charges made by Anita Hill against Judge Clarence Thomas. Lots of thanks to Brant Houston, who provided the chapter on computer-assisted reporting. We very much appreciate the help of John Stoltz, an executive with Global Communications, for telling us all about how the new satellite phone systems (videophones) work.

I received a great deal of assistance from colleagues at radio and TV stations throughout the country. Much of that help was provided by stations in Baton Rouge, my home base. Special thanks to friend and colleague John Spain, former station manager of WBRZ-TV, who has provided extraordinary information about a variety of aspects of broadcast news.

Management and staff at WAFB-TV, the other major station in Baton Rouge, were equally cooperative. My thanks to Station Manager Nick Simonette and WAFB-TV anchor-reporter Paul Gates, who provided excellent examples of his work.

Thanks also to former *60 Minutes* producer Chris Szechenyi and Mark Lagerkvist of News 12 Long Island for providing details on how they wrote and produced their excellent investigative reports.

Many thanks to John Stoltz for his excellent explanation of how the video phone works.

My appreciation to Will Wright, former news director of WWOR-TV in New York, for recalling how he rose from desk assistant at CBS to become one of only a handful of African American news directors at major TV stations. Wright and African American journalist Sheila Stainback provided valuable information and advice for minorities who hope to succeed in broadcast news.

Others at local stations who provided information and scripts include: Jack Atherton; Jerry Bell, news director of KOA-TV, Denver; news director Chris Berry and reporter Kris Kridel of WBBM Radio, Chicago; Tom Bier, news director of WISC-TV, Madison; Jerry Brown, weathercaster for KUTV, Salt Lake City; Christine Devine, anchor for KTTV-TV, Los Angeles; Ed Godfrey, news director of WAVE-TV, Louisville; Gordon Peterson of WUSA-TV in Washington; anchor Jerry Turner of WJZ-TV in Baltimore; and John Bobel, president of Talentbank.

Many thanks to the crowd at KPNX-TV, Phoenix including producer Mary Morse-Lay; and my appreciation also to those at KTSP-TV in Phoenix including investigative reporter Steve Kraft. Thanks also to News Director Dennis O'Neil, and Producer Lisa Hudson and Kathy Matz of KTVK-TV, Phoenix.

I received a lot of help from the late Marty Haag, former vice president of News and current consultant for the A. H. Belo Corporation, which owns several stations, including KHOU-TV in Houston and WFAA-TV in Dallas. Penny Scott and reporter Don Wall of WFAA-TV were a great help, as was Bill Bauman, news director at KCRA-TV, Sacramento.

Special thanks and a hug for friend and colleague Nan Siemer, who provided students with information on how to survive in our business. We remember another friend, John Lynker, who passed away in 2003.

Thanks also to the many journalism professors who shared information with me, including several at the University of Missouri: Rod Gelatt, John Ullmann, and Vernon Stone, former research director for the Radio and Television News Director's Association (RTNDA).

Another colleague and giant among us who will be deeply missed is Ed Bliss, a Professor Emeritus at American University and another transplanted *CBS News* writer and editor. He left us a marvelous book about the profession he loved, *Now the News.*

Other professors who made contributions to the book include: Robert Mulholland, former chair of Broadcast News at the Medill School of Journalism at Northwestern University and former president of the NBC network; Lou Prato, who heads Northwestern's program in Washington, D.C. And, of course, we'll all miss the smiling face of Travis Linn of the University of Nevada at Reno, and a former *CBS News* bureau chief in Dallas, who also passed away in 2003.

Thanks also to Bill Small, a former senior vice president of *CBS News;* Paul Thaler, author of *The Watchful Eye;* and Stephen Doig of Arizona State University; we also appreciate the assistance and photo from Charlie Bose and assistant, Sharon Tounley; thanks also to Ken Mellgren of Associated Press.

Special thanks also to my good friend and former student, Lennie Tierney, who has learned so much about TV news photography that he can teach his old mentor a few tricks, which he explains in chapter 24 (Using the Hardware). Thanks also to all the other students, too many to name, who have made me proud by becoming successful in news.

Lots of people shot photos for us, and many others dug pictures and scripts out of files and archives. These people include Kathy Ozatko of Madison, Wisconsin, and Marty Silverstein of CBS. The shooters included James Terry and Christopher Rogers of Baton Rouge and Mike Coscia of WFAA-TV, Dallas; thanks also to former CBS colleague Mike LUDLUM, now a professor at N.Y.U.

Special thanks to Carol Lichtenberg, curator at the Historical Photograph Collection at Washington State University, for finding photos of Edward R. Murrow. Thanks to Catherine Heinz, director of the Broadcast Pioneers Library, for telling me where to look for things I needed.

Help also came from Richard Lobo, president and general manager of WTVJ-TV in Miami, and from Carmen Perez, PR director for that station; and we thank Jeff Burnside for his environmental report.

My appreciation also to Mata Goodwyn and Margery Sly, archivists at Smith College, for locating a script written by the late Pauline Frederick.

I am indebted to voice coaches Carol Dearing, Mary Berger, and Jeff Puffer for providing excellent information on voice control and other aspects of anchoring and reporting for radio and TV, and thanks also to NPR's Loren Jenkins, and Jeff Hoffman of WAVE-TV.

During the several years of writing and research for this new edition, I attended many conferences and meetings of broadcast groups (particularly those held by the Radio and Television News Director's Association and the Association for Education in Journalism and Mass Communication) and reviewed many journals and magazines such as *The Communicator* and *Broadcasting and Cable TV* so that I could include the comments and observations of many whom I was unable to interview. A special word of thanks at RTNDA for their assistance, especially Noreen Wille.

Here's a list of those I have quoted, in one way or another, throughout the book: investigative reporters David Anderson, Jack Anderson and Peter Benjaminson; *ABC News* correspondents Sam Donaldson and Judy Muller; *NBC News* commentator John Chancellor; Bob Engleman of Scripps-Howard; former *CBS News* Vice President Peter Herford; *CBS News* anchor Dan Rather and correspondent Leslie Stahl; *Wall Street Journal* reporter Robert Goldberg; Craig Le May, editor of the *Freedom Forum Journal;* Robert Logan, director of the Science Journalism Center at the University of Missouri; former CNN environmental reporter Deborah Potter who is now executive director of the RTNDA Foundation; Bill Kovach, chairman, and Tom Rosensteil, vice chairman, of the Committee of Concerned Journalists; Walter R. Mears, vice president and Washington bureau chief of the Associated Press; Professor William Metz, University of Nevada; attorney and former reporter Bruce Sanford;

Penny Parrish, news director of KMSP in Minneapolis; Doug Ramsey of the Foundation for America Communications; network news veterans Liz Trotta and Ed Fouhy; the staff at Brill's *Content* magazine, which we miss; Christopher Dickey of *Newsweek*; George C. Wilson of The National Journal; Mark Fisher and Michael Getler of *The Washington Post*; Alicia C. Shepard and Mark Lehorn; weathercaster Jerry Brown of KVVU in Las Vegas; photographer Eric Foerch; professor Robert Logan of the University of Missouri; professor Hubert Brown of Syracuse University; Mark Lisheron and sports commentator Bob Costas; *NBC News* president Andrew Lack; Hendrick Smith, PBS producer and former *New York Times* correspondent; Karen Foss of KSDK; and Seymour Topping, former managing editor of *The New York Times*, now an administrator of the Pulitzer Prize.

I also received help from Tom Goodman, director of media relations for CBS, and PR associate Eldra Gillman; Lynn Ross of AARP in Washington; Charlie Folds, PR director for WSVN-TV in Miami; the Gallup and Roper research and polling organizations; Magid Associates talent coach, Jeff Puffer; and Marvin Kalb, former network news correspondent and director of Harvard's Shorenstein Center on the Press, Politics, and Public Policy.

A number of people were helpful in the report on the Oklahoma City bombing, including Bill Perry, who was working for the Oklahoma PBS network when the blast occurred; his colleague, reporter Charles Newcomb; Joyce Reed, the news director of KWTV; news director Jim Palmer and reporter Billy Rodely of WKY radio; Susan Kelley, news director of KOCO; Melissa Klinzing, news director at KFOR-TV; and KTOK-TV news director Jerry Bohnen. We also received lots of help in our coverage of school violence from the Freedom Forum and, in particular, Robert H. Giles, a senior vice president of the Forum, and Bob Haiman, a Freedom Forum fellow. Assistance was also provided by KUSA-TV's Ginger Delgado.

I also thank Stephen Gorelick of the City University of New York; Nell Hancock, an assistant professor at the Columbia University Graduate School of Journalism; James Garbino of Cornell University; Richard Wald, senior vice president of *ABC News;* James Glassman, a fellow of the American Enterprise Institute; Sig Bedingfield, vice president of CNN; and the *American Journalism Review* writer Sherry Richiardi. Also contributing thoughts to our news coverage of violence were Chris Cramer, president of CNN's international division; psychiatrist Frank Ochberg; Roger Simpson of the University of Washington at Seattle; and Michael Sorkin of the *St. Louis Post Dispatch*.

Thanks to Bob Papper of Ball State University for his research on minorities and women in broadcasting.

Helping us to try to sort through the events of the Waco, Texas, conflict were Anson Shupe and Jeffrey K. Hadden, authors of *Armageddon in Waco*; James T. Richardson, an expert in new religions; Shelly Katz, a *Time Life* photographer; attorney Dick de Guerin; and James Wood, editor of the *Journal of Church and State*.

Sharing information with us on a variety of subjects were Michelle Kosinski of WSOC-TV in Charlotte; Peter Landis, director at NY1; Barbara Cochran, president of RTNDA; Chuck Peters of the Gazette Company of Cedar Rapids; Rick Ragola, president of WFLA-TV; *Tampa Tribune* reporter Lisa Greene; Greta Van Susteren, legal correspondent for CNN; James Rosen, a Washington correspondent for *Fox News;* Steve Sweitzer, news operations manager at WISG-TV in Indianapolis; Jim Disch, director of news and pro-gramming for CLTV in suburban Chicago; Jack La Duke of WCAX-TV in Burlington, Vermont; CBS spokesman Kevin Tedesco; *New York Times* media critic Caryn James; *New Yorker* writer Jeffrey Toobin; attorney Raoul Felder; *The New York Times'* Jim Rutenberg; John Moody, vice president of Fox TV channel; Steve Capus of MSNBC; reporter Edna Buchanan of *The New York Times;* Karen Foss of KSDK-TV; Christopher Dickey of *Newsweek*; news directors Andy Ludlum of KFWB, Ed Pyle of KNX, Tom Shield of WCBS; Ben Mavorach of WINS and Cliff Williams of WFAA-TV.

Thanks also to Brian Bull of KSUD; Don Dillon of KFDI/KFTI; WATD owner Ed Perry and disc jockey Ted McGaw.

Thanks also to colleagues Frank Coakley, Dr. Howard Jacobson, and to the late Dr. William Turpin, Professors George Crutchfield and Bill Giles, and attorney Dan Schaneville for their friendship and support over the years.

Finally, thanks to Marie Lee, Amy Jollymore, Cara Anderson, and Dan Stone at Focal Press. Without their assistance, this book would not have been possible.

Acknowledgments

Aaron, Betsy, "Marines in Lebanon," September 14, 1993. Transcript from *ABC News*, reprinted by permission. Copyright 1983.

Atherton, Jack, "The Price of Fame" transcript, December 5, 1989, and "Ford Follow" transcript, July 16, 1991. Excerpts courtesy of National Broadcasting Company, Inc. All Rights Reserved.

Bloom, David, script from Iraq excerpts and photo. Courtesy of National Broadcasting Company.

Burnside, Jeff, script on ocean/medical research. Used with permission of WTVJ-TV, Miami.

Hodding Carter, Assistant Secretary of State for Public Affairs/Department Spokesman.

Devine, Christine, "Deadly Fires" newscast, KTTV-TV, Los Angeles. Script excerpts courtesy of Fox Television Stations, Inc. © 1992 Fox Television Stations, Inc.

Dotson, Bob, "Cave Rescue." Excerpts courtesy of National Broadcasting Company, Inc. All Rights Reserved.

Ellerbee, Linda, *NBC News Overnight*. Excerpts courtesy of National Broadcasting Company. All Rights Reserved.

Frederick, Pauline, report from United Nations, December 5, 1963 story. Excerpts courtesy of National Broadcasting Company, Inc. All Rights Reserved.

Gates, Paul, lead story on weather. Used with permission of WAFB-TV, Baton Rouge.

Gordon, Dick, script from Iraq. Permission of WBUR, Boston.

Harvey, Paul, "Rebirth of a Nation." Used with permission of Paul Harvey News.

Kirk, Bruce, marked script. Used by permission of Bruce Kirk, KPNX-TV Broadcasting, Phoenix, Arizona.

Kridel, Kris, David Chreck murder story. Used with permission of Kris Kridel, WBBM-AM, Newsradio 78, Chicago.

Kuralt, Charles, "On the Road in Montana," 1975, and "On the Road in Vermont," 1976. Used with permission of *CBS News*.

Lagerkvist, Mark, Series on HMOs, 1995. Used with permission of News 12 Long Island.

Murrow, Edward R., "Orchestrated Hell," "Permit Me to Tell You," and "The Fault, Dear Brutus," from Ann M. Sperber, *Murrow: His Life and Times*, New York: Bantam Books, 1986. Originally published by Frendlich Books.

Olmstead, Jill, excerpts from "How to Find a Job in Radio/TV." Used with permission of Jill Olmstead, The American University.

Osgood, Charles, "Obituary for Dr. Seuss" and "Newsbreak." Used with permission of *CBS News*.

Parker, Nancy, story on prison visit. Used with permission of WAFB-TV, Baton Rouge.

Rodgers, Walter, script from Iraq. Used with permission of CNN.

Introduction

Much of the earlier edition of this book was written during the conflict in the Persian Gulf and its aftermath. The timing offered a variety of opportunities to observe the broadcast media as they moved into a new role: the live reporting of a war on television. For the first time, the American people, along with most of the world, thanks to CNN, watched a war much as they would a Super Bowl. The instant coverage of rockets falling on Israel and Saudi Arabia brought the war into living rooms as never before. This coverage of the war showed us how dramatically electronic journalism had matured technically. Yet it also showed us many other things that were not as positive and were, in the minds of many, controversial. For, unlike the Super Bowl, the "replays" that Americans were seeing on their screens were censored and controlled by the military while frustrated journalists were often restricted to the "bench" or forced to take part in orchestrated pool coverage. As we mentioned in the Preface of this book, on the eve of the publication of the earlier edition of the book, terrorists attacked the World Trade Center buildings and the Pentagon. Because that earlier edition was already at the printers when the attack occurred, the author was limited in writing about how journalists covered the biggest story of their lives. But, in this new edition, the author was able to revisit that awful day on September 11, 2001, and research in more depth how broadcast journalists performed. This new edition also gave the author an opportunity to observe and report in great detail on a new landmark in American history, a preemptive attack on Iraq that included a dramatic new relationship between the military and the media, the so-called embedding of journalists. The author examines all the ramifications of this new policy, including the impact it had on the media coverage of the war and the effectiveness of the reporting for the American people. As in the earlier edition of the book, the invasion of Iraq provided an opportunity to examine some of the positive and negative aspects of electronic journalism, including the new technical advances, such as the videophone, which brought the war into American homes on an even more personal basis than the previous Gulf War. Another interesting development is how the new technology has provided a growing amount of independent TV stations and network affiliates to provide on-the-scene reports from their own reporters in Iraq. Because of the printing deadline problem mentioned earlier, the author was limited on what he could write about the December 2004 Indian Ocean tsunami, but, that report in Chapter 11 (Reporting Assignments) will be updated continuously on our web site (http://www.broadcastnewsbook.com).

Unfortunately, the author also found it necessary to continue his examination of the media excesses in the coverage of high profile crime cases, including the Washington, D.C.-area sniper killings, and a variety of other murder cases, that continued the alarming drift toward increased tabloid journalism among certain segments of the media, particularly cable TV. In the past two years, there also has been an increase in convergence in the media, the practice of combining broadcast, print, and online news coverage, with an accompanying move toward using the same reporting staffs to provide the products for these combined operations. We'll look at the impact all this is having on the employment picture.

This new edition also required that we examine a frightening increase in journalism plagiarism, fraud, and deceit. We also looked at the disastrous media coverage of the 2000 presidential election and the problems with exit polling that occurred in 2004. And since our last edition, we also have added information on a story that has been demanding more attention, new gay and lesbian demands for more equal rights, particularly the right to same-sex marriage, and how the news media are adjusting to the coverage and assignment of reporters to these stories.

A Changing Industry

Long before the war, many TV stations had expanded their newscasts from 30 minutes to an hour or more in the evening, and some added an additional hour at noon and an other hour of news in the late evening. So, as we said earlier, it was not unusual, especially in the larger markets, to see local reporters competing with network journalists during the war in Iraq.

The significance of this trend for journalism students is that as more local TV stations begin to rely on their staffs to cover events outside their listening areas, more jobs will become available for people breaking into the field.

One of the most significant developments in broadcasting in the last few years has been the growing influence of Rupert Murdoch's Fox Network and its all-news operation. Also adding to the problems for CNN, which had a lock on the all-news business, was the emergence of NBC's all-news channel, MSNBC.

The expansion of all-news networks is good news for students coming out of J-schools. It means more jobs.

Another positive factor is the growing profitability of local TV news. But unfortunately less than 40 percent of radio stations are showing a profit. Competition from a variety of new sources has cut deeply into audiences for traditional broadcast stations and networks.

The explosion in cable and satellite dish programming has taken a heavy toll on broadcasters. Another threat is interactive news services, which make it possible for viewers to watch programs, news stories, and background reports whenever they want. Broadcasters fear that the saturation of information and news added to other programming could have a negative impact on both the networks and local stations. (There will be more on the changing industry later in the book.)

For now, at least, the job market shows signs of expansion. But also remember that competition for jobs in broadcast news is keen, and that is not likely to change. The field is crowded because the profession is a dynamic one. It's exciting, colorful, mostly rewarding, and often glamorous, attracting many people who want to be part of the action. But do not be overly alarmed. There always is room for the achievers. If you are determined to be among those broadcast journalism students who "make it," you will need plenty of determination, motivation, and hustle.

You do not have to be a born genius to become a good broadcast journalist. It never hurts, of course, but it's certainly not a requirement. As in all professional fields, you must be intelligent. However, there are other characteristics and skills that you must have or develop as well. These include: (1) an insatiable curiosity about the world around you; (2) a desire to change those things and circumstances that you perceive to be unfair, improper, or unlawful; and (3) persistence and aggressiveness in discovering the truth.

Is Journalism for You?

The late Frank Graham, a sports columnist, once observed that journalism will kill you, but it will keep you alive in the meantime. An exaggeration, perhaps, but the lifestyle does not encourage a healthy or emotionally stable way of life. As one broadcast reporter puts it, "You have to be a little crazy to want to spend your life working lousy hours, eating bad food, probably drinking too much, and fighting with your wife or girlfriend because you had to miss dinner for the 99th time or had to break a date."

ABC News correspondent Barry Serafin says the broadcast news business is "just awful" on family and married life. "You must have a very understanding, tolerant wife or husband. They must be very supportive." He adds, "It is not the glamorous life that most people think. Last night I had a hotdog at an airport. After 25 years in the business, you wouldn't think it would be that way, but it is—that's the nature of the business." Serafin recalls that earlier in the week he stayed up all night working on a complicated story. "We spent most of the next day on the story just to get it on the air," Serafin adds, repeating, "That's just the way the business is."

The late veteran broadcaster and commentator John Chancellor noted that journalism is difficult work. "It's often frustrating, frequently exhausting, not the way to get rich." He said, "Every slip is out there in print or public view, to draw scorn, wrath or lawsuits." In *The News Business* (which Chancellor co-authored with Pulitzer Prize-winner Walter R. Mears of the Associated Press), the authors also wrote that journalism is "exciting, fascinating, constantly challenging and changing work."

What Role to Play?

Do you hope to be in front of the cameras or behind them? Most journalism students want to be on camera as TV anchors. The odds are not quite as bad as for college quarterbacks making it to the NFL, but the competition is still formidable. Fortunately, there are more TV stations—and an even greater number of radio stations—than there are pro football teams

If you are determined to be an anchor, keep in mind that it takes more than a college degree or time spent as an intern. Most anchors earn their spot in front of the cameras by putting in their time as reporters. In time, and with appropriate skills, a reporter may be given a shot at anchoring on weekends and/or holidays when the "stars" have a day off. If you are intent on being an anchor, then work hard at developing your reporting skills. If your goal is to be a broadcast reporter, sharpen your writing skills because they are the essence of good reporting.

Many of you will say, "I don't want to write or report, I want to be a producer." But when asked what kind of producer, most responders show an interest in *The Tonight Show* or some other area of entertainment. There are some talented people producing those shows, but their work is far removed from producing TV news, a more serious aspect of broadcasting.

TV news producers also pay their dues. They frequently start out as writers and associate producers, sometimes as researchers and even as desk assistants. Like the other people in broadcast news, producers get their jobs because they demonstrate many different skills. News judgment (i.e., the ability to sort out what should and should not go into a newscast, and what should be highlighted and what downplayed) is one of the most crucial skills. If the producer's news judgment is not sound, the program will not be successful.

One concern for producers is ratings. A news manager whose newscasts are constantly running third in the ratings in a three-station market will probably be looking for a new producer. If that doesn't help, the news manager, too, will be looking for a new job. Reaching the top of the ratings chart is only part of the challenge in broadcast news. Staying there is even harder. A good producer knows how to attract and hold a large audience by keeping news programs interesting.

Whatever role you hope to play, this book will help you achieve your goals. It concentrates on three areas—writing, reporting, and producing—which are the cornerstones of broadcast journalism. If you are successful in finding a place in the broadcast news industry, you will probably find yourself using these skills daily. Before you start work on developing these skills, however, let's examine some other fundamentals that will help prepare you for a career in broadcast journalism.

Your College Education

There is a continuing debate among news executives over the value of a journalism degree. Many professional journalists argue that a liberal arts education is more important than a program in journalism. "Give me young people with a well-rounded liberal arts education," say many news executives, "and I'll teach them how to be journalists."

It is a strong argument, which is why a great many college broadcast journalism programs require students to take most of their credits in liberal arts.

While you may want to focus solely on your journalism courses, keep in mind that all the history, economics, political science, and language courses you are required to take will inform you as a journalist and will enrich your life as well.

An increasing number of job advertisements placed by news directors seek journalists who have some strong interest or background in such areas as health, business, or law. Almost any concentration in a secondary area, including political science or sociology, may improve your chances of finding a position in broadcast news.

Another advantage for those entering the broadcast news market is a second language. Spanish is particularly useful for journalists working in markets in the Southeast, Southwest, and West and also in major northern cities, such as New York and Chicago, which have large Spanish-speaking populations.

Internships

Never pass up a chance to work as an intern for a radio or TV station while you are in school. Such work can be a tremendous advantage because it gives you an opportunity to observe firsthand what you are learning in your classes. Interns are often asked to write and work at the assignment desk or to help the producer. Yes, there will probably be a lot of coffee runs, and you will take many calls from complaining listeners, but anything you do that gets you inside a radio or TV station is well worth it even if you do not get paid. However, interns sometimes do receive minimum wage, if not more.

One of the greatest advantages of an internship is that you meet the people who do the hiring. Many students, after graduation, remain with the stations where they worked as interns. Many become reporters, producers, and assignment editors. Even if there is no job waiting for you at the station after your internship, you have something substantial to put on your resume. If you performed well, you have some good references too.

An internship also allows you to see what broadcast news is really like. You may discover that it is not what you want to pursue as a career. Some students discover during an internship that it's not for them. If you are not "pushy" by nature and are not comfortable with pressures and deadlines, it is better to discover that as quickly as possible.

Your First Job

Like entry-level positions in many fields, your first job will not pay much. One disadvantage of working in broadcast news is that a lot of other people want to do it. News directors know that and pay accordingly. They also know that if you have what it takes you will not be staying with the station for long.

There is not much union representation except in larger markets, and you are unlikely to begin in one of those. However, for most people who end up in broadcast news, money is secondary. There is always the hope of ending up in New York, Chicago, or Los Angeles, where salaries are substantial, but you cannot depend on that happening. So, most people work in broadcasting for the very reasons that they got involved in the first place: it's fun, exciting, and yes, sometimes glamorous. There also is the satisfaction of knowing that you are doing your part to keep people informed, sometimes making things better in your community and correcting injustices.

Responsibility and Accuracy

The two most important words in your vocabulary, starting right now, are *responsibility* and *accuracy*—the cornerstones of ethical journalism. To be a successful journalist, you need to learn to be responsible and accurate in everything you write or report. There is a well-worn phrase known to every journalist: "Getting it fast is no good unless it's right."

The responsibility and accuracy of the news media became serious problems during the murder trial of O. J. Simpson. Many news organizations were guilty of a variety of inaccuracies during the trial and in the months before the case came to trial. The need to be first, and the frequent manipulation of the media by the prosecution, defense, and police, all played a part in erroneous reporting. The media was guilty of another serious blunder when they all got the results of the 2000 presidential election wrong. Again, their mistakes were caused by an overwhelming desire to be first instead of right. We will discuss these matters in detail in other chapters of the book.

Responsibility is not just limited to checking information to ensure accuracy. It also means being fair. Journalists must learn to write and report without prejudice, despite their own personal views on a subject or an issue. To do otherwise is to betray the trust that is placed in them by the public. There will be much more on ethics throughout the book.

This introduction is designed to give you a brief overview of some of the important requirements and rewards of a career in broadcast journalism. The remaining chapters focus on the process of developing the writing, reporting, and producing skills and techniques necessary to succeed in broadcast journalism.

At the end of each chapter, there are exercises to help you and your instructor determine how well you are absorbing all this new information. If you find that you are having trouble, go back and review the material. Much of the information you need to complete the assignments successfully is detailed in the chapter itself, but at times you will also have to use other resources. Locating outside information is the first step in a research process that will become a part of your everyday life if you become a broadcast journalist.

1   Broadcast News Writing Mechanics

Before you can get a driver's license, you have to learn how to drive a car. Before you write broadcast news, you must learn good grammar and know how to use a computer. You also must understand what news is and how writing broadcast news copy differs from other types of writing. As noted in the Introduction, you must quickly learn about accuracy and responsibility. You also need to learn the vocabulary of broadcast journalism, terms such as *wrap*, *voice-over*, *standup*, and *cutaway*.

Before you have finished working with this book, you will have learned about all these things and many more. This chapter starts with the mechanics of broadcast news writing, the small but essential details of preparing a script correctly. Learning these mechanics is like learning how to use the controls on a dashboard.

Some Basics

Computers have replaced typewriters in newsrooms and classrooms, but the formats for typing scripts still closely resemble those used for typewriters. Your computer-produced scripts will still be printed on 8 1/2 by 11-inch paper, so for radio scripts you should set your margins so that you have approximately an inch on each side of the page that will remain blank. (Television newswriters work with what is called the split page, which will be discussed later in this chapter.)

You also should type your copy double- or triple-spaced to make it easier to read on the air and also to allow room between the lines for last minute corrections. (Ask your instructor about this setting.)

Correcting Copy

Before computers, corrections on a typewritten script had to be made with great care. The words being changed had to be completely crossed-out, and the words being substituted were written clearly just above the crossed-out words. If the required corrections were too elaborate, the script became difficult to read and had to be retyped. Now, of course, on computers, corrections are made electronically but there is still a frequent need to make additional changes by hand once anchors are on the set, or are about to do so, which is why we need the double or triple line spacing, mentioned previously.

By the way, standard newspaper copyediting symbols are not permissible in broadcast copy. Here are two examples of corrected copy. The first is edited for print, the second for broadcast.

The mayor says he's binging the two sides in the newspaper strike to the bargaining table today and is hopeful that an agreement can be reachd before the end of the week. The strike is now in its 3rd week. The major issue are job security and the newspaper's demand that the union accept a 20% reduction in wages.

The mayor says he's ~~binging~~ *bringing* the two sides in the newspaper strike to the bargaining ~~talbe~~ *table* today and is ~~hupeful~~ *hopeful* that an agreement can be ~~reachd~~ *reached* before the end of the week. The strike is now in its ~~3rd weeek~~ *third week.* The major ~~issiue~~ *issues* are job security and the newspaper's ~~demnand~~ *demand* that the union accept a 20% *percent* reduction in wages.

Poorly corrected copy increases the possibility that an anchor will make a mistake. As might be expected, anchors are particularly sensitive about stumbling over a word or sentence, and if the mishap is the writer's fault, you can be certain that the newscaster will let someone know about it as soon as the newscast is over or, more likely, during a commercial break.

Slugs

Every page of the news script must be identified. These identifications are called slugs, and they are placed in the upper left-hand corner of the page. The slug includes a one- or two-word description of the story, such as Fire, Newspaper Strike, or Missing Boy. The slug also includes the date, the time of the newscast and the writer's initials. Here's an example:

Fire
2/10/04
9 a.m.
TW

Slugs are important because they allow the writer, producers, anchors, director, and a variety of other people involved in putting a newscast together to quickly locate a particular story in the script. This can be vital when, for example, the position of the story in the script must be changed or the story must be dropped just as the newscast begins or when it is already on the air.

The Split Page

Preparing a TV script is somewhat more complicated than preparing a radio script. A TV script is divided into two vertical sections and is known as the split page. All technical instructions and identification of video and graphics appear in the left portion of the split page, and the script to be read by the anchor or reporter appears in the right column along with sound bite outcues and times. There will be a number of examples of split pages, and how they are used, throughout this book.

As you examine those scripts, you will notice that each station has its own way of using the split page. Experienced broadcast journalists adjust easily to the slight variations as they move from station to station.

Avoiding Abbreviations

All words in broadcast news copy, with a few exceptions, must be spelled out. Abbreviations are not permitted because they would force anchors to interpret their meaning, thus inviting confusion and mistakes.

Wrong	*Right*
Lt. General	Lieutenant General
Ass't. Sec. of State	Assistant Secretary of State
Union Pres. Felix Jones	Union President Felix Jones
John St. and Norfolk Ave.	John Street and Norfolk Avenue

Abbreviations are used if the names of organizations are better known by their initials than by their full names—for example, FBI, NBC, and CIA. However, to make it easier for anchors to read, place hyphens between the letters.

F-B-I

N-B-C

C-I-A

Avoiding Split Words and Sentences

If there is not enough room on a line of copy to complete a word, the entire word must be carried over to the next line. Words should not be hyphenated because splitting words at the end of a line could confuse the anchor.

The same is true with sentences that cannot fit on one page. Part of a sentence should not be carried over from one page to another. Forcing anchors to jump from the bottom of one page to the top of the next when they are in the middle of a sentence invites trouble. It cannot be stressed too often that writers must avoid anything that increases the chance that anchors will stumble over copy.

If a sentence cannot be completed on a page, it should begin on the top of the next page. Type the word MORE at the bottom of the page so the anchors know that there is more to the story on the next page. Otherwise, they may pause unnecessarily, believing a new story starts on the following page. Some newsrooms prefer to use an arrow at the end of the page to indicate more copy is coming.

Punctuation

While the opening of this chapter stressed the importance of using correct grammar in broadcast copy, be aware that there are certain exceptions to standard grammatical rules. For example, use commas to indicate a pause, not simply for grammatical reasons. Some writers use a dash instead of a comma to indicate a pause, but dashes should be used sparingly, usually to indicate longer pauses. Unless you are writing for yourself (when you can do whatever is comfortable for you), you should not use an ellipsis (three dots) to indicate a pause or as a signal that you have eliminated part of a quotation because those dots could confuse anchors. Never use a semicolon.

Capitalize certain words, like Not and other words you think the anchors should emphasize. This is especially helpful when the anchors might not have an opportunity to go over the copy before they read it on the air. Keep such emphasis to a minimum, however, for the anchor is usually the best judge of which words to stress.

Names and Titles

Titles are always used before a person's name in broadcast copy; never after it. For example, Secretary of Defense John Smith should be used rather than, as newspapers write, John Smith, Secretary of Defense. Using the title first alerts the listener to the name that will follow, and it also reflects conversational style.

It is acceptable to break up the name and the title. For example:

> The secretary of the Navy said today that joint maneuvers would begin in the Atlantic next week. John Smith told reporters that Canadian and British vessels would join part of the Atlantic fleet in the maneuvers.

If you use names in your copy, make sure you double-check their spelling and pronunciation. If you are reporting an accident or a fire in which there are injuries or deaths, ask the police officer or fire chief to confirm any names you're unsure about. Wire services are a good source for checking names and

Figure 1-1 David Nussbaum, meteorologist; Sylvia Weatherspoon, co-anchor; and Todd Ross, co-anchor, WBRZ, Baton Rouge, LA. (Photo by James Terry)

pronunciations. (More discussion regarding that in Chapter 8, "Delivering the News.")

Names are not always essential to a story. Scripts written at a small-town radio or TV station should certainly include the names of those who were killed or injured in a fire at the local paper plant. However, the names of three people from another state who were injured on the freeway would be of little interest to the local audience. It would be sufficient to say:

> Three Florida residents suffered minor injuries after their car spun out of control on the freeway and hit a guardrail.

If those three people live in a small town in the station's listening area, however, then the names and addresses should be mentioned. The story might read:

> Three Centerville people are recovering from minor injuries suffered this afternoon when their car went out of control on the freeway and hit the guardrail. Police identified the injured as Pam and John Rose of the 300 block of Blackwell Avenue and Peter Noyes, who lives at 177 Sunshine Road.

Some news directors prefer to omit the house numbers, limiting the address to the street. In many cases, the determining factor is the size of the community. A radio station in a community of 5,000 will give more details about the injured than a station in a city of 100,000. A newscast in a larger city might merely identify the neighborhoods in which the injured people lived.

But in that community of 5,000, the second paragraph of the story might give more details:

> The injured were on their way home from a P-T-A meeting. The Roses both teach at Johnson High School. They were giving Noyes a ride home when the accident took place.

The added details are of interest because in a small community the chances are that many of those listening to the newscast know the three people. If they do not, they may still be interested for other reasons: most of the audience will be familiar with Johnson High School, they may be members of the PTA, and some may have attended the PTA meeting.

Middle Names and Initials

Do not use middle names or initials unless they are part of the name a person is known by or they are needed in a story to identify people with similar names. For example, some politicians and celebrities, like the following, always used their middle initials, so you would be correct to use them in the story:

Edward R. Murrow

The late President John F. Kennedy

Dr. Martin Luther King

Foreign Names

It was sometimes amusing, but more often embarrassing, to hear radio and TV anchors trying to pronounce all the foreign names during the Gulf and Iraqi Wars. Everyone quickly learned the name and pronunciation of the president of Iraq, Saddam Hussein. The king of Jordan was easy: King Hussein. But anchors used a variety of pronunciations for the president of Syria, Hafeez Assad, and the emir of Kuwait, whose full name is Sheik Jabiral-Ahmadal-Sabah. Most of the time the emir was referred to simply as Sheik al-Sabah, and the Saudi Arabian monarch was usually called just King Fahd.

There will be more discussion on pronunciation in Chapter 8, "Delivering the News," but for now remember that foreign names are used in broadcast copy only if they are essential. The names of foreign heads of state, ambassadors, and foreign ministers who are frequently in the news must be mentioned, but secondary foreign officials can usually be identified by title alone.

When a foreign name is used, it must be used according to custom. In some foreign countries, such as China, the first name is the surname and important one, not the last. For example, the late Chinese leader Mao Tse-tung is referred to as Chairman Mao.

Ages

A person's age should be used in a news story only if it is significant for some reason. Most of the time it is irrelevant. There certainly would be no need to give the ages of Pam and John Rose or Peter Noyes, who were involved in the earlier accident example. However, if the Roses' 5-year-old daughter had been involved in the accident, her age would be worth mentioning because she is so young; likewise, if Noyes' 87-year-old mother was in the back seat, her age should also be given.

Sometimes it is also acceptable to give ages in crime stories. If two teenage boys were involved in a hit-and-run accident, their ages should be reported. If an 80-year-old man tried to hold up a bank, his age is the most interesting part of the story because it's unusual to hear of a senior citizen committing such a crime.

If a 75-year-old woman's vehicle crossed a divider and collided head-on with another car, give her age. It could have been a factor in the accident. Perhaps not, but until police determine the cause of the accident, the woman's age should be included. It also should be noted if, for example, police said one of the tires on the woman's car had blown out and possibly caused the accident.

Other reasons for giving ages include exceptional accomplishments or unlikely occurrences. For example:

A 16-year-old graduates at the top of her law school class.

A 60-year-old Hollywood actor marries a 22-year-old woman.

A 44-year-old woman gives birth to quadruplets.

Marital Status

It is not necessary to specify whether someone is married, divorced, or single unless the information directly relates to the story in some way. There would be no reason to say whether someone who was arrested for driving while intoxicated is single or married. However, when a candidate is running for mayor most people want to know whether he or she is single or married. It may influence how some people vote.

During the Iraqi War, a soldier usually was identified as a married woman when the reporter discovered that her husband was also in the service, or, perhaps, was home looking after the children. For the most part, however, reporters were more concerned with servicewomen's role in the war, not their marital status, and that was appropriate.

Race

As with marital status, race should be noted only if it is relevant to the story. For example, you would mention race or ethnicity if a city elected its first Hispanic member of the city council or if an African American graduated at the top of the class in a predominantly white college. But a person's race should be mentioned in a crime story only if it is necessary for identification

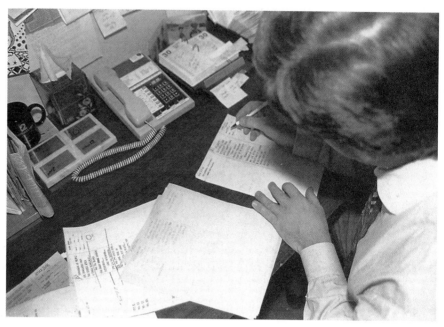

Figure 1-2   An anchor reviews copy.

purposes while police are still looking for a suspect. If a person has already been arrested for a crime, there is no reason to indicate the person's racial or ethnic background.

Numbers

The fundamental rule regarding the use of numbers in broadcast copy is that they should be rounded off and spelled out when there is any chance for confusion. For example, a budget figure of $60,342,960,000 should be rounded off to "more than 60 billion dollars." Such a figure is spelled out because it would be virtually impossible for a newscaster to deal with all those numbers in the middle of the copy.

The convention is to spell out single-digit numbers, and eleven, and to use figures for 10 and for 12 through 999. For larger figures, use words or word-figure combinations. Here are some examples:

There are only eleven days left until Christmas.

There were 45 students in the class.

There were three people at the table.

There were 600 prisoners of war.

There were 75-thousand people in the stadium and another 15-thousand were turned away.

Single-digit numbers with million, billion, and so on are expressed in words, such as: It will take another three million dollars to complete work on the project.

Some figures reaching the news desk are expressed in decimals.

The stock market was up 6.88 points.

Unemployment was down .01 percent for the month.

The Navy asked for an additional 5.5 billion dollars.

Some newscasters will say the stock market was up "six point 88," but most prefer to eliminate the decimal and round off the figure to "almost seven points." As for the other examples: recast them for broadcast copy to read, "Unemployment was down one tenth of one percent for the month," and "The Navy asked for an additional five and one-half billion dollars."

Timing Stories

It is essential to know how to time copy. If you are writing for yourself, use a stopwatch as you read each page of copy aloud, and then write the time on the page. Be sure to read the copy aloud because the timing would be different if you read it silently.

If you are writing the copy for someone else, it is more difficult to estimate time because everyone reads copy at a different pace. On average, newscasters read at a speed of about 15 or 16 standard lines of copy per minute.

For television, because of the split page and the use of bold type for the teleprompter, most newscasters take about one second to read each line of copy. When computers are used to write TV scripts, the timing may be different. (Some computers will time each story.) As you become familiar with the equipment you use to write scripts, you'll learn how best to time the material. You must know this information so that you will be able to estimate how many lines of copy you need to write for a given story. You may often be told by a producer, "Give me about 20 seconds."

Review Questions

1. Why can't you use standard newspaper copyediting techniques when you are correcting mistakes in broadcast copy?
2. What is a slug, and where does it go on your copy?
3. Most abbreviations are not permitted in broadcast copy. Give examples of some exceptions.
4. What should you do if you cannot complete a sentence on one page?
5. Do titles go before or after a name in broadcast copy?
6. Explain when you should and should not give the street address of someone involved in a car accident.
7. Should you ever give a person's middle name or initial in broadcast copy? Explain.
8. When is it proper to give a person's age in broadcast copy?
9. When should you mention a person's racial or ethnic background?
10. How would you express the following sentence in broadcast copy?

    The Centerville School Board approved a budget of 1.5 million dollars.

11. How would you express the figure in the following sentence?

    There were 49,883 people at the game.

Exercises

1. Photocopy the following broadcast copy or retype it exactly as it appears and then, with a pen or pencil, correct the errors.

   The President said the United States would continue its course in Iraq until that nation is secure but he refused to predict just how long American troops would have to remain in that country.

   Donald Rumsfeld, Secretary of Defense, said he was impressed by all the dramatic improvements in Iraq since he last visited the war-torn nation and he repeated his belief that there were enough American troops in that nation.

2. Rewrite the following to reflect good broadcast style:

   Ted Kennedy, the Democratic senator from Massachusetts, said he would vote against the Supreme Court nomination.

   Colin Powell, Secretary of State and former Chairman of the Joint Chiefs of Staff, was scheduled to address the U.N. Security Council tomorrow.

3. Read through your local newspaper until you find three stories that use numbers that would have to be changed for broadcast. Type the material so that it reflects proper broadcast style.

4. Using the same newspaper, find three examples of names and titles that would have to be rewritten for broadcast. Type the material in broadcast style.

5. Rewrite a one-page story from a newspaper and, after you have corrected the copy, time it and note the time on the page.

2   Broadcast News Writing Style

Chapter 1 helped acquaint you with some of the rather tedious but necessary basics of broadcast news writing. The next step is to learn broadcast news writing style. Broadcast style is very different from other styles of writing, principally because, unlike most other writing, broadcast copy is written for the ear, not the eye.

Much of the news "writing" heard on radio and television is actually "rewriting." Although broadcast news reporters write original copy when they are covering a story, a considerable portion of the news on radio and television is gathered from the news wires and rewritten in broadcast style or taken off the broadcast wire and read on the air without a rewrite. This chapter focuses on rewriting the wire.

Rewriting Wire Copy

One semester, a student stopped me at the end of a class and said, "Professor White, I need some help. I have an internship and an opportunity to write some broadcast copy. Can you give me some tips?"

I was puzzled and amused. He was carrying a copy of my textbook under his arm. "It's all in the book," I told him. "Everything I've learned about writing is there. I have no secret, no 'quick fix.' It's all important."

He looked at me, nodding his head in agreement. "I know," he said, "I've read it all, but isn't there something special, something particularly important that I should remember when the editor gives me a piece of wire copy and says, 'rewrite this'?"

I was still amused by his question and his apparent panic at the idea of having to write a story from a piece of wire copy in an actual broadcast newsroom, rather than in the classroom. Then suddenly I remembered being in a similar situation before this young man was even born. There was, indeed, one essential point to learn about rewriting wire copy.

"Look," I said, "there actually is one thing that you can do when you are given that wire copy, that you must learn above all else. Get rid of it as fast as possible. Read it, digest it, and then discard it. After that," I said, "write what you remember and don't look at the wire copy again until it's time to check your facts."

You may find it difficult to surrender the wire copy and rely only on memory, but that is the only way to be certain that you rewrite what is basically newspaper-style wire copy into conversational broadcast copy. The wire

Figure 2-1   Newsroom at WAFB-TV, Baton Rouge. (Photo by Christopher J. Rogers)

services do offer a broadcast wire written in a conversational style, but we are not concerned with that wire. This book prepares you to do what the broadcast news service writer does with the service's newspaper wire copy.

Getting accustomed to reading and absorbing material and then expressing it in your own words takes practice. Once you have conquered the temptation to refer to the original wire or newspaper copy as you write, you will discover that your broadcast copy will be easy and natural for you, or anyone else, to read on the air.

Conversational Style

Writing in conversational style means writing for the ear. Newspapers, obviously, are written for the eye, which means that if readers do not understand something, they can return to the paragraph or sentence and read it a second time. In broadcast news, however, the audience has no such luxury; they hear the copy just once. So, broadcast copy must be written clearly and simply. Thoughts must be expressed quickly with brief, crisp, declarative sentences. They must be aimed at ordinary people, which means the words must be understood immediately, without second thought. If the audience does not understand the copy, nothing else matters.

Contractions

Broadcast newswriters must write the way most people speak. When we have a discussion with another person, we automatically do a number of things of which we usually are not aware. For example, we almost always use contractions. We are more likely to say "I'm going to work now, Frank," than "I am going to work now, Frank." And we might add, "Let's get together for lunch again soon," instead of "Let us get together again soon." In other words, if we contract our words in conversation, we should do the same in broadcast copy. Here are some other examples:

Good Morning, I'm Jack Jones with the late news.

Here's a rundown of the top stories we're covering.

We've just received word that teachers are walking out of classrooms at Willow Street High School. . . .

If you're driving to work, expect serious delays on the freeway because of an accident at the James Street exit. . . .

There's no word from the mayor yet on rumors he'll resign. . . .

Those are the headlines. Now here are the details. . . .

In the above copy, most pronoun-verb combinations have been contracted. However, sometimes—for emphasis—it is better not to contract words. For example:

The mayor says he will seek reelection.

Because the word *will* is key to this particular sentence, it would be better to avoid the contraction *he'll*. The newscaster would want to emphasize the word *will*.

Reading Your Copy Aloud

Reading copy aloud helps you determine when words should be contracted, which words should be emphasized, how clear the sentences are, and how well the copy flows from sentence to sentence. Writers should not be embarrassed about reading copy aloud in the newsroom. The ear, not the eye, is the best judge of well-written broadcast copy. It is almost impossible to catch some poorly written phrases or sentences without testing them on the ear. In particular, you may not realize how complicated a sentence is until you read it aloud.

Avoiding Information Overload

Often, copy that is difficult to understand contains too much information in any one sentence, a situation known as information overload. Some of the nation's finest newspapers are guilty of overloading sentences, but, as mentioned earlier, readers can always reread complicated passages. Here's an example of some copy from a major city newspaper and how it could be simplified for broadcast:

Two weeks into the Congressional debate on taxes, and with at least two more weeks to go, it is clear that Congress will eventually approve a big tax cut, smaller than the $726 billion, 10 year reduction President Bush proposed but still the third largest in history, on top of the largest, enacted just two years ago this month.

Quite a mouthful. It is not well written even for a newspaper, but in its present form, it would be outrageous to read on the air. For broadcast, we must chop that unmanageable paragraph into separate new short sentences that can be easily understood by the listener.

Our first sentence could start out this way: "Two weeks into the Congressional debate on taxes, it is clear that Congress will eventually approve a big tax cut." Next we could point out that the debate will go on for at least two more weeks. Our third sentence could deal with the amounts of the proposed tax cuts: "The amount approved by Congress is expected to be smaller than the $726 billion, 10-year reduction proposed by President Bush." The next and final sentence would give these additional details: "The final tax cut is expected to be the third largest in history, on top of the largest, enacted just two years ago this month."

This copy, rewritten for broadcast, can now be easily understood. It would have been virtually impossible to understand the original newspaper copy if it had been read on the air as it appeared in print.

Here's another newspaper lead that needs revising for broadcast:

> The Energy Department proposes to spend $2.4 billion next year and up to 53.7 billion in each of the following four years to bring the nation's paralyzed nuclear weapon production plants into compliance with environmental and safety laws, according to Energy Secretary James D. Watkins.

If you read that sentence to some friends, and then ask them to tell you what it says, you would probably find that unless they have unusual abilities of concentration and recall, they would be unable to repeat all the details. That lengthy, involved sentence could be turned into good broadcast copy:

> The Energy Department wants to spend almost two and one-half billion dollars next year to improve the nation's nuclear production plants. The funds would be used to bring the paralyzed plants into compliance with environmental and safety laws. Energy Secretary James Watkins says the government is willing to spend almost 15 billion dollars over the next four years to continue the cleanup and safety checks at the nuclear weapon production plants.

If you read the new sentences to your friends, they would probably remember more about the story than they did when you read the newspaper version. Let's examine how the newspaper copy was rewritten.

First, it was broken into three parts to reduce the number of details in one sentence. It is easier for listeners to understand the information if they hear it in small doses. The newspaper version mentions two large figures, $2.4 billion and $3.7 billion. In the broadcast version, the first figure was explained in the first sentence, and the second figure was mentioned in the third sentence.

The first figure, $2.4 billion, was rounded off to "almost two and one-half billion dollars." It is best to round off figures and to eliminate use of the decimal in broadcast copy because the result is easier for most people to understand. The second figure, "up to $3.7 billion in each of the following four years," was totaled and rounded off. The result, "the government is willing to spend almost 15 billion dollars over the next four years," is easier for listeners to grasp because they don't need to do the math in their heads. Notice, too, that dollars is spelled out in broadcast copy.

No attempt was made in the first sentence to discuss exactly how the Energy Department plans to spend the money. It was enough to tell the audience that the department wants to spend this money to improve the plants. Now that the audience has digested that information, it is told how the money is going to be used, "to bring the paralyzed plants into compliance with environmental and safety laws." And then, in the third sentence, the audience learns that the energy secretary wants even more money in the coming years to complete the job. Just in case the audience was not paying complete attention, how the money is to be used was mentioned again in the closing words "to continue the cleanup and safety checks" at the plants.

Last, the middle initial D was dropped from Secretary Watkins' name because the secretary does not use the initial consistently.

Avoiding Relative Clauses

Other sentences that produce information overload are those that contain relative clauses. Relative clauses are introduced by the relative pronouns *who, which, that, what, whoever, whichever,* and *whatever* and add information to simple sentences. Newspapers often use relative clauses to stress one point about a person or thing over another in a particular sentence. Because relative pronouns refer to nouns that precede them, TV and radio audiences may have trouble identifying the noun and pronoun as the same person or thing. Take this example found in a newspaper:

> The comments from the State Department spokesman came in response to a report in the English-language Tehran Times, which quoted a source as saying Iran would definitely intercede to gain the release of the hostages if Washington gave assurances it would release frozen Iranian assets.

Whereas newspaper readers would immediately know that *which* refers to *Tehran Times* because the words are next to each other, a broadcast audience might have to stop and think about what *which* refers to. When this copy was rewritten for broadcast, the relative pronoun *which* was removed and the sentence was cut in two. The noun *newspaper* was used again instead of the pronoun:

> The State Department spokesman made the comments after a report appeared in the English-language newspaper The Tehran Times. The newspaper quoted a source as saying Iran would definitely help win release of the hostages if Washington promised to release frozen Iranian assets.

Other changes included recasting the passive construction in the first sentence as active and replacing the phrase *intercede to gain* with the single word *help*. Likewise, *gave assurances* was simplified to *promised*. The second version is better for a broadcast audience because it does not use pronouns or wordy phrases that could cause misunderstanding.

Which, when used as part of a clause that adds descriptive detail about a noun, also presents unnecessary problems for broadcast writers. Take this print copy:

> Two people were killed today when a small plane, which was on a flight from Key West to Miami, crashed into the ocean off the coast of Key Largo.

All these details will be simpler for your audience to digest if you give the number of dead and where the crash took place in the first sentence and explain the departure and destination of the plane in the second sentence. Here's a broadcast version:

> Two people died today when a small plane crashed into the ocean off the coast of Key Largo. The plane was on a flight from Key West to Miami.

Relative clauses introduced by *that* contain information important to the meaning of a sentence, not just additional details. For example:

> The truck that jackknifed on the freeway today was carrying flammable liquid.

The *that* clause identifies which particular truck was carrying flammable liquid.

In some sentences, *that* can be omitted because the sentence sounds more natural and is clear without it. For example:

> The governor says that he'll leave the capital by plane this evening.

Dropping *that* makes the sentence more conversational:

> The governor says he'll leave the capital by plane this evening.

Eliminating Long Words

Short words are usually easier to understand than long ones and, crucially for broadcast news, where time is precious, they take less time to deliver. For example:

> Police *abandoned* the search.

is more difficult to say than

> Police *gave up* the search.

Here are examples of long words and some shorter ones that could replace them in broadcast copy:

AVOID	USE
extraordinary	unusual
acknowledge	admit
initiate	start, begin
transform	change

Certain words should be avoided because they are difficult to pronounce on the air. Here are some examples:

AVOID	USE
burst into	broke into
coaxing	tempting

recrimination	countercharge
autonomy	independence
deteriorate	grow worse
allegations	charges
intermediaries	go-betweens; negotiators

If you are unsure about other words you find yourself using, remember that reading them aloud is the best way to decide whether they are appropriate broadcast words. If a word is difficult to say or sounds strange or confusing to the ear, don't use it.

Conjunctions

Coupling pins such as *but* and *and* are often helpful in connecting sentences or parts of sentences. Using conjunctions to link ideas to one another can often help broadcast copy sound more conversational. However, do not overuse conjunctions. Remember also that some conjunctions that work in print, such as the *however* in the previous sentence, do not always work as well in broadcast copy. Use *but* instead of *however* in broadcast copy.

Prepositions

Prepositions can also help make copy more conversational, particularly when used to eliminate the possessive, which tends to make listeners work harder to follow the meaning. Here are some examples; the first uses the possessive:

> The Senate Armed Services Committee's spokesman announced a series of new hearings on budget cuts.

Here is a preposition used in the same sentence:

> A spokesman *for* the Senate Armed Services Committee announced a series of new hearings on budget cuts.

See how much easier it is to read the version with the preposition. It is more natural. The preposition is more likely to be used than the possessive in conversation.

Pronouns

We use a lot of pronouns during conversation, and they serve a useful purpose in broadcast copy. They eliminate the need to repeat a person's name. Some difficulty arises, however, when pronouns are used too far from the person's name or when more than one name is mentioned in the sentence or paragraph. Examine this troublesome use of a pronoun:

> The Boy Scout of the Year award was given to Frank Jones by Mayor Harris. Immediately after the presentation he slipped and fell on the stage.

Who slipped and fell on the stage, the mayor or the Boy Scout? The pronoun _he_ does not work here because two males are mentioned in the sentence. The person who fell should be identified by name.

Modifying Phrases

Some writers, in their eagerness to tell the story, often get the details right but put the words in the wrong order, thus changing the meaning of the sentence. Look at the following example:

> Russian officials said political prisoners arrested by the KGB during former communist regimes have been released at a news conference today.

Because of the placement of the modifying phrase at a news conference, this sentence implies that the prisoners were released at the time of the news conference. What the writer meant to say is:

> Russian officials said at a news conference today that political prisoners arrested by the KGB have been released.

When you use modifying phrases, be sure to place them as close as possible to the word(s) they describe or identify. Here's another example:

> The two cars collided in heavy rain on Interstate 95 during the rush hour.

It's true that the "heavy rain" did fall on the highway, but it also fell elsewhere. When recast to be less ambiguous, the sentence would read this way:

> The two cars collided on Interstate 95 in heavy rain during the rush hour.

Avoiding Clichés

In preparation for writing this book, I watched television news in a variety of major cities. The reporting was often good, but the writing was just as often horrible. When you watch and listen to news for hours at a time, you realize how badly broadcast copy can be written, not only on local stations but on the networks as well.

Newspaper writers, including those working for such distinguished publications as _The New York Times, Washington Post,_ and _Los Angeles Times,_ turn out a lot of long, cumbersome copy that sometimes takes several readings to digest. But, to these newspaper writers' credit, their writing is rarely as cliché-filled as the copy produced by broadcast writers and reporters.

Broadcast news managers often argue that their writers do not have as much time as newspaper writers to produce copy, which is often true. They also point out that some of the cliché-filled copy I complain about is not very different from the way people talk. "We're writing conversational copy, aren't we?" asked one news director, "so what's wrong with a few clichés? We use them all the time in conversation."

Some people might find that argument persuasive, but writing in a conversational style does not mean adopting all the bad habits of conversation. Many people hold conversations without using clichés.

The American College Dictionary defines a cliché as "a trite, stereotyped expression." In his book *Newswriting,* William Metz says a cliché is "a phrase that has been used so often that it has no zip, has outlived its usefulness. A cliché is a worn-out phrase." He adds, "These barren, impotent word combinations are used by careless and lazy writers."

We all use clichés from time to time, but you should avoid using clichés in broadcast copy as much as possible, even though some clichés are heard every night on news programs. For example, killers are often "cold-blooded"; "slaughter" is always "bloody"; and events "come on the heels of" other events. Broadcasts during political campaigns in particular inundate listeners with clichés, such as "hats in the political ring," "campaign trails," "political hay," and "political footballs."

Here are some more clichés that should be (if you will excuse the cliché) "deep sixed":

Airliners that become "ill-fated planes" after they crash

Politicians and others who "take to the airwaves"

Lobby groups and others who "are up in arms"

People who end up "in the driver's seat"

Facts that are "difficult to swallow"

Plans brought to a "screeching halt"

Comments or actions that add "fuel to the storm" (a mixed metaphor)

Troublesome situations that are a "can of worms" or a "Pandora's box"

Why are so many things "put on the back burner"? What is wrong with "delaying action" or referring to something as having "a low priority"? Say simply that people are "delaying" or "avoiding" something, rather than "dragging their feet." Police should be "searching for" or "looking for" or even "hunting for" a missing person, not "combing the woods" for him or her.

Broadcast writers who use "cooling their heels," "tight-lipped," and "Mother Nature" should be "tarred and feathered." Although some news makers insist on referring to something as being "miraculous," do not use the word to describe some spectacular escape from death or injury unless you are quoting the newsmaker. Use instead "unbelievable," "amazing," or "incredible."

"Rampage" is another "worn-out" word that will never go away. Instead of using the cliché to tell a prison riot story, describe what's actually going on inside the prison. For example:

> Prisoners at Center City jail this afternoon took five guards hostage, burned cellblocks, and demanded that Governor Wilson come to the jail to hear their demands.

A Miami TV station, in its story about the arrest of a suspect in the Florida State University serial killings, reported the following:

> People are breathing easier tonight because a suspected serial killer is behind bars.

As it turned out, the suspect was then released for lack of evidence, so we can assume that the breathing in the community became heavier again.

A network sportscaster reporting about a series of injuries in the NBA wrote this sentence:

Officials are scratching their heads for an explanation.

All of the above are examples of "lazy" writing. Whenever you are tempted to use a cliché, make the extra effort to think of a fresh way to express your point.

Writing What You Mean

During the Gulf War, the English language also came under attack. It was not an Iraqi boat that was sunk in the gulf, it was a ship. A boat is something you paddle or sail. If you are referring to anything larger, use ship.

In writing broadcast copy, be precise. Use the right word. If you do not, your credibility, a key factor in building a career, comes into question.

Here are a few words and phrases commonly used incorrectly on the air:

The consensus of opinion is that the war will be over within a few months. [*Of opinion* is redundant; consensus means "general agreement."]

There was bad weather over the gulf due to a fast-moving storm front. [*Due to* means "owing to"; use *because of.*]

The fighting is different than last week's. [*Different* here takes the preposition *from.* However, it is correct to say: The fighting is different than he expected.]

The number of people injured was over a dozen. [*Over* implies a spatial relationship; use *more than.*]

The house is further down the road. [*Further* means "in addition to"; use *farther* to refer to distance.]

Since you are going downtown, please get me a newspaper. [*Since* refers to a relationship of time; use *because* to indicate a causal connection.]

These are just a few examples of improper word usage. A good background in English grammar is important. Most college journalism programs insist that you take one to two years of English, but it is not always easy to find classes that focus on grammar. Ask your adviser to recommend a professor who teaches courses on grammar.

Good Grammar and Some Exceptions

The same rules of grammar apply to both print and broadcast copy, most of the time. Writers do take a few liberties in broadcast copy because of its conversational nature. You'll recall that commas can be omitted from broadcast copy unless they indicate a pause and that subordinate clauses should be avoided in broadcast writing. Another exception: verbs can be dropped from some sentences, as is frequently done in conversation.

For example, if you are talking to your letter carrier and say, "Looks like snow today, Helen," no one is going to object because you did not say, "It appears as if we are going to get snow today, Helen." Therefore, it would be natural for a newscaster to say, "Three injuries tonight on the turnpike, that story when we return." Few people will take offense because the newscaster did not say "*There were* three injuries tonight on the turnpike." Verbs will be discussed further in Chapter 3, "More Style Rules."

Summary

This chapter suggests that you use conversational style in writing broadcast copy. The material in the chapter is meant to help you learn to write as you speak. Most of us use brief sentences, with few subordinate clauses, and choose easy-to-understand words in everyday conversation. Communicating information to a radio or TV audience is best done in everyday language, simply and with sincerity.

Keep in mind that reading your copy aloud is the best way to test how well you are using conversational style. Your ears, not your eyes, will tell you if your copy is good.

Review Questions

1. Where would you use contractions in the following sentences?

   The governor says he will leave on vacation tomorrow.
   There will be a dozen people at the reception.
   The workers say they will walk off the job at noon.
   Here is the latest word from the Weather Bureau.
   Now let us take a look at what happened in baseball tonight.

2. Would you use a contraction in the following sentence? Explain.

   The president says he will sign the bill.

3. What's wrong with the following sentence, and how could it be improved for broadcast?

   Two years after the crash of a helicopter into the Washington channel, the D.C. Fire Department has not provided scuba equipment and training for its fireboat personnel, despite an order from Congress to do so accompanied by an appropriation to pay for it.

4. Here is another complex sentence. How could you improve it for broadcast?

   Higher rates for electricity could be one result of the miners' strike against the Pittston Coal Company, which has forced some utilities to curtail sales of power to neighboring companies and to buy more expensive types of fuel, according to an industry spokesman.

5. Here is a list of words that are not particularly good for broadcast. Think of an appropriate substitute for each.

emblazoned	facilitate
ascent	perquisites
capitulation	stupefied
exodus	disperse

6. Keeping in mind the suggestions for using prepositions and conjunctions, how could the following sentence be improved for broadcast?

The circus' chief lion trainer did not take part in the show because he was sick. However, the apprentice trainer took over and his performance was loudly applauded.

7. There's a pronoun problem in the following sentence. Identify it, and explain how the sentence should read.

    The governor accused his opponent, Frank Smith, of mudslinging. After the exchange, he predicted he would win the election.

8. What words and phrases might you use to replace the clichés in the following sentences?

    The prisoners rampaged for more than an hour.
    The White House announcement came on the heels of Iraq's invasion of Kuwait.
    The Republican candidate said he had no doubt that the tax issue would become a political football.
    The gun lobby was up in arms because of congressional approval of the Brady bill.

Exercises

1. Correct any misused words and phrases in the following sentences:

    The consensus of opinion was that the Republicans would gain control of the House.
    Due to the bad weather, we decided not to go boating.
    There were over a thousand people in the ballroom.
    The car rides like an expensive one should.

2. Rewrite the following wire-service sentence for broadcast.

    Thunderstorms that raged through the South, and bad weather elsewhere, have been blamed for at least 23 deaths and the presumed drowning of a North Carolina man swept away by a swollen creek the night before he was to be married.

3. Take a story from the wires or a newspaper. Read it carefully, and then put it aside. Now rewrite the story in broadcast style without looking at the copy again. When you have finished, look at your copy, and make a note of anything important that you forgot or any information that you wrote incorrectly.

4. Watch a program of any kind on television, and then write a story about it, describing it as you would to a friend.

5. Read over your story from exercise 3 or 4, and make any changes you think will improve the copy. Then read the copy aloud, and note any changes you would make that you did not notice when you read the copy to yourself.

6. Find a newspaper story that has at least one subordinate clause in the lead, and rewrite it in broadcast style.

7. Look through your newspaper for words that you feel are too long or might be difficult for a broadcast audience to understand. Look them up in a dictionary or thesaurus to find synonyms that would be more appropriate for broadcast copy.

3   More Style Rules

Like Chapter 2, this chapter focuses on broadcast style rules. Much of this chapter is devoted to the use of verbs, adjectives, and other parts of speech. It also examines the various ways broadcast writers express time, quote people, and attribute information.

Verbs

Present Tense

Broadcast news must always present an image of immediacy. Without deceiving an audience by treating an old story as if it were fresh, the broadcast news writer's job is to tell the news as though it is in progress or has just recently happened. If a story is still developing or has just cleared the wires, a newswriter should make it sound as new and exciting as possible because most of the audience will be hearing the story for the first time. Use of present-tense verbs, particularly present-progressive verbs, which suggest ongoing action, adds to that immediacy. For example, in covering a meeting at the White House that is still in progress, a writer would best say:

> The president is meeting with his cabinet this morning to discuss the budget.

Only if the meeting had ended by the time of the newscast would the writer use the past tense:

> The President met today with his cabinet to discuss the budget.

When writers use the past tense, they tell the audience that the event has already taken place, even though some aspect of it may actually still be in progress. Look at the following examples to see how the use of present-tense verbs focus on the continuing action:

Poor: Members of Congress ended their session today and headed for home.

Good: Members of Congress are on their way home today after ending their session.

Poor: A hurricane warning was issued tonight for Florida and Georgia.

Good: A hurricane warning is in effect tonight for Florida and Georgia.

Present Perfect Tense

Another verb tense that gives a sense of immediacy is the present perfect, which suggests that an action started in the past and is continuing into the present. For example:

> The president has left Camp David for Andrews Air Force Base.

The present perfect tense is useful when the status of the story is not certain. In this case, it may be known that the president left Camp David, but it may not be clear when he is going to arrive at Andrews Air Force Base.

Mixing Tenses

Because a news story may mention events that happened at different times or may report a statement that still holds true but was made earlier, it is acceptable to mix tenses in broadcast copy. For example, a story may begin with the present tense and then change to the past tense in later sentences so that the story makes sense. Here's an example of changing tenses:

> Mayor Jones says he hopes to keep property taxes at their present level.
> He made the comment during a speech earlier today before a meeting of
> the Chamber of Commerce. The mayor told the group he expects an
> improving economy and a reduction in city expenses will eliminate the
> need for higher property taxes.

The first sentence uses the present-tense verb *says*, but the rest of the paragraph uses past-tense verbs because it would sound strange to continue the present tense once it is established that the mayor made the comments earlier in the day.

But suppose the mayor has not yet delivered the speech. The story might be handled this way:

> Mayor Jones says he hopes to keep property taxes at their present level.
> Jones will say this tonight in a speech to the Chamber of Commerce. The
> mayor says he believes that an improving economy and a reduction in city
> expenses will eliminate the need for higher property taxes.

In this case, the present tense is used to describe opinions the mayor holds now, and the future tense is used to describe when he will express those opinions. The fourth and fifth sentences might continue with the future tense:

> The mayor will also tell his audience that he expects to attract new
> business to the city. He'll say he has a promise from Governor Williams for
> extra state funds to take care of the city's needy.

Active Verbs

Good broadcast copy also uses active verbs, not passive ones. Active verbs speed up copy and give it more punch because they focus on the action rather than the receiver of the action.

Poor: Three buildings were destroyed by the fire.

Good: The fire destroyed three buildings.

Poor: The Dow Jones was pushed up 30 points today after buyers took over on Wall Street.

Good: Buyers took over today on Wall Street, sending the Dow Jones up 30 points.

Says Is a Good Verb

Don't be afraid to use *says*. Many writers think they have to find different ways to avoid using a form of *say* because they think it is a boring verb. As a result, they will use forms of *exclaim, declare, assert, announce,* and other words that they believe mean the same thing as *say*. The problem is that these other words are not synonyms for *say;* each has a different connotation.

Strong Verbs

Although these verbs should not be used in place of *say*, sometimes they do accurately describe the situation. For example:

> The United Nations Security Council declared today . . .

> The White House announced that Peter Grant would become the new Secretary of the Interior.

> "We'll walk this picket line 'till hell freezes over!" exclaimed union leader Frank Chilton.

As for *assert,* it is difficult to think of an occasion when it would be appropriate to use that word in broadcast copy.

In writing broadcast copy, look for strong verbs that vividly describe the action:

smother, rather than *put down,* an uprising

snuff out, rather than *defeat,* a rebellion

echo, rather than *repeat,* an opinion

clash, rather than *disagree,* over strategy

lash out at, rather than *attack,* opponents

muster, rather than *collect,* enough votes

When choosing verbs, think about the image you want to create. For example, a tornado *roars,* but it also can *sweep* through a neighborhood. A hurricane can *destroy* a beachfront, but *demolish* gives a stronger picture. A high-school student might be *expelled,* but a deposed leader would be *exiled.* Battalions can *move* through the desert, but if they are doing it quickly, as they were in the war in Iraq, they might be said to *race* through.

Limiting Use of Adverbs and Adjectives

Like good verbs, adjectives and adverbs sometimes add color to broadcast copy, but for the most part they should be avoided. Many adjectives add unnecessary detail, and rather than enliven the copy, they weigh it down. Here's an example of a sentence with too many adjectives and adverbs:

> The *diesel-powered* train was quickly moving around the *very sharp* curve when suddenly there was a *loud, screeching* noise and the cars near the *very* front of the train *rapidly* started to leave the track.

The sentence would be more effective without most of these adjectives and adverbs because they add little meaning. It is not important to know that the train is *diesel-powered,* because most are. *Quickly moving* could be replaced by the strong verb *racing,* and the adverb *very* could be omitted because intensifiers are "filler" words that rarely add meaning. *Rapidly* could be eliminated because it is a given that the cars would leave the tracks quickly if the train was *racing* around the curve. Finally, *started to leave* could be replaced by the more vivid *jumped.* The cleaned-up sentence would read:

> The train was racing around the sharp curve when suddenly there was a screeching noise as the cars near the front of the train jumped the track.

Screeching was left in the sentence because it is a strong, colorful adjective that describes the noise. *Loud,* however, was eliminated because a screeching noise is, by definition, loud.

Attribution

Proper attribution is one of the basic requirements of good news writing and reporting, whether for newspapers or broadcasts. The chapters on reporting will deal with the various types and methods of attributing information. For now, let's examine the proper style of attribution used in broadcast scripts, which differs from the style used in newspapers and newspaper wire copy.

For the most part, newspapers use attribution at the end of a sentence, what is called *dangling attribution.* For example:

> Hundreds of people have been killed in Russian army attacks, according to The Associated Press.

Attribution in broadcast copy, if used in the lead sentence, is always at the top of the sentence. For example:

> The Associated Press reports hundreds of people have been killed in Russian army attacks.

The attribution can also be *delayed;* that is, it can be mentioned in the second sentence. For example:

> Hundreds of people reportedly have been killed in Yugoslav army attacks on Croatia. The report comes from The Associated Press.

Using Quotes

Most of the time, quotes are paraphrased in broadcast copy. Newspapers have the luxury of providing long, detailed quotes of politicians, government officials, and other newsmakers. But broadcasting time restrictions require a distillation of such information. There will be times, because of the importance of statements, when direct quotes can be used. Even then, however, the writer must keep them to a minimum.

Here is a sample of a quote that appeared in a newspaper:

"This is an example of the worst brutality I have ever come across," was the way the judge described the beating of a man arrested by police.

The broadcast version would read:

The judge said the beating of a man arrested by police was—in his words—"the worst brutality I have ever come across."

The quote also could have been paraphrased:

The judge described the beating of the arrested man as the worst brutality he had ever come across.

If a quote is too important to paraphrase, the actual words must be used. Most writers and broadcasters avoid using the terms quote and unquote at the beginning and end of a direct quote, but you will occasionally hear them on the air. There are better ways to handle a direct quote.

Here's one way:

The Senator said the Republican sponsored welfare reform bill would— and this is a direct quote—"take food out of the mouths of poor children."

Some newcasters will use a direct quote after saying "and these are the president's exact words." Other anchors will simply pause a second before a direct quote and change the inflection of their voices, but not all newscasters do this effectively. If you are writing the script, be explicit and use an introductory phrase to indicate you will be quoting someone directly.

Expressing Time

Because broadcast news usually reports or describes events that are currently happening, it is not always necessary to use the word *today* in broadcast copy. If events are not current, point that out quickly.

If a story says that 18 people have been injured in a train crash in Center City, listeners are going to assume that the accident occurred today unless the broadcaster explains that it happened last night or at some other time. Repeating the word *today* throughout a newscast, then, would become tiresome.

Those writing or reporting for an evening or late-night newscast should be specific. If the story is about something that is happening while the newscast is on the air or took place a short time earlier, the copy should stress the word *tonight* or use a phrase such as *at this very moment, a short time ago, within the past hour,* or *earlier this evening* to alert the audience that this is fresh news.

A story should never lead with the word *yesterday*. If a story happened the day before, something new must be found to freshen the story and

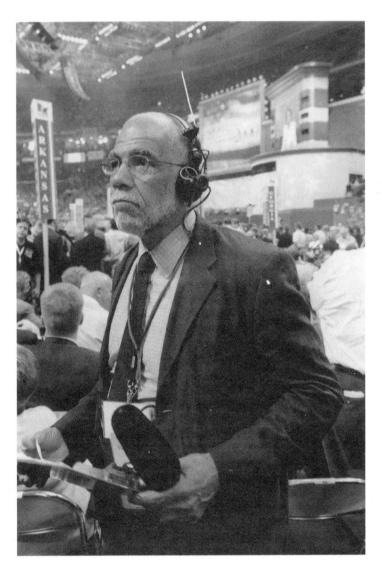

Figure 3-1
60 Minutes correspondent
Ed Bradley. (Courtesy of *CBS News*)

eliminate *yesterday* from the lead. There will be details on the subject of updating leads in Chapter 4, "Writing Broadcast Copy."

Looking Ahead

Some newscasts alert the audience to events that are expected to happen in the future. The information should be as specific as possible. An example:

> The president is expected to leave the White House in the next 15 minutes or so for Andrews Air Force Base, where he'll board *Air Force One* for the trip to London.

Another example:

> At any moment now, members of the United Nations Security Council will be considering new proposals on the crisis in the Middle East. We were

told a few minutes ago that members were already beginning to arrive at the Security Council chamber.

This sort of specific time reference adds immediacy and drama. It's much better than saying:

The Security Council meets today to consider new proposals on the Middle East.

One final note: Whenever you use a specific time reference, such as *tonight* or *a few minutes ago,* place the reference as close as possible to the verb whose action it describes.

Transitions

Transitions are phrases and words that signal relationships between sentences. Some broadcast news writers use transitions to carry listeners from one story to another; but in a newscast, transitions should be used with care and in moderation. If a transition is natural, it can be effective, but most transitions tend to sound contrived.

Here's an example of good use of a transition:

Centerville Mayor Frank Jones is flying to New York City at this hour to take part in talks with other mayors on how to deal with Washington's cut in funds for American cities.

Also traveling today is Centerville Police Chief Robert Potter. He's on his way to Chicago to meet with officials in that city to discuss the fight on drugs.

The transition *also traveling today* works here because it links stories about similar events of equal importance. But here's a bad example:

Centerville Mayor Frank Jones is flying to New York City at this hour to take part in talks with other mayors on how to deal with Washington's cut in funds for American cities.

Also traveling tonight, Hurricane Dorothy. It's headed our way at about 10 miles an hour and could slam into the mainland in the morning.

In this example, the transition is forced. Unlike the natural connection of two city officials who are traveling on government business, there is nothing logical about connecting the movement of the mayor and that of a hurricane. That example was not made up. The names have been changed, but the transition tying together the movement of an official and a hurricane was actually broadcast.

Here is another example of an effective transition:

The Justice Department wants to know if there are patterns of police brutality anywhere in the country. The Department has ordered a review of all police brutality complaints filed with its civil rights division during the last six years. The order comes amid an outcry over the police beating of motorist Rodney King in Los Angeles—an attack videotaped by a witness and aired across the country.

Los Angeles isn't the only place where authorities are investigating allegations of police brutality. In Georgia, witnesses say more than a dozen police officers pounced on a suspected prowler they caught after a chase from Atlanta to Stockbridge. The Atlanta and Clayton County police departments are conducting internal investigations. (*AP Radio*)

The transitional sentence *Los Angeles isn't the only place where authorities are investigating allegations of police brutality* is quite logical.

The prize for bad transitions must go to a Miami TV station:

The pope wasn't the only one celebrating a birthday today. Five years ago today, Mount St. Helens volcano erupted.

People, Not *Persons*

Our final style note concerns the use of the term *people* as opposed to *persons*. When more than one person is involved in a story, it is more conversational to refer to them as *people*, even though some style books continue to insist that a small group should be referred to as *persons*. For example, in conversation we are more likely to say that "five *people*" are going to join us for dinner than we are to say that "five *persons*" will be joining us.

Summary

Verbs play a vital role in broadcast newswriting. One of the most important messages of this chapter is to use present-tense verbs in broadcast copy as much as possible. People turn to radio and television because they want to know what is happening *now*. When you write broadcast copy, try to make the news sound fresh without being dishonest or misleading.

Using the *right* verb is also crucial. Remember that you don't always need to look for ways to replace *says*. It's a good verb. Look for strong verbs that vividly describe the action, but make sure they don't send the wrong message.

This chapter also discusses attributing information in broadcast copy. If you *need* to include an attribution, always place it at the beginning of your sentence.

Review Questions

1. How could the verb tenses in these sentences be improved for broadcast?

    The President said he would veto the tax bill unless Congress made some major changes.
    He spoke to reporters at the White House a short time ago.
    Rescuers went through the wreckage looking for more bodies. They said they expect to work all day and night.
    The hurricane slammed into Hollywood, Florida, a few minutes ago, and our reporter had this report from the beach area.

2. What's wrong with the verbs in these sentences?

    There was applause when the birthday cake was brought out by the chef.
    The robber was grabbed by the sheriff as he tried to run from the bank.

3. How could the verbs in these sentences be improved for broadcast?

    The teacher declared that the student outing was postponed because of rain.
    The mayor asserted that she would seek another term.
    The president exclaimed that he would go to Camp David for the weekend.

4. What's wrong with the attributions in the following sentences?

    The nation's economy is going to get worse before it gets better, according to a leading economist.
    Hundreds of people were injured in rioting in Los Angeles, according to the police.

5. What's wrong with the transition used to link the following sentences?

    Forest fires swept through a number of states on the West Coast today, destroying hundreds of thousands of acres of trees. Also under fire is our town's police chief, who is accused of failing to control some of his officers.

Exercises

1. Using stronger verbs, rewrite the following copy.

    An earthquake has hit San Francisco. Police say several people may have been killed. There is no report on injuries. But rescue workers looked through several wrecked buildings for possible victims. Hundreds of frightened residents left their homes. It was the strongest quake to hit the city in several years.

    Power lines were down in some areas. Police say they fell when cracks developed in the pavement.

    Utility company officials are in the area to examine damage. They said some power lines were broken during the quake and present a danger.

2. The following remarks were made by President Bush. Write a story showing how you would use them in broadcast copy:

    WASHINGTON-President Bush said yesterday that "now may be the time to revamp and reform our intelligence services," opening the way for consideration of changes at the C.I.A., the F.B.I., and other agencies.

    The Bush administration has not acted on a number of far-reaching proposals to reorganize the government's intelligence organizations, including recommendations made last year by a Congressional inquiry into the attacks of September 11, and other independent intelligence panels.

    Expanding the powers of the director of central intelligence and establishing a domestic intelligence agency like Britain's M15 are among ideas circulating in Washington as the independent commission looking into the attacks holds hearings and prepares to make its own recommendations.

3. Find two related stories on the wires or in the newspaper. Rewrite them in broadcast style, and use a transition to tie them together.

4. Using wire copy or newspaper stories, find three sentences that use the passive voice, and rewrite the sentences in broadcast style.

5. Find as many verbs as you can on the front page of your local newspaper that you feel could be stronger or more colorful. Replace them.

4 Writing Broadcast Copy

The hardest part of writing broadcast copy is getting started. There are times when you will have difficulty moving your fingers. Your brain will seem dead. You may feel hypnotized by the white paper in your typewriter or the glow from your computer screen. Break the spell! Type the first thing that comes into your mind. Don't worry whether it is good, just write. Get started. It will get easier.

You may find that the first sentence you write works as an opening for your story, or you may need to write a few sentences before you come up with one that you like. This chapter focuses on writing an effective opening sentence, or lead, for a news story.

Leads

The lead is the most important part of a news story because it sets the tone for all that follows. The lead must grab or "hook" the audience's attention in as few words as possible. The hook can be an exciting or dramatic sentence, a clever phrase, an intriguing fact, or a provocative quote.

The "Five W's and H Rule"

Unless the story is a feature, the lead must include an element of news. It must begin to address the traditional journalistic concept of discovering information. To guarantee that all of the important news elements are reported in a story, journalists have devised a rule that requires newswriters to answer six basic questions: *who, what, where, when, why,* and *how.* This rule is referred to as the *"five W's and H rule."*

At one time, most newspaper editors expected every lead to answer all of these questions. But few newspaper editors still require this, and broadcasters never follow the rule. However, at least one or more of the questions must be answered in the lead of the story for it to be news. By the end of the story, most—if not all—of the questions should be answered.

An opening sentence that contains no news is referred to as a *non-news lead,* and such leads are unacceptable in a news story. Here's an example from the Gulf War:

> The chairman of the Joint Chiefs of Staff Colin Powell has met with reporters.

This lead could become news by answering some of the journalistic questions. *Why* did the chairman meet with reporters? *What* did he tell them? For example:

> The chairman of the Joint Chiefs of Staff **Colin Powell,** told reporters this morning that the United States would probably continue to keep troops in Iraq for a number of months.

This revised lead does not deal with all five W's and the H, but it is a start. The *who* is the chairman of the Joint Chiefs of Staff. The *what* is the issue of maintaining troops in Iraq. The *where* is Iraq. The *when* is for a number of months. Still unanswered are the *why* and the *how*. These questions would be answered in the balance of the story—if the answers are available. This revised lead is an example of a *hard lead*. Such leads address the most important aspect of a story immediately. There are a variety of ways to lead your story, and all of them will be examined in the following sections. The decision about which kind of lead to use depends on a number of factors; the most important is the nature of the story. Is it a feature or breaking news? Is the story sad or upbeat? Is it about people or an event? Is the story about politics, a war, a medical development, or the kidnapping of a child? Is the story brand new or a continuing one? The lead is like the foundation of a house. How the foundation is built determines how the rest of the house will look. The lead sentence determines how the rest of the story should be constructed.

Hard and Soft Leads

In choosing a lead, decide first whether it will be hard or soft. As you saw in the previous example, a hard lead tells the audience the vital details of the story immediately. Hard leads are usually used for breaking news:

> At least 30 people were injured in the collapse of the building.

> More than a dozen people were arrested in the drug bust.

> The government announced today that 150 thousand more Americans were employed in November.

A soft lead takes a more subtle approach; it alerts the audience to the news that is to follow. This approach is sometimes called "warming up" the audience. The following soft leads could be used for the above stories:

> A building collapses in Center City. At least 30 people have been injured.

> A major drug bust in New York City. More than a dozen people are under arrest.

> Improvement in the unemployment figures. The government announced that 150 thousand more Americans were employed in November.

The soft leads may not sound as exciting or dramatic as the hard leads, but they do invite the audience to keep listening. Notice that two of the example soft leads are not full sentences but phrases that serve the same purpose as headlines in a print story. Soft leads can be helpful to listeners carrying out

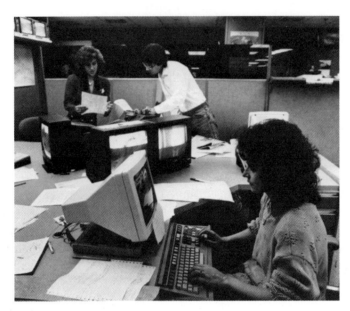

Figure 4-1   An anchor and producers go over a script at WTVJ-TV, Miami.
(Courtesy of WTVJ-TV, Miami)

other tasks or fighting traffic on the way to the office, by giving them time to shift their attention to the news.

Many editors discourage soft leads because they tend to slow down a newscast, particularly if used too often. But used in moderation, soft leads add variety to broadcast copy. Experienced editors tend to be flexible in dealing with a writer's style, including the kinds of leads writers choose. Good editors recognize that there is not just one way to write a story. They might say, "Well, it's not the way I would have written it, but it's not bad."

The "Right" Emotion

One challenge in writing a lead is deciding on the appropriate emotion, or tone, to express in the story. The tone depends mainly on the kind of story you are going to tell. For example, if the story is about something amusing, you would establish a lighthearted tone in the lead. Let's look at an example:

> A Center City schoolteacher got enough kisses today to last—well, maybe not a lifetime, but a few weeks, anyway. Kathy Long kissed 110 men at the annual fund-raiser for the local zoo. At ten bucks a kiss, Long raised eleven hundred dollars for the zoo, and when she turned the money over to zoo officials she joked that all the animals were not behind bars.

Even stories about accidents can sometimes be treated lightly:

> "I'll never drink hot coffee in the car again." That's what Tony Nieves said when he left the Center City hospital. This morning, his car struck a fire hydrant, bounced off a tree and smashed into the window of a flower shop.

> Nieves said he had bought a container of coffee at a McDonald's drive-through, and as he tried to add sugar and cream he lost control of the car when the hot coffee fell between his legs.

Stories about tragedies, as you would expect, require a more serious, straightforward approach:

> It's now believed that the death toll in the earthquake in Mexico has reached more than 50.

or

> At least three people are reported dead in the collision this morning of a half-dozen cars on the freeway.

For these leads, the writers chose to give just the facts; a decision that creates a quiet tone that underscores the loss of life described in the stories.

While every story requires the writer to choose a certain tone, features and nonbreaking news stories allow more flexibility than does breaking news. Some writers are very effective at evoking joy, pathos, and other emotions from an audience through the tone they create. Look, for example, at these leads written by former CNN anchor Reid Collins. His story about the invasion of Kuwait began: "A rich little country died at dawn today." On the rioting at the Viennese Opera Ball, Collins wrote: "A night at the opera in Vienna was a Marxist nightmare—part Karl, part Groucho." And his lead on a story about Mikhail Gorbachev's busy day was: "Like a juggler with too many plates in the air, Mikhail Gorbachev was stage right, stage left, and stage center today. So far, no breakage."

Notice that Collins creates an air of sadness in his Kuwait lead, whereas he suggests the chaos and confusion of the riot in his lead about the Vienna Opera. Similarly, his image of Gorbachev as a juggler effectively elicits a picture of Gorbachev frantically rushing around trying to hold his country together. These leads tell the audience not only what the stories are about, but how the writer wants the audience to feel about them.

The Quote Lead

Sometimes a *quote*, like the "hot coffee" example used earlier, can provide an excellent hook for a story:

> "Life is short and life is sweet. So take time to enjoy what you have." Marine Captain Russell Sanborn says that's one of the lessons he learned as a prisoner of war in Iraq. He and some other former P-O-W's told their stories today at news conferences in the Washington area. (*AP Broadcast Wire*)

Here is another example:

> "The first thing I'm going to do is quit my job and take a trip around the world." That's what lottery winner Bill Turpin said when he redeemed his ten million dollar winning lottery ticket.

Quote leads should be used sparingly, however. Unless the quote is comparatively short, the listener may miss its connection with the rest of the story.

The Shotgun Lead

The *shotgun,* or *umbrella,* lead can be effective for combining two or more related stories:

> Forest fires continue to roar out of control in California, Oregon, and Washington State. The drought that has plagued the three states is now in its second month. Fires have scorched more than a million acres of timberland in California and another half million acres in Oregon and Washington.

The advantage of the shotgun lead is that it allows the writer to eliminate the boring alternative of reporting the fires in three separate, back-to-back stories.

Here is another example:

> Congress today is looking at administration proposals that would increase the number of crimes punishable by the death penalty and make it easier for police to collect evidence.

The writer would then devote a few sentences to each of the White House recommendations.

The Suspense Lead

The object of the *suspense lead* is to delay telling the key information until the end of the story.

National Public Radio's Susan Stamberg used an effective suspense lead in her story about a famous photographer:

STAMBERG: Edith Shane had run over to Times Square from her job at Doctors Hospital. She wanted to be part of the celebration. Off duty, she wasn't supposed to be in her uniform, but she was. The sailor, Bill Schwhitzgood—all these names popped up years later, by the way, and the two never did meet formally—the sailor grabbed the nurse in glee just as he had grabbed all those other women, but this was different. The nurse is caught gracefully in the sailor's arms. Her body twists a bit in his embrace. They look as if they could be dancing. It's the Eisenstaedt moment.

EISENSTAEDT: If this nurse in white would have been in a dark uniform, wouldn't have been a nurse, wouldn't have been a picture or vice versa. If the, if the nurse was in white and he would be in white, wouldn't be a picture either. It was just a coincidence that he was in navy blue and she was in white and she was thin. If she would have been fat, it wouldn't have been a good picture either.

STAMBERG: Alfred Eisenstaedt was one of the original staff photographers for Life magazine, not a person to snap

Figure 4-2
V-J Day Times
Square, New York
City, August 14, 1945,
by Alfred Eisenstaedt.
(Alfred Eisenstaedt/
Life Magazine © Time
Inc.)

five rolls of film to get the single perfect shot. He has
been seen standing absolutely motionless for an hour
or more, waiting for a sailboat to move to exactly the
right spot before he released the shutter. That August
day in 1945, the day of the Eisenstaedt moment, he
took more pictures than usual and knew he had
something.

EISENSTAEDT: I know this was the best picture I took on that day. I
knew that.

STAMBERG: What Alfred Eisenstaedt didn't know then is that of
all the thousands of images in his long career, this one
of the sailor and the nurse would be the one he's
known for.

EISENSTAEDT: When I someday go to heaven and I'm not living
anymore, maybe probably everybody will say, "Oh, this
is the photographer who took that picture," and
everybody remembers that picture.

STAMBERG: Photographer Alfred Eisenstaedt just celebrated his
92nd birthday. He lives in New York, still goes into the
Life magazine offices every day and still takes

> photographs, Eisenstaedt moments. U.S. troops
> continue coming back from the Persian Gulf, and it is
> possible one of the homecoming photographs will
> capture the end of Operation Desert Storm, but in this
> age of the moving image, it's unlikely that the picture
> will mean to future generations what V-J Day Times
> Square has come to mean in the past nearly half
> century. In Washington, I'm Susan Stamberg.

Stamberg does not tell her audience until the final paragraph that Eisenstaedt has just celebrated his 92nd birthday and that this is why she is talking about him and his work on this particular day. She decides to grab her audience with a story about a sailor and a nurse. The listeners have no idea why she is telling them the story, but it is bound to get the audience's attention. And the picture Stamberg paints is a colorful one:

> . . . the sailor grabbed the nurse in glee just as he had grabbed all those
> other women, but this was different. The nurse is caught gracefully in the
> sailor's arms. Her body twists a bit in his embrace. They look as if they
> could be dancing. It's the Eisenstaedt moment.

The last sentence of Stamberg's opening introduces Eisenstaedt for the first time, but listeners still do not know who Eisenstaedt is unless they guess he is the famous photographer. Then, Stamberg intrigues listeners some more by letting Eisenstaedt speak for himself. At that point, the audience realizes that the story is about Eisenstaedt the photographer and about a famous picture he took more than 45 years earlier.

Stamberg doesn't fill up her script with a lot of details about the career of the famous photographer. She decides to remind listeners of the man by telling about his most famous picture—one that captured a moment in history at the end of World War II.

The Delayed Lead

Instead of saving the most important information until the end of the story, as in the case of the suspense lead, the *delayed lead* just withholds the most important details for a few sentences.

> The scene in the locker room of the Center City Rockets was quieter than
> usual last night although the team won by three goals. There also was a
> lot less swearing than usual and no nudity. Also new in the locker room
> last night was Heather Tierney.
>
> The sports reporter for the Center City Times is the first woman to be
> allowed in the team's locker room. Club officials broke the female ban
> after Tierney threatened to go to court to win the right to enter the locker
> room after games.

If the delayed lead had not been used, the story probably would have started out this way:

> For the first time, last night a woman reporter was allowed in the locker
> room of the Center City Rockets.

The delayed lead gives writers another option for adding variety to a script, but, like some other leads mentioned earlier, it should not be overused.

Negative Leads

Negative leads, which include the word *not,* should be avoided. A positive lead can easily achieve the same result. There is always the chance someone in the audience might miss the word *not* and reach the wrong conclusion about what is happening. Here are some examples:

> *Avoid:* Striking newspaper workers say they will not return to work.

> *Use:* Striking newspaper workers say they will continue their walkout.

> *Avoid:* The mayor says he will not raise the city sales tax.

> *Use:* The mayor says he will keep the city sales tax at its present rate.

Updating and Reworking the Lead

One of the most effective ways to attract and hold listeners is to convince them that the news is fresh. There will be days when news is plentiful, but on slow days newswriters need certain skills to make the news sound exciting and timely. One skill is the ability to *update* leads, which means finding some- thing new to say in stories used in an earlier newscast. Another is the ability to *rework* the original lead to include new developments. For example, take a story about the arrest of a dozen men on narcotics charges. Police say the men were found in a cocaine "factory" where they were "cutting" more than one hundred million dollars' worth of cocaine.

Here's the first version of the lead:

> Police have arrested a dozen men during a raid on a cocaine factory in Center City. They say the men were cutting more than 100 million dollars' worth of cocaine.

An hour later, the lead might say:

> A dozen men are under arrest after police raided a building in Center City. Police say the men were cutting more than 100 million dollars in cocaine.

Still later, the lead might read:

> Police are guarding an estimated 100 million dollars in cocaine that they scooped up in a raid on a Center City building. A dozen men are behind bars in connection with the raid. Police say the men were cutting the cocaine when the raid took place.

Another possible updated lead might say:

> A dozen men are being held for arraignment on narcotics charges following a raid on a Center City building. Police say they found about 100 million dollars' worth of cocaine in the building. Police say the men were in the process of cutting the cocaine when the officers broke into the building.

As new developments occur in the story, there will be added opportunities to rework the lead. Within a few hours, detectives may reveal details about how they found out about the cocaine factory. They also may give more details about the raid. For example:

> Center City police now say that their raid on a cocaine factory that resulted in the arrest of a dozen men came after two months of surveillance by detectives.

A skilled writer will be able to tell the story many times without making it sound stale.

Constructing the Rest of the Story

Once you have the lead of a story, its foundation, you are ready to construct the rest of the story by building on the lead. The audience has been prepared for what is to come. Now you must provide the details in a clear and logical manner.

In broadcast news, you can use more than just words to accomplish your goal. You can employ sound on radio and use both sound and pictures to help tell the story on television. Those techniques will be examined later. For now, let's just deal with words, returning to the story on General Colin Powell mentioned earlier in the chapter. We'll start with a hard lead:

> The chairman of the Joint Chiefs of Staff, General Colin Powell, says U.S. troops will stay in Iraq for a number of months.

The listeners now know part of the story. It's not much, but it is sufficient to grab interest. A general whom they have come to know over the months is telling them something important: that their sons, daughters, husbands, wives, and other relatives and friends—at least some of them—are not coming home right away. The audience will want to hear the general's explanation:

> General Powell says American forces will stay in Iraq to enforce provisions of a pending U.N. cease-fire agreement. He says the troops would also prevent Iraq from using chemicals and air strikes to defeat rebels trying to overthrow President Saddam Hussein.

Now the audience knows why troops will remain in Iraq. What it does not know yet is how the troops are going to prevent Iraq from using chemical weapons and air attacks against the rebels. The next sentence addresses the question:

> General Powell did not explain how U.S. forces would prevent Iraq from using chemicals and air attacks against the rebels.

Once the general made reference to the chemicals and air attacks, the statement had to be explained to the audience even if the general did not elaborate. Otherwise, the audience might have been asking the question and accusing the newscaster of withholding the information. What next? Because the third sentence mentions the rebels, that aspect of the story could be expanded:

General Powell also said he was surprised by the strength of the revolt against the Saddam regime. He also denied that the U.S. forces are trying to play a role in influencing the outcome of the rebellion.

The general had much more to say to reporters, and newspapers carried the story in greater detail. But the broadcast newswriter, who had eight other stories to cover in a three-minute newscast, told the Powell story in just 20 seconds. The essential details were given; nothing vital was left out. This is key to broadcast newswriting: condense the important material and eliminate the unimportant without distorting the story or the facts.

Summary

Writing broadcast copy is like building a house. This chapter focuses on the foundation—the lead. You now know many different ways to open your story. Some leads may be more appropriate than others, depending on the nature of the story, but remember that there is always more than one way to lead your story.

In the first four chapters, the emphasis has been on the basics of broadcast newswriting. Now that you know how to construct a news story and include all the important details in your story in a logical manner, you are ready to learn about what many believe is the most important aspect of newswriting: color, the subject of Chapter 5.

Review Questions

1. Many writers have problems writing the first sentence of a story. How can they overcome this block?
2. What is the most important part of a news story? Why?
3. Although the five W's and H rule is basically a print journalism concept, it does have application for broadcast journalism. What are the five W's and H, and what is the major difference in the way they apply to print and broadcast journalism?
4. What is the difference between hard and soft leads?
5. How does emotion play a role in determining the lead sentence and how the rest of the story is written?
6. Do quote leads work for broadcast? Explain.
7. What is a shotgun lead?
8. What is a delayed lead?
9. How do you update a lead?

Exercises

1. Using the following information, write both hard and soft leads:

   A tanker registered to the Zabo Oil Company of Panama has run aground. This happened off the coast of Charleston, South Carolina. One half million gallons of oil already have spilled into the Atlantic. It is believed that another half million gallons are still on the ship.

2. Write a quote lead based on the following information:

    A man on welfare, Bill Nelson, found a purse on the street. When he opened it there was $5,000 inside. Nelson counted it a dozen times. After two hours, he went to the police station and turned over the money to the officer at the desk. When questioned about his honesty, Nelson said, "I may be poor but I am honest."

3. Using the information from Exercise 2, write a delayed lead.

4. Write a shotgun lead using the following information:

    Forest fires in Oregon have burned more than 10,000 acres of timberland and the flames are threatening thousands of additional acres. In California, firefighters are battling flames that already have destroyed 15,000 acres of woodland.

5. Use your imagination to figure out ways to update these leads:

    The president is scheduled to leave this afternoon for a vacation in Florida, where he will work on a new budget.

    The hurricane is off the coast of Jacksonville, Florida, and could hit the mainland within the next three hours.

    Striking autoworkers are meeting at this hour to decide whether to accept the auto industry's latest contract offer.

    The countdown has begun at Cape Canaveral for the launching of the space shuttle *Atlantis*.

6. Using any of the types of leads discussed in this chapter, write a story from the following information:

    Lori and Kevin were married today. It was exactly 30 years ago to the day that they met. When they were teenagers the two had dated for about a year after meeting on a blind date in 1963. "I remember the date, of course, because it was my birthday," said Lori Scott. Lori and Kevin Rowce broke up following a fight. They both married and had children and had not seen each other for 29 years. Kevin contacted Lori when he heard from a friend that her husband had died. Kevin had been divorced a number of years ago. They decided to marry after dating for the past year. They were married on New York's Staten Island ferry. "That's what we did on our first date," Kevin said.

5 Color: The Key to Good Writing

The last few chapters stressed that broadcast news writing should be conversational—written the way we would speak with a friend at a restaurant or on a street corner. What makes such conversations memorable? An element known as *color*.

Who are the people who most hold our attention in social conversations? Interesting people, of course; people who can tell a yarn with a flair; people who make us laugh; people who sometimes shock us and on occasion make us cry. They may be people who fascinate us because of the way they use the language or the way they dress or because they just act differently. The people we like to meet are colorful people. They may not know it; that's just the way they are. Their style comes naturally. Color in broadcast copy should be just as natural.

Color Should Be Natural

Color should not be forced or achieved with clichés or hype. Strong verbs, and adjectives used in moderation add color, but they must be selected carefully. Poorly chosen verbs and adjectives can destroy copy. "Colorful" words do not always produce colorful copy.

The people involved in a story, and what they have to say, are likely to add color. Broadcast writing should honestly reflect the feelings and emotions of those people. Sound bites and pictures of the newsmakers themselves often provide the humor, pathos, and other emotions that make the story a success. But using the voices and pictures of colorful people to provide the color for the story is almost a given. The real challenge is bringing color to the script through words, much as a good painter adds the proper strokes to a canvas to bring it to life.

Color is provided by observing and paying close attention to details, and using those details in your copy. Listen to and watch carefully people engaged in conversation. Does John use his hands like an orchestra leader to make his point? Does Mary whisper and look away in embarrassment when she tells her story, as though she's afraid someone will hear her? Is there a hole in the sole of Frank's shoe? Does Ann look directly into Pat's eyes as she speaks? Do Paul's hands shake? These are the things that good writers look and listen for if they hope to let the audience know and understand Paul and Ann and John and Mary.

Ernest Hemingway's name often comes up during a discussion of good newswriting. Hemingway was one of America's best storytellers, and as one of his biographers noted, Hemingway's work as a journalist taught him "certain lessons in verbal economy" that he carried over to his novels. It was Hemingway's short, crisp, uncluttered, journalist-like sentences that marked his career as a novelist—skills he learned as a newspaperman for the *Kansas City Star.*

Here's a sample of Hemingway's writing from "The Old Man and the Sea":

> He was an old man who fished alone in a skiff in the Gulf Stream and he had gone eighty-four days now without taking a fish. In the first forty days a boy had been with him. But after forty days without a fish the boy's parents had told him that the old man was now definitely and finally salao, which is the worst form of unlucky, and the boy had gone at their orders in another boat which caught three good fish the first week.

Consider what Hemingway tells us in only three sentences. We know that the fisherman is old and that he fishes in the Gulf Stream and that he certainly is very unlucky. We also know that he had a young companion in his boat until the boy's parents also reached the conclusion that the old man was unlucky. The old man is now fishing alone.

Hemingway tells us more about the character of the boy in the next sentence:

> It made the boy sad to see the old man come in each day with his skiff empty and he always went down to help him carry either the coiled lines or the gaff and harpoon and the sail that was furled around the mast.

And we quickly learn about the condition of the boat:

> The sail was patched with flour sacks and, furled, it looked like the flag of permanent defeat.

Hemingway's description of the old man is next:

> The old man was thin and gaunt with deep wrinkles in the back of his neck. The brown blotches of the benevolent skin cancer the sun brings from its reflection on the tropic sea were on his cheeks. The blotches ran well down the sides of his face and his hands had the deep-creased scars from handling heavy fish on the cords. But none of these scars were fresh. They were as old as erosions in a fishless desert.

In only two paragraphs we already have a clear picture of this fisherman and his young friend. We can see them together by the sea, the young boy sad with worry about the old man and the fisherman weary and broken by age and bad luck.

Consider Hemingway's detail—the kind of detail mentioned earlier that is so important in the development of colorful copy:

The old man was thin and gaunt with deep wrinkles in the back of his neck.

The brown blotches of the benevolent skin cancer . . .

The blotches ran well down the sides of his face.

. . . his hands had the deep-creased scars . . .

But none of these scars were fresh. They were as old as erosions in a fishless desert.

We know more about this old man in just two paragraphs than most writers could tell us in two pages.

Emulate the Best

A good way to learn how to use color in a story is to look to the masters of the craft. Read E. B. White, James Thurber, and other good essayists and examine closely the words of such distinguished broadcast journalists as the late Charles Kuralt of *CBS News,* and other outstanding broadcast writers such as Bill Moyers, Cokie Roberts, Diane Sawyer, and Susan Stamberg. Examine the writing of the late Pauline Frederick of *NBC News* and the late Edward R. Murrow of *CBS News*—the most distinguished of all broadcast journalists. One of the best ways to practice good techniques is to adopt the styles of successful writers.

Kuralt, a master of colorful writing, suggested that you also look in style manuals and usage guides—"browse through Fowler or Eric Partridge or Bergen Evans from time to time." He wondered how many people keep Otto Jesperson's seven-volume *Modern English Grammar* on a shelf in the bathroom.

CBS News correspondent Charles Osgood, also known for his colorful writing, is "fascinated by the writings of people like John McPhee and Loren Eiseley, both wonderful craftsmen and artisans in their use of the language, who like to deal with subjects that have to do with science." He also says, "You can get a lot out of reading novels simply because we refer to every news story that we do as a story."

Osgood notes that all stories, whether they are novels or news, have to be constructed "according to some kind of logical plan with a beginning, a middle, and an end." He comments that if there has to be development and character and other elements in a novel, writers "should at least pay some homage to it in doing a news story."

Interestingly, both Osgood and Kuralt spoke of rhythm and music when they talked about writing. Osgood says language starts with the ear: "A child learns the language by hearing people speak it. He hears words. He learns to say words long before he learns to read them. There's music in language." Osgood says that, like music, language has rhythm: "There's a shape, form and character to it. It's language, it's music, it's a noise." Kuralt said, "I know that I hear the rhythms of writers I have read and admired in my head. Sometimes," he added, "I can even remember which writer's rhythm I am feeling. I think good writers hear the music of good writing they've read. The great writers compose new music for the rest of us to hear when we sit down to type."

Kuralt also said that good writing "takes patience." He added, "it's worth sitting there until you remember the right word," recalling that Mark Twain once said that "the difference between the right word and the nearly right word is the difference between lightning and a lightning bug."

Kuralt On the Road

Many of Charles Kuralt's colleagues would say that his name should be added to the list of great writers. Kuralt was by everyone's definition a "writer's writer." Many successful network correspondents acknowledge that they have learned from him.

Kuralt's *On the Road* TV series brought joy to millions. In 1975, he did a special series called "On the Road to '76" to mark the upcoming 200th anniversary of the nation's independence. Kuralt did a historical story from each of the 50 states, and one of his stops was Little Bighorn, Montana.

MONTANA
Kuralt-Bleckman-Colby-Quinlan
September 4, 1975
Kuralt on camera SOF

This is about a place where the wind blows, the grass grows, and a river flows below a hill. There is nothing here but the wind and the grass and the river. But of all places in America, this is the saddest place I know.

SOF pull back from
sparkle on river

The Indians called the river the Greasy Grass. The white men called it the Little Bighorn.

Saddle gap in mountains,
pull back to wide
grassy plains

From that gap in the mountains to the east, Brevet Major General George A. Custer's proud 7th Cavalry came riding early in the morning of June 25th, 1876, toward the Little Bighorn.

Looking down at river

Custer sent one battalion, under Major Marcus Reno, across the river to attack what he thought might be a small village of hostile Sioux. His own battalion he galloped behind the ridges to ride down on the village from the rear.

grassy valley

pan down from hill . . .

When at last Custer brought his 231 troops to the top of a hill and looked down toward the river, what he saw was an encampment of 15-thousand Indians stretching for two and a half miles—the largest assembly of Indians the plains had ever known—and a thousand mounted warriors coming straight for him.

. . . to broad plain below
(right after slate in roll
2)
zoom back from river

view of hills . . .

Reno's men, meantime, had been turned, routed, chased across the river, joined by the rest of the regiment,

. . . pull back to Meador's
grave on hill
pan from grass . . .

surrounded, and now were dying, defending a nameless brown hill.

. . . to post with cross on it

In a low protected swale in the middle of their narrowing circle, the one surviving doctor improvised a field red hospital and did what he could for the wounded. The grass covers the place now, and grows in the shallow rifle trenches above which were dug that day by knives and tin cups and fingernails.

shallow rifle trench . . .

. . . and peer over side
Kuralt on camera

Two friends in H Company, Private Charles Windolph and Private Julian Jones, fought up here, side by side, all that day, and that night stayed awake, talking, both of them scared. Charles Windolph said, "The next morning, when the firing commenced, I said to Julian, 'We better get our coats off.' He didn't move. I looked at him. He was shot through the heart."

camera tilts down
to gravestone
view from hilltop

Charles Windolph won the Congressional Medal of Honor up here, survived, lived to be 98—he didn't die until 1950—and never a day passed in all those years that he didn't think of Julian Jones.

wide shot showing
white stones in distance

And Custer's men, four miles away? There are stones in the grass that tell the story of Custer's men.

one you can read

The stones all say the same thing. "U.S. Soldier, 7th Cavalry, fell here, June 25th, 1876."

montage of grass and
and stones first one or
two, then—

The warriors of Sitting Bull under the great Chief Gall struck Custer first and divided his troops. Two Moon and the Northern Cheyenne struck him next. And when he tried to gain a hilltop with the last remnants of his command, Crazy Horse rode over that hill with hundreds of warriors, and right through his battalion. The Indians who were there later agreed on two things—that Custer and his men fought with exceeding bravery, and that after half an hour, not one of them was left alive.

Another bunch of stones,
larger group
Then a big group

Zoom through grass . . .

. . . to stone that has
Custer's name on it.

WS battlefield, stones in
distance

The Army came back that winter. Of course, the Army came back—and broke the Sioux and the Cheyenne,

	and forced them back to the starvation of the reservations, and in time murdered more old warriors and women and children on the Pine Ridge
More grass and stones	Reservation than Custer lost in battle here.
Kuralt on camera	That is why this is the saddest place. For Custer and the 7th Cavalry, courage only led to defeat. For Crazy Horse and the Sioux, victory only led to Wounded Knee.
Saddest shot of battlefield, maybe backlit stone with grass	Come here sometime, and you will see. There is melancholy in the wind, and sorrow in the grass. And the river weeps.
Maybe one last zoom to river.	Charles Kuralt, *CBS News*, on the road to '76 in Montana.

Kuralt once commented that the Little Bighorn story was a challenge: "There was really nobody to interview there. There's nothing there but grass, water, and gravestones, but I wanted to do a story anyway. We were not in a hurry to do this one; we had a whole day to walk around the battlefield and think. We didn't shoot anything."

Figure 5-1
CBS News correspondent Charles Kuralt and his camera crew work on one of his *On the Road* reports. (Courtesy of *CBS News*)

Kuralt said he had been reading about the battle and had several books about the Little Bighorn battlefield. After the daylong tour of the battlefield, he said, "I went back to the bus and wrote the story, and afterwards we went out and shot it." Kuralt admitted, "We broke my rule and reversed the order, but I was writing to pictures I knew we were going to shoot." Kuralt said it was one of the few times that he worked "almost like a movie script writer."

Kuralt said that when the story went on the air, "it was beautiful . . . all mood, all writing and some beautiful photography." He added, "You can fill the story with words and not do any interviews at all if you have a good story to tell and a skillful photographer at work."

Kuralt stressed how important it is to write to the picture. "Write something that will add to the experience of the viewer in seeing the picture," he said, "but when you can, have the courage to remain silent and let the picture tell the story. Give people time to feel something."

There is another Kuralt script in Chapter 14, "Putting the Television Story Together," in which he discussed the importance of pictures.

"A Postcard from Nebraska"

Colorful writing and good pictures make good TV news. *CBS News* special correspondent Roger Welsch's success in marrying the two elements has made him a frequent contributor to the *Sunday Morning* program. Here is the script of one Welsch story, with Kuralt's introduction:

Kuralt O/C	To prepare us for Thanksgiving, the great harvest festival we celebrate this Thursday, Roger Welsch has sent us another postcard from Nebraska. This one is reverent. Between the lines you can hear Roger giving thanks.
V/C Video of corn fields	(Welsch) It won't be long before these fields are empty. The corn picked, the squash tucked away in the cellar. Well, we managed to get some sweet corn into the freezer. It'll be a long time before we taste the sweetness of corn dripping with butter right off the
Video of melons and Placke's Market	cob. As for the melons, there's no saving them. They're here . . . and then they're gone. But it wasn't long ago back in Dannebrog, when Dan or Eric, maybe it was Harriet, said, "Hey, Roger, Placke's has sweet corn and melons for sale, let's go." It doesn't take me long to respond to an

	invitation like that. It's a special time of the year. An ephemeral moment that has to be grasped right now before it's gone and the fields are empty and cold.
Video of people at Placke's	(SOT Unidentified Person) "That ought to do it."
Video of highway and produce places	V/O Highway 281 near Saint Libory is peppered with produce stands. Some little more than rustic sheds, some fairly fancy–markets where local farmers sell their squash, tomatoes, peppers, onions, and sweet corn. This is my idea of a supermarket.
Video of people at market	There's no question that the merchandise here is fresh. It was picked this morning from fields within
Video of produce picking	walking distance of where we're standing right now.
SOT	(SOT Unidentified person) "Those have got a high sound to them. You've got to have a low sound."
V/O Market footage	V/O Personal service? Well, the family that's selling me my groceries this morning picked it and planted it, watered it and weeded it. In every sense of the word this watermelon is the Plackes' watermelon, until I pay for it. Then in every sense, it's mine.
Video of watermelons and watermelon eating	(SOT Unidentified person) "You guys going to eat that?"
V/O	V/O And taste? Nothing beats the taste of melon straight out of the field.
SOT	(SOT Unidentified person) "That's good, waited all summer for that."

V/O Video of Welsch at market	V/O Spaghetti squash?
SOT	(SOT Unidentified person) "Yes, they're very good."
V/O Video of market	V/O Well, I'm going to try some of those.
SOT	(SOT Unidentified person) "OK."
V/O	Sure, part of the attraction of buying produce like this is the price. It's not expensive and the Plackes usually consider 13 ears of corn a dozen and round off the total of your bill from $9.37 to $9 even. I don't know what I'm going to do with these red peppers, but they're too pretty to pass up.
SOT	(SOT Salesperson) "OK . . . a dollar, 78, 40."
V/O Video of people picking produce	V/O But, do you know what I think makes this food taste especially good? Handing over my money to the very folks who grew the sweet corn and who picked the watermelon and know the peppers by name. Sure the food is cheaper. But frankly I'd pay more knowing that the money goes to the farmers. And, of course, it's better tasting, but I attribute part of that to the fact that the folks who sell it to me want it to taste better.
Welsch O/C at market	O/C They have to look me in the eye when they sell it to me and when I come back the next week and next year. I've been buying produce at the Placke stand now for 15 years. One of the Plackes' nephews was a classmate of mine at the University of Nebraska 10 or 20 years ago or so. Thanks a lot, Marilyn. I appreciate it.

SOT	(SOT Unidentified person) "Yeah."
V/O Video at market	V/O These folks are not just businessmen, they're friends and neighbors. There are a lot of reasons to complain about the weather out here on the plains. Sometimes it seems as if complaining is our favorite of all season sports. But when the heat of summer is gone and before the winter's blizzards sweep across these fields . . . at that short and lovely moment when the sweet coolness of autumn is evident, it's then that the Saint Libory produce stands remind us how good things out here can be. How rich and how full and how tasty.

Welsch's story relies heavily on words as well as pictures. Welsch had only a few short sound bites to punctuate the narration, which meant the narration had to be longer, particularly because the stories on *Sunday Morning* usually run at least twice as long as the two-minute stories on most other news programs.

The story succeeds only because the script is so well written. Normally, without interviews it is difficult to sustain so much copy. But the combination of excellent pictures and colorful words allowed this story to run as long as it did. In the hands of a less talented writer, the story most certainly would have been shorter.

Crisp and Clear

Welsch's writing style is crisp and clear. He picks short sentences and phrases and makes each word work for him. His sentences are conversational and often incomplete.

> It won't be long before these fields are empty. The corn picked, the squash tucked away in the cellar.

The squash could have been stored in the cellar, but tucked away is so much more colorful.

The first section of this chapter discussed the importance of using your senses in writing broadcast copy. Welsch uses his senses well:

> It'll be a long time before we taste the sweetness of corn dripping with butter right off the cob.

Welsch also involves the audience. He brings the viewers into the story with lines such as:

I don't know what I'm going to do with these red peppers, but they're too pretty to pass up.

Most of us have said the same thing at one time or another as we shopped and spotted food that we just could not resist buying. We identify with Welsch's feelings, and that makes his writing effective.

He involves the audience again later in the script:

But, do you know what I think makes this food taste especially good? Handing over my money to the very folks who grew the sweet corn and who picked the watermelon and know the peppers by name.

Welsch speaks *with* us, not *to* us. It's *conversation,* not *narration.* His script effectively mixes strong and tender thoughts:

But when the heat of summer is gone and before the winter's blizzards sweep across these fields . . . at that short and lovely moment when the sweet coolness of autumn is evident, it's then that the Saint Libory produce stands remind us of how good things out here can be.

And then he reinforces the thought with the final line of the script:

How rich and how full and how tasty.

If you spot some similarity between the writing styles of Roger Welsch and Charles Kuralt, you may see why so many Welsch stories wound up on *Sunday Morning.*

Use Your Senses

The novelist William Burroughs once observed that if a writer "can't see it, hear it, feel it, and smell it he can't write it." You will not be able to use all of your senses every time you sit down at a typewriter or computer. But on most occasions, you should be able to draw on the two senses most useful to a journalist—seeing and hearing.

Here's an excellent example of how a writer used those senses, a script written by *NBC News* Correspondent Bob Dotson about a cave rescue in Carlsbad, New Mexico. The actual script is produced in its entirety because it shows an unusual technique employed by Dotson. In the left-hand column, among the video notes, Dotson tells in great detail what he is seeing and hearing.

SLUG	SHOW	WRITER	DATE	TIMING	LC
Cave	= NN/DD =	dotson	Thu May 16	HOLD	2:11 260
Rescue =			10:48 1991		

```
"NN CAVE" 4/4/91
W/BOB DOTSON
CARLSBAD, NEW MEXICO
SPOT RUNS: 2:31
SUPERS: BOB DOTSON
CARLSBAD, NEW MEXICO
(_:_–_:_)
[LEAD INFORMATION]
```

Imagine slithering through a block of swiss cheese a mile and a half long. Climbing up a thousand foot maze dragging a broken leg. That's what it was like for Emily Mobley. She clawed her way beneath the earth for 4 days, after an 80 pound boulder slipped and crushed her in a cave. It took 60 people to rescue her. Emily's ordeal ended at 3:15 EDT this morning.

ANCIENT INVASIONS OF ICE HAVE CREATED AN ENORMOUS UNDERGROUND CATHEDRAL. ONE LONE CLIMBER—HIGH ABOVE— CLINGS TO ITS SPIRE. THE LIGHT FROM HIS HELMET LAMP DABS THE CAVERN WITH COLOR.

NAT SOT: (RESCUER)
"IS THE WHOLE TEAM READY?"

OTHER RESCUERS APPEAR IN THE BEAM OF LIGHT. THERE IS A SQUEAKING OF PULLIES AND ROPES. RESCUER IS RAPPELLING DOWN.

V/O
Shadows chase shadows. Now and then a whisper of sliding rope.

ONE RESCUER SLITHERS IN AND OUT, MOMENTARILY LOSES CONTROL. TUMBLES, BUT RIGHTS HIMSELF.

NATSOT: (RESCUER)
"OKAY, EASY, EASY!"

A THIN LINE OF RESCUERS, CARRYING EMILY, HUFF THEIR WAY THROUGH A TIGHT OPENING, THEN PICK CAUTIOUSLY ALONG LOOSE GRAVEL.

V/O
The anxious, uneven breathing
of 60 people lugging one of their
own.

MOBLEY IS LASHED TO A
MAKESHIFT STRETCHER.
ONLY THE RESCUERS'
WITS AND A LENGTH OF
ROPE KEEP HER FROM
PLUNGING INTO ETERNAL
FREE FALL.

NATSOT: (RESCUER)
"I GOT IT!"

V/O
Emily Mobley was at the bottom of
the deepest cave this country has
ever seen. In a cavern so big there
are explorers at the opposite end that
don't even know the 4-day rescue
took place.

A RESCUER SQUINTS ACROSS
THE BLANK STONE, TRYING
TO SEE THE CRACKS HE
HAD MEMORIZED THE
NIGHT BEFORE, THEN
COMMENCES AGAIN THE
STEADY ROUTINE OF THE
CLIMB.

NATSOT: (RESCUER)
"MUCH BETTER! MUCH
BETTER!"
V/O
The darkness would have been total
without her friends.

NATSOT: (RESCUER)
"LOOKING GOOD!" "MOVE A
LITTLE FASTER." "KEEP HER
COMING!"

RESCUERS MUST BE MORE
THAN BRAVE. THEY MUST BE
METICULOUS AND ABOVE ALL
ORDERLY. EACH STEP MUST
BE THE SAME. EXACTLY THE
SAME. AGAIN AND AGAIN.

	V/O They tugged her to the top an inch at a time. One-and-a-half miles.
	NATSOT: (RESCUER) "KEEP ON MOVING."
EMILY IS BREATHING OUT THE PAIN.	
	(MOBLEY) "YEAH, I'M FINE. JUST KEEP MOVING ME."
THE RESCUERS LIE ON THEIR BACKS AND PASS THE STRETCHER OVER THEIR HEADS.	
	V/O In places they cushioned her weight with their own bodies. And always kept a light for her to see above.
	NATSOT: (RESCUER) "REAL SLOW AND EASY GUYS."
EMILY'S SMILE SHOWS THROUGH THE DUST AND GRIME ON HER FACE	
	V/O Emily showed her appreciation with a grin . . . lit from inside.
	SOT: (MOBLEY) "UM, IF I HAVE TO BREAK MY LEG, I CAN'T THINK OF BETTER PEOPLE I'D RATHER BE AROUND."
SHE IS HOOKED TO ROPES THAT WILL LIFT HER INTO DARKNESS. SHE SPINS UP AND AWAY.	
	NATSOT: (RESCUER) "ON THREE . . . ONE, TWO . . ." NATSOT: [THE CLANKING AND HUFFING BELOW CONTINUES UNDER DOTSON's STANDUP]
CUT TO DOTSON ON CAMERA WITH RESCUE TEAM NEAR MOUTH OF CAVE. SUPER: BOB DOTSON CARLSBAD, NEW MEXICO	

[Standup] The ordeal below did not build character, but it revealed it. What matters down there are energy, muscle and will. Qualities her friends had in abundance. Otherwise she would not have survived.

TEAM STRUGGLES FOR FOOTING AT THE BOTTOM OF A TALL STACK OF LOOSE ROCKS.

NATSOT: (RESCUER)
"OKAY, WE CAN CARRY HER ON OUT."

EMILY'S WORDS ARE BRAVER THAN SHE LOOKS.

SOT: (MOBLEY)
"AS LONG AS I DON'T STEP ON MY LEG, I'M FINE."

THEY FACE THIS LAST CHALLENGE WITH HOPE AND A CERTAIN HORROR. RISK IS AS MUCH A CLIMBER'S TOOL AS A ROPE.

V/O
They are all expert climbers. So is Emily. She was mapping this new cave when a loose rock started this test of friendship.

NATSOT: (RESCUER)
"ALL RIGHT. . . ."

EACH CLIMBER STEADIES THE NEXT. HAND HOLDING HAND, THEY LIFT EMILY OUT OF THE DARKNESS.

V/O
Pals came from all around the country. A cry of need seems to carry further in darkness. Or perhaps we listen closer.

THEY SCRABBLE UP, HUNGRY NOW TO REACH THE TOP.

NATSOT: (RESCUER)
"HOLD ON!"

THE COMMONPLACE HORIZONTAL WORLD OF

MORTGAGES, GIRLFRIENDS
AND FAMILY SEEM FAR
AWAY. THEY HAVE FORGED
AN INTENSE RELATIONSHIP
WITH EACH OTHER AND THE
ROCK.

NATSOT: (EMILY)
"AM I EXCITED! YOU BET I AM!"

AT LAST! THEY ARE OUT.
UNDER A FULL MOON, HUGS,
HANDSHAKES, CONQUEST!

V/O
Finally, the light above did not need
batteries.

NATSOT: (RESCUER)
"CHEERS FOR EVERY BODY!"
NATSOT: (CROWD WHISTLES
AND APPLAUSE)
Emily's friends felt as old as thick
mud. Nearly 100 hours in that pewter
world.

RESCUER ON CAMERA
TURNS AND SPEAKS FOR
ALL WHO LABORED SO
LONG.

SOT: (RESCUER)
"WE'RE REAL PLEASED TO GET
HER OUT ALIVE. AND GET HER
OUT IN ONE PIECE. IT WAS REAL
SPECIAL TO ALL OF US."

EMILY'S FRIENDS GENTLY
SLIDE HER INTO A
WAITING AMBULANCE. SHE
GIVES THEM A THUMBS UP
THROUGH THE WINDOW AS
IT DRIVES OFF INTO THE
NIGHT.

Deep within themselves they had
discovered the people they wanted to
be. Bob Dotson, *NBC News*, Carlsbad,
New Mexico.

If you go back to the Welsch script, you will note that there is limited information in the video column. The Dotson notes, in contrast, are so literary,

Figure 5-2 *NBC News* correspondent Bob Dotson. (Courtesy of *NBC News*)

and include such detail, that they could have easily provided a second script for the story.

Dotson's broadcast script is lean by comparison with the notes. You may find yourself wondering why Dotson did not use more of the well-written notes in the actual script. One very important reason is time. The story that was broadcast ran 2 minutes and 11 seconds. Dotson did not really have the option of adding more narration because of the time constraints placed on him by his producers. And second, although Dotson is a splendid writer, he is primarily a "picture person." He selects his pictures first and then writes his script to the pictures. Some reporters believe that the script should be written first and then the pictures selected to support the words. That long-standing debate will be discussed later in detail, in the reporting section. For now, let's examine Dotson's writing style.

Dotson gives his script a lean, almost poetic quality. He captures emotion and color by selecting his words carefully:

Shadows chase shadows. Now and then a whisper of a sliding rope. . . .

The anxious, uneven breathing of 60 people lugging one of their own. . . .

The darkness would have been total without her friends. . . .

In places they cushioned her weight with their own bodies. . . .

Emily showed her appreciation with a grin . . . lit from inside. . . .

Pals came from all around the country. A cry of need seems to carry further in
   darkness. Or perhaps we listen closer.

Dotson's words—like Emily's rescuers—are strong, caring, and proficient. Both got the job done.

Now examine the words that did not get into the script. They tell us that their author, although a "picture person," has mastered the skill and art of good writing:

Ancient invasions of ice have created an enormous underground cathedral.
   One lone climber—high above—clings to its spire. The light from his helmet
   lamp dabs the cavern with color. . . .

Only the rescuers' wits and a length of rope keep her from plunging into eternal free fall.

A rescuer squints across the blank stone, trying to see the cracks he had memorized the night before, then commences again the steady routine of the climb. . . .

They face this last challenge with hope and a certain horror. Risk is as much a climber's tool as a rope.

Remember that these words are not written for a broadcast audience but for Dotson's and the editor's reference. He and his co-workers are the only people who will read the video notes. We will examine Dotson's work in more detail in Chapter 14.

Color Comes in Many Shades

You have read some examples of outstanding, colorful writing by top broadcast journalists. All of the scripts display an element of entertainment, humor, and enlightenment. They may have brought a smile to your face and, perhaps, even a tear or two. But color comes in many shades; it is not just humorous or entertaining.

Color can be expressed in writing about dramatic or frightening situations:

> The man held his gun to the side of the woman's head and you could see that both of them were scared. Her eyes were bulging. So were the veins on her neck as she looked down at the grey steel barrel moving down to the side of her neck. The gunman's hand shook nervously and menacingly.

Color can appear in the middle of a report on a congressional debate:

> The senator's face was beginning to turn red. His fists were tight and you could see he was about to give in to the anger that was swelling within him. I don't think I have ever seen the senator from Oregon as angry as he was at that moment.

Color can be used to describe an FCC hearing:

> Neither side was happy about the decision. The networks warned they could go broke and the Hollywood producers said the decision could mean the public would see fewer creative programs. Someone said it was a battle between the rich and the wealthy.

In discussing color in broadcast copy, *NBC News* correspondent Roger O'Neil says, "If I am successful it's because I take a great deal of pride in telling a story rather than giving people facts and figures, most of which no one remembers anyhow. It seems to me," he continues, "the great failing of local reporters that I watch across the country is that they are not good storytellers."

For a story to be successful, O'Neil says, an audience "must be provoked" by the story or "moved by it, or be happy or sad about it." He adds that he is talking about a human interest story, not a news story from the White House.

Colorful Obituaries

Just about any event or situation that is worth news coverage has potential for colorful writing—writing that influences and affects an audience in a dozen different ways. This is true even of obituaries. Former *CBS News* correspondent Richard Threlkeld has written many obituaries over the years. Here is an example that displays his special talents.

V/O	Threlkeld
Montage of Dr. Seuss characters	Dr. Seuss wasn't a real Seuss doctor, but he was at least as instrumental in the upbringing of a couple of generations of kids as Dr. Spock.
Clips from various Seuss videos	And not just American kids. Everywhere, in 18 languages, they know about ziffs and zuffs and nerkles and nerds.
Seuss video clips and kids reading books	They called his books "children's books," but the children knew better. "Children like my books," said Dr. Seuss, "because I treat them as equals."
SOT of kids reading books and commenting on them. Video of Cat in Hat	(SOT . . . kids) V/O And the books are about grownup things, after all. About taking responsibility.
PIX of Cat in Hat book	"I know it is wet and the sun is not sunny, but we can have lots of good fun that is funny."
PIX of Horton Hatches the Egg	About loyalty. "I meant what I said and I said what I meant. An elephant's faithful, one hundred percent."
Seuss movie	About prejudice.
SOT	(SOT) "Ronald, remember when you are out walking, you walk past a sneetch of that type without talking."
V/O Seuss video	V/O So, Dr. Seuss wasn't all stuff and nonsense, even though creatures in his world were pretty weird and called each other funny names. When you grew up, you were always

amazed at how many people in
the real world reminded you of
somebody you met in Dr. Seuss.
Somebody asked him once, who was
his favorite?

SOT T. S. Geisel

(SOT)
"I think the Grinch, maybe."

SOT Grinch video

"I'll be coming back someday."

V/O Grinch movie

V/O
The Grinch has been coming back
to our living rooms every holiday
season for 25 years now, trying and
failing to steal Christmas.

SOT END of Grinch Xmas
movie, sad kids in window
and cat walks by

(SOT)
Dr. Seuss never had any children
of his own. But he is survived by
millions of children, past and present,
all over the world. Richard Threlkeld,
CBS News, New York.

Threlkeld says that he tried, in his obituaries, to capture the "essence" of the
particular person. He says that because of time limits in broadcasting, "You
aren't able to include all the nuances as you would in a newspaper obit. But,"
he adds, "the advantage in broadcasting is that the nuances, quite often, come
in the pictures and sound."

For the Dr. Seuss (T. S. Geisel) obit, Threlkeld said, "I got every piece of
information in print that I could find and culled through it looking for
particular things that would lead me to the essence of the person and his
work." Threlkeld said that he was fortunate to have the Dr. Seuss TV special
that is broadcast every Christmas, and he bought all the Dr. Seuss books
available.

Threlkeld said that he had the advantage of living through two genera-
tions of Dr. Seuss—as a child himself and as a parent reading the stories to
his children. "As I looked at all the visual material," he said, "I thought of the
things that affected me when I was a kid. I realize now, of course, that Dr.
Seuss was not only entertaining but also teaching children things. I asked
myself what was he trying to teach and, in the case of Horton the Elephant—
'an elephant's faithful one hundred percent'—he was teaching loyalty to children." Threlkeld said that in the Dr. Seuss books he was able to find three or
four examples to demonstrate "these principles of good, decent living that
[Dr. Seuss] was trying to teach."

Threlkeld said that it was not easy finding sound bites because Geisel was
something of a recluse. But he was able to find one bite that worked. As for
the readings from Dr. Seuss' books, Threlkeld said he decided he was the
right one to read them because he had "read them out loud" to his children.
"I tried to let the viewer look at the life's work of this man," he said, "that's
what you do in an obituary."

Figure 5-3
Former *CBS News* correspondent
Richard Threlkeld prepares to do a
report. (Courtesy of *CBS News*)

Dr. Seuss was special—and an inspiration—to another *CBS News* correspondent, Charles Osgood, who likes to use rhyme in many of the stories he writes for the *Osgood File* on CBS Radio. The title of Osgood's first book is *Nothing Could Be Finer Than a Crisis That Is Finer in the Morning,* and he dedicated the book to Dr. Seuss, who, he said, "gave me a new way to look at the *neuss.*" Dr. Seuss sent Osgood a note in reply saying, "Nothing could be finer than to be an Osgood inspiriner."

In his script about Dr. Seuss' death, Osgood used his marvelous flair for rhyme to express some "personal thoughts about inspiration . . . and immortality."

And now the news . . . what can I say? My inspiriner passed away?
That he just died and went to heaven . . . at the age of 87?
I do not like that . . . sad I am
For in his books . . . Green Eggs and Ham . . .
The Cat, the Grinch, and Lorax too . . .
There's something that keeps coming through.
It's there, if anybody looks
In 47 of his books.
The ones that kids enjoy so much . . .
His play with words, his special touch.
And yet in just that way he told
Of war and peace . . . and growing old . . .
From the sublime to the absurd . . .
He always picked the perfect word.
And if no perfect words were known . . .
He made up new ones of his own.
You read his stuff . . . I'm sure you did
And as you read it to your kid
You smiled because you really knew
That it was also meant . . . for you.
Your kids will read those books again

As grown-up women . . . grown-up men.
And their kids also will enjoy . . .
Reading to THEIR girl and boy.
Although it's true the MAN is gone . . .
His genius will go on and on.
A spark that was much more than clever
Dr. Seuss will live forever.
So tell the kids they shouldn't cry.
Inspiriners never die.

Osgood says that one of the nice things about radio is "you don't have the problem of fighting pictures, because there you're creating a picture from the very beginning." He adds, "I think radio is a superior visual medium because the picture is not literal."

Osgood recalls that when the late Rod Serling made the move from radio to television he wrote a line for a drama that said, "'Once there was a castle on a hill' and he was asked 'What kind of a castle do you want? Do you want ramparts? Is this a medieval castle? What kind of castle is it?' Serling answered, 'I don't know. Let each person build his own castle.'"

Osgood says, "That's what you do in radio. The listener fills in. But you have to help him, you have to give him enough information so that he can build his castle. You give him materials to build with."

Frederick, Ellerbee, and Aaron

No discussion of good writing would be complete without examining the writing of one of the nation's best journalists, the late Pauline Frederick, who was the United Nations correspondent for *NBC News* for many years. Following is the script of a broadcast from December 5, 1963, two weeks after the assassination of President Kennedy.

FREDERICK: This is Pauline Frederick, *NBC News*, New York, with United Nations. The rifle shots that were heard around the world, reverberated through the halls of the United Nations.

Then came a time to weep, a time to mourn and a time to be silent. Slowly the tempo of living resumed—the carrying out of assigned duties— the pleading for and against causes—the passing and defeating of resolutions.

Even though it could be assumed that all was the same, it was not. An accustomed underpinning was gone, a certainty that permitted assault on the accepted, a questioning of the unquestioned. There is a new subdued quality about business here.

One important Western Delegate says that Africans who were once talking freely about drastic measures have lost their fire. They seem frightened, not because they fear the tangible but because suddenly where there was the known there is the unknown. As when a father drops the hand of his child in the dark. This feeling has been particularly evident in the Security Council.

The Africans had demanded an urgent meeting of the Council to take new steps to force South Africa to free all of its people or be read out of the community of nations. The Council was called for Monday morning, November 25.

Instead, this became a time to be silent.

When the Council did convene a week ago, President Sir Patrick Dean gave voice to the sudden realization of members of a change that affected them all, afflicted them with a sense of uncertainty because there was change. Sir Patrick said: "Inevitably, and rightly, the United States assumes a large share of our total responsibility under the Charter of the United Nations for the continuing peace of the world. President Kennedy was second to none in his recognition of that fact and in the steadfast support he gave, in word and deed, to the purposes of the United States and to the authority of the Council."

After all the urgency for Council action, only two visiting African foreign ministers were ready to speak. After their words, the Council adjourned until Friday.

The debate since then has repeated most of the words that have been said many times on the subject—there have even been suggestions that South Africa should be deprived of its privileges in the General Assembly. But they were spoken with less zeal than has marked the African demands heretofore. And when Norway's Sievert Nielsen proposed a compromise to bridge the demands of the Africans for sanctions and the more moderate views of the western industrial powers, he succeeded in gaining African support.

The resolution would deny materials for arms-making to South Africa, and the Secretary-General is asked to set up a group of experts to work with South Africa in peacefully according human rights to all of its people.

Not that the Africans have given up thoughts of extreme pressure against South Africa eventually, if necessary.

But the moment appears to be a time to heal.

This is Pauline Frederick, *NBC News*, United Nations.

Frederick began her career with ABC, where she became the first woman correspondent with the networks. She went on to spend 22 years with NBC. She retired at 65. She continued to work for National Public Radio and was the first woman to moderate a presidential debate. She died in 1990.

Another respected woman journalist is Linda Ellerbee, who also spent many years with NBC before moving to ABC. Here is one of her stories, written for *NBC News Overnight*:

Doing something just because you really want to do it can make trouble. Especially if you're about the only one who does it. Consider the case of Roy Warren and Elizabeth Sargeant of Massachusetts.

They got married on June 12. Mr. Warren has six brothers. Miss Sargeant has none. For that reason, Roy Warren took her surname and became Roy Sargeant. The priest, said Mr. Sargeant, freaked out. The Department of Motor Vehicles told the ex-Marine it was illegal to change his name on his license. It wasn't. The Social Security office considered the name change for three days.

Figure 5-4   The late NBC correspondent Pauline Frederick files her report from the United Nations. (Sophia Smith Collection, Smith College)

> Mr. Sargeant is still carrying his marriage certificate to prove he is not Mr. Warren. Perhaps we ought to be more easy about something that is really a simple thing, but we're not.
>
> On the other hand, we may take pride in being somewhat more advanced in our notion of equality than the Irish government. The European Economic Community, or Common Market, pointed out to the Irish government that it had not yet implemented the agreed sex-equality legislation. The Dublin government immediately advertised for an equal-pay enforcement officer to correct the situation. The advertisement offered different salary scales for men and women. And so it goes.

Another woman who managed to break through the "women need not apply" attitude at the networks in the 1940s and 1950s was Betsy Aaron. She had too much talent to be ignored. Before moving to CBS, Aaron worked for ABC. Here's one of her reports from Lebanon:

Marines in Lebanon
9/14/83
Aaron/Irving
NATL SOT: POEM

> What Lebanon Means To Me: I lay on the ground with my face in the dirt and wonder what I'm doing here. The bullets go by, the mortars explode, the rockets scream in my ear.

V/O

> Corporal Thom Stephenson. Hometown Cherry Hill, New Jersey. In Beirut since May . . . and now much older than his 23 years.

NATL SOT: STEPHENSON	How has this changed you? I think about what's going on in the world now.
V/O	The Americans occupy three positions protecting Beirut's airport. Alpha . . . hugging the runway . . . the company with four men killed in action. Bravo . . . overlooking the airport. The company taking the most shelling. And Charley . . . way out at the end of the runway. The company closest to the Lebanese Army troops. The company hit with the heaviest artillery.
SOT: POEM	I wait for a minute and I run for my hole and dive for the comfort inside. Sand in my tee shirt, sand in my socks, and the temperature's at least 105.
V/O	He's not kidding. It's just plain hot here . . . all the time. Hot and dirty.
SOT: SGT FOSTER HILL	Most everybody is used to the luxuries of home and it's hard when it's taken away from you.
V/O	Just over a week ago it rained shrapnel all over Charley Company . . . for most of a day and a night. There's only one way to handle shrapnel.
SOT: SGT HILL	We got an old saying here in the first platoon. If you want to hide behind the wall you must dig behind the wall.
V/O	So that's what they do . . .
SOT: LT ARTHUR HARRIS	The deeper the better. And we're trying to make it a little more comfortable in our bunkers because it looks like we'll be there for a while.
V/O	And when they're not digging, they're filling sandbags . . . more bags than they'd ever dreamed they'd fill. Walls of sandbags lining bunkers dug deeper since the Marines began taking casualties.

NATL SOUND SEQUENCE
WITH GUNFIRE =
OBSERVERS IN BUNKERS
ON BINOCULARS AT MAP
... ON PHONE
V/O

    It's a front row orchestra seat to a show where the plot unfolds daily.

CONTINUE NAT SOT:
V/O

    The Marines call them men. They are very young men.

SOT: POEM

    As I sit here melting, sweating away, I'll remember her voice on the phone ... She said keep your head low, don't be a hero, we all want you home in one piece.

NAT SOT: PROMOTION
CEREMONY
V/O

    A month ago all 165 men in Charley Company would have turned out for this promotion ceremony. But it's dusk now, and the fighting in the mountains is picking up. It always does ... in the evening.

CONTINUE CEREMONY
V/O

    There is a tradition in a Corps long on tradition. For officers above the rank of those promoted to pin the stripes on ... so they'll stick.

CONTINUE SLAPPING
SEQUENCE
V/O
ATL SOT:
V/O

    And at sunset ...
    Lowering of the colors.
So far just another day in Lebanon ... a place where Marines are glad to get eggs and pancakes for dinner ... when it's the first hot meal they've had in 9 days.

NAT SOT: W/ SOT HILL

    Oh goody—give me the one with the big bug.

V/O

    Meals and mail-pretty big items in a Marine's day. Time to try and forget the fighting. But then there is news of shelling at company headquarters. There are casualties ... but no details.

SOT: SGT HILL

    We haven't done anything to hurt anybody. We just trying to keep the peace and somebody just wants to hurt us and provoke us into violence against whoever is doing this to us. EDIT What's going through your

V/O

SOT: TAPE 5 5:00

SOT: TAPE 5 4:30

V/O

NATL SOT GUNFIRE IN
DARK
V/O
NAT SCENES OF UP AND
AT 'EM. END SEQUENCE
WITH NAIL SOT:
V/O

NATL SOT:
SOT: POEM

STANDUP

mind? Just praying we get through
the night.

Charley Company is now
operating under Condition One. No
lights . . . everyone under cover. The
men in headquarters sit in the dark
and talk.

I wanted to see what it would be
like in a hostile environment. This
was the most hostile you can get.

There was so much incoming and
they dropped boom, boom, boom. All
you could see of the three of us was
the tops of our boots. I just dove for
my life.

And finally with the Druze and
the Lebanese Army still going at each
other . . . Charley Company goes to
sleep.

Reveille is 4:30 a.m. An ungodly
hour to get up save for one thing: It
is clear . . . and cool.

First shot of the morning."
The monotony of the routine can get
to you . . .
a little breakfast . . .
a little work . . .
write a letter . . .
chase your dog . . .
blow off steam.
There is no more jogging . . .
no more basketball.
listening post . . . gunfire.

I can't help but wonder why these
people fight. I guess diplomacy isn't
their style. Bombs and grenades,
death and destruction. We'll keep our
heads low for awhile.

Despite the casualties . . . despite
the sitting duck conditions, despite the
debate in Washington . . . the Marines
who are here say they should be here
and they're convinced that, no matter
how bad things get here, they'd be
worse without the Marines. Now the
Marines are supposed to say that.
But they say it as if they really
believe it.

NATL SOT: PVT MICHAEL MCCARTY	". . . we have a job to do."
V/O	And yet both enlisted men and officers freely talk about the problems of this peacekeeping mission, especially the problem of staying on the defense when you're being attacked.
CAPT CHRIS COWDREY CHARLEY COMPANY COMMANDER	We are not out here banging away at the drum and trying to start something up, or trying to take lives unnecessarily. We are here really taking more licks than we really deserve, or are justified in receiving.
SOT: MCCARTY	If they would let us get out and fight and move around or if they would take us out of here. The choice doesn't really matter. But it's just a fact sitting here in this particular area it's like we're trapped down.
SOT TO STEPHENSON	Should you and the Marines be in Lebanon? I don't know . . . that's a tough one I think about all the time.
V/O	Betsy Aaron for Nightline with Charley Company in Beirut.

Aaron said the package was designed to accomplish several goals: to show the American people what it was like in Lebanon for Marines and to reveal that the Marines didn't understand why they were there and what they were supposed to accomplish. "They had a little boy attitude," she said, "they thought that they were there to do some good." Aaron said that some of the Marines in her story were later seriously wounded in the bomb attack on the barracks that killed 220 Marines.

"We were the first reporting team to spend the night with the Marines," she said, "and we wanted to know how they felt because we were convinced it was an ill-fated mission. You could look at the mountains and the sea that surrounded them," Aaron said, "and you knew they were sitting ducks. That was important for Americans to see, to let them know what we had stepped into."

Aaron said that wasn't the first war she covered. She reported on the Six Day War in the Middle East and the war on Cyprus between the Greeks and Turks, which she said was the worst "slaughter" she had ever covered.

Murrow and His "Boys"

You have read scripts written by some of America's top broadcast journal-ists—communicators effectively using language in a colorful, eloquent,

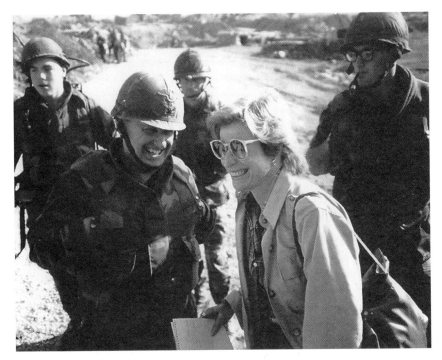

Figure 5-5 Former *CBS News* correspondent Betsy Aaron reporting from Lebanon while she was still with ABC.

and sometimes classic manner. The best of these men and women point to one individual who set the standard on a rooftop in London more than 50 years ago.

Shortly before World War II, the head of CBS, William S. Paley, decided that he wanted the nation's top broadcast news operation. Edward R. Murrow would get it for him.

Murrow was already on the payroll, working in London for CBS, when he was told by his New York office to start hiring the best reporters he could find to work in the key capitals of Europe. He did, and "Murrow's Boys," as they came to be known, did give Paley the best broadcast news team in the nation. It also established a dynasty that would allow CBS to dominate broadcast news for more than 40 years.

Among the "boys" were Bill Downs, Charles Collingwood, Richard C. Hottelet, Alexander Kendrick, Larry Le Sueur, David Schoenbrun, Eric Sevareid, William L. Shirer, and Howard K. Smith. The team was to broadcasting what the Babe Ruth Yankees were to baseball. CBS would continue its successful recruiting, adding to its roster the talented Winston Burdett, Walter Cronkite, Douglas Edwards, Robert Pierpoint, Harry Reasoner, Daniel Schorr, and Robert Trout.

"This Is London"

In the 1940s, Murrow quickly established a reputation as the most notable broadcast journalist covering the war in Europe. His nightly reports from

London rooftops—with sounds of bombs and anti-aircraft and sirens in the background—became a ritual for millions of Americans.

It was Murrow's skill with words that set him apart from other broadcast journalists. Here are some excerpts from some of Murrow's reports:

> There are no words to describe the thing that is happening. [But he found them.] A row of automobiles, with stretchers racked on the roofs like skis, standing outside of bombed buildings. A man pinned under wreckage where a broken gas main sears his arms and face . . . the courage of the people; the flash and roar of guns rolling down streets . . . the stench of air-raid shelters in the poor districts.

> The fires up the river had turned the moon blood red. . . . Huge pearshaped bursts of flame would rise up into the smoke and disappear. The world was upside down.

This rooftop report was delivered as anti-aircraft fire lighted the sky:

> Out of one window there waves something that looks like a white bedsheet, a . . . curtain swinging free in this night breeze. It looks as if it were being shaken by a ghost. . . . The searchlights straightaway, miles in front of me, are still scratching that sky. There's a three-quarter moon riding high. There was one burst of shellfire almost straight in the Little Dipper.

One of the best examples of Murrow's writing is a report he made after flying on a combat mission to Berlin aboard a British bomber called "D for Dog." Here are excerpts from Murrow's script that display his extraordinary use of words to capture the mood and drama of everything that passed before him:

Figure 5-6
The late *CBS News* correspondent Edward R. Murrow risked his life to go on a bombing raid over Germany during World War II. (Historical Photograph Collections, Washington State University Libraries)

We went out and stood around a big, black four-motored Lancaster, D for Dog. A small station wagon delivered a thermos bottle of coffee, chewing gum, an orange and a bit of chocolate for each man. Up in that part of England the air hums and throbs with the sound of aircraft motors all day. But for half an hour before takeoff, the skies are dead, silent and expectant. A lone hawk hovered over the airfield, absolutely still as he faced into the wind. Jack, the tail gunner, said, "It would be nice if we could fly like that. . . ."

The take-off was smooth as silk. The wheels came up, and D-Dog started the long climb. As we came up through the clouds, I looked right and left and counted fourteen black Lancasters climbing for the place where men must burn oxygen to live. The sun was going down, and its red glow made rivers and lakes of fire on the tops of the clouds. Down to the southward, the clouds piled up to form castles, battlements and whole cities, all tinged with red.

We were approaching the enemy coast. The flak looked like a cigarette lighter in a dark room—one that won't light. Sparks but no flame. The sparks crackling just above the level of the cloud tops.

The blue-green jet of the exhausts licked back along the leading edge, and there were other aircraft all around us. The whole great armada was hurtling towards Berlin.

We were still over the clouds. But suddenly those dirty gray clouds turned white. We were over the outer searchlight defenses. The clouds below us were white, and we were black. D-Dog seemed like a black bug on a white sheet.

The same moment the sky ahead was lit up by bright yellow flares. Off to starboard, another kite [plane] went down in flames. The flares were sprouting all over the sky—reds and greens and yellows—and we were flying straight for the center of the fireworks.

Suddenly a tremendous big blob of yellow light appeared dead ahead, another to the right and another to the left. We were flying straight for them.

And then with no warning at all, D-Dog was filled with an unhealthy white light. I was standing just behind Jack and could see all the seams on the wings. His quiet Boots voice beat into my ears. "Steady, lads, we've been coned." His slender body lifted half out of his seat as he jammed the control column forward and to the left. We were going down.

Jack was wearing woolen gloves with the fingers cut off. I could see his fingernails turn white as he gripped the wheel. And then I was on my knees, flat on the deck, for he had whipped the Dog back into a climbing turn. . . .

The small incendiaries were going down like a fistful of white rice thrown on a piece of black velvet. . . .

The cookies—the four thousand pound high explosives—were bursting below like great sunflowers gone mad. . . .

I looked down, and the white fires had turned red. They were beginning to merge and spread, just like butter does on a hot plate. . . .

We flew level then. I looked on the port beam at the target area. There was a sullen, obscene glare. The fires seemed to have found each other—and we were heading home. . . .

Two other journalists, on other Lancasters in that raid over Berlin, did not return home. Murrow had the incredible ability—and it was the reason he was so effective—to use words to transport the listener onto a plane or a London rooftop or into an air-raid shelter.

Listen also for the rhythm of Murrow's words in the "D for Dog" report:

. . . the skies are dead, silent and expectant. A lone hawk hovered over the airfield, absolutely still as he faced into the wind. . . .

The sun was going down, and its red glow made rivers and lakes of fire on the tops of the clouds.

. . . clouds piled up to form castles, battlements and whole cities, all tinged with red. . . .

The flak looked like a cigarette lighter in a dark room—one that won't light. Sparks but no flame. The sparks crackling just above the level of the cloud tops.

The blue-green jet of the exhausts licked back along the leading edge. . . .

It was no wonder that Murrow won great respect from his audiences and peers. Traveling on a near-death ride through hell, Murrow captured and held pictures of everything that was going on, including details like Jack's "woolen gloves with the fingers cut off." Then, like a composer, he put a score to the word pictures he brought back to the studio: he added the dozens of different sounds and sights that were exploding around him, the "fistful of white rice thrown on a piece of black velvet" and the fires that were "beginning to merge and spread, just like butter does on a hot plate." The broadcast became known as "Orchestrated Hell."

"Permit Me to Tell You"

One of Murrow's most moving reports from Europe came from his visit to the infamous Buchenwald concentration camp after the fighting was over.

Permit me to tell you what you would have seen, and heard, had you been with me on Thursday. It will not be pleasant listening. If you are at lunch, or if you have no appetite to hear what Germans have done, now is a good time to switch off the radio, for I propose to tell you of Buchenwald. It is on a small hill about four miles outside Weimar, and it was one of the largest concentration camps in Germany, and it was built to last.

There surged around me an evil-smelling horde. Men and boys reached out to touch me, and they were in rags and the remnants of uniforms. Death had already marked many of them, but they were smiling with their eyes. I looked out over that mass of men to the green fields beyond where well-fed Germans were ploughing.

A German, Fritz Kersheimer, came up and said, "May I show you around the camp? I've been here ten years. . . . I asked to see one of the barracks. . . . I was told that this building had once stabled eighty horses. There were twelve hundred men in it, five to a bunk. The stink was beyond all description.

When I reached the center of the barracks, a man came up and said, "Remember me? I'm Peter Zenkl, one-time mayor of Prague." I remember him, but did not recognize him. He asked about Benes and Jan Masaryk. I asked how many men had died in that building during the last month. They called the doctor; we inspected his records. There were only names in the little black book, nothing more—nothing of who these men were, what they had done, or hoped. Behind the names of those who had died there was a cross. I counted them. They totalled 242. Two hundred and forty two out of twelve hundred in one month. . . .

As we walked out in the courtyard, a man fell dead. Two others—they must have been over sixty—were crawling toward the latrine. I saw it but will not describe it.

In another part of the camp they showed me the children, hundreds of them. Some were only six. One rolled up his sleeve, showed me his number. It was tattooed on his arm. D-6030, it was. The others showed me their numbers; they will carry them till they die.

An elderly man standing beside me said, "The children, enemies of the state." I could see their ribs through their thin shirts. The old man said, "I am professor Charles Richer of the Sorbonne." The children clung to my hands and stared. We crossed to the courtyard. Men kept coming up to speak to me and to touch me, professors from Poland, doctors from Vienna, men from all Europe. Men from the countries that made America.

We went to the hospital; it was full. The doctor told me that two hundred had died the day before. I asked the cause of death; he shrugged and said, "Tuberculosis, starvation, fatigue, and there are many who have no desire to live. It is very difficult. . . ."

We went again into the courtyard, and as we walked we talked. The two doctors, the Frenchman and the Czech, agreed that about six thousand had died during March. Kersheimer, the German, added that back in the winter of 1939, when the Poles began to arrive without winter clothing, they died in Germany; they had had some experience of the others. . . .

There were two rows of bodies stacked up like cordwood. They were thin and very white. Some of the bodies were terribly bruised, though there seemed to be little flesh to bruise. Some had been shot through the head, but they bled but little. All except two were naked. I tried to count them as best I could and arrived at the conclusion that all that was mortal of more than five hundred men and boys lay there in two neat piles.

I pray you to believe what I have said about Buchenwald. I have reported what I saw and heard, but only part of it. For most of it I have no words. Dead men are plentiful in war, but the living dead, more than twenty thousand of them in one camp. And the country round about was pleasing to the eye, and the Germans were well fed and well dressed. American trucks were rolling toward the rear filled with prisoners. Soon they would be eating American rations, as much for a meal as the men at Buchenwald received in four days.

If I've offended you by this rather mild account of Buchenwald, I'm not in the least sorry.

"The Fault, Dear Brutus"

One of Murrow's programs was *See It Now,* a weekly 30-minute examination of often-controversial subjects. The most memorable episode was the one in which Murrow took on Senator Joseph McCarthy, who had established a national reputation with his anticommunist witch-hunt. McCarthy had charged that the State Department and Pentagon were riddled with communists. Murrow challenged McCarthy's tactics. At the end of the program, Murrow concluded with a biting attack on the senator:

> This is no time for men who oppose Senator McCarthy's methods to keep silent, or for those who approve. We can deny our heritage and our history, but we cannot escape responsibility for the result. As a nation we have come into our full inheritance at a tender age. We proclaim ourselves, as indeed we are, the defenders of freedom—what's left of it—but we cannot defend freedom abroad by deserting it at home. The actions of the junior senator from Wisconsin have caused alarm and dismay amongst our allies abroad and given considerable comfort to our enemies. And whose fault is that? Not really his; he didn't create this situation of fear, he merely exploited it and rather successfully.

> No one familiar with the history of this country can deny that congressional committees are useful. It is necessary to investigate before legislating. But the line between investigation and persecution is a very fine one, and the junior senator from Wisconsin has stepped over it repeatedly. His primary achievement has been in confusing the public mind as between the internal and external threat of Communism. We must not confuse dissent with disloyalty. We must remember always that accusation is not proof and that conviction depends upon evidence and due process of law. We will not walk in fear, one of another. We will not be driven by fear into an age of unreason if we dig deep in our history and our doctrine and remember that we are not descended from fearful men, not from men who feared to write, to speak, to associate and to defend causes which were for the moment unpopular.

> Cassius was right. "The fault, dear Brutus, is not in our stars but in ourselves."

Because of Murrow's great popularity with the American people, his criticism of McCarthy is considered by many to be an important factor in the eventual downfall of the senator.

Murrow's influence on broadcast journalism was overwhelming. Eric Sevareid, one of the first "boys" to be hired by Murrow, was impressed by his boss from the beginning, and the admiration never ended: "He could absorb and reflect the thought and emotions of day laborers, airplane pilots, or cabinet ministers and report with exact truth what they were. . . . One can read his broadcasts now, years later, in the printed form for which they were never intended and find London all around—its sights and sounds, its very smells and feeling through the changing hours, all brought back."

Murrow, who died in 1965, would have liked that tribute. He probably would have replied that Sevareid was no "slouch" either.

Figure 5-7
The late *CBS News* correspondent
Edward R. Murrow on the set of an
early TV show, *See It Now.* (Historical
Photograph Collections, Washington
State University Libraries)

Eric Sevareid: **Writing with Class**

Many adjectives have been used over the years to describe the splendid
writing of the late Eric Sevareid during his almost 40 years with *CBS
News*. His writings have been described as "majestic," "magnificent," and
"elegant." His colleague Walter Cronkite spoke of Sevareid's "beautifully
chosen words of wisdom," which made him "one of the finest essayists of the
century."

There is no doubt that Sevareid's reports and commentaries stood a
notch above most of the writing heard on the air. What he had to say
was always important. Sometimes he expressed his strong feelings about
the responsibilities of journalists, as he did in a commentary on the
CBS Evening News on the night of his retirement. Here is part of that
commentary:

> Mine has been here an unelected, unlicensed, uncodified office and
> function. The rules are self-imposed. These were a few: Not to
> underestimate the intelligence of the audience and not to overestimate its
> information. To elucidate, when one can, more than to advocate. To
> remember always that the public is only people, and people only persons,
> no two alike. To retain the courage of one's doubts as well as one's
> convictions, in this world of dangerously passionate certainties. To comfort
> oneself, in times of error, with the knowledge that the saving grace of the
> press—print or broadcast—is its self-correcting nature. And to remember
> that ignorant or biased reporting has its counterpart in ignorant and
> biased reading and listening. We do not speak into an intellectual or
> emotional void.

In another commentary, speaking specifically of electronic journalism,
Sevareid wrote:

It is a marvelous and frightening instrument, broadcasting, as part of this marvelous and frightening century. But ordinary men must use it as ordinary men have made this century what it is. Bad men can use it to their advantage, but in free societies, only for a time—and a shorter time, I think, than in previous eras. The camera's unblinking eye sees through character faster than the printed word.

And on the subject of democracy, Sevareid wrote:

Democracy is not a free ride. It demands more of each of us than any other arrangement. There can be no rights and privileges without responsibilities. My forebears here were at ease with the word "duty." They knew that self-denial was not just a puritanical test of character, but a social necessity, so that others, too, might have elbow room in which to live. They believed, as I do, that civilized life cannot hold together without these old and now sometimes derided values. The reason is simple: only people with a sense of personal responsibility can help others or, for that matter, be helped. There can be no final solutions. From solutions arise new problems, of lessened severity, we are entitled to hope. Time is life. If one uses it to ameliorate the problems, he has lived successfully.

No other people have that chance more than do Americans. The world still looks to this country as the critical experiment in the relations of man to man. This is a fabulous assignment history has given us. From what I have read of the past, and from what I remember of my own generation's beginnings, I believe we are not failing in this assignment, and will not.

At Sevareid's retirement, the late NBC correspondent, John Chancellor said, "With his colleague Edward R. Murrow, he [Sevareid] brought a level of excellence and distinction to broadcast journalism it had not enjoyed before."

The late Charles Kuralt said that Sevareid "was one of the better writers who ever worked around here, one I always admired and whose work I used to read." Kuralt added, "When I got to know him I discovered that he was never entirely comfortable with the lights and the cameras and the makeup and all of the things you have to put up with in television. He said working in television is 'like being nibbled to death by ducks.'"

Kuralt also said that once when Sevareid was "feeling particularly grumpy about television [Kuralt] heard him murmur, 'One good word is worth a thousand pictures.'"

Good Things from Local Stations

All of the scripts that you have read so far have been by network journalists. Usually, they have more time to tell their stories than do their counterparts at local radio and TV stations. As a beginning journalist, you can also benefit from examining the work of fine local broadcast writers, who are working within the time constraints you will probably face in the early part of your career.

Well-written scripts do not have to be long. The challenge will be to tell your stories quickly without sacrificing quality. Here are examples of good writing from local journalists.

SLUG: GRANDMA 2
DATE: Wed Oct 30, 1991
REPORTER: NP
NEWSCAST: 5P
ON CAMERA

PARENTS OFTEN FIND THEMSELVES
SHOULDERING THE BURDENS OF
THEIR CHILDREN LONG AFTER
THOSE CHILDREN BECOME ADULTS
... AND WHEN PARENTS BECOME
GRANDPARENTS ... THE EMOTIONAL
LOAD CAN BE EVEN HEAVIER ... IN
OUR SERIES GRANDMA'S HANDS ...
WAFB'S NANCY PARKER REPORTS
ON A GRANDMOTHER WHO'S
TAKEN HER GRANDSON INTO HER
HOME ...
WHILE <u>HIS</u> PARENTS ARE BEHIND
BARS.
(SOT PKG)

Opening shot of Paul and
grandmother walking into
prison

V/O

(V/O)
It's visiting day at Saint Gabriel
Prison. Judy Hill and her 9-year-old
grandson Paul come here a couple
times a month.

Nat sound up

(SOT)
Door slams shut as Paul and his
grandmother sign prison visitors'
book.

(V/O)
This is where Paul's mother, Dotty
Hill, is serving time.
(nat sound)

Dissolve to Paul's mother
entering the room and nat
sound of Dotty Hill saying
"Paul" and hugging him

(V/O)
The reunions are always sweet for
Dotty and her son. For three years
now Paul has been in his
grandmother's care. His
mother watches him grow, visit by
visit.

SOT Dotty	(SOT)
	"Let me see how big you've gotten . . ."
Mug shot of mother full screen	(V/O)
	Dotty Hill and her son were separated in May of 1989 when she was brought to Saint Gabriel on a drug distribution conviction, facing an eight-year sentence.
SOT Fade to Dotty bite, music up softly (love theme from "Dying Young")	(SOT)
	"I was arrested and they brought me to jail and I took it hard. The first thing that came to mind was where I was going to put my son. I'm going to be in prison the rest of my life."
Full Screen Font: 530 INMATES 397 HAVE CHILDREN 12% OF CHILDREN IN FOSTER CARE 88% WITH FRIENDS AND FAMILY	(V/O)
	But she's not alone. St. Gabriel officials say of the 530 inmates at the prison, 397 have children. Twelve percent of these are in foster care, 88 percent are with friends and family.
Fade music out SOT Dissolve to grandmother bite	(SOT)
	"I pray a lot. I tell her to pray a lot, that she's gonna get out. I want him to be with his mother. He needs to be with her."
Fade to Dotty bite	"She is the mother to him instead of me. Even when I was out she was a mother to him. I loved him and gave him material things. I didn't give him the mother's love, but she did."
Fade to Parker asking question and Paul responding	Parker: "What's the worst part about not having your mom around?" Paul: "I missed her."
O/C standup	(O/C)
	Paul's grandmother not only has to raise him but she has to deal with his emotions as well. Not only is his mother in prison here at Saint Gabriel but his father is also behind bars.

SOT
Fade to bite of
grandmother
Music up
Nat sound of woman
guard slamming jail door.
Dissolve and freeze
and then slo mo of Paul
and mother hugging
and saying goodbye.

(SOT)
"I try to explain to him that
they did something wrong and when
you do something wrong you have to
pay for it. But as long as she needs
me, I'll be there. Even when she gets
out, I'll be there for both of them."

V/O

(V/O)
Nancy Parker, Channel 9 News, Baton
Rouge.

The 50th anniversary of Pearl Harbor was a special occasion, so Executive
Producer Rod Haberer of station KPNX-TV in Phoenix was given more air
time than usual for this story, which he wrote and produced for anchor Kent
Dana. (Note that Haberer's script format is somewhat different from the
earlier one by Parker.) He identifies, by number, the tapes he is using and at
what time on the tape the sound bites are located. As is the case in many
newsrooms, Haberer also uses the symbol VG (video graphic) instead of Font.

PEARL HARBOR
ANCHOR LEAD-IN:
50 YEARS AGO TONIGHT . . . MUCH OF THE WORLD WAS AT WAR. BUT
AMERICA WAS SITTING THIS ONE OUT. THAT IS, UNTIL THE
FOLLOWING MORNING. AMERICA'S ILLUSION OF PEACE WAS
SHATTERED ALONG WITH THE HULL OF THE BATTLESHIP ARIZONA.
MORE THAN A THOUSAND MEN WERE KILLED WHEN A JAPANESE
BOMB EXPLODED ABOARD THE SHIP . . . DURING THE AIR RAID ON
PEARL HARBOR. KENT DANA REPORTS.
(SOT FULL RP)
(ALL GRAPHICS PRE-PRODUCED)
END TAPE 5:42 OUT: CALLED A MAN (FADES TO BLACK)

TOMORROW MORNING, AT 7-55 A-M . . . PRESIDENT BUSH WILL BE
ABOARD THE USS ARIZONA MEMORIAL . . . TO LAY A WREATH
OVER THE SHIPWRECK THAT STILL HOLDS AN ESTIMATED 900
MEN ENTOMBED SINCE DECEMBER 7TH, 1941.

TAPE 29A 20:07
VG: LORRAINE MARKS
USS ARIZONA
HISTORIAN

(NAT SOT EXPLOSIONS)
IN: On that day, 1177 men were
killed, the largest single naval
disaster in United States history.

LORRAINE MARKS LIVES IN
PHOENIX, AND IS THE OFFICIAL
HISTORIAN FOR THE USS
ARIZONA REUNION ASSOCIATION.

HER HUSBAND, WHO DIED FIVE
YEARS AGO, SERVED ON THE
ARIZONA. A SURVIVOR, ED
MARKS WAS ASHORE WHEN THE
ARIZONA WAS ATTACKED.

TAPE 29A 3:50   (SOT FULL)
MARKS   IN: In 1985 he went back to the last
reunion that he could attend. And a
television reporter asked him why,
after all these years do you attend
these reunions? And for the first
time, I saw him cry . . . because he
said we can't forget those guys.

TAPE 29B 3:07   (SOT FULL)
MARKS   IN: I know my husband suffered all
those years, he wouldn't talk about it.
There's a lot of women I know who
say their husbands just won't talk
about it.

TAPE 28A 5:40   (SOT FULL)
STRATTON   IN: Kind of a tough day.

STILL STRATTON   DONALD STRATTON, WHO NOW
TAPE 28b 26:30   LIVES IN YUMA, WAS ABOARD THE
ARIZONA ON DECEMBER 7th, 1941,
AT HIS BATTLESTATION ON THE
ANTI-AIRCRAFT DIRECTOR ABOVE
THE BRIDGE.

TAPE 25A 3:50   (SOT FULL)
STRATTON   IN: General quarters sounded and
VG: DONALD STRATTON   everyone was on their battlestations
USS ARIZONA BB39   as far as I knew.

TAPE 28A 4:44   (SOT FULL)
STRATTON   IN: When the bomb hit, it shook that
33-ton ship like you'd shake a piece
of paper.

TAPE 28A 5:26   (SOT FULL)
STRATTON   IN: The people in the number one and
number two turrets and those
manning stations to bring ammo
from up below and all that, that was
in the forward part, never had a
chance.

TAPE 29B 1:00 MARKS	(SOT FULL) IN: The Japanese planes came, battlestations sounded, the band threw down all their instruments and went to their battlestations.
TAPE 29B 1:30 MARKS	(SOT FULL) IN: And their battlestations were in the bowels of the ship, passing ammunition, and everyone in the band that day was killed.
STILL USS VESTAL TAPE 26 16:12 & 17:00	WHEN THE ARIZONA EXPLODED, THE U-S-S VESTAL WAS STILL TIED UP ALONGSIDE, AND THE VESTAL WAS THE ONLY WAY OFF THE ARIZONA FOR STRATTON AND OTHERS STILL STRANDED.
TAPE 28A 7:53 STRATTON	(SOT FULL) IN: I would say 50 to 60 manned that station, but there was only six of us went across this . . . as you know, the Vestal was tied up alongside.
TAPE 29A 16:12 MARKS POINTING TO PAINTING	(SOT FULL) IN: This is the Vestal tied up alongside . . . the repair ship . . . and this is the ship that threw a line over the aft section of the mainmast where Don Stratton was.
TAPE 28A 8:10 STRATTON	(SOT FULL) IN: We pulled over the heavier messenger line, and tied if off to the Arizona, and we crawled across to the Vestal.
TAPE 28A 8:54 STRATTON	(SOT FULL) IN: I was burned over 60 percent of my body.
	STRATTON SURVIVED . . . BUT SO MANY OTHER YOUNG MEN DIDN'T. LIKE JAMES RANDOLF VAN HORNE.
TAPE 29C 4:50 MARKS	(SOT FULL) IN: He was a sophomore in Tucson High School and he heard Admiral

Kidd, rear Admiral Kidd, talk about
the navy.

TAPE 29C 5:18   (SOT FULL)
MARKS   IN: He quit school, and he joined the
navy, both he and the admiral died
just a few months later.

TAPE #1 17:43   (SOT FULL)
VG: PAUL STILLWELL   IN: I talked to the son of the ARIZONA
AUTHOR/BATTLESHIP   admiral who was on board, and in
1942 his mother got a package from
Hawaii that had in it her husband's
naval academy ring, and that had
been found fused to the conning tower
right in front of the bridge, and
apparently that was all that was left
of Admiral Kidd.

STILL ROBERTS   ANOTHER 17-YEAR-OLD KILLED
TAPE 29D 47:30   THAT DAY . . . WAS WALTER SCOTT
ROBERTS.

TAPE 29B 14:03   (SOT FULL)
MARKS   IN: The navy department deeply
regrets to inform you that your son,
Walter Scott Roberts, Junior
Radioman First Class US Navy, is
missing following performance of his
duty and in the service of his
country.

STILL BRITTON   AND 17-YEAR-OLD CHARLES
EDWARD BRITTON OFTEN WROTE
HOME . . . ON JULY 19TH, 1941, THIS
NOTE TO HIS MOTHER.

TAPE 290 14:08   (SOT FULL)
MARKS   IN: I was not able to send you the
five dollars I got off you . . . a 17-year-
old boy borrowing money from his
mom.

PHOTOGRAPHS OF HER SON AND HIS
LETTERS HOME ARE ALL THAT
CHARLES EDWARD BRITTON'S
MOTHER HAD TO REMEMBER HER
BOY. BUT SHE WOULD BE PROUD,
AND MOST LIKELY MOVED TO
TEARS, TO HEAR THE WORDS

LORRAINE MARKS HAS WRITTEN
INTO THE HISTORY BOOKS OF THE
USS ARIZONA.

TAPE 290 12:48   (SOT FULL)
MARKS   IN: Where his remains are now are
                               uncertain, but the soul of this 17-
                               year-old departed that day, December
                               7th, 1941, from the starboard side of
                               the quarterdeck of the burning and
                               sinking battleship USS Arizona BB39.
                               His name is engraved in stone along
                               with 1176 of his shipmates on the
                               wall of the USS Arizona memorial
                               that spans the sunken hull in Pearl
                               Harbor, Hawaii. His service to his
                               country and ultimate sacrifice earned
                               him the right at the tender age of 17
                               to be called a man.

Haberer was asked how he felt about doing all the work on the Pearl Harbor story, while Dana simply anchored the story. His reply: "It's the way TV has evolved. It's much more anchor driven than it used to be. People like the anchors and they want to see and hear more of them. It's our job to make the anchors look as knowledgeable and as strong as we can make them look." He said he accepts that the anchors are going to get credit for the work he does; "it's just part of the job." More discussion on this in Chapter 18, "Ethics and the Law."

Figure 5-8 Kris Kridel of radio station WBBM in Chicago. (Courtesy of WBBM, Chicago)

The following story was written by Kris Kridel of radio station WBBM in Chicago.

David Chereck Murder/Kris Kridel

[neighborhood traffic sounds]

In the three weeks since the murder of their son, Alan and Esther Chereck's brick home in Skokie has been filled with people: investigators and reporters, family friends, and . . . most important to David's mother . . . his friends.

AUDIO: His friends came. They just kept coming and they keep coming and, uh, and it just shows how much he was loved.

KRIDEL: Esther Chereck says David's friends sit in his room and talk about him.

AUDIO: More kids than I realized really knew and cared about David. The cards that we've gotten tell us memories of David and they fill in those blank spots that you don't share with your teenager.

KRIDEL: The Checks have learned, for instance, how David once helped a grammar school classmate.

AUDIO: One year she wouldn't have made her math class, if he hadn't helped her through it, she wouldn't have passed. He never boasted. We never knew these things about him.

KRIDEL: On the piano and in the nearby etagere in the Checks' living room are David's academic awards, his artwork, and pictures of him at all ages.

AUDIO: In fact, I put more of them up. Having him around, especially when I was sitting shiva, was a comfort. As you see, he has a bright smile and, uh, he's there with me. I don't think he'll ever leave us.

KRIDEL: It is a great comfort to the Checks that David's classmates at Niles West High School are organizing an art scholarship fund in his honor.

AUDIO: We just love them for what they want to do for David.

KRIDEL: David's parents are appealing to people who may have any information about his murder to step forward and help.

Kris Kridel, WBBM Newsradio 78

[neighborhood traffic sounds fade]

Summary

No one expects you to turn out copy of the quality shown in this chapter right away. Working color into your stories effectively will not come easily or quickly. At the outset, the real challenge will be to write respectable broadcast news copy with speed. You will not have days (unless you are working on a documentary or special report) to write your story. Often you will be dealing in minutes and, at best, an hour or so if you are working on a TV script. But there will be enough time for you to write clearly and accurately while you are developing the skill of writing colorfully.

Don't wait until you are covering a story to develop your observation skills. Start to watch people and take notes about their appearance, how they talk and look, and anything unusual or different about them. Observe people the next time you go to the cafeteria or a ball game. Also start to develop your other senses. If you are in a crowded, smoke-filled room, think about how you feel. There are special smells just about everywhere: in a gym, in the corridors of a high school and a hospital, in a church, How many times have you entered someone's home and said, "Something really smells good . . . what's cooking?" Let all your senses work for you full-time, and put what they tell you into your copy.

Review Questions

1. List the various ways you can bring color to your copy.
2. Why do so many broadcast news professionals recommend that aspiring journalists read the works of Ernest Hemingway?
3. Give the names of other well-known nonbroadcast writers who might help develop your writing style.
4. Why is the writing of Charles Kuralt so admired? Give some examples of sentences or phrases in his *On the Road* script that you particularly like, and tell why you like them.
5. What is it about the stories of *CBS News* Correspondent Roger Welsch that makes them so successful? Give some examples.
6. Give some examples of color in the writing of NBC's Bob Dotson. How would you describe Dotson's style?
7. Is color restricted to feature stories? Discuss.
8. Why is Edward R. Murrow's writing so well respected? Give some examples of the style that made him famous.

Exercises

1. Examine one of the biographies of Edward R. Murrow, and summarize some of the statements made about his writing.
2. Listen to NPR's *All Things Considered*, and make notes on stories that you think are colorfully written.
3. Watch a network newscast and the local newscast that precedes or follows it. Keep notes on the stories that you believe are well written, and why.
4. *Sunday Morning* on CBS is considered by many to be the best news program on the air. Watch it, and report on the stories that you like most. Explain why.
5. Describe, in as much detail as possible, your closest friend. Include the individual's physical appearance and any habits or mannerisms he or she might have. Tell what you like and/or dislike about the person and why you consider him or her to be your closest friend.

6   Radio News

It is difficult to generalize about radio news operations and news programs because they seem to be constantly changing. One statement that can be made, however, is that newscasts on most local radio stations are getting shorter and less frequent. The demise of the significant role that radio had traditionally played in covering the news began with the unfortunate decision by the Federal Communications Commission that radio stations did not have to provide news as a public service. So, hundreds of radio stations decided they could save a lot of money by ending their news operations, and they did. The majority of those stations are either playing music or are in the "talk" business, and that business is, for the most part, conservative. The easing of ownership restrictions over the years also played a large role in destroying the close relationship that radio stations traditionally had with their listeners because those landmark stations stressed public service and took pride in serving the community and keeping it well informed. People turned to their radio sets to find out about disasters such as tornadoes and hurricanes, and routine matters such as school closings and traffic conditions. The short-sightedness of the FCC and the power of the broadcast industry's lobbyists to influence Congress have put a great number of the nation's radio stations in the hands of a small group of media giants such as Clear Channel which owns more than 1,200 radio stations. It dominates the audience share in 100 of 112 major markets. Another giant, Infinity Broadcasting, operates 185 radio sta-tions, mostly in the nation's top 50 markets. It reaches more than 76 million listeners a week in 40 markets in 22 states. The most positive thing to be said about Clear Channel is that it has become a darling of Wall Street because of its ability to make lots of money from entertainment and conservative talk while providing little in the way of pubic service. By eliminating many of the news jobs that once existed at the acquired radio stations and replacing the local talent with syndicated sound-alike package programming, Clear Channel has been able to keep its costs to a minimum. Quite frequently, there is no journalist working full-time at the radio stations during the day, and this is even more likely to be true at night.

Clear Channel came under fire in January of 2002 in Minot, North Dakota, when authorities tried without success to reach someone at six of the seven radio stations Clear Channel owns in the town, to warn residents that a train carrying 10,000 gallons of anhydrous ammonia derailed in the area, causing a toxic cloud. When authorities called the six stations, no one answered the phones.

Senator Byron Dorgan of North Dakota used the incident to warn FCC Chairman Michael Powell that as large media companies like Clear Channel buy up the last remaining independent media outlets, the public suffers. As previously noted, the FCC has shown a bias toward helping the broadcast industry while frequently forgetting the interests of the public. The Center for Public Information (CPI) hints that this FCC bias in favor of the broadcast industry and its lobbyists is a result of the very cozy relationship that has developed between them. The organization's Chuck Lewis noted, for example, that FCC Commissioners made 1,400 trips—all expenses paid by broadcasters. Lewis asked, "how can the FCC judge and discuss media ownership if they're taking trips from these guys?" As for the impact of all this on local news, in a research survey conducted by the Radio and Television News Directors Association and Ball State University, Professor Bob Papper noted that radio consolidation makes it almost impossible to compare news operations over time. He said more than 95 percent of radio news departments handle the news for more than one station. In fact, he said, the average news department runs news on three stations in the same market. He added that more than four in ten radio news departments say they do news for one or more stations outside their own market.

Papper says there are now four places where you still hear radio news: real all-news stations in major markets; some news/talk stations in some major and large markets; some public stations in a wide variety of market sizes; and finally, in some small and medium stations where news has remained a key part of their programming. Papper adds that the typical radio newsroom has one person. As for Clear Channel, its penetration into the national radio market is overwhelming, with eleven stations in Los Angeles, nine each in San Diego and Jacksonville, seven in Cincinnati, five in Little Rock, and four in Poughkeepsie, New York, a city of less than 30,000 people. In Wheeling, West Virginia, another relatively small city of about 30,000 where Clear Channel owns six radio stations, it made major cuts in its local news programming and personnel at WWVA, a 50,000-watt station with a strong history of news coverage. It fired the news director and a reporter with the station, Dave Demerest, resigned on the air in disgust because of the cutbacks, which he described as the elimination of seven-and-a-half hours of local programming. Demerest said the changes have left the public with practically no forum for discussion of local interest.

He also said that Clear Channel demonstrated no concern for the station's listeners when it decided to try to move the station to a suburb of Ohio. The host of one of the eliminated talk shows, George Kellas, called the cutbacks "a prime example of corporate greed. Demerest said that among the devices used by Clear Channel to save money is to have one of its disc jockeys do a program on one of the stations and then later in the day do another program on another of its stations, using a different name.

You Need A Scorecard

The old cliché about needing a score card to keep up with the players is definitely true when it comes to understanding what's been happening in broadcast ownership for the past two decades. Even with a scorecard, which we'll try to provide, the situation is, at best, very complicated.

For those of you who have not taken a course in the history of broadcasting, the story pretty much started in 1920, when the Westinghouse Corporation's radio station KDKA started scheduled radio programming with the Harding-Cox Presidential election. In 1928, William S. Paley bought the Columbia Broadcasting System for $400,000.

In 1995, after a long history of success in news, CBS was sold to Westinghouse for $5.4 billion. A year later, in 1996, Westinghouse/CBS purchased Infinity Radio broadcasting, a deal that was mainly a result of the Telecommunication Act of 1996, which heavily deregulated the media industry and allowed a company to significantly increase the number of radio stations it could own. A year later, Westinghouse changed its name to CBS and unloaded its hardware and manufacturing operations. Two years later, in 1999, Viacom and CBS announced a merger. The $50 billion deal came one month after the FCC gave its approval to duopolies, the owning of three stations in the same market. The FCC limits such duopolies to large markets. Meanwhile, Viacom has acquired 33 television stations, eclipsing the FCC's 35% ownership cap, which is based on the number of stations one company owns that reach 35% or more of the nation's television households. A U.S. Court of Appeals gave Viacom temporary approval to exceed the 35% ownership cap. Meanwhile, in 2004, a new effort by the FCC—with the support of the Bush Administration—to allow conglomerates to buy even more radio stations, ran into a buzzsaw of anger in Congress and in the public. So, the blood-letting has ended, at least temporarily, while some in Congress try to restore sanity to the situation.

The other broadcast giant, Infinity Broadcasting, also makes tons of money. But Infinity accomplishes more than just offering music, entertainment, and so-called "hot talk" jockeys. It's deeply imbedded in news and talk and all-news stations, owning and operating the top two billing AM stations, WINS and WFAN. WINS, the number one news station is also the most-listened to station with more than 2.5 million listeners each week. Infinity also operates eight of the nation's top-ten-rated news stations and eight of the nation's top-ten-rated oldies stations, which certainly qualifies it as arguably the most eclectic broadcasting network. Infinity also has a long-standing alliance with Westwood One, which provides some 7,700 stations with news, sports, weather, and a variety of other programming. Also in the Infinity stable is the CBS Radio Network, which is managed by Westwood One. CBS provides hourly newscasts to more than 1,500 news and talk-formatted stations. Infinity also has the distinction of owning two all-news radio stations in both of the nation's largest cities, New York and Los Angeles.

That's an interesting story in itself, which we will examine shortly. So, despite some very negative things that are going on in radio news, particularly in small communities where news certainly is in deep trouble, there are still many news and all-news operations in some big cities.

And, thank goodness, there's still National Public Radio, and many of its affiliate stations that provide significant news programming. There also is CNN Radio News and ABC Radio News with its 4,500 affiliates. NPR, of course, stands out. Its longer-form radio news thrives in a way that is virtually unknown on the commercial side. Much of its success is the result of its strong commitment, which includes fifteen domestic bureaus, nine foreign correspondents, and a total staff of about 60 reporters.

Writing about the accomplishments of NPR in the American Journalism Review, Lori Robertson says the radio network "has evolved from a lone man in London to a leading source of foreign news, from a pack of revolutionary radio artists to a cadre of journalists, from an alternative outlet to a primary news provider."

Robertson notes that listenership more than doubled between 1993 and 2003, and more than 22 million people tune in to NPR programming weekly.

But, as *Washington Post* columnist Marc Fisher pointed out in another article for *American Journalism Review*, in most big cities and in an increasing number of middle-sized markets, the only radio news operations that bother to send reporters out on stories, besides NPR affiliates, are all-news stations. On most music stations, he notes, news is limited to morning drive time and is delivered from a single centralized newsroom belonging to either Metro Networks or Shadow Broadcast Services. In most of the top 75 markets, Fisher notes, Metro or Shadow or some combination of the two provide not only traffic and weather reports, but also the newscasts on virtually all the stations in town. Metro began as a traffic service, putting planes and choppers aloft to monitor commuter jams, but eventually Metro and Shadow realized they could also save stations money by providing them with news services. Today, Metro delivers newscasts for 490 stations in 62 of the country's top 75 markets and Shadow serves more than 125 stations in 15 markets. And, as Fisher reported, the two services do not charge stations a penny for their efforts. Stations simply give a couple of minutes of time to Metro or Shadow, and they fill it with a few headlines. The news providers, if you can call them that, make their money by tagging on ten-second commercials at the end of the newscasts. In the Washington D.C. area, for example, twelve stations take newscasts from Metro and nine from Shadow. Fisher noted that most Metro and Shadow newscasts do not even rise to the level of traditional rip and read journalism made possible by the AP broadcast wire. Neither Metro nor Shadow take the AP wire, the mainstay of many news operations. Fisher said both Metro and Shadow rely heavily on what radio people call "published reports," which means mellifluous voices reading a digest of the morning paper. Fisher said that in one news summary, Metro had six stories, three of them barely rewritten from the *Post*, and three paraphrased from the suburban Journal newspapers. To their credit, Metro and Shadow are apparently trying to improve their image. After taking a lot of heat for laying waste to an entire news profession, Metro and Shadow did add news gathering activities to their product. As we noted earlier, there are still many stations in medium sized and large size markets that take pride in their news operations and maintain writing and reporting staffs. Some of these stations, particularly those that provide "all news," have extensive news staffs.

One of these news operations, the WBUR Group provides programming from NPR, the BBC and a variety of its own locally produced news and feature programs to more than a half million people in Boston and another 43,000 listeners in Providence through its sister-station WRNI. The two stations have won more than 20 awards for excellence in reporting. Among the stations' most popular programs are *The Connection* and *Talk of the Nation*, which engage its listeners each weekday live from the WBUR studios. The programs feature intelligent discussions and debate about issues that affect our lives. The shows' hosts, Dick Gordon on *The Connection* and Neal Conan *on Talk of the Nation*, encourage listeners in the 63 markets they reach to join the conversation. Gordon's Connection, in December of 2003, became the first American radio show to sign on live from Baghdad. Then, in November of 2004, WBUR sent Gordon back to Iraq for another series of daily live reports. Here's one of them.

It was kind of a rough day and evening here for the staff at the Al Dar Hotel. About half their guests moved out and then their hotel's diesel generator had a tantrum. Early in the morning, Peter, Willem, and Tim with Dutch television headed back to Amman, Jordan, and on to Amsterdam. As well, a number of the newspaper reporters here, mainly American correspondents who made their way south from Mosul, Kirkuk and Tikrit, had spent a week or so here, but they're beat. They've been on the road nearly two months. They too left for Jordan. That left Marc Allard. He's the freelance producer that WBUR hired to help make this happen, and me, the Irish crew, German TV, and Paul from the Asia Times. (Actually I'm not sure about the Irish, I saw Tony giving leftover tinned food to the guards, and that's a sure sign someone's packing up to go.) As you can tell, you get to know people covering a story like this. You have to. You rely on them for contacts and safety information and they rely on you.

Marc and I have one more night here and then we are heading back. I'll miss room 208. Did I tell you that I've been sleeping in *The Connection* studio as well? Don't tell our senior producer, Tara. She might get ideas about re-configuring my accommodation in Boston. Actually, aside from the mosquitoes coming in off the Tigris now that it's the start of the hot season . . . and aside from the oversize cockroaches that come out of a hole in the wall of Marc's room, and aside from the creative means necessary to perform daily ablutions. I am sooo happy we've been here instead of living with the mass media petting zoo down the street at the Palestine and the Sheraton. That place is an armed camp. There are thousands of hacks living there, and hundreds of U.S. soldiers with tanks and miles of concertina wire encircling the compound.

There are also thousands of Iraqis there now, great crowds on the street, exchanging money, selling cigarettes, or just sitting on the traffic circle median, looking up at all the TV lights on the fourth floor patio where CNN, CBS, ABC, and all the other TV networks do their "live shots."

Each morning at the Al Dar, we wake to a city that's usually quiet. There's still no electricity, so we hear the roosters and the dogs barking and the sound of distant gunfire, and most of the time we don't live with the hammering of all those generators around the other hotels. Speaking of generators, the Al Dar has one as well. They use it for lights, and when they get some food in, to cook eggs and chicken. Bread, they buy on the street. There are now cucumbers and tomatoes and some very old looking olives.

The generator died last night. Marc and I had to work by candlelight, but the people who run this hotel are delightful.

They help out whenever they can. There was a flurry of activity around the machine, which is directly below my window. Pails of diesel were slopped about (the fumes were somewhat overpowering) and the cranky starter was ground further and further toward the end of its life.

Figure 6-1 Reporter Dick Gordon of WBUR Radio in Boston finishes a script by candlelight when the generator in his Iraqi office quit one night. (Courtesy of WBUR Radio, Boston, MA.)

Eventually though, they got it going. Kind of like Baghdad. Eventually they'll get it going. But it's going to be a long, slow job. You feel a bit melancholy when you see all the reporters packing up, just watching all the Iraqis who can't. Our translator, Ahmed, was going to come to Jordan with us, to help on the trip and do a bit of shopping himself before returning to Baghdad. We made the request. The Jordanians said, "no chance." The people who live here are stuck here.

Twelve years of sanctions kept them virtually prisoners in a country run by Saddam Hussein. Today, under a rule of law imposed by the U.S. military, they are still stuck (and this is liberation?). It will be months, perhaps years, before there is enough of a civilian infrastructure to even think about passports for ordinary Iraqis. Even then, they wonder, will the world trust us Iraqis to travel? Will we be forever marked as dangerous, and unwanted? That will be in their minds when they watch us pack up the truck for the first leg of the trip back to Boston tomorrow.

All News Radio Stations

Among the interesting developments to come out of the mergers and take-overs cited earlier were two unique situations in New York City and Los Angeles. The two all-news stations in each of these cities found themselves owned by the same corporation, Infinity. When Westinghouse bought CBS, that put WINS-All News and WCBS-All News into the same corporation. KNX and KFWB in Los Angeles found themselves in the same boat. So, how does this work? Two competing all-news stations which are traditional rivals for listeners in the New York and Los Angeles markets find that they are getting their paychecks from the same company while they continue to compete for listeners? We found it fascinating and spoke to the news directors involved.

They told us that before the four stations were bought by Infinity they competed under all news program styles that are very much the same today. The Westinghouse approach, developed at WINS in New York City, *"give us 20 minutes and we will give you the world,"* is still basically the format at WINS (which, as we mentioned earlier, is the most-listened-to AM station in the nation) and at KNX in Los Angeles, a 50,000-watt giant that reaches not only Los Angeles but a major part of the surrounding communities. Meanwhile, KFWB in Los Angeles, part of the original CBS empire, continues to offer what it calls a more in-depth news approach, with the traditional CBS newscasts at the top of each hour and 30-minute blocks of news. That formula also continues, of course, at WCBS Radio in New York City. Andy Ludlum, the News Director at KFWB, notes that while he and KNX's news director, Ed Pyle, run operations that are walking distance from each other, and share the same general manager and program director, they have separate editorial staffs. Management never gets involved in how Ludlum and Pyle run their news operations. Ludlum says one of the major differences between the two stations is that his station focuses more on spot news (a headline sound), while KNX, as we indicated earlier, does more stories in depth, and more stories of a national and international nature, relying heavily on the CBS stable of reporters like Dan Rather and Bob Schieffer, who frequently pop up to do radio versions of the stories they're covering for TV. Ludlum says his station's strength lies more in local news. When there's a major local story, he says, like an earthquake, more people are probably going to tune to us. Breaking news is our strong point, he added, while KNX is more likely to give you longer stories. Both stations have large news staffs, but KNX relies more on its anchors to do the writing while KFWB has writers and editors to handle most of the copy.

The situation in New York is very similar, again, because the two competing stations came out of the same Westinghouse and CBS environments before Infinity acquired them. As indicated, WCBS News has access to the network's reporters while WINS, interestingly, has access to ABC correspondents. To muddy the waters even more, WCBS News Director Tim Sheld said WCBS-TV might allow WINS to use some of its sound bites to achieve additional exposure. As is the case in Los Angeles, WINS is considered to be more of a local station, while WCBS News spends more time covering news in the suburbs than does WINS.

Good News Teams Are Also Found in Small Places

South Dakota Public Radio has won the top prize in the regional Associated Press awards for the past three years, as well as numerous regional and national Edward R. Murrow awards from RTNDA. Also picking up prizes for outstanding news coverage are small-market radio stations in Kansas and Massachusetts. KFDI/KFTI in Wichita, Kansas, the 95th market, won three national Edward R. Murrow Awards in 2003. News Director Dan Dillon says, "the recipe for success hasn't changed much over the years. We've always been good covering the weather and breaking news and we improved our coverage to include the state legislature, the city council, and the county commission."

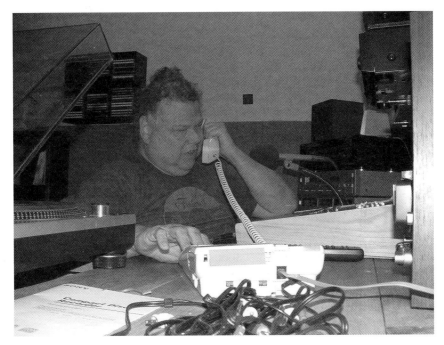

Figure 6-2 Blind disc jockey, Ted McCaw, at radio station WATD, Marshfield, MA. (Courtesy of WATD, Marshfield, MA.)

Dillon, who also serves as the morning anchor, has four full-time staffers. He said the stations also have someone who works overnight in the newsroom who is free to leave the station to cover breaking news. "Because of that," Dillon said, "we call ourselves 'The 24-Hour News Center.'"

WATD Radio in Marshfield, Massachusetts, has only 3,000 watts, but they are powerful watts. With its 12 full-time, 4 part-time staff, the station has won a national Murrow award for each of the past five years. WATD is unique in many ways.

"My wife and I own the whole thing," says Edward Perry, proudly. He adds that he's not very good at much of anything except picking out good people to work for him.

For 20 years, WATD has had a blind disc jockey, Ted McCaw, who works from his house. Perry says "the young man used to come to the station to do his shift, but after his parents died and getting to the station became more difficult, we built a studio at his home."

Perry also prides himself on giving aspiring journalists a chance. "We have volunteers who come in overnight," Perry said, "who don't get paid, but they get experience on their resumes. Every once in a while, somebody hits it big," he added.

In the Sioux Falls, South Dakota, market, the 10-kilowatt Public Radio Station, KSUD, won an RTNDA/UNITY award in 2003 with six reporters each day trying to cover an entire state that sprawls over 76,000 square miles. There are about 700,000 people, the population of Milwaukee, living in that expanse, and their interests are almost as diverse as their numbers. News Director Brian Bull says his reporters have to deal with, and know about, economic development, agriculture, race relations, education, and the advent of technology in South Dakota and the plight of Indian reservations. Bull says the station passes on a lot of news that other stations routinely cover. "We deprioritize traffic accidents, most suicides and celebrity news. I mean, who really cares who Jennifer Lopez marries this week." Bull said, "We seek out the stories that you aren't normally going to hear on the air on other stations."

In some small markets, where radio news is still produced locally, it's often the product of a one-person news staff. Young people still interested in a career in radio news will probably work in that environment, which has some advantages. It's an opportunity to develop the skills that you learned in school: writing, reporting, interviewing, working with sound, and editing. It also offers time to develop that most important of broadcasting skills—news judgment. But working alone also has some disadvantages. No one will be there to help correct and guide you when you need it most.

This chapter discusses the factors you should consider when preparing for and writing radio newscasts. Getting to know the audience is the first consideration.

Your Audience

One of the continuing debates in both print and broadcast news is whether the news should provide the kind of information that people need to know or the information they want to know. Most journalists agree that the answer lies somewhere in the middle. People must be informed, but it also makes sense to tailor the news for the audience. A station programming easy-listening music probably would not want to provide the same kind of news as a rock station. The rock station would have a relatively young audience, and the easy-listening station would have an older audience. If you were the news director at the rock station, you would be looking for stories that might appeal more to young people. The writing style also would be lighter and less formal than it would be, for example, for the audience of that easy-listening station.

The story selection also would be different for news delivered in urban and rural areas. Stories about the weather would be important in farm country, whereas stories about traffic congestion would be important in the city.

Although you need to consider all these factors, your main concern in putting a news report together is the news itself. A story of overwhelming importance, whether it is local, national, or foreign, always takes precedence over the rest of the news.

Organizing Material

Before a radio newswriter decides which story should lead a newscast and which stories should follow, he or she must know what news they have to work with. A good way to start is to call the police and fire departments to see if anything is going on and then if you have a wire service, read it carefully, along with the local newspaper. Serious newsrooms keep a file marked "futures" that alerts the staff to special events scheduled in the listening area that day and during the upcoming month or later. Check this file next. In a small community there may not be much going on, and, if that community is served by an equally small station, any material in the futures file was probably put there by the newsperson who will be covering the event.

If the station can afford a wire service, the most important items are often those that the wires periodically move about events in the local area. After you have read the copy, the newspaper, and any other sources available, you decide which stories you want to use, and in what order.

Most newspeople list on a pad all the stories they have to work with and try to figure out a tentative order in which the stories will appear in the script. Other writers print out the stories on the computer they wish to use and arrange the stories in the order they wish to use them, so that the most important stories are at the top and the less important ones at the bottom. There is no right or wrong way to organize copy, so look for the method that is the most comfortable for you.

Writers using computers organize their copy in a variety of ways. Some move the stories they wish to consider for their newscast into a separate computer file. Later, when they are ready to rewrite the stories, they split the screen so that they can look at the wire copy on one side and use the other half, the blank side, to rewrite the copy.

Once that story is written it is saved, and the writer moves on to the next one, and so forth. When all the stories are written, the writer prints them out and puts them in the order in which they will be read on the air.

Writing from the Back

One thing that just about all newswriters agree on is that the first stories they write are those that will not change. Working in this way is called *writing*

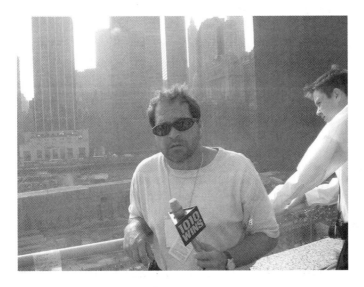

Figure 6-3   WINS Reporter John Montone covering the one year anniversary of the World Trade Center attack.

from the back because the stories that are not likely to change are usually those that are read in the latter part of the newscast.

"Breaking" stories, as their name suggests, will probably change considerably before air time, so they should be written last.

The Lead Story

The method for selecting the first story in the newscast—the lead story—may sound simple: Just pick the most important story. But how do you decide which story is most important? Should a local, national, or international story be the lead? Does the time of day affect the decision? Will any of the stories affect the local audience in some way? The answers to these questions can help you determine which story should lead the newscast.

Most of a station's listeners will be more interested in what is happening in their community than in the rest of the world. There are exceptions, of course, as during the terrorist attacks on the Trade Center in New York on 9/11 and the tsunami catastrophe in December of 2004, when most Americans turned on their radio and TV sets to get the latest on the disasters. But now, let's examine how we decide what's news to a local audience on a relatively normal news day. News in a town of 5,000 is not necessarily news in a city of 50,000. And what is considered news in that medium-sized city may not be too important in a city of a million or more. Here are some story choices on a particular day at a radio station in the hypothetical town of Centerville, population 10,000.

1. The president says he is encouraged by the progress being made in the baseball strike negotiations.
2. The Labor Department says unemployment rose another one-half of one percent.
3. The governor says he will make major cuts in services and state workers' jobs rather than raise taxes.

4. The wife of Centerville's mayor gives birth to triplets.

The story of most interest in Centerville, and the story that most listeners would be talking about that day, is the birth of triplets to the mayor's wife. But 100 miles north, in the state capital, the birth would be less important, and the governor's comments on cuts in jobs and services would be the top story. The network newscast would lead with the jump in unemployment because that story holds the most interest for a national audience.

Suppose we add another story to the list: a three-car accident on the freeway near the state capital. While the story may not sound too important, suppose the accident was at 8 A.M., and those three wrecked cars had created a gigantic traffic jam. It most certainly would be the lead story on the 8 A.M. news for stations in the capital because that is "drive time," the highest-rated listening period for radio. The people listening to their radios on the way to work are more concerned about when they will get to the office than they are about the governor's comments on taxes and jobs. How about the audience in Centerville? Because the accident took place over 100 miles away, the

Centerville listeners would have no interest in it. The network radio audience would not even know about the accident because it would not be important enough to make the A.P. wire.

Keep in mind that when you start to prepare your newscast, you should not be overly concerned about which story will lead it. The chances are that what appeared to be the most important story an hour earlier may be overshadowed by a new story that broke before air time. That is the nature of the news business. On some very busy news days—unlikely in Centerville—a story that was considered the lead at one point may not even get into the newscast. That's why each story should be on a separate sheet of paper to allow for a quick reshuffling of the script.

The Rest of the Newscast

You can use the formula you established for choosing the lead story to pick the rest of the stories in the newscast. Once you have selected the lead, determine which of the remaining stories would hold the most interest for your audience, then the next most interest, and so on. The stories would then be broadcast in that order.

There are important exceptions to this formula, however. Sometimes it makes sense to place stories back-to-back because they have something in common. During the war in Iraq, for example, it was not unusual for newscasts to carry a report of the fighting and then follow it up with a story from the White House or Congress concerning some political aspect of the military action. Those two stories were often followed by a third that might have been a reaction-type report to the invasion of Iraq from Congress or even a poll of American opinion on the invasion.

Another example would be the linking of weather-related stories. If part of the nation is suffering a drought and another section is in the middle of serious flooding, it would be logical to report those two stories together in the newscast. Without such logical connections, the rule is to report the news in its order of importance.

Localizing the News

When writing for a local station, always look for some local angle in national and international stories. If a British airliner crashes in Europe, the first thing to check is whether any Americans were on board and, if so, whether any were from the local listening area.

During the first Gulf War and the war in Iraq, local radio and TV news directors were always interested in getting interviews with service personnel who were from their area. When casualties were reported, it was the responsibility of news organizations to find out if any local men and women were killed or injured.

If a person wins a million-dollar lottery it's a good story, but if the person happens to be from the listening area, it's a "great" story.

Story Length

The length of a story is determined by the length of the newscast, the importance of the story, and the availability of news at that particular hour. If there is not much news to report, the stories may have to be longer than they would be normally. If there is a lot of news, most stories should be short to allow sufficient time for the major stories.

Before you start to write, you must determine how much time you actually have for news in a newscast. In Chapter 1, you learned that most newscasters read approximately 15 or 16 lines of copy per minute. So, for a three-minute newscast, you would need approximately 45 to 48 lines of copy.

But is the newscast really three minutes long? Probably not. Let's say there are two commercials, each running 30 seconds, in the newscast, which leaves two minutes of news. If there is a 10-second weather report, and maybe five seconds for stocks, and another five seconds to sign off, the two minutes have been reduced another 20 seconds. What is left is one minute and 40 seconds. If that time is converted to lines, you have about 25 lines in which to cover all the news. That is why you must learn to condense your stories. You may have as little as three lines to tell some of those stories.

Actualities

The voices of the newsmakers are called *actualities* or *sound bites*. They are the heart of radio news.

In Chapter 5, you learned that color is often provided by the voices of the people in the story. A good writer can tell the story without the actual voice, but he or she faces a greater challenge. Even the best newswriters would tell you that if given a choice, they would rather have the actual sound bite provide the color than their paraphrase of what was in the sound bite. Regardless of the writer's and newscaster's talents, it's not possible to capture all of the nuances in a sound bite with a paraphrase and the newscaster's voice. How can anyone better express the remarks of New York City cab drivers than they themselves? And how would the newscaster make up for the missing sounds of the city in the background—the natural sound—without the tape? Good tape is essential.

Wraparounds

The combination of sound and words is known as a *wraparound*. This technique, as the name suggests, uses the voice of the newscaster or reporter at the beginning and end of a story or report and the voice of the newsmaker in the middle. You might want to think of a wraparound in terms of a sandwich. There can be more than one thing between the two slices of bread. Wraparounds often have more than one sound bite in the middle. The anchor or reporter may wrap several different pieces of sound with script. Here's an example:

A Conrail freight train today left the tracks near Centerville, causing some major problems for passenger trains that also use the tracks. Railroad officials say the locomotive and eight of the train's 14 cars were derailed. They blamed a broken rail.

Remarkably, there were only two injuries—to the engineer and his assistant—and they were not serious. Engineer Brian Potter spoke to us at the hospital.

(sound bite)

15 sec.

Outcue: "... I was plenty scared."

Conrail engineer Brian Potter. He's in good condition at Centerville General Hospital.

The train was on its way to Southern California with a load of steel and lumber when the accident took place shortly before midnight. Freezing temperatures—dipping into the teens—will make the job of cleaning up a very unpleasant one and will hamper efforts to get service back to normal. But Conrail spokesman Mark Florman is optimistic.

(sound bite)

20 sec.

Outcue: "... we will know more in a few hours."

Conrail spokesman Mark Florman.

He also said that Conrail passenger trains will be detoured, causing some delays probably for 48 hours.

Lead-Ins

Every sound bite, wraparound, and report from the scene included in a news script must be introduced by a line or phrase known as a *lead-in*.

Here is one possible lead-in the anchor could have used to introduce the train wreck wraparound if it were done by a reporter at the scene:

A train wreck in Centerville during the night.

Reporter Dayna McDonald has the details.

(Take wraparound)

Runs 1:10

Outcue "...Dayna McDonald reporting for KTHU Radio."

The most important thing to avoid when writing a lead-in is redundancy. One of the worst style errors is a lead-in that says exactly the same thing as the first line of the wraparound or sound bite. The way to avoid this problem is for the writer or anchor in the newsroom and the reporter at the scene to discuss in advance what each is going to say.

Teases

The short sentences used in a script to hold the audience's attention just before a commercial break are called *teases*. The idea of a tease is to give the audience some reason to keep listening, rather than turning the dial. This is best accomplished by giving just a hint of what is to come after the commercial. The cleverer the tease, the greater the chance the audience will put up with the commercial.

If the train wreck wraparound were to follow a commercial, this is the way it might be teased:

Freezing temperatures add to the problems of a Centerville train wreck. That story after this.

(Commercial)

If the news is long enough, or being written for an all-news station, it's effective to tease two or more stories before going to a commercial. Such a tease gives the writer more opportunities to hook listeners. If they are not interested in the first story that is teased, they might go for the second or third one.

Headlines

Headlines are another form of tease. Headlines come at the top of a newscast and should reflect the most interesting and exciting stories to be covered in the upcoming newscast. Often, a headline for an offbeat story is an effective tease. Here is a sample:

A tornado rips through a small Kansas town, killing six people.

The cost of living climbs for the third straight month.

Governor Jones says he will veto legislation that would restore the death penalty.

And a pet cheetah scares a lot of people when he decides to take a walk down Main Street.

Those stories and more on the six o'clock news.

Good evening, I'm Bill Giles

Some radio newscasts start with only one headline:

Six people die in a tornado in Kansas.

Good evening, I'm Bill Giles with the six o'clock news. The tornado ripped through Centerville, Kansas ...

Many stations, particularly those that have shortened their newscasts, have eliminated headlines completely on the grounds that they are redundant and take up too much time. On many other radio stations, the only news is the headlines.

Pad Copy

Copy written for protection against mistakes in timing and unexpected changes in the newscast that could affect the timing is called *pad copy*. Most of the time, such copy will not get on the air, so the stories that are selected as pad copy should be relatively unimportant.

Because most radio newscasts are relatively short, pad copy normally consists of only a few short pieces totaling perhaps between 30 seconds and a minute. More pad copy might be written for longer newscasts.

Note that the chief reason for pad material is to avoid one of the scariest situations in broadcast news: running out of something to say before the program is scheduled to end.

Back Timing

Getting off the air on time takes some planning. If a newscast runs over, or is short, it sometimes can create problems for the programs that follow the news. This is particularly true if network programming comes after the newscast.

One way to guarantee that this situation does not happen is called *back timing*. The final segments in the newscast are timed and then deducted from the length of the newscast. Let's look at an example. Suppose the last two items in a newscast are the stocks and weather. Both are timed. It will take 10 seconds to read the stocks and another 20 seconds for the weather. The standard close for the newscast takes another five seconds to read. The newscaster will need 35 seconds, then, to read the last three items. So, 35 seconds are deducted from the total time of the newscast. The newscaster now knows that he or she must begin reading those three final items at exactly 2:25 into a three-minute newscast. The three final items should be placed in a separate pile within easy reach on the studio table. The time 2:25 should be written boldly on the top page of this back-timed copy. When the clock reaches the 2:25 mark in the newscast, the reader simply picks up the three pages and begins reading them, regardless of where he or she is in the newscast. Some stories may have to be dropped, and often they are, but that is the only way to guarantee that the newscaster gets off the air on time. In newsrooms that are computerized, the timing and backtiming are done by the computer itself.

Summary

Working in a radio operation in a small market has always been a good way to break into broadcast news, although many people seem to find the glamour and the pay of TV more appealing. At a small radio station committed to news, you do get a wonderful opportunity to learn how to do everything; you might end up being the writer, reporter, announcer, and technician. In these days of automation, you might be the only "live" person in the building.

As the only member of the news staff, you would quickly learn how to organize your time and effort because you would have little or no help. Your news judgment would be tested every day. You would get an excellent opportunity to hone your writing and reporting skills. You would also be preparing yourself for the next job in a bigger market.

Even if your main interest is television, the things that you learned in this chapter are important because radio news provides an important foundation for work in television news. The principles of radio newswriting and reporting also apply to television news, which is discussed in the next chapter. You will be required to make some adjustment because of pictures, but if you have absorbed the material in this chapter, you are well prepared to move along.

Review Questions

1. Why is it important when you are writing broadcast news to know about your audience?
2. You are the only newsperson working at your radio station. When you arrive for work, you have two hours before you read your first newscast. Explain how you would get prepared.
3. Explain the meaning of the term *writing from the back*.
4. If you were writing news in Centerville, Kansas, a market of 10,000, which story would you pick for the lead of your newscast? (a) United States forces drop emergency relief supplies to flood refugees in Mozambique; (b) Ten thousand autoworkers go on strike in Detroit; or (c) Centerville welcomes home ten of its service men and women who served in the NATO air attacks on Yugoslavia. Explain your choice.
5. If you were writing for a radio station in Ann Arbor, Michigan, which of the stories in Question 4 would you lead with? Why?
6. After you have selected the lead of your newscast, how would you determine the order of the rest of the stories?
7. What does localizing news mean? Give examples of how you could localize a story about a fire at a rock concert that caused some deaths and injuries and a story about the National Basketball Association draft.
8. If you were writing a two-minute newscast for radio, approximately how many lines of copy would you need?
9. If you have three commercials in the two-minute newscast, one of them 30 seconds and the other two 10 seconds each, how many lines of copy would you need to write?

Exercises

1. Using the stories reported on the front page of a newspaper, prepare headlines for a radio newscast.
2. Using those same headlines, write teases for two of the stories that will appear later in your radio newscast.

3. Read the front page of the newspaper, and decide which of the stories you would lead with in a newscast.

4. What other stories on the front page, and in the rest of the newspaper, would you use in your newscast, and in which order?

5. Go to a local radio station that has a news operation, and watch how they put a newscast together. Prepare a report on what you saw.

7　Writing for the Television Newscast

The major difference between radio and TV news is, of course, pictures. When you write for television, pictures are always crucial to a story. In radio, you must create pictures in your mind—as did Edward R. Murrow and other great broadcasters who used the medium effectively—and then find the words to paint those pictures for your audience. In television, you can show the actual pictures.

Combining Words and Pictures

The battle over which are more important in television news—the words or the pictures—is endless. There is no doubt that words are vital and that some broadcast writers use them more effectively than others. The late Charles Kuralt is an example of a writer whose words rival the pictures for prominence in a story. But even Kuralt would have been hard pressed to tell his stories without pictures. His talent was in his ability to strengthen the pictures with words. *Great* pictures and *great* words make great television news.

The beauty of good pictures is that they do not need a lot of words—just some good ones. The challenge for TV writers is to avoid clashes with the video. Do not tell viewers what they are seeing. Instead, support the video by saying what the video does not or cannot reveal. Fill in the blanks, but do not overpower the video. Give your viewers time to savor the pictures.

Such advice assumes that you have good pictures to work with. If you don't, then the words do become crucial because they are needed to prop up the video. But because TV news is not about using poor video, stories with bad pictures are likely to be dropped for more appealing ones unless the messages they convey are too vital to be eliminated completely.

If the pictures are poor, however, you can be sure you'll be asked to tell the story quickly. A common criticism of television news is that it relies on the pictures too much, but right or wrong the formula is not likely to change: poor pictures, short stories; good pictures, long stories.

Sound Bites

As in radio, sound bites, the words of newsmakers, are key to telling a good TV news story. An advantage for TV writers is that TV sound bites feature the faces of the newsmakers as well as their voices. Good TV newswriters weave their copy between and around the sound bites, much in the way that radio writers create wraparounds. This combination, called a *package*, is the best way to tell a news story on television. The chapters on reporting will deal extensively with building packages.

The Television Newswriter

In television, as in radio, a writer's duties depend on the size of the newsroom. In a small market—and even in some medium-sized markets—no one is assigned solely to writing. The anchors, reporters, producers, and perhaps an intern from a local college write the news. Television newsrooms in big markets and at the networks usually have several writers and, perhaps, associate producers who also write. Those who write television news have three basic writing tasks: read stories, voice-overs, and lead-ins.

Read Stories

Read, or *tell,* stories are read by the anchors without the use of pictures except for those that usually appear next to the anchor's head. Visually, read stories are the least interesting in TV news. They are virtually the same as radio copy. They are, however, a necessary part of the TV newscast because they give the anchors exposure to the audience. Anchors are paid well, and the audience expects to see their faces on camera at least part of the time.

Sometimes, read stories are used because no video is available. Read copy might even lead the newscast if it is about a breaking story that is just developing. We all are familiar with the phrase *film at eleven,* which usually indicated that it was too early for video, but it would come later. Often it meant the film needed to be developed, a problem eliminated, of course, with video tape and the ability to go live with microwave and satellite capability.

Read stories are most often those that are not important enough to require video or whose video would be dull. At the same time, read stories play a major role in the TV newscast—they break up the other types of material. Too much of anything tends to be boring, so the read stories provide a change of pace.

Finally, read stories are easiest to work with in a newscast because they are flexible. They are the putty that fills in the holes of the newscast. Read stories often play the same role as radio pad copy; they provide an opportunity to make adjustments that guarantee that the newscast gets off the air on time. If the TV newscast is long, the read stories are the likely stories to be dropped. If the newscast is short, more read stories are likely to be used.

Voice-overs

The second type of assignment given to TV newswriters is the voice-over (V/O), copy that the anchor reads while video or other visuals are shown. The video can either be silent or have a soundtrack that is kept low for natural effect, a technique referred to as *sound under* or *natural sound.*

Remember: The copy must complement the video. It should not duplicate what is obvious to viewers. Avoid phrases such as "what you are seeing here" unless the video is difficult to understand. For example, if you are showing video of a train derailment, rather than tell your viewers "What you are seeing is the derailment of a Conrail freight train that left its tracks last night," you would say "A Conrail freight train left its tracks last night," and let the pictures show the derailed train.

To write voice-over copy intelligently, you need to look at the video and take notes. When viewing the video, use a stopwatch to time each scene. The cameraperson sometimes shoots a series of short shots that may require little editing, but individual shots are often too long to use without editing. Let's consider the train wreck story discussed in the last chapter.

The cameraperson shot a long, continuous *pan* of the wrecked cars that lasts about 30 seconds. There's another shot of a derrick hovering over the scene for 20 seconds and a third 20-second shot of railroad workers huddled around a hastily made trashcan fire to ward off the frigid weather. Finally, there's an additional 30 seconds of video that shows some of the train's wrecked cargo—an assortment of steel rods and girders and lumber. The total running time of the video is one minute and 40 seconds. The producer asks the writer for a 20-second voice-over. The writer, then, must lift an assortment of brief shots from the video that can be strung together in some logical order that will make sense when the narration is added. (In a small newsroom, reporters often write the script and edit the videotape. In a large operation, a tape editor follows the writer's or reporter's instructions.)

Now that the writer has notes on the length of each scene, she must decide how to *edit*, or *cut*, the video. (*Cut* is a film term that has carried over to video. All editing is done electronically; the videotape is not physically cut.) The writer decides to use part of the long pan of the wreck scene first. The

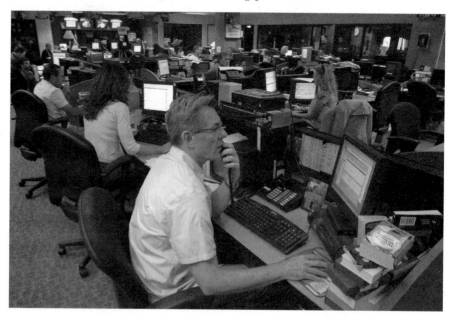

Figure 7-1   WCBS-TV producer Dennis White prepares an evening newscast. (Courtesy of WCBS-TV, New York, NY)

cameraperson held steady on the scene at the end of the pan, knowing that the writer might wish to use part of it. It is poor technique to cut into a pan, but it is acceptable to use part of it as long as it comes to a stop before the next shot. The writer uses eight seconds of the pan. Then the writer selects five seconds of the wreckage video that shows the steel girders and the lumber spread over the tracks and terrain. Four seconds of the derrick at work follow, and the voice-over closes with three seconds of the railroad workers around the trashcan fire.

The writer gives her instructions to the tape editor, and then returns to her desk to type out the script from her notes and wire copy. In preparing the script, the writer uses a format different from that used in radio.

The Split Page

In Chapter 1, you learned that TV scripts differ from radio scripts because they contain both the newscaster's words and an explanation of how the video is to be used. The format for a TV script is known as the *split page.* In Chapter 5, you saw examples of many such scripts.

The split page is divided vertically so that about 60 percent of the page is in the right column and about 40 percent is in the left. Those writing TV news do so on computers. Although their product is often sent electronically to the teleprompters, scripts also are normally printed out from the computers, as a backup, in case the computers malfunction.

The right side of the split page is reserved for the copy that will be read by the anchors, the running times (which also appear on the left), and the outcues (final words) of any videotape that has sound. The anchors—and this is important to remember—will be able to see only the right side of the script on their teleprompters. It is also important that you write only in the column on the right side. If you write outside the column, the words will not appear on the teleprompter screens.

Video Instructions

The left side of the script is set aside for the slug and for video and audio instructions and tape times for the director. Because of the limited space on the left side of the script, abbreviations are used for the various technical instructions. Here are some common ones:

1. O/C, "on camera," tells the director that at this point in the script the anchor will be on camera.
2. V/O, "voiceover," means the anchor is reading copy while the audience is seeing something else, such as silent videotape or graphics.
3. SIL indicates "silent" videotape and is used in combination with the V/O symbol.
4. SOT lets the director know that there is "sound on tape." It could be a sound bite with a newsmaker or a report from the field that was taped earlier.
5. ENG, "electronic news gathering," tells the director that the video is on a videocassette.

6. FONT, an abbreviation for the manufacturer Videfont, indicates that names, titles, and other information are superimposed over videotape or graphics to identify newsmakers, locations, and various other pictures appearing on TV screens. Many stations use the term *super* or the abbreviation VG (video graphic) instead of FONT.

7. SL, ESS, or ADDA indicate that pictures or graphics of some sort will be shown next to the anchor. SL stands for "slide"; ESS refers to Electronic Still Storage, an electronic graphics and video computer system; ADDA is the name of a computer system that also provides electronic storage. If the word *box* appears next to any of these abbreviations, the graphic will be enclosed in a box next to the anchor rather than fill the entire screen. Other technical abbreviations are used by writers to help the director. You will learn them once you start working with video on a regular basis.

Here is the split-page script used for the train wreck story discussed earlier:

TRAIN WRECK 3/15 6pm tw O/C Smith Box ADDA	SMITH A Conrail freight train today left the tracks near Centerville, Kansas, causing some major problems for passenger service trains that also use the tracks.
V/O SIL (TRT: 40 sec.)	V/O Railroad officials say the locomotive and eight of the train's 14 cars were derailed. They blamed a broken rail. Remarkably, there were only two injuries—to the engineer and his assistant—and they were not serious. The train was on its way to southern California with a load of steel and lumber when the accident took place shortly before midnight. The wreckage was scattered over a wide area. Within hours a derrick was sent to the scene to help clean up the mess. Officials say the job will take days. Freezing temperatures—dipping into the teens—will make the cleanup difficult and unpleasant.
Smith O/C Tag	O/C Railroad officials say that while the wreckage is being removed and repairs made to the tracks, Conrail passenger trains will be detoured. This probably will cause delays for at least 48 hours.

If you examine this script, you will see that the slug *TRAIN WRECK* is in the upper left-hand corner along with the date, the time of the newscast, and the writer's initials.

On the next line in the right column is *SMITH*, the name of the anchor. Because most newscasts have two or more anchors, the name of the anchor reading the copy must always be displayed at the top of the right-hand column.

On the next line at the left is *O/C Smith*, which lets the director know which anchor is on camera. Underneath that are the words *Box ADDA*, which tell the director that a picture will be displayed in a box next to the anchor's head. In this case, it could be a generic train wreck graphic that TV newsrooms keep on hand along with scores of other such graphics. (It also could be a freeze frame of part of the video that would be shown with the voiceover. But if that were the case, the writer would have to indicate it by typing *SIL/FF* ["silent/freeze frame"] next to *Box ADDA*.)

The anchor's script continues on the right side. Below the first sentence, you see the V/O symbol, which means that at this point in the script the video will be shown. The anchor continues reading, but the audience no longer sees his face.

The V/O symbol is also displayed in the left-hand column with the abbreviation for silent videotape, *SIL,* for the benefit of the director. In parentheses is the total running time of the videotape (TRT: 40 seconds), which tells the director that there are actually 40 seconds of wreckage footage on the videocassette. Because the V/O copy should take only about 30 seconds to read, the director has a 10-second cushion to avoid going to black, which is something of a nightmare for directors and their bosses. To avoid that problem, tape editors always "pad the tape"—cut more tape than the writer requests.

When the anchor has finished reading the V/O copy, he returns on camera (which is why we show *O/C* in both columns) to read a final sentence about delays in rail service brought on by the wreck. That final sentence is called a *tag,* and the writer of this script has added the word *tag* after O/C in the left column just to remind the busy director that this is the end of the story.

Sound on Tape

Those writing news for TV must also learn to write voice-over scripts that include sound on tape (SOT). Because the voices and pictures of newsmakers are a vital part of TV news, a great deal of the sound on tape is provided in the middle of reporter packages and is of no real concern to the newswriter. But sound is often worked into the anchor's script without the help of the reporter, and that is the newswriter's function.

Let's go back to the train wreck story and suppose that there is some sound on tape of one of the workers trying to keep warm around the trashcan fire. The writer decides to add that sound on tape to the script at the end of the voice-over before the anchor comes back on camera. A sound bite used at the end of a voice-over is abbreviated VO-SOT or V-SOT. The script would look like this:

SOT :15 FONT: Mark Florman	TRACK UP OUTCUE ". . . get any railroad worker warmer." Time :15
O/C Smith	O/C Railroad officials say that while the wreckage is being removed and repairs made to the tracks, Conrail passenger trains will be detoured. This probably will cause delays for at least 48 hours.

The sound-on-tape symbol and the time appear in the left-hand column to indicate that sound on tape will be used at this point in the script. The director now knows that when the anchor reads the last words of the voice-over, ". . . difficult and unpleasant," it is time to bring in the sound on tape.

The terms "Track Up" and "Time 15" also appear in the right-hand column along with the outcue, the final words of the sound bite. This lets the anchor know that a 15-second sound bite comes up before he returns on camera to read the last sentence in the story. The abbreviation *FONT* in the left column means that the name and identification of the railroad worker is to be superimposed over the lower portion of the screen while the railroad worker is speaking. The director will signal the font operator to punch up the information approximately three seconds into the sound bite.

After the sound bite instructions, the symbol O/C is written on both sides of the script to indicate that the anchor returns on camera to wrap up or "tag" the story or to begin a new story.

Lead-Ins

The third common scripting chore for the TV newswriter is preparing *lead-in* lines for sound bites and reporter packages. Writing television lead-ins is similar to writing lead-ins for radio wraparounds but is slightly more complicated. As with radio lead-ins, the information in the first line of the report or sound bite cannot be repeated in the lead-in.

Unlike radio lead-ins, those for television require some additional instructions for the director because while the anchor is leading into the report or sound bite on camera, some visual is usually shown in a box next to the anchor.

TRAIN WRECK 3/15 6pm tw O/C Smith	SMITH A Conrail train has derailed in Kansas and we have a report from the scene from our reporter Frank Coakley.

SOT :55   TRACK UP
FONT: Frank Coakley   Outcue: "... Frank Coakley reporting."
                                               Time :55

The writer used a soft lead-in because she knew that Coakley would provide the hard-news lead. He started his report this way:

> The engine and eight cars of the Conrail train left the tracks around midnight near the town of Centerville. Fortunately only two people were injured slightly.

This lead-in is effective because it allows the reporter's opening words to build on it as he tells the rest of the story.

Headlines and Teases

Depending on the size of the news operation, headlines and teases usually are turned out by the writer, the editor, or a producer.

As always, the major difference between headlines for television and those for radio is that headlines and teases on television are normally supported with pictures. Some network newsrooms forgo the traditional headline approach, preferring to have the anchors talk briefly about the top story before going to a reporter for details. But local news almost always leads the newscast with headlines, which are most effective when used with flashes of video. Here's a sample of how one local newsroom scripts headlines:

HOWARD (DEE)   (HOWARD)
                                               Coming up on Action News at Six...

V/O #5 (liquor store)   Police search for two men who killed
                                               a liquor store owner during a holdup.
RUNS :04
WIPE TO V/O #3   (DEE)
(Mayor shaking hands)   Mayor Thompson honors a citizen
                                               who rescued a child from a burning
                                               building.

RUNS :04
WIPE TO V/O #2   (HOWARD)
(Unemployment office)   And unemployment in Center City
                                               reaches a new high.

RUNS :03
O/C Howard (Gail)   Good evening, I'm Howard Pass.

                                                 (DEE)
                                               And I'm Dee Danaher. Those are some
                                               of the stories we're covering on
                                               tonight's Action News.

In the left column, *HOWARD* indicates that one anchor reads the opening line of the newscast and the first headline, while *(DEE)*—note the parentheses—

indicates that the other anchor is also on camera. Both anchors quickly disappear from the screen, but Howard is heard reading the first headline over video showing the scene of the liquor store holdup. The video runs about four seconds. After the first headline, the video wipes to a shot of Mayor Thompson shaking hands with a hero while Dee reads that headline. The second voice-over also runs four seconds. The video wipes a third time to a three-second shot of workers standing on line at an unemployment office. Howard reads that headline, as indicated, over the video. Then both anchors return on camera as Howard says "good evening" and identifies himself. Dee does the same and reminds the audience that the stories just teased would be covered in the upcoming newscast.

The numbers next to the voice-over symbols indicate which playback machines are used in the control room, information that is vital to the director. If the director or his or her assistant calls for the wrong machine, the wrong video would appear, and the newscast would get off to a confusing start. Some stations give numbers to the tapes instead of the machines. In that case, the tape numbers would be placed on the scripts so that the director could call for the proper one.

Later in the newscast—before the commercials—teases are used in an effort to hold the audience. The same voice-over technique used in headlines is used for teases. Many producers also include fonts over the video to give it extra punch. For example, these words might appear at the bottom of the appropriate video:

Police hunt killer . . .

Hero honored . . .

Unemployment climbs . . .

The point of such teases is to hook viewers, to keep their interest in the news during the commercial. Teasing three stories increases the chance that your audience will be interested in at least one of the upcoming stories.

A Team Effort

As you can see, writing television news is more complicated than writing radio news. Although one individual writes the television story and may even edit the videotape used in the story, the final product involves other people in the newsroom.

In radio, writers usually pick the stories they wish to tell their audience. In television, those who write the stories are told what to write and how long the stories should be. In radio, one person may do it all—record interviews on the phone, cover a news conference, and include in the newscast some of the tape he or she has edited. There are no one-person newsrooms in television, although at small stations you may be expected to play more than one role.

As in radio, television affords opportunities to learn how to do several different jobs. Writers often go on to other positions as reporters, anchors, and producers. Some move over to the assignment desk, where the people "find the news," a subject discussed in Chapter 9.

Summary

This chapter introduces a variety of terms used in television news, such as *split page, voice-over, package,* and *font,* and describes a television writer's most common writing assignments.

In carrying out these assignments, you need to learn to work with both words and pictures; broadcast news professionals have strong views on which is more important—the words or the pictures. The truth, of course, is that *both* words and pictures are critical to a successful TV news script. Television is a visual medium, and the pictures must be effective, but if the words that go with those pictures are unclear, confusing, or contradictory, the story will fail because no true communication will take place.

Choose your pictures carefully, and do the same with your words.

Review Questions

1. What is the major difference between writing for radio and writing for television?
2. How will poor pictures affect TV news stories?
3. How important are sound bites to a TV news script? Why?
4. What is a read story?
5. Why are read stories important to a TV newscast? List the different ways they are used.
6. What is a voice-over? Describe what the audience sees and hears during a voice-over.
7. Describe some of the things to remember when writing for pictures in a voice-over script.
8. Is it better to have too few or too many words in a voice-over? Explain.
9. Explain the steps that a writer takes in selecting videotape to be used in a voice-over.
10. Explain the term *split page,* indicating the dimensions and how the page is used.
11. Why must you be careful in observing the margins on the split page?
12. Explain the purpose of fonts and give some examples.
13. Explain the following abbreviations: SL and ADDA.
14. What does *SL Box* in a script mean?
15. What does *TRT* mean, and why is that term important for a director?
16. What is an outcue, and why is it important to the director and anchor?
17. What is the most important thing to remember when writing a lead-in to a sound bite or a correspondent's report?

Exercises

1. Take a story from the wire or a newspaper and rewrite it on a split page as a read story. It should be 20 seconds long.
2. Using the same piece of copy, prepare a V-SOT. Suppose that you have a sound bite from someone who is involved in the story. Using the split page, indicate the proper symbols and time for a 10-second sound bite. You have 30 seconds for the entire story.

3. Suppose that you have a reporter covering a story about a tornado hitting Centerville, Kansas. Three people have been killed, and more than a dozen have been injured. Write a lead-in for a live report, also indicating what the reporter's first sentence will say.
4. Using wire copy or the front page of a newspaper, script three headlines for a TV newscast.
5. Using the same copy, script two teases that will come before your first commercial break.
6. Go to a local TV station and observe who is doing the writing. Talk to either a writer or a producer on how the writing is assigned, and report on what you discover.

8   Delivering the News

Many of you have hopes of anchoring news. How long it takes you to end up at the anchor desk depends mainly on two factors. The first one is talent—your ability to deliver the news. The second consideration is the size of the market in which you begin your career.

If you have talent and start working in a relatively small market, you may reach the anchor desk quickly. You will still, however, have to prove you are ready for that job by impressing the news director with your reporting ability. Also, remember that not all reporters become anchors; some good reporters do not have the special talent required to anchor news. Similarly, some anchors make awful reporters. This chapter discusses the qualities you need to anchor or report in front of a camera or microphone.

Credibility

Ask news directors what they look for in reporters and anchors and most will tell you *credibility*. They want people who are believable, people who come across as knowledgeable about and comfortable with what they are doing.

Jeff Puffer, a voice coach for one of the nation's major broadcast consulting firms, Frank Magid Associates, says he knows many "reliable anchor-reporters with good potential who just don't seem comfortable in the anchor chair. In person they're spontaneous and charming. But on the air they're wooden, with unnatural speech rhythms and awkward inflection."

Puffer says that when he's instructing anchors and reporters, he expects them "to show two qualities in their reading: intelligence and genuine sensitivity." He says he looks for "emotion that is appropriate for the story, the person, and the occasion. I want them to demonstrate that they know what they're reading and that they're thoughtfully weighing the facts as they speak." Puffer says: "I always want them to say it with feeling, not artificially, but with sensitivity and maturity."

It is not always easy for anchor-reporters to accomplish these goals, and those who coach people in delivery techniques use a variety of methods. Puffer says he doesn't concentrate on speech pathology material such as breathing, diction, and resonance. "We're involved in matters relating to interpretation, making the voice sound spontaneous and conversational, like an ad-lib."

Puffer admits that his methodology could be called "unconventional or unorthodox," but, he says, "given what we have been finding in neuroscience research, we know that the whole of human intelligence is not just the left side of the brain, the intellectual side. It's also intuition, artistry, abstractions, pattern recognition, and the like."

One-Way Communication

Puffer says the difficulty in broadcast training is the "noninteractive environment." He points out that there is "no give and take, it's largely one way. The result of that strained environment is that the communicators do not automatically use all their self-expression when looking into a camera or speaking on mike as they would in a face-to-face dialogue." Puffer adds: "What we try to do is restore that quality and feeling in the delivery. We try to trigger that part of the brain that is responsible for artistry, abstraction, etc."

Puffer also notes that he's not trying to make a person's voice sound like someone else's. "We all have developed and cultivated a wealth of knowledge regarding what is appropriate interpersonal communication over the years," he says. "We all know the tools; we know how loud to speak; how to emphasize and articulate our words; how to use our face and eyes with accompanying gestures; no one has to tell us how to do these things. The idea," Puffer adds, "is to tap into those resources and help bring them into the environment that is not interactive, like the broadcast studio."

Puffer says he typically begins a talent coaching session by indicating (in these exact words) "I am not going to teach you today anything you don't already know." I believe, he says, "to the core of my being that for a young adult to have achieved success in relationships with others throughout his or her life, that person has developed considerably useful instincts regarding the ways to use volume, pitch, pacing, inflections, emphasis, eye contact, etc. to gain attention, hold interest, and create an atmosphere of good will and trust." Puffer goes on, "The difficulty occurs when that same person moves into the sequestered environment of a studio to anchor or into an edit suite to record the voice track for a package." He says without the benefit of direct contact with the receiver, the speaker automatically faces a disadvantage.

He says any number of unintended peculiarities can begin to creep into the delivery, making that person's speech sound stilted. Puffer adds that this is where talent coaches like him come in, they help anchors and reporters, "translate to the broadcast not only the behaviors and mannerisms consistent with conversation but also the attitudes and frames of mind that invite lively, expressive conversation with your best friend or your mom." But Puffer says it's not as easy as telling the student to pretend that you're talking to your friend or mom. He says there is an intermediate step that sets the exchange of conversation between two people in motion, and it's understanding those subtleties involved in getting started that proves to be the most effective in getting the authentic self to come forward.

Puffer also discusses what he describes as the "single, most common delivery trap that broadcasters fall into—the pattern characterized by lifting or raising the inflections at the end of sentences which is referred to as "comma splicing" or "circumflex."

To illustrate the problem, Puffer offered this exercise: Read the following sentence the same way you would if you were to say, "I dunno," as you finish the sentence.

"The state board of regents voted not to increase tuitions at their final budget meetings yesterday."

Puffer says the inflection pattern not only is inconsistent with the way a person speaks in an actual explanation, but it also risks hurting one's credibility in either of two ways. First, he said, it can register in the ears and minds of the audience as being dismissive. He says the rising intonation is the same that most typically occurs when someone says (shrugging) "you can listen if you want, but you don't have to." Or Puffer adds, alternatively, the intonation can suggest ambivalence—uncertainty. He says it's the same sound you hear when you or someone else says, "may-BE." Puffer concludes, "learn not to speak this way so as not to compromise your credibility through indifference or ambivalence."

Getting Help with Your Delivery

If you are having problems with your voice, diction, and delivery, it's a good idea to deal with the problems while you are in college. Speech and debating courses sometimes help, but if you have serious problems, you may need a voice coach. Voice coach Carol Dearing Rommel advises students who are intent on being in front of a microphone or camera to Rommel "do all they can to prepare themselves before they leave college." She says that without professional help, some students "fall into habit patterns that will work against them."

Dialects

Traditionally, station managers and news directors look for people who speak "standard American speech" when they hire on-air personnel. That's another way of saying they like Midwestern voices, which are considered "neutral."

Figure 8-1
Former *CBS News* correspondent Walter Cronkite was among the most respected anchors in TV news. (Courtesy of *CBS News*)

Don't count yourself out if you were not born and reared in South Dakota. Some dialects can be eliminated with good coaching. If they cannot be corrected, it's still possible to work in an area where your dialect is the primary one. "If you have a Southern dialect you can work in the South," says coach Rommel, "but you are not likely to get on the air in Chicago." She said that same rule applies to people who were born and reared in Chicago. "If they have a strong big-city dialect they are not likely to make it in Dallas."

Mary Berger, a speech pathologist and author in Chicago who works with young people, says it's important to let students know, if they have a dialect that reflects a minority racial or ethnic background, that there is "nothing wrong with them. Many have been told that they are stupid because of the way they speak. Once you tell them that you do not intend to change the dialect but develop a new 'style' for use in the work place, they relax." Berger explains her methods in her book *Speak Standard, TOO.*

Like Jeff Puffer, Berger says many of her colleagues may consider her approach to speech problems "unorthodox." She recalls that she was asked by Columbia College, in Chicago, to design a course after the college got feedback from graduates indicating that they were having trouble finding work because of voice problems.

"What we find in our classes," she notes, "are a lot of students with high-pitched, nasal-sounding, unpleasant voices not acceptable for air. We don't try to correct those problems in the traditional way, working on pitch and inflection, etc. What we do is give them an 'indirect hint' that says, 'Your voice is different but you can change it without too much help from us.'"

Berger says the first thing she has the students do is record their voices and then listen to them. "They detect immediately the high pitches and other things that they would like to change. Then we say, 'OK, now pretend that you are someone else, like newscaster Bill Curtis or a general giving orders to troops.' Amazingly, their voices suddenly get deeper."

Berger stresses that there are times when students obviously cannot change their readings. "When their voices are straining, for example, when they try to change their pitch, we direct them to people who deal with such problems."

Voice coach Rommel says that pitch is one of the most troubling problems for young people. "Young ladies," she says, "usually have too high a pitch. When they read their copy, it sounds as if they are much younger and less credible than they really are." But Rommel warns young women that trying to change the pitch of their voice dramatically without professional help can be dangerous.

Rommel, an adjunct at Southern Methodist University, says another common problem is articulation. She says many people going into broadcasting have a minor lisp. But Dearing says this problem is easily correctable and should not prevent anyone from moving forward as a reporter or an anchor.

Listening to Yourself

In the chapters on style, you learned that it is always a good idea to read your copy aloud because your ear catches mistakes and detects poorly constructed copy that your eye misses. Similarly, reading aloud alerts you to any prob-lems you have with pronunciation, articulation, and awkward speech patterns.

Getting Pronunciation Help

Newscasters should avoid using words that are difficult to pronounce. The mind understands the meaning of many words, but sometimes it has trouble relaying the pronunciation to the tongue, which causes newscasters to stumble over their copy. Tricky words and phrases invite trouble.

Sometimes writers and anchors have no choice, however. Proper names, for example, cannot be changed. Spelling them correctly does not guarantee that they will be pronounced correctly. The writer of a newscast must identify the correct pronunciation of any difficult names in a script. Reporters should ask the people whom they are interviewing for the proper pronunciation of their names. Names of towns also should be checked if there is any doubt. For example:

> Biloxi in Mississippi is pronounced Bi-lok'-si. Acadian in Louisiana is pronounced E-kay'-di-en. Kankakee in Illinois is pronounced Kang'-ka-ke. Cairo in Illinois is pronounced Ka'-ro.

If a job takes you to a new part of the country, it is a good idea to seek out someone who has lived in the area for some time. Colleagues who have been working at the station will be able to help, and someone at the local library or historical society will probably be happy to answer questions about the pronunciation of nearby towns or local family names.

The wire services send out pronunciation guides to their customers (see Figure 8-2). These are particularly useful when covering national and international stories. If your news operation is computerized, these guides should be stored for future use.

In cities large enough to have a wire service bureau, the staff will help its clients find the proper pronunciation of a name or place in the city or state. The wires also have a phonetics desk that helps with hard-to-pronounce names in national and international news stories.

In Chapter 1, you learned that it is not always necessary to use the names of foreign dignitaries. If you do use them, it is a good idea to refer to the dignitaries by their titles during the rest of the story, particularly if the names are unusually difficult to pronounce.

When using difficult names, write them phonetically in the copy to help the person who will be reading the script. (See Figure 8-2 for an example of how to spell phonetically.) The phonetic spelling can be given after the word or written above the word. Writers working on a newscast should ask the anchors which style they prefer. Here are examples of the two methods: Cayuga (Ka-yoo'-ga) Indians still live on the land. Cayuga (Ka-yoo'-ga) Indians still live on the land.

Dictionaries, which give the proper pronunciation of words as well as their meanings, are invaluable tools. Several dictionaries of pronunciation are also available for purchase, and most newsrooms keep copies on hand. If you are unsure about the pronunciation of a word, look it up.

K
Ahmed Tejan Kabbah—AH'-mehd TEH'-jahn KAH'-bah
Kabul—kah-BOOL' (though the pronunciation KAH'-bool is also common)
Farouk Kaddoumi—fah-ROOK' kah-DOO'-mee
Akhmad Kadyrov—kuh-DEE'-ruhv
Thomas Kaenzig—KEN'-zig
Kalai-Zal—kah-LAY'-zahl
Peter Kalikow—KAL'-ih-koh
Elaine Kamarck—KAY'-mahrk
Melina Kanakaredes—kah-nah-kah-REE'-deez
Kanawha—kah-NAH'
Kandahar—kan'-duh-HAHR' (slight stress on first syllable; stronger
    stress on third syllable)
Karachi—kuh-RAH'-chee
Radovan Karadzic—RA'-doh-van KA'-ra-jich
Karbala—KAHR'-bah-lah
Islam Karimov—EES'-lahm kah-REE'-mahv
Mohamed Abdirahman Kariye—ahb-deer-uh-HAHM' ky-EED'-eh
Mel Karmazin—KAHR'-muh-zin
Raed Karmi—RAH'-ed KAHR'-mee
Karnei Shomron—kahr-NAY' shahm-ROHN'
Hamid Karzai—HAH'-mihd KAHR'-zeye
Qayum Karzai—ky-OOM' KAHR'-zeye
Kaspiisk—kahs-PEESK'
Mikhail Kasyanov—kah-see-AH'-nahf
Moshe Katsav—KAHT'-sahv
Jorma Kaukonen—YOR'-mah KOW'-kah-nen
Yoriko Kawaguchi—yoh-ree-koh kah-wah-goo-chee
Kazimiya Shrine—KAH'-zi-mee-yah
Thomas Kean—kayn
Bernard Kerik—KEHR'-ihk
Teresa Heinz Kerry—teh-RAY'-zah
Khaldiyah—KAHL'-dee-yah
Zalmay Khalilzad—ZAHL'-may kah-LEEL'-zahd
Ali Khamenei—hah-meh-neh-EE'
Abdul Qadeer Khan—ahb-DOOL' kah-DEER' khahn
Khaneqin—hah-nah-KEEN'
Mohammad Khatami—HAHT'-ah-mee
Essid Sami Ben Khemais—EH'-seed ... keh-MEES'
Khobar—KOH'-bahr
Mikhail Khodorkovsky—mih-hah-EEL' khoh-dohr-KAHV'-skee
Ayatollah Khomeini—ah-yah-TOH'-lah hoh-MAY'-nee
Khost—hohst (heavy stress on first "h")
Mwai Kibaki—mwy kih-BAH'-kee
Kim Jong Il—kihm jawng eel
Kiowa, Kansas—KY'-oh-wah
Kiribati—keer-ih-BAH'-tee
Kirkuk—keer-KOOK' or keer-KUK'
Heidi Klum—kloom
Junichiro Koizumi—joon-ee-chee-roh koh-ee-zoo-mee

Figure 8-2   Sample of an AP pronunciation guide.

Valery Korzun—val-uh-ree kohr-ZOON'
Vojislav Kostunica—voh-YEE'-slahv kosh-too-NEET'-zuh
Frank, Martha (Stewart) Kostyra—kah-STY'-rah
George Kouloheras—koo-loh-HEHR'-us
Dennis Kozlowski—kahz-LOW'-skee
Ray Kubilus—koo-BIL'-uhs
Robert Krughoff—KROO'-gahf
Ryszard Krystosik—RIH'-shahrd krih-STAW'-sehk
Kok Ksor—kahk kuh-SOHR'
Dennis Kucinich—koo-SIN'-ich
Andre Kuipers—KEYE'-purz
Kunar—ku-NAHR' (The vowel sound in "ku" is similar to the double-o
    sound in "took")
Kunduz—KUHN'-dooz
Kushiro—koo-shee-roh
Kut—koot
Aleksander Kwasniewski—kvahsh-NYEV'-skee

L
Hemant Lakhani—HEH'-muhnt luh-KAH'-nee
Landstuhl—LAHND'-shtool
Anthony LaPaglia—luh-PAH'-lee-uh
Amel Larrieux—lahr-RYOO'
LaSalle County, Illinois—luh-SEL'
Lashkar-e-Tayyaba—LAHSH'-kar ay TEYE'-buh
Jorge Lazareff—HOR'-hay
Lee Hoi-chang—lee hweh-chayng
LaSalle Leffall—leh-FAWL'
Leganes—leh-GAN'-ehs
John Lehman—LAY'-man
Leipzig, Germany—LYP'-sihg
Camp Lejeune—lih-ZHOON'
David Lereah—lur-RAY'
Mark LeTexier—lah-TEKS'-eer
Katrina Leung—lee-YUNG'
Daniel Libeskind—LEE'-behs-kihnd
Lien Chan—LEE'-ehn jan
Likud—lee-KOOD'
Lindsay Lohan—LOH'-han
Jose Lopez Portillo—hoh-say loh-pehz pohr-TEE'-yoh
Los Olivos—lohs oh-LEE'-vohs
Kim Louagie—LOO'-wah-jay
Loya jirga—LOY'-uh JEER'-guh
Richard Lugar—LOO'-gur
Constantine Lyketsos—ly-KEHT'-sohs

M
Dan Macagni—muh-KAHN'-yuh
Macclenny, Florida—MAK'-klen-ee
Madhya Pradesh—MUH'-dyuh PRUH'-desh
Imam Mahdi—EE'-mahm MAH'-dee

Figure 8-2 cont'd   Sample of an AP pronunciation guide.

RYMg

Pacing

What else can you do to improve your delivery? *CBS News* correspondent Charles Osgood says pacing is important. Osgood advises using a pause to get attention when you want something you just said "to sink in. . . . A pause can be very telling, provided you know something." He says the "most remarkable pacer in our business is ABC newscaster Paul Harvey. You can drive a truck between 'Paul Harvey' and 'good day.' He's doing that for a reason."

Osgood recalls times when he's been traveling with a news crew and everyone is talking among themselves until Harvey begins broadcasting. "When Paul Harvey comes on the radio," Osgood says, "everybody stops [talking] and listens to Paul Harvey. You cannot not listen to that man."

Osgood says: "You can hate him. You can think he's terrible. You can disagree with him completely as far as his politics are concerned. But you can't not listen to him, because he has got you. He has found out how to say, 'Hey, shut up. I'm talking now.'"

Here are excerpts from a *Paul Harvey News* broadcast titled "One Vote," which aired on April 4, 1996:

> One voter in each precinct in the United States will determine the next President of the United States.
>
> One vote. That's a big weapon you have there, Mister.
>
> In 1948, just one additional vote in each precinct would have elected Dewey. In 1960 one vote in each precinct in Illinois would have elected Nixon. One Vote.
>
> One morning in 1844, a grain miller from DeKalb County, Indiana, was walking toward his mill. It was election day but he had work to do and did not intend to vote. Before he reached the mill, however, he was stopped by friends who persuaded him to go to the polls. As it happened, the candidate for whom he voted won a seat in the state legislature . . . by a margin of one vote.
>
> Now . . . when the Indiana Legislature convened, the man elected from DeKalb cast the deciding vote that sent Edward Allen Hennegan to the United States Senate. Then, in the Senate, when the question of statehood for Texas came up, there was a tie vote. But who do you suppose was presiding as President pro tempore? Hennegan. He cast the deciding vote from the chair.
>
> So Texas was admitted to the Union because a miller in DeKalb County, Indiana, went ten minutes out of his way to cast . . . one vote.
>
> More?
>
> Thomas Jefferson was elected President by one vote in the Electoral College. So was John Quincy Adams. Rutherford B. Hayes was elected President by one vote. One vote gave statehood to California, Idaho, Oregon, Texas, and Washington. The Draft Act of World War Two passed the House by one vote.

Figure 8-3   News commentator Paul Harvey. (Courtesy of Paul Harvey News)

Almost two hundred million Americans are eligible to vote this year. Fewer than half will.

Plato said it: "The penalty good men pay for indifference to public affairs is to be ruled by evil men."

So your one vote is important. Historically you use it . . . or you will lose it.

Tell the world if you don't want to vote, but don't pretend it makes no difference. Tell the world you no longer want to think and act for yourself, but don't figure you can relax and let George do it. Because sometimes George sells his vote for a bottle of cheap booze to the very men who stand for everything you are against.

If you're not sure for whom you should vote, turn to a newspaper you can trust. Because everything we've won in 10 wars at the point of a gun can be taken away a vote at a time.

Edmund Burke said it another way: "All that is necessary for the forces of evil to win in the world is for enough good men to do nothing."

Osgood says that when he writes for himself he uses a lot of ellipses (series of three dots). "I want to remind myself that that is supposed to be a pause. I will also capitalize certain words . . . because I want to hit that particular word for it to work."

The *CBS News* correspondent also says it's important to remember when you are on the air that "you're talking to somebody, which means that you have to be conscious at all times that there's somebody there." Osgood notes that you can't assume people are listening; you "have to get their attention, you don't automatically have it."

Marking Copy

Most newscasters mark copy to help them remember when to pause or to emphasize certain words. They mark the copy as they read it aloud, which

B)
THE SALT RIVER PROJECT'S WEST VALLEY
SERVICE CENTER/ HAS BEEN CLOSED AFTER
TESTS SHOW THE PRESENCE OF
LEGIONNAIRES' DISEASE

TAKE 1/2" VO :00   S-R-P CLOSED THE CENTER AT TOTH
AVENUE AND VAN BUREN. . . (AS A SAFETY
PRECAUTION.)

VG: 79TH AVE & VAN   THAT'S AFTER THE PRESENCE OF A
BUREN SRP CENTER   WATER-CARRIED BACTERIA/ THAT CAUSES
CLOSED   LEGIONNAIRES' (WAS FOUND.)

THE COMPANY DID NOT WANT TO
ENDANGER ITS 200 EMPLOYEES AT THE
CENTER /. . SALT RIVER SAYS IT EXPECTS
TO REMOVE THE BACTERIA AND RE-OPEN THE
END TAPE :20   BUILDING TUESDAY.

LEGIONNAIRES' IS A RARE DISEASE
NORMALLY FOUND IN HUMID CLIMATES . . .
BUT THERE WERE 17 CASES REPORTED IN
ARIZONA.

also helps them control their breathing. Long sentences require extra breath, so newscasters must either pause more often or rewrite the sentence. Otherwise, they sound as though they are running out of breath. Often, inexperienced newscasters try to speed up their delivery when they realize that they might have trouble getting through a complicated sentence, but that's a poor solution. If you find yourself leaning toward this solution, rewrite your copy until you can read it at a normal pace.

Here is an example of copy marked by a newscaster.

Bruce Kirk, a former anchor at KPNX-TV in Phoenix, who marked the example script, uses slash marks to indicate pauses and underlines words that he wishes to emphasize. Some anchors use a double underline for words that require extraordinary emphasis. Other anchors use all caps for words they wish to stress. Some anchors use ellipses to indicate pauses, and still others use dashes. Some anchors like their scripts typed in all caps while others prefer upper- and lowercase (which, according to studies, is easier to read).

Christine Devine, an anchor for KTTV in Los Angeles, who marked this next example, says she doesn't always have time to mark her script, but when she does "it results in a better show." Devine uses a bracket to let herself know she's starting to read a new paragraph and a new thought, and after a sound bite so she doesn't lose her place. She uses an ellipsis to signify the end of a phrase, but not the end of a thought.

Devine underlines key words for emphasis, which seems to be standard practice among anchors. She also routinely underlines "not." In addition, Devine says she underlines for contrast when, for example, contrasting Republicans and Democrats.

ANCHOR	**(CO)**
I-DEADLY FIRES	<u>TWO</u> PEOPLE ARE DEAD TONIGHT AFTER <u>SEPARATE</u> FIRES IN <u>TWO</u> SOUTHLAND CITIES.
	A BLAZE SWEPT THROUGH A <u>HOME</u> IN <u>ORANGE</u> EARLY THIS MORNING . . . <u>FATALLY</u> INJURING AN <u>ELDERLY</u> WOMAN AND LEAVING HER <u>HUSBAND</u> <u>CRITICALLY</u> <u>INJURED</u>.
	OFFICIALS SAY THE FIRE WAS SPARKED BY A <u>NATURAL</u> <u>GAS</u> <u>EXPLOSION</u> IN THE COUPLE'S KITCHEN.

Characteristics of Successful Anchors

Jim Boyer, the former news director of WWL-TV in New Orleans says that "people watch people. They don't watch helicopters or satellites and they prefer to watch anchors they like and are comfortable with." Boyer recalled the work of one of his anchors, the late Bill Elder, who worked for WWL for 20 years. Boyer said Elder was like an old friend telling them what's going on and it's very easy for them to watch. Speaking about his career a few years ago, Elder stressed that it is also important for anchors to be involved in the production of the show. He liked to boast that he would write a third of the news, even on days when he was working on special projects.

A number of anchors we spoke with also stressed how important it is to keep up with things, even if they are not part of their own culture, like the rock band scene and other things that appeal to younger people.

News directors we spoke with say it is important for anchors to understand that there is more to the job than looking and sounding good on the air. They also say anchors should be involved in the community through personal appearances or charity work. They also stress that it's important for anchors to be working journalists, who should be able to handle a school board meeting or a foreign story with equal ease.

Most news directors use the same language when they speak about successful anchors, and words like *credibility, honesty,* and *genuine* keep cropping up, along with concern and caring about what's going on in the community. Another common denominator is that successful, top-rated anchors are all genial people who are well liked by their co-workers and their viewers.

Diane Doctor, the news director of WCBS-TV in New York, says it's difficult to define why some anchors are more successful than others, but she also used the words credibility, on-camera presence and a comfort level that good anchors share with the audience. Obviously, she said they have to be intelligent to begin with and the audience has to believe that what the anchors are telling them is true. Doctor, who worked in a number of local markets, and for NBC and WNBC in New York in both management positions and as a reporter and producer, before joining the CBS organization, agreed that it's also important for anchors to be active in the community, so the viewers tend to think of them not so much as performers but as part of the family.

Ratings Wars

Of course, what keeps anchors in their jobs, particularly for long periods, are ratings and the numbers. These factors are especially important for the celebrity-type anchors who come into our homes every morning to provide entertainment in addition to news. Almost every local TV station has programs now that copy the network shows like *Good Morning America* and *Today*. The local shows often complement the network productions.

Nowhere on television is the battle for ratings and survival as keen as it is in the morning, with CBS, ABC, and NBC trying to come up with fresh approaches to news and entertainment. On the plus side, this mixture is more palatable than the stuff that often tries to pass as news in the late evening hours—a subject that we have discussed in great detail, particularly in Chapter 22, "Tabloid Journalism."

Those who produce the morning shows rely more on personalities than anything else, although some of the anchors have strong news backgrounds. Morning anchors have changed frequently, and the ratings have flip-flopped over the years, but *Today* has been dominant most of the time, with *Good Morning America* in the second slot. CBS has had trouble finding the right formula and the right anchors for *The Early Show*. It consistently finishes third in the ratings.

Cosmetics

It has always been true that anchor people, in addition to having good voices, also must be attractive on camera. Fortunately, the problem of "looks" is not quite as bad as it once was when it was virtually impossible to get on camera unless you were beautiful or handsome. News managers still want people with pleasing faces, regardless of race or gender, but we do see anchors wearing glasses, and wrinkles are not outlawed, as they once were. But those who select their on-camera talent often want to change their looks and delivery, even though they liked them well enough to hire them.

Among the absurdities that anchors must sometimes put up with from their bosses is this particularly amusing one related by *ABC News* correspondent Judy Muller when she was still at CBS. According to Judy, her boss called her into his office to complain about the way she was saying the traditional cutaway phrase before a commercial break—"Now this." At the time, Muller didn't think the criticism was very funny. She said it is memorable to her because it "took aim at possibly the only thing I was secure about at the time: my on-air delivery."

Muller was puzzled because she asked herself: How many ways can you say "Now this"? But she said she dutifully practiced different inflections: with authority, drawn out in a provocative manner, queried in an inquisitive manner, "every way until I had it just right, which is basically the way I was saying it before, but with a touch of suspense."

This encounter with a boss over such a petty issue is described by Muller as a lesson in understanding that, just when you think you've got a thing wired, something comes along to short-circuit that notion, to pull you up short and remind you that now, of all things, you "must deal with *this*. It may be something petty, or improbable, or unpredictable, but you cannot proceed without dealing with it."

Muller obviously did not forget the lesson. Many years later when she wrote her memoirs she called the book: *Now This* (Putnam Publishing Group, 2000). In her book, Muller also recalls an incident when she moved into TV reporting for the first time and was given some advice on how to improve her appearance.

A consultant hired by *ABC News* to help new correspondents took Muller into a screening room where they looked at some of the correspondent's stories. After viewing a few of them, the consultant told Muller that she obviously did not need any help with her writing or delivery. Muller then asked about her looks. "Well," the consultant replied, "I really only have one word for you." Muller asked: "And what would that word be?" The consultant leaned close to Muller and whispered in her ear: "*Scarves.* I think they will help soften your angular face." Muller said that during her radio career she didn't have to worry about her angular face. She said that she never realized that she *had* an angular face.

Muller said she began to understand that the "face" thing is important to the people who hired you, like the day she arrived at the Los Angeles Bureau with a new, very short haircut, and the person on the newsdesk said with a shocked expression: "Did you talk to *New York* before doing that?" Muller replied: "No, I didn't know I had to." As for the consultant, Muller said despite the advice she never managed to get into scarves, much less figure out how to tie them.

Muller says despite all the attention given to cosmetics by TV producers and managers, she still believes that, scarves or no scarves: "A reporter's best accessory is the string of words that, like so many pearls, can make for a beautiful story."

Muller added that good camera presence has always been an asset for television reporters, but more and more, at least at the magazine shows, correspondents are increasingly valued more for that attribute than their writing skills.

In her memoir *Reporting Live* (Simon & Schuster, 1999), Lesley Stahl, a long-time *60 Minutes* correspondent, recalls that when she was hired for the job by executive producer Don Hewitt, he told Stahl that there was just one thing that he wanted her to change. Sensitive to what he was about to tell Stahl, he prepared her: "I have to do something that I'm afraid is going to make you angry," he went on. "You're going to be really upset with me. I hate to say this." Stahl replied: "What already?" Hewitt blurted out: "I hate your hair, you have to change it, it's too stiff."

Stahl writes that if she had been younger, "I would have chafed at the insult—how dare he." But she wasn't offended. She told Hewitt that because she couldn't be futzing with her hair in the middle of covering the White House, with everything that was going on, she teased her hair and sprayed it and forgot about it. But she told Hewitt: "If you want me to change it, no problem, I'll change it." Stahl said that she spent as much time as she could spare on her appearance. She got her hair done twice a week and bought enough makeup "to open my own boutique."

Stahl recalled another occasion when she and a group of correspondents were meeting with the former President of *CBS News*, Eric Ober, and he complained that there seemed to be a reluctance at the network to discuss cosmetics. He noted that one of CBS' finest correspondents, Bob Simon, needed voice lessons. Stahl said eyes met in horror, and she yelled out: "Guess it's time for my facelift!" "No!" said Ober. "Older is more authoritative. People want their news from older-looking people." "Thanks," replied Stahl.

Stahl also admitted that there were many times when she was anxiety-ridden on the air when she was co-anchor of *CBS Morning News*. "I never froze," she said, "but I tightened up when the camera light went on. I did this strange thing," she continued, "that showed some teeth that was supposedly my smile, but I couldn't look into that camera and be me." She added: "That's the most important thing for anybody on television. The audience can sense when you're not relaxed, and they don't like it." Stahl said her mother called her to say that she had found a teacher for her—to teach her how to smile. Stahl said she had a lesson and "had to find 'me' in there, and that took a long time."

Asked if working as an anchor made her respect the work that network anchors do, she replied that she had always respected their work; not because they read well, but because of the way they perform in a crisis: "A space shuttle disaster, the President's been shot—when they're thrown on the air and don't know the complete story and are flying by the seat of their pants. This is when they earn their money," she added. "The anchors remain calm and set the tone for the public so they don't panic."

Jill Geisler, a former anchor and news director who now heads the Leadership and Management program at the Poynter Institute, says that because anchors are "the face of the news, the voice they carry forward needs to be an informed one." Geisler adds that the informed voice is best achieved when anchors are active leaders rather than passive participants in the editorial process. "To be a successful leader," she says, "anchors must develop the ability to influence those around them." She says the three key elements to having real influence on others are competence, integrity, and empathy. Geisler notes that the best anchors get involved in the editorial process early in their day, usually with the editorial meeting. "The process works well," she says, "when reporters in the field will talk to the anchors as well as the producers and managers as they develop their stories."

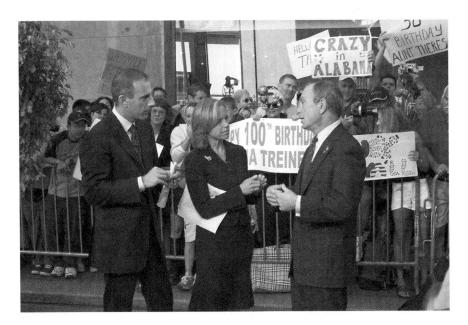

Figure 8-4 Matt Lauer and Katie Couric interview New York City Mayor Michael Bloomberg on NBC's *Today Show*. (Courtesy Max Franklin, Getty Images)

Geisler points out that this approach creates a connection between the on-and-off air staffs that results in better stories and, ultimately, a better newscast. Writing in the RTNDA magazine, *The Communicator*, Geisler quotes an anchor at KPRC in Houston, Khambrel Marshall. "It sets a better tone in the newsroom," he says, "when the anchor is willing to roll up his sleeves and work on the programs." But, he adds, it's also important to work as an equal with the production team. Marshall cautions, "you have to be careful to strike a balance so that you don't irritate the producers and the others who work hard on the news." He adds, "the goal is to contribute, not to 'big foot' the process."

In a roundtable discussion that Geisler conducted with a group of network and local anchors, there was agreement that anchors, to be successful, must be leaders in the newsroom. Anchor Karen Foss of KSDK in St. Louis told her colleagues that "the sleight of hand that makes an anchor's job look easy masks the effort it takes to put together a confident, coherent broadcast." She added, "as an anchor you are the lead journalist in your newsroom and your standards influence ... the tone of many in the newsroom."

Barbara Cochran, President of RTNDA, listed some common qualities among some of the stand-out anchors she has known, including Bob Schieffer, Tom Brokaw, Dan Rather, and Peter Jennings. She noted that "they all consider themselves reporters, not anchors . . . they're curious and really put a lot of emphasis on their own writing, and on good writing, appearing in their newscasts."

Summary

If you wish to report or anchor for radio and television, you must analyze your voice as soon as you can. One of your instructors may be able to tell you if you need help and where you can get it. If speech courses are not offered in your journalism program, seek out the speech department. Consider the help of a coach if you have some special problems with your voice or diction.

Remember that a regional or cultural dialect will not necessarily eliminate you from contention as a reporter or anchor. Many of those problems, if they can't be eliminated, can at least be modified sufficiently for you to work in the area where you were born and reared.

If you have a good voice, learn to use it properly. Get accustomed to reading your copy aloud before you go in front of a microphone. In addition to alerting you to grammatical errors or awkward phrases you may have missed, reading your copy aloud will help you discover that certain words and names in the copy are hard to pronounce. If so, add the phonetic spellings next to or above the difficult names and places. Last, reading your copy aloud gives you the opportunity to determine what words you want to emphasize and how you can use pacing effectively.

Review Questions

1. Name some of the talents you must develop if you wish to become a radio reporter.

2. What additional talents will you need if you wish to report or anchor for television?
3. If you are having troubles of any kind with your voice, how soon should you get an evaluation?
4. If you have problems with diction, breathing, or dialect, what kind of help can you get?
5. What are some of the approaches to solving voice problems?
6. Two of the voice coaches quoted in this chapter say some of their techniques might be considered unorthodox. Discuss.
7. The wire services offer some pronunciation assistance to their clients. What kind of help?
8. Why is Paul Harvey so effective in getting and holding an audience's attention?
9. Why do anchors mark their copy? What are some of the symbols they use?

Exercises

1. Read a few newspaper stories silently and then read them into a tape recorder. Make a note of the things you discovered were a problem in the copy only after reading it aloud. After making appropriate changes in the copy, read it into the tape recorder a second time, and note any improvements.
2. Write a one-minute radio script based on information from a newspaper or newspaper wire. Then read the script into a tape recorder. Listen to the recording, and make notes on anything that you did not like about your reading, such as inflection, breathing, pitch, or pace.
3. Do a second reading, but this time mark your copy before doing so. After reading, note whether there was an improvement in your delivery.
4. Go through a newspaper or newspaper wire copy, and find words that are unfamiliar to you. Look up the words in a dictionary for meaning and pronunciation and in a pronunciation guide if one is available. Write the words phonetically along with the rest of the sentences, and read them into a tape recorder. Then replay the tape for other members of your class, and note whether they understood the meaning of the words.
5. After you have noted the words that fellow students did not understand, find synonyms for them and rerecord the sentences with the new words. See if the students understand the copy this time.

9 Finding the News

Most national and international news comes into a newsroom from the Associated Press. Most local news comes from a combination of sources and activities, including the police and fire departments, the courts and various other municipal institutions, and community and business organizations. Local news also is generated by the routine follow-up of the leads and tips that pour into the assignment desk on a continuing basis from beat reporters, tipsters, and even non-news personnel who work for the station. This chapter and Chapter 16, "Collecting Information from Documents," examine all these news sources.

The Wires

The term *wires* is still used to describe the services offered by news-gathering organizations such as the Associated Press, United Press International, and Reuters, a British firm. United Press, which was once a formidable competitor to AP, is only a shadow of its former self, giving AP a virtual lock on this news delivery system. The word *wires* refers to the telegraph cables that were originally used to transmit the news to newspaper clients. Today, the wires feed news to some 5,000 radio and TV customers, as well as newspapers. The news is distributed not by wires but via satellite to computers. The old clattering typewriter-type machines that were in every newsroom have been converted to systems that allow the news to be fed directly into computers in the newsrooms and at the anchor desks. Writers, producers, and anchors can print out stories that interest them, and if they wish, the anchors can read the material live from the video screens at their desks.

Most small-market radio stations use the AP broadcast wire that transmits hourly summaries of the news. The broadcast wire is designed for those stations with little or no news operation. The broadcast wire is popularly referred to as the "rip-and-read" wire because that is the way these summaries are most often used at stations lacking staff to rewrite news copy. The stories are designed to be read without any rewriting.

Some radio and TV stations, usually in large markets, also subscribe to an AP newspaper wire, called the *A Wire*, which provides considerably more detail about national and international news than the broadcast wire because A Wire stories are written primarily with newspapers in mind. The A Wire also moves many more stories than the broadcast wire. Because the A Wire stories are written in newspaper style, however, they are virtually impossible to read on the air without a rewrite (see Chapter 6). So, there is little purpose in subscribing to the A Wire unless someone is available to rewrite the copy.

The AP also provides *splits* on the broadcast and main wires throughout the day and night. Splits are stories of state and regional interest sent to radio and TV customers from bureaus in your state and surrounding states.

In addition to the various wires, the AP also provides a variety of audio feeds via satellite, including news on the hour and the half-hour, special reports on the hour's major stories, and an hourly feed of actualities and natural sound. The AP also provides scripted national and international news, agricultural reports, business news, sports, entertainment news, special features, and a headline service designed for what the AP describes as stations with "a limited news appetite."

The AP also provides several photo and graphics services, including an interactive database that supplies thousands of head shots, maps, and images of breaking news and a high-speed, digital photo network that delivers color photos to TV stations.

Television Satellite Feeds

Television stations also receive a steady stream of sound bites and reports via closed-circuit feeds, usually referred to as *newsfeeds*, by the networks and various independent producers. Although satellite technology has changed the way newsfeeds are transmitted, the networks have been feeding local stations with additional news for years. Other companies offer custom-made newscasts throughout the day.

Radio and TV stations also can buy satellite-delivered information about health and medicine, finance, weather, sports, consumer news, and numerous other subjects. Multiply the paid syndication services by 25 and you probably have a figure close to the number of organizations and companies that dump free information, called video news releases (VNRs), on satellites each day. The information is free because it's promoting an organization or a cause. Among those making use of satellites are associations representing the chemical, gas, sugar, and scores of other industries; the American Legion; the FBI; various religious and health-related organizations; public relations companies; and a variety of universities. Some of the free material is produced as a public service, but most is pure public relations. VNRs became front page news during the 2004 presidential campaign when the White House began distributing its own VNRs to promote some of the things it was taking credit for, such as Medicare reform. The Democrats cried foul, charging American taxpayers were paying for what really amounted to a political statement and not a legitimate message explaining how the new Medicare law works, as the White House insisted. The Republicans fired back, saying that President Clinton also used VNRs to promote his accomplishments while in the White House.

Figure 9-1   (Foreground) Photographer Rick Portier and (Background) Photography Editor Patrick Perry checking video at WBRZ, Baton Rouge, LA.

The Internet

Radio and TV stations rely heavily on the Internet for news and research; however, anything taken from the Internet must be used with caution and attribution because a lot of the information is not reliable. (For more discussion on the Internet, see Chapter 17, "Computer-Assisted Reporting.")

Newspapers

Many broadcast news managers do not like to admit it, but they often rely on newspapers as a source of news. Because they have much larger news staffs and more room for news, newspapers often have stories that broadcast newsrooms miss or do not bother to cover.

Some stations rely on newspapers more than others. Stations with enough reporters to do a good job covering the local scene are less dependent on newspapers than are stations with small news staffs. Some stations are constantly playing "catch-up" because they cannot compete with the newspaper's beat system.

Broadcast newsrooms often find themselves trying to figure out ways to take a good newspaper story and *advance* it. Advancing the story—finding some new development to make it appear new or at least fresh—is often considered a justification for "borrowing" the information developed by the newspaper. It's important to remember, however, that if a newspaper is the *only* source for a story, it is ethically proper—and a necessary protection in case the information is not accurate—to attribute the story to the newspaper. Remember also that most newspapers copyright their material. Few papers object when their stories are broadcast, as long as credit is given. Some news directors take the position that once the accuracy of information first disclosed in a newspaper has been independently verified by the station, it is no longer necessary to credit the paper.

Although good broadcast news operations should rely as little as possible on newspapers for story ideas, papers should be mandatory reading for everyone in the broadcast newsroom. Broadcast editors and writers find that reading newspapers is often a good way to double-check the facts in a wire story. Also, it is not unusual for national papers such as *The New York Times* and *The Washington Post* to have details or new angles on a story that are not included in the wire versions.

Monitoring Radios

Every newsroom should have radios that monitor police and fire department channels that broadcast every fire or police call that is being answered in the station's immediate area. Someone should monitor the radios constantly. The station that ignores the radio gets scooped by the competition.

Scanning devices on radios can monitor police and fire channels at the same time. The scanners hop back and forth, pausing whenever anyone starts to speak. The chatter is difficult to hear at times, but with practice it becomes easier to decipher, particularly if you learn the special codes used by authorities. One of the most common systems used by police is known as the 10-code, which uses *signal codes* that vary from city to city. For example, in New Orleans, 10–55 means a police officer needs assistance. In Baton Rouge, that message is a signal 63. A robbery in progress in Baton Rouge is a signal 42, but in New Orleans it's a 65. Some cities, including New Orleans, use the state's criminal code numbers. A homicide is a signal 30, a driving while intoxicated (DWI) incident is 599, and a hit-and-run is 100. Because cities use different systems, you'll need to learn the codes when you enter a new market. They should be posted near or on the radio.

None of the information obtained from these radio scanners is ever to be used alone in writing a story for broadcast; the incidents must be checked out by phone. The police and fire reports often turn out to be unfounded or less serious than one might expect from the code. It is also a violation of Federal Communications Commission (FCC) regulations to rebroadcast any material heard on police, fire, or ham radio broadcasts.

Making Phone Calls

Unless a station has someone on duty overnight, which is not that common except in large markets, the first member of the news staff to arrive at the station each day should call police and fire department headquarters. Large cities provide a special phone number and public relations staff just to handle the media. For the most part, however, reporters deal with the police and fire dispatchers.

News staffs, particularly in medium-sized and large markets, routinely make other telephone calls. Before and during rush hours, they check on auto traffic and commuter train and bus service to see if any major delays are present, and, of course, in many of the markets choppers are used to monitor traffic. During bad weather, such information becomes more critical. Trains and buses may not be moving. The roads may be treacherous. School officials may call in to report closings, and that information is important in *every* market.

During bad weather, the news staff also takes calls from the Parent-Teacher Association (PTA), the Rotary Club, the YWCA, the local theater group, and numerous other organizations that may cancel events because of the weather. The newsroom should have a complete list of emergency telephone numbers on rotary files, clipboards, or in the computer. The local gas and electric companies will have information on disruptions of service and potentially dangerous situations brought on by snowstorms, tornadoes, and earthquakes.

A serious snowstorm turns a routine weather report into a lead story. News staffs check with the local weather bureau at least every hour, and perhaps more often during a potentially disastrous weather situation.

Stringers

Many stations—both radio and television—have working relationships with *stringers,* people who are not on the payroll but who are paid for stories that they develop, or who cover breaking news at night when no one is working at the station. Stringers often help a station avoid the embarrassment of missing a story that breaks overnight. Some stringers have their own camera gear, and some TV stations provide gear to stringers who are productive.

Many news directors also have arrangements with firefighters or police officers on duty overnight who agree to call the news director at home if an important story breaks. Some stations encourage viewers to submit stories shot on home video recorders if the stories have news value. Such video must be aired with extreme caution, however, because of the potential for deception, libel, and other problems.

Tipsters

Most stations also encourage people to call with news tips. Some even pay for such information. It is surprising just how much news is generated this way.

All tips should be taken seriously. Many are about breaking news stories—a shooting heard from the listener's bedroom window or a fire spotted by someone walking the dog. Other tips come from people who are upset for some reason. It may have to do with something going on in local government or at the plant where they work. If possible, get the caller's name and phone number. Tipsters often refuse to identify themselves, but assignment editors should not make the mistake of thinking that most people who call a radio or TV station are cranks. Stations do receive a lot of crank calls, but newspeople must consider every phone call to be potentially important.

One of the news producers for a network investigative unit made the mistake of telling a tipster to "write a letter," which is one of the worst ways to deal with someone who calls with information about a story. Instead of writing a letter, the tipster called another network, which assigned a producer to check out the information. The story attracted national attention when it was broadcast. (The topic of tipsters is discussed further in Chapter 18, "Developing Sources.")

Employee Input

Story ideas often come from people on the news staff—reporters, producers, anchors, desk assistants, and others—and some ideas even originate with secretaries and people in the mailroom.

People working in news seem to develop a sense that alerts them to news in all sorts of places. A producer waiting to cross the street near a bus stop suddenly got a blast of soot in her face. As she recovered, she noticed that a passing city bus continued to emit a steady stream of pollutants as it moved down the block. Standing next to the angry producer was a police officer. "Did you see that?" yelled the producer. "What?" replied the officer. "All that pollution!" The police officer looked a little confused by the observation and shrugged his shoulders as if to say, "So what?"

The producer could not wait to get to the newsroom to share her experience with the assignment editor. The editor listened intently and agreed that the producer might be on to a story. A couple of telephone calls later, the assignment editor strolled over to the producer's desk and said: "The reason that cop gave you a blank stare is because we don't have any laws that cover air pollution in this city." That was the start of a good series on pollution.

Everyone on the staff should be encouraged to develop story ideas. One news director uses the station's newsletter to encourage non-news employees to stop by the assignment editor's desk if they see or hear anything that might make a news story.

Assignment editors do listen to a lot of stories, and some of the stories do generate news, but assignment editors do more than just listen. They are responsible for collecting and organizing most of the source material that comes into a newsroom.

Sometimes the assignment desk is small. There may be one person in charge of assignments, and then only during the daytime. Assignment editors are found mostly in TV newsrooms, but some large radio news operations in major cities also employ them. At many radio stations, and some small TV stations, the news director or perhaps an assistant news director functions as

Figure 9-2   Assignment desk at WBZ-CBS 4, Boston. (Courtesy of Viacom Boston)

an assignment editor but does not have that title. Large-market TV stations normally have at least two assignment editors—one for the morning and one for the evening. In the largest newsrooms, the assignment desk operates around-the-clock.

Almost everything starts at the assignment desk because that is where all the information enters the system. Assignment editors are the "keepers" of the news wires. They monitor the wires constantly, looking for stories that will be of interest to producers who are responsible for putting newscasts on the air. Some of these stories are assigned to reporters. Others are given to writers for read stories or, perhaps, to be used for V-SOTs. Still others need follow-up by the assignment editor. In a breaking story, that follow-up is immediate.

Sounding the Alarm

A desk assistant is the first to hear the fire department advisory. It's obviously a bad one. He tells the assignment editor, and she listens for about 15 seconds, long enough to know that she has to get people moving on it. She calls the crew room. As she waits for an answer, she calls to the reporter who is listening to the radio: "Frank, let's go." Frank heads for the door.

By the time Frank reaches the microwave truck, the assignment editor has figured out exactly where the fire is and the best way to get there. She gives the information to the cameraman on the two-way radio and turns up the volume on the scanner. The producer of the six o'clock news notices all the sudden activity and is quickly informed that a reporter and a photographer are already on the way to a major fire.

On a fire story, especially in the middle of the afternoon, the microwave truck is used for a variety of reasons: to get some live reports on the air before the evening newscast, if warranted, and to go live from the scene during the newscast.

As soon as the truck arrives at the scene, the microwave rod is set up to make sure that a picture can be sent back to the station. A monitor is set up at the assignment desk, as well as in the master control room where the actual feed comes in, so that the assignment editor will know if it's possible to get a live shot. The producer will also be waiting for that information.

Meanwhile, the assignment editor and her desk assistant are working the phones. The desk assistant says he caught something on the scanner about two hospitals—City General and St. Joseph's. Another reporter has been waiting at the assignment desk for orders, and now she gets them: "Go to City General Hospital." Another photographer is already sitting in the station's other microwave truck, waiting to roll.

And so it goes for the rest of the afternoon and into the late evening. A third reporter, who has been covering another story, is pulled off it by the assignment editor and sent to the second hospital. The assignment editor and her desk assistant get as much information about the fire and injuries as they can from the scanner and the telephones to support what the reporters are finding out at the scene.

Conversation is almost continuous among the reporters and those at the assignment desk as they all share this information. The assignment editor and the desk assistant also take notes for the producers on everything from font information to the number of deaths and injuries and the status of the fire.

The assignment editor's desk is also the clearinghouse for exchanges between the reporters and the producers. After the first report is finished at the top of the six o'clock news, the producer may tell the assignment editor he wants an update in 20 minutes. That information is relayed to the microwave truck, and in a few minutes the producer is told: "You got it!"

As things settle down, a reporter checks in from the scene saying fire officials suspect arson and will hold a news conference in 20 minutes. There is an unconfirmed report that someone may already be under arrest. Next, the editor is on the radio with the crew at St. Joseph's, telling them: "Break down and get to fire department headquarters immediately for a news conference. Tell John [the reporter] that I will talk to him when you get rolling."

Meanwhile, the desk assistant has tried to get more information on the advisory. A call to fire department headquarters confirms the report on the news conference, but the official refuses to say anything about an arrest.

"Tell the producer," says the assignment editor, and the desk assistant takes off. Within minutes, the producer has the new copy on its way to the anchor desk. The newscast will be over before the news conference gets under way, but the anchor reads the new copy and promises the viewing audience: "We'll have details on the news conference at 11 o'clock and, of course, we'll break into our regular programming with any new details on the fire as soon as we receive them."

Developing Story Ideas

Fires and crimes do get a lot of coverage on local newscasts, but assignment editors have to look for other, nonbreaking news to fill an hour or longer newscast. To accomplish this goal, they must be part journalist and part detective.

They must examine every wire story to see if any possible angle can be developed into a good local story. Chapter 6 mentioned how important it is to look for a local angle in national and international stories. This search is constant at the assignment desk. For example, if the unemployment figures out of Washington are bad, the assignment editor tries to develop a story about local effects. Have the local unemployment figures gone up too, or did the community do better than the rest of the nation? What are the opinions of the people at the unemployment office—those on line and those behind the desk? How are shop owners doing? If local unemployment has worsened, has it had an effect on their businesses?

What about inflation? If Washington reports an increase, how has it affected shoppers? The assignment editor might send a reporter to a supermarket. The manager might admit that prices have been going up, and you can bet the people at the checkout line will speak out.

The assignment editor also looks for ways to update a story. The fire story detailed earlier presents lots of opportunities. There will be interviews at the hospitals with the injured as their condition improves. The arson investigation will provide updates, and if someone is arrested, that would provide another update.

Interaction

Assignment editors probably interact with more people than anyone else in the newsroom, which is why they are so essential to a good news operation. In the fire story, you saw the assignment editor's interaction with producers, photographers, and reporters. A close, harmonious working relationship must exist between those at the assignment desk and all these people. During a breaking story, the assignment editor must control the coverage of the story firmly from the start. The news director usually keeps a close eye on what is going on, but more often he or she allows the assignment editor to run the show.

When things are quieter, more dialogue is likely to take place between the producer and those at the desk. The producer often influences assignment decisions on nonbreaking stories. If the producer is not interested in a story, the assignment editor may think twice about giving it to a reporter, but many assignments have to be made before the producer even arrives in the newsroom. The producer has to accept the assignment editor's judgment in covering stories. Once reporters have been assigned to stories, the producer has to try to work most of them into the newscast. Otherwise, there would not be enough material for the newscast.

As you learned earlier, once reporters are on the road, the assignment editor keeps the producer informed about their progress. Some stories may not work and will be killed. A reporter may inform the desk that his story is not as strong as it first appeared and so will be shorter than anticipated. Another reporter may say her story will be longer. Producers must know all this in planning for the newscast.

Interaction with the camerapeople also takes much of the assignment editor's time and tact. A good relationship is vital. Generally, local stations assign just one photographer to a microwave truck. When a story is breaking, as in the case of the fire we just discussed, a station sometimes assigns a two-person crew (if an extra person is available) so that the photographer can shoot without worrying about setting up and monitoring the live shot. This is particularly true if the story breaks just before airtime. Some stations in large markets and at the networks have unions that determine the size of the crew.

An important part of the assignment editor's job during a breaking story, as you read earlier, is to get the reporter and crew to the scene as soon as possible. The assignment editor also needs to schedule reporters and crews so that they arrive on time for nonbreaking news conferences and other planned events. The assignment editor must provide accurate street and room numbers and the names of contacts.

Like many people in the newsroom, crews often work long hours and are under a great deal of pressure. They may miss lunches and dinners and be required to work overtime at the end of an already full day. Showing them the respect they deserve usually motivates tired crews more than do screams and demands. So, assignment editors, who are under a lot of pressure themselves, need to keep their cool. They also need to be organized.

Insights

Assignment editors play a major role in determining what the newscast looks like. Although the producers make the final decisions about what goes into newscasts, they must rely on the assignment editor's judgment in the collection process. That process works best when it is organized.

Earlier sections of this chapter discussed the responsibility of the assignment editors to go over the AP wire carefully and to check the newspapers to see if something is going on that the wire might have missed. The assignment editors must also look through the *futures* file discussed in Chapter 6. The file contains information about news conferences and other events and feature stories that are set up in advance.

Once all this has been digested, the assignment editor must prepare a menu—sometimes called *insights* or *outlooks*—of all of the news possibilities for the day, along with evaluations and recommendations as to which stories should be assigned to reporters and which should be covered only by a cameraperson.

This document is distributed to the entire news editorial staff and discussed at a meeting, usually scheduled in mid-morning, that is attended by the news director, various producers, writers, and any reporters—especially beat reporters—who have not already been sent out on stories. The meeting determines the "battle plan" for the day. As with any battle, it is impossible to predict the outcome. What appears to be news in the morning may not be so in the middle of the afternoon. That is the nature of news.

Assignment Boards

In addition to the written assignment outlooks, the assignment desk staff must maintain an *assignment board* that lists all of the stories that have been assigned for that day. The board shows the names of the reporter and crew, the location of the story, the time it is scheduled, and, usually, the time the crew is expected back. There also should be room for additional notes on the progress of the story.

A chalkboard or a white plastic board with dry erase markers is used so that changes can be made throughout the day. Because the board is usually located right behind or to the side of the assignment desk, it should be big enough so that producers, reporters, and others do not have to crowd around it to read the information. Keeping the board up to date is usually the responsibility of the desk assistants, who also answer the phones, distribute copy to anchors and teleprompter operators, and perform many other chores that are asked of them as they gain experience working in a newsroom.

This job is one of the best ways to get started in broadcast news. Desk assistants who work hard and impress the staff and bosses soon find that they are given more responsibility, which may include writing an occasional story and going out on assignments with reporters.

Summary

If news staffs didn't know where to look for news and how to gather it, there would be little news on radio and TV. Most collecting is done by assignment editors, while the gathering is done by the reporters.

The assignment desk is where most information enters the newsroom. The assignment desk staff monitors the news wire, the police and fire radios, and the telephones and receives an endless assortment of news releases by mail and email. Assignment editors also look for story ideas from reporters, particularly those with beats, as well as from stringers, tipsters, and other newsroom employees. The assignment editor, who may be the news director as well in some markets, makes the initial decisions about which material should be considered for coverage. He or she also assigns reporters and photographers to stories.

Assignment editors and news directors also rely heavily on the rest of the news team, especially producers. The producers select material and decide what goes on the air; they are responsible for the look of the news. Most newsrooms hold daily meetings to plan the newscast and maintain assignment boards to keep staff members apprised of their duties for the day. Broadcast news is a team effort. Without harmony and togetherness, the newscasts will not succeed, and the ratings will fall. That's bad news for everyone because when ratings fall, owners usually look for a new team. The team that works together will live to see another "sweeps."

Review Questions

1. What is the name of the most widely used news wire service?
2. Which wire is used most often by small radio stations? Why?
3. What is the A Wire, and what kinds of stations usually subscribe to this service? Why?
4. What other kinds of products do the wire services offer radio stations? Describe them.
5. TV stations have access to feeds from the networks and other sources. How do they arrive at the TV stations? Explain how material is used.
6. Why are there special radios in broadcast newsrooms? How are they used? Are they important?
7. It is routine for many broadcast news staffs to make certain telephone calls each morning. What kinds of calls? Why are they important?
8. Who are stringers, and what do they do? Why are they important?
9. Explain why the assignment desk is an integral part of a news operation.

Exercises

1. Part of the assignment editor's job is to look for updates on stories. Look at the wire or your newspaper, and pick stories that have potential to be updated. Explain how you would update them.
2. The assignment editor is always looking for local reaction-type stories to national and international developments. Look at the wire and newspapers for stories that might provide local reaction. Tape a reaction from someone.
3. If there is a news wire bureau in your area, visit the office, and write a report on what you observed. If there is not, visit your local newspaper office, and see how the wire is used by the staff. Then write a report.
4. Visit a local radio or TV station and see who is monitoring the police and fire radio. Take notes on what you heard, and turn in a report.

10   Broadcast News Reporting

Good reporters first must learn to write, which is why the first part of this book was devoted mostly to writing. But just being able to write well does not guarantee that a person will make a good reporter. Many additional skills and abilities, unrelated to writing, are required.

Although print and broadcast reporters need many of the same skills, broadcast news reporters face challenges not encountered by their print counterparts, or even by broadcast journalists of the recent past. Electronic news gathering (ENG), which relies on videotape or digital equipment and microwave technology, places demands on TV reporters that were unknown when reporters filmed stories and had the luxury of writing their scripts while the film was being developed. Broadcast journalists today need to think faster and to prepare their reports more rapidly, often while the story is still going on around them. They also need to learn about the different types of assignments they are likely to cover and the best way to perform them.

The next several chapters describe these needs and offer suggestions for developing skills to meet them. This chapter begins with the basic skills required of successful reporters.

Basic Skills

As noted in Chapter 1, the most important skill a reporter needs is accuracy. At first, this may not appear to be a skill, but being accurate requires a lot of attention—checking and double-checking information demand concentration. Errors usually creep into copy when reporters become too relaxed. Nothing should be assumed or taken for granted. If information cannot be confirmed, it should not be used without some kind of attribution.

Reporters also must develop news judgment. They must understand what news is and be able to recognize that certain stories are more important than others. That skill sometimes takes time to develop. Later in this chapter, professional journalists offer their views and advice on what makes news and how you can develop news judgment. Reporters must also be curious, showing an interest in everything and everyone making news—whatever the reason.

Reporters must be concerned, sometimes alarmed, often angered, and always caring about the major problems that face the communities and world in which we live. Reporters often can do little to correct injustice or unfairness, or the misery, suffering, and critical problems of certain segments or groups in our society, but they should have a desire to do so. Their weapons are enlightenment and information.

Reporters must be determined and persistent in their search for facts and details. Reporters must be aggressive, walking a thin line between tenacity and belligerence. For many people entering journalism, some of these characteristics seem to come naturally, whereas others need to be developed. Let's look at these qualities in detail.

Accuracy

The introduction to this book mentioned the importance of accuracy and the difficulties that arose in this regard during a number of major stories, including the O.J. Simpson murder trial, the JonBenét Ramsey murder case, and the Clinton-Lewinsky sex scandal.

Most of the blame for the inordinately high level of inaccurate reporting during these events was placed on (1) the record amount of media coverage; (2) the apparent need to be first with every bit of information, regardless of its value and questionable accuracy; (3) the new technology that encourages broadcast journalists to go live before they have sufficient time to think; (4) the manipulation of the media by a variety of entities, including but not limited to the prosecution, police, and the defense; and (5) the incredible, unprecedented use of unidentified and unreliable sources. The attitude during coverage of these stories appeared to be: "If the story is wrong, we'll correct it later . . . but let's air it before someone else does"—a certain formula for disaster.

Election 2000: It's Better to Be Right Than First

Before Election Night 2000 was over, the networks and cable news channels had to eat their words twice. First they called Florida for Al Gore, only to retract that call later. Then they declared Florida and the election for George W. Bush, only to also retract that call. Declaring Gore the winner in Florida came *before* the polls closed in the Republican-dominated Florida panhandle. That misstep may have cost Bush up to 10,000 votes, a Yale researcher told *Newsweek*.

But *CBS News* correspondent Dan Rather, appearing on CNN's *Reliable Sources*, said that study after study shows that no empirical evidence proves that projections made before the polls close affect the outcome of the election. Most of Florida is in the eastern time zone, except for the panhandle, which lies in the central time zone. So the polls there remained open an hour later. ABC officials noted that it was the only network that did not call Florida for Gore until after the polls closed in the panhandle.

Election night coverage was a humiliating experience not only for the broadcasters, who flip-flopped twice, but also for many newspapers that declared Bush the winner in their early editions, before it became clear that the outcome was still undecided. It also caused havoc for Al Gore, who called Bush to concede, and then later retracted his concession.

The first gaff came early on when the networks declared Al Gore the winner in Florida, with its crucial 25 electoral votes. But two hours later, the networks and the Associated Press began taking back their projections, stating that the vote was too close to call. It remained that way for several hours. At 2 A.M., it became clear that whoever won Florida would win the election. Sixteen minutes later, the Fox News Channel declared Bush the winner in Florida and hence the presidency. Within minutes, in lock step, the networks, CNN, and Reuters followed suit, but they were wrong *again*.

The AP didn't go along with the Bush win declaration, and at 2:37 A.M., it put out an urgent message stating: "The race was still up for grabs and it all came down to Florida." At 3:11 A.M., the AP put out an advisory that Bush's lead in Florida had dwindled to about 6,000 and warned that with the counting of two heavily Democratic counties to go, the lead could change. Shortly before 4 A.M., the networks were forced to retract their earlier prediction and began placing Florida and the national election outcome in the "undecided" category. More than a month later, the election was still undecided.

Election Night 2000 was "probably the worst moment in the 50-year history of television coverage of politics," said Bill Kovach, chairman, and Tom Rosensteil, vice chairman of the Committee of Concerned Journalists, in an op-ed piece in *The New York Times.* "Misleading coverage not only failed to report what happened on election night, but created . . . the suggestion of an election that was called back and might be stolen," adding, "when the truth is simply that a very narrow election is late on being decided."

Marvin Kalb, former *CBS News* correspondent and director of Harvard's Shorenstein Center on the Press, Politics, and Public Policy, said, in the past, the networks had been "remarkably reliable" in their calling of elections. But on Election Night 2000, Kalb added, "Television news flubbed its lines big time." Those comments appeared in op-ed pieces in the *Boston Globe* and *New York Daily News.* "These editorial blunders," he said, "quickly created a political crisis filled with uncertainties and suspicions."

Kalb further stated: "Americans, already skeptical about network coverage of politics, may now wonder whether they can trust the networks to be fair and accurate in their calling of presidential elections."

Why did the errors occur? Kalb said that the trouble lies in having one source of polling data. In years past, the networks each performed their own election research. But in recent years, to save millions of dollars each, they decided to use one service, the Voter News Service (VNS), to conduct research for all the outlets. "If VNS was wrong, all the networks would get and distribute the wrong information," Kalb said. VNS relied on interviews with voters at selected precincts as they left the polls, known as exit interviews, and actual vote counts.

Ironically, early during election night coverage, *CBS News* anchor and managing editor, Dan Rather, announced to his TV audience: "Let's get one thing straight, right from the get go. We would rather be last in the reporting returns than be wrong." And he continued: "If we say somebody carried a state, you can pretty much take it to the bank, book it that it's true." Of course, he had to eat those words later in the evening.

A few days after election night, Rather, appearing on CNN's *Reliable Sources,* said: "We were wrong, we need to stand up and to take the responsibility for it." He added that "this is not an exact science, but *CBS News* has by far the best record in the business on election nights." In addition, Rather said, "we're taking steps to make sure it will happen as little as possible in the future," adding, "but it will happen."

He also said that, when making projections in an election, "one of the things we can do better is to underscore more often to the viewer that while we believe we're right, *making these calls . . . we can be wrong*. I think credibility is the most important thing we have. Accuracy is job one," Rather added.

ABC News correspondent Sam Donaldson, also appearing on CNN's *Reliable Sources,* said: "We have egg on our face, no question about it," adding, "it's not a good system for all the networks to get their information from the same place." He said that much of the problem is caused by competition, the desire to be first. But Donaldson further said: "If we waited until all the votes are counted before declaring a winner, you'd say, 'Congratulations ABC' and the next time around no one would watch us because the other networks would beat us by projecting winners much earlier."

Some network executives acknowledged that the miscues resulted from faulty data and misleading returns fed into the VNS computers. Rather called for a 24-hour voting period and a uniform poll closing law that he said would "wipe out the possibility" of this happening again. The networks quickly launched investigations into what went wrong and how to prevent such a debacle from happening again.

Even before we knew who won the election, *ABC News* announced preliminary results of its investigation saying it will no longer call a contest in any state until all the polls have closed. And it added that it will attempt to "insulate" its analysts from competitive pressure to call a state prematurely.

Issues raised by the election were heard in several Florida district courts, the state Supreme Court, and the U.S. Supreme Court. In the aftermath of the election coverage, Arizona State University journalism professor Stephen Doig wondered if the networks were right, in the first place, when they called Florida for Gore early on election night. Professor Doig completed a computer analysis of voting patterns in the election for the *Miami Herald*. He concluded that Gore would have beaten Bush in Florida if all the state's ballots for the presidency had been error free and completely counted. He said the networks' call for Gore, which was based on exit polling, "I suspect, was pretty accurate."

He believes that in the exit polls, the VNS found out who each person they interviewed voted for, but the machines missed some votes; however, Doig said, "I think [the networks] screwed up" by calling the election results before all the polls had closed. "[The call] might have affected the voting," he added. He was also critical of the networks for using the same research service. "Having more than one," he said, "allows the opportunity to see if others agree with you."

New Problems in 2004

Although the networks kept their promise, and did not project any winners of states in the Bush-Kerry presidential race, or the race itself until all the polls clsoed, another problem did develop with exit polling. Early exit polls indicated that John Kerry would do much better than he appeared to be doing as actual vote counts came in. News organization promised shortly after the election was decided in Bush's favor to look into why their election day exit polls showed an initial surge for Kerry. Initial evaluations blamed bloggers for spreading news that gave a misleading view of the presidential race. To help eliminate the blunders of the 2000 race, an organization called the National Election Pool, was created to deliver exit poll data to the traditional networks and those on cable. The first wave of such polling showed Kerry with a lead of three percentage points in Florida and four points in Ohio, both battleground states won by Bush when the votes were actually counted, giving him the margin of victory. One of those complaining about the early exit polling showing Kerry leading the President was Marty Ryan, Fox News Channel's executive producer for political coverage. "It was disappointing," said Ryan, noting that the new system worked OK during the primaries, but it was "not good on election night." But other network representatives said their confidence in NEP remained unshaken. As for the websites, the Florida and Ohio exit polls and in other states where Kerry was strong, were quickly disseminated on such sites as Slate, The Drudge Report, Wonkette.com. Although they were criticized by the main-stream media for posting the supposedly early exit poll lead for Kerry, the Slate and Drudge did caution that the reports were early and should not be used to conclude that Kerry would win. However, CNN's poling expert, Bill Schneider, noted that people who read the website numbers—especially those with an intense interest in the election—put too much faith into them and leaped to conclusions. One of the two men who ran the exit polling for NEP, Joseph Lenski, charged that the bloggers picked out different numbers to use for their purposes, but as the day wore on, later waves of exit polling showed the race tightening. He said that "doing an early poll is like reporting the results of the game at halftime—you only have about a third of the information." The Associated Press reported that some of the speculation about the early exit polling that showed Kerry ahead, indicated that maybe Democrats were more eager to speak with pollsters than Republicans, or that Kerry supporters tended to go to the polls earlier in the day than Bush voters. Others suggested that pollsters spoke more to women voters than men and that might have skewed the early results in Kerry's favor. The good news is that none of the exit polling was used by the networks wrongly to call a state for a candidate, as was done in 2000. However, some correspondents apparently were sufficiently impressed by the early exit polling to hint that trends might be developing. For example, NBC's David Gregory said Bush "appeared subdued," and ABC's Terry Moran noted that the president had expressed a "rare sense of doubt." A Fox News analyst, Susan Estrich, said "The view in Boston is that if the exit polls are right, it's going to be very difficult for George Bush to win tonight." As we learned later in the election night, those polls—or the reading of them—proved to be incorrect.

The O.J. Simpson Trial

Another classic example of broadcasting irresponsibility was KNBC-TV's report that DNA testing showed that Nicole Brown Simpson's blood was discovered on one of O.J. Simpson's socks found in his bedroom. Everyone connected with the case—the prosecution, defense, police, and Judge Ito—said the report was false. That assertion did not convince the television station, however; it reported the same story with some new false details the next day, causing the livid Judge Ito to consider discontinuing all TV coverage of the trial. An anchor for the station, questioned at a round-table broadcast, explained that "the source for the story had always been accurate in the past." Later, KNBC-TV did admit that its report contained some inaccuracies.

The report, unfortunately, was picked up throughout the nation. The headlines that night said something like "A bloody sock ties O.J. closer to the murders" or "Nicole Simpson's blood found on O.J. sock."

Those headlines point out a continuing problem in both the broadcast and print media. The people writing the headlines do not always understand the story as well as they should, and there often appears to be an attitude that says, "It's only a headline." Sometimes you have difficulty finding anything in the story that supports the headline. In the Simpson case, viewers were led to believe that scientific tests showed that Nicole Brown Simpson's blood was found on one of O.J.'s socks. Ironically, months later, DNA experts for the prosecution would testify that Nicole Simpson's blood *was* found on one of O.J.'s socks; however, when KNBC-TV aired its report, those DNA tests had not yet been performed.

That was only one of several serious mistakes broadcast and printed by the media. Here are the worst of the others regarding that case:

Police had found a bloody ski mask.

The murder weapon was found on the plane that Simpson took to Chicago.

Simpson kept one of his hands in a bag during the flight to Chicago so no one would see he had an injury.

Police found a bloody golf bag belonging to Simpson.

Police have a shovel used to decapitate the victims.

Defense attorney Marcia Clark was videotaped at the crime scene 15 minutes before a warrant was issued.

Lawyer and Professor Charles Ogletree commented that so many stories were generated by the media "that it is difficult to say which ones are true or false." Howard Kirch, media writer for *The Washington Post,* accused those reporters covering the O.J. Simpson story of "second-hand journalism gradually turning rumor into fact."

The same situation was true in the tragic murder case of 6-year-old JonBenét Ramsey and the sex scandal involving the President of the United States and White House intern Monica Lewinsky. (These two cases are discussed more fully in Chapter 22, "Tabloid Journalism.")

The news coverage was not all bad, of course. A great amount of accurate and fair reporting took place during all of these events. Accuracy is essential in every story, not only in sensational murder trials and national scandals. And it does take a lot of hard work. Every detail in a news story must be checked and rechecked.

It does not matter how well a story is written or whether it has a clever lead or a snappy ending if it is not accurate in every detail. News managers have little patience with reporters and writers who cannot get the facts straight. Inaccuracy on a continuing basis can end a career quickly.

Names are particularly important. It was a time-consuming, painful job trying to sort out those who were injured and lost their lives in the collapse of the World Trade Center towers after the terrorist attacks on 9/11. The names came slowly, as you would expect, because there was a great deal of confusion at Ground Zero. That confusion lasted for weeks as rescuers looked for victims. That particular identification problem was enormous. Because of the devastation caused by the attack, there was little remaining of many of the victims, making their identification a nightmare. And, of course, some of the dead were never found. Throughout that long process, it was critical for the media to report the names, and other details about the victims, with extreme caution.

Names not only have to be spelled right, but you must also know how to pronounce them, as was pointed out in Chapter 8. If you are on the air, you would not wish to be embarrassed by pronouncing a person's name incorrectly; and if you are writing for an anchor, you wouldn't want to embarrass that individual either. The chances are that if you do pronounce someone's name incorrectly, you will hear about it from the person or someone else.

No one is perfect, of course, and journalists do make mistakes. But the responsibility for accuracy demands that such mistakes be kept to a minimum. When they are made, they must be corrected as quickly as possible.

News Judgment

In the Introduction, the idea that news judgment is something "you are born with" was dismissed. It can be developed. But how?

First, perhaps news judgment should be defined, which isn't easy. Even professional journalists have difficulty explaining the term. CNN correspondent Jeff Greenfield says people have different news judgments, which he believes is desirable. He noted that *Nightline* anchor Ted Koppel is a "foreign policy freak" and tends to "see more value in an international story," whereas Greenfield himself is a "political freak."

Greenfield said news judgment can also be related to the audience you are trying to serve. "The editors of *The New York Times* and *The [Washington] Post* will see news differently," he said. "They each will ask, 'Is this a story my readers will care about and want to know about?'"

Greenfield cited as an example the story of Kimberly Bergalis, a woman who died from AIDS after being infected during oral surgery performed by her HIV-positive dentist. "Why is that a news story?" asked Greenfield. "Because something terrible happened to her. She never used drugs and never had sex of any kind. Yet, this beautiful young woman was dying of the disease."

The ABC correspondent said it was a news story for two reasons. First, he said, "We resonate to the story . . . it's a 'there but for the grace of God' story." Second, he added, "It raises a public-policy debate. Should medical professionals have to be tested for HIV?" Greenfield said that while people react differently to that story, news judgment dictates, "We've got to cover it."

2. *NBC News* correspondent Bob Dotson says that when he thinks of news judgment, he thinks of fairness. He believes reporters must ask themselves if there is more than one side to a story and try to present all sides. Dotson says he views ethics as an important part of good news judgment.

3. Former *CBS News* correspondent Richard Threlkeld believes news judgment is "in the eye of the beholder. If you are going to put on a newscast and want people to watch it," he says, "you have to give them stories that they ought to know—important developments overseas and how the mayor and governor are doing their jobs at home. They also want to know if there was a bad fire in the neighborhood. News judgment comes into play in giving the public the proper mix of things they should know and want to know."

Dotson says one of the best ways to develop news judgment is to learn from one's mistakes and try to avoid them in the future. He remembered working as a young newsman and being asked to do a story about the anniversary of Pearl Harbor. "I was only 22 at the time and didn't know a heck of a lot about Pearl Harbor," Dotson recalled, "but I had a handout film that had sprockets on both sides of the film. I had a master's degree in cinematography," Dotson said, "but I forgot to check which side was up. So during the newscast the planes attacking Pearl Harbor came in upside down."

Dotson said that because he didn't know any better, he thought maybe the Japanese had actually done it that way. "But when the flag came on upside down I knew I was dead meat," said Dotson. "The news director always had a critique after the news, and he would tell you what you did wrong and often make you do it over again. Well," Dotson continued, "you didn't do that too often before you started thinking of ways to improve what you were doing."

4. Former *ABC News* correspondent Morton Dean says he developed news judgment "by just working in the field . . . by doing it and working with some very good people and learning from them. You have to pay attention to people around you, and if you are fortunate enough to have good, solid, professional people to work with when you start out, that's a great help. It's like being in a perpetual classroom." Dean adds: "It's important in this business to keep your eyes and ears open all the time. . . . You can always learn new things, not only about the world but about yourself. It's important to look at yourself and listen to yourself to pick up on whatever communication problems you have."

NBC correspondent Roger O'Neil notes that when he was a local reporter he "always paid attention to every network correspondent on the air." He "studied them, analyzed what they said and learned a lot."

Richard Threlkeld also says reporters always have to remember—regardless of their age—to be concerned about things that are of interest to people outside their age group. "Young reporters just starting out," he notes, "must realize that there are people out there who are over 35 and have different interests and concerns." Threlkeld adds that even he has to keep asking himself: "What are my daughters, who are in their 20s and 30s, interested in? What would they want to watch? The same goes for people who are my seniors. Is this a story that would interest them?" Threlkeld advises reporters to remember that broadcasting is "mass media, and that means everybody— little kids, and old people, and black and white and brown people. They're all watching, and they all deserve the best that you can give them."

Curiosity

For curious people, one of the rewards of reporting is the joy of discovering things. Discovering something "first" is the best reward of all. But discovering information is not always as exciting as depicted on the TV programs based on broadcast news. To hold a network prime-time audience, these programs must come up with some imaginative story ideas each week. In the real world, few reporters get caught up in the kind of sensational situations and intrigue depicted on sitcoms and TV dramas.

Most reporting assignments are fairly routine. Reporters spend a lot of time covering murders, lots of fires, plenty of elections, more news conferences than they would care to remember, accidents of all kinds, and hundreds of feature stories. That is the *real* world of broadcast news.

The fact that most reporters do not deal with crooked politicians, track down terrorists, or go to bat for someone on death row who they are convinced is innocent does not mean that reporting is dull. There is an endless assortment of stories to satisfy most people's curiosity, and there are opportunities to explore previously unknown subjects. Getting the answers, finding out about things—and learning and growing along the way—are part of the excitement of reporting. These are some of the reasons why the profession is so compelling.

When reporters arrive at the newsroom for work, they never know what stories they will be covering, and that is an exciting concept for curious people. Most reporters will tell you that they could not imagine any kind of work that they would rather do. Former *CBS News* correspondent Betsy Aaron agrees: "It keeps you young. We're in this business because we are nosy, and curious, and angry and we want to change the world. If you lose this edge," she says, "then it's hard to put in the 90 hours a week and mess up your family life and the other things that go along with it."

Concern and Caring

There is never a shortage of news about people who need help. People in many parts of the world are dying of hunger and disease. Thousands are dying as a result of evil and political strife in various countries. At home, unemployment, homelessness, and poverty continue to be major problems. Tuberculosis, a disease that at one time was thought to have been eradicated, at least in the United States, has again become a threat. AIDS is not only a serious medical emergency but a subject of national debate regarding whether the government is doing enough to combat the disease.

These are just a few of the tragedies and distressing stories making news. All such stories raise concern, as they should, for those hearing the news. Those reporting the news must be equally concerned. Part of the job of reporting such stories is providing information that may enlighten the audience. A radio or TV reporter may not be able to do much about the plight of civil war or famine victims except to report the story in a thoughtful and caring manner. In the case of domestic problems such as homelessness, AIDS, and unemployment, a reporter often can provide information that may help those affected deal with the problem or may call others' attention to it.

Persistence

A good reporter hates taking "no" for an answer. Learning how to get people to talk to you when they may not want to is a skill. Getting them to tell you things they don't want to requires even more skill.

ABC News correspondent Barry Serafin says that he usually does take "no" for an answer when someone does not wish to speak with him, but he says that he also mentions in his report that the individual refused to be interviewed. Serafin says that the situation is different when a public official is involved. "Then," he adds, "I try not to take 'no' for an answer."

Jeff Greenfield has a similar view. "If it's a private individual who doesn't want to talk to you," he advises, "get out. But if it's a public or government official, you are entitled to keep banging on the door as much as you like. It's not a privacy issue."

Greenfield notes it takes a "combination of aggressiveness and guile" to get someone to talk when they are reluctant. He says he has had some success by telling people: "Look, I can't really force you to talk to me, but I am not out to prove a point or make a case. There is an issue at stake here, and your side is important to us. It is absolutely up to you whether you will talk to us."

Greenfield says he also makes this promise: "I'll give your side of the story fairly." He adds, "I then ask the person, 'Exactly what is it that you are most afraid to discuss with me?' Sometimes it works, and sometimes it doesn't."

Aggressiveness

Most reporters seem to agree that they try to be aggressive without being obnoxious. They criticize reporters who shout and shove microphones into people's faces, demanding answers to their questions. Unfortunately, some news directors insist on such behavior—they expect to see microphones with the station call letters on the six o'clock news as much as possible even if the only voices heard on the microphones are the reporters'. News directors also listen to hear if their reporters asked questions, which is a reasonable expectation. But these scenes can get ugly. For decades, Hollywood filmmakers have portrayed reporters as rude and arrogant—and often stupid—in movie scripts. The Hollywood stereotype of the dumb reporter has been overdone but not entirely.

Most politicians, police officials, lawyers, and others who deal with the media on a daily basis are accustomed to a certain amount of badgering from the press. They would probably be disappointed and feel neglected if the news corps was not surrounding them when there's a story to tell. But the reporter who runs down the street after a newsmaker's car and shoves a microphone into the open window is out of line. More than one reporter has lost a microphone that way when the irritated person rolled up the window.

Fairness

Reporter behavior is discussed in great detail later in the book when we take a closer look at some of the news stories already mentioned, such as the high school shootings and the JonBenét Ramsey murder case. It is often argued that it is not possible for anyone to be completely objective. This may be true. Everyone has certain biases and prejudices, but reporters must learn to leave out their personal feelings when they start writing or delivering news. Objectivity for a journalist really means "fairness"; it means honestly giving both sides of an argument, controversy, or debate.

Reporters can tell when their report on a controversial issue has been successful because both sides of the issue accuse them of being partial to the other.

Diversity

Part of *fairness* also is learning to deal with diversity in a fair manner—accepting that all races are equal and should be treated equally whether it be in the newsroom or in a news story.

Earlier in the book, we explained that race should only be referred to in a crime story if the suspect is wanted by police. That's true, but to be of any use to police or to citizens who may run into the suspect, knowing that he is African American is of little use. Even if he is identified as a six-foot male with braided hair, that description would fit literally hundreds of blacks in a large community.

Keith Woods, a member of the Ethics and Diversity faculty at the Poynter Institute, says such vague descriptions of wanted persons are familiar to anyone who has ever watched the nightly news. He said that this sort of description passes for information in too much of American journalism today, part of a dysfunctional racial discourse that doesn't always mean what it says and seldom says what it means.

Woods recalled a sports headline that read: "Indians extend Boston's massacre" [after the Cleveland Indians defeated the Boston Red Sox]. This treatment may not have intended to evoke the racist stereotype of the savage American Indian, but it hurts just the same. Woods added that the mangled language of race is punctuated with descriptions that underscore ethnicity but describe nothing. He said it is "mired in euphemisms and the tortured, convoluted syntax that betray America's pathological avoidance of straight talk about race relations."

Woods said put it all together and you get stereotypes, dangerous misinformation, half-truths, and daily proof that when it comes to race, journalists are "chained to habits that defy the cornerstone principles of solid journalism." He noted that the word minority, a numerical term, is often used when the journalist actually has a specific racial group in mind, allowing for the ridiculous oxymoron, "majority minority." Poor, he noted, is euphemized as "disadvantaged" and often used as a synonym for people of color.

Woods gave as an example of the dysfunctional racial discourse he spoke of, this paragraph from an actual story:

> Incongruous as it seems, designer names that once were best known among the traditional preppy set are now the highly coveted *must have* items of black teenagers all over the country.

Woods asks us to consider the way race, class, and fashion are handled in that example from a story about teenagers' love affair with brand-name clothing. What, asks Woods, does "traditional preppy" mean? He says if you use the dictionary's definition (a student or former student of a private secondary school that prepares students to enter college), "preppy" and "black teenagers" would not be as incongruous as the writer says. More likely, Woods says, the writer meant "white and well-off" when she wrote "traditional preppy." Woods says the paragraph could be challenged for accuracy and completeness, two cornerstones of solid journalism.

He cites another example about a Florida woman shot in her jewelry store that said "her husband arrived and reported that the 28-year-old Vietnamese woman had been murdered." Why, asks Woods, is it relevant to identify the woman as Vietnamese? Woods says that maybe the woman was a Vietnam native working toward American citizenship. But he says that from the sentence construction, we don't know. The story did not provide the context that solid journalism demands. What we are left with, says Woods, is a story that singles out a person's race or ethnicity for no apparent reason.

Racial identifications do carry information about geography, bloodlines, and heritage but don't describe much of anything. Woods asks, for example, what does a Hispanic man look like? Is his skin dark brown? Reddish brown? Pale? Is his hair straight? Curly? Coarse? Fine? Does he have a flat, curved nose, or is it narrow and straight? Telling the public that he's 5-foot-8, 180 pounds, with a blue shirt and blue jeans says something about the person's appearance. But what do you add to that picture, asks Woods, when you say Latino?

Woods takes the question a step further: "What is black," he asks. "It's the color of pitch." But he notes that the word is used to describe people whose skin tones can cover every racial and ethnic group in the world, including white people.

Woods agrees that all racial and ethnic groups do share some common physical characteristics. But, he says, the media doesn't use the phrase "Irish-looking man," although red hair and pale skin are common Irish characteristics. And Woods asks what image an audience might conjure if an anchor said the suspect appeared to be Italian or that police were looking for a middle-aged man described as "Jewish-looking." The point is, of course, that all Irish Americans don't look alike and neither do blacks. Why then, asks Woods, do we accept a description that says a suspect is African American. Woods points out, as we have elsewhere in the book, that unless the story is specifically about race, it has little descriptive value in a story.

Here are some excerpts from Woods' guide to fairer journalism:

> When the scope of coverage shows communities in their fullest complexity —all classes, religions, races, ethnicities, men and women, gay and straight, all political persuasions—then there is greater chance that all groups will feel valued and will respect your organization.

> How we refer to people or incidents can speak volumes to the public. Each adjective, phrase, or inflection, either verbal or written, has the power to signal to the audience that the reporter has a particular point of view. He warns about single-word descriptors—radical, hysterical, separatist—that are used as labels by one person or group against another.

Images shape impressions, and their effects, positive and negative, are long lasting; they work when they portray a diversity of people and offer a range of perspectives—they take the public where they might not ordinarily go.

The most abiding and most immediate values transmitted from journalists to their public arrive via the "play" a story gets; journalists tell people who and what is most important, which stories must be told now, and which can be relegated to the news briefs and the back pages. Play works best when all people are valued equally. Breast cancer stories get the same play as prostate cancer stories. Success and tragedy stories about people of color receive the same prominent play as those about white people.

Covering Stories about Gays and Lesbians

Although the gay and lesbian fight for equal rights has been waged with increasing vigor over the past decade, it reached a climax in 2004 when gay and lesbian couples stepped up the fight, insisting on the right to marry; and the Episcopal Church of America approved the confirmation of an openly gay bishop. The same-sex marriage issue became front page news when the Massachusetts Supreme Court ruled that the legislature had to amend the state law to allow same-sex marriages. At the same time, on the west coast, the mayor of San Francisco defied the State law forbidding same sex-marriages. Hundreds of same-sex couples rushed to city halls in Massachusetts and San Francisco to get married but the fight had just begun and continues today. President Bush quickly announced that he was against same-sex marriages, and many members of Congress began calling for a Constitutional amendment to restrict marriage to a man and woman. The Democratic candidate for the White House, Senator John Kerry, took a less dogmatic position without actually endorsing same-sex marriage. A movement also was launched in Massachusetts for a similar amendment to the state constitution to ban same-sex marriages. There certainly was plenty of news to cover about these issues and news managers began to reexamine whether their coverage and the staff they assigned to cover such stories were correct. Just for openers, some news executives wondered whether it posed a conflict of interest for gay and lesbian reporters to cover stories about gays and lesbians.

In the forefront of this reexamination has been the Poynter Institute, often referred to as a journalism think tank on journalism, with headquarters in St. Petersburg, Florida. One of the ethics faculty members at the Institute, Kelly McBride, did a series on gay and lesbian issues. She noted that since the same-sex marriage issue started making headlines there was a good deal of discussion and debate in newsrooms and within the national Lesbian and Gay Journalists Association which has some 1,200 members. Among the developments being examined is a decision by the editor of the *San Francisco Chronicle* that a city hall reporter and a photographer could no longer cover marriage for gays and lesbians because they were among the thousands of same-sex couples who received marriage licenses in the city after Mayor Gavin Newsom advised city marriage clerks to ignore the state law forbidding same-sex marriages.

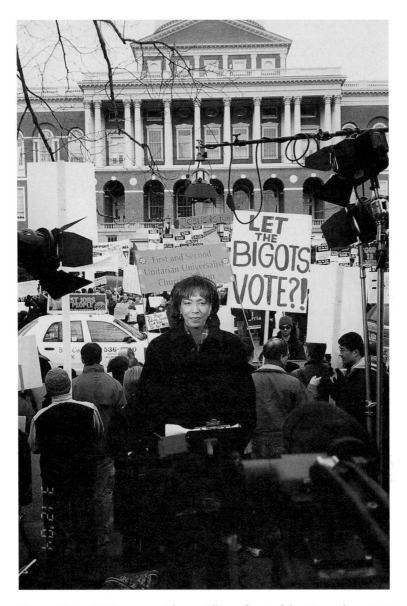

Figure 10-1 NBC reporter Rhema Ellis in front of the Massachusetts State House during a demonstration regarding gay marriage. (Courtesy *NBC News*)

McBride noted that after all the debate and discussion about who could and couldn't cover same-sex marriages, one thing was clear, a majority of editors involved in the story and discussions were in agreement that "*Chronicle* journalists directly and personally involved in a major news story—one in whose outcome they also have a personal stake—should not also cover that story." But McBride, in agreeing that there was a unique conflict in gay and lesbian journalists covering same-sex marriages, said it does not mean that the conflict is necessarily greater than for straight journalists.

She said that shining a spotlight on the journalists who are by their very identity related to the story ignores the fact that everyone has a stake in this issue. McBride points out that the journalist who gives money to a church where the minister preaches for or against marriage for gays and lesbians has a stake, as does the reporter whose sister or daughter is a lesbian. In most cases, the Poynter faculty member said, it takes more than a person's identity to disqualify him or her from covering a particular story. Usually, she adds, it takes a specific action, like giving money to a cause or taking a public stance by signing a petition or putting a bumper sticker on your car.

McBride agrees that journalists should avoid becoming part of the story, but when newsrooms worry only about the most evident conflicts, she says, "we sew a flimsy safety net."

McBride noted that the *Chronicle* editor, Phil Bronstein, made it plain that his decision not to allow the two lesbian staffers to cover same-sex marriages had nothing to do with gay and lesbian rights, even as the story itself is. He said it's about what the public thinks. "Are we willing to accept," he said, "the public perception that results when two lesbian staffers get married?" He also asked, "if the public perception is that the *San Francisco Chronicle* is in favor of legal marriage for gays and lesbians, could we live with that?"

McBride also devoted a column to how newsrooms deal with a person's sexual orientation in a news story. In other words, when is it okay to identify a person as being gay or lesbian? McBride admits that she doesn't have a good answer to that question but she did offer what she called "these rough thoughts":

> Identifying someone who is gay or lesbian against his or her will i.e., "outing" someone, should be avoided.

> When discussing sexual orientation with a source, precise language is important to avoid errors and to obtain informed consent For example, you could ask the individual "what would you think if I describe you as gay?" or "How should I describe your partner?" or "Do you describe yourself as transgendered?"

She added journalists should not use public forums, like school board meetings and court hearings to "out" an individual.

McBride says that if a person's sexual orientation or habits become a news issue (say parents ask a local school board to fire a gay teacher), great care should be taken to make sure sexual orientation is germaine to the story. If it is, McBride says, the individual in question should be contacted and allowed to clarify or correct the public record. "Journalists," she says, "should make a sincere effort to listen to the people most likely to be harmed by such stories and search for alternatives when possible."

Another consideration raised by McBride: How do journalists decide if sexual orientation is relevant to the story? She says in most cases the source in question has the answer. When a person tells you her sexual orientation is not part of the story, McBride says respect is in order most of the time. Conversely, she says, "when a source indicates her sexual orientation is important to a news story, don't dismiss the notion."

Finally, McBride writes that "identifying a gay teenager in the news should be done with great care and in consultation with a parent or other caregiver." She says it's hard to know which teens might be mature enough to understand the consequences of agreeing to a news report. "It's better," McBride adds, "to take a cautious approach to informed consent."

One of the dilemmas facing editors and news directors during the gay and lesbian rush to marry was whether to print or show video of same-sex couples kissing at their marriage ceremonies. Randy Cox, the senior visuals editor for *The Oregonian* newspaper, said there was concern about the kissing photos. He noted that same-sex kissing is "a powerful image, and we decided we would not use such a picture on the front page." In the end, the story dominated three-fifths of the front page and several inside pages. As for the kissing photos, Cox said they "evoke a reaction that further polarizes the debate." He added that none of the hundreds of photos the photographers took that day, when 400 couples were married, including same-sex kissing, "cried out for front-page treatment."

Cox said kissing photos may have become a cliché in the month when the marriage story started to grab so much attention, as images from San Francisco and Massachusetts traveled the wires, but he pointed out that "pictures are just an iconic representation of an event, they can't possibly tell the whole story."

The newspaper's online partner, *Oregon Live,* published a photo gallery of 12 pictures and seeing the same images in slide show format, said Cox, changes their impact.

Staying Well Informed

Reporters cannot function well unless they are well informed. Being well informed does not mean just having a good education; it means taking the time to know what's going on around you. Journalists must constantly add new material to their knowledge. One of the best ways to stay well informed is to read.

Reading the news wire and the Internet extensively is an immediate way to know what is going on. Reporters should also read the local newspaper (or all of them if they work in a city with more than one) and at least one national paper every day. Weekly news magazines are a useful source of additional information, as are books, particularly nonfiction bestsellers.

It is also a good idea to observe the competition. Reporters who watch and listen only to their own station's newscasts miss an opportunity not only to find out what the competition is saying, but also, on occasion, to improve on their own techniques.

Research

All good reporters do research because they want to know as much as possible about a story before trying to cover it. The Internet has made the research task tremendously easier than when reporters had to dig through libraries and morgues to find information. (Research is discussed further in Chapter 17, "Computer-Assisted Reporting.")

It is also a good idea to get on mailing lists. Many organizations are happy to add a reporter's name to their lists, and just getting on some mailing lists automatically places your name on many others. Much of the information distributed by these groups has limited news value because it is public-relations material, but it is useful for alerting you to the positions certain organizations take on issues. Many of the groups are dedicated to worthwhile causes. Almost all of them, and thousands of other organizations, too, will have Websites.

Manners and Sensitivity

Reporters often cover unpleasant stories. They are expected to interview people who are involved in a variety of tragedies—to talk, perhaps, to the parents or relatives of a homicide or accident victim. It is important for inexperienced reporters to learn how to handle such interviews with tact and sensitivity.

There have been so many bad examples of tactless interviews that the question "How do you feel about your daughter being murdered?" has become a stereotype of the insensitive reporter. It is an insensitive question. News directors should quickly discipline reporters who display such bad taste.

NBC News correspondent Bob Dotson says part of the problem is that "people don't want you there, and you don't want to be there." Dotson recalled covering a tornado story in Small Town, South Carolina, where several fatalities had occurred. "It was the day after the tornado struck, and we made sure that we got there before nine o'clock in the morning," recalled Dotson, "because anyone who is affected by a hurricane or tornado is not going to be at home later. They are either going to be at the hospital checking on loved ones or at the mortuary. So we got there before nine o'clock because the one thing people always do in tragic situations is come back and look for pictures. They don't care about stereos or TVs," Dotson noted, "but they are looking for pictures."

Dotson recalled that they found a man and his son digging through the rubble. "The son came up to us and jumped in my face, and rightfully so, and said, 'What are you guys here for . . . you're vultures,' and so forth. And I looked at him and said, 'You know it's Sunday morning, and there are a lot of folks getting up and asking themselves why . . . why did this happen?' And that is all I said, I didn't ask him a question. And then the father came over and he said to me, 'I'll tell you why.' "

"Well," Dotson said, "we started shooting what he had to say. But he became overcome with grief thinking about the loss of his wife and daughter, and he walked away. Then—because of the kind of person he was, and because he said he would tell us—he came back and finished the story."

Dotson said the story ran on *NBC News*, including the 10 or 12 seconds when the man walked away to compose himself and then walked back to the camera. "A week later I got a letter from him, and he said he had received thousands of letters from people around the country saying that he had helped them put tragedy into perspective, and he thanked me. And then I got a Christmas card from him. So," Dotson observed, "it doesn't necessarily mean that just because you are working on an emotional edge you are not going to be able to handle that situation properly."

He added that it is important in such situations to make it plain that you are representing yourself and not your company, and "If that means not having your camera rolling when you walk up, then so be it. If someone is experiencing great grief and doesn't want you there, fine, there's another story somewhere. But nine out of 10 times you can stay if you come along and talk to them as an individual first and don't ask questions—just commiserate. Then," Dotson added, "if they take a liking to you, someone will stop and tell you, and that's when you turn the camera on. But," Dotson stressed, "you never go up to someone who has great grief and act like a stereotypical journalist or you are going to go out on your ear, or worse."

Former *ABC News* correspondent Morton Dean says, "You have to think carefully about what you are going to ask. You can't rush into it. Ask yourself, 'What would make me react the best way if, God forbid, I were in a situation like this?' I sometimes say, 'This has got to be a terrible moment for you,' and I know there are people out there who, having heard that question, will say, 'No kidding, dummy, of course it's a terrible moment.'" But, Dean adds, sometimes those "dumb" questions have to be asked. He recalled that when he returned from reporting in the Persian Gulf, friends and even relatives often asked: "How could you people ask so many dumb questions at those news conferences? You know they are not going to answer a question about when the ground war is going to start."

Dean said his response was: "I've made a career out of asking dumb questions. I mean, that's our job—not to prove how smart we are but to elicit answers, and I think you sometimes have to ask what appears to be a dumb question. I am not out there to impress the audience that I have brilliant questions all the time. I am old-fashioned enough to believe that the idea is to get some news at the other end of the question."

As stated earlier, many Americans have a negative image of the news media. The polls show that a large part of the people believe that the news media as a whole is biased and negative, influenced by powerful organizations, and unwilling to admit mistakes. A poll conducted in 2004 by the First Amendment Center in collaboration with American Journalism Reveiw, shows that more than 60 percent of Americans polled believe that making up stories is a widespread problem and only 39 percent thinks news organizations try to report without bias. More alarming, said the pollsters, was that four in 10 Americans believe the press has too much freedom. The poll found that in the minds of "too many Americans," freedom of the press is the least popular of the five freedoms protected by the First Amendment. There was some good news for journalists, however, 77% of those polled agreed that the news media should act as a watchdog on government. Fifty percent said that they have too little information about the government's war on terrorism.

CBS News correspondent Mike Wallace also is concerned about the media's image. He noted that confidence in the news media "has fallen below confidence in the government." He said part of the reason for the mistrust of the press corps is that many people consider us "unnecessarily negative . . . insensitive . . . irresponsible . . . and arrogant." Wallace reminds us that back in 1971, a public opinion poll showed that Walter Cronkite was the most trusted man in America. Today, the trust of the media is at an all-time low.

Cronkite himself, who is not completely happy with the media, says that "newspapers and, to a degree, TV are doing a much better job of investigative reporting than they used to. With each of these [investigative] stories," he says, "we alienate a portion of the population. They fail to understand the importance of a strong, tough-minded press."

Cronkite says that if reporters do not do investigative reporting, "our democracy is in much greater danger than it would be even from an irresponsible press." He says it would be much worse if the press didn't have "the guts and determination" to report the truth. (The responsibility of the press—and sometimes the lack of it—is discussed further in Chapter 20, "Ethics," Chapter 21, "More Ethical Issues," and Chapter 22, "Tabloid Journalism.")

Working with Colleagues

Reporting the news is a team effort. Getting along with colleagues is essential. Young reporters just beginning their careers should watch and listen to the seasoned staff members. Seeking their advice lets them know that they are appreciated. When that happens, there is little that they will not do to help a reporter, which is important when the reporter needs a cameraperson to skip lunch or a tape editor to spend an extra 30 minutes in the morgue looking for "just the right file footage" for a story.

It is also important to remember that reputations follow reporters from station to station. News managers like team players. They hire reporters who have demonstrated in previous positions that they are cooperative and eager to learn and grow.

Summary

This chapter describes the skills and character traits of a good journalist. Although few reporters have all of the qualifications, the most successful ones strive toward them.

Here is a list of those skills and character traits:

accuracy	good research habits
aggressiveness	news judgment
concern and caring	persistence
curiosity	sensitivity
fairness	

Developing such skills will make your life, as well as your career, more interesting and rewarding.

Review Questions

1. What is the most important skill required of a reporter?
2. News judgment is a difficult concept to express even for veteran journalists. How would you explain it?

3. Can news judgment be developed? Explain.
4. What other character and personality traits should a reporter possess?
5. How aggressive should reporters be when they are trying to get a story?
6. Reporters should always strive to be fair when they are covering stories. What does that entail?
7. Reporters are sometimes accused of being insensitive. How should reporters ask questions of someone who is involved in a tragedy?

Exercises

1. Switch from station to station at the top of the local news, and note whether the stations are leading the news with the same or different stories. Which story would you have led with? Defend your choice.
2. Accompany a radio or TV reporter on a story, and observe how he or she handles an interview and works it into the story.
3. Interview a radio or TV reporter, and find out how he or she prepares for an assignment before leaving the newsroom.
4. Visit a newsroom, and find out what kind of research books, audio or video morgues, and computer resources are available for writers and reporters looking for background information. Turn in a report on your findings.

11   Reporting Assignments

Reporters spend most of their careers covering spot news, which dominates the contents of all radio and TV newscasts. Spot news includes fires, accidents, holdups, and other incidents that occur every day, with varying frequency, in every city and town in the nation.

As mentioned in Chapter 9, reporters learn about most spot news stories from the police and fire radio advisories. Tips from viewers and listeners can also provide the first word on a spot news story.

This chapter discusses the most common types of spot news stories, and Chapter 12, "Covering Planned Events," examines a variety of other typical assignments. The purpose of these two chapters is to describe the various types of assignments and to highlight the things that reporters must remember to do in covering them.

Most of the discussion focuses on editorial decisions. Remember, however, that television is a visual medium, and the success of reporting for television depends mainly on the pictures taken by camerapeople. Establishing a good working relationship with a cameraperson is also discussed in this chapter.

Fires

The decision regarding whether to cover a fire usually is based on the amount of destruction it is causing. Sometimes a relatively small fire can have tragic results if it occurs in an occupied house, particularly in the middle of the night when people are asleep.

These considerations are on the news director's or assignment editor's mind when news of a fire first breaks. In a large city such as New York, there would not be enough reporters to cover other news if reporters were assigned to every fire. There are just too many of them. A cameraperson may be sent to cover a burning, empty warehouse, and the video may provide 20 seconds of footage on the six o'clock news. In the same city, such a fire may not even be mentioned on radio newscasts unless the blaze lasted for hours or caused some tie-up in traffic or injuries to firefighters. In a small town, a fire of any kind may be a major story and may need a reporter at the scene. A fire in a residential area is almost always news, regardless of the size of the community, once it has been determined that the dwelling is occupied and lives are in jeopardy.

Once at the scene, the radio and TV reporters look for the same kind of information: Have any injuries or deaths occurred? Are any people in the

Figure 11-1   A fire in this warehouse in Madison, Wisconsin, caused tens of millions of dollars in damage and kept broadcast news organizations busy for days. (Photo by Kathy Ozatko. Used by permission of the *Capital Times*)

building? If it's an industrial building, what is burning? Is the material hazardous? How many firefighters and pieces of equipment are at the scene? How did the fire start? And finally, is arson suspected?

Reporters get most of this information from the fire official in charge. The official doesn't always know the answers to some questions, but they must be asked anyway. The radio reporter gets the answers on a tape recorder, and the TV reporter's cameraperson videotapes or beams the interview back to the station via microwave or satellite. Because of new technology, radio reporters also can go live from a scene without depending on the phone or two-way radio in the mobile unit. Using a cellular telephone, the reporter can move about at the scene and file the report whenever it's ready. By plugging a tape recorder into the phone jack, the reporter has the ability to go live with a previously recorded interview or to isolate an actuality for use in the middle of a live open and close (wraparound).

The radio and TV reporters at the fire scene also look for other people to interview—those who escaped from the building, those who might have seen the fire start or, in the case of fatalities, friends or relatives of those who died in the building. The radio reporter also records the natural sound of the fire and the battle to put it out, and the TV cameraperson does the same on videotape.

Station WISC-TV in Madison, Wisconsin, won a Radio and Television News Directors Association first-place award for spot news for its coverage of a most unusual fire. Here's the station's 10 o'clock news report on the fire, which was still in progress at the time.

	(Beth V/O)
WIDE LIVE SHOT	An enormous four-alarm fire is
	still raging on Madison's east side,

	seven hours after it began. The warehouse owner came home from vacation tonight:
SOT Kenny Williams Warehouse Owner RUNS :03 TWO SHOT	SOT "I just can't believe it. It's taken a lifetime of work."
	(Beth O/C) Good evening, everyone. Dozens of firefighters are still trying to put out the fire at the Central Storage Warehouse on Cottage Grove Road.
FILE TAPE #1009	(John) And tonight they're having limited success. The three buildings are the size of two football fields. Tonight two of them are ruined and dozens of firefighters are battling to save the third. The blaze broke out when a forklift battery exploded in mid-afternoon. It set off what likely will go down in history as this city's costliest fire, in the tens of millions of dollars for the building alone. That doesn't count the 51 million pounds of food stored inside that is causing environmental concerns. News Three's Joel DeSpain begins our coverage.
Package Font: Joel DeSpain Reporting Font: 4309 Cottage Grove Rd.	(SOT)
O/C TWO SHOT	(Package outcue: Standard) John O/C The fire isn't the only huge concern tonight . . .
	Beth There's also a big environmental impact, and it deals with a river of food washing down the street.

Key Live/Remote	News Three's Roger Putnam joins us live with the story.
Remote	(Roger remote)
	City crews are keeping waist-deep grease from clogging city lines.
Package	SOT
	(standard outcue)
Question after package	Roger, how are they doing battling this melted butter and hot dog problem?
Roger remote continues	(Roger remote)
O/C	John O/C
	At least two Madison-area companies had products in the warehouse. Oscar Mayer lost about four million dollars worth of meats but says the loss won't have much of an impact.
	Certco, a grocery delivery company, had frozen foods stored there—it's not known how much. And Swiss Colony has used the warehouse before, but it wasn't confirmed that products were there today.
O/C	(Beth)
	Several accidents tonight as a result of the fire, but nothing serious.
V/O (NAT/SOT)	(V/O)
	Stoughton Road was blocked off for more than four hours. Debris from explosions at the fire was falling onto Stoughton Road creating a safety hazard. Dempsey and Atlas Roads were also congested.

WISC-TV continued its coverage throughout the night.

Accidents

Accidents are another common type of spot news stories. Reporters cover a variety of accidents during their careers. When people talk of accidents, they tend to mean traffic accidents, which certainly do provide a lot of news. But many other accidents occupy a reporter's time as well: trains jump tracks, cranes fall at construction sites, children fall out of windows, small planes collide, and buildings collapse. Most of the time, such accidents—and many others—require reporter coverage.

Traffic accidents do get the most attention, however, even when they do not result in deaths or injuries. A chainlike collision involving a dozen or more cars on a snow-covered major highway is certain to attract reporters. Radio reporters know that drive-time audiences will be interested because of the effect such a pile-up may have on getting to and from work, and TV reporters and crews want to be at the scene for pictures and interview possibilities. TV audiences, at least in the minds of news directors and assignment editors, are fascinated by the sight of a dozen cars wrecked on a highway. Fortunately, most of those chainlike accidents produce more totaled cars than deaths and injuries. The drunk-driving accidents are the deadly ones, and reporters find little joy in covering them.

Crime

Depending on the size of the city or town, reporters spend a lot of time covering crime. Wherever police turn out, at gang battles, homicides, drug busts, and numerous other criminal activities, you will find reporters and cameras.

The crime that gets the most coverage is homicide. Americans kill one another more than people in any other country, and most of the killings will be reported on radio and TV.

Reporters working nights in a large city often get "burned out" covering murders night after night. The scripts all tend to sound alike after a while. Reporters talk to police in an effort to find out what happened and, more often than not, the word *drugs* is in the sound bite. There are sound and video of crying relatives, questions to witnesses, and shots of the body bags.

The O.J. Simpson murder trial was, of course, something unusual, and the media coverage was beyond comparison with any other homicide this century, as evidenced by the trial. The case was so unique because it involved a well-liked sports and entertainment celebrity who was married to a beautiful woman whom he allegedly abused physically. Simpson hired a so-called dream team of attorneys whom most Americans believed would win an acquittal or, at least, a hung jury. Later in the book, we take a look at the live TV coverage of the trial, which took nine months to try and only about three hours of jury deliberation to acquit Simpson.

Our discussion of the O.J. Simpson case includes a debate on whether the story received too much attention by the media and the impact that live cameras had on the trial. There is also a discussion of other high-profile murder cases (Congressional intern Chandra Levy and pregnant housewife Laci Peterson) that also received excessive and often tabloid-like attention.

Crimes other than murder are also news. The decision whether to cover other crimes, such as holdups and gang battles, depends mainly on the circumstances. In a large city, a holdup would only bring a reporter to the scene if people were seriously injured or taken hostage or if an enormous amount of money was involved. In a small community, even an injury-free holdup of a convenience store might attract a broadcast reporter to the scene.

It may sound obvious, but reporters must always remember that a person charged with a crime is considered innocent until proven guilty. The fact that someone is charged with a crime does not mean he or she is guilty; police make mistakes. It's up to a judge or jury to decide whether someone is guilty or not guilty. It is important to remember that many accused people walk out of court free.

Before the courts reach a verdict, a reporter must always say the defendant is "accused of" or "charged with." A reporter must never take on face value what a police officer or detective says at the scene of a crime. A reporter may be told that John Doe was stopped in his car and a pound of heroin was found in the trunk. It is irresponsible reporting to go on the air and say: "Police find a pound of heroin in a Center City man's car trunk. Details in a moment." The words *police say* or *police charge* are critical, even in a headline. The reporter must ensure that the defendant is treated fairly in any broadcast about a crime.

Rape

The crime of rape became a national headline story in 2004 when one of the top stars in the NBA, Kobe Bryant, was accused of sexually assaulting a young woman in Colorado. That story is discussed in detail in Chapter 22, "Tabloid Journalism," because of all the media attention that was given to the case. We also are examining the subject in this chapter because the Bryant case raised a variety of issues that journalists must be concerned with in the coverage of such stories, particularly how to protect the rights of the alleged victim and the defendant. Over the years, it has been common practice for journalists and the courts to protect the identity of the alleged rape victim. That effort was made in the Kobe Bryant case, but it was far from successful. Information about the woman, including a phone number and email address, photos, and even tax information on her parents' home could be found on the Internet and in tabloid magazines. Some news analysts say it is naive to believe that it's possible any longer, with the media expansion to the Internet and 24-hour cable news, to keep the rape victim's name a secret. Shortly after the charges were filed against Bryant, a Website calling itself the "Binary Report" set out to discredit the young lady.

Some in the media also question whether it is fair to the rape defendant when the name of the victim is not published and the defendant's is. In Colorado, as in many states, state law also makes it difficult to bring up the sexual history of the alleged victim at trial. Bryant's defense attorney, Hal Haddon, argued in a court filing that people accused of sex crimes in Colorado are deprived of their right to equal protection because two state laws set a "blatant and fundamentally unfair double standard."

One law says a defendant's sexual history is typically considered to be valuable information and should be presented to a jury. The other "rape shield" law says the defense has to prove an alleged victim's sexual history is relevant in order to present it to the jurors.

Haddon won a victory in pre-trial motions when the Colorado Supreme Court cleared the way for him to ask the 19-year-old woman detailed questions about her sexual past in a pre-trial hearing. The judge in the case ruled later that the defense could use information about the woman's sexual past in the trial itself.

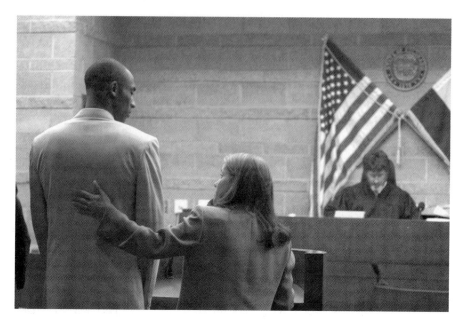

Figure 11-2   Kobe Bryant and his lawyer Pamela Mackey. (Courtesy Barry Gutierrez-Pool, Getty Images)

The prosecutor in the case, Mark Hurlbert, said he was dismayed by the ruling. He said, "We continue to have great concern about the humiliation the victim is being asked to endure at the hands of the criminal justice system." He added, "we also fear future victims may not report their victimization for fear of similar humiliation."

Cynthia Stone of the Colorado Coalition Against Sexual Assault agreed with Hurlbert. She said the loss of privacy is one of the key reasons assault victims don't pursue charges. She said Bryant's accuser would be the subject of a "horrendous 'fishing expedition' at the hands of the defense."

Writing about the Bryant case in the Poynter Institute's Ethics Journal, Kelly McBride, a faculty member at the Institute, says that concealing the victim's identity in the name of sensitivity, then reporting every other identifying element of her life is hypocritical. She says, either you do or you don't believe that she deserves anonymity. If you do, writes McBride, then grant it. If you don't, she adds, then be bold enough to say so. "It's confusing to claim you are protecting her identity, and then reveal enough information to make her identifiable to anyone in the state of Colorado."

The woman herself ended the debate, of course, when she suddenly dropped the criminal charges against Bryant, telling the district attorney that because of the "cumulative stress" of the case she would no longer be able to cooperate.

Be a Watchdog

On the subject of how reporters should cover rape cases, Poynter's McBride says they should be watchdogs to make sure the system is fair. Here are some of her suggestions:

Examine the ability of law enforcement to investigate sex crimes.

Be a historian. For much of the last century, the only sexual assaults that garnered much public reaction were those where a black man was charged with attacking a white woman. But research shows us that in most cases, the assailant and the victim are the same race and ethnicity. Race brings a historical charge to this modern-day case.

Be a sociologist. Rape and sexual assault are common in the United States. Rape can be measured by counting the victims or the assailants, by calculating the financial impact or the emotional devastation. This may be the occasion to document exactly how common rape is and to explore the toll the phenomenon is exacting.

McBride also writes, don't follow the *Globe*. Stand for the principles of a noble profession rather than racing your competitors to the depths of an anything-goes-as-long-as-it-sells contest. There is still no justification for journalists to deviate from the standard practice of granting this particular woman anonymity along with millions of other rape victims. Nor, she adds, is there any reason to show the *Globe's* cover photo in the name of reporting the controversy.

The Poynter faculty member suggests that if journalists are intent to better the public's understanding of the crime, they should look for stories about rape where the victims agree to be named. She says, approach victims or their representatives and ask if they would be willing to be named. She also has this advice: We should dedicate ourselves to reporting on the judicial process. Recognizing the different stigma that comes with being falsely charged with rape, journalists should strive for balance and accuracy in stories about cases where the court system has yet to determine guilt or innocence.

The Courts

Those arrested by police wind up in criminal court unless the defendants are younger than 16 years old, who are then handled by the juvenile courts. Domestic relations courts also get some cases involving marital disputes.

A second court system, the civil courts, handles noncriminal matters—civil suits between individuals, between individuals and corporations and other institutions, and between two or more companies. These suits, for the most part, are about money. Someone wants payment for damages. It could be for libel, an unpaid bill, shoddy workmanship, an auto-accident injury, or numerous other reasons.

Federal courts deal with matters that in one way or another involve the federal government or federal laws.

This section concentrates on the courts that most reporters cover—criminal and civil.

Criminal Courts

Depending on the state, city, or town involved, a variety of court procedures takes place before a defendant comes to trial. In small communities, a defendant may appear first before a justice of the peace, or he or she may appear in a county court. The defendant could be released on bail or remanded to jail to await a court hearing. In minor cases, a judge may hear the case and render a verdict, unless the defendant requests a jury trial.

In cities, the defendant usually is brought first to a police station, where he or she is *booked*—formally charged, photographed, and fingerprinted. Depending on the time of day of the arrest and booking, the defendant appears in court the same day or the next, where he or she enters a plea and is released on bail or sent back to jail to await arraignment and the setting of a trial date. More serious crimes are sometimes turned over to a grand jury, which examines the evidence and decides whether the accused should be indicted and stand trial or be released.

If the defendant is a celebrity, radio and TV reporters usually cover the court appearances, even if the charge is relatively minor. More serious crimes—such as rape or homicide—draw a crowd of reporters. As noted earlier, because so many killings take place in large cities, radio and TV reporters virtually ignore many of them. Assignment desks send reporters to homicide arraignments only if there is something unusual about the killing or if the defendant or victim is well known.

Reporter Access

Although many courts are easing restrictions on cameras and recorders in courtrooms, many still bar such equipment. When they are allowed, access is usually obtained on a pool basis. Some courts allow reporters with cameras and tape recorders to question lawyers, prosecutors, defendants, and others in the corridors, whereas others restrict the media to remaining outside the courthouse.

Good reporters attend the court hearings and trials even if the equipment is barred. They take detailed notes on what goes on for use in their reports. The reporter not only looks for important remarks and choice quotes from the judge, prosecutor, defense counsel, and witnesses but also makes note of facial expressions and other signs of emotion. If it's a jury trial, the reactions of the jury members are particularly important because they may give some clue about how the case is going.

When cameras are not allowed in the court during an important case, an artist is usually assigned along with the reporter to render sketches of the principal figures. Chapter 21 has more discussion about cameras in the courtroom.

Civil Courts

When people believe that they have been damaged in one way or another by individuals, professionals, or companies, they may seek redress by suing in civil court. The suit may be for libel, malpractice, failure to live up to a contract or to pay a bill, or divorce (just to name a few). The loser in civil court usually ends up paying money. No one goes to jail as they once did when debtor prisons existed; however, refusal to pay court-ordered alimony or child support would be considered contempt of court, and that could put the guilty party in jail.

Radio and TV newsrooms do not assign reporters to many civil court trials or hearings because most of the cases tend to be dull and relatively unimportant; however, an unusual malpractice case involving millions of dollars or a class action suit against an automobile company for allegedly building an unsafe vehicle attracts broadcast media to the courthouse. Reporters also cover civil cases when celebrities are seeking damages for libel or are involved in a scandalous divorce or paternity suit.

As far as reporting assignments go, the rules are the same as those for covering the criminal courts. Attend the hearings and trials, take notes (particularly if you can't use equipment inside), and try to speak with both sides outside the courthouse.

Demonstrations

The right to demonstrate is a freedom enjoyed by all Americans, and hundreds of thousands of us, maybe more, take advantage of this freedom each year. Radio and TV reporters do not cover every demonstration, but if the organizers know their business, they can almost always orchestrate a demonstration to guarantee media coverage. Regardless of the nature of the demonstration, the primary responsibility of the reporter is to avoid being "used."

With the possible exception of issues of civil rights and U.S. involvement in the Vietnam War, the battle over abortion has brought out more protesters than any other controversy. Americans on both sides of the issue are dedicated to their cause, and they spend a great deal of time defending, or trying to close, abortion clinics. The picture and sound possibilities are always good at such demonstrations, so a high percentage of them get radio and TV coverage. The right-to-life demonstrators are likely to have their children in tow and an assortment of picket signs accusing abortion clinics of murder; often they may be carrying a fetus in a jar. The pro-choice advocates have their share of signs and are extremely vocal in pleading their case that a woman should have control over her body.

Reporters cannot allow themselves to get caught up in this frenzy. Once the media arrive at the scene, the crowd gets louder and more agitated; the arrival of the TV cameras brings the noise to a peak. If you see this happening, wait until the crowd gets back to normal or near normal. Turning the camera off, and moving away from the crowd for a few minutes, is often effective.

The reporter should find a spokesperson in the group and get a statement. It is not the reporter's role to debate the merits of the controversy with the individual. The reporter should also knock on the door of the clinic and try to talk with someone inside.

Often, both sides show up at the same site. That makes the reporter's job of being fair even easier. Remember that regardless of what the demonstration is about, the reporter must always get the views of both sides.

Riots

Demonstrations sometimes get out of hand and turn into riots. And sometimes riots just break out on their own—in prisons, among workers involved in a strike, or on city streets following a racial incident. The most sensational rioting in recent years followed the verdict in the Rodney King trial in California. Four Los Angeles police officers were accused of beating King repeatedly with their batons following a high-speed chase in March of 1991. King suffered a fractured skull and internal injuries. When the officers were cleared of the charges a year later, violence erupted across the city's black neighborhoods. Fifty-five people were killed in several days of rioting and more than one billion dollars worth of property was damaged. The National Guard was deployed to restore order. A year later, the four officers faced a second trial on federal charges of violating King's civil rights and two of them received 30-month jail sentences. As for the rioting that occurred, there are special rules for covering such events.

The most important one is that reporters should never put themselves or their crew in unnecessary danger. It is impossible to determine, or even guess, what an unruly mob will do, and it could just as easily as not turn its anger on the media.

Nighttime is particularly dangerous. Camera lights invite trouble, and most news directors tell their crews not to use them. Today's cameras do a credible job with just streetlights. News managers suggest that crews use tele-photo lenses if the situation shows the least sign of becoming dangerous.

Helicopters have eliminated some of the danger from covering potentially explosive situations. All seven VHF-TV stations in Los Angeles had helicopters in the air videotaping the looting and rioting that followed the Rodney King trial verdict.

Disasters

Webster's dictionary defines a *disaster* as "an occurrence causing widespread destruction and distress." Hurricanes and tornadoes often produce disasters. A plane crash or the sinking of a vessel is also a disaster, if many lives are lost. Most certainly, the terrorist attacks on the World Trade Center towers in New York and the Pentagon on September 11, 2001, which killed more than 3,000 people and the bomb that killed 168 people in the Oklahoma City federal building were all disasters. The Indian Ocean tsunami that struck in December 2004 might have been the worst disaster in history, killing over 210,000 people.

Some reporters never experience a disaster; however, those reporters working in tornado or hurricane areas and in cities with major airports will probably cover one eventually. The horror of disasters creates an emotional and trying experience for reporters.

Although it's often difficult, reporters covering a disaster must get the facts straight. That may sound obvious, but because of the magnitude of a disaster, a lot of confusion ensues. All sorts of people will be talking to reporters, and it is often difficult to tell which version is accurate. A reporter must check and double-check all information. If something sounds suspicious, it should be reported with specific attribution. If there are two versions of casualty figures, for example, the reporter should give both figures, with attribution, and advise the audience of the discrepancy. This approach is better than trying to guess which figures are accurate and running the risk of having to make a correction later. The key point: When in doubt, be cautious.

Figure 11-3   The World Trade Center south tower (L) bursts into flames after being struck by hijacked United Airlines Flight 175 as the north tower burns following an earlier attack by a hijacked airliner in New York City, September 11, 2001. (Courtesy Reuters/Sean Adair)

The Terrorist Attacks of 9-11

On September 11, 2001, terrorists hijacked four airliners and flew two of them into the World Trade Center towers, one into the Pentagon, and one into a field in Pennsylvania. In the following pages, I have attempted to describe, as much as possible, the media coverage of the terrorist attacks. I have tried to show what was being reported and broadcast by major national news organizations and some of the local radio and TV stations in New York at the time the terrorism began and for the next few hours after the disaster. I have included some broadcast segments with dramatic reports from eyewitnesses and journalists who were at the scene, not only to convey the horror of the events, but also to show how the news media functioned during the worst terror attack in the nation's history.

Most Americans can recall what they were doing when President Kennedy was assassinated, and it appears the same is true about the day terrorist attacks killed thousands of people following the coordinated hijacking of four airliners.

Like millions of Americans, the author was on his way to work, listening to National Public Radio, when news of the disaster first broke.

NPR's Carl Kassell had this to say:

Details are sketchy but it appears a plane has crashed into the upper floors of the World Trade Center in New York City. CNN is quoting witnesses as saying it was a two-engine plane that flew right into the Trade Center. Witnesses report hearing a huge explosion and heavy smoke can be seen billowing from the building at the moment. Otherwise, witnesses said they saw a small commuter plane smash into the building, so it appears that a plane has crashed into the upper floors of the World Trade Center in New York.

Kassell read some other news stories and a few minutes later recapped his earlier information and added that there was a new report saying that an explosion had rocked the second Trade Center building.

Meanwhile at 8:52 A.M. on CBS's *The Early Show*, Bryant Gumbel was saying, "We understand that there has been a plane crash on the southern tip of Manhattan. You're looking at the World Trade Center. We understand that a plane has crashed into the building. We don't know anything more than that. We have no idea how many were on board or what is the extent of the injuries." Gumbel then spoke to an eyewitness, identified only as Stewart, who was working at a restaurant near the Trade Center. He told Gumbel, "I literally saw what—it seemed to be a small plane bounce off the building, and then I saw a huge ball of fire on top and a lot of smoke was coming out." As Gumbel spoke to the man, the audience was looking at a picture of smoke coming out of the Trade Center building. Stuart continued, "I heard a sort of crashing sound and looked up quick enough to actually see something go into the building. But everything happened so fast, I wasn't quite sure what I was looking at."

Another eyewitness, Wendell Klein, a doorman at the Marriott World Trade Center, told Gumbel he was standing right in front of the hotel across from the Trade Center when he heard an explosion. Then he said, "all of a sudden stuff just started falling, like bricks and paper and everything, and so I ran inside to get away from the debris and glass and so forth, and cars were crashing into each other." Klein said that when the falling material "kind of stopped" he heard a man screaming. "When I looked over there was this guy on fire so I like ran over and tried to put the fire out on him. And he was like screaming and I told him to roll and roll and he said I can't. And then another guy came over with his bag and kind of put the flames out on him."

Gumbel then spoke to another witness, Theresa Renault, who told him about ten minutes earlier there appeared to be an explosion at about the 80th floor of the Trade Center building. Looking out of her apartment window, Renault said, "major flames are coming out of the fire and it looks as if the building is still on fire inside." At that point, Renault saw the second plane hit the other tower. She told Gumbel, "Oh there's another one. Another plane just hit right, oh my God, another plane has just hit. It hit another building; it flew right into the middle of the building." She added, "it definitely looked like it was definitely on purpose." When Gumbel asked Renault why she said definitely on purpose, she responded, "because it flew straight into it." Renault said both buildings were completely on fire.

Almost in disbelief, Gumbel announced that they were rewinding the video tape to see if a second plane had hit. Seconds later Gumbel told his audience, "Yeah, we see it right now. We see a plane now coming in and impacting on what would be the north side of the tower." Next, Gumbel was connected with a man who was on the 24th floor of a building with a view of the Trade Center who also saw the planes hit the buildings. Fredrick Snyder

Figure 11-4 FBI agents, firefighters, rescue workers, and engineers work at the Pentagon crash site on September 14, 2001, after a hijacked American Airlines flight slammed into the building on September 11. (Courtesy Cedric H. Rdisill/DOD/Getty Images)

said his 51-story building shook when a plume of flame shot out of the Trade Center. He then saw the plane that crashed into the building fall down. "There was a tremendous amount of smoke and then it started to rain huge pieces of paper, and the paper continued to come down." Snyder added, "I was sitting at my desk when a second jet, a fairly large plane, flew in over the south end of Manhattan and deliberately flew directly into the Trade Center." Gumbel asked Snyder why he said the plane deliberately flew into the building. He responded, "because there was no doubt in my mind that both planes were using the Trade Center as a target. They weren't in trouble, they weren't in distress, and they weren't falling from the sky. They aimed for it. And they did a very good job." While Gumbel was on the air, another commercial airliner had plowed into the Pentagon in Washington, D.C., but that would not be confirmed for more than an hour. At 9:43 A.M., Gumbel reported and showed pictures of smoke coming out of the Pentagon.

"Oh my goodness, we're looking at a live picture from Washington and there is smoke pouring out of the Pentagon. It appears that there has been another major explosion. You are looking at the scene of an apparent blast aftermath . . . we don't know whether this is the result of a bomb, or whether it is yet another aircraft, but there is smoke pouring out of the Pentagon."

A short time later, Gumbel informed the audience that all airports and all tunnels and bridges leading into New York City had been closed. Shortly after this report, President Bush spoke to the nation from Florida, where he was promoting the education program.

CBS News correspondent Bill Plante reported from Washington that the entire White House staff was evacuated. He said the Secret Service "had moved everybody away from the White House grounds, and kept telling us that we have to remain a block away."

While Gumbel was carrying much of the burden of covering the story in New York for CBS, Dan Rather was making his way to the studios. Gumbel turned over the mike to Rather after reporting that there had been a second explosion on Trade Tower 2. After taking over, Rather said that there was an unconfirmed report that a portion of one of the trade towers had collapsed. Rather was able to reach correspondent Harold Dow who was near the trade towers. He reported that there had been another explosion and that literally the top of the building came down, sending smoke and debris everywhere. Dow added, "I had to do all that I could to run away from the debris. I and a number of other people are trapped in a subway here, in a shoe store actually, trying to get away from most of the debris." He continued, "it is a surreal and devastating scene over here, something like I've never seen before." Rather then reached another correspondent at the scene, Mika Brzezinski. Here is part of his report:

> I was standing with *CBS News* correspondent Byron Pitts when the collapse occurred. And literally plumes of smoke and gases as the collapse happened began to roll our way, and that is when the crowd went wild. People just began to run. Our live truck shut down, crews were running, reporters were running and the cops were literally just waving their arms, saying "go, go, go."

Following this report, correspondent Jim Stewart told Rather and the nation that police in Washington had closed down the Capitol, the House, the Senate, and the Justice Department. One building that was not closed down, Stewart said, was the FBI. He said the FBI had established an emergency command post in the center of the building.

At NBC, *Today Show* hosts Katie Couric and Matt Lauer were interviewing an author when the attacks occurred. Lauer interrupted to say, "we're going to go live now to show you a picture of the World Trade Center where I understand a plane has crashed into the Trade Center here in New York City. Like the other networks, NBC also was able to get eyewitnesses on the air quickly while showing pictures of the Trade Center buildings on fire. Eyewitness Jennifer Oberstein said, "I have to tell you it's quite terrifying, I'm in shock right now. I came out of the subway and was heading to work when I heard a big boom, looked up and there was a big ball of fire. . . . I've never seen a fire like this before in the air and the pieces of building were flying down. . . . It looks like the top, maybe 20 floors . . . it's horrible . . . I can't even describe it."

Moments later, at 9:00 A.M., Lauer said, "we're back with dramatic pictures of an accident that happened a short time ago. You're looking at the World Trade Center in lower Manhattan where just a few minutes ago, we're told, a plane crashed into the upper floors of one of the trade towers. You can see fire and flames, or smoke billowing from that tower." The anchors continued to interview witnesses. Dan Dietrich said he saw one plane crash into the middle of the top floors of one of the towers, and 10 minutes later he saw another plane crash into the other tower. "There was a huge fireball and a gaping hole in the side of the tower," he said, adding, "As we were looking at it, another plane came in low, I believe from the other side, and hit the middle of the other tower. I saw both planes, two separate planes, crash into each tower."

MSNBC reporter Ashleigh Banfield told a dramatic story of being engulfed in a cloud of debris so thick that she had to kick in two glass doors to an apartment building just to keep from suffocating.

Will Wright, the news director for Fox station WWOR-TV, which is on the New Jersey side of the Hudson River, said he was about to leave for the station when he received a phone call from one of his producers saying a plane had just crashed into the World Trade Center. The producer told Wright that she had already reached the station and was dispatching crews to the scene. Wright said some of his crews were able to hire pleasure boats to take them across the river because the tunnels and the George Washington Bridge had been closed. He said other crews walked across bridges to get to the scene.

Meanwhile, at 8:51 A.M., after the first plane hit, ABC's *Good Morning America* went from a Charles Gibson interview with the Duchess of York to a picture of the World Trade Center. Gibson and Diane Sawyer were on the air when the second plane hit. ABC quickly began a special report that included a live shot of the second plane hitting the trade center. Correspondent Dan Dahler called in from the roof of his apartment building four blocks away from the Trade Center on his cell phone—the first network correspondent to do that. By 10 A.M., Peter Jennings took over. An ABC spokesman said Jennings walked right into the building and sat down in the anchor chair. The network's three-day coverage of the disaster was the longest continuing coverage of any story in the history of ABC.

Shortly after the crash, local stations in New York began calling up reinforcements from co-owned stations outside the city. WNBC-TV, for example, called in reporters and crews from sister stations in Philadelphia, Providence, and the Hartford-New Haven markets. NY1 cable station pulled in reporters from a similar Time-Warner cable operation in Tampa. Because CNN lost its microwave facility on the Trade Center, it was forced to set up a temporary receiver on the roof of its New York headquarters. An official noted that the network had never had to do that before, but as he put it, "Desperate times call for desperate measures."

Radio coverage of the disaster also helped millions in New York City and the neighboring area to know what was going on, because all but one local TV station, WCBS-TV, were knocked off the air when their transmitters were destroyed at the Trade Center.

At the all-news radio station, WINS, sales account executive Joan Fleisher went to the roof of her apartment building at 8:50 A.M. and described what was going on at the Trade Center. News Director Ben Mevorach was walking across one of the bridges to Manhattan and reported live on his cell phone as the second trade tower collapsed. He said 15 of his reporters finally got to the Trade Center, City Hall, and area hospitals.

ABC News Radio aired its first special report at 8:52 A.M. and provided its stations with 91 hours of anchored coverage through the first weekend. CNN Radio delivered 96 newscasts per day.

During the two years after the 9/11 tragedy, a lot has been written and broadcast about the worst terrorist attack on the nation, and there has been time to revisit in more depth the roles that journalists played that day—roles that often tended to go unnoticed at the time because, after all, they were just doing their job. Here now, are more of the dramatic moments that reporters, producers, camerapeople, and others in the journalism profession remember about how they did their job on 9/11.

Trying to Find a CBS Crew

That's what *CBS News* correspondent Carol Marin said she was doing when one of the Trade Center buildings started to collapse. She recalls asking a fireman if he saw any CBS crews and he told her to walk down the middle of the road. "All of a sudden there was a roar, an explosion and we could see coming toward us a ball of flame, stories high." Marin said the fireman and others screamed "run" and she ran. When she fell, one of the firefighters picked her up. "We ran as fast as we could," she said, and then the firefighter threw her into the wall of a building and covered her with his body. Marin said, "I know firefighters do incredible work all of the time, but this exceeded anything I can imagine. He threw me into a wall and covered me with his body. I could feel his heart banging against my back; we were both so sure we were going to die."

Marin said, "I made my way somehow through the smoke, into the light to our crew."

Marin's story was described in one of those books referred to earlier, a collection of journalists' stories of 9/11 gathered by *CBS News* called *What We Saw*.

Another *CBS News* reporter, Pamela McCall, recalled this experience on 9/11:

"It is a scene of utter devastation before my eyes. The second World Trade Center Tower is demolishing." She added, "people are screaming in the streets here in utter disbelief, clutching their heads. There are plenty of tears. People cannot believe that these towers have come down."

"I've seen a lot people running for their lives. The people who get to this point are very tired, about half a mile away, and they can't believe they are lucky enough to have gotten out of there. A lot of people heard one explosion, ran outside or looked out their windows and saw the aircraft crash into the tower. They immediately tried to get out of the area as best they could, especially before one of the towers collapsed, or a good portion of it. The devastation that is before us right now is unbelievable in terms of an entire World Trade Tower collapsing. There's nothing left of this thing. All we see is a calm billow of smoke, which marks where this building once stood."

CBS News correspondent Scott Pelley remembered this: "At ground zero, as the area around the site of the World Trade Center disaster came to be known, firemen dug with their hands, searching for any sign of life. There were one and a half million tons of ruins and nearly 3,000 people inside. 'It's just incredible, indescribable,' as an exhausted fireman told me. 'We are standing on the roof of the building and as we're digging out, all you see is the tops of fire engines and cars, there's stuff and people everywhere.'"

"Everybody's working together," another fireman said, "piece by piece, hand by hand. The whole city is trying to get people out."

"Volunteers marched in off the street, including retired firemen, iron-workers, nurses, and tourists. They set up bucket brigades to move the wreckage, hand over hand, a few pounds at a time. In the first hours, I saw a great deal of hope. 'Rescuers climbed the mountain of debris expecting miracles.'"

CBS News Correspondent Byron Pitts who also was at the trade center on 9/11 recalled this scene:

"My colleague, Mika Brzezinski, and I ran inside Pubic School 89 to escape the collapsing towers. It was the first open door we came across as smoke, ash, and fire chased us up the West Side Highway. As we ran in the back door, teachers were calmly evacuating schoolchildren out the front door."

"When I first stepped out from the elementary school, I couldn't breathe and I couldn't make sense of what I was seeing. It looked like it was snowing. Everything was light gray, the street, the sidewalk, and the cars, even the few people walking around. I ran back in to take a deep breath and to process what I had just seen. I peeked in on Mika, told her things looked relatively safe and that I'd be back in a few minutes.

But as I turned to leave, I bumped chest first into a fireman. He was covered from head to toe in a thick layer of ash.

I asked him if he would mind being interviewed live via telephone for *CBS News*. He didn't answer so I took that as a yes, or at least not a no.

Once on the air, I asked the fireman what had happened and what he had seen. 'I lost all my men. When the building came down, I got separated from my men,' he said.

'How many men?' I asked.

'At least ten,' he said, 'and there are hundreds more missing.' He asked us to call his wife to let her know that he was okay."

Women Journalists at Ground Zero

You already have read about what some women journalists were doing on 9/11 and now we know that there were an unusually high number of female journalists covering that story. So many, it turns out, that a book was devoted to their efforts, called *Women Journalists at Ground Zero.*

Here's what some of those journalists saw and heard:

"A plane has crashed into the World Trade Center. You have to get here right away. I'm going to need you to find the mayor or the police commissioner." The words were those of WNYC Radio acting news director, Kevin Beasley, and he was speaking on the phone to a very shocked reporter, Beth Fertig, at her apartment in Greenwich Village, a short distance from the Trade Center. "I was completely taken by surprise," she said, "I didn't know what he was talking about." She turned on the radio and heard an anchor at her station repeating what she heard on the phone, a plane had indeed struck the World Trade Center but nothing else was known. Fertig said her boyfriend then called and told her to turn on CNN. She did and saw the Twin Towers burning.

Fertig ran downstairs and outside, where she had a perfect view of the Trade Center. She saw a group of people in the street, staring. "I looked south, and the Twin Towers were clearly visible to me with holes in them and burning—these big, black holes in each tower and flames shooting out. It was a perfect blue sky day and the towers were perfectly illuminated by the sun— sparkling, silver towers with these holes in them and with flames jumping out. It was the most striking image; I didn't think it was real. I was looking at it like a surrealist painting. Then I realized, oh my God, this is real, I could smell the smoke." She realized in that instant that she was witnessing a huge tragedy.

With her bag of equipment, Fertig ran to her train station on Bleeker Street, three stops from her radio station, or about a mile and a half away. When she arrived at her stop, the air was thick with smoke and little bits of stuff were floating around her. Fertig ran up to the newsroom but no one was there except an anchor and a couple of managers who said the building was evacuated. Since she was assigned to find the mayor or police commissioner, Fertig ran over to One Police Plaza, a short distance from the radio station.

But the building had been evacuated. Then she ran to City Hall and was told that building also had been evacuated. She learned that the mayor had gone to a bunker next to the Trade Center buildings. "I'm thinking," she said, "that he wouldn't be crazy enough to go to his bunker if the towers are burning." Fertig returned to her radio station and saw her program director and a cluster of people and she said, "I don't know what's going on but I'm just going to go." He told her not to do anything crazy. She added, "I go running down the street, and I'm pushing through this crowd of thousands of people standing in the middle of the street just staring at the towers burning." She said she heard a sound truck say that the Pentagon also had been hit. "By then I realized that it had been terrorism but I didn't know it was beyond New York."

Fertig said she remembered pushing through the crowd and looking up at the the southern tower which she said "looked like a candle melting." She said the building looked a little shorter because the flames were eating it away.

The reporter got to within a block of the Trade Center and then was turned back by a woman police officer. She showed the officer her press pass, but she still wouldn't let Fertig pass. "I'm like all indignant and shouting, I've got to get there, the mayor is there. . . . I've got to cover this. . . . As if on cue," Fertig said, "the first tower came down. I hear this huge rumbling noise like an elevated train above my head. I'm staring at this in disbelief. I just held my microphone out to get the sound of it and began narrating what I'm seeing, the building is falling, people are running, there's smoke . . . whatever was happening, I just started narrating. Then I realized everyone is running." Beth decided to run also.

But she didn't know where to run because she didn't know which way the building was falling. "It just descended like a timed implosion—like they are deliberately bringing a building down. It was the strangest thing to see," she said, "It was coming down so perfectly that in one part of my brain, I'm thinking, They got everybody out and now they're bringing the building down because they have to. . . ." Fertig said she thought for the first time that her life was in danger. She said she knew she had better run.

When she stopped running, Fertig continued to do her job, interviewing people and doing reports for her station. It was 4:30 A.M. the next day when she finally headed for home. She couldn't get a cab, so had to walk about a mile. "That was the worst experience of my life," she recalled. "I was walking home alone in the dark, looking toward the Twin Towers. They were gone. It was just the saddest thing in the world."

Another WNYC Radio reporter, Amy Eddings, was doing a story in Brooklyn, a 20-minute subway ride from the Trade Center when her pager went off. It was someone in her newsroom telling her to go to the Trade Center. She took the subway back to Manhattan and got off at a stop several blocks from the towers. When she was on the subway she knew only that one plane had hit a building, but by the time she got off the train, the second plane had struck. Eddings described what she saw when she reached the street:

> People were clustered on the sidewalk and in the streets, watching the towers. She said lots of people were streaming out of the towers. Several were crying and visibly upset.
>
> One man was lying on the street, unconscious, with a gash on his forehead. Blood was running toward the gutter and Eddings stepped over it. She asked those who were attending him whether he had been hurt by falling debris. A bystander said "no, it was from all the people." Eddings said she kept looking for big parts of the planes but instead saw lots of shoes, nuts and bolts, headphones, and a book. She said she then started to interview people at the scene. Three men told her they saw at least ten people jump from the towers. Another man told Eddings that cars parked along one of the streets near the Trade Center were exploding. Still another man told her that he had run down 73 flights of stairs in the south tower. "We saw lights flicker, and then a ton of debris came over the side," he said, "and then smoke . . . and the smell of aviation fuel." He was soaking wet from sweat.

As Eddings stood there looking up at the north tower, she could see the mark of the wing where it had sliced into the building. She said she remembered thinking, "How in the heck are the firefighters going to get the fire out?"

It was very frustrating for Eddings trying to report. Her cell phone was out so she walked to a nearby pay phone where she had a clear view of the burning building, but when she called her newsroom, there was no answer. The building, as noted earlier, had been evacuated, although it was seven blocks from the Trade Center. She then called NPR in Washington (WNYC is an NPR affiliate) and she said she was about to be patched through to the news program when a plain clothes detective asked her to relinquish the phone for security reasons. Eddings flashed her press pass and explained she was filing a story, but the man insisted she give up the phone. She spent the next ten minutes going from corner to corner trying to find another pay phone without success. Finally, she ran into a shoeshine store and offered a man 20 dollars to use his cell phone. But the battery had already died—a result of other people making the same request. Eddings decided then to run back to the station, some six blocks away so that she could get her taped interviews on the air. When she arrived, a security guard tried to keep her from the building, but an official cleared the way for her and when she got to the studios, she found her fiancé, anchor Mark Hilan, and a management official still broadcasting despite the evacuation order. Although it had transmitter problems like other stations because its FM antenna was destroyed, WNYC was able to broadcast until 6:00 P.M. on its AM frequency because that antenna was in New Jersey.

How Not to Spend the Last Day of a Vacation

NBC correspondent Rehema Ellis planned to spend the day just enjoying New York City.

But shortly after 9:00 A.M. on 9/11 her pager started to beep. She called her office and was told to turn on her TV set. What she saw she couldn't believe, and it would start for her the longest working day of her career. What Ellis saw on TV horrified her. She said she really didn't believe what she saw. But when she looked out the window of her high-rise apartment on the upper East Side and saw a thick cloud of smoke coming from downtown she knew something was terribly wrong, in addition to the television pictures confirming it for her. She rushed out the door and caught a cab. She said the driver was so upset he could hardly drive but they did make it to an NBC live satellite truck about ten blocks from the Trade Center. "People were running away and I was running to the Ground Zero.

She noted that New York City is a city of ten million people and it was as if all of them were in the street. Everyone was in a state of confusion with a look of what do we do and where do we go.

Initially, Ellis was frustrated as she tried to locate the crew. Her cell phone was not working, and the pay phones were either not working or had long lines of people waiting to use them. She managed to convince people inside a closed *Victoria's Secret* shop to let her use their phone. She called the newsroom and asked where the crew was. She was told to go to the Trade Center area.

When the first tower came down, Ellis was still walking alone and trying to make her way to the live shot location. She recalled that "it was not a good feeling to be alone because people were running and crying. It was strange because I was afraid too, but I also thought I had a crew closer than I was at that point, and I had to get to them." She added, "To tell you the truth, I just didn't think. If I'd given everything a whole lot of thought, I might have turned around and run in the other direction, too." But she didn't and kept trying to find her crew. Ellis said she really didn't have a sense of the magnitude of what had happened. She said, "It was a day when everything was upside down—my own sense of what was going on was upside down."

By the time Ellis reached the crew, the second plane had hit. She said it was raining paper and dust, and even before she got into the middle of the disaster, it already covered everything on her—her hair, face, purse, everything. It was just that heavy, even ten blocks away, she said. While she was looking for the crew she saw a producer, Mary Beth Toole, who happened to be shopping in the area when the planes hit the towers. Together, they decided to start videotaping whatever they could. She said, "We literally inched our way into Ground Zero, taking pictures, talking to people." She started doing standups, talking into the camera about what they were seeing. They stopped at a hospital and then went to city hall, which is only a few blocks away.

Then they walked to the nearby Brooklyn Bridge where they saw a sea of people walking over it, not on the sidewalk but in the road where vehicles are supposed to be. Ellis wanted to get a picture of that scene but when police turned them back, they climbed over a fence and worked their way up the backside of the bridge to get the pictures they were looking for. Ellis said, by willing to step into places we wouldn't advise others to go, we managed to make our way around the police. Ellis said she saw shoes in the street, and she wondered if they literally ran out of their shoes, or . . . —she didn't complete that thought. Ellis didn't do an on-camera live shot until later that night. She and her producer fed their video tape in so they could do a report for *Nightly News with Tom Brokaw*, a special edition that went from 6:30 until 8 P.M. Ellis had worked nonstop from nine that morning until eight that night. She had no food and very little water all day.

Just Go . . . Go . . . Go!

It was primary day in New York City on 9/11 and CNN producer Rose Arce was planning to vote that morning but decided to get coffee first at a deli across the street from the polling site when she heard an NPR broadcast saying that something had happened at the World Trade Center. She said it sounded ominous and immediately used her cell phone to call the CNN office. She asked where they wanted her to go because she planned to just start running downtown. The reply was "just go, go, go and call us when you get there." Arce said she did just that and when she had gone about two blocks she could see the building on fire. She hitched a ride that took her only a few blocks from the Trade Center. She kept trying to reach CNN but the line was constantly busy. She saw a woman standing outside an apartment building and asked her if she lived there. She said yes and that her husband was on the top floor, so Arce ran to the top and found the man, and said she was with CNN and would like to use his apartment. He agreed. As it turned out, Jim was a photographer of children and he loaned Arce his DVD camera which she used to magnify the burning buildings. Jim had a portable phone in the apartment, which she used to call CNN and give reports on what she was seeing.

While she was doing that, CNN was showing live pictures of the towers smoking in the distance. Arce noted that normally anchors would be asking her questions, but not this time. She said "I would just keep talking and there would be silence on the other end. It was like they couldn't believe what I was saying."

Then Arce said she saw the most horrific scene she had ever witnessed. "All of a sudden one person came to the window, and it looked like he was helping people jump.

One by one they started jumping. Then from a variety of windows, a bunch of people started jumping. They were flailing against the wind as they fell down. Some of them were holding hands."

As people were jumping, Arce said, the building was crumbling, almost like a deck of cards.

Arce decided that she had to get out of the building and look for a CNN cameraman. She said she started running and stopped at pay phones trying to reach the bureau. She said her eyes were burning and she was coughing really hard at this point.

When Arce found the cameraman, they tried to get closer to the buildings, which were completely on fire and in danger of collapsing. "At that point," she said, "I was more in a state of shock than I realized. Once or twice my cameraman grabbed me and said, "Hey Rose, we've got to get out of here.""

Arce finally made it back to the office with the tape and did a story about what she had seen. She didn't go home until about 4 or 5 A.M. the next day for a quick nap. Then, she said, she went back to work for a few more hours, about fourteen.

Broadcasting and Cable magazine, in an issue devoted to the disaster, noted that much of the live coverage and dramatic pictures came from traffic reporting helicopters ringing Manhattan. Those choppers delivered live pictures of the second passenger jet plowing into Tower 2. The magazine also noted that as the Twin Towers stood for their final hour, TV crews had time to capture images of frightened evacuees pouring through the streets, trapped office workers clinging to the outside of the buildings, and—most chillingly—terrified jumpers choosing to plunge to their deaths rather than face the 2,000-degree flames consuming the upper floors. The magazine said of the news coverage: "Considering the wall-to-wall coverage, radio and television reporting was remarkably informative, maybe even calming."

In a special report on the media coverage in the *Communicator*, the magazine published by the Radio and Television News Directors' Association, Gil Geisler wrote that when life in the United States was at its worst, broadcast journalism was at its best. She said the story was chaotic, but the storytellers were calm. She said television made every citizen an eyewitness.

Geisler, who is with the Poynter Institute in St. Petersburg, Florida, wrote that you could see "the conscious decision of TV directors to stay with the pictures during the coverage. This was not a day to see the faces of anchors; their voices sufficed." Geisler added, "Viewers needed to see the towers, the Pentagon. The sheer magnitude of the damage needed to be on screen for all to see."

Geisler also pointed out that at a time of budget strain, layoffs, and cutbacks, "Networks took the high road and dropped commercials, foregoing millions of dollars in revenue, and poured untold dollars into overtime, satellite bills and the care and feeding of crews."

Newsweek magazine's special report on the disaster noted that television doesn't always get tragedy right, but, "The media's work on the terrorist attacks did something that seemed nearly impossible considering the disastrous coverage of election night 2000." The magazine said the media exercised commendable caution and rightfully kept the grisliest images from the public. But it noted one unfortunate exception, what it called the "seemingly endless" video of someone plunging from the Trade Center. CBS, Fox, and CNN showed the footage repeatedly, though NBC wisely aired it only once.

Oklahoma City Bombing

Covering the Oklahoma City disaster was, of course, complicated by the criminal aspect of the bombing. Reporters spent as much time, probably more, trying to keep up with the police and FBI investigation of the bombing as they spent trying to sort out the number of dead and injured.

A broadcast journalist who was in the middle of the news coverage of the bombing says it was "like Pearl Harbor" in that it scored a direct hit on the hearts of Americans and prompted a surge of sympathy from around the world. Bill Perry was working for the Oklahoma PBS network when the blast occurred. He said that unlike Pearl Harbor, modern news technology allowed information from the blast to be distributed within seconds of its devastating detonation.

Perry said that when the yellow Ryder truck exploded at 9:02 A.M. on April 19, 1995, all of Oklahoma City's network-affiliated stations were beginning their morning meetings to plan the day's news coverage. All of the stations are clustered in the same area of the city, about eight miles from the bomb site, and when the explosion occurred, everyone in the newsrooms heard and felt it.

According to Perry, the CBS affiliate, KWTV, already had two crews downtown for other stories, and the helicopter was warming up to go to Kansas for a spot news story. That chopper was redirected to the federal building, and the station had pictures of the site quickly. The news director, Joyce Reed, said her photographers take cars and gear home from work, and most of them were headed in to the station when the bomb exploded. Many of them, she said, went directly downtown. Others picked up reporters and headed for the scene.

Two other stations, the NBC affiliate KFOR and the ABC affiliate KOCO, also sent choppers to the scene, but the FAA quickly closed the air space, and no other aerial images could be obtained for a month, until demolition crews collapsed the building completely. All the news reports and pictures after the first hour were taken from the ground.

A reporter for WKY radio, Billie Rodely, said she was driving downtown when the blast occurred. She said she jumped out of the car and started running when she suddenly realized there was glass everywhere. Rodely said she was still several blocks from the scene and continued running until she got about a half block away. That's when she saw the bombed-out building. Rodely said she was shocked at what she saw. Nobody knew what had happened. She said, "The blood was incredible." Rodely said she saw things up in the trees that she never reported. She said the other reporters who got there early were the same way. "It wasn't necessary to talk about body parts and tissue," she added.

One of Perry's colleagues, reporter Charles Newcomb, said his first view of the bombing scene far exceeded what he had expected to encounter. "We were a half mile away from the building," Newcomb said, "and it already looked like a war." He said bricks and broken glass were everywhere.

As microwave links were established, reporters at the scene and anchors at the studios were reporting over raw videotape of the bombed-out building. Susan Kelley, the news director at KOCO, recalls that some photographers struggled at first with whether they should be shooting footage of the scene or helping the victims. Photographers would later say that they continued shooting because there was such a strong response by medical personnel that they thought they might just get in the way. But Kelley said that crews still helped even while doing their job, whether it was loaning people a cell phone or literally giving them the coats off their backs because someone was cold.

KFOR news director, Melissa Klinzing, said that within two minutes of the explosion, the station was getting calls from around the country from stations wanting video. She said they uplinked their local coverage for NBC stations, and that eliminated a big headache. She said, "What we sent up was exactly what everybody wanted, and most of them re-broadcast it as it came down." Klinzing said that at one point when she was in the control room, she looked at the various monitors and saw that her station's video was not only on the Oklahoma City station but also on CNN and NBC at the same time.

Perry said that's the way it all began—what was probably the longest local newscast in broadcast history. It would be five days, he said, before any of the Oklahoma City stations played a commercial or aired anything but around-the-clock news coverage.

Bill Perry, who provided this description of the early news coverage of the disastrous bombing in Oklahoma City, is a former News Director at NBC and ABC television affiliates. He's currently Executive Producer of Documentaries for the Oklahoma PBS network.

The 2004 Tsunami

The estimated death toll in the earthquake and tsunami which struck eleven countries in South Asia on the day after Christmas of 2004, is estimated to be more than 210,000, making it one of the worst disasters in modern history, but the actual number of people who lost their lives may never be known. What we do know is that this catastrophe has received more news coverage than any previous disaster, thanks to new technology like videophones and jets, which now allow reporters to go to any part of the globe in a day or two. As columnist John L. Smith of the *Las Vegas Review–Journal* pointed out, an earthquake in Tangshan, China in 1976, killed 242,000 people but it did not receive as much news coverage as the South Asia tsunami for the reasons I just cited. Smith said the Asian tsunami is without question the greatest natural disaster we have watched unfold before our eyes through nonstop television news coverage.

Smith added that there have been world wars, great floods, devastating plagues and, more recently, news readers have learned the AIDS epidemic in Africa kills hundreds of thousands a year and the Rwanda genocide killed millions, but "unless we experienced those stories up close, they somehow manage to remain distant." Smith said that as disturbing and terrible as all these calamities are, they are not as shocking because we are seeing the tsunami for ourselves through the mass media news coverage. "The scenes of devastation are overwhelming," Smith writes, "the loss impossible to fathom, but to see such devastation, to listen to survivors tell their stories, to shed tears along with the parents whose children remain missing, that is something real and human. That makes it a local story."

Smith also notes that there are many downsides to the culture of constant television coverage. It can fray the senses, push other important stories into the shadow, and sometimes focus the masses on stories of great interest but little consequence, like the story of Laci and Scott Peterson. Smith also cited the constant TV coverage about whether the United States was doing enough to help the victims of the tsunami, and for about 48 hours, was being depicted in the media as being "stingy".

Although there has since been an outpouring of both government and private donations for the victims, Smith says the complaints that we are still not doing enough continues to be grist for political pundits and talk show hosts who spin it to fit their own agendas. Smith says he has no doubt that America will be immensely generous, but that the constant TV coverage has something to do with that, too.

Although the traditional networks and all news cable networks did not realize the enormity of the story right away, and initially were slow to cover it,

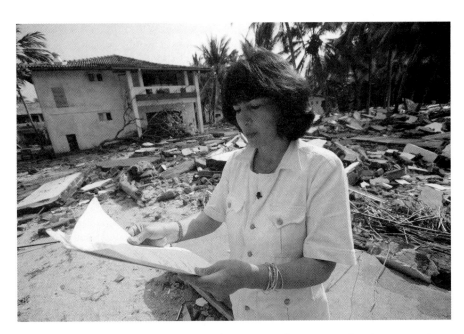

Figure 11-5 CNN's Christiane Amanpour covering the 2004 South Asian tsunami. (Courtesy of CNN)

they recovered rapidly and were soon dispatching their star reporters to the scene, to begin around-the-clock live reports that would continue for weeks. All the news outlets reported increased ratings during the tsunami coverage. CNN dispatched 80 reporters, camera operators and a variety of others to the area. Correspondent Anderson Cooper led the CNN team, and Dan Rather of CBS and Brian Williams of NBC traveled to the region to cover the story for their networks. Writing in *The New York Times*, Jacques Steinberg notes that TV news executives have long viewed natural disasters as offering a rich back-drop against which to showcase the skills of their top talent. Steinberg added that the networks were mindful that whatever the drop in network TV view-ership in recent years, people tend to flock back at times of crisis and this story offered them a rare chance to try to recapture their interest.

NBC's president, Neal Shapiro said that "the horrible images in this story remind you that there is no glee we take that this story happened, but given all the interest, it reminds us of all responsibility we have to cover it." He added, "We would be letting people down if we didn't get all the places we needed to get." *The New York Times* story quoted Dan Rather as saying that "it's very difficult, perhaps impossible to understand the conflicting undertows that go through a journalist, when covering such a story." He said that while "you are aware of headlines that talk about death tolls that are practically impossible to imagine, at the same time you are saying, 'what a story'."

ABC's Peter Jennings was stuck at his anchor desk in New York, sidelined by a respiratory ailment. *The Times*'s Steinberg noted that for ABC, which had spent tens of thousands of dollars in recent weeks on a promotional cam-paign intended partly to emphasize Jennings experience as a foreign corre-spondent, the situation was agonizing. In Jennings' absence, ABC highlighted the contributions of Diane Sawyer who had arrived in the region New Year's weekend. While co-hosting *Good Morning America*, she was filing reports to Jennings's *World News Tonight*.

Fox News sent none of its anchors, and of all the traditional and cable networks, it had the leanest operation, with a staff of about 25 in Asia. In predictable fashion, Fox's vice president for production, William Shine, attempted to justify his networks apparent lack of commitment to the story, saying "I think there's a knee-jerk reaction to get the star there. We try to do things differently here." Its decision did not especially hurt Fox's ratings. For the week after the tsunami struck, Fox's ratings were up 17 percent over the same period last year. But CNN, though a distant second to Fox, improved far more, drawing an increase in viewers of 64%.

Steinberg wrote that CNN's Anderson Cooper spent most of his time with a camera crew visiting devastated seaside villages along Sri Lanka's west coast. But that he also shot digital video images himself. Cooper was also the anchor for several additional hours live each night from Sri Lanka. In his *New York Times* story, Steinberg noted that NBC's Brian Williams, the father of a 16-year old daughter and 13-year-old son, found that bearing witness to seemingly endless scenes of abandoned children made it especially difficult for the NBC anchor to do his job at times.

Important new developments concerning the news coverage of this tragic story will be added to our homepage: broadcastnewsbook.com.

Tragedies

A tragedy is a form of disaster but on a smaller scale. For the friends and relatives of a couple and five children who were killed in a fire, however, the event is no less a disaster. For reporters, tragedies are often more difficult to cover than full-blown disasters because they become more personal. Regardless of how tough a reporter thinks he or she is, the sight of five small body bags being removed from a burned-out building has a strong emotional impact. Reporters can cry, and sometimes do, alone. They must, however, report such stories as dispassionately as possible and move on to the next one. For some, the emotion is too strong; more than a few reporters quit as a result.

Violence

It sometimes seems as though violence is an inescapable part of our lives. In one form or another, violence touches on the lives of many thousands of Americans each year. And when we escape such horror, it appears that we often miss it narrowly or know some friend or relative who is a victim of it.

There have been many reports about violence and television, and sometimes it seems as if the two words are synonymous. The debate about too much violence on TV has been continuing for more than two decades. Although most of it deals with violent entertainment and the impact such programs have on children, there is great concern among journalists and nonjournalists that television news also shows too much violence.

News directors defensively point to society and argue, as we pointed out earlier, that the world is violent and journalists are just reporting what is going on. Much of that argument is valid, but critics maintain that too much emphasis is placed on violence in the news and that it is not necessary to report every violent incident, as it sometimes appears to TV viewers.

News directors counter that they do not cover all violence, and if they did, there would not be enough room in the 30-minute newscast to cover any other news. It is true that, particularly in many large markets, there may be multiple murders on any given night, and as the author recalls from his days as an assignment editor in New York City, reporters often covered murders almost every night of the week. I recall one reporter complaining that she was going to go crazy if she had to cover one more murder during the week. There were 571 murders in New York City in 1999, and Chicago had 645. Even in smaller markets, like Louisiana's capital city, Baton Rouge, there were 43 murders in 2003. Sadly, we live in a violent world, and the United States is more violent than the rest of the world's nations, at least in crime-related violence.

This section examines the problem of violence in the news and how journalists try to deal with it—not only the reporting of it but also how they handle the often gruesome details of the crime, those who commit the violence, and the often-forgotten victims.

The past decade was violent. Much of it was brought about by wars in the Middle East, Europe, and Africa, and that violence, including Iraq, is covered elsewhere in the book. This section deals with domestic violence, much of it about the shocking series of school shootings that occurred from 1997 to 1999.

Schoolyard Shootings

The school violence began in Pearl, Mississippi, in October 1997, when a teenager killed two students and wounded seven others at a high school. Two months later at a high school in West Paducah, Kentucky, a 14-year-old student killed three students and wounded five others. Then on March 24, 1998, in Jonesboro, Arkansas, two boys, ages 11 and 13, shot to death four girls and a teacher and wounded 10 others.

A month later, on April 24 in Edinboro, Pennsylvania, a 14-year-old boy shot and killed a science teacher in front of students at a graduation dance. A month later, on May 19 in Fayetteville, Tennessee, a high school senior fatally wounded a student in the school parking lot. Only two days later, in Springfield, Oregon, a 16-year-old killed his parents and then went to Thurston High School, where he killed two students and wounded 25 others.

The final school shooting tragedy in the series was the deadliest. On April 20, 1999, two students at Columbine High School in Littleton, Colorado, shot and killed 12 students and a teacher before turning the weapons on themselves. It was the worst school violence in the nation's history.

The impact of these tragedies on the nation was overwhelming. The incidents also tested journalists' ability to deal with juvenile violence at a level never experienced before. The magnitude of the violence also brought media coverage of an unequaled level to the communities in which the tragedies took place. National media gave the stories saturation coverage. Some of it continues even today as anniversaries serve as reminders of those grim days and give cause for revisiting the stories.

Much of the news coverage of the school shootings has been praised but, as might be expected, many examples of bad journalism were also witnessed.

Most of the analysis of news coverage centered on the most violent of the shootings—Jonesboro, Arkansas, and Littleton, Colorado.

Media Invade Small Community

Approximately 200 journalists invaded Jonesboro, Arkansas, in the days after the tragedy. Before the week was out, CBS had dispatched 17 reporters and support staff to the scene. CNN had 30 people there, and ABC and NBC added another 37.

One of those who analyzed TV coverage of the Jonesboro shooting was the late Ed Turner, a Freedom Forum Senior Fellow and Editor-at-Large for CNN. Turner was a former Executive Vice President for the Cable News Network. He said that in covering the Jonesboro shooting, television scored few major hits, but it didn't commit any major blunders either. He said the nightly newscasts were thorough, if lacking real depth. He added that the morning talk shows provided informed, interesting guests, but the magazine shows generally were disappointing.

Figure 11-6 SHOOTING: LITTLETON, COLO, 20 APR 99—Columbine high school students run from the school after gunmen opened fire on terrified students, killing up to 25 people before taking their own lives. Jeff Stone, sheriff of Jefferson County, said the students were found dead in the library on what he called a "suicide mission." (Reuters/Gary Caskey/Archive Photos)

Turner said that the local and regional late-night coverage, while less sophisticated and polished, was nonetheless solid in almost all respects. He said the network evening newscasts did not delve deeply into the broader issues of gun control, parental responsibility, and school responsibility. He said NBC allotted the most time to the story, and its coverage seemed the broadest.

Turner praised the relatively small staff of TV station KAIT in Jonesboro, which, he said, produced solid reports on what happened. He said the reports were "often long on emotion but did not embarrass, mislead, or inflame." He said that in a sense the station served as a place where the community could grieve and that the newscasts undoubtedly were appreciated for their sensitive tone.

Turner concluded that the quality of TV journalism ranged from average to good. Turner's analysis was part of a report prepared by the Freedom Forum, examining Jonesboro's coverage. It was part of a series examining fairness in the news media. As part of its investigation, the Freedom Forum collaborated with the College of Communication at Arkansas State University and the *Jonesboro Sun*. They invited residents of the community to a "speak out." Approximately 300 people showed up to share their thoughts and, in some cases, to criticize the media coverage. Some said journalists were intrusive, invaded the privacy of victims, and relied on children as news sources.

Criticism of Media

The Freedom Forum report said that many citizens believed that the media were too quick to draw conclusions about the character of life in a rural, southern town—a perception that was deeply resented as a stereotype. In the weeks that followed the town meeting, the Freedom Forum sent a team of reporters to Jonesboro to check out the comments made by those at the meeting. Robert H. Giles, a Senior Vice President of the Freedom Forum and director of the Free Press/Fair Press project, said the team of reporters spoke to victims and their families and reporters and editors involved in the story and "tracked down reports of inappropriate behavior by individual journalists."

The Freedom Forum reporters sent to Jonesboro said that virtually everyone they interviewed gave most reporters relatively high marks for accuracy and fairness, taste, and sensitivity. But the investigators said the roughly 10 percent of the reporters who "pushed too hard" or behaved callously are the ones who are remembered. They noted that people who were interviewed remembered the conduct of the media, rather than the content of their reports. The Freedom Forum report said it found few instances of misinformation in news reports, and almost all of them came early on, when the story was first breaking.

Jonesboro Police Chief Floyd Johnson had mixed reactions to the reporters who came to his community. He said that before the shooting, he thought he'd seen it all in terms of the media because when he was a sheriff in 1968 he dealt with the media when a tornado struck Jonesboro and killed 34 people. But he admitted he was wrong. He was not ready, he said, for the wave of journalists who turned up after the shooting. "For the most part," he said, "when you were dealing with a reporter one on one, they were very sympathetic, seemed to have a lot of sympathy for the folks. But," he added, "I would have to compare them with a bunch of animals whenever they all get together with their cameras." He said, "They'll run into each other, run over you, park in streets, and block others."

Although inaccuracies in reporting the story apparently were few, one broadcast said that Shannon Wright, the teacher who was fatally shot as she protectively draped her body over a student, had died when she actually did not die until many hours after the erroneous report. Still other reports incorrectly said the woman was pregnant.

The husband of the hero-teacher, Mitchell Wright, also had mixed views about the media. He said that he is convinced that photographers climbed his fence and tried to get into his yard one night and that a TV crew set up a camera across the street from his house, focusing a camera on his front door. Wright said a neighbor warned the crew that if they did not get their equipment out of the road he was going to run over it.

Wright did commend the media for their constant referrals to his wife as a hero. He consented to interviews with ABC and NBC to talk about his wife. But he said a CBS representative tried to pressure him into doing another interview against his will, claiming that it would not be fair because he had talked to other networks. The CBS representative allegedly tried to sway Wright by saying that her boss was going to be upset with her if she didn't set up the interview.

Another resident of the town, Gretchen Woodward, says she was hounded by two reporters who accosted her when she left her house, demanding to know if she was Mitchell Johnson's mother and refusing to leave when she told them she had nothing to say to them. The woman said the reporters hid in her yard through the night and that she had to call police at 1 A.M. and again at 3 A.M. to get them off her property.

A sheriff said he had many complaints about media peeking through windows and knocking on doors. He said that some people claimed that if residents opened their doors some crews would walk in and reporters would start asking questions, saying that "they're live on 'Action News' or what have you."

The Freedom Forum report also said that some people were approached by news organizations with offers of money for exclusive interviews. The sheriff said one offer was for substantial cash payments to deputies monitoring the cell blocks if they would take a picture of the two boys in custody. The sheriff said he warned his deputies that if they took the pictures, or allowed them to be taken, they would be fired.

The mother of one of the children killed in the shooting, Suzann Wilson, said she only got upset once with the media, when a photographer stepped out in front of the hearse on its way to her child's funeral to take a picture. The woman had requested that no cameras of any kind be at the funeral. She said when they got to the cemetery there were hordes of reporters and cameras at the graveside, some hanging from trees. But both Wilson and Michael Wright agreed that some news coverage of their loved ones helped with the healing process.

Analysis of media performance during the other school shootings was similar to those in Jonesboro. For the most part, it appears journalists acted responsibly, but there were some "bad apples."

There also were some interesting contrasts. For example, in the Columbine school shooting, the residents of the community appeared more willing to talk to the media, often searching out reporters and producers for an opportunity to discuss the tragedy. "It was bizarre," said KUSA-TV's Ginger Delgardo. "When in your life," she asked, "have you seen so many victims and families come forward? So willing to talk." She said maybe students and families just accepted the axiomatic wisdom of our talk-show culture: talking heals pain.

Delgardo said that many of these sources were teenagers who "seemed so self-possessed, looking directly into the cameras, spouting pithy sound bites." She said they soon learned to query reporters, "Are you national or local?"

One of the students who narrowly escaped the bullets but saw the tragedy close-up, Bree Pasquale, was one of those who apparently found relief in talking about the attack. She described to reporter Delgardo how one of the gunmen "put a gun to my head and asked if we all wanted to die." She said, "I just started screaming and crying and telling them not to shoot me. The shooter turned to another girl," Bree said, "and shot her in the head in front of me, and he shot the black kid because he was black." The KUSA interview with Delgardo was broadcast over and over again on CNN and NBC.

ABC News correspondent Judy Muller, who was pulled off a story suddenly in New England and dispatched to Littleton, says she also was surprised when people involved in the tragedy were willing to talk to her. In her memoir, *Now This* (Putnam, 2000), she recalled striking up a conversation with a woman who was standing by herself near the school library and discovering that the woman was a teacher. Muller said that even as she was empathizing as a former teacher and mother, she identified herself as a reporter and somehow, as she put it, "I found the courage to ask her if she could talk to me on camera." The woman frowned, looked down at the ground, and then agreed to do the interview. Muller said it was not the only time during her stay in Littleton that she was surprised that people were willing to talk to her. Muller said it seemed to her that people, almost in a mass wave of catharsis, were unfailingly polite in their responses to reporters as they shared their experiences.

Throughout the week that followed the shooting, soaring network news audiences pumped up ratings for school-shooting specials such as *Dateline* on NBC and ABC's *20/20*. That Thursday night's edition of *48 Hours*, which included the interview with Bree, marked the first time that the *CBS News* magazine ever beat NBC's *ER* in the ratings.

Writing in Brill's *Content*, contributing editor Jon Katz called the media coverage of the Colorado shooting and its aftermath "grotesque, even outrageous." He said journalism, even its most serious practitioners, accepted and transmitted the idea that two students turned to mass murder because they played nasty computer games or had access to Internet bomb-making sites. Although approximately 20 million Americans, mostly kids, are into video and computer gaming, Katz said this idea was so widely disseminated and discussed by journalists that most Americans actually came to believe it.

The week after the massacre, a Gallup poll showed that more than 80 percent of Americans agreed that the Internet was at least partly responsible for the Columbine killings. "And," asked Katz, "who could blame them?" CBS's *60 Minutes* devoted an entire segment to this question: "Are video games turning kids into killers?"

Katz noted that hundreds of newspapers and TV stations ran stories linking computer games, Websites, and other "aberrant, abnormal, or weird behavior to mass murder." Katz added that these messages were almost guaranteed to panic parents and students and stampede educators into overreaction. "Instead of being a force for truth," Katz observed, "many in the media became transmitters of hysteria."

Veteran reporter Bob Steele, director of the ethics program at the Poynter Institute for Media Studies, praised media outlets that looked at the broader issues in the shootings as well as the violence. He said opening up the coverage of the shootings to include the broader aspects of the nexus of children and violence is key. Stephen Gorelick, a sociologist who teaches communications and journalism at the City University of New York, said journalists should give the public as much information as they can in such situations, without feeding the public desire for salacious material.

ABC News correspondent Judy Muller recalls that the first morning after the shooting, she was assigned to do a profile of the victims, what she described as "a reporter's worst nightmare: asking impossibly intrusive questions in order to get seemingly impossible answers, aimed at summing up a life in a matter of seconds, and all this against terrible deadline pressures." Muller says she and her producer started the day with a feeling of dread. She said there had been no official word yet on who the victims were, so they had to try to find out who they were and ask someone, a family member or friend, what they were like.

Muller found her assignment "emotionally wrenching." She recalled how she and her crew went to the school library where parents were waiting to hear whether their children were safe. She said she watched the faces of the parents as they searched the list that had been posted telling which students had been located and which were still inside the school. At that moment, Muller said, I was not a reporter, I was a parent. "I could no more have walked up to one of those people, who clearly were experiencing one of the worst moments of their lives, and ask them questions than I could have driven a knife into my own heart."

Muller said her camera crew stood back from the scene, filming quietly and from a distance, but she knew that it also was hard for them because they, too, were parents. "But," the correspondent added, "we had to do our jobs, to tell the story to a nation that waited, horrified, for the facts of yet another school shootout."

Why Such Killings?

LynNell Hancock, director of the Prudential Fellowship for Children and the News, and an assistant professor at the Columbia University Graduate School of Journalism, says that journalists dealing with high school shootings "should just get the facts out first and not try to weigh in with 'why' so much." On that note, James Garbino, director of the Family Life Development Center at Cornell University, says that the real reasons—the "whys"—are often difficult to pinpoint and sometimes just not possible to decipher. He said the media need to explore many possible "whys."

Sometimes those trying to find out the causes of the shootings focus on guns. The media was often accused of using the gun issue to explain many of the shootings; however, Garbino notes that journalists cannot ignore the role that guns play in youth violence. He says that granting too much attention to the opposite view that "guns don't kill, people do" is also a mistake.

Garbino says that journalists also should avoid referring to schoolyard shootings as "senseless" acts of violence. He said school shootings do "make sense inside the head of the kid who did them." In fact, he added, most of these kids commit these acts as a culmination.

Don't Forget the Victims

Most analysts of the school shooting coverage agreed that while discussions of motives of the killers cannot be excluded, it's important to give a significant amount of coverage to the victims. One observer pointed out that in tragedies such as school shootings, a whole town or community is affected, not just the victims. Bob Haiman, a Freedom Forum Media Studies Center fellow, agrees that stories detailing the grief of families and the community are important. He said that other stories dealing with fund-raising for victims, counseling sessions, and vigils also are of value. As the editor of the *Jonesboro Sun* put it, "the victims are not just the 25 people who were shot. Everybody is in pain."

Was the Reporting Excessive?

A negative view of the media coverage of the school shootings came from James Glassman, a fellow at the American Enterprise Institute. He called the news coverage "inordinate," saying that the media chose "to blow individual incidents in small towns into national crises."

Richard Wald, Senior Vice President of *ABC News*, thinks that the communities involved in such tragedies tend to have a higher regard for the work of local media than the networks. He said: "If you live in the community and watch the local news and read the newspaper, there is a tendency to view [those reporters] as being more sensitive." The national media is viewed, more often than not, as outsiders.

ABC News correspondent Judy Muller says that when she and her crew drove up to the school parking lot in Littleton, her worst fears of media excess were realized. She found the following scene: "Sprouting like overturned toadstools in the mud, satellite dishes pointing at the sky as far as the eye could see, part of a media encampment that was growing by the hour." Muller says she thought to herself, "Surely we can find a better way to cover these stories in the future, perhaps pooling our efforts to the point where no family would be requested to speak more than once." Muller says such ideas "pop up after each of these shooting incidents but are quickly forgotten as those media outlets weigh anchors and sail away to other troubled waters."

Some analysts believe that in the news coverage of high school shootings, too much emphasis may have been placed on discussing whether schools are safe, creating fear among Americans about their own children's safety. According to the National School Safety Center, schools are relatively safe.

One survey notes that teens are far more likely to commit suicide than homicide with guns.

Sid Bedingfield, Vice President of CNN, agrees that school violence has to be put into perspective. "Finding balance in any crime story," he said, "is important." He said you have to look at the many schools where the children are safe.

Another controversy that arose out of the school shootings was the identification of the young people who did the shooting. Many news organizations have long-standing policies of not identifying juveniles until it is determined that they will be tried as adults. But some exceptions are made, and decisions often can be influenced by what other members of the news media do.

ABC News says it chooses to release the names of minors accused of crimes on a case-by-case basis. In the shooting cases, ABC said it released the names when relatives of the suspects made statements to the media. CBS said that while it does not usually identify minors allegedly involved in crimes, "the boys had been identified by other news outlets, including their hometown newspaper and TV station, before we were going on the air." CNN and NBC spokespersons made much the same argument for releasing the names.

At the conclusion of its report on how the media performed during the shooting coverage in Jonesboro, Arkansas, the Freedom Forum offered the following "lessons for the media":

1. Be wary of unsubstantiated information. Anything not observed by a reporter should be scrupulously attributed.
2. Avoid demonizing or glorifying suspects or victims.
3. Correct errors promptly and prominently in full detail.
4. Obey the law, don't trespass on private property, and respect the privacy of those involved.
5. Appreciate the value of veteran journalists who know the community and who have built relationships over the years based on trust.
6. Remember that when a disaster or tragedy occurs, coverage should reflect the fact that the entire community may feel victimized, not just those directly affected.
7. Understand that viewers are better able to handle the grim details when they are reported in a larger context of sympathetic and extensive coverage that embraces the experience of the entire community.
8. Don't hype an already powerful story or tell it in florid language.
9. Avoid drawing quick conclusions, making unsubstantiated assumptions, or creating stereotypes.
10. Never misrepresent yourself or engage in deception to get the story.
11. Report on what went right and what worked when government and the public responded to a major, newsworthy event.
12. Remember that trust is the bedrock in the relationship between the news media and the community. It enables public officials to deal openly with the media by providing information that allows the story to be told quickly, completely, and accurately. Trust also helps the community understand the purpose, needs, and duties of the news media

Violent Stories Also Cause Stress for Journalists

Some news managers said that during and after the coverage of the school shootings they suggested to reporters and other staff members that they might wish to take advantage of station-provided counseling. The horror of the story took its toll on many journalists.

Covering tragedies can create immense psychological stress for journalists, according to the *American Journalism Review* (AJR), and sometimes it makes sense to get help. AJR cited one example of an *Arizona Republic* reporter, Katrina Bland, who was transfixed by a Polaroid photo attached to a police file showing a small pink coffin containing the body of an 8-month-old child who had been killed by an adult. In a story that she wrote about the tragedy, Bland wrote that the coffin was the size of a dresser drawer. Later, the reporter said that the photo of the coffin surfaced in her dreams, in which she would spot the doll-sized coffin at her office, in a convenience store, or nestled among her belongings in a drawer at home. The reporter said the nightmares triggered more such sleep-halting dreams about young children burned, beaten, and sexually molested. When the dreams persisted, Bland finally turned to a crisis counselor.

Writing about Bland's experience in AJR, Sherry Ricchiardi said the reporter's dreams pointed out the dilemma for journalists confronting horror, whether in a police file, on highways, or at house fires or the bombed ruins of a federal building. The AJR writer noted that although such coverage can create intense psychological stress, the standard newsroom script calls for stoicism. She said admitting to emotional fallout collides with the detached, dispassionate demeanor on which the profession prides itself.

Chris Cramer, President of CNN's international news division, says "some journalists do shy away from the stress issue and 'pooh-pooh' it, fearing being exiled as some kind of wimp." Ricchiardi says some journalists apparently fear that if they admit to any mental trauma, it may be viewed as weakness or even spark editors to pull them off important projects. Psychiatrist Frank Ochberg finds that surgeons and journalists have most strongly resisted outside help.

Coverage of automobile accidents and other emergencies often falls to rookies, according to Ricchiardi, and to deal with the stress, a Journalism and Trauma Program was established at the University of Washington in Seattle. According to program director Roger Simpson, the program aims to inoculate journalism students via role-playing and discussion. "I guess it's like a vaccination," he says. "If you do this in the classroom, it may be somewhat easier at a crash."

Although some journalists apparently are seeking psychological help for the effects of frequent exposure to tragedy, others such as Michael Sorkin of the *St. Louis Post-Dispatch* decided to try to avoid such trauma. After several years of covering corruption and murder in East St. Louis, Sorkin asked his editors not to tap him for any more "blood stories."

The Waco, Texas, Conflict

On February 28, 1993, the U.S. Bureau of Alcohol, Tobacco, and Firearms (BATF) launched the largest assault in its history against a small religious group, near Waco, Texas. The raid was a disaster: six Branch Davidians and four agents were killed. That tragedy was then followed by a 51-day standoff. Then, the U.S. Justice Department approved a plan that sent tanks carrying CS gas into the compound where Branch Davidian leader David Koresh and his followers were holding out. After the gas was shot into the building, a fire broke out and all 74 men, women, and children were killed.

The tragedy provoked much criticism against both the Justice Department and the BATF. But the media also was accused by some for allowing itself to be manipulated by government agencies, for not being aggressive enough in trying to put the conflict into perspective, and for not giving the public sufficient information about the Branch Davidians, who were blamed from the start by the government as a dangerous "cult" that was responsible for triggering the assault on the compound that took so many lives.

Some of the criticism against the media was that it was too quick to accept the government's explanation for the standoff and never made a serious effort to explain the Branch Davidians' side of the story. The media was charged with going along with the orchestration of public relations by government officials and not trying harder to talk to Davidian leaders.

Finally, the media was criticized for accepting the conflict as just another "cult" story about people who were strange, different from most, and probably dangerous. Before the Waco tragedy, the American people were unaware of the Branch Davidians, and even those living near the compound said they knew little or nothing about the religious sect. But after the compound went up in flames, the Davidians were known to millions around the world.

Public opinion polls in the United States showed little sympathy for the Davidians but substantial support for the actions of federal agents in handling the siege.

Was News Coverage Fair?

In the book *Armageddon in Waco,* Anson Shupe and Jeffrey K. Hadden say the absence of public criticism of the federal agents' behavior is not surprising because from the onset, the mass media substantially reported the story without much scrutiny of the details of the raid and siege as these were presented to them in government press briefings in Waco. Shupe and Hadden, who have written extensively on religious sects and cults, say that in presenting the story largely without criticism, the media contributed significantly to legitimating the government's role and portraying the federal agents as properly assuming responsibility for abused and endangered children; with responsibility for bringing to justice a band of criminals who had assembled an enormous cache of illegal weapons; and finally, portraying the agents as guardians of a community at risk from the followers of the fanatical and dangerous cult leader and his brainwashed followers.

In the same book, James T. Richardson charges that the media have contributed directly to development and promotion of the anticult ideology. But, he adds, the media cannot be blamed for the specific way the tragedy developed. "The several authorities in charge, from beginning to end," he writes, "must be held responsible for the many bad judgments and misguided plans that were developed before, during, and even after the fire at the compound." But, Richardson notes that a key element of the strategy taken, particularly by the FBI, was to exercise total control of the media. He said the authorities treated the media simply as a resource to be allocated and used

Figure 11-7 Overhead of smoking fire consuming David Koresh-led Branch Davidian cult compound, believed set by cult after FBI/ATF teargassing in an effort to end the siege. (Courtesy Time Life Pictures/FBI/Time Life Pictures/Getty Images)

as desired and as a nuisance to be dealt with severely if they refused to comply.

Government Control of Media

Some reporters at Waco said there was more government control during the conflict than they had ever experienced during their careers. Richardson, who has written extensively on new religions, says that federal officials made an early decision that reporters would not be allowed access to Koresh and his followers.

A total ban on communication with those inside the compound was established, and reporters, of whom there were hundreds, were moved progressively back from the front lines until they were some three miles from the compound. Richardson charges that the government agencies used the media for their own ends, inhibiting and restricting information and preventing any sympathetic account from the residents in the compound. He noted that the FBI was upset at one point when Koresh called CNN directly and cut all phone lines except the one they wanted kept open.

Richardson says that when reporters did try to get closer than the three-mile limit, they were treated harshly. Some were summarily arrested, thrown to the ground, handcuffed, and taken to jail. Shelly Katz, a *Time Life* photographer, said that in more than 30 years, "I have covered everything from wars to riots but was never restrained as I was in Waco." Richardson says that Koresh and his followers knew they were losing the media war, for they continually requested access, sometimes even unfurling homemade banners made from bedsheets saying: "God Help Us, We Need Press."

Koresh's attorney, Dick de Guerin, told a Freedom of Information conference that it now seems plausible that had the media been allowed better access to the Branch Davidians, it might have resulted in a different outcome.

Could Media Involvement Have Changed the Outcome?

But Richardson charged that this would have had the effect of humanizing Koresh and his followers and that would have undercut the authorities' seemingly official policy of demonizing the religious sect. Richardson said the media might even have served as third-party negotiators with Koresh, not an unprecedented occurrence in such situations. But, notes Richardson, none of this happened. Instead, FBI tactics and Koresh's reactions to them moved the situation tragically toward the conflagration that occurred. Richardson concluded, "The effort at managing and controlling the media was virtually a total success, but the *operation* itself was a complete failure: most *patients*, including the children, died."

James Wood, editor of the *Journal of Church and State*, observes that "if the state had intervened elsewhere in the world against a religious group as it happened at the Branch Davidian compound, it would have been reported in the U.S. as an act of oppression."

War Reporting: The Rules Have Changed

Most journalists will never be required to cover a war or other military action, so offering advice on how to do so might not seem necessary but there were a number of young journalists on the Iraqi battlefield and they were not all from the networks and cable news stations. The veteran journalists who reported from Vietnam, Korea, and during World War II would probably say there is not much advice they could give about the war in Iraq, other than the obvious about reporting accurately and objectively, because the "rules" had changed. They had changed also in Grenada, and even more drastically in the Gulf during Operation Desert Storm. But the most dramatic changes in the "rules" for covering a war occurred when the so-called "Coalition of the Willing" invaded Iraq and occupied that country, taking along with them some 700 reporters who came to be known as "embedded journalists."

Historically, war correspondents have been permitted to walk onto beaches with U.S. Marines and to sit in the belly of a bomber flying on a mission over an enemy target if they wanted to risk their lives in such endeavors. Many did, and some died. That kind of reporting allowed the people at home to know firsthand how the war was progressing and what happened to their loved ones. But during the Vietnam War, the first war to be brought into American homes via television, something else happened. Americans saw, more dramatically than ever before, what war was really like. They would eventually see, despite the efforts of the military and various administrations to keep it from them, that the United States was losing the war.

Many generals and politicians still blame the media, particularly television, for causing the withdrawal of U.S. forces from Vietnam. Many journalists maintain that the military learned a lesson in Vietnam: never again to allow the media the kind of unrestricted access they were permitted in Vietnam. The invasion of Grenada was virtually complete before the media were allowed to report from the island. National security was cited as the reason for the secrecy. As for Desert Storm, Doug Ramsey of the Foundation for American Communications said there were "two great victories in the Gulf War: the allies decisively defeated the Iraqi military and the American military decisively defeated American news organizations."

Ed Fouhy, a 25-year network news veteran, said that as a result of Vietnam, the military not only instituted pool coverage of wars, but they also "sent their officers to charm school, and to make sure the briefers were people with stars on their shoulders—not bars as they were in Vietnam." Fouhy said the Pentagon made a political decision to control information.

Jeffrey Marks, the former chairman of the Radio and Television News Directors association, said the military engaged in "news management." He said, "We were maneuvered away from the stories we wanted to cover. Trips into the field were orchestrated to show only what the military wanted America to see and hear. Reports were censored for reasons of pride, not security."

Former *CBS News* anchor Walter Cronkite told Congress that "with an arrogance foreign to the democratic system, the U.S. military in Saudi Arabia is trampling on the American people's right to know."

Former *CBS News* correspondent Robert McKeown (now with *Dateline NBC*), who was the first journalist to report from the front lines on the night the ground war began and the first reporter to report live from Kuwait City (arriving even before allied troops), said there was "greater manipulation of the press than there had ever been before." McKeown said the censorship affected the networks overall and the war was covered "to only a fraction of what it should have been, given the technology."

McKeown disputed the Pentagon's claim that pool coverage was necessary because of national security. He said that he saw many things in the desert that could have presented a security problem if he had reported them, but that he didn't, even though he had the ability to go live at any time because he was equipped with a mobile satellite dish.

McKeown further said, "It is not our job to compromise national security. The system always has been built on a system of checks and balances and a responsible press. A responsible TV reporter would not report stories that jeopardized national security, and we didn't."

Embedded Journalists

So what happened to the Pentagon philosophy toward the media between the military victory in the Gulf and the decision to invade Iraq some 12 years later? What brought about its complete reversal in policy that moved from

Figure 11-8   Members of the U.S. media embedded with U.S. Marines. (Courtesy Richard Ellis/Getty Images)

the tight control it enforced on the media in the Gulf to its decision to "embed" journalists with the military when it invaded Iraq?

The popular explanation was that the Pentagon thought it might be able to better control the news coverage and also create a certain degree of support from journalists by making them, in effect, part of the team—a kind of pre-verse version of the old saying, "if you can't beat 'em, join 'em."

In another unexpected move, the military also arranged to send those who wanted to be embedded to go to "combat school," training programs run by former military personnel to teach journalists how to avoid danger-ous situations and to protect themselves against chemical attack. The jour-nalists also were taught how to handle themselves if they were captured and held hostage.

CBS and CNN sent more than 500 people to the so-called media boot-camp and ABC and NBC also sent some of its people. Only about 100 jour-nalists from other parts of the world were allowed to cover the war, and there were only a handful of independent American journalists covering the war and the occupation that followed.

Although the idea of "embedding journalists" was the brainchild of the Pentagon, it was generally welcomed by media organizations which com-plained, as previously noted, that they were denied access to battlegrounds of the first Gulf war in 1991.

Clarence Page, a Pulitzer-Prize-winning journalist for the *Chicago Tribune*, said he doesn't think there is a problem with embedded journalists as long as it's only one part of the source of news. A Reuters editor, Michael Scott, agreed that an over-dependency on embedded reporters could seriously affect the objectivity of the coverage. He said, "While we certainly have a greater access to the military, the main thing is to be aware that we are only seeing snippets of the battlefield and that is only part of the overall picture."

Boston Globe media analyst, Mark Jurkowitz, said the coverage provided by embedded journalists is like "looking through a soda straw—there is plenty of information, but it only allows us to see a narrow slice of the war." Sociology Professor at Tufts University, Henry Rubin, noted that when other countries cover the war they focus more on the damage and civilian casualties of the war, while the U.S. emphasis is different—"we have reported a war of triumph." He cited the example of the rescue of seven American prisoners of war and the special attention given by the media to private Jessica Lynch.

The Private Lynch Fiasco

The personal story of Private Jessica Lynch was hyped by the Pentagon because the rescue was a bright spot in an otherwise grim story of setbacks in Iraq. Initial stories of the rescue reported that Private Lynch had been shot and stabbed and that she had fought fiercely, firing on Iraqi forces before being captured. Lynch did suffer some injuries but the broken bones and other injuries were apparently caused when her vehicle overturned, not at the hands of Iraqis as originally reported. Overshadowed in the reporting was the fact that in the ambush of Lynch's company, eleven other soldiers died and nine were wounded.

Professor Rubin pointed out that the Lynch story, while not the biggest event in the war that particular week, nevertheless dominated the news all week and continued to be a major story for many additional weeks, partially because of the continuing media attention it received, particularly from CBS which suggested, in writing to Private Lynch, that in exchange for doing an interview with *CBS News*, the network might do a two-hour documentary about her story, and also suggested the network's owner, Viacom, might produce a movie about her. CBS chairman Leslie Moonves reacted to the negative publicity the proposed deal brought from critics by saying the suggestion of a movie deal "may have gone over the line." There also was criticism of *The Washington Post*'s handling of the story by the newspaper's own ombudsman, Michael Getler. The *Post* was the first to report the heroic version of Lynch's capture. Getler questioned why the newspaper's story, which was "wrong in its most compelling aspects, remained unchallenged for so long?" He said the "story had an odor to it almost from the beginning." It wasn't long after the accurate story of the rescue surfaced that Private Lynch, recuperating at home, announced her resignation from the army, apparently to pursue a book deal.

Professor Rubin also was critical of the round-the-clock television coverage of the war which he said "takes away the impact of actual death and destruction and makes it seem like a video game." Other critics have raised the issue of objectivity, noting that embedded reporters must rely on the troops for their own protection.

Dr. Rita Kirk Whitlock, chairwoman of the Division of Corporate Communications and Public Affairs at Southern Methodist University, said ethical issues arise when reporters get too close to soldiers. "If you're an embedded

Figure 11-9   PFC Jessica Lynch waves to crowd on the last leg of her journey home as she rides beside her brother Gregory Lynch Jr. (Courtesy John Himelrick/Getty Images)

reporter and you have no gun, you develop friendships with the troops. How much criticism are you going to do?" she asked.

Norman Solomon, the executive director of the Institute for Public Accuracy, was much stronger in his criticism of the embedded program, describing it as "not a great moment" for journalism. He said "They're so embedded with the troops, they may as well be getting a P.R. retainer from the Pentagon."

But a spokesman for the Pentagon, deputy assistant secretary of defense Bryan Whitman, defended the policy. He asked, "what better way to counter some of the disinformation coming from the enemy than to have a large contingent of reporters that are out there alongside our troops reporting what actually occurs in near real time, to the extent that we can, without compromising the missions or the safety of the people that are doing the reporting."

Phil Nesbitt, a journalist for 34 years, noted that the military and the media are "embarking on a grand experiment" in making journalists a part of a combat unit. In a commentary for the American Press Institute, he said embedded journalists are seeing the war unfold up close and it appears they are unfettered by military intervention, and confined only by the signal of their satellite phone. Nesbitt says he doubts the embedded program is providing slanted coverage. What we will get, he said, is better coverage, more accurate and immediate coverage.

David Carr of *The New York Times,* noted that the decision to embed journalists has produced both compelling video and suggestions that the

American news media have become a defacto part of the coalition forces. What has been created, he said, is a new "standard of openness and immediacy . . . raising the question of whether reporters, soldiers or news consumers will ever be satisfied with less." He also observed that reporters say they can be objective in their coverage, but their ability to remain detached is being tested every day by this new level of engagement.

The *Times* journalist said that some critics have suggested that it has been difficult to "tell journalists and military apart." He quoted a professor of journalism and sociology at Columbia University, Todd Gittlin, as saying, "I am discouraged by reporters' willingness to swallow most of what is being told to them."

But Carr also quotes Ted Koppel of *ABC News*, who has spent time with troops in Iraq. Koppel said he does not think he or other journalists have gone native. "I am an American citizen, and I love these young men and women for what they are doing," he said. "But that doesn't mean that as a journalist I can't maintain my objectivity."

"In a strange way," Koppel continued, "this has come full circle for me." When I was covering the Vietnam War, we had a lot of access, as well. But this time," Koppel said, "we have the kind of access to leadership that was not possible back then, and now we have an intersection between absolute access and the ability to send images instantaneously."

But Alan Murray of the *Wall Street Journal* asks this question: "Has embedding improved our understanding of what's really happening in Iraq?" He says, "As both a consumer and a purveyor of war coverage, I doubt it. . . . The fog of war seems as thick as ever—maybe thicker."

Are Reporters Acting Too Much Like Soldiers?

Howard Kurtz of *The Washington Post* asks this question: "are reporters in Iraq acting too much like soldiers?" He says that a number of incidents in Iraq seem to have blurred the lines between combatants and chroniclers and he recounted this scary episode on the battlefield involving CNN's Brent Sadler who had his bodyguard return fire when he and his crew came under Iraqi attack. Kurtz says this was an entirely reasonable response, considering the alternative, but "Why," asks Kurtz, "was Sadler storming into Tikrit before American soldiers got there? If reporters with armed escorts go into battle zones on their own," he notes, "is it any wonder that they will be treated as little different from soldiers?"

The *Times* writer also notes that such activity may jeopardize other journalists who ride around dangerous places with press signs on their car, hoping to be treated as neutral observers.

Cheerleaders for the Military?

Embedded journalist George C. Wilson of the *National Journal* said that he felt some pressure to be a cheerleader for the units he was with in Iraq. "I think the Pentagon set it up that way." During a PBS discussion on the issue, Wilson said that he enormously admired the grunts, the marines and the conditions they put up with and the junior officers, but it was "like being the second dog on a dogsled team. You saw a lot of the dog in front of you and a little bit to the left and the right, but if you saw an interesting story you couldn't break out of the dogsled team without losing your place because we were moving all the time."

Wilson also said he felt he was something of "a willing propagandist" for the military. He said you were put into a position where you would certainly not be antagonistic to the kids that you were involved with and admired and "I didn't have the ability like I had in other wars to check out things for myself."

Michael Getler of *The Washington Post*, who also took part in the PBS debate, thought the embedded media performed very well, giving consumers an amazing actual look at what goes on in the battlefield. But he cautioned, like Wilson, that they were narrow slices of what was happening. He said that when you took all the pieces they came out to be quite an accurate and very timely picture. But he added that news organizations had to have "other people, who were not embedded, who were on their own, if you wanted a broad picture of the war."

Barbara Cochran, president of the Radio-Television News Directors Association, said she believes television is doing a good job in Iraq, considering it is coping with "a view of the conflict that we've never had before." Cochran, *CBS News'* Washington Bureau Chief during the first Gulf War, said that handling huge amounts of up-to-the minute information "requires really a lot of care, and that underscores the need not only for experienced reporters but for experienced editors capable of standing back and taking a broader view."

Some journalists were especially critical of the way the networks handled the intensive bombing of Iraq. In an *American Journalism Review* article, Christopher Dickey, Middle East regional editor for *Newsweek*, was quoted as saying that "night after night, rooftop cameras linked to satellites beamed long shots of explosions and fires to viewers around the world . . . and when mixed in with intricate graphics of the bombs and missiles in the U.S. arsenal, the technological display contributed to this notion of war as a video game and strips the war of its humanity."

But some embedded journalists found they could not escape the humanity, particularly when they were personally caught up in the action. One of the best examples of this was an incident involving *Atlanta Journal Constitution* reporter Ron Martz. Writing about it in the *American Journalism Review*, Sherry Ricchiardi described how Martz, after surviving a hail of bullets on the way to Baghdad, found himself cradling the head of an American soldier in his hands, imploring him not to black out before medics could repair the hole in his chest. Later, the reporter collapsed against an army vehicle, drenched in sweat, mouth dry, and his clothes sticky with blood.

Journalist Deaths in Iraq

As of this writing, in October of 2004, 20 American journalists have died in Iraq. Some were caught in the actual exchange of fire, and others died in car and helicopter crashes. There's some evidence that 17 of the journalists were targeted because of their reporting. Among the dead are two outstanding award-winning journalists, *NBC News* reporter David Bloom and *Atlantic Monthly* editor-at-large Michael Kelly.

Bloom had become one of the most colorful and resourceful of the embedded journalists, riding in an M-88 tank that had been customized by NBC to include a gyro-stabilized camera—the kind used on helicopters—to eliminate the lurching as the vehicle bumped through the desert. The tank, dubbed the *Bloomobile*, even had special tires that were made especially soft so they could move through the sand. But it wasn't the strange vehicle carrying Bloom through the desert that was the real story—it was his brilliant reporting. Bloom was only 39 and his death came suddenly and unexpectedly from an illness, not bullets. He was traveling with the Army's 3rd Infantry Division outside Baghdad when he suddenly collapsed. Bloom had complained earlier of cramps behind his knees, probably brought on by the days and nights crouched in his vehicle. Doctors believed the pain was probably brought on by deep venous thrombosis and advised him to seek medical treatment, but Bloom did not want to take the time out and did not seek medical help. After collapsing, he was airlifted to a field medical unit but never regained consciousness. Doctors said his death was caused by a pulmonary embolism.

Bill Wheatley, Vice President of *NBC News* said Bloom was "a person who combined an extraordinary amount of talent with boundless energy. He liked nothing better than to be out front on a big story and often was, never more so than the last few weeks."

Bob Dotson, NBC National Correspondent, whose own extraordinary work is displayed earlier in this book, said of Bloom's work, "He connected so well with viewers because he learned something very rare in TV journalism: how to talk " 'people talk.' " Dotson said his colleague took writing very seriously. He was attentive to details and would ask out loud—to himself and others—"How does it sound to the ear . . . How do you write pictures in your head first?" Dotson added, Bloom "never put his pencil down until he absolutely had to, he would polish, polish, and polish."

CNN correspondent Walter Rodgers, who went to the media boot camp with Bloom, noted that the NBC correspondent had given up a cushy *Weekend Today* anchor job because he wanted to cover the war. Rodgers said it was fun to watch a young journalist with so much enthusiasm. He said Bloom was determined to make his mark in Iraq. Rodgers said, "This is where David was going to really show what a fine journalist he was, but" Rodgers added, "that his colleagues at NBC already knew he was."

Here is a report that Bloom did from Iraq for *NBC Nightly News*:

Bloom: There are supply problems, Tom, but not of a critical nature. They've been somewhat low on water, a little bit low on MREs. They're getting ammunition up here, they're getting fuel up here, but clearly the supply line is stretched very thin. And these soldiers and their commanders concur with what General Wallace said in terms of the opposition that they faced being more intense. As a result they've dug in here. I mean, keep in mind, we arrived here Tuesday morning local time. It's now Friday night local time. They did not expect to be here that long. So those problems with the supply lines are also creating problems in terms of this force, which had anticipated going on the offensive against the Republican Guard very quickly, now digging in more defensive positions, Tom.

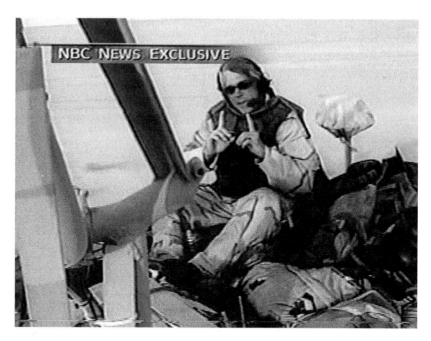

Figure 11-10   The late David Bloom reporting from Iraq. (Courtesy *NBC News*)

Brokaw: And in those defensive positions are they making any runs at you, either from the regular Iraqi army or those so-called militia that we've been hearing so much about?

Bloom: They are, Tom. Pretty much every night, there are incursions both by Iraqis who are dismounted infantry. They don't know whether they're regular army soldiers or if they're just Fedayeen Saddam soldiers, the militia, the paramilitaries. They've also had tanks making incursions. They've definitely stepped up the perimeter security here. There are now passwords. The soldiers are now told not to go out of the encampments at night alone. I mean, they're just being much more cautious because, as I said, this is the force that anticipated going up against tank brigades, immediately, and instead it's dug in here, having to go, or at least prepare, to have hostile forces coming at it from all directions.

Brokaw: All right. Thanks very much. NBC's David Bloom with the 2nd Battalion, 3rd Infantry near Karbala.

Another embedded journalist, Michael Kelly, who was *Atlantic Monthly* editor-at-large and a *Washington Post* columnist, became the first American journalist killed in the war. He died in a Humvee accident, also while traveling with the army's 3rd Infantry Division.

The last column he wrote for the *Post* before his death demonstrates his excellent writing skills. It started this way:

Near the crest of the bridge across the Euphrates that Task Force 3-69 Armor of the 1st Brigade of the 3rd Infantry Division seized yesterday afternoon was a body that lay twisted from its fall. He had been an old man—poor, not a regular soldier—judging from his clothes. He was lying on his back, not far from one of the unwilling irregulars employed. The tanks and Bradleys and Humvees and bulldozers and rocket launchers, and all the rest of the massive stuff that makes up the U.S. Army on the march, rumbled past him, pushing on.

Kelly wrote stories for the Post for almost two weeks before he died. While traveling with the 3rd Division, on the way to Baghdad they suddenly came under fire from Iraqi soldiers using AK-47s and rocket-propelled grenades. The driver swerved to avoid the fire and rolled into a canal. Both men were dead when soldiers reached them 25 minutes later.

Kelly never did get to Baghdad.

Considering the short duration of the war, the campaign had been the deadliest for journalists in modern history. When the war began, it was believed that reporter casualties might be high because of the unusually high number of them embedded with troops and the dangers of covering the war on the front lines, but the death toll surprised many. In just three weeks of conflict the journalist death toll was roughly 16 times that of coalition troops.

No casualty rate for journalists in any recent conflict compares. The four reporters killed in the 1991 Gulf War did not die in combat, but in the chaos that followed the withdrawal of U.S. troops. In November of 2001, eight journalists were killed in Afghanistan during 16 days in the month of November. That was the highest number of journalists killed in combat since the Vietnam War.

Tragically, some of the reporter deaths were the result of *friendly fire*. One such incident caused a bitter dispute between journalists and the military, after soldiers shelled a hotel in Baghdad, killing two of nearly 100 journalists staying there. The military claimed it shelled the hotel after someone in the hotel fired on the troops. But a journalism advocacy group said there was no evidence that troops were fired on from the hotel. The group noted that the military was well aware that the hotel was full of journalists and was determined not to hit it, but it added, senior field commanders failed to convey their concerns to a tank commander who fired on the hotel. After the Committee to Protect Journalists issued a report saying that interviews with a dozen reporters who witnessed the event confirmed that no shots were fired from the building, Secretary of State Colin Powell and a Pentagon spokeswoman, Victoria Clarke, insisted that the shelling was justified because there *was* firing coming from the hotel. But the journalist committee bolstered its report by pointing out that American commanders themselves were angy over the shelling and criticized the lieutenant who ordered it. A Ukranian-born cameraman working for Reuters and a Spanish cameraman were killed by the fire. Among the other journalists killed in action were a number of foreign citizens working for American news organizations.

The Tip of the Spear

CNN correspondent Walter Rodgers, who was embedded with the Army's 7th Cavalry of the 3rd Infantry Division, said the high casualty rates for journalists was a direct consequence of the embedding process because the Pentagon allowed many reporters to come up to the "tip of the spear."

Rodgers, himself, came close to that spear. Here are excerpts of one of the reports he filed while he was moving with troops toward the Iraqi capital.

Rodgers: You are watching the leader of the Apache troop, the 7th Cavalry Abrams tank. It is a very tight shot. We can not get too broad on this because we would be revealing the kinds of topographical features about the location of the 7th Cavalry, which we are forbidden to reveal.

They've been rolling down a road moving closer and closer to Baghdad. We can hear shooting all about us, particularly the 25 mm cannon aboard the Bradley fighting vehicles. The Cavalry, along with its parent unit, the 3rd Infantry Division, is definitely pushing in the direction of Baghdad, and is much, much closer than yesterday.

About two hours ago we crossed the Euphrates River at a crossing that had been earlier taken by the 1st Brigade of the Division. That brigade had to fight its way through the territory. They are not encountering large Republican Guard units. But there are freelance Iraqi fighters out there, and they are firing at the convoys.

Mostly what they've encountered besides the small arms fire from the sides of the road . . . are small foxholes and small bunkers at intersections on backcountry roads.

The Iraqi soldiers would dig into those holes, but they are no match for the heavy armored column ahead of us now.

We have seen quite a few dead Iraqi soldiers by the road. What we noticed was all of the dead Iraqi soldiers had gas masks. They are moving in anything but what you would call an organized formation. The Iraqis we see are generally driving pickup trucks, or they are riding about in old Soviet Union vintage armored vehicles, which are no match for the armor-piercing shells that the tanks are firing.

This armored column has been under almost constant fire. When we first crossed the Euphrates River, it was pretty barren in terms of not much of a civilian population. As we pushed closer to Baghdad, we began to see that the Iraqi population was indeed welcoming the U.S. Army convoy and welcoming them northward.

The men were cautious about waving. But increasingly, young women and children were waving almost enthusiastically, and eventually some of the men began to flash a "V" sign or flash a thumbs up as the troops moved forward.

Unfortunately, in the months following Rodgers' report there were less and less thumbs up and fewer and fewer friendly Iraqi crowds in the streets. What were in the streets for the most part were car bombings and the killing of hundreds of Iraqi civilians, coalition forces, businesspeople and diplomats. In short, in the Fall of 2004, the situation was chaotic.

The occupation of Iraq was going badly. The deaths of American servicemen and women were growing dramatically totaling more than 1,400 and more than 7,700 U.S. troops have been wounded in action. The American people and the rest of the world also were shocked by a new terrible development—the abuse of Iraqi prisoners by U.S. guards and possibly interrogators who were attempting to pry information from the prisoners. Ironically, the

Figure 11-11 CNN correspondent Walter Rogers reporting from Iraq. (Courtesy CNN)

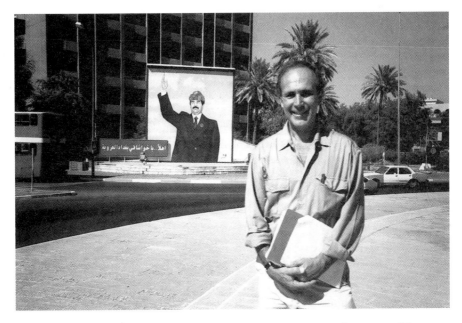

Figure 11-12 Former ABC correspondent Mort Dean reports from Iraq. (Photo courtesy of *ABC News*)

Figure 11-13   Iraqi prisoner abuse.

abuse took place at the same infamous Abu Ghraib prison where the regime of Saddam Hussein tortured and killed thousands of Iraqis. The explosive new development was revealed by *CBS News* on an edition of *60 Minutes*. It showed photos of Iraqi prisoners being sexually embarrassed and abused by those who were supposed to be guarding them. CBS delayed broadcasting the story for a period, at the request of the Defense Department in the national interest, but aired the story when it was plain that other news organizations were about to publish the same information. The *60 Minutes* broadcast launched a series of investigations within the military, in both houses of Congress, and the condemnation of the United States from the rest of the world. As of this writing, new photos of the prisoner abuse were being released and the government admitted that there were hundreds of additional photos and videotape of the abuses that were being withheld on the grounds that they were evidence in the prosecution of a number of soldiers accused of the abuses.

The photos, grotesque and sexually graphic, raised all sorts of concerns among the print and broadcast media about whether they should be shown to the public and, if so, in what manner. The Radio and Television News Directors Association released guidelines for airing the photos of the prisoners and other photos of the execution of an American businessman, Nick Berg, at the hands of his Iraqi captors. RTNDA's Ethics Committee offered a number of suggestions for news managers for their consideration in deciding whether to use the photos and, if so, how. Here are some of the highlights of the guidelines:

1. What is the journalistic purpose behind broadcasting the graphic content? Does it materially clarify and help the audience understand the story better?

Is there an issue of great public importance involved such as public policy, community benefit, or social significance?
2. Is the use of the graphic material the only way to tell the story? What are your alternatives?
3. If asked to defend your decision to show the pictures to your audience, such as family members or stakeholders in the story, how will you justify your decision?
4. When is the story important enough to justify replaying graphic material?
5. Should you have guidelines or discussions about how to use the graphic material in promos and teases?
6. When is a notice to the audience warranted that they are about to see or hear graphic material?

The Poynter Institute's Ethics Journal also offered its views and observations on the photos. Ethics faculty member Kelly McBride noted that if the images weren't journalism they would be pornography. She said she empathizes with the many people who complained to newsrooms around the country about the showing of the photos.

But McBride said she's not angry with the media for showing them. She said the pictures serve the highest functions of journalism. They tell a truth in a way that can't be argued. They hold the powerful accountable. They are part of democracy in action. And McBride noted that the release of the pictures is what sparked the wave of congressional inquiries.

McBride also pointed out that the photos of the prisoner abuses and the beheading of Nick Berg create similar emotions of disgust because both are shocking portraits of war, but journalists need to discuss their use as related, but ultimately separate, decisions. Each set of pictures, she writes, holds the potential for a different set of harm.

She notes that in the prison photos, men and women on a mission for this country, being paid by our tax dollars, are doing horrible things. But the video of Nick Berg's execution, she adds, while more horrific, has less purpose. It tells a story, but the only people held accountable are hiding behind masks.

Poynter ethics fellow Robert Steele called the abuse coverage "measured and thoughtful," but cautioned editors to make sure they used the images in context, not merely as the "great" picture element. He added, "they should be used if they provide factual, authentic pieces of a larger puzzle."

Ted Koppel, of ABC's *Nightline*, defended criticism from Republican conservatives that the media's continued coverage of the prisoner scandal was part of an anti-Bush political agenda and could endanger U.S. troops. Koppel said it must sadden our troops to see these accounts of prisoner abuse, and make them angry and may even expose them to greater danger, but he added, freedom of the press "is part of what they're fighting for. Our forefathers wanted an informed electorate."

A former managing editor of *The New York Times*, Seymour Topping, now an administrator of the Pulitzer Prizes, called the prisoner abuse coverage "balanced and penetrating." And even the publisher of military newspapers, Tobias Naegele, said he doesn't think the coverage has been inappropriate. People in the military themselves are outraged, he said, adding that the story "already is sensational because it's so patently offensive." Naegele, the editor-in-chief of the *Military Times*, pointed out that "history

Figure 11-14   Christiane Amanpour of CNN reports from Lebanon.

tells us that government officials sometimes withhold facts, and you want the media there to scratch below the surface."

And scratching below the surface is what the media did. In addition to CBS, *The Washington Post* was on top of the story, and the *Denver Post* and *Newsweek Magazine* reported new developments in the scandal. The *New Yorker's* Pulitzer Prize-winning journalist Seymour Hersh, was the first to report that Defense Secretary Rumsfeld made the decision himself that led to the scandal, reportedly authorizing a Defense Department operation that widened the hunt for al-Qaida terrorists in Afghanistan to interrogation of prisoners in Iraq which, in effect, encouraged much harsher interrogation of prisoners. The Defense Department denied the Hirsh report.

However, the Pentagon was forced to reveal that it knew of the abuses at the Iraqi prison and the existence of the photos and videos months before CBS released the story. It also was forced to acknowledge that it had received reports of prisoner abuse from the International Red Cross months before the scandal broke and did nothing about the reports. The administration also acknowledged that it had failed to share any of the abuse information that it knew with congressional committees during appearances by Rumsfeld and other officials even on the eve of the *60 Minutes* report.

Writing in the *American Journalism Review*, the magazine's senior writer Sherry Ricchiardi reports that the media took too long to break the prisoner abuse story even though "there was no shortage of signs that something was amiss." She noted that for two years Amnesty International and Human Rights Watch repeatedly warned of mistreatment of detainees in the hands of Americans in Afghanistan and at Guantanamo Bay, Cuba. Ricchiardi also pointed out that two years before the abuse story finally surfaced, the *Washington Post* published a piece on the CIA's "brass-knuckled quest for

Figure 11-15   Former *CBS News* correspondent Bob McKeown reports from Kuwait during the Gulf War. (AP/Wide World Photos)

information," and three months later, a cover story in *The Nation* said that torture was gaining acceptance in the Bush administration. She also said that the Associated Press was among the first to raise concerns about the abuse at Abu Ghraib, but that few of the AP's clients showcased the story or ran it at all. Several more months went by before CBS's *60 Minutes* aired the photos that finally put the abuse on the front pages and the top of newscasts. "Why," asks Ricchiardi, "did it take the news media so long to uncover the story?" The Washington Bureau Chief of *The New York Times*, Philip Taubman says "we didn't do our job until the photos appeared on CBS and Seymour Hersh's story hit the Internet" Taubman added, "It was a failure of newsgathering." Ricchiardi added that there's a strong consensus that the administration's skill at information management also played a major role.

The foreign editor for National Public Radio, Loren Jenkins, said "I have never seen greater news management in 30-plus years in this business." But, he added, that should not have prevented the news media from doing its job—"that's what the Fourth Estate is all about—poking holes in news management." He said "it's our job to find out whether we are being told the truth or not."

Ricchiardi writes that several media experts hypothesize that since 9/11, the government has played on the patriotism of journalists, raising the terrorism banner to deflect press criticism. She adds, "that could make a difference in how reporters pursue a story that might embarrass the U.S., particularly when soldiers are dying in a foreign land."

Marvin Kalb, a senior fellow at Harvard University's Shorenstein Center on the Press, Politics, and Public Policy, and former network TV correspondent, says there is an awareness on the part of the White House that this tendency exists, so they go for it, exploit it Kalb adds, "It isn't that the government beats somebody over the head. They don't have to," he, "that's what makes it so much more painful."

It was not long after the original photos horrified the world that a second set, described as worse than the first group, was shown to congressional committees behind closed doors. Soon after that, *The Washington Post* released new photos along with eye-witness accounts from prisoners. The newspaper said the documents it obtained included hundreds of new photos and short video clips of torture by the U.S. military. It said it also had access to testimony of abuse from 13 Iraqi detainees—all part of evidence gathered by army investigators for the court martials of seven U.S. soldiers charged with abusing the prisoners.

The photographs and videos showed detainees cowering before unmuzzled dogs, being forced to masturbate, being hit or sexually assaulted by guards, and being threatened with a shotgun.

The *Denver Post*, simultaneously, released its own front page story detailing investigations of military personnel in connection with the deaths of at least five Iraqi prisoners. The deaths include the killing of a high-ranking Iraqi general who was shoved into a sleeping bag and suffocated, according to the Pentagon report obtained by the newspaper. The *Post* said another military officer was asphyxiated after being gagged, and his hands tied to the top of his cell door. The newspaper said the documents it obtained show wider problems beyond the Abu Ghraib prison and demonstrate that some coercive tactics used at that prison have shown up in other interrogations in other prisons. The *Post* also said that the documents show that twice as many detainee abuse cases are being investigated by the military than was previously known. The *Post* said that 75 abuse cases are under investigation and that 27 of them involve deaths, at least 8 of which are believed to be homicides.

There is no doubt that this prisoner abuse story will be major news for some time and, as indicated elsewhere in the book, when stories continue to be in the news, important new developments will be added to our homepage: www.broadcastnewsbook.com.

Beats

During their careers, reporters cover most of the types of news stories just discussed. Some reporters may have one particular type of story assigned to them as their *beat*. Unfortunately, not too many radio and TV newsrooms use the *beat* method of reporting, which was developed by—and its still a tradition at—newspapers. Most broadcast managers argue that they do not have the budgets necessary to assign reporters to beats. They note that news is only a small percentage of what is viewed on television every day, while newspapers devote most of their attention to it. Many people believe broadcast news suffers because it does not have enough beat reporters, who can concentrate on and become expert in a particular subject such as health and medicine and the environment.

The networks and some large-market stations, however, do have beat reporter-journalists assigned to such special areas.

Cliff Williams, managing editor of WFFA-TV, Dallas says his station is dedicated to beat reporting. "It's very much a part of who we are," he said. It "builds relationships" with news sources. We get to know the news sources

Figure 11-16 The newsroom at WFAA-TV, Dallas. (Courtesy of Don Wall, WFAA-TV)

better and don't miss big stories, he says. The beat reporter develops an expertise and cultivates sources in the area he or she covers which gives them a leg up when competing with general assignment reporters on breaking news stories.

A disadvantage to beat reporting, Williams says, is the reporter gets locked in, "too comfortable" and doesn't want to go outside the beat. Another disadvantage is the reporter can get too close to the people on the beat he or she is covering and lose objectivity and only want to put the source in a good light for fear that to do otherwise, would adversely affect the relationship he or she has cultivated.

WFAA-TV beats include police, city and county government, the state capitol, transportation, education, economy-business, the environment, health and entertainment. Even for a large-market station, that's an impressive assortment of beat reporters, and not that common. In addition, WFAA has two investigative reporters.

The beat system at the station was developed by the late Marty Haag, who was Vice President of News for the A.H Belo Corporation, which owns WFAA and four other stations. Haag also said he believed in the beat system because the world is getting too complicated. The beat reporters know what they're writing about; you have reporters who are familiar with the players." Haag said the beat system also allows stations to compete with newspapers. We don't want to be clipping stories out of newspapers and then covering them," he said, "we want to be ahead of them, not behind them."

Another believer in the beat system is Jeff Hoffman, News Director of WAVE-TV in Louisville; however, his station's reporting staff numbers only 11, half the number of WFAA. Of course, Louisville is much smaller than Dallas. Hoffman has beat reporters covering city hall, medicine and consumer news. He agrees that beat reporters give a news operation two important advantages: they can enterprises and cultivate sources.

Former WAVE news director Ed Godfrey, now retired, who was also very supportive of the beat system also noted that such reporters sometimes "get too close to their beats and wind up with stories not interesting to a general audience or get too close to their sources and can lose their objectivity. But he quickly added that the advantages of beat reporting "far outweight the disadvantages."

Diane Doctor, the News Director at WCBS-TV in New York has a flock of beat reporters, along with bureau chiefs in New Jersey and Long Island. Her beat reporters cover education, technology, and consumer issues, and she has an investigative reporter and two people assigned to political reporting. She's very supportive of the beat concept, stressing that such reporters are able not only to focus on a particular subject, which makes them more effective, but also are able to enterprise more stories because of the contacts and sources they develop.

Beat reporting is discussed further in chapter 20, "Speciality Reporting." Both general assignment reporters and beat reporters need to be concerned with two aspects of broadcast reporting: advancing the story and avoiding the pack.

Advancing the Story

If news were a commodity, it would be a bad investment because it doesn't last long—it's perishable. So, reporters must keep looking for new angles to try to update, or *advance*, the news. Chapter 4 discussed the need to update the lead of the story so that the news sounds fresh, even if it is not.

Updating a story—putting a new lead on it—is only part of what is involved in advancing a story. A new lead reporting, for example, that the death toll in an air disaster climbs from 100 to 115 does advance the story, but it is a rather routine update. In the more traditional sense, this story could be advanced if, for example, the cause of the crash was determined or it was suddenly discovered that a famous person was on the plane. The story also could be advanced if a reporter learned that this particular type of aircraft had been involved in a series of similar crashes in recent months or if a reporter discovered that the FAA was about to ground all planes of the same make.

Avoiding the Pack

Good reporters are always looking for an unusual angle for their stories. Sometimes it is difficult to report a story differently from other reporters because the lead seems so obvious; however, finding a new twist to a story is what distinguishes some reporters from the rest of the pack.

Former *ABC News* correspondent Morton Dean says he tries to get "an edge" on his colleagues by doing research before he goes out on a story. "I try to get as much background and history as I can," says Dean. "I try to find my own sources. I try to make an extra phone call. One way or another I try to find a nugget of information that might give me an edge."

NBC's Robert McKeown notes that "good reporters aren't to be found" in the pack. They are out seeking people other than officials. He also says it's important to "know the beat and become familiar with it so that you sound like you know what you are talking about when a story develops. You should have a sense of what is really happening."

Keeping in Touch

The news director and the assignment editor always must know what's going on "out there." If, for example, a demonstration is getting out of hand and is turning into a riot, the newsroom must be told. Any changes in stories, even routine ones, should be reported. Nothing irritates an assignment editor more than a crew and reporter who "disappear."

Reporters must keep the newsroom informed as much as possible about the status of a story. Is it running late? Is it falling apart? Is the video poor? All of these things and more must be shared so that those working on the newscast in the newsroom know what to expect. They also have the right to expect the reporter and crew to return early enough so that the story can be edited and aired on time. The team in the field should decide on a cutoff time—the time at which they must stop shooting and start to pack up their gear and head for home.

Establishing Rapport with the Cameraperson

The beginning of this chapter mentioned that a good relationship between a reporter and cameraperson is essential. Here are some suggestions and observations on how to establish that relationship.

Morton Dean says it is always a good idea "to discuss with the cameraperson what you are looking for, what your expectations are, and what you plan to do with the story."

NBC's McKeown gives much of the credit for his successful reporting during the Gulf War to his cameraman, David Green, and his satellite technician, Andy Thompson. McKeown and his crew had a high-tech mobile unit that allowed them to set up a transmitter that sent a live TV signal to a satellite, which relayed the signal some 23,000 miles to CBS studios in New York. McKeown says most people are not aware of the cooperative effort that goes into the news that they see on their screens.

NBC News correspondent Bob Dotson tells reporters to look for help and advice from the cameraperson. "They should have a shorthand, kind of like what a married couple would have," he says. "If you have this sort of camaraderie, the cameraperson is going to think, maybe for the first time in his life, that somebody thinks what he's doing is important."

Dotson credited Tom Zannes, a freelance cameraman for NBC, for the outstanding video used in Dotson's excellent package about a woman trapped in a cavern in Carlsbad, New Mexico. (The script for this package appears in Chapter 5.) Zannes was in the cavern with the team that was exploring it for the *Encyclopaedia Britannica* when a member of the team slipped and broke her leg. When Dotson arrived at the scene to cover the story, Zannes was still in the cave. Dotson said Zannes was allowed to remain there during the rescue because he is a world-class caver and because "he knew when to take pictures and when to put the camera down and help with the rescue."

Former *CBS News* correspondent Ben Silver says that if there is not a close working relationship between the reporter and the cameraperson, each may go off in a different direction, and they won't end up with a good product. "If you want camerapeople to get good video for your story," he says, "they have to know where you're going with the story."

Silver, now professor emeritus at Arizona State University, says reporters should remember that camerapeople often have journalism backgrounds and have good ideas too. "Two sets of eyes are better than one," he says, "and three sets of eyes are even better." Silver notes that when reporters are working on a story, strangers sometimes approach them with information. "Listen to them," Silver advises. "They may have seen something you and the cameraperson missed because you were busy doing something else. You always have to keep an open mind."

One-Person Band

If you start out in a small market, which is where most young people right out of college do begin their careers, you may not only be reporting the news. You may be shooting it as well. To save money, more and more small stations—and even some bigger ones—are hiring people who can "do it all."

Thanks to lighter cameras, digital technology, and tighter budgets, some stations are employing people who know how to write, report, and handle a camera in the field. At some stations, those same people edit the stories when they return to the station. Many of the people who are working alone seem to enjoy the freedom of doing everything by themselves. Does the quality of the product suffer? Probably, but those writing the checks often are willing to accept less if it costs less. On the positive side, it means that there may be more opportunities for young people who have learned the basic skills—writing, reporting, and videography.

Michelle Kosinski, the bureau chief in Salisbury-Piedmont for WSOC-TV in Charlotte says working alone helps her get better stories. "It's just me and my camera," she says, "so people tend to tell me more. They feel closer to me." Kosinski says she writes her story while she shoots. "There's a beauty in seeing something and making it look the way you want it to look."

Lisa Goddard, who worked on her own in Myrtle Beach, South Carolina, before moving on to another reporting job, agrees. She liked having control over her packages. "You can shoot based on how you want to write," she says. But Goddard admitted that being alone was difficult when she had to do stand-ups. She said that for the first two weeks on the job she kept cutting off her forehead.

Peter Landis, News Director at NY1, the 24-hour cable news operation, has 23 people who both shoot and report. He says economics force newsrooms to do more with less. He asks: "Why pay for two people to do the job one person can be trained to do?"

Convergence

In addition to the comeback of the "one-person band," another trend in broadcast news is *convergence*. With convergence, reporters cover a story for one medium, do the same story for other media owned by the same company, or they may simply share information. As with the "one-person band," convergence is also dictated by economics. One person does the job that used to be handled by two or three. In addition to saving money, advocates maintain that convergence results in a better product.

Here's how it works: A television reporter's company also owns other media in the same market, such as a radio station, a newspaper, a Website, or all of the above, in the same market. The reporter writes his story for television, then does radio and newspaper versions of the same story. Or the newspaper reporter could start the ball rolling, and the process can involve other media, such as cable and the Internet.

Just as the "one-person band" is not new, neither is a marriage between different media. While these concepts are not new, they're developing at a "much more rapid pace than ever," according to Barbara Cochran, president of the Radio and Television News Director's Association (RTNDA). She noted a number of such cooperative efforts.

- In Tampa: WFLA-TV, the *Tampa Tribune,* and Tampa Bay On Line (TBO.com)
- In Chicago: WGN radio, WGN-TV, and the *Chicago Tribune*
- In Cedar Rapids, Iowa: KCRG radio, KCRG-TV, and the *Cedar Rapids Gazette*
- In Orlando: the *Orlando Sentinel* shares content with the Florida Cable News Channel

Not only are different media owned by the same company converging, but media owned by different companies are also forming partnerships, although limited ones, in which they tap into each other's expertise. Some examples are NBC and *The Washington Post* and their Internet resources; CBS and *The New York Times;* and WBZ-TV and the *Boston Globe.*

How serious is the endeavor? In Tampa, a television station, newspaper, and Website are working side by side in a Media General $40-million complex devoted to convergence, reports the *RTNDA Communicator.* "They share news tips, resources, and reporters in a convergence effort far more ambitious than anyone else has ever tried."

Editors from the various media sit next to each other on the assignment desk, which is the "nerve center" of the converged operation. A camera is set up near the *Tribune* newsroom. It enables newspaper reporters to tell about stories they covered during the television newscasts. The company, Media General Inc., has built a $40-million, four-level, state-of-the-art news complex devoted to convergence, called the News Center.

The Gazette Company of Cedar Rapids, Iowa, also converged some of its operations, but not all. It originally intended to construct a new building to house all its news operations but instead settled for two newsrooms, one to house both radio and TV and the other for print and online operations. Chuck Peters, the company's chief operating officer, said the Gazette Company did converge six different subsidiaries into the two operations just mentioned.

But, he said, that while the print and broadcast people are committed to sharing information, the news director and newspaper editor exercise independent judgment but cooperate where they can.

Rick Ragola, president of WFLA, told the *Communicator* that convergence combines the immediacy of the Internet, the urgency and emotion of television, and the depth of the print media. How is the concept working in actual practice? Some worry that quality suffers when reporters spend so much time shifting gears as they prepare stories for the various media. Another criticism is that a reporter who serves more than one medium can't cover as many stories as a reporter who serves just one medium. *Tampa Tribune* reporter Lisa Greene told the *Communicator* that presenting her story on more than one platform gives her greater reach, but she fears it takes time away from reporting on other topics.

And there are other problems with convergence: Reporting for print and radio and TV require different skills. Print reporters must learn how to integrate pictures and sound into a television story and how to perform in front of a camera. Broadcast reporters have to learn to write for the print media. And still photographers must learn how to tell a story with motion pictures and sound. That's no easy task. It's much easier for videographers to take still pictures than for still photographers to handle a motion picture camera.

One newspaper reporter said convergence has improved his writing, forcing him to be more concise when writing for television. A television reporter says she can write concisely for television and use more depth in the newspaper version of the story and still greater depth—or at least length—in the Internet story.

The Internet version often includes not only the complete stories used on the air and in print but also facts edited out of the broadcast and print versions of the story, or "outtakes" as they are referred to in broadcast parlance. With convergence comes greater impact, or exposure. Stories that might normally appear only on television, for example, with convergence might also appear in the newspaper, on the radio, and on the Internet. Convergence enables the viewer or reader to go to the Internet for more details on the same story.

So, if you are planning to go into broadcast news, here's a word to the wise: In addition to broadcast journalism courses, take courses in print reporting and even the Internet. You may have to work in all three mediums. A print reporting course not only helps you master a different medium, but because you're required to do more reporting and writing in print than in broadcast reporting courses, it also greatly adds to your reporting and writing skills.

Shortly after America Online (AOL) absorbed CNN-Time Warner in 2001, CNN announced a layoff and redefined the role of its reporters. Both actions were designed to cut costs. Reporters were ordered to learn how to use lightweight digital cameras and editing equipment. In addition, they would also be expected to file their stories on the Internet at AOL and on CNN radio. So, the question was asked, were convergence and the "one-person band" hitting the big time? Convergence seemed to be in, as was at least a modified form of the "one-person band."

Top CNN executive Eason Jordan was quoted as saying, "Correspondents whose expertise is TV reporting must know how to write for interactive and provide tracks for radio and deliver them as needed." The *Wall Street Journal* quoted another executive as saying that the merger provides "significant cross-promotional opportunities" because AOL reaches 27 million homes. Jordan said deploying compact digital cameras and editing equipment "will allow us to deploy smaller reporting teams of one or two people, at times when it makes sense." He added that "larger teams will be with us for some time to come."

Reporters were less than excited about doing camera and editing work. Legal correspondent Greta Van Susteren was flabbergasted, the *Wall Street Journal* said. "I would certainly like to learn to do it, but I'd like to learn to speak French," she added. "For this reason, they don't ask me to do makeup in the makeup room, I don't think they'll ask me to do this."

Quality Suffers

James Rosen, a former one-person shooter-reporter, sometimes referred to as a video journalist, says, "I loved shooting but hated the *schlepping*." He recalls when he was working for News 12 in the Bronx, he once covered a college graduation speech by Bill Cosby and had to park 10 blocks away. He says he left the tripod behind and blew his stand up. "The quality of the piece suffers," he added, "when you work alone." Rosen says he was grateful for the challenge and opportunity to learn the skills. Rosen is now a Washington correspondent for Fox News Channel and has a photographer, editor, producer, and makeup person.

Steve Sweitzer, News Operations Manager at WISG-TV in Indianapolis, doesn't think that video photographers should be worried about losing their jobs. He says the photographer's job may be redefined somewhat, but there is still plenty for two people to do when out on a story. "Two minds are still better than one," he adds. Sweitzer says news operations that value quality will hire pros to operate the cameras and get the most out of the equipment. That feeling is shared by Jim Disch, director of news and programming for CLTV in suburban Chicago. "We prize our photography," he says. "We use tripods unless we're running after something." And he adds that he believes the station will best serve its viewers by hiring both photographers and reporters.

Jack La Duke, New York state bureau reporter for WCAX-TV in Burlington, Vermont, has been going solo for 35 years and loves it. But he admits it is not a perfect way to cover the news. He says you are shooting the interview and thinking about the questions, listening, and asking follow-up questions while worrying about the focus and the batteries. He says he enjoys working alone, but it's not for everybody.

Some critics also raise safety issues about working alone. In breaking news, the reporter often watches the photographer's back and helps protect that person from danger. Sweitzer notes that good reporters stand right next to the photographer. Other news directors worry about theft of equipment when only one person is doing the job. Still another news director was concerned about stand up shots, which he described as "often god-awful when only one person is trying to shoot and talk at the same time."

Despite the criticism of "one-person bands," Michael Rosenblum, a former producer at *CBS News*, is busy training them. He said his consulting firm has trained more than 1,000 people to be shooter-reporters in the past 10 years.

For young people in school, we advise you to learn how to do it all as well as you can, not necessarily because you may have to do everything in your first job but because if you know how to write, shoot, and report, you will know what everyone else in the team has to know. That background will make you better at your job, whatever that job may be.

Summary

Most reporting jobs in radio and television are general assignment positions. Reporters with these jobs cover everything they are told to cover, but most of their stories are spot news stories. Spot news deals with everyday breaking stories—fires, accidents, crimes, disasters, and so on. Some stations and the networks use beat reporters, who are assigned to specific topics, such as education, politics, and health.

Whether you cover general assignments or a beat, remember that good reporters learn how to advance a story, how to find new information to keep a story fresh, and how to find a new angle from which to develop a story.

Review Questions

1. What are spot news stories? Give some examples.
2. What factors are considered when deciding to cover a crime or a fire?
3. Journalists must be especially careful with stories about defendants in a criminal case. How is that done?
4. Why does an assignment editor or news director decide to cover some court cases and pass up others?
5. What precautions should reporters and crews take to ensure that a demonstration is covered fairly?
6. What precautions should reporters and crews take in covering a riot?

Exercises

1. Arrange with a news director or assignment editor to follow a reporter when he or she is assigned to a breaking news story. Report on what happened at the scene and how the reporter covered the story.
2. Attend a pro-life or pro-choice demonstration, and report on how the media covered the story. Make note of the radio and TV reporters who covered the demonstration and monitor their wraps and packages to see if the reports were balanced and fair.
3. Check the local newspaper(s) to see how the demonstration was covered by print reporters. Write a report comparing the print and broadcast coverage.
4. Monitor a local TV newscast, and see how many spot news stories were reported. What other types of stories were in the newscast?

12 Covering Planned Events

There are literally thousands of corporations, politicians, special-interest groups, nonprofit organizations, government agencies, and other individuals and groups looking for exposure on network and local newscasts. Assignment desks are inundated with news releases and telephone calls from public-relations firms and publicists working for these various groups. And, of course, most of these organizations have Web pages on the Internet where newsrooms can reach them and vice versa.

Every one of these publicists tries to persuade the assignment staff that there is something special or important about the product, company, issue, or individual they represent. The assignment desk rejects most of these news releases and telephone calls for a variety of reasons—usually because they are too commercial or have little or no news value, or because there just isn't enough airtime available to go around. But some of these releases and telephone calls alert the assignment staff to events that are important and warrant coverage.

Gathering a crowd of journalists with tape recorders and cameras in one room is a triumph for anyone working in public relations. The number of journalists who attend such news conferences depends on what is being "sold." Make no mistake about it, that is what we are talking about—"selling."

It makes no difference whether the news conference is called by a government official, a Broadway producer, a major corporation, or the Red Cross; each news conference has a message to sell to the American people. For example, the district attorney may call a meeting with the news media to announce the arrest of several organized-crime bosses. The arrest is news, of course, but the district attorney also wants to let everyone know what a good job she and the department are doing.

News Conferences

The Broadway producer is betting that the media will turn out to hear about a new show because the release just happens to mention that the chorus line will be there in full costume.

The Red Cross is hoping for the best but knows that it may have difficulty getting reporters to show up at its news conference to discuss a blood shortage because it's not likely to provide good pictures for television or exciting sound bites for radio. The conference may get a 20-second read story on the

Figure 12-1   Setting up for a news conference. (Photo by James Terry)

six o'clock news. You might wonder why a blood shortage is not considered an important story. It is, but it probably will get more attention from newspapers than from radio and television. It just isn't a "good" broadcast story, a point of view that elicits a lot of criticism of broadcast news, much of which is justified.

That same morning, General Motors is holding news conferences in the convention center in your city and in various key locations throughout the country to display its new line of cars, including, as its news release boasts, a compact car that gets 40 miles to the gallon. As you might expect, every radio station, TV station, and newspaper, as well as several magazines, will send reporters, and the story will make most local and network newscasts.

How do reporters get ready for news conferences? Let's look at a reporter preparing for the conference being held by the district attorney. Depending on the sophistication of the newsroom, the reporter starts with the clips and video morgue, which may be computerized, to see what's available on the arrested organized-crime figures. If there is video of them, she asks for it to be pulled. She reads carefully any clips on the arrested men and checks the Internet and Websites for local newspapers. Before she leaves for the news conference, she also might make a quick check with other reporters in the newsroom to see if they have any additional information they gathered while covering other stories involving the men.

The reporter and her cameraperson arrive at the news conference early because it will be crowded and she wants to get a good position for the camera and herself. When the conference begins, the DA reads a prepared statement. The cameras and tape recorders will be rolling, although little of the statement— and maybe none of it—will get on the air. The question-and-answer period following the opening statement usually produces the best sound bites.

The reporter keeps notes on the opening statement, in any case, so she will know where the best bites are if she decides to use any of them. She does the same when the question-and-answer period begins, keeping track of the time when the best comments are made. While she was reading the clips in the newsroom, the reporter noticed that the organized-crime leaders were arrested five years before. The DA—the same one—got a conviction, and the men were sentenced to 5 to 10 years in prison. The reporter hopes that no one else beats her to the question she is ready to fire at the DA: "How come these guys aren't still in prison? It's only five years since you grabbed them and put them away the last time." The question would surely be provocative; perhaps the answer would be one of the highlights of the news conference. In all likelihood, the DA would respond with something like, "I just convict them; ask the judge and the parole board why they are back on the street so quickly." The DA, who had been critical of the judiciary on several other occasions, provided anchors with the headline, "DA Criticizes Judges and Parole Board."

Sometimes it is important to ask tough questions. News conferences should not be just a forum for those calling them. It's also important to ask follow-up questions, particularly when the individual holding the news conference is evasive or unclear. Techniques for asking good questions are discussed in Chapter 15, "The Interview."

Many broadcast reporters like to interview individually the person holding the news conference when the conference is over. Former *ABC News* correspondent Morton Dean said he did this if he didn't hear what he wanted during the news conference or if he wanted to go in a different direction. "Otherwise," he says, "I would pull a bite from the news conference."

Reporters often call in advance to arrange an interview with the person *before* the news conference. Some people agree; others refuse because they know it sometimes irritates other members of the media. This is particularly true when the reporter is still conducting the interview when the rest of the news corps arrives in the room. Other broadcast reporters, seeing what's going on, tell their camerapeople to set up and start shooting. Suddenly, there's a mini-news conference going on before the regular one starts. Such occurrences are particularly offensive to the print reporters, who must then wait for the scheduled news conference to begin. Once the broadcast people have their interviews, it is not unusual for them to pack their gear and be on their way, leaving the person holding the news conference with just the newspaper people. Many broadcast reporters cover news conferences this way because their assignment editors tell them to be in and out of the news conference quickly so they can move on to other stories.

Doing an interview before a news conference has its risks. Another reporter may know something important that the early reporter missed in the one-on-one; or a confrontation may occur when one of the print reporters asks an embarrassing question that catches the news conference host by surprise. The early reporter who came and went will not have this confrontation on tape.

Hard Questions

For a relatively small number of reporters, the most important questions they will ever get a chance to ask will be at a presidential news conference. The Washington press corps didn't get much of an opportunity to exercise their skills during the administration of President George Bush because during his first two years in office he only held three of them. In the third news conference, the president started out with a lengthy statement that was described by many of the assembled reporters as a speech defending his administration's policies at a particularly difficult period in his presidency, when the occupation in Iraq was going badly; the death toll of American servicemen and women was growing at an alarming rate, and some best-selling books were questioning the president's decision to go to war instead of focusing on terrorism.

And then there were questions about how the reporters themselves questioned the president. Writing about the news conference in a Poynter Institute online newsletter, faculty member Chip Scanlan said the event was an "example of missed opportunities and a lesson in the power of questions." He added, "Most of the questions provided vivid and dispiriting evidence that White House reporters sorely need a lesson in interviewing."

Scanlan suggested that the best person to give the lesson would be John Swatsky, a Canadian journalist and teacher who, Scanlan said "has made a science of identifying the kind of questions that produce answers and those that are invitations to obfuscate."

Scanlan said that students of Swatsky could easily spot the warning signs during the presidential news conference. He said the transcripts show that President Bush took questions from about 15 reporters, and most of the questions were double-barreled and/or closed-ended. Scanlan cited an example in which a reporter asked the president if he believed he made any errors in judgment during his presidency, which the president ducked. He also singled out a question to the president that asked him if he was falsely comforted by the FBI, and another that asked him if he thought the American people deserve an apology from him similar to the one offered by his former counter-terrorism chief. The president skillfully tip-toed around that shotgun question.

Scanlan said he can understand the impulse behind this kind of approach: I'm only going to get one crack at the president so I better load up and ask more than one question. "The problem," according to Scanlan, "is that double-barreled questions let the subject decide which, if any, question he wants to answer."

Scanlan also criticized the reporters for asking closed-ended questions which are designed to produce brief, unequivocal responses. He describes such questions as a "guaranteed conversation stopper." They gave the president three choices: yes, no, or dodge the question.

Scanlan was troubled by the lack of open-ended questions at the presidential news conference. That sort of question, that starts with a how, why, or what, encourages a subject to describe, explain, and amplify.

Scanlan cited an open-ended question to the president that worked: *Mr. President, April is turning into the deadliest month in Iraq since the fall of Baghdad, and some people are comparing Iraq to Vietnam and talking about a quagmire. Polls show that support for your policy is declining and that fewer than half of Americans now support it. What does that say to you and how do you answer the Vietnam comparison?*

Scanlan acknowledged that the question was front-loaded and double-barreled, but it worked. He noted that the question produced one of the few exchanges where the president answered the question he was asked, which "made it a tough question."

Scanlan said the news media needs to be asking tough questions, whether you're in the East Room of the White House or the mayor's office. He added, "you don't need editorializing, grandstanding, or filibustering to get meaningful answers, you just need to ask good questions."

There is a whole chapter devoted to interviewing (Chapter 15) that goes into these issues in more detail).

Local Government

The work of city and town government is extremely important, but it also can be one of the dullest assignments radio and TV reporters must cover. The problem for broadcast reporters is that the deliberations of the city council, the board of supervisors, and other local officials often take hours. The debated issues, however, often affect many people. An increase in local taxes, a curfew for teenagers, or a company's effort to locate a waste disposal plant in a community brings out a big crowd and lots of journalists. Because such meetings can go on for hours and days, what do radio and TV reporters do?

Let's suppose that the Centerville town supervisors are considering an out-of-town company's offer to build a waste-burning incinerator in the town. The company claims that the facility will employ 100 people and that it will be completely safe. Centerville could use another 100 jobs. Basically, Centerville, a dairy-farm community of about 5,000 people without much industry, is hurting financially; however, these people are farmers because they appreciate the earth and clean air, and they are suspicious of anyone or anything that might damage the environment. A local newspaper has already reported that the company wants to burn medical waste.

More than 100 people show up at the high-school auditorium to hear exactly what the company has in mind. There is a radio station in town but no TV station. A TV reporter from a nearby city shows up along with a local radio reporter and print journalists. TV cameras and tape recorders are rolling as town officials introduce a spokesperson and an engineer from the waste-disposal company. After some lengthy statements by the two representatives—complete with charts and statistics—a heated debate begins. The broadcast reporters take detailed notes, keeping a record of who is speaking and when. A local real estate agent says the plant would hurt property sales. "People escape the city to get away from pollution. They won't buy here if you build the plant," the agent says.

A parent questions the effect of toxic fumes on the town's children. The company official tries to reassure the crowd, which clearly is reacting negatively to the idea of building this plant in town. "There is absolutely nothing dangerous about anything we will be burning," the spokesperson says.

A man stands up holding a newspaper clipping. "Wasn't your company cited for not burning things right in the Carolinas?" he asks. "This story says your company left a real mess around and you were burning all sorts of dangerous things improperly."

The company official tries to explain away the story, saying, "We had a few workers who weren't doing their jobs the way they should have, but they've been replaced and things are all squared away now."

The man with the paper is still standing. "And this story says that you only employ about a dozen workers at that Carolina plant. You claim the plant here would mean 100 jobs for our town."

The debate went on for two hours, but the story prepared by the TV reporter would probably last no more than 90 seconds, maybe a little longer if the meeting took place on a slow news day. The local radio reporter would devote more time to the story because the issue is big news in Centerville. The radio reporter might do a special in-depth wrap-up of the meeting in addition to some one-minute wraparounds during newscasts throughout the day. There is no local daily newspaper, only a weekly, so the townspeople are anxious to hear as much as they can on the debate.

The cameraperson with the TV reporter picked up the heated debate and stopped shooting during the dull periods. After a while, a cameraperson develops a sense for knowing when to start and stop shooting a story like this one. Because the cameraperson knows that less than a minute of sound bites will make the news, it is unnecessary to shoot continuously.

After shooting the highlights of the debate, the reporter and cameraperson moved outside and interviewed some people as they left the building. Everyone they spoke with was opposed to the incinerator. In an effort to be as fair as possible, the reporter continued interviewing until she finally found a man who said he was "keeping an open mind on the matter" until he heard more. "If there really would be an extra 100 jobs," he said, "I'd want to think about it."

The reporter decided they had enough material. She would have liked to do a separate interview with one of the company representatives, but there was no time. The debate had continued for almost two hours, and the ride back to the station would take 40 minutes. She decided to use part of the official's remarks for balance and to include some of the debate along with the interviews she conducted outside the building. She also decided to use some of the crowd shots to go along with the sound bites. The company had provided her with a video of the South Carolina plant.

The reporter opened her package with a sound bite—a *cold* open—as follows:

SOT Woman yelling at meeting	SOT runs :04 "I'm not going to let you put anything in my backyard that's going to poison my children!"
V/O Crowd debating NAT SOUND UNDER	V/O This woman was one of almost 100 people who showed up at a meeting in Centerville tonight to listen to a

proposal that would establish a waste-burning incinerator in this predominantly dairy farm community of five thousand people.

SOT MAN TALKING IN CROWD. HE'S WAVING A NEWSPAPER.

SOT :12
"I don't trust your company. This story says your company left a real mess around and you were burning all sorts of dangerous things improperly . . ."

V/O SHOTS CE S.C. PLANT

The company that this man is referring to is the Medvac Waste Disposal Corporation out of Greenville, South Carolina. And there have been published reports that Medvac was fined for not properly disposing of medical waste at its plant outside Greenville.

SOT
FONT:BOB SMITH
CEO, MEDVAC
WASTE DISPOSAL

SOT :06
"We did have some trouble for awhile, but we've corrected all those problems." (protest from crowd)

V/O ANGRY CROWD

(V/O)
There was no doubt about the sentiments of most of the people assembled here tonight. These are farm people and the environment—the land they work and the air they and their cows breathe—is precious to them. But many young people have left the farms and are desperate for work in Centerville. Medvac claims it would hire 100 people at the incinerator it wants to build.

Video of farms and rolling hills

SOT ANGRY MAN

SOT :08
"And what about these 100 jobs you're talking about? This story says that you only employ about a dozen workers at that Carolina plant."

V/O CROWD LEAVING HALL

V/O
The debate lasted almost two hours and we only found one man who had

SOT O/C TWO SHOT

anything positive to say about the proposed plant.

SOT :05

"Well, if it's true that the plant would bring 100 jobs to town, I'd want to think about it."

V/O VIDEO OF TOWN
OFFICIALS AND OTHERS
TALKING OUTSIDE HALL

V/O

Town supervisors told Medvac that they would have a decision for them within 30 days. But from the tone of tonight's meeting, it seems unlikely that the project will be approved. This is Jackie Johnson reporting from Centerville.

This package is a good example of the proper way to cover a local government meeting. Unfortunately, many local reporters cover such stories from the back of the meeting room or on the steps of city hall. In such stories, the opening shot shows the reporter and then the camera moves from the reporter to the members of the city council or other governing body. In dull fashion, the camera pans from one member to another while the reporter voices the report. There usually are no sound bites in the story, just the voice of the reporter and the nameless faces and voices of the town officials. Former *CBS News* correspondent Ben Silver calls such reports "video clichés."

To avoid such uninteresting stories, the reporter covering local government meetings should find out in advance what is going to be discussed and select the most interesting subject and, if possible, one that lends itself to video footage. For example, let's consider a story about the extension of sewers to a certain part of town. Before the debate, the reporter and cameraperson should go to the location, take pictures of the area, and speak with some residents. Some might like the sewer idea, but others might oppose it because it would mean higher taxes.

Now when the reporter attends that public meeting and reports that the town supervisors voted to extend the sewer system, she can say, "Earlier in the day we spoke to some residents of that area, and here's what they had to say." The taped comments and video of the area make better news than pictures of the reporter announcing the supervisors' decision and shots of the members voting.

Political Campaigns

Covering politics can be one of the more interesting stories that reporters cover, although sometimes the politicians themselves are less than inspiring and the issues sometimes not very stimulating. Also, covering politicians can be frustrating because the candidates often skirt the real issues and get into

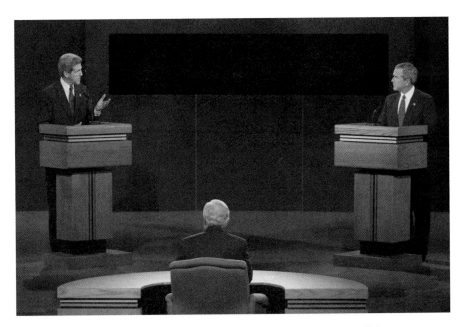

Figure 12-2 U.S. President Bush and Democratic presidential candidate Senator John Kerry participate in a 90 minute debate on the campus of Arizona State University. (Courtesy Joe Raedle, Getty Images)

name-calling and personality assassination. Compounding the problem is that the public is often indifferent to politics, ranking the subject fairly low, below topics such as education, crime, and the environment.

A group at Harvard University measured voter interest in the 2000 presidential campaign and found that two-thirds of the public were paying little or no attention. This apparent indifference of the public to such an important subject that impacts so keenly on their lives presents a real challenge for journalists—to make their coverage of politics as interesting and stimulating as possible. And covering politics is not just an assignment for top journalists covering the race for the presidency.

People are running for some political office just about everywhere. Most reporters find themselves covering a political campaign early in their career. Even relatively small communities hold elections—for mayor, sheriff, town supervisor, and numerous other positions. Reporters also cover the campaigns of candidates for the state legislature, for Congress, and for the presidency when those candidates visit the area.

The most important requirement for reporting on politics is remaining neutral. Regardless of how reporters feel personally about the candidates, they must maintain their objectivity. Assignment editors and news directors are not going to ask reporters what their politics are when they're assigned to cover the campaign of a state assemblyperson. The reporters are expected to report fairly, without any bias, even if they think poorly of the candidate. On the other hand, it is not unusual for reporters to find that they like some candidates after they have been on the road with them; however, reporters need to watch that this admiration doesn't creep into their scripts. When it does, the reporter might not even be aware of it, but sometimes it is visible to the audience and other journalists.

ABC News correspondent Barry Serafin says it is a challenge sometimes to hide personal feelings when assigned to cover one candidate. "After a while the candidate will be calling you by your first name and so will his wife. It is particularly difficult to maintain your objectivity," says Serafin, "when you like the person. It's not so bad," he adds, "if you don't like him because all your training automatically comes into effect and all the safeguards drop down. If you like him it's harder but you absolutely, positively have to keep that arm's length—that journalistic objectivity."

Serafin recalled covering Ronald Reagan during two campaigns. "I got to know him better than any other candidate, and afterwards I was happy when some of the people around him said, 'We didn't always like the stories you did, but we think you were fair. We never thought you cheap-shotted us.'" Serafin said, "I decided that if after two campaigns they didn't like every story I did and thought I was fair, then I probably didn't do a bad job."

CNN correspondent Jeff Greenfield also notes that a reporter runs the risk of getting to like the candidate he or she is following and sometimes "has a

Figure 12-3   Ted Koppel with Colin Powell. (©2004, ABC, Inc.)

professional reason for wanting the candidate to do well, including taking him to the White House with him." Serafin says, however, that that danger has been minimized because the networks now tend to rotate their political reporters.

Putting Comments into Perspective

When covering a candidate during a campaign, a political reporter should not just parrot the candidate's speeches. If the candidate says the same things every place he or she goes, it would be appropriate for the reporter to point that out. It would be equally important for the reporter to note when candidates change their positions on the issues depending on the kind of group they're addressing.

The reporter should also tell the audience things about the location of the speech and the crowd. Was the candidate speaking in a predominantly Republican or Democratic area? Was the crowd mostly white-collar or blue-collar? Obviously, if the candidate was Republican and she was addressing a crowd in an affluent area of the city, her reception could be expected to be warmer than in a ghetto. Likewise, the opposite could be expected if the candidate was a Democrat.

The crowd's reaction is important. Was it enthusiastic or relatively quiet? Was the crowd large or small? If the weather affected the turnout, that should be noted. Did people challenge the candidate's remarks? Did they seek out the candidate to shake his or her hand?

Former CNN correspondent and anchor Bernard Shaw suggested that the broadcast media should be doing more to put political statements and claims into perspective. He questioned whether radio and TV stations really want to stop "attack ads." He noted that millions of dollars in ad revenue are at stake and that sales departments "are loaded with people who have never seen an ad they didn't like. But isn't there a higher calling? A higher need?" asked Shaw. He added that attack ads have become news stories, and it is the responsibility of news directors to point out the distortions and to expose candidates who "work harder at ducking than discussing issues."

Shaw also suggested that the news media should let candidates know that the voters are not more interested in a "staged picture than a thousand words of discussion of issues on their minds." He spoke of the "arrogance of the candidates and their managers and their media manipulators who fly into an airport, speak for five minutes, pose for pictures for 10 minutes, and get back in the plane and move on to another location."

Shaw said that when a candidate does that, there is nothing wrong with leading the newscast that night by saying, "Democratic candidate Tom Harkin thought enough of San Jose voters to spend 22 minutes at the airport today before going on to a Los Angeles fundraiser tonight. The senator said nothing he did not say before, but he did note that our weather was the best he had seen in days."

Shaw cited another way to put a political story into perspective:

> The president took his election campaign to the Centerville nursing home for the elderly today, promising that he would not allow Congress to tamper with Social Security. But when he left, the president used a side

Figure 12-4
CBS News correspondent Charles Osgood. (Courtesy of Charles Osgood/*CBS News*)

door and his motorcade went the wrong way on a one-way street, apparently to avoid some two thousand unemployed workers whose benefits had run out.

Shaw said audiences are "keen for those kind of reporting distinctions. They need them for perspective on the sleights of hand that they are subjected to by politicians lusting for votes but lacking in so many ways."

Shaw also attacked some "sins" committed by politicians, citing as an example the arrogant refusal to answer reporters' questions on the issues. "But worse than the candidate's refusal to answer the question," he said, "is the news media's complicity by generally failing to point out and underscore that the politician did not answer the question."

Shaw said that every time this happens it reinforces "the politician's misguided belief that he can get away with it and voters don't care." The former CNN anchor said he believes it's time to stop the exploitation of the news media by politicians. "If what politicians are saying and doing is not news, why put it on the air?" he asked. Some reporters privately agreed with Shaw's criticisms and suggestions, but others doubted most political reporters would change. One political reporter said his boss wouldn't be very happy if he told him he wasn't going to do a package that evening because the candidate didn't say anything new.

Some stations are to be commended for examining politicians' paid campaign spots and analyzing them for content and inaccuracies and pointing out flaws in them when appropriate. During the 2004 Presidential campaign, several networks offered so-called "fact-checking" segments on a regular basis to correct inaccurate statements made by the candidates.

Feature Stories

Covering hard news—whether spot news or planned events—is the "meat and potatoes" of broadcast journalism, whereas feature stories are the "dessert." Those are the stories that often bring a smile and sometimes a tear to our faces.

CBS News correspondent Charles Osgood is a master of the feature story. He says he gets many of his ideas from unimportant-sounding stories on the wires. For example, he once found a three-line story about the Navy's considering a change in the rank of admirals. Osgood said: "You just suck the rest of it out of your thumb." His thumb gave us this:

The U.S. Navy wants to establish a new rank to distinguish one-star rear admirals from two-star rear admirals. They thought about it and thought about it and the proposed name for the new rank that they've come up with is "Rear Admiral Lower Half." Now if President Reagan approves "Rear Admiral Lower Half" then "Rear Admiral Lower Half" it will be. Let's consider if this is such a good idea.

Military ranks are sort of baffling to the layman to begin with. We all know that generals and admirals are big deals, but there are many gradations inside the general and admiral category; and these are not always what you would think they would be. Major outranks a lieutenant, but a lieutenant-general outranks a major-general. A very model of a modern major-general only has two silver stars. A lieutenant-general has three. Both of them are outranked by the just plain general who has four silver stars. All three are addressed as "general" and so is the brigadier-general who has the one star. These are a dime a dozen at the Pentagon, as are admirals, of course. And there are different kinds of admirals, too. The admiral who corresponds to a four-star general is called an admiral. The admiral who corresponds to a three-star or lieutenant-general is called a vice admiral. And the one who corresponds to a major-general is called a rear admiral. The next naval rank down corresponding to a brigadier or one-star general is now called a commodore.

The U.S. Navy has now decided that its commodores should be admirals too, just as the Army's brigadiers are generals, and so the Navy has proposed a new rank called "Rear Admiral Lower Half." You would address such an officer as admiral so-and-so, not rear half so-and-so, by the way. The abbreviation for the new rank—they have thought of everything—would be "R.A.D.M. lower half," not "R.A.L.H.," as you might think. Too bad, because then if your first name was Ralph you could be R.A.L.H. Ralph. Sort of like Major Major Major in *Catch-22*.

I'm sure "Rear Admiral Lower Half" is very nautical and a great naval tradition and all of that, but what I question is whether "Rear Admiral Lower Half" brings the right sort of image to mind. The concept of rear is already somewhat puzzling, since the aft section of a ship is not called the rear, but the stern. There are a lot of stern admirals. Some of them are rear admirals and some are not. Once our attention has been called to a rear, it seems an unfortunate added indignity to specify that one is referring specifically to the lower half thereof.

How about you? Would you rather be called a commodore or a rear admiral lower half? Commodore is a little dated, admittedly. Even the Hotel Commodore isn't called the Commodore anymore. No, it isn't the Hotel Rear Admiral Lower Half either. It is now the Grand Hyatt Hotel. How about grand hyatt for the name of a new rank? Instead of rear admiral lower half so-and-so, the officer would be grand hyatt so-and-so. Grand hyatt has a certain brassy Gilbert and Sullivan flair to it. "Captain Jones, you're being promoted to the rank of grand hyatt." None of that stuff about rears and lower halves. You see what I mean?

Osgood said the nice thing about writing such stories is that "you don't have to know a lot . . . I go to the almanac and find the different ranks in the Army and Catch-22 Navy and how they correspond to one another. I don't know that stuff," he added, "but you can get your hands on it easily and it's right there in the newsroom."

Features also receive a lot of attention on NPR's *All Things Considered* and *Morning Edition*. Reporter Cokie Roberts wrote and produced a feature about the Congressman Morris Udall for "Morning Edition." Here's the way the anchor led into the report:

ANCHOR: One of the most respected and best-loved members of the House of Representatives is expected to announce his resignation today. Arizona Democrat Morris Udall has been suffering from Parkinson's disease for many years but in January a serious fall incapacitated the 68-year-old Congressman, leading to his likely resignation. NPR's Cokie Roberts reports:

ROBERTS: Mo Udall came to Congress 30 years ago as a reformer out of the West, ready to take on the structures and seniority of what was then a hidebound House of Representatives. He leaves as a senior statesman who earned the admiration and affection of his political friends and enemies through his hard work and, especially, through his humor. Mo Udall is not only a very funny man himself, he is a connoisseur and custodian of American political humor, compiled a number of years ago into a book.

(sound bite)

UDALL: I was doing a chapter the other day on politicians' mixed metaphors and bloopers. I'll share a few with you today as a sort of preview if I can push the book a little bit (laughter). I'll start with Gerry Ford, who said in that famous speech on the House floor, "If Lincoln were alive today he would be turning over in his grave." And somebody said, perhaps it was I, "we honor Lincoln because he was born in a log cabin which he built with his own two hands." (Laughter)

ROBERTS: The occasion of this spate of storytelling was Udall's 1984 announcement that he would not run for president again. He said the presence of other liberals in the race made his candidacy unnecessary but, in fact, Udall was already suffering from the Parkinson's disease that has made the last several years so difficult for him. The decision not to make the run was a tough one because Udall had long before been attacked by the political malady of presidentitis. He went for the White House in 1976 but after coming in second in seven straight primaries, Udall concluded that he drew more laughter than votes, causing columnist James Kilpatrick to declare the Arizona Democrat too funny to be president. That eventually became the title of Udall's book, which was finally published in 1988. When

Figure 12-5   ABC correspondent Cokie Roberts. (©1998 ABC, Inc.)

NPR's Scot Simon interviewed the Congressman on his collection of political anecdotes, Udall—as usual—praised John Kennedy and Adlai Stevenson as the masters of the political quip.

(sound bite)

UDALL: Stevenson had a natural sense of humor—a sense of the ridiculous. A good example: Stevenson went to one of the women's colleges up in New England and made a big hit and as he was leaving this woman shouted, "Great going, Governor Stevenson, you got the vote of every thinking person." And he said, "It's not good enough, I need a majority." (laughter)

ROBERTS: It could have been his own story. Udall was never able to attract a majority for president or for a House leadership position, although he ran for Speaker in 1989 and for majority leader in 1971. But he did wage a successful attack on the House seniority system, pushed through a landmark campaign finance bill, and as chairman of the Interior and Insular Affairs Committee he shepherded several major environmental measures through Congress, including the Alaskan Lands Act. Udall succeeded legislatively by pulling together sometimes impossible coalitions, often using humor as his thread. To Udall, the ability to amuse was essential for a committed politician.

(sound bite)

UDALL:　Politics used to be entertainment. If you lived in a little town in South Carolina 100 years ago, you never saw a presidential nominee on TV or otherwise. They were names in a newspaper and when the politicians came to town, they were expected to make two-hour speeches that would entertain the troops, and now we have speech writers and gag writers in great profusion. The mere act of hiring a gag writer says I don't understand myself and the issue enough to make people laugh legitimately, I have to hire somebody to give me a false line.

ROBERTS:　Today's generation of politicians, lamented Udall in his book, "is less seasoned, more serious, richer, and less humorous. The ability to deliver a riveting speech, rich in substance and leavened with humor and anecdotes, is a declining art in Washington today." It would have died a lot faster had Mo Udall not been here for the last three decades, savoring his stories and telling his tales.

(sound bite)

UDALL:　I grew up between the Navajos and the Apaches. I worked on Indian problems all my life and the Indians really appreciate this story: A politician goes to an Indian village and gathers the Indian voters around and says, "You like me, you vote for me, and we get schools and hospitals for little Indian children." And they shouted, "Gooma, gooma." And he said, "You vote for me and we will put gas heat in every tepee." And they shouted, "Gooma, gooma." And the chief said, "You white man great friend of Indian, you must come down to the corral where we are going to give you an Indian pony. But," he said, "be careful you don't step in the gooma, gooma." (laughter)

ROBERTS:　(music under) Arizona Democrat Morris Udall, retiring today. I'm Cokie Roberts.

Features also are a basic part of local TV news, and to a lesser degree, to network TV news. Every local news producer schedules a variety of features throughout the newscast to give it balance. (More discussion on that subject is presented in Chapter 21, "Producing.")

Summary

Reporters spend much of their time covering planned events. Unlike spot news, which is unpredictable, most planned events are known about by the assignment editors days and weeks in advance. These events fill part of the newscast almost every night. A good percentage of planned events are news conferences. Because news conferences are called by people trying to "sell" something, reporters must be prepared to ask tough questions; they cannot allow themselves to be used.

Other common planned events are those provided by the workings of government—town and city council meetings and, in state capitals, meetings of the legislature. Research is important. Reporters must be familiar with the issues under discussion and be ready to ask intelligent questions about them. Planned events are not always exciting; they often have few or no picture opportunities. They are, however, an important part of covering the news, even if they wind up as a 20-second voiceover.

Another type of nonbreaking story is the feature story. Feature stories give reporters more opportunity to display their creative talents. Every reporter has his or her favorite type of story, but you must remember that you have to learn how to cover them all, not just the colorful and exciting ones.

Review Questions

1. Name some of the planned events that broadcast reporters cover.
2. How do assignment editors determine which planned events they will cover?
3. What are the chief reasons that people and organizations call news conferences?
4. How does a reporter prepare for a news conference?
5. What is the best way for broadcast reporters to cover a town or city council meeting?
6. What is the worst way to cover such a meeting?
7. What are the most important things to remember when covering a political campaign?

Exercises

1. Cover a city council or town meeting with a tape recorder or video camera. Prepare a wrap or package.
2. Attend a news conference, and prepare a wrap or package.
3. Attend a morning news meeting at a TV station, and write a report on how decisions were reached on which stories would be covered that day.

13 Reporting Live

Chapter 10 mentioned some of the differences between broadcast reporting and newspaper reporting. This chapter discusses one of the most profound differences—the ability of broadcast reporters to deliver live reports. This chapter offers some suggestions for handling the special pressures and responsibilities that reporting live places on broadcast journalists.

Reporting live from a mobile unit has always been routine for a radio reporter. Immediacy has been radio's big advantage. Since the early days of radio, Americans have been accustomed to getting the first news of an important story from that medium. Often, the news has come from a radio reporter at the scene.

Radio has lost some of its advantage as new technology has made it possible for television to put a live signal into homes almost as quickly and easily as radio does. Radio continues, however, to be first in reaching a large portion of the listening audience—those traveling on the highways.

Organizing Thoughts

Because they broadcast live so often, radio reporters learn early in their careers how to organize their thoughts quickly. They also develop the skill of ad-libbing. Radio reporters are often expected to report from the scene of a breaking story for much longer periods than their TV counterparts because radio is normally not under the same time limitations as television. It is much easier to interrupt a music format on radio with a breaking story, for example, than it is to interrupt a soap opera on television. Lost advertising revenue is far less expensive for a radio station than for television, and it is much easier for a radio station to make up lost commercials.

The best way to organize material for a live report is to use a reporter's notebook. This device is particularly handy because it fits into a handbag or jacket pocket. Always take more than one pen or pencil. (In freezing weather or pouring rain, a pencil works a lot better than a pen.)

In anticipation of going live from the scene, broadcast reporters must keep notes on a variety of happenings. First, they must keep track of important comments that are made, whether during a news conference or a one-on-one interview. They must note exactly when the remarks were made so they can be located quickly on the videotape or audiotape. Some reporters take courses in speedwriting; others develop a system of their own. Experienced reporters learn that they cannot get so involved in taking notes that they lose control of the interview. They make entries only

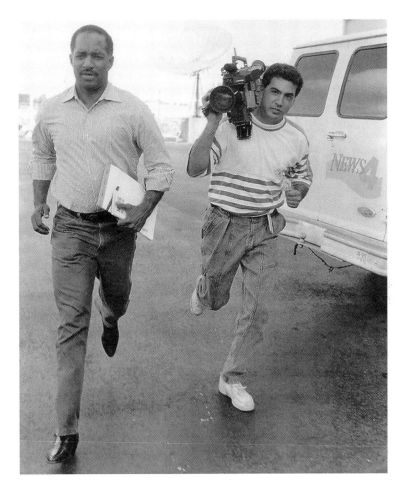

Figure 13-1 WTVJ-TV Reporter Ed O'Dell and Cameraman Pedro Cancio rush to the scene of a story in Miami. (Courtesy of WTVJ-TV, Miami)

when comments are important enough to be used as a sound bite or in the narration that will surround it. TV reporters who have a camera with a time code recording system that shows the actual time of day that each scene is recorded only have to note the time when they hear something important.

Reporting live presents different problems for radio and TV reporters. For starters, radio reporters work alone, whereas TV reporters have at least one and sometimes two people with them in the microwave truck.

The production of the live report also is handled differently by a TV reporter than by a radio reporter. Sometimes the news conference or individual interview is microwaved back to the station while it is in progress. An associate producer or a writer at the station may monitor the feed and make notes. When the feed is over, producers can quickly confer with the reporter on which sound bites he or she wishes to use and then instruct the tape editor to cue them up. The reporter then does a live open from the scene, and the sound bites are played from the station. The reporter returns after the bites to do a live close.

It is also possible to do everything from the mobile unit. New technology allows TV crews to record and edit video in the truck, add the reporter's narration, and actually play the story from the truck without using any of the support equipment at the station. This type of sophisticated equipment is usually found only in larger markets.

Another major difference between reporting live for radio and TV is obvious: The audience does not see the radio reporter. It does see the TV reporter, which adds some complications. The radio reporter can get comfortable in the front seat of the mobile unit, cue up her tape, spread her notes out, and concentrate on delivering her narration without worrying about anyone seeing her. Meanwhile, her TV colleague may be memorizing his script so that he is not constantly looking at his notebook during his time on camera.

Let's examine a typical live report filed by a radio reporter from the scene of a fire:

Two people are known dead in a fire that swept through an apartment house on Rose Avenue in the suburban West End community of Center City. Fire Chief John O'Hara says he doesn't know if everyone else in the building escaped.

(sound bite)

"We think everyone but the one couple got out of there, but it's too early to tell. So far no one has reported anyone missing, so we are hopeful."

(reporter)

The dead have been identified as Barbara Swift and her husband Robert. It's believed the fire started in their apartment shortly after midnight and spread to the rest of the building. So far, there's no information on what caused the fire, which was brought under control about an hour after it started. More than two dozen people were in the building. One woman who escaped, Val Hills, said she is happy to be alive:

(sound bite)

"There was so much smoke, that's what scared me the most. When I heard some shouting, I got up and I knew there must be a fire. Fortunately, I was able to get to the stairs and get out."

(reporter)

Some 50 firefighters and 10 pieces of equipment are still at the scene. Some of the firefighters are still hosing down the building and others are going through the debris just to make sure no one else is in there.

Once again, two people are dead in this Rose Avenue fire in the West End. It's believed that everyone else escaped from the building. This is Frank Sneed. Back to you, Bill.

Meanwhile, a TV station was carrying this story from its reporter at the scene via microwave. The story opens up with the reporter on camera and the fire scene behind her:

O/C Heather

Two bodies have been removed from this burned-out apartment building on Rose Avenue, and it's not yet known if there were any other fatalities.

The fire started around midnight in one of the apartments and spread quickly through the rest of the building. Earlier, we spoke with a couple who escaped from the burning building.

SOT
Font: Frank Lewis

SOT
"We were asleep when we heard shouting and jumped out of bed. I could smell smoke. I grabbed some trousers and my wife tossed on a robe and we got the hell out of there."

Font: Laura Lewis

"I was scared stiff. I'm just happy to be alive."

(Heather)

O/C two shot

With me now is Fire Chief John O'Hara. Chief, do you think everyone is out of there?

(Chief)

"Well, we're hopeful. So far no one has reported anyone missing so that's a good sign. But you never can be sure."

(Heather)

Do you know how the fire started?

(Chief)

"Well, we think it started in the apartment of the couple who died in the fire and then spread to the other apartments, but so far we aren't sure how it started."

	(Heather) Thank you, Chief.
O/C tight shot of Heather	The couple who died in the fire have been identified as Barbara and Robert Swift. There was no other information available about them.
V/O Shots of building and firefighters wetting it down	V/O As you can see, this building is completely gutted, and if everyone else got out alive it would be amazing. Apparently some two dozen other people were in the building. About 50 firefighters have been battling the blaze. They brought it under control around one o'clock—about an hour after it began. Some of the firefighters
Shots of smoldering building	have been moving slowly through parts of the burned-out building in an effort to determine if anyone could have been trapped inside. Meanwhile, other firefighters continue to hose down the smoldering remains of the building.
O/C Heather	O/C Once again, two people dead and apparently everyone else escaped from this apartment complex on Rose Avenue in the West End section of the City. This is Heather Nelson, KTHU News.

After the radio and TV reporters finished their live reports, they would probably be asked a few questions by the anchors. Sometimes it is possible for the anchors and reporters to confer in advance on what questions the anchors will ask. The reporters often try to field whatever questions come their way without any advance preparation. That's when ad-libbing ability is important.

Ad-Libbing

Certain methods can help reporters improve their ad-libbing ability, or speaking without a script. Word association is one common method used by reporters to make sure they do not run out of things to say during a live remote. Many reporters write down a list of key words or phrases in the order in which they want to cover their material. When they exhaust all the information dealing with a key word, they move to the next one on the list until they have covered everything. Good ad-libbing reporters need only that one word or phrase to keep them going, which is important because reporters are often forced into remote situations that require a considerable amount of ad-libbing.

ABC News correspondent Barry Serafin says the best way to learn how to ad-lib is by doing it. He says he never thinks about reporting to an audience of 20 million people but concentrates on the idea that he is conversing with a single person in a "natural and human manner." Serafin praises *ABC News* anchor Peter Jennings' ad-libbing ability on what Serafin calls a "we're not sure what's going on here folks" kind of story.

Serafin notes that Jennings is not afraid to say, "Well, we're not quite sure where we are going here, but we'll let you know when we are, and in the meantime I'm going to do this." "Jennings doesn't try to be a superman—he tries to be calm and composed," says Serafin. "He lets the audience know he's following the story with them—that he's human." Serafin adds, "The main thing about ad-libbing is not to sound perfect . . . Don't try to tell what you don't know. Don't speculate."

The Challenges of Electronic News Gathering

A great way to prepare for the world of electronic news gathering (ENG) is to do radio remotes. It is easier for TV reporters to handle the challenges of live television if they have a radio background, but not as many reporters are making the transition from radio to television as in the past.

Most TV reporters now start their careers in television, and they have to learn how to do remotes from the start. During the transition from film to videotape and microwave in the mid-1970s, many TV reporters found it difficult to make the adjustment. They were accustomed to having 45 minutes or more to write their scripts while the film was being developed. The only time TV reporters went live was when the station or network bought a telephone line, and that was reserved for important occasions. Many TV reporters were unable to handle the pressures of going live and thus changed jobs.

Former *CBS News* correspondent Betsy Aaron made the transition but recalls the luxury of the film days when a reporter might have from 3 o'clock in the afternoon until airtime to write a script. "You had time to think," she said. "The time for reflection and making phone calls about your story has disappeared. The deadline is always immediate," she added, "and often the product suffers."

Serafin also recalls making the transition: "In the days of film you couldn't be changing, writing, and producing the piece 10 seconds before it ran." Serafin remembered going live at the end of the Falklands War when an angry demonstration started outside the palace in Buenos Aires. "Because of technology," Serafin said, "I was really forced at the last minute to make some editorial decisions about what was going on. Was it just a little spasm of public opinion or was it the beginning of the end of the government . . . or none of the above? I had to report to a network audience [without really knowing the answer] and it was difficult."

Former *ABC News* correspondent Morton Dean agrees. He says it is "scary" when you have to go live and you are not quite sure what is going

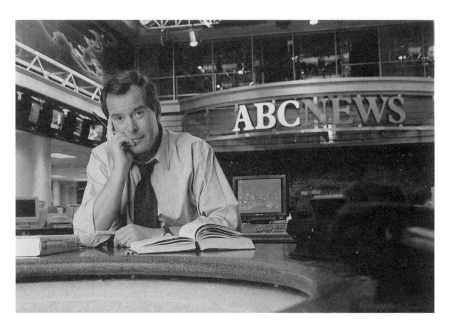

Figure 13-2   ABC anchor and correspondent Peter Jennings on the set of *World News Tonight With Peter Jennings*. (Michael O'Neill/*ABC News*. © 1999 ABC, Inc.)

on. "I think that is the most difficult part of this business—covering a breaking story live," Dean says. "You are often out there 'naked' and you have to resist the pressure to give information that you're not certain of and to give your own personal thoughts as opposed to what's really going on." Dean says he's often asked to give his opinion about "what is going to happen" at the scene when he really does not know.

Dean recalled his reporting experience in the Gulf War when he was going live, and Iraqi Scud missiles were zooming overhead, and people were putting on their chemical outfits, and troops were running around with guns and taking their positions. "It's really very difficult to keep your wits about you," he said.

When asked if he was ever uncomfortable about his live reporting during the Gulf War, Dean said only to the extent that he developed a habit that may be considered bad in television: saying "I don't know" when he really doesn't know. "I think there's a terrible temptation to be glib," said Dean, "and just talk nonstop and maybe not say anything. You must have the courage to say 'I don't know,' and some people think that's a sin when you are on television."

Dean said there are times "when your mind is not working that quickly . . . and you have to feel secure enough to say 'I'm not sure about that' . . . or 'I have to think about that.'" He also said there have been times when he refused to go live, telling his producer he really had nothing to say.

Aaron is concerned that some people in the field are so involved in the technology that they do not care about what reporters are saying. The result, she says, "is that you have people who will say 'only time will tell' in a hundred different ways. They say it very smoothly, but they don't know how to say anything else. They don't know what they're covering, or why, or the history or implication . . . They just know it's a great picture and they make air. Sometimes," she says, "dead air is better than making air."

ABC *Nightline* anchor, Ted Koppel, says that the ability to go live often gets in the way of good journalism. "Putting someone on the air while an event is unfolding is clearly a technological tour de force, but it is an impediment, not an aid, to good journalism."

Koppel also recalled that when he was in Vietnam, "we focused far more on the journalism and far less on the distribution mechanism." He said satellite transmission had become an option, but "only in the rarest instances." Most of the time, he added, the film had to be shipped to the States. "You write differently when you know that your piece won't make air for another day or two."

The same concerns about technology were expressed 12 years earlier by the late veteran newswoman Pauline Frederick of NBC. She noted that technology has "given our profession marvelous tools with which to work. But, the question that should forever confront us is whether in our eagerness to use these instruments, the import of the message may become confused with the messenger, who could be perceived as trying to make and shape the news."

Former *CNN News* anchor and correspondent Bernard Shaw also raised some questions about the new technology. "We can fire up, and fly in or roll in portable satellite earth stations, slap on a wireless mike, report live, and not wait for tape at 11. We have digital this and digital that, telephones that connect to a satellite, fiber optics in the wings, and technology that will provide even smaller satellite dishes and antennas that will fit in an oversize briefcase. But," asked Shaw, "how are we using this stuff?"

Shaw went on to suggest several situations that raise the question of whether broadcast news technology offers balanced and fair reporting. "If in covering a nation at war, a correspondent shows pictures of devastation without pointing out that the host government is severely restricting the movement of reporters and showing only what that government wants shown, is the crucial element of perspective for the viewer or listener well served?" asked Shaw. "If there are no pictures to videotape and no sounds to record but only shreds of information gained from listening and observing, is expensive live capability that impressive?" he asked. "If you are a reporter covering a protest around a nuclear power plant and you have the cameraperson shoot, say, 50 demonstrators tight so that it looks like 500 demonstrators, and if the reporter decides not to interview a plant spokesman because it's too close to satellite feed time, has that technology yielded better balance and a fair report?" asked Shaw.

All the correspondents agree that ENG has increased the risk of inaccuracy. As stressed in earlier chapters, nothing is more important for journalists than accuracy. Reporting live to a community, to the nation, and often to the world carries with it a tremendous responsibility. There have been some notable cases of live reports that gave inaccurate accounts. For example, it was reported that presidential aide James Brady had been killed during the assassination attempt on President Reagan in 1981; in fact, Brady survived his traumatic head wounds.

As with any story, but particularly when covering a story live, reporters must check and double-check their information and must rely heavily on attribution when the slightest possibility exists that the information may not be accurate.

Keeping Cool

The Scud attacks during the Gulf War demanded a lot of "cool" on the part of network reporters. Some correspondents were reluctant to leave the roofs until they were ordered to do so by anchors and network officials. The matter-of-fact, low-keyed reporting of CNN correspondents Peter Arnett, John Holliman, and Bernard Shaw from a hotel room in downtown Baghdad was certainly one of the highlights of the Gulf War reporting. The trio said that watching the air raids on Iraq from their hotel windows was "a little like watching a fireworks display." To their credit, their calm and responsible reporting could have been compared to the way they might have handled an assignment at the Statue of Liberty during a Fourth of July celebration.

Peter Arnett, in particular, kept things in perspective, discouraging speculation about what was and was not going on when it was obvious that such speculation would have served no useful purpose.

The only time a correspondent seemed to lose composure was when some technical problem prevented the reporter from being heard or seen during the middle of a missile attack. Technical problems are often the cause of reporters losing their cool during less dramatic live reports.

All of us have seen a TV reporter in trouble during a live remote. The scene usually goes something like this: The reporter is standing in front of a camera getting ready to report live and something goes wrong with the ear-piece system that allows the producer or cameraperson to speak with the reporter. The reporter ends up looking mystified because she does not know whether she is on the air. A cameraperson may be trying to signal what's going on, but sometimes this person is also in the dark. A worst-case scenario is when the reporter actually says, "Are we on?" when in fact she is.

Sometimes these mishaps can be avoided if a TV monitor is available for the reporter. That way, the reporter would know if she is on the air without having to wait for verbal instructions. These situations are trying for reporters, who understandably do not like to appear foolish in the eyes of the audience, but the TV audience has become so sophisticated that it tends to ignore such mishaps or, at worst, to chuckle a little over the breakdown in communications. It's best for reporters to accept the fact that mistakes are going to happen and equipment is going to malfunction.

Memorizing and Delivering Live Reports

Some reporters have an amazing ability to memorize scripts. For most reporters, however, memorizing one minute of copy presents a problem. Because all TV reporters are asked to do live reports, they must either develop the ability to memorize their material or use some tricks to help them. Most stations and networks have no problem with reporters glancing down at their notes during live reports, particularly during a breaking story. It's less acceptable, however, especially in a routine live report outside a city-council meeting

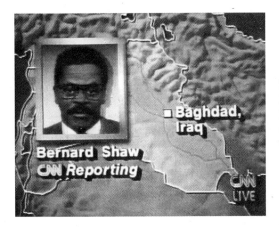

Figure 13-3
Former CNN correspondent
Bernard Shaw reports from the
scene during the Gulf War. (1992
CNN. All Rights Reserved.)

or the mayor's office, to see a reporter's head bobbing up and down every few seconds to read notes.

Former *CBS News* correspondent Ben Silver says it sometimes helps "to just throw the script away." Silver recalls: "I was having trouble memorizing the close to a story and I must have done it 10 times when the cameraman finally said, 'Give me the script.' He took the clipboard from me and I did the close without any problem."

Changing Lens Shots

On particularly long, taped standups, some reporters have the cameraperson change the shot during the delivery. The opening camera shot might be wide as the reporter delivers the first part of the standup. Then, the reporter can pause while the cameraperson moves in for a tight shot. The reporter then delivers the second half of the script, and the audience is unaware that any break in the delivery occurred. The two shots have to be drastically different to avoid a *jump cut*—the jerking of the head that would be seen if the camera shots were too much alike.

Summary

The biggest challenge that most broadcast reporters face is reporting live. Radio reporters have always faced that challenge because they could be on the air from the scene of a breaking story in minutes with the use of a two-way radio. TV reporters relied on film for their coverage until the 1970s, when two technologies were developed: small, portable videotape cameras (minicams) and microwave. Reporters suddenly lost the luxury of preparing their reports while they were traveling back from the scene of a story and while the film was being developed. Suddenly, reporters found that with microwave technology, they were often asked to go on the air immediately, while their videotape was being rewound and edited or cued up within minutes of being shot. They discovered that most of their thinking time had disappeared.

These developments brought about not only new challenges but also new risks. When thinking time is reduced, the chance of inaccuracy is increased. As a result, TV reporters have two concerns: (1) to collect information and sort it out quickly, and (2) to ensure it is accurate. The immediacy of the new technology also requires that reporters learn to ad-lib, making their improvised speech look easy and comfortable.

Review Questions

1. New technology permits broadcast news reporters to go live from almost any part of the globe with short notice. But these technological advances also place new burdens and responsibilities on journalists. Explain.
2. Before the arrival of microwave technology, TV reporters used to have more time to collect their thoughts. Why?
3. Good organization and note taking are important when a reporter covers a story live. How can these skills be developed?
4. Reporters who hope to be successful reporting from the scene of a breaking news story must develop certain skills. What are they?
5. How can reporters improve their ability to memorize and deliver live standup reports? Explain.

Exercises

1. Cover some event in the community, and then arrange for another student in the school's broadcast lab to videotape your standup report on the story you covered. After you have given your report, have the other student question you on tape. Return to the lab, and watch the tape.
2. Cover a news conference with either an audiocassette player or video equipment. If you are using an audiocassette player, pick a sound bite and cue it up so that you can play it over the phone in the middle of a wraparound. If you are using a video camera, do an open and close at the scene without preparing a script. Return to the lab, and insert a sound bite between the open and close that you recorded at the scene.
3. Have another student read a lengthy story to you from a newspaper. Make notes as he or she reads the story. Study your notes for two minutes, and then record a report either on audiotape or on video. Play it back for other students and your professor, and ask for an evaluation.

14 Putting the Television Story Together

When reporters leave the newsroom on assignments, they never know how their stories will turn out. The producers and assignment editors may be looking for a package—a story that includes one or more sound bites, the reporter's narration, and video. Sometimes they must settle for less, however, because the story itself turns out to be less important than they originally thought or because the interviews are not strong or the video is weak. When that happens, the story often becomes a voiceover-sound on tape (VO/SOT), or is relegated to the simplest type of picture story, a voiceover (V/O).

There also are times when the assignment editor knows in advance that a story is not worthy of a package. A cameraperson may be sent on a story without a reporter just to shoot video and natural sound. The producer will be made aware of that situation and will plan on covering that story in the newscast as a VO/SOT or V/O. This chapter discusses these types of television stories.

The Package

A TV newscast is mostly made up of packages. That's because, if they are done well, packages have all the elements that bring a story alive: good pictures, interesting sound bites, and a well-written script. As mentioned, if any of these elements is weak, the story may be downgraded or kept short. In other words, the quality of the video and the sound bites often determines the length of a package. But even great video and excellent sound bites do not always guarantee a long package. It depends on what else is going on in the news that day. Even on slow days, packages rarely run longer than a couple of minutes.

At the Scene

Good organization is essential in putting together a successful package. Reporters try to decide quickly how they are going to produce the package. They may not have every detail pinned down, but they generally decide on some fundamentals, such as whether they are going to do the open, the close, or a transition in the middle on camera. If one of these on-camera options may be needed, it should be shot just in case.

Taking Notes

Good organization requires good notes. *NBC News* correspondent Bob Dotson says he uses his notebook "like a pilot's checklist." He says he never finds the creative part of reporting to be a big problem. "I always find that the obvious is overlooked, like I forgot to get the wide shot or I forgot to ask the mayor whether he was going to run for another term."

Dotson notes that as soon as he knows he is going to do a story, he starts putting little boxes in his notebook with "thoughts, ideas, pictures, anything" he thinks he may need. "And then I scratch off what I don't need as I go along," he adds, stressing, "I do not leave a story until I have checked all the boxes that I do need so I don't overlook anything."

Opening the Story

NBC correspondent Roger O'Neil says, "If I can't get you with the first pictures and the first sentence, I've lost you. So, I may spend several hours writing the first sentence, and the rest falls into place."

That luxury of time, however, is usually available only to network correspondents. Reporters at local stations would soon be looking for other jobs if they took two hours to pick their first shots and lead sentences. O'Neil's comment does, however, point out how important it is to get a good lead and strong video at the top of a story.

O'Neil notes that the first sentence is dictated by the first pictures, and the first pictures are dictated by the best pictures. "I can write a story a hundred different ways," he says, "but I'm going to find the best pictures and find a sentence that fits those pictures."

Good Pictures

O'Neil takes issue with those who believe that words are more important than the pictures. He says those who believe that the script should be written first and the pictures added to support the words "should be in the newspaper business. We're in the business of pictures," he adds, "not the business of words."

He notes many reporters "fail to tell the story with pictures and then fill in the words" because they believe they don't have enough time to look at the pictures. "That's an excuse," O'Neil says. "I never write a script until I have looked at the pictures."

O'Neil's colleague, *NBC News* correspondent Bob Dotson, also looks at his pictures before he writes. He described how he and his editor worked on the Carlsbad Cave rescue story (see Chapter 5) in a recreation vehicle that was equipped with editing equipment: "We spun through the tapes as they came up, and I would make log notes . . . in the left-hand column of the script. What I start to do is tell the story visually in my mind—this is what happened, this is where it went, and this is how I finish it. Once I've got that set in my mind, I can sketch that out pretty quick."

Dotson said it then was relatively easy to go over to the right side of his script and write what viewers will not be able to see. "The problem with writing your script first and then trying to paste the pictures to it," he said, "is you end up with wallpaper and it doesn't flow. Suddenly you have a paragraph and no pictures to cover the paragraph."

Dotson said that even when he worked as a local reporter and had to do a couple of stories a day, he still chose his pictures before writing his script. He said it's a "little like learning jujitsu. You learn the system and philosophy of how to approach a story and learn how to do it quickly and well. If you 'write your pictures' first, your story is going to stand out from all the others [reporters] who don't."

60 Minutes correspondent Ed Bradley believes TV news has been "driven too much by pictures and what's available in telling picture stories rather than information." *60 Minutes*, because of its format, relies on a lot of "talking heads" and, Bradley says, "there's nothing wrong with a talking head . . . as long as it's shedding some light on something." Most television reporters and producers find talking heads to be dull and replace the face with video relating to the story. When Bradley was reminded that *60 Minutes* is full of talking heads, he responded: "God bless talking heads."

Good Writing

Former *CBS News* correspondent Richard Threlkeld noted that all good reporters have something in common—they are good writers. "If you are a good writer," he said, "you also must be a good reporter."

Threlkeld believes that to be successful as a TV reporter you "almost have to relearn what you have been taught in school when you had to do term papers and put all your thoughts down on the printed page for people to read." Threlkeld said that it might be obvious that television is a different medium from others but, unfortunately, "this doesn't sink into the brains of most broadcast journalists."

Threlkeld noted that everyone works differently; for example, according to Threlkeld, *CNN News* correspondent Bruce Morton gets "everything together in his head and then he'll sit around for a bit and then he will simply write a script about as fast as it takes me to tell it to you." Threlkeld said the late Charles Kuralt "agonized more," whereas he himself is somewhere in between: "I get all the pictures together and all the printed material I need, and then I write fairly fast."

As for the debate on which is more important, the words or the pictures, Threlkeld said both are important. But, he adds, "I think what most reporters in TV fail to see—and never do see with some exceptions—is how important pictures are to writing." Threlkeld said that while it's important to write well—in a conversational and colloquial style—the pictures, in most cases, must come first. "When you look at them, you must ask yourself 'how can these pictures tell the story?'"

The end result of all this, said Threlkeld, is that reporters end up "underwriting. And most of the best prose in both broadcasting and print is underwritten." Then, like so many others, Threlkeld reminds us that "one of the finest writers of this century, an old journalist named Hemingway, was a master at under-writing." "If you can under-write and let the pictures tell the story," he adds, "you are ahead of the game."

Former *ABC News* correspondent Morton Dean says his approach depends on the story. His approach differs, for example, if he's working on a story and reporting from the scene or has a chance to come back to the studio to work on it. "My preference," he notes, "is to look at the footage and then write the script and make the pictures and sound work for me and inter-ject myself only when necessary."

Dean says that when reporters work with a complicated story, they some-times can't limit it just to the pictures they have. He notes: "You sometimes have to write material for graphics or include standups. You may have infor-mation that is essential to the story that you must get into your script one way or another."

The late Charles Kuralt said, "I believe in never writing a line without knowing exactly what picture I am writing to; so when the script is finished, the story is edited—at least in my head." Kuralt said that during his *On the Road* series, his cameraman Izzy Bleckman "knew never to shoot anything unless I was there taking notes, because we shipped the film unprocessed with the narration, and never even saw it until it was on the air." Kuralt added, "This worked fine, as long as I was there to imagine the shot as Izzy was making it, so I could be sure to work it in."

The following is the script Kuralt wrote in Strafford, Vermont, and sent to his editor at CBS in New York. Along with the narration, he provided direc-tions on the left side of the script and a separate *dopesheet* telling the editor what was on the film. Kuralt said all this detail proves that the "hardest part of every story is putting it together on paper."

pan village Kuralt SOF	This one day in Vermont, the town carpenter lays aside his tools . . . the town doctor sees no patients . . . the shopkeeper closes his shop. Mothers tell their children they'll have to warm up their own dinner. This one day, people in
. . . to Kuralt on camera SOF	Vermont look not to their own welfare, but to that of their town. It doesn't matter that it's been snowing since 4 o'clock this morning. They'll be here. This is town meeting day.
people walking up hill to town meeting	Strafford, Vermont, has grown to a population of 536 since it was char-tered by King George the Third in 1761. Its first town meeting was held in the freedom days, March 1779. And every March for 175 years, the men and women of Strafford have trudged up this hill on the one day of the year

...and pan with one group up to town hall as people pass sign	which is a holiday for democracy. They walk past a sign that says, "The Old White Meeting House. Built in 1799 and consecrated as a place of public worship for all denominations, with no preference for one above another. Since 1801, it has also been in continuous use as a Town Hall."
snow outside, pull back from window to high, wide shot of hall	Here, every citizen may have his say on the question. The question is, will the town stop paying for outside health services. The speaker is a farmer, an elected selectman—David K. Brown, and Farmer Brown says "Yes."
Brown voice under	
Brown on camera...	BROWN SAYS: "I'll tell you the select-men have had some, what I consider unsatisfactory service from them. Last year, we had an individual in town that was in a very deep depres-
faces of people listening	sion and he did not have any immediate family in town and they called upon us to do something about it, and we went and he was trying or
Brown on camera again	thinking about committing suicide. So we called the Orange County mental health, and this was I believe on a Friday night. They said they'd see him Tuesday afternoon. And if we had any problems, take him to Hanover and put him in the emergency room. Now I don't know if we should pay $582.50 for that kind of advice."
others on feet, voice under	They talked about that for half an hour, asking themselves if this money would be well or poorly spent. This is not representative democracy. This is pure democracy, in which every citizen's voice is heard.
moderator	"ALL THOSE IN FAVOR, SIGNIFY BY SAYING 'AYE.'" "AYE." "ALL THAT ARE OPPOSED" "NAY" "I'M GOING TO ASK FOR A STANDING VOTE. ALL THOSE IN FAVOR, STAND PLEASE."

As they stand	It is an old Yankee expression, which originated here, in the town meeting, and has entered the language of free men: "Stand up and be counted." And,
moderator prepares to announce	when the judgment is made, and announced by James Condict, maker of rail fences and moderator of the meeting, the town will abide by the judgment.
he does	THERE ARE 100 VOTES CAST . . . 61 IN FAVOR AND 39 AGAINST. IT THEN BECOMES DELETED FROM THE TOWN BUDGET.
faces in meeting as somebody speaks voice under about street lights	This is the way the founders of this country imagined it would be, that citizens would meet in their own communities to decide directly most of the questions affecting their lives and fortunes. Vermont's small towns have kept it this way. Will or will not Strafford, Vermont, turn off its street lights to save money?
man in audience	PAPER BALLOT! PAPER BALLOT! ANY MEMBER HAS THE RIGHT TO DEMAND A PAPER BALLOT! IS THAT SECONDED? DOESN'T HAVE TO BE SECONDED!
moderator	"PREPARE AND CAST YOUR BALLOTS FOR THIS AMENDMENT."
line of people coming up . . . . . . handing paper ballots to deputy sheriff	If any citizen demands a secret ballot, a secret ballot it must be. Everybody who votes in Vermont has taken an old oath, to always vote his conscience without fear or favor of
CU's hands and ballots	any persons. This is something old, something essential. You tear off a little paper, and on it, you write "yes"
Ballots being counted. We see "Yes" and "No"	or "no." Stafford voted to keep the street lights shining.
Somebody takes a piece of pie	There is pie, baked by the ladies of the PTA. There are baked beans and brown bread, served at Town Meeting

woman dishing up beans (little woman standing beside line of taller people)	by Celia Lane as long as anybody can remember. Then, a little more wood is added to the stove, and a dozen more questions are debated and voted on in the long afternoon. What is really on the menu today is government of the people. Finally came the most routine of all motions, the motion to adjourn.
wood in stove WS meeting	
moderator and crowd	ALL THOSE IN FAVOR SIGNIFY BY SAYING "AYE" (LITTLE AYE). ALL THAT OPPOSE (BIG NAY) . . . THEN WE DON'T ADJOURN AND THE NAYS HAVE IT.
somebody else on feet talking, voice under people out of building into snow . . .	It is heady stuff, democracy. They wanted to go on enjoying it for a while in Strafford today. When finally they did adjourn, and walk out into the snow, it was with the feeling of having preserved something important, something more important than their street lights—their liberty.
. . . downhill . . .	
. . . and camera pans to village	Charles Kuralt, *CBS News*, On the Road to '76 in Vermont.
	dopesheet (The references to ROLLS and feet, and ASA, and STOPS are film terms; film was still being used when Kuralt did this story.)

SOF

Roll 1—Kuralt open, people arriving, about 200 feet.

ALL REMAINING SOF ROLLS ARE PUSH ONE STOP ASA 250

Roll 2—400 SOF—Registering to vote at Town Meeting, Strafford, Vermont . . . call to order by Moderator James Condict . . . pledge of allegiance . . . voting in booths, presidential primary . . . WS room over moderator's shoulder . . . faces . . . one of the selectmen, David K. Brown, farmer, reports on town budget . . . more faces.

Roll 3—400 SOF—crocheting red white and blue sweater . . . Selectman David Brown says Mental Health gives poor service . . . debate on $1,179 for Community Health Services . . . etc.

Roll 4—400 SOF—Ayes and nays can't be distinguished . . . which leads to a standing vote . . . announcement of vote: 61–39 against spending the money . . . nice intercut of wandering child being snatched away from front of room by mother . . . debate on street lights, $1,900 budget item. Farmer Jerry Smith (with beard) says one shines in his eyes at night . . . etc.

Roll 5—400 SOF—On street light question, call for a paper ballot on whether to cut street lighting in half. Details of balloting, hands CU, etc., then counting paper ballots and announcement of result, 59 yes, 82 no, so motion to reduce street lighting defeated . . . break for lunch, pies in foreground . . . home-cooked baked beans and brown bread being dished out by Celia Lane, who has served baked beans at the Town Meetings since anybody can remember . . . high shot of room with eating going on . . . neighborly floor-level eating and chatter . . .

Roll 6—400 SOF—More chit-chat during lunch break . . . janitor feeds more wood into the stove . . . high shot thru window of snow falling, pull back to meeting, repeat several times . . . counting ballots from above . . . faces in audience . . . Gile S. Kendall, farmer, selectman reelected . . . people coming forward to vote, faces in and out of frame.

Roll 7—400 SOF—Vote for second constable. Bob Nutting defeats Lois Smith and Gerald Smith . . . faces in crowd, rack focus young face to old face, etc. discussion of reappraisal of property values . . .

Roll 8—400 SOF—More reappraisal discussion. Girl, pull back to feeding fire. Jerry Smith makes a "You don't need government agencies in Vermont" speech . . . discussion of $750 appropriation to senior citizens center in neighboring town . . . and of radio for car of "civil defense" director . . . voting down adjournment! Sign: "The Old White Meeting House. Built in 1799 and consecrated as a place of public worship for all denominations, with no preference for one above another. Since 1801, it has also been in continuous use as a Town Hall." with people coming and going in front of sign. People leaving, pan down steeple. People down hill and pan to village. Empty town hall after they've all left.

Phil Scheffler, a senior producer for *60 Minutes*, says Kuralt had a "particularly fine eye. He saw things others didn't and saw them very clearly. That's also why he was such a good reporter." Scheffler says the thing that struck you about Kuralt's writing was "how simple it is. It's unadorned. He was able to create a very clear picture in your mind as to what he'd seen."

Organizing the Story

One of the most frustrating orders for most reporters is "keep the story short." *NBC News* correspondent Roger O'Neil says he finds it more challenging to do a short story than a long one. O'Neil believes that the key to writing a tight script is *organization*. He says he is often accused of being "cold or mad at people, or the world," because he is quiet on the car trip back from a story. "I am quiet," O'Neil says, "because I'm thinking about the pictures I saw the photographer take—trying to arrange those pictures in my head. I am quiet because I am thinking about what I have to do when I get back to the station."

O'Neil says too many reporters do not take advantage of that trip back to the station. "They don't think about what they are going to do with the story until they sit down at the typewriter," he notes. "Then they complain they don't have enough time to tell the story because they haven't thought it out."

Reporters certainly should be using that time in the car to organize their thoughts, and it helps to have interviews on audiotape. Every broadcast reporter should carry an audiocassette recorder for this purpose. It is not necessary to have a good-quality recording because the audiotape will not be used for broadcast, only to help the reporter select sound bites. This tip is a great timesaver.

NBC News correspondent Bob Dotson says he uses the car ride both to and from the scene to get organized. "The minute I know that I am going to do a story," he notes, "I start thinking in terms of how I am going to develop it, what questions I would ask, where I would go from point A to B." Dotson adds that on the way back from the scene he listens to the audiotape and selects the sound bites long before he returns to the studio.

Selecting Sound

Dotson says that in addition to good sound bites, he is always looking for good *natural sound*—what a novelist might call mood setters. "What you are really doing in TV is not showing or telling but trying to have people experience what it is like. Sound can help you experience it, and sound can bring your audience back to the TV screen because so much of what we call news just washes over us all the time. But if you stop talking, and you hear a rooster crow, people are going to turn to see the rooster. They will put down the spoon, stop eating dinner, and come to the TV set."

As for sound bites, Dotson says, "I always use sound as an exclamation point. I do not use sound to explain. There just isn't enough time to let the subject explain. In a minute and a half, you have to use several voices to tell all sides of the story. So you, as a professional writer, give the basic information and use the sound bite for emphasis."

Dotson gives this example: "You have a sound bite from someone talking about a picnic. The person says, 'We're going to have a picnic on Friday at one o'clock and we are going to have a band there and it's going to be a great time and we hope you all will come and it's sponsored by the Kiwanis Club.' You take the bite, which is really like an exclamation point—'We're going to have a great time'—and you, as a professional writer, fill in the information that leads up to the sound bite. And the sound bite proves what you just said."

Working with the Video Editor

Dotson compares video editing with rewriting. "It's like a catcher on a baseball team. That's the backstop, and all the other things you have done during the process of putting that story together can either be lost or saved in the editing room. Sometimes the fantasies you had as you were writing your story can be saved by the editor. That's where you are putting it all together—your sound and pictures and words—and editors have to be very hard on the process." They must say: "These symbols move the story forward, and these symbols you put in the basement and show your parents later on, because we don't have time for them."

Dotson adds, "I always look at a news story as a kind of good jazz ensemble. At some point there is a trumpeter, and at some point there is a drummer, and each person has his soul and it's important sometimes that they all play together. That's the same way with a story, and the editor helps reinforce that."

The Voiceover

In a voiceover (V/O), the newscaster or reporter reads copy as the video appears on the screen. Normally, voiceovers are not long because they are usually used to break up a series of packages or to give the anchors some exposure. The following is the script for three short voiceovers used in a newscast produced by WBRZ-TV in Baton Rouge, Louisiana:

Two shot O/C Margaret and Andrea	(Margaret) Updating some of the other stories making news across the nation . . . authorities in Newport News, Virginia, are investigating an accident involving an Amtrak train.
Roll Sony V/O Video of derailed train	(V/O) A dump truck collided with this train at a railroad crossing. The force of the collision sent the engine and all five passenger cars off the tracks.
Video of injured people	The driver of the truck died in the accident . . . about 50 people on the train were hurt, but not seriously.
Wipe to Sony Video of plane wreckage Font: Blevelt Falls Lake Lilesville, N.C	(Andrea V/O) And divers in North Carolina are searching for the bodies of nine people who died when a military transport plane crashed into this lake in North Carolina.

More video of wreckage	The victims were stationed at Fort Polk. They were on a training mission. So far, the cause of the crash is unknown.
Wipe to Sony Kennedy and wife shaking hands with people in Dallas Kennedy motorcade in Dallas Video of people on lawn as Kennedy motorcade goes by	And a citizens' group called Public Citizen is demanding the National Archives release nearly 200 autopsy photos and X-rays of President Kennedy.
	A bill in Congress would require the release of documents pertaining to the assassination, but excludes the autopsy material to protect the Kennedy family's privacy.
ON CAMERA TAG	(Andrea O/C) A spokesman for this citizens' group says the materials should be public record.

Most newscasts use voiceovers along with read stories to fill in the time around packages; voiceovers seldom run longer than 20 or 30 seconds. The first voiceover in the example ran 24 seconds; the second ran 16 seconds; and the third ran 27 seconds. They were separated by *wipes*, an electronic technique that slides one video picture off the screen and replaces it with another—in this case with the opening video of the next story.

The use of the word *Sony* in the left column lets the director know that the video material is in the Sony tape decks. The director's copy of the script would indicate by number which deck plays which tape during the newscast.

The Voiceover-Sound on Tape

As discussed earlier, when a voiceover is used to lead into a sound bite, it is called a V-SOT or V/O-SOT. Here's an example of a V-SOT script:

	Newscaster
V/O Video of police officers at graduation Video of female graduates	Central City's fight against crime got a boost today with the graduation of 45 new officers from the police academy. Among the officers—eleven women. One of them is Ann Black,
Video of Black and family	and she had her own cheering section: her mother and father, her husband, and her three-year-old
Video of Black holding daughter	daughter, Sally. Black's father also is a police officer.

SOT: 05

(SOT/Ann Black)
"It's just a wonderful time . . . to
finally be on the force, like my dad,
and to have everyone I love here to
cheer me on . . . it's just great."

At this point, the anchor could return on camera to do a *tag* to the story or
go back to a *voiceover*, as is the case here:

ANCHOR

V/O
Video of graduates
tossing hats in air

The 45 new officers will not have too
much time to celebrate. They report
for duty in the morning.

V-SOT stories are usually used when a reporter was not assigned to do a
package or the producer decided that the material was not strong enough,
or of enough interest to the audience, to warrant the time necessary for a
package.

Reporter Involvement

Many news directors want to see their reporters' faces in their stories. They
encourage reporters to appear on camera either at the end or in the middle
of their packages. The theory is that the audience should think of the reporters
and anchors as "family," and the more on-air exposure these family members
get, the better management likes it.

NBC correspondent Roger O'Neil says: "It's stupid for network and local
stations to require standups just to get their reporters on the air." The always
outspoken O'Neil adds: "It's ludicrous to take good pictures away just to put
some ugly reporter's face on the air." ABC's Morton Dean and former *CBS
News* correspondent David Culhane agree. Both say they like to stay out of
their stories as much as possible, preferring instead to let the pictures and
other people's words tell the story.

The best reason for a reporter to appear in a story is to help explain it.
Some reporters would argue that should be the only time a reporter is seen
on air. On occasion, a reporter can help the viewer better understand a situation by appearing on camera in the middle of the story. Such a standup
bridge is sometimes useful in tying together two parts of a complicated story,
but it can also be disruptive when a reporter suddenly breaks up the flow of
the story for no practical reason.

Some of the worst examples of reporter involvement occur when the
reporters become a part of the story. Unfortunately, many news directors
have no problem with reporters sledding down hills during a snowstorm or
eating a hot dog at a street festival or lifting weights at the opening of a new
health spa. The late Charles Kuralt, in his book *A Life on the Road*, wrote this
about reporter involvement:

> With respect to my own appearances on camera, we have adopted the
> Tricycle Principle. We were somewhere in the Midwest, watching the local

news on the TV set in the bus before going out to supper. There was a feature about a children's tricycle race, cute little toddlers pedaling away and bumping into one another, an appealing story pretty well-filmed and edited.

Izzy said, "You know what? Before this is over, the reporter is going to ride a tricycle."

"Oh, no" I said. "That would ruin the whole thing."

Sure enough, the reporter signed off in a closeup with a silly grin, the camera pulled back to show that he was perched on a tricycle, and he turned and pedaled clumsily away, making inane what had, until then, been charming. The anchorpeople came on laughing to sign off the show.

The Tricycle Principle is simple: "When doing a tricycle story, don't ride a tricycle." The story is about CHILDREN, dummy, not about you. Keep yourself out of it. Try to control your immodesty.

Some TV audience members think such reporter involvement is cute, however, and that's enough for many news managers. On the other hand, most news directors I've spoken with agree with Kuralt. They will tell you that they discourage such behavior and want reporters involved in their stories only when there is a legitimate reason. For example, it would not be inappropriate for a reporter to demonstrate how to use a new at-home device that measures blood pressure. Doing so could be the best way for the reporter to explain how the new device works.

Summary

One thing reporters find exciting about their job is that they rarely know what's going to happen when they get to work or how the story they've been assigned to cover will turn out. The sound bites may be fascinating and the video colorful, so that the story becomes a good package. But covering news also has its frustrations. An interview may be weak, or some promised video opportunities may not materialize. The story then becomes a voiceover-sound on tape or a voiceover.

Good organization and notes improve the chances that a package will be a success. Reporters should not try to predict the outcome of the story they're working on, but rather should know as much as possible about the subject and the players involved in their assignment when they leave the newsroom. Before they leave the scene, reporters should be certain that they have covered everything they need.

Review Questions

1. Discuss the differences between read stories, voiceovers, voiceover-sound on tape, and packages.
2. Discuss some of the considerations that determine which of the described techniques in this chapter are used to tell certain stories.
3. What are the most popular ways to open and close a package? Discuss the merits of each technique.

4. What do most top broadcast news reporters say about the relative importance of pictures and words in packages?
5. Richard Threlkeld says that all good reporters have something in common. What is it?
6. What factors determine how long a package runs?

Exercises

1. Pick a story out of the newspaper or from the wires, and write a 20-second voiceover. Record the voiceover at your school lab.
2. Pick another story that has some quotes, and script a 30-second V-SOT.
3. Prepare a package about a feature story. Limit it to one minute and 45 seconds and include two talking heads. If your school has the equipment, produce the package.

15 The Interview

One basic method used by reporters to gather information is the interview. Newspaper, radio, and TV journalists use different techniques, but they generally all try to achieve the same end: to find out as much newsmaking information as they can from the person they are interviewing. In broadcast jargon, the interviewee usually is referred to as the talking head, or simply the "head."

Newspaper reporters have the luxury of going into depth in their interviews. Because radio and TV reporters have limited time on the air, they have less time to conduct their interviews. Therefore, they must be selective in their questioning and must be well prepared. This chapter discusses techniques for conducting successful interviews.

Lesley Stahl, co-editor of *60 Minutes* and former chief White House correspondent, was asked if there were any questions that she would never ask and she replied "delving into officials' personal lives." She added, "I've never been convinced that the way a person conducts his personal life has a direct bearing on how he's going to conduct whatever office he's been chosen to fulfill."

TV Guide once described Stahl as "a watchdog with perhaps a streak of pit bull somewhere in her ancestry." When asked why more reporters do not ask difficult questions, she said some think they're in a popularity contest with the public and the most important thing is that the audience likes them. She added, "You're not going to win a popularity contest if you ask questions like, 'Are you a crook?'"

Preparing for the Interview

Reporters should always research the subject and find out as much as possible about the person to be interviewed. Good places to start your investigation are the radio or TV newsroom clip files and audiotape and videotape libraries. Some news organizations also have access to computer database services such as LexisNexis, which indexes national and some regional newspapers, the wire services, and more than 100 magazines and journals. And, of course, there are Google, Yahoo, and other information-providing services on the Internet.

Reporters also must decide before the interview what kind of information they want. Interviews are not always expected to produce news. Some are designed to solicit emotional responses, such as those conducted for a

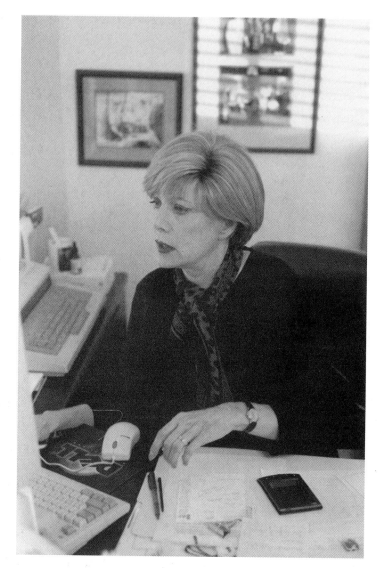

Figure 15-1   Lesley Stahl, *60 Minutes* co-editor and *CBS News* correspondent. (Photo Patrick Pagano/CBS Photo Archive)

human-interest story. Other interviews are attempts to find out more about the newsmaker or, perhaps, his or her family. Reporters might seek such information if, for example, the interviewee had been appointed to some public post or as head of the local hospital.

If a reporter is interviewing the winner of a congressional seat, she is going to be looking for information that is different from what she sought the day before when she interviewed the mother of quadruplets. The reporter will want to ask the congresswoman-elect about her priorities when she gets to Washington, why she thinks her campaign was a success and, perhaps, whether she believes her victory indicates some sort of national trend. When the reporter spoke to the mother of quadruplets, she asked questions about the problems of taking care of four babies, about whether the house is big enough to accommodate the family, and so on.

Phrasing Questions Carefully

Many people interviewed by reporters are shy by nature or intimidated by microphones and cameras. Many others just seem to measure their words carefully. In order to prevent one- and two-word responses, reporters must phrase their questions so they are impossible to answer with a "yes" or "no" or by just a shake of the head.

If you ask a person, "Do you like farming?" you are bound to get a "yes" or "no" answer, but if you ask "What do you like about farming?" you should get a sound bite. If you ask a witness to an auto accident "Did you see what happened?" you might, again, end up with a one-word response. If you ask "What did you see?" you'll most likely get a longer response. Children are particularly likely to give "yes" or "no" answers, so ask them open-ended questions and be patient.

Avoiding Leading Questions

Do not lead the interviewee toward giving a particular response. Some of the best reporters are sometimes guilty of this bad habit. During the Gulf War, a nationally known TV reporter asked a Bush administration official if he was "upset" after viewing pictures of an air raid that showed heavy destruction to a civilian target. The reporter herself clearly *was* upset by the pictures, and phrasing the question in that manner was a disservice for two reasons: (1) it probably influenced many viewers' feelings about the video, and (2) it put the administration official in an uncomfortable situation. If he had said he was *not* upset, he would have appeared callous; if he had said he *was* upset, he might have sounded critical of the military, which may or may not have been fair or accurate. The reporter allowed her personal feelings about the air raid to influence the question. It was a leading question. She should have asked the administration official, "What did you think about those pictures?"

Listening Carefully

Reporters should arrive at an interview with a list of questions that they intend to ask the newsmaker; however, they also must develop a keen habit of listening carefully to the answers and asking follow-up questions. Many inexperienced reporters are so intent on asking their prepared questions that they fail to listen to the answers. They often do not realize that their previous question was not answered fully, or at all. Sometimes, to the embarrassment of all, the reporter asks a question that already has been answered. The astute newsmaker—often anticipating the reporter's next question—sometimes adds additional information to an earlier response. The rude awakening comes when the reporter asks another question on the list and the newsmaker says, "I just answered that."

To avoid falling into such traps, the reporter should put the list of questions to one side and refer to them only when necessary. *CBS News* correspondent Ed Bradley says he always has a list of questions but does not get locked into using it. He says that if he's interviewing someone and that person moves to a subject farther down on his list, he goes with the interviewee because he can then go back and pick up where he was.

The *60 Minutes* correspondent notes that some reporters "come in with an agenda, a list of questions, a predetermined mindset as to where the interview is going to go; they don't hear what it is that people say." He believes listening is important because too many reporters have "a tendency to try to fill space . . . instead of listening to what it is that a person says." Bradley advises interviewers to allow some silence and let the person fill it instead of trying to fill it by themselves.

Another effective technique is to establish direct eye contact with the person being interviewed. It's easier for reporters to concentrate on what people are saying if they look them right in the eye. This habit also establishes good rapport. Maintaining eye contact with newsmakers lets them know that the reporter is listening and interested. If the reporter's eyes drift toward the list of questions, or to the cameraperson, the newsmaker might take that as a signal that he or she has said enough and wait for another question even though he or she might not have finished answering the previous question.

Warming Up the Head

Reporters differ on just how much they should disclose to the interviewee about the line of questioning before the interview starts. The advantage of *warming up* the head is that it gives the person time to collect his or her thoughts, usually ensuring a smoother interview. Without a warm up, the interviewee might be caught by surprise. The person might say, "I had no idea you would ask that; I really don't know the answer" or try unsuccessfully to fake an answer. Warming up an interviewee also tends to put the person more at ease. A relaxed head usually provides a better interview.

Sometimes, however, reporters do not want the interviewee to know the questions in advance because they plan to ask questions about a controversial topic designed to catch the person by surprise. There is no rule against warming up the interviewee, but some reporters are opposed to it. Almost all agree that it should be restricted to situations in which the reporter is looking for noncontroversial information. For example, a reporter would not warm up the head if the questions dealt with charges the person misappropriated funds during an election campaign.

The Tough Questions

Susan Morris, who conducts workshops on interviewing techniques, believes that "no one enjoys asking embarrassing questions. It's uncomfortable and difficult." But she adds: "I've learned that a certain toughness is required. While excessive pressure can destroy an interview, it's important to keep in mind that you are there to get answers, not to create a good impression. After the interview," she points out, "you have to write a news story, not a press release."

Morris also says it helps to blame the tough questions on other people. For example, questions can be phrased as follows: "Today's newspaper reports that . . . What is your response?" or "Some of your critics say . . . Could you clarify the situation?" She says that "by attributing the charges to another source, you make it clear they are not coming from you personally."

CBS's Lesley Stahl, as we mentioned earlier, established a reputation over the years, particularly when she was a White House correspondent, of asking tough questions. She says her attitude is that public officials in our system are obliged to explain and justify their policies, decisions, and actions. She says she is proud of being tenacious. "I liked being called tough. But," she added, "I also was being called impolite and I didn't like that." She says the pressure of the clock is why so many interviewers get the reputation for being discourteous. Stahl said the time is being eaten up (by the interviewees' filibustering) and you're still on question two. "It's a constant balancing act between moving it along and being rude."

TV Guide once ran a picture of Stahl sneering with a line saying, "Her questions range from sharp to stinging." Stahl says she developed a lot of her interviewing skills when she was anchoring *Face the Nation*. She says she and the producers would try to guess what the newsmaker might say to various questions, then fashion comebacks. Stahl said she never went on the air without a thorough blueprint. The trick, though, she added, was not to stick with the blueprint but to use it as a backup security system that would leave her free to listen and point out when a question was ducked. Stahl said that many officials actually took lessons in how to avoid answering, how to wriggle out from under tough questions. Stahl says administration officials often admitted that their goal in coming on *Face the Nation* was to escape without making any news.

The Surprise Questions

CBS News correspondent Mike Wallace is probably the reporter most identified with surprise questions—those that catch the interviewee off guard. Wallace's seemingly relaxed, easygoing style tends to disarm the individual he's questioning. His look of apparent bewilderment and confusion should, by now, warn interviewees that Wallace is ready to spring a trap, but the people he interviews keep taking the bait. The scene is familiar: There's a pause while the individual tries to figure out how Wallace knew enough about the person or the subject matter to ask the question that now must be answered.

Is such interviewing fair? John Spain, former station manager for WBRZ-TV in Baton Rouge, Louisiana, who has a distinguished record for investigative reporting, says, "I try to be honest and fair, but I'm not obligated to tell someone we are investigating everything we have come to talk about. If we did, he probably wouldn't do the interview."

Spain says that if the individual says he or she will only talk about certain subjects, then Spain has to decide if he still wants the interview. "But most people will talk to you," says Spain, "because they don't think they have done anything wrong and everything will be OK as long as they can tell their side of the story. They do, and that's when we ask them the tough questions that they didn't know we knew."

Spain said the long-standing rule followed by lawyers, "Don't ask any questions unless you already know the answers," also applies to reporters. "We go as well prepared as we can," he says.

Spain adds that people "generally underestimate our knowledge, resources, and ability to look into their actions. Why," he asks, "do people continue to talk to *60 Minutes*? It's because they totally underestimate what the media has been able to obtain in terms of research and background."

Questions to Ask Before the Interview

In a noninvestigative situation, the main reason for interviewing people is to get information that is generally not known to the reporter and the public. Once the cameras and audio recorders are rolling, reporters shouldn't spend time asking people how long they have been employed, where they were educated, whether they are married, or whether they have any children. If that sort of information is important, it should be learned informally before the actual interview begins. You might want to include such information in the introductory sentence of your story, but you would rarely waste valuable air time with video- or audiotaped responses on these subjects. The recorded questions and answers should be restricted to those that gather information about what the newsmaker knows or thinks about an idea or issue or, perhaps, to those that capture emotions.

Keeping Control of the Interview

Sometimes reporters inadvertently allow newsmakers to take control of an interview. Politicians are particularly skilled at manipulating interviews. For example, some politicians take a couple of minutes to answer a question, whereas others ask reporters how long a response they want and then give an answer of exactly that length. Because politicians and others accustomed to working with broadcast journalists know that reporters think in terms of sound bites, they usually try to express their views in about 12 seconds to make sure their answers are not edited.

A problem arises when the newsmaker takes too long to respond. The choice then is either to interrupt or to allow the head to finish the answer and then re-ask the question, saying, "That was great, but could you cover that same ground again in about half the time?" Most often the individual is happy to comply, which simplifies the editing process and results in a more natural-sounding response. Editing a sound bite down from a minute to 20 seconds sometimes alters the speaker's inflections.

Some newsmakers try to mislead reporters. They avoid answering some questions and skirt around others. Unless challenged, newsmakers often dominate interview situations. If the head doesn't answer the question or gives only a partial answer, the reporter should try to follow up. The news-

Figure 15-2
Mike Wallace reports for CBS's weekly news show *60 Minutes.*

maker often then gives largely the same answer phrased differently. The reporter then needs to decide whether to ask the question a third time, or perhaps to say to the newsmaker, "I'm sorry, but you still have not answered my question." When the response is, "That's all I'm going to say on the subject," that in itself makes a statement. The reporter might then note in the story, "When pressed to answer the question several times, he refused to elaborate on the original answer."

Asking Enough Questions

It takes time to develop the skill of knowing when you have asked enough questions during an interview. Reporters just entering the field tend to ask too many questions, usually because they are understandably insecure. As reporters gain experience, however, they usually start to develop a feel for when they have collected enough information.

Because time is precious to a broadcast reporter, asking too many questions means that the reporter spends more time than necessary at the scene or on the phone. That leaves less time for working on other stories and complicates the editing process.

Successful reporters who have researched the topic and the newsmaker know when they have just the right amount of material on tape. Because they have an idea of what information they hoped to hear, they know which sound bites they will probably end up using, and they also have a fairly accurate idea of how long those bites will run.

Experienced broadcast journalists often know immediately after the interview is over how they are going to put their stories together. With practice, reporters develop a habit of mentally processing information, sound bites, and pictures in a way that allows them to organize their material quickly.

"Did I Forget Something?"

The pressure of conducting interviews quickly can sometimes cause reporters to miss important information. It is often a good idea for the reporter to ask the interviewee if he or she would like to add anything or to ask candidly if the reporter might have missed anything important. It is surprising how often the response is, "Well, as a matter of fact, I probably should tell you . . ."

Off the Record

One frustration of being a reporter is being told: "I'll discuss that with you only if you promise not to use it." When the tape recorders and cameras are turned off, the newsmaker sometimes reveals what turns out to be the best part of the interview. That information—even if it is off the record—is often useful to reporters because it can put them on a trail that might lead to other people who will reveal the same information for the record.

Reporters *must* honor any off-the-record agreement. A reporter who breaks that promise is guilty of a serious breach of ethics. This long-held tradition was tested in January 1995 on the *CBS News* magazine, *Eye to Eye*, hosted by Connie Chung. During an interview with 68-year-old Kathleen Gingrich, the mother of the House Speaker, Newt Gingrich, Chung "tricked" Mrs. Gingrich into admitting that her son once referred to First Lady Hillary Clinton as a "bitch."

Chung did not actually tell Mrs. Gingrich that they were "speaking off the record," but it was close enough to cause a major debate among journalists. During the interview, Chung asked Mrs. Gingrich what the Speaker thought of President Clinton. "What has Newt told you about President Clinton?" was the actual question, and Mrs. Gingrich responded "Nothing. And I can't tell you what he said about Hillary."

That remark was too good to be true, and Chung could not resist following it up, as any good reporter would do; however, the ethical issue came into play when Chung told the elderly woman: "Why don't you just whisper it to me, just between you and me." Some people maintain that when Chung said "just between you and me," she made an off-the-record contract with Mrs. Gingrich even if she did not use those specific words. Mrs. Gingrich took the bait and whispered, "[Hillary Clinton's] a bitch. About the only thing [Newt] ever said about her. I think they had some meeting, you know, and she takes over." Chung asked, "She does?" and Mrs. Gingrich continued, "Oh, yeah, but with Newty, she can't."

A large segment of the journalism community and journalism educators believe that Connie Chung should have known better than to ask Mrs. Gingrich to share this information with millions of Americans when she thought she was having a "just between you and me" discussion. As bad as Chung's behavior was, however, it was not nearly as irresponsible as the actions of the show's producers. The so-called whispered conversation between Chung and Mrs. Gingrich was actually amplified in the control room, so there was no doubt what was said. But the real travesty came later when the executives in control of *Eye to Eye* decided not only to leave the offensive remark in the taped interview but also promoted it on CBS before the program actually aired.

Commenting on Chung's tactics, the *Sacramento Bee* asked, "Remember when CBS covered news?" The paper said that Chung obviously "set up Mrs. Gingrich . . . and Hillary Clinton was done a great disservice."

Chung defended herself by claiming that Mrs. Gingrich should have known better than to make the comment because of the obvious cameras, lights, and microphones; however, the *Sacramento Bee* said that even if that was true, "such a blatant abuse" of the off-the-record arrangement that was implied "mocks the process." The paper added, "As it is, reporters are ranked with used-car salesmen and ambulance-chasing lawyers . . . thanks, Connie, for enhancing our stature within the tar pit."

The *Bee* said that it's not that Chung does not know better because "she has been at the game too long and she got where she is because she's good. . . . It's distasteful to see her so willing to cross the line between news and entertainment."

Curbing Nods and Smiles

Television reporters must be concerned about their facial expressions and head movements during an interview, particularly in a studio situation when two or more cameras are being used. Limiting this natural tendency is also important in field situations when listening shots of the reporter (called *reversals*) are being taken for editing purposes. It's permissible for reporters to smile or to nod their heads in agreement during an interview about a non-controversial subject; however, when the issue is controversial and involves a subject with more than one point of view, a reporter cannot be shown expressing agreement or disagreement. A smile or frown or nod could send a wrong signal to an audience. The question of credibility and objectivity immediately comes into question.

For example, to protest the Gulf War, some students managed to get onto the CBS *Evening News* set with Dan Rather. To Rather's credit, he ignored the whole incident and went on with the newscast; however, at one affiliate station that replayed the incident, the anchor shook her head in obvious disgust as she came back on camera. She compromised her objectivity. Regardless of how she personally felt about the invasion of the CBS studio, she should have kept it to herself.

The Phone Interview

Radio reporters have the option of conducting many of their interviews on the phone. TV reporters use the phone only as a last resort because interviews without pictures are weak.

One disadvantage of the phone interview is that it's sometimes difficult to know when the newsmaker has finished giving an answer. Unless reporters listen carefully, they might interrupt the answer before it is complete, which sometimes makes editing the sound bites difficult. When you realize you might have missed something, apologize and ask the person to repeat the answer.

Phone interviews should only be used when it is impossible to interview the individual in person. It sounds unprofessional to conduct an interview on the phone with the mayor or someone else in your city or town when you could hop in a car and go to the person's office. Phone interviews are most effective when used to reach newsmakers in another part of the country or overseas. Such interviews demonstrate to the audience that the station is making a special effort to cover the news.

Checking Facts

Some responses during an interview may not sound right. If that happens, reporters should tell the newsmaker that something is puzzling them or that they do not quite understand the answer. If the answers still do not sound true or are confusing, the reporters should check the information as soon as possible. Reporters could try contacting other sources who might have the same information or be doing some research in the newsroom files, the library, or computer databases. If the information cannot be verified, reporters should explain that in the story. For example:

> The head of the Newtown Power Company said there had never been an accident at the plant in the two years since it opened until today, when four people were seriously injured. We were unable to reach a union representative to verify the statement.

Some Other Tips

Susan Morris of the University of Pittsburgh has these other interview suggestions:

1. Develop a technique of asking short questions that get right to the point.
2. Phrase the questions without apologies and in a matter-of-fact manner. Avoid beginning a question with "I hate to ask you this, but . . ."
3. Pause between questions even when dealing with less volatile subjects. You are likely to get more thoughtful answers.
4. If a person is hedging, take time to explain what the information is being used for. Explain that you do not have an editorial position.

Check Out Charlie

Students and beginning reporters who want to learn how to improve their interviewing skills should watch Charlie Rose at work. His hourly weeknight interview program on PBS is the best of its kind on television. Rose, an Emmy Award-winning interviewer, who also takes on assignments for *60 Minutes Two*, entered television journalism full-time in 1974, when he became man-

Figure 15-3   Charlie Rose with Rudolph Giuliani, Former Mayor of New York City. (Courtesy Shaun Townley/"Charlie Rose")

aging editor of the PBS series *Bill Moyers' International Report*. He continued to work with Moyers on several more of the veteran journalist's highly regarded PBS programs, and then in 1984 he began anchoring the *CBS News* late night program *Nightwatch* and hosted that show for six years.

Rose said that if it were not for that show he would not have his current program on PBS. He admits to making a mistake in 1990 when he left CBS to anchor *Personalities*, a syndicated program produced by Fox. He quit after six weeks when he realized that his producers were mostly interested in tabloid-type news.

After that unfortunate experience, Rose lucked out, signing on with PBS's affiliated station Thirteen/WNET-TV in New York City.

He recalled how he sold his concept for a talk show to CH 13 management: "My mission is that talking heads, done well, can be engaging television and can attract an audience." Management went along. The formula worked and his program is now broadcast on more than 200 PBS affiliates.

Rose says he "sort of came of age as a broadcaster in local television in the 1970s when he worked for WTTG-TV in Washington and WLS in Chicago, and finally, at KXAS in Dallas-Ft. Worth where he actually was hired as program manager. Although the station had no budget for a talk show, Rose was offered a time-slot for what was to become *The Charlie Rose Show*. Recalling those days, Rose said all the responsibility for the program was on him. He was working alone; he produced the show, found the guests, and did all the research. He called it "an extraordinary time." Rose eventually moved the program to the nation's capital where it was broadcast on the NBC station, WRC-TV and was nationally syndicated. As the cliché goes, the rest is history.

It's obvious to those who watch *The Charlie Rose Show* that those days in the 1970s when he mostly had to rely on himself to do his interview program provided an excellent foundation for what was to come. The techniques demonstrated each night exemplify what is obviously a lot of serious reading and research along with a strong curiosity about the various worlds he finds so enjoyable in exploring. Whether it be a top politician, scientist, movie star, or musician, Rose keeps the audience engaged. The fact that he is extremely intelligent, of course, doesn't hurt.

Summary

To conduct a good interview, you must prepare for it. Do some research to find out as much as you can about the person you will be interviewing. Decide on the kind of information you want, and choose your questions accordingly.

Remember to listen carefully during an interview. Make sure your questions are answered to your satisfaction. If they aren't, say so, and follow up on your questions. Don't be used. Try to maintain control of the interview. If you permit it, the interviewee will often take over. Keep to your objectives; don't let the head go off on tangents.

Finally, the most important thing to remember about interviews is that they are not necessarily a reliable source of accurate information because those being interviewed want to be perceived in the best light. Often, interviewees are hiding something from you. Within reason, you should try to find out what they're hiding and be sure to check all facts they do disclose.

Review Questions

1. Why must radio and TV reporters be more selective than their newspaper colleagues in choosing questions to ask in their interviews?
2. How should you prepare for an interview before you leave the station? Give some examples.
3. It's always a good idea to prepare a list of questions for an interview, but there also are dangers. Explain.
4. How should you phrase questions to make sure you get complete answers?
5. What kind of trouble can reporters fall into if they do not listen intently to the person they're interviewing?
6. Discuss the pros and cons of warming up the person you're interviewing.
7. Discuss tough and surprise questions.
8. What are the advantages and disadvantages of off-the-record comments?
9. Why must reporters be aware of their body language during an interview?

Exercises

1. Interview a faculty member in a department other than your own. Before doing so, however, find out as much as you can about the individual, and turn in those notes, along with a story based on your interview.

2. Introduce yourself to a student whom you've never met, and conduct an interview. Write a story or produce a package about the person.

3. Read through your local newspaper, and pick someone in your community who is in the news. Interview the person, and then produce a wraparound report or package.

16 Collecting Information from Documents

Although the interview is the most common method of gathering information, it is not always the most reliable. Most spot news stories—fires, accidents, natural disasters, crime—usually can be covered with a few quick sound bites and video that support the reporter's story. But if the story is more complex or interviews fail to provide all the answers, reporters must look to other sources of background information. This chapter explores the many documents available to reporters to provide such information.

Public Records and the "Sunshine Laws"

One freedom people enjoy in a democracy is the openness of society. Very little goes on in public life that is not recorded in one way or another. At times, however, those in public office attempt to cover up some of their activities. They can, and often do, complicate the reporter's efforts to uncover information. Persistent journalists are often able to circumvent such attempts at secrecy by examining public records. Reporters also have another strong weapon—the Freedom of Information Act (FOIA).

Congress passed the FOIA in 1966, allowing the public access to records held by federal agencies of the executive branch. Since then, all 50 states have passed similar laws that permit the public to examine most records maintained by state and local governments. The freedom of information laws have been dubbed the "sunshine laws" because they are designed to shed light on the workings of government; however, that light hasn't always shined brightly. Government agencies often refuse to disclose public records to private individuals or to journalists. The federal government, for example, has often claimed that revealing certain information would threaten national security. The issue was usually not the nation's security but information that would prove embarrassing to the agency or bureaucrat involved.

With that in mind, Congress amended the FOIA in 1974 and 1976, requiring federal agencies to release documents to the public unless the agencies could show some valid reason for not doing so. Nine exemptions were added to the FOIA, but the ones used most pertain to national security and foreign policy, advice and recommendations made within a federal agency, unwarranted invasion of privacy, files dealing with criminal cases that are current or pending, and trade secrets.

Because state "sunshine laws" vary, reporters seeking information from a state or local government office must examine that state's law before filing.

Filing an FOIA Request

The first thing a reporter must do when seeking government information is determine which federal agency has the information being sought. Sometimes, a telephone call to the agency is enough to produce the information. If not, the reporter must then file an FOIA request in writing. The request should be written on the news organization's letterhead, and it should include the following:

1. An opening sentence making it clear that the letter deals with a Freedom of Information Act request.
2. An offer to pay reasonable fees for reproduction of records. (Some news organizations prefer to list an amount they are willing to pay, say $50, rather than use the term "reasonable amount.")
3. A request that the fees be waived because the information would benefit the public. (An optional statement indicating how the information would be beneficial increases the likelihood of the waiver being granted.)
4. A specific description of the documents being requested, including the actual titles of the documents, if they are known.
5. A reminder that, by law, the agency has 10 days to provide the information requested or to explain why it is denying the request.
6. Some reporters like to inquire whether any other government agencies have requested the same information. This "fishing expedition" sometimes provides some unexpected information that's helpful.

It is a good idea to send the letter by certified mail and to request a return receipt. The envelope should indicate "FOIA Request" or "To the Attention of the FOIA Officer." Although the FOIA states that the agency has 10 days to respond to the request, it also allows the agency to take more time as long as it informs the reporter. Many agencies assign a number to the request, which should be used in any future contacts with the agency. A telephone call to the agency sometimes speeds up responses. If the agency does not reply within a reasonable time—two or three weeks—the reporter should send another letter, again reminding the agency of the time limits.

If an FOIA request is denied, the requester can file an appeal with the agency, which must be answered within 20 days. If that fails, the reporter can go to court to try to obtain the information—a costly and often lengthy endeavor; however, the threat of a lawsuit sometimes can convince an agency to release the information.

FOIA requests filed by investigative reporter Mark Lagerkvist, formerly of News 12 Long Island, are reproduced in Figures 16-1 through 16-6.

The information obtained by Lagerkvist required an exchange of 10 letters with the New York State Department of Health; however, the correspondence made it possible for him to break a story about certain health maintenance organizations (HMOs) that reward doctors who do not refer patients to specialists, hospitals, and other providers.

Lagerkvist said a family physician in one major HMO can "earn" more than $50,000 a year in bonuses by restricting referrals. "These 'bargains' may compromise the medical decisions that affect millions of Americans and their access to health care services," writes Lagerkvist.

The News 12 Long Island reporter worked six months on the secret deals of HMOs. The result was a four-part series and half-hour documentary revealing that 11 of Long Island's 12 HMOs reward doctors who limit referrals or penalize those who do not. Because of space constraints, only one part of the four-part series is reproduced in this book.

Lagerkvist won first place in the National Press Club Consumer Journalism Award competition for the series. For earlier reports, he won major national journalism awards from United Press International (UPI), Investigative Reporters & Editors (IRE), and the Scripps-Howard Foundation. He has also received more than 30 regional and state awards from the Associated Press (AP), the Radio and Television News Directors Association (RTNDA), and a variety of major press clubs. During his 20-year career, he has enjoyed equal success as a television and newspaper reporter.

Lagerkvist said the one thing that concerned him most about the HMO story was that patients rarely were informed of the financial incentives that doctors received. He also noted that patients were not warned about how the arrangements could affect the judgment of their physicians.

You will notice that Lagerkvist's script format is just the opposite of the traditional split page—the technical information on the left and the narration on the right. Because Lagerkvist's stories are all prepackaged, this script is used only by the reporter in putting the story together; it's not used by a director in the control room. It is not shown on the teleprompter, which, of course, could not handle a script in which the narration appears on the left side.

HMO #1	
Lena Lange of Deer Park had cancer . . . She says her doctor told her no test was needed . . .	Lange
LANGE: "You know, they were playing with my life . . ." (:03)	Lena Lange HMO patient
(BLIP) Hazel Taus of East Islip was in danger of going blind in one eye . . . She says her doctor said the condition was not serious . . .	*HMO-47/13:18 H. Taus
TAUS: "They would let me lose the sight in my eye rather than give me a referral . . ." (:03) (BLIP)	Hazel Taus HMO patient HMO-39/12:51
As a newborn, Luke Kube had a serious infection . . . Doctors told the family not	Luke Kube

to worry . . . But by the
time Luke received the
care he needed, it was too
late . . .

D.KUBE: "I think it could   Diane Kube
have been totally avoided   HMO patient's mother
by a simple blood test."   HMO-41/19:19
(:04)

(BLIP)
These are more than just   STANDUP
three isolated cases of
questionable medical care
. . . They are clues to a
hidden danger that may
affect you and millions of
other Americans . . .
Under the guise of health
care reform, many doctors
can profit by restricting
the care their patients
receive . . . And for
patients, the bottom line
may be deadly . . .

(FLATLINE)
On Long Island, more   Clinic footage
than a half-million
patients belong to HMOs,
health maintenance
organizations . . . But few
are told of the secret
deals between HMOs and
their doctors . . . For six
months, News 12   Graphic #1 w/font
investigated those deals . . .
We found that 11 of the
12 HMOs on Long Island
reward doctors who limit
the cost of medical care
provided to their
patients . . .

In some HMOs, doctors   Graphic #1
may earn bonuses by   w/1st effect
keeping their patients
away from expensive tests
and medical services . . .
In other HMOs, doctors   Graphic #1
may be financially   w/2nd effect

penalized for sending
patients to specialists or
hospitals . . .

RELMAN: "It's certainly   Arnold Relman, M.D.
unethical. And I think it   N. Engl. J. Med.
ought to be made illegal.   HMO-15/5:25
I think arrangements of
that kind ought to be
against the law because it
provides powerful economic
incentives for doctors to
act in an unprofessional
way." (:15)

News 12 discovered those   U.S. Healthcare
incentives can change a   charts
doctor's income by
10,000, 20,000 or more
than 50,000 dollars a
year . . .

HIMMELSTEIN: "Patients   David Himmelstein, MD
ought to know that when   Harvard Medical School
they don't get to see a   HMO-23/1:27:05
specialist, the doctor
makes more money. They
ought to know exactly
how much money that is."
(:09)

Instead, patients know   HMO-doctor contracts
little or nothing about
these deals . . . There are
no laws requiring New
York HMOs or doctors to
tell patients about the
incentives . . .

J. KUBE: "The brochures   James Kube
make it sound like the   HMO patient's father
service is excellent. But,   HMO-42/36:55
of course, they don't
mention anything about
bonuses or kickbacks or
whatever it might be."
(:07)

The Kube family belonged   HIP I.D.
to the Health Insurance   (footage or graphic)

Plan of Greater New York—better known as H-I-P or HIP . . . With nearly one million members, it is the state's largest HMO . . . HIP is a non-profit company . . . But the care is provided through for-profit groups of doctors that work exclusively for HIP . . .	HIP docs at work
JAMPOL: "It's a very close and symbiotic relationship." (:03)	Jesse Jampol, M.D. HIP HMO-35/2:56
HIP offers bonuses to the medical groups . . . It is a cash incentive for the doctors to limit the amount of hospital care that patients receive . . .	HIP docs at work
JAMPOL: "When the group meets or beats its targets, it is entitled to get a portion of the savings." (:07)	Jampol SOT HMO-36/19:10
The bonuses can equal up to 10% of the doctor's income . . . A doctor with a $100,000 salary can make an extra $10,000 a year . . . The key is to keep HIP patients out of the hospital . . .	$$$ graphic w/fonts
J. KUBE: "I can't believe they get paid bonuses for stuff like that." (:04) Like most HMOs, HIP does not tell patients about its private deals with doctors . . .	J. Kube SOT HMO-42/36:25 HIP at work
LAGERKVIST: "Is there any direct disclosure of that?"	Jampol SOT HMO-36/32:19

JAMPOL: "No, there isn't.
That's an internal
functioning of the plan . . ."

JAMPOL: "I don't see   HMO-36/32:44
that it would do anybody
any good."

J. KUBE: "I wouldn't have   J. Kube SOT
taken the insurance if I   HMO-42/36:10
had known that at the
time." (:04)

Seven years ago, Luke   STANDUP
Kube was born at Syosett   at hospital
Community Hospital . . .
The parents soon realized
something was wrong with
their newborn son . . .

D. KUBE: "I noticed he   D. Kube SOT
was jaundiced. And I   HMO-41/2:25
mentioned it to the nurse,
and she said she would
check with the doctor
and have the doctor come
and look." (:06)

But without test or   Luke Kube
treatment, Luke was
discharged from the
hospital by an HIP
doctor . . .

D. KUBE: "I think they   D. Kube SOT
should have done the   HMO-41/18:46
blood test before we left
the hospital . . ." (:02)

During the next week,   HIP clinic at
Luke's condition did not   Ronkonkoma
improve . . . According to
the parents, a doctor at
this HIP center was
reluctant to send Luke
back to a hospital for the
test . . . After two office
visits and several phone
calls, the Kubes finally

refused to take no for an
answer . . .

D. KUBE: "At that point, I had to insist that they do this test because I couldn't take him home that way anymore." (:09)	D. Kube SOT HMO-41/13:16
The hospital test showed that Luke's blood contained dangerously high levels of a toxic pigment called bilirubin . . . In newborns, too much bilirubin can destroy brain cells . . .	Blood test shots
The Kubes believe that's why Luke has cerebral palsy . . . The infection was not treated until their son was 10 days old . . . And now he is unlikely to ever lead a normal life . . .	Luke Kube
J. KUBE: "With a simple blood test, I think this whole situation could have been avoided . . ." (:06)	J. Kube SOT HMO-42/32:04
HIP and the doctors refused to comment on this case . . . In court, the doctors denied any blame . . . But they paid a large malpractice settlement to pay for Luke's future needs . . .	Luke Kube
HIP denies that its bonus system compromises the medical care its doctors provide to patients . . .	Jampol B-roll
JAMPOL: "We have in place a number of mechanisms to make sure the patient gets the appropriate care." (:06)	Jampol SOT HMO-36/27:22

And HIP contends it only gets more complaints because it has more patients than other HMOs . . .	
JAMPOL: "I don't think that the number of complaints against HIP are unusual."	Jampol SOT HMO-36/35:32
But according to state records, HIP gets more than its share of complaints . . . One-fourth of the HMO members in New York belong to HIP . . . Yet last year, HIP was cited for two-thirds of all HMO violations and deficiencies issued by the state health and insurance departments . . .	Complaint files
If this looks bad on paper, you should see it in real life . . . And how it affects real people—like Luke Kube and his family . . .	Luke Kube & family
D. KUBE: "This is the way he is. And 'what if'? I can't think about 'what if' anymore . . ." (:06) HMO-41/23:29	D. Kube SOT HMO-41/23:29 D. Kube SOT

Lagerkvist said the HMO investigation could not have been done without public records. He said that some of those records were found with the help of the FOIA, but "we also got some without using the law. They give us certain documents," he said, "because they know that we can get them . . . so they give them to us."

Lagerkvist conducted other investigations on HMOs in Florida and New Jersey. "Over the years," he said, "I learned about secret deals and conflicts of interest in HMOs, and my news director wanted to see if we could duplicate what we did elsewhere." As investigative reporters are quick to tell you, if you can find out about the "bad guys" in one market, there's a good chance you can find them in other communities. Lagerkvist did.

But he said it was "like pulling teeth. Everyone was uncooperative . . . it took weeks and months to get information from them . . . the HMOs did not want to discuss anything." He said the New York State Department of Health did give him some basic information filed by HMOs, but they also "held back a lot."

LONG ISLAND

One Media Crossways
Woodbury, New York 11797

Telephone: 516/496-1766

April 28, 1994   *TRANSMITTED BY FAX*

Don McDonald
FOIL Officer
NYS Dept. of Health
Albany, NY

Dear Mr. McDonald:

Under the provisions of the state Freedom of Information Law, I am seeking access to the following records:

All Statements of Deficiency and Plans of Correction from 1990 to present for the following Health Maintenance Organizations: Aetna, ChoiceCare, CIGNA, Empire, HIP, Managed Health, Metlife, Oxford, Prudential, Sanus, Travelers and U.S. Healthcare.

Please call me at 516/496-1299 when the files are available for review. Upon review, I may request photocopies of certain records.

Sincerely,

Mark Lagerkvist

c. Peter Slocum

Figure 16-1 FOIA request filed by investigative reporter Mark Lagerkvist of News 12 Long Island.

STATE OF NEW YORK
DEPARTMENT OF HEALTH

Corning Tower   The Governor Nelson A. Rockefeller Empire State Plaza   Albany, New York 12237

Mark R. Chassin, M.D. M.P.P., M.P.H.
  Commissioner

May 3, 1994

Paula Wilson
  Executive Deputy Commissioner

Mark Lagerkvist
NEWS 12 - Long Island
1 Media Crossways
Woodbury, New York 11797

Dear Mr. Lagerkvist:

RE: 94-05-023

This will acknowledge receipt of your April 28, 1994 request for copies of documents under the Freedom of Information Law regarding SODs/POCs from 1990 to the present for select HMOs.

We have forwarded your request to appropriate Department program units to identify documents that are responsive to your request and which can be made available under the provisions of the New York State Freedom of Information Law.

We estimate that it will take approximately 20 days to complete your request or determine the availability of documents responsive to your request.

A fee of $.25 per page has been established by the New York State Department of Health for photocopies and/or data printouts.

When the information or documents have been obtained, we will call and make an appointment for you to come in for access. When you come in for access, you should arrange to make the copies yourself and make payment that day. At that time, you can also look over the documents we had previously copied for you regarding FOIL #94-04-200.

Sincerely,

Donald Macdonald

Donald Macdonald
Records Access Officer

Figure 16-2   Response to Lagerkvist's FOIA request from New York State Department of Health.

NEWS 12 LONG ISLAND

One Media Crossways
Woodbury, New York 11797

Telephone 516/496-1766

May 24, 1994   *TRANSMITTED BY FAX*

Donald McDonald
Records Access Officer
NYS Dept. of Health
Albany, NY

Dear Mr. McDonald:

Under the provisions of the state Freedom of Information Law, I am requesting access to certain contracts between HMOs and primary care providers.

I've previously discussed the logistics of this request with Elizabeth McFarland, Bureau of Alternative Delivery Systems. And in an attempt to avoid an unnecessarily burdensome request, I am narrowing the scope to the following HMO/primary provider contracts:

HIP: Three recent contracts between HIP and its primary physician-group providers in Nassau or Suffolk counties.

SANUS: Three recent contracts between Sanus and primary care providers for the HMO's "Sanus 65" Medicare plan in Suffolk or Nassau counties. Plus two recent contracts between Sanus and primary care providers for its "commercial" plans in Suffolk or Nassau counties.

MANAGED HEALTH: The most recent contract between Managed Health and CHP, its sole group-provider.

U.S. HEALTHCARE: Three recent contracts between USHC and primary care providers in Suffolk or Nassau counties.

Page - 1

Figure 16-3 Lagerkvist's follow-up letter seeking additional information under the FOIA.

HEALTHNET (EMPIRE): Three recent contracts between Empire's HealthNet and primary care providers in Suffolk or Nassau counties.

AETNA: Three recent contracts between Aetna and primary care providers in Suffolk or Nassau counties.

CHOICECARE: Three recent contracts between ChoiceCare and primary care providers in Suffolk or Nassau counties.

CIGNA: Three recent contracts between Cigna and primary care providers in Suffolk and Nassau counties.

METLIFE: Three recent contracts between MetLife and primary care providers in Suffolk and Nassau counties.

OXFORD: Three recent contracts between Oxford and primary care providers in Suffolk and Nassau counties.

PRUCARE: Three recent contracts between PruCare and primary care providers in Suffolk and Nassau counties.

TRAVELERS: Three recent contracts between Travelers and primary care providers in Suffolk and Nassau counties.

In all, this request encompasses a sample of three dozen HMO/primary care provider contracts. My original idea was to request access to all HMO/provider contracts, but my conversations with Ms. McFarland led to this proposed compromise.

Please call me at 516/496-1299 to let me know when some or all of these records are available for inspection. If you have any questions or suggestions, please don't hesitate to call.

Sincerely,

Mark Lagerkvist
News 12 Long Island

Figure 16-3 (continued)   Lagerkvist's follow-up letter seeking additional information under the FOIA.

STATE OF NEW YORK
DEPARTMENT OF HEALTH

Corning Tower   The Governor Nelson A. Rockefeller Empire State Plaza   Albany, New York 12237

May 27, 1994

Mark R. Chassin, M.D. M.P.P., M.P.H.
Commissioner

Paula Wilson
Executive Deputy Commissioner

Mark Lagerkvist
News 12 - Long Island
One Media Crossways
Woodbury, New York 11797

Dear Mr. Lagerkvist:

RE: 94-05-176

This will acknowledge receipt of your May 24, 1994 request for access to documents under the Freedom of Information Law.

We have forwarded your request to appropriate Department program units to identify documents that are responsive to your request and which can be made available under the provisions of the New York State Freedom of Information Law.

We estimate that it will take approximately 30 days to complete your request or determine the availability of documents responsive to your request.

A fee of $.25 per page has been established by the New York State Department of Health for photocopies and/or data printouts.

When the information or documents have been identified, you will be advised of the cost and how payment should be made.

Sincerely,

Donald Macdonald

Donald Macdonald
Records Access Officer

Figure 16-4   Response from New York State Department of Health to Lagerkvist's second FOIA request.

NEWS
12
LONG ISLAND

One Media Crossways
Woodbury, New York 11797

Telephone: 516/496-1766

June 10, 1994   *TRANSMITTED BY FAX*

Donald McDonald
Records Access Officer
NYS Dept. of Health
Corning Tower - Room 2230
Albany, NY

RE: 94-05-023

Dear Mr. McDonald:

I appreciate your office's effort to provide access to the requested records
during my visit to Albany this week. However, it appears that a large portion
of the records were inadvertently omitted from disclosure.

My request dated April 28 included "all Statements of Deficiency and Plans
of Correction from 1990 to present" for 12 HMOs (copy attached).
However, after careful review, it is apparent that I was only provided access
to the SODs and POCs that resulted from the Department's periodic
inspections.

Overlooked were the SODs and POCs that resulted from complaints received
by the Bureau of Alternative Delivery Systems. As part of #94-05-023, I
expect access to those records without the delays of processing a new FOIL
request.

Page - 1

Figure 16-5   Lagerkvist's letter to New York State Department of Health complaining that he did
not get all the records he requested.

Cynthia Weber Glynn of BADS suggested that I could access a regional subset of the "missing" SODs and POCs at the Department's office in New Rochelle. At this point, I would consider that to be an acceptable solution. If that is not acceptable to you, I am willing to inspect the full set of complaint-initiated SODs and POCs when I return to Albany for request #94-05-176.

I do appreciate your office's efforts and hope that you will give this matter prompt attention. If you have any questions, comments or suggestions, please call me at 516/496-1299.

Sincerely,

Mark Lagerkvist
News 12 Long Island

c. Peter Slocum

Figure 16-5 (**continued**) Lagerkvist's letter to New York State Department of Health complaining that he did not get all the records he requested.

NEWS 12
LONG ISLAND

One Media Crossways
Woodbury, New York 11797

Telephone: 516/496-1766

June 10, 1994   <u>*TRANSMITTED BY FAX*</u>

Cynthia Weber Glynn
Bureau of Alternative Delivery Systems
NYS Department of Health
Corning Tower - 19th Floor
Albany, NY

Dear Cynthia:

Thank you for taking time to meet with me earlier this week. Your
input and assistance were greatly appreciated.

As we discussed, I am seeking statistical information from BADS
for 1993 on the number of complaints, the number of substantiated
complaints and the number of complaints that resulted in
Statements of Deficiency for each of the 12 HMOs that serve Long
Island.

Those HMOs are: Atena, BCBS HealthNet, ChoiceCare, Cigna,
HIP, Managed Health, MetLife, Oxford, PruCare, Sanus, Travelers
and U.S. Healthcare.

Page - 1

Figure 16-6   Lagerkvist's additional follow-up letter requesting more information under the
FOIA.

Once again, thanks for your help. When the information is
available, please call me at 516/496-1299.

Sincerely,

Mark Lagerkvist
News 12 Long Island

Page - 2

Figure 16-6 (continued)   Lagerkvist's additional follow-up letter requesting more information
under the FOIA.

Figure 16-7   Mark Lagerkvist, former investigative reporter for News 12 Long Island. (Courtesy of News 12 Long Island)

Lagerkvist said that sometimes he visits the government agency to look at their files to find out what they have. In this case, Lagerkvist drove from Long Island to Albany, the state capital, and after conversations with officials, he realized they had not given him everything he wanted.

"In some cases," Lagerkvist said, "they were not keeping records because they did not think it was important to do so." The reporter cited an example in which the Department of Health told him that it did not keep records of contracts between HMOs and the doctors they hire. Lagerkvist said, "Sometimes you can learn a lot from the fact that they don't keep certain records." He added, "It tells me that they are not monitoring the deals because they don't think it is significant enough to merit their attention."

Although he was not able to see signed contracts between the HMOs and doctors, the Department of Health did provide Lagerkvist with blank contracts that indicated that "deals" were being made. With that information and other public records, Lagerkvist was able to confront HMO officials and found out more details on the arrangements they were making with physicians, which became the focus of the reporter's investigation.

Supporting Video

As is often the case in investigative reports, finding enough good video can be a problem, but Lagerkvist said he was happy with the way the story looked visually. He said, "We didn't have any video of doctors huddling in corners making deals . . . no secret cameras . . . but you can't let the video dictate what we do. If we did," he added, "that would be pandering."

So, what did Lagerkvist do? He relied on a lot of generic footage of doctors at work in the HMOs without showing any closeups, which could cause legal problems (see the section "False Light" in Chapter 20). He also used some graphic material; however, the most important element, he said, was creativity. "If you tell the story right," he said, "you can get the video to work. If the story is important and compelling . . . and you have good, clean, and concise sound bites, it will all come together naturally."

When asked if the HMO story had caused any changes in the system, Lagerkvist said not as yet, but he suspects the "other shoe has not dropped." He said there was a tremendous amount of requests for tapes of the series, and some of those requests came from local and state legislators. Lagerkvist was quick to point out, however, that while it is nice to bring about change and to win awards for such reports, the "bottom line is to serve and inform the people . . . to provide a public service by telling them things that they did not know before."

After leaving News 12 Long Island in late 2002, Mark Lagerkvist tackled an investigation close to home—and discovered his relationship to "the most gruesome murder in the history of northeastern Michigan." On Christmas morning 1921, Lagerkvist's real grandfather killed his grandmother in the presence of their nine children, including Mark's infant mother. The crime shocked the small farming community of Wolf Creek, which exiled most of the unfortunate orphans to another state. To investigate the 80-year-old homicide and find a lost family that had been concealed from him, the veteran journalist used every trick, technique and resource available—including obscure records, archives, interviews and even DNA testing. The result of his exhaustive two-year investigation is a compelling non-fiction book—*In My Blood: The Secrets of Wolf Creek*. Details and updates on Lagerkvist and the book will be posted at www.broadcastnewsbook.com.

Another FOIA request filed by producer Chris Szechenyi, who was with WRC-TV in Washington, D.C., at the time, made it possible for him to break a story involving the unreliability of defibrillators (i.e., high-tech medical equipment designed to shock a failed heart back to life). The producer discovered that during a six-year period, such equipment malfunctioned 512 times. He also discovered that the product made by one company, Physio Control Corporation, a subsidiary of Eli Lilly, accounted for 442 of those malfunctions. The company has about 80 percent of the defibrillator market. Szechenyi decided to find out all he could about Physio Control Corporation. He filed an FOIA request with the Food and Drug Administration (FDA). By law, medical-device manufacturers must report deaths to the FDA within 15 days if there is a reason to believe that the deaths were caused by a medical device.

Szechenyi said he thought about doing a story about faulty medical equipment after Congress held hearings regarding problems with heart valves. "I was aware that there was a database for all that information provided to the FDA on malfunctioning equipment by hospitals and manufacturers. But when I went to the government's National Technical Information Service (NTIS) to check on the information, I found thousands of pages of reports. I knew there was no way to successfully gather all the information and come up with any intelligent evaluation. I realized I needed a computer to collate the information to find out which devices were causing the most problems."

Szechenyi then discovered that for $350 NTIS would provide a computer tape that would give him the information he needed. He also realized that he would need help to decipher the tape and thus joined forces with the Missouri Institute for Computer-Assisted Reporting (MICAR). The investigation took four months, and when it was over, Szechenyi and WRC-TV produced a four-part series on medical-equipment problems. The probe was not limited to the Physio Control Corporation. Szechenyi said the defibrillator failures are "only a fraction of the [death] toll caused by a variety of defective medical devices." The investigative team discovered that there were 3,328 deaths and 52,000 injuries associated with medical devices during a six-year period. Szechenyi said, "We discovered that pacemakers, ventilators, heart valves, and other devices designed to save lives are in fact losing lives."

Szechenyi noted that the story, which won the National Headliner Award in 1991, could not have been done without the information produced by the FOIA. Computer technology was also important to the investigation. Since 1984, the FDA has entered into its computers the investigation of more than 100,000 cases of medical-equipment failure. For each case, the computerized record contains the name and address of the manufacturer, the kind of medical device that was involved, a description of the problem, and a statement detailing whether the device merely malfunctioned or caused an injury or death. The record also states whether the FDA has finished its investigation and whether the device was determined to be at fault.

Szechenyi said that computer analysis "is only the first step in the reporting process. Once you have identified a product that is causing problems, you have to find out if there were any recalls." Information about recalls can also be obtained from the FDA under the FOIA. The recall notices say what's wrong with devices, how many were distributed, and what the company is doing to correct the problem.

Szechenyi said FDA inspections of a company's plants also are available under the FOIA. He noted that "it paid to be friendly" with the FOIA officer at the FDA field office in Seattle, who sent a stack of documents only three weeks after Szechenyi made the request. The producer said he got about 600 documents from the field office; it also waived all fees.

Szechenyi said that "behind the statistics and records are tragic human stories, and court records are the best source to find the victims." He also got results by contacting some top litigation lawyers. "I found one lawyer who handled a medical-equipment malfunction case," Szechenyi said, "and he told me about other attorneys who had similar cases, and that's how we got the human stories used in our reports."

A Neglected Tool

Szechenyi says that he avoids using the FOIA, if he can, because filing a request is so much trouble. Perhaps that is why few journalists use the FOIA. Only a small percentage of broadcast journalists have filed FOIA requests. Actually, prisoners and businesses have used the FOIA more than any other group. Although some information obtained through FOIA requests can be found in other places, there are times, as Szechenyi admitted, when there is no way to do the story without the FOIA.

The Privacy Act

Some members of Congress were concerned that the FOIA would impinge on one of Americans' most treasured freedoms—privacy. In 1974, Congress passed the Privacy Act in an attempt to protect individuals from unwarranted invasion of their privacy. The act forbids the government from disclosing information in its files pertaining to individuals. Many journalists, however, argue that the government uses the act to keep important information from the public.

Government Reports

Ironically, while the government often fails to disclose certain information to the public, it publishes volumes of manuals and directories that are important sources of information for journalists. Sometimes, the information found in these government publications is as embarrassing as the material an agency does not disclose.

The government publications found at public and university libraries that are particularly useful to journalists are the reports issued by the General Accounting Office (GAO)—a congressional agency. The GAO issues more than a thousand reports per year, and its recommendations to Congress often provide interesting and sometimes provocative story ideas for journalists. The now famous stories about the Pentagon paying 20 and 30 times what it should for hammers and other basic tools came from GAO reports.

Other government publications that are useful to reporters include the following:

The Code of Federal Regulations—which describes how laws and regulations are enforced.

The Congressional Record—which offers a daily report of congressional debate and other business. It also lists most agencies and high-ranking government officials, including members of Congress, of its various committees, and of the judicial and executive branches.

The Federal Regional Directory—which lists federal offices that have records on local programs and activities involving the government.

The Federal Register—which gives a daily account of federal-agency activities and executive orders from the White House.

The Federal Regulatory Directory—which describes the 15 major regulatory agencies and lists the more than 60 lesser-known regulatory bodies. It also lists the names of top officials.

The U.S. Bureau of the Census publications—which provide statistical information on almost every aspect of life in America.

The U.S. Government Manual—which outlines the responsibilities and organization of the federal government. It includes all types of valuable information, including addresses, phone numbers, and names of officials at various government branches.

The Washington Information Directory—which provides additional nongovernment sources not shown in the Government Manual.

All of these publications—and a great many more—are also housed in Government Depository Libraries located throughout the United States and on many university campuses.

Business Publications and Indexes

Reporters working on complex or investigative stories about business can find a variety of useful publications in the library, including Dun & Bradstreet's directory of companies worth a million dollars or more. *Standard & Poor's Register of Corporations* is also useful because it not only lists the corporations but also includes background information on major business leaders.

Reporters looking for information on specific products use the *Thomas Register of American Manufacturers* series.

Magazines and newspapers also write about business and industry. The most respected of these sources are the *Wall Street Journal, Forbes, Fortune,* and *Business Week*.

Trade Publications

The story of American industry is also told in hundreds of magazines and publications available in libraries. Many of these publications are biased because they speak for the industry they represent. Nevertheless, reporters often find useful information in such publications, which can provide leads for reporters seeking industry spokespeople. Trade publications are also an important source for information on what position various industries are taking on an issue.

Database Services

We have made numerous references in this book to the information explosion—the so-called information super highway—which has had a major impact on all types of communications. It already is a boon to journalists. The Internet, in particular, has invaluable tools for searching all types of subjects.

Many libraries have computerized the catalogue of the information that's housed in them, which makes locating the information much faster. Many libraries subscribe to database services such as LexisNexis, InfoTrac, and others that index hundreds of newspapers, magazines, academic and scientific journals, and trade publications.

Many broadcast newsrooms that acquired computers for word processing, assignment lists, producer rundowns, and various other news activities also subscribe to database services, particularly LexisNexis, the largest and broadest of all the services. LexisNexis is also available at 75 percent of American colleges and universities.

In addition to its retrieval service, you can get assistance from a "live person" 24 hours a day and you can consult with specialists in law, finance, and taxation free of charge. LexisNexis offers thousands of sources of news and business information, including many that appear in full text. It includes virtually all the major newspapers, wire services, CNN, and major networks. Foreign newspapers and wire services also can be accessed.

Reporters routinely use LexisNexis for the following tasks:

- background and document stories
- identify contacts and experts

- formulate interview questions
- verify facts obtained in interviews and news conferences
- verify quotes for accuracy
- obtain quotes they missed
- see how others covered the story
- develop different angles
- obtain story ideas
- gather statistics

Great for Running Stories

Retrieval services like LexisNexis are a major help in covering stories such as the O. J. Simpson trial and the Oklahoma City bombing. The company provided complete transcripts of both the trial and sidebar conferences (between the attorneys and Judge Ito) within an hour after the morning and afternoon sessions. Reporters also were able to research prospective witnesses before they took the stand and read case law cited by the lawyers.

After the Oklahoma City bombing, reporters were able to quickly access a history of bomb attacks in the United States and obtain lists of experts on bomb attacks and building blasts. LexisNexis also provided texts of FBI news briefings and President Clinton's news conferences.

Investigative reporters also use the retrieval services. Reporter David Farrell of the *Detroit News* said that after gathering extensive information on the service, he uncovered a network of dummy corporations with the sole purpose of depositing checks authorized by two top police officials. Farrell's story generated a full-scale investigation that resulted in prison sentences.

So why not use the Internet, which is free, instead of LexisNexis? Wendy Beecham, LexisNexis' senior vice president says, "LexisNexis provides important business resources and information that cannot be found on the Web for free." Also, she says, "tools are designed to aggregate the date and speed up the search process so you're not endlessly searching through irrelevant information or missing critical information." Beecham adds that "If you're a journalist you know that in many cases, it's the obscure information not found through a free Web search that could be the next breaking news story."

Most importantly, she said, having access to this information before anyone else is key—the advantage that the LexisNexis services can provide.

For stations that cannot afford LexisNexis, there are a variety of free retrieval services on the Web, including Yahoo and Google.

Other Public Files

Reporters have another useful method of locating information, particularly information about individuals' government files. Governments at all levels maintain files on numerous activities that happen within their borders. When a baby is born, or when someone dies, or is married or divorced, or registers a car, or opens a liquor store, or buys a piece of land, or is arrested, or sues somebody, or opens a restaurant, someone issues a document that is kept on permanent record. Anyone who wishes to do so may look at and copy such documents.

Police Records

The amount of information that reporters can obtain from police records varies from community to community. Reporters who establish a good rapport with a police desk sergeant often get the information they want with little trouble. Technically, any information on the police log or blotter should be available to reporters. Without a good rapport, however, it sometimes takes the threat of court action to get the information. The records include the name of the individual, the date of the arrest, the charges, and the disposition of those charges. Once a person is behind bars, that information is normally available where the individual is being held.

Court Records

Information about the court cases most reporters deal with—criminal and civil cases—is available at a court clerk's office. In a civil case, anyone can obtain information about the complaint or petition brought by the plaintiff. The complaint usually describes what the defendant has allegedly done and why the plaintiff wants the court to award damages.

In criminal cases, reporters also have access to the charges brought against an individual. The records list the name of the complainant, most often a police officer, and the name of the defendant. The records cite the charge and describe what allegedly occurred that led to the arrest and court action. Reporters soon learn that it's a lot easier, and quicker, to find these records if they are on a first-name basis with the court clerks.

Birth and Death Records

The facts of a person's birth often can be important to a reporter. A birth certificate lists the names of the parents, the date of birth, the name of the doctor who delivered the child, and the name of the hospital. Death certificates also provide information that may be important to a story. They show the cause of death and the date and time it occurred; however, such records are not

Figure 16-8
NBC News correspondent Roger O'Neil. (Courtesy of Ray Farmer/*NBC News*)

always public. If an individual left a will that involved real estate, reporters may also obtain a copy of the death certificate attached to mortgages and deeds found at the property tax office.

Being friendly and showing respect often make it easier to find some of these records or, perhaps, to get a quick look at those that are not supposed to be open to the public.

Licenses

Nearly every community issues licenses of many kinds, and sometimes knowing who received a license can be important to a newsperson. In a large city, little goes on in business that does not require some sort of a license—even selling hot dogs on the street. Such licenses list names and other personal information about the grantee. Such information would be valuable, for example, if a reporter was working on a story about a junkyard that was an environmental or safety hazard.

The licensing of guns has been an ongoing issue throughout the nation. Because there is no national gun-control law, the ability to check on people who may own guns depends on where the reporter is doing the checking. New York has strict gun laws; Virginia does not. In 1995, Virginia passed a law making it legal to carry a concealed weapon. This bothers many people who live just across the border in the nation's capital, which has one of the worst crime and homicide records involving guns in the world.

Driver's license records and car registrations are also easily available in some states and can be obtained with a minimum amount of coaxing in most others if the reporter can provide a good reason for wanting the information.

Many professional people, such as doctors, architects, and engineers, also must hold licenses. The state agencies or boards that issue those licenses have biographical information, including education and the applicant's specialty.

Land Records

The property tax office can provide a lot of information to an investigative reporter. It has records on who pays the taxes on property and, presumably, but not always, on the owner of the property. The records also reveal the former owners' names and the purchase price of the property, as well as who holds the mortgage on the property, if there is one. The names of the real-estate brokers and lawyers who were involved in the sale are also indicated. This information might be important to know if, for example, a reporter was checking on a city judge who seemed to be lenient with drunk drivers and it was discovered in the property tax records that the judge was living in a million-dollar home in the suburbs.

Financial Records

It is easy to check a person's financial record. Many people, except perhaps reporters looking for such information, believe that it's too easy to find out how Americans handle their finances. Reporters need only ask the station's business office to call TRW or some other credit bureau, and the person's computer-produced financial record will be on the reporter's desk in minutes. The record shows credit histories for 10 years or more, the names of those holding mortgages, where individuals shop, and whether they pay their bills on time. The report also shows any bankruptcy declared during the past 10 years.

Anytime an individual moves and establishes credit of any kind, the new address is recorded, which can be useful to a reporter trying to find the person. Other firms provide a person's new address as long as the reporter supplies a Social Security number.

Tax Records

Tax records are among the most difficult documents to obtain. Reporters do, from time to time, obtain information about a person's tax returns from the Internal Revenue Service (IRS), but almost always as the result of a leak initiated by someone inside the agency. Some reporters manage to develop sources inside the IRS, but it is not easy.

City Directories

The city directory is often helpful if you want to find out where a particular individual lives. The directory lists a person's name, address, spouse, children, employment, and several other useful pieces of information. The directories are particularly helpful when a reporter is trying to talk to relatives of someone who is in the news.

Telephone books are also useful; they would be the first place to look when trying to locate someone if you know the town or city in which he or she lives. In some communities, the telephone company also prints telephone books that list people and companies by their addresses. They are extremely useful, for example, if a major fire breaks out on the 1500 block of Main Street. There are listings for all of the phones on Main Street that are not restricted, so all the reporter or assignment editor has to do is try to locate a phone near the 1500 block. A call to a phone listed at 1550 Main Street, for example, might find someone who can see the fire from an apartment window. It's then simple to put the person on the air while he or she describes the fire and answers the reporter's questions.

Summary

Unfortunately, most radio or TV news organizations do not give their reporters enough time to use the various information sources described in this chapter. Reporters spend most of their time working on breaking news stories. Investigative stories require a lot of research time and are expensive to produce. Most stations want at least one story a day from their reporters, which doesn't allow much time for checking court records or filing FOIA requests.

If you do have an opportunity to work on stories that require in-depth research, the information in this chapter should be extremely helpful. The FOIA is an important asset if you want to examine the actions of government at any level—town, city, state, or federal. The library at your college or university has numerous documents that will reveal more about the federal government, how it works, and what mistakes it makes. The report of the GAO, a congressional watchdog, and the Congressional Directory are also useful.

You should also familiarize yourself with the various business publications, indexes, journals, and magazines in your library and learn about the ability of the Internet and databases such as LexisNexis, which have cut reporter research tremendously.

This chapter also describes how to use the various government files maintained by police and the courts, tax and land offices, and bureaus that keep records on births, deaths, licenses, and numerous other activities.

Review Questions

1. What is the Freedom of Information Act?
2. Why is it so important to journalists?
3. Does the FOIA apply only to the dealings of the federal government?
4. List the different points that should be made in a letter requesting information under the FOIA.
5. Journalists can learn about the government and how it operates through various records and publications. List some of the most important ones, and explain how they are useful.
6. How can computer databases be useful to reporters?
7. What kind of information can reporters obtain from police and court records?

Exercises

1. Suppose that you are filing an FOIA request with the Defense Department because you have a source that claims that when he worked for the Acme Tool and Dye Company in Centerville, a government contractor, as many as 60 percent of the products produced in the plant were rejected for various reasons. Prepare the FOIA request.
2. Pick three corporations among the *Fortune 500* list, and find out the names of the top officials who run them. Also list any other companies that are owned by one of these parent corporations, and find out the names of any corporations or individuals who own a substantial number of shares in a parent company.
3. Use a database service to find out how many articles were published last year about Dan Rather. List the names of the publications along with the titles of the articles and the dates they appeared.
4. Visit the local courthouse and find out the names of those who were convicted of drunk driving during the past month.

17 Computer-Assisted Reporting for Broadcast

*By **Brant Houston** (© 2000 by Brant Houston)*

In the past decade, computer-assisted reporting (CAR) has become part of many journalists' day-to-day work and aided those journalists in creating high-impact, public-service stories.

CAR is the acquisition and analysis of electronic information and databases. It is the natural extension of using hard-copy (paper) documents, and many records described in Chapter 16, "Collecting Information from Documents," have become electronic.

Although journalists need training to use CAR, the result—once they have had the training—is that they become proficient at finding, filtering, sorting, and analyzing public records. In the past, journalists might have taken days to look at a few hundred records; now they can examine tens of thousands of records in a few hours.

A few years ago, CAR was a skill reserved for a few expert reporters and research librarians, but it has now been rapidly integrated into deadline, daily, and beat reporting. For example, many journalists routinely use databases and the tools of CAR whenever covering a plane crash.

With knowledge of CAR, a journalist has a distinct advantage over the competition. The journalist with CAR skills can bring more depth, context, and credibility to a story. CAR often provides a journalist with an exclusive story. In addition, the explosion of public information on the Web, the simplification of software, and the increased speed in computer processing permits a CAR journalist to outdistance others on breaking stories.

This chapter provides an overview of the basic tools of CAR and the kinds of stories that broadcast journalists have reported with the help of these tools. This chapter also refers to the books and online resources that offer much more detail about research on the Web and on performing data analysis.

The Three Basic Tools

The three basic software tools of CAR are online resources, spreadsheets, and database managers. These three are not exclusive, and often a CAR journalist employs all three while working on a story.

Online resources include the Internet and commercial databases. Reporters use them to find people, background businesses, monitor discussion groups on special topics, and acquire relevant data for a story. The effective use of the Web is a critical skill because, as everyone knows, it's possible to "surf" for hours without results. Equally important is the focused use of commercial databases because of the potential high cost of their services.

With spreadsheet software, such as Microsoft Excel, a reporter can quickly calculate, sort, and filter electronic data. Tabular data (i.e., data in columns and rows like a stock table or sports rankings) can be efficiently downloaded into a spreadsheet from the Internet. A reporter also can easily enter data into a spreadsheet. Reporters often use spreadsheets to examine budgets, salaries, population figures, and housing costs.

A database manager (e.g., Microsoft Access) lets a reporter quickly search, summarize, and compare public records. Although a database manager is more difficult to learn to use than a spreadsheet, it is a powerful tool. A database manager can search hundreds of thousands of electronic records for a specific item, summarize those records to determine if patterns exist, or compare separate files of information to find records that match. Broadcast reporters have used database managers to discover the day of the week that public employees most often call in sick, to identify dangerous bridges and dams, or to find teachers who are also convicted felons.

Online Resources

Commercial databases are available online and on CD-ROMs. (Never forget to check the local library for what might be available for free on CD-ROMs.)

For online pay services, many journalists use LexisNexis, which has news stories and many legal resources. They also buy Autotrack services from Database Technologies or CDB Infotek services to get information about corporations or individuals that is not on the Web or that is not easy to find on the Web. But until a journalist becomes skilled at searching commercial databases, it is wise to ask an experienced research librarian for help rather than waste time and money.

Regardless of how the information is obtained, a journalist should know what information is offered through these services. Nora Paul, an expert researcher, provides a valuable review and comparison of commercial services in her book *Computer-Assisted Research* (4th edition, 1999, Bonus Books and the Poynter Institute for Media Studies). This book is a good starting guide to what is available at different commercial databases and on the Web.

Search Engines and Guides

The Web can be frustrating for a journalist, especially if he or she is utilizing search engines (automated indexers of Web pages) that return hundreds or thousands of "hits" when a journalist enters one keyword. Tom McGinty, training director for Investigative Reporters and Editors, Inc., gives one of the simplest pieces of advice on search engines: Read the help files. Those help files will teach you Boolean logic, which involves narrowing or widening your criteria through the words "and," "or," and "not" (see Figure 17-1).

Many reporters find the Web subject indexes (particularly Yahoo.com) and the directories offered on the home pages of the search engines to be more helpful. Better yet—because they are aimed at journalists—are the "homegrown" guides created by journalists. The Reporter's Desktop, www.reporter.org/desktop, authored by Duff Wilson of the *Seattle Times*, and the Net Tour, www.ire.org/training/nettour, offered by the National Institute for Computer-Assisted Reporting, authored by McGinty and Sarah Cohen of *The Washington Post*, are efficient places to start (see Figure 17-2).

Finding People

Many Websites offer ways to find people's addresses and phone numbers. Most of them are like a reporter's tip sheet, however, in that they give possible answers, but they must be checked out and verified—like everything on the Web. If a journalist can't find a person by looking at the service www.switchboard.com, then he or she could try Yahoo's People Search at

Figure 17-1   Altavista.com (a commercial search engine) provides a clear description of how to look for a recipe with its "search box."

Figure 17-2
The welcome screen for the Net Tour Website.

Location: http://www.switchboard.com/bin/cgiqa.dll?LNK=3:11

Internet   Lookup   New&Cool

Switchboard.Find a Person

First Name: [William]

Last Name: [Clinton]

City: [Washington]

State: [DC] (State List)

[Search]

Figure 17-3
Entering a search for President Clinton on www.switchboard.com, www.people.yahoo.com, or one of the many other "people finders" available, such as www.whowhere.lycos.com.

Nearby^SM
* Clinton, WIlliam Jefferson
1600 Pennsylvania Ave.,
Washington, DC 20003

Is this an old classmate?

update/remove

TRIP.com

Email, Maps, and What's Nearby^SM

* Denotes a Switchboard User

Figure 17-4 The results for a search for President Clinton on www.switchboard.com.

www.people.yahoo.com, or one of the many other "people finders" available, such as www.whowhere.lycos.com. For example, a search for President Clinton at www.switchboard.com is shown in Figure 17-3.

The service returns his basic information that in the year 2000 he lived on Pennsylvania Avenue, but no further information is provided, although it does appear he is a Switchboard user. (Note the asterisk in Figure 17-4.)

Backgrounding Businesses

The Web has become an excellent resource for conducting research about businesses. First, many businesses have their own Websites on which they reveal much about themselves. Second, you can find basic business information at services like Switchboard.com with maps to the business locations. Third, businesses must file information with the government. Many states are placing corporate records and licensing records up on their Websites.

If a company has publicly traded stock, then they appear on a site all journalists should use routinely—the U.S. Securities and Exchange Commission Website, www.sec.gov, where filings by companies are kept in a database called "EDGAR" (see Figure 17-5).

Figure 17-5   The welcome page for the U.S. Securities and Exchange Commission Website.

The EDGAR site contains information that tells you about the company's earnings and losses, subsidiaries, lawsuits, officers, strategies, and many other useful bits of information. Journalists often go to other sites, including www.hoover.com (as in vacuum cleaner, not the dam or president), which gathers extensive information about businesses.

Information on Disasters

The Web also plays a crucial role for journalists covering disasters. Whether you're looking for information on bombs, explosions, hurricanes, or floods, both breaking news and context are available. Many journalists log onto electronic discussion groups to get material and tips they may not hear at the scene of a catastrophe. After the Oklahoma City bombing, many journalists learned about the rise of "militia groups" by reading e-mail postings to newsgroup discussions. Both the Web and in-house databases have become a standard resource when covering airplane crashes.

Andrew Lehren, who does the CAR work for *Dateline NBC,* has not only used CAR for in-depth projects, but also has demonstrated the effective use of databases on deadline or for quick-turnaround stories. When TWA Flight 800 went down over Long Island in 1998, Lehren, who at that time was database administrator at the National Institute for Computer-Assisted Reporting (NICAR), swiftly showed the fallacy of the theory that the plane had been shot down by a Stinger missile. Lehren found the altitude of the plane when it exploded and then went to a Website that had information on Stinger missiles, which revealed that those missiles could not reach that altitude.

More recently, Lehren did work on the crash of John F. Kennedy Jr.'s plane, using both online resources and aviation safety databases. Lehren ana-

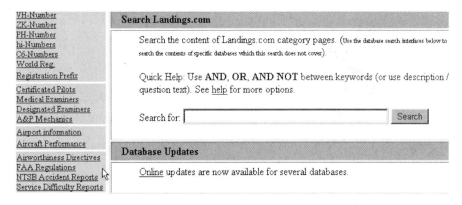

Figure 17-6 The search screen for the Landings.com Website.

lyzed data from the National Transportation Safety Board. He said the data provided "a wealth of information about those who have died" in Piper Saratoga planes.

In an article for NICAR's newsletter, *Uplink*, Lehren said the data "allowed comparisons of crashes involving instrument-rated versus visual flight-rated pilots." Kennedy was only visual flight-rated. Lehren also analyzed service difficulty reports for planes from the Federal Aviation Administration (FAA), including air-worthiness directives, ownership records, registration records, and Aviation Safety System records.

While this sounds like a tremendous amount of material to check, Lehren said he worked with *Dateline* producers and correspondents to come up with breaking news and relevant information in the two days immediately following the crash.

Lehren also noted that an important lesson from this story is not to rely solely on Websites, but to make sure to have complete databases already in-house. He said several critical Websites were down or missing crucial reports and records at the time he was conducting research about the JFK Jr. plane crash.

One of the best starting points for air safety is a site called www.landings.com, which provides a gateway into many databases (see Figure 17-6).

Notice the reports available pointed out by the cursor in Figure 17-6. These are the reports that Lehren examined, but Lehren also had ordered and received complete datasets before the crash and had learned how to analyze them. Journalists must be prepared ahead of time to cover an event on deadline.

Covering Beats

Many reporters check daily on Websites that relate to their beats or topics they cover. For example, a journalist reporting on Congress would make http://thomas.loc.gov a daily stop. That site carries extensive information on legislative bills and other information on Congress. To keep track of campaign contributions, the interested journalist would also check the Federal Election Commission site, www.fecinfo.com, to keep track of campaign contributions, and other nonprofit sites, such as the Center For Responsive Politics at www.crp.org. Broadcast journalists with CAR skills download information often on campaign finance to monitor and report independently on local politicians and their supporters.

A journalist interested in the environment and health would check the Environmental Protection Agency site, www.epa.org, and the nonprofit Natural Resources Defense Council site, www.nrdc.org. These sites contain information on pollution and efforts at cleanup. Reporters can also go to these sites to check on the environmental records of local companies.

If a journalist were keeping track of crime, he or she would routinely check the Federal Bureau of Investigations (FBI) site, www.fbi.gov, and the Bureau of Justice Statistics site, www.ojp.usdoj.gov/bjs, for perspective and to look for trends and possible stories. Crime data is often downloaded and entered into a spreadsheet to calculate percentage increases and decreases in the kinds of crime.

Downloading Databases

A journalist should routinely download information from Websites. For example, journalists should regularly obtain information about their states and local communities from the U.S. Bureau of Census site, www.census.gov, and have that information on hand for stories. This site is a good place to find data for a multitude of stories, and it makes much of its data easy to download.

A search for median incomes for families of four in each state led to this location at the Census Website, shown in Figure 17-7. This information is in

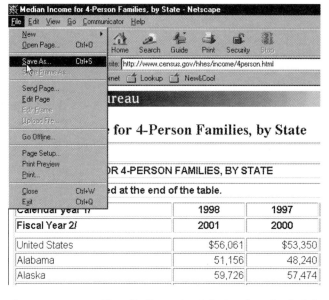

Figure 17-7 A table of information is being downloaded from the U.S. Census Website by going to "File" and clicking on "Save As."

a particularly friendly format—an HTML (hypertext markup language) file that can be readily opened by Microsoft Excel. (We will return to this file in the spreadsheet section of this chapter.)

Spreadsheets

Spreadsheets can help a journalist monitor changing information, look at salaries and budgets, analyze crime statistics, and track population figures. A journalist can quickly perform calculations with a spreadsheet because a spreadsheet can copy and apply the calculation to other numbers. A spreadsheet also can store the information, unlike a calculator, for later use.

Journalists often need to add a column of numbers such as salaries. With a spreadsheet, a journalist can type in a series of numbers and add them up with a formula. The spreadsheet makes this possible to do by giving every number an address like a map. The address is composed of the letter of the column and the number of the row in which the number itself is located.

In the example in Figure 17-8, the formula "= SUM(A3:A11)" was typed in A13. That formula means that all the numbers from A3 to A11 are added. Notice both the total and the formula that was typed to get the total. (The formula is just above the cursor in Figure 17-8.)

This capability is especially useful when a journalist is adding up hundreds of numbers. A spreadsheet has many ways of speeding up calculations, but one of the most valuable is the ability to copy a formula. If all the salaries in Figure 17-8 were to be increased by 5 percent, the total salary after the increase could be calculated by multiplying the number in A3 by 1.05 as shown in Figure 17-9. (The 1.05 gives the previous salary plus the 5 percent increase.)

Note both the formula and the number in B3. Also, note that the cursor has been turned into a narrow cross when placed in the lower right-hand corner of B3. By double-clicking on the narrow cross, the formula is automatically copied down the column. This shortcut saves journalists

A13		=	=SUM(A3:A11)
A	B	C	D
1 Salaries			
2			
3 $ 43,235			
4 $ 63,448			
5 $ 22,931			
6 $ 67,309			
7 $ 56,317			
8 $ 66,559			
9 $ 94,234			
10 $ 19,112			
11 $ 40,667			
12			
13 $ 473,812			

Figure 17-8
Adding figures in a Microsoft Excel spreadsheet.

Figure 17-9
Performing a percentage
increase formula in a
Microsoft Excel spreadsheet.

Figure 17-10
Duplicating formulas
throughout a column in a
Microsoft Excel spreadsheet.

(or anyone else, for that matter) an incredible amount of time (see Figure 17-10).

Using Downloaded Data

A journalist often doesn't have to type in numbers, but can download them from the Web or receive them on a diskette. Let's look at the downloaded U.S. Census Bureau data on the incomes of four-person families in the United States.

When the file is opened in a spreadsheet, rows and columns can be deleted or added. Then calculations can be done to put the data in perspective. In the worksheet in Figure 17-11, the increase from 1997 to 1998 has been calculated and copied for every state. The percentage change also has been calculated. Note that the increase in Arkansas (15 percent) was higher than in other states. The formula for that calculation (D15/C15) can be seen at the top of the worksheet.

To see the many other uses of Excel for journalism, we refer you to Chapter 3 in *Computer-Assisted Reporting: A Practical Guide*, by Brant Houston (2nd edition, 1999, Bedford/St. Martin's Press).

E15 ▼ = =D15/C15				
A	B	C	D	E
1 Census Bureau				
2				
3 **Median Income for 4-Person Families, by State**				
4				
5				
6				
7 **MEDIAN INCOME FOR 4-PERSON FAMILIES, BY STATE**				
8 **Footnotes are located at the end of the table.**				
9 **Calendar year 1/**	**1998**	**1997**	**Change**	**Percentage**
10				**change**
11 United States	$56,061	$53,350	$2,711	5%
12 Alabama	51,156	48,240	$2,916	6%
13 Alaska	59,726	57,474	$2,252	4%
14 Arizona	49,397	47,133	$2,264	5%
15 Arkansas	44,471	38,646	$5,825	15%
16 California	55,209	55,217	($8)	0%
17 Colorado	63,428	58,988	$4,440	8%
18 Connecticut	75,534	72,706	$2,828	4%

Figure 17-11 Creating a composite spreadsheet for data analysis in Microsoft Excel.

Database Managers

A database manager takes more time to learn than a spreadsheet, but it is a powerful tool used by businesses and government agencies and now more often by journalists. With a database manager, a journalist can search tens of thousands of electronic records, summarize the records in seconds, and compare or match those records to records in another file.

Searching

To search in a database manager such as Microsoft Access, a journalist must "query" the database. A query can be done by filling out the equivalent of a form and specifying the criteria by search—very much like using a keyword on an Internet search.

Journalists often use databases for political campaign finance records. In this example, contributions in 2000 to U.S. Senator John Ashcroft, a Missouri Republican, were downloaded from the Web and placed in Microsoft Access. The data included the name of the contributor, the amount contributed, the contributor's city and state of residence, and the contributor's occupation. Note the names of columns of information in Figure 17-12.

One routine search that can be applied to this database is to see which contributors are not from Missouri. Rather than scanning through the data, a "query form" can be used to find everyone not from Missouri. The query form also allows a journalist to select which columns, known as "fields," to look at. In Figure 17-13, the columns for name, amount, and state have been

NAME	DATE	AMOUNT	CITY	STATE	ZIP	EMPLOY/OCCU
ABERNATHY, DEBORAH	10/14/99	500.00	JOPLIN	MO	64801	SOFTWARE
ABILHEIRA, ELIAS	5/3/99	1000.00	ENGLISHTOWN	NJ	07726	SCHOEFELD AND
ABLES,	1/24/00	250.00	OLATHE	KS	66061	PHYSICIAN
ABRAMOFF, JACK	6/22/99	1000.00	WASHINGTON	DC	20006	PRESTON GATES &
ABRAMOFF, PAMELA	6/22/99	1000.00	SILVER	MD	20901	HOUSEWIFE
ABSHEER, LARRY	4/13/99	250.00	ST LOUIS	MO	63119	MISSOURI ATHLETIC
ABSHEER, LARRY	6/30/99	250.00	ST LOUIS	MO	63119	MISSOURI ATHLETIC
ABSHEER, LARRY	11/23/99	200.00	ST LOUIS	MO	63119	MISSOURI ATHLETIC

Figure 17-12   Excerpt from a campaign contribution database created in Microsoft Access.

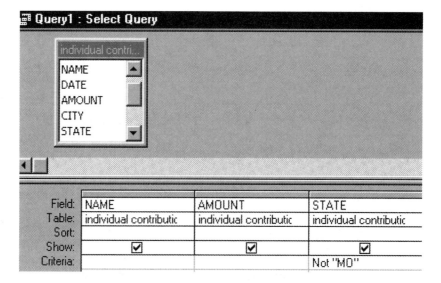

Figure 17-13   Excerpt from the query form for a Microsoft Access database.

selected from the possible choices above, and the criteria "not MO" (meaning not from Missouri) has been typed in the state column.

The result when the query is "run" is a list of non-Missouri contributors, as seen in Figure 17-14.

Summarizing

A query in a database manager can also powerfully summarize data. Although it can be helpful to find individual contributors, trends can be spotted by obtaining total contributions from each state that is not the home state of the candidate.

Figure 17-15 shows an example of such a query. In this case, the contributions are "grouped by" each state and then totaled with the word "sum." The result is also sorted by the highest amount to the lowest amount (in descending order).

The result of "running" this query shows that the largest amounts from out-of-state contributors came from Kansas and Texas (see Figure 17-16).

NAME	AMOUNT	STATE
ABILHEIRA, ELIAS	1000.00	NJ
ABLES,	250.00	KS
ABRAMOFF, JACK	1000.00	DC
ABRAMOFF, PAMELA	1000.00	MD
ACCARDO, NATE	1000.00	KS
ACKERMAN,	500.00	MI
ACKERMAN, EDITH	1000.00	PA
ADAM, P	1000.00	KS
ADAMANY, FRED	1000.00	IL
ADAMANY, FRED	1000.00	IL
ADAMS, MILDRED	1000.00	OR
ADAMS, MORGAN	200.00	CA

Figure 17-14 Results of a query run on a campaign contribution database in Microsoft Access.

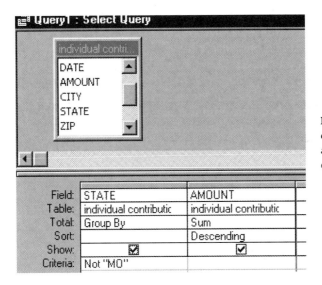

Figure 17-15 Excerpt of a summary query in a Microsoft Access database.

STATE	SumOfAMOUN
KS	195975
TX	116663
CA	76727
IL	70200
VA	62850
NY	57900
PA	57350
MI	50100

Figure 17-16 Results of a summary query run on a campaign contribution database in Microsoft Access.

With this information, a reporter can now start asking why contributors from another state would give so much to Senator Ashcroft's campaign.

Comparing and Matching

The ability to compare and match information from different files is the third major advantage of a database manager. The database manager can make matches depending on one or more criteria. In enterprise stories, journalists generally have to rely on several criteria to find possible matches.

In a query, matches of files of school staff and convicted felons would probably look like Figure 17-17, where the first names, last names, and dates of birth are matched to find possible felons working in a school system. The lines between the two files in the query are created by clicking on one column header and dragging it to the similar column header in the other file.

Building Your Own Database

Sometimes there is no data available, only hard copy. In this case, broadcast reporters have successfully built their own databases and entered data into them. One classic story was done by Karl Idsvoog and Corky Johnson when they worked for WCPO in Cincinnati. They constructed a database on time and attendance records of county election employees in Ohio. The reporters entered the data and found that Friday was not only the most popular day for employees to be absent, but that employees were often absent on that day.

It is not difficult to construct a database and enter data. In Microsoft Access, a "design view" window allows a journalist to give names to columns and decide what kind of data—text, numbers, or dates—can be entered into the database (see Figure 17-18).

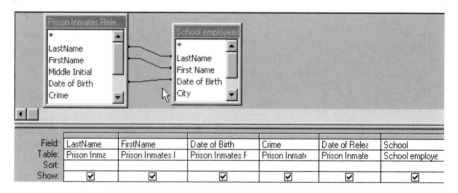

Figure 17-17 Excerpt of a query comparing school staff and convicted felons in a Microsoft Access database.

▦ City employees : Table		
Field Name	Data Type	Description
▶ Lastname	Text	Employee's last name
Firstname	Text	Employee's first name
Salary	Number	Amount of sarly
Date of Hire	Date/Time	Date employee was hired
Title	Text	Job title of employee
Department	Text	Department in which employee works

Figure 17-18 A "design view" window for building a Microsoft Access database.

Acquiring Data

The federal government has an electronic Freedom of Information Act (FOIA), and most state and local governments have similar acts or laws that permit the distribution of electronic information in the same manner as the distribution of hard-copy information.

When seeking electronic databases, however, a journalist needs to obtain some technical information. This includes a record layout (which looks like the database design in Figure 17-18), the format or language the data is in, the size of the data in megabytes, the number of the records, and the kind of medium (e.g., diskette, CD-ROM, computer tape) in which it will be delivered.

CAR Stories

Broadcast journalists have reported hundreds of news stories, many of them dramatic, using these techniques. Some CAR stories particularly lend themselves to high impact because the data can be summarized with a single shot, chart, or interview.

In 1999 in Atlanta, WSB-TV and the *Atlanta Constitution-Journal* joined forces and found almost 3,000 convicted criminals working in Georgia schools. Using the Georgia Open Records law, the station and newspaper obtained a database of school employees and of criminals. With the guidance of long-time CAR practitioner David Milliron at the *Constitution-Journal*, they matched names and dates of birth between the two databases and then used social security numbers to confirm the matches. To give the story a human angle, they began by focusing on the case of a football coach.

Here's a transcript of the beginning of the story:

PART 1

LEAD:

Channel Two Action News has learned that teachers or teachers' aides in several metro area school systems have felony convictions on their records—and yet we found them still working directly with students.

These are just a few of the nearly three thousand school employees statewide we found with felony and misdemeanor records.

One is at a metro school already embroiled in a controversy involving charges against the head football coach.

[1] (ANCHOR)

Channel Two's Richard Belcher has spent months investigating the backgrounds of teachers throughout the metro area.

He's here with the results of his Whistle Blower Two special assignment. Toss:

(RICHARD) When the head football coach at Dekalb County's Avondale High School was arrested on charges of sexual assault on a student, it turned out that Billy Ray Smith had already been criminally prosecuted.

Another story that cross-referenced two files to create a disturbing finding involved dangerous Emergency Medical Technicians (EMTs). At WBNS-TV in Columbus, Ohio, Paul Adrian, a CAR specialist, compared a database of all certified EMTs in Ohio to a database containing drunk-driving convictions in the state and another database of prison inmates. Adrian and his colleagues found 82 certified medics who had three or more drunk-driving convictions and a smaller group that had serious felonies.

State law prohibited people with alcohol problems or who had serious felonies from becoming medics, but officials did not check the backgrounds of applicants—despite a state law requiring background checks. WBNS-TV began its piece by looking at one medic, Jeffrey Crain, who had drunk-driving convictions and disciplinary problems. It continued by building its case:

And Crain is not the only medic getting DUIs on a regular basis. The I-Team found 6 EMTs in Ohio who have 5 drunk driving convictions . . . We discovered 3 with 6 DUIs . . . And when we asked the computer . . . How many medics have received 3 or more DUIs? The answer . . . 82.

One out of three of them does not currently have a valid driver's license.

And it doesn't stop there.

Our analysis also uncovered five people, able to get their EMT certification, who have been convicted of killing somebody on the road.

The story resulted in the removal of some EMTs from their jobs and a revamping of regulations.

Resources Needed

To start making use of CAR techniques, a reporter needs only a good personal computer with software that includes a Web browser, a spreadsheet, and a database manager. The reporter should begin with smaller stories as he or she works on building up CAR skills. The reporter also should find a colleague who is interested in these techniques and who is willing to check the calculations and queries done by the reporter.

For ideas about how to use CAR techniques, the reporter can check the Resource Center of Investigative Reporters and Editors, Inc., www.ire.org/resourcecenter, where examples of hundreds of stories that have used CAR are electronically indexed (copies of those stories can be ordered).

Summary

The use of CAR techniques has been steadily rising among both print and broadcast journalists. The techniques can be employed on most stories and add more context and depth to those stories. In some cases, CAR techniques allow journalists to come up quickly with new information on breaking stories.

Journalists need training to make sure that they understand how to apply these skills with accuracy, but they should not be afraid to use tools that improve their credibility.

Review Questions

1. What are the three basic tools of computer-assisted reporting?
2. For what kinds of tasks should a spreadsheet be used?
3. What tasks does a database manager perform?
4. Name two Websites that help journalists find people or research information about businesses.
5. Name four Websites from which journalists can download information.

Exercises

1. Find information on your community from the Environmental Protection Agency Website regarding pollution.
2. Go to the Census Website and find data about your community. Download data relating to population estimates and open them in a spreadsheet. Calculate the change from one year to another.
3. Enter five salaries in a spreadsheet. Using a formula shown in this chapter, calculate the total of those salaries.
4. Download campaign contribution information on a local congressman and identify the highest contributor.
5. Find five examples of broadcast stories that used CAR techniques.

18 Developing Sources

As reporters and anchors become known and respected by their audience, they receive telephone calls, e-mails and letters about a variety of subjects. Some are letters of praise; some are complaints. Also included among those calls and letters are some news tips. Some of the most important stories aired by radio and TV stations come from tipsters. Others come from sources cultivated at public agencies and insiders at corporations and other institutions. This chapter discusses how to develop relationships with such sources.

Tips

Stations that establish reputations for doing investigative stories are more likely to get tips than others. Astute news directors encourage tipsters, often setting up private telephone lines just for that purpose. Most calls involve breaking news—fires, accidents, crime—but sometimes the caller has information that leads to an investigative story.

Tips are usually the result of stories that were reported earlier by the station. For example, a story about a politician using public funds for a personal trip to Las Vegas may attract calls from viewers who know about similar trips by other politicians. Who makes such calls, and why? The calls and letters are often from people who have been working closely with the wrongdoers. They may be annoyed because of the misuse of public funds, because they lost their jobs, because of jealousy, or because of a long-standing grudge. The caller then becomes a source who might provide additional information on other stories or the names of additional sources. The way the phone conversation might go is: "I don't know all the details, but I can give you the name of someone who can, as long as you don't reveal my name." The phrase "don't reveal my name" is key to developing and keeping sources.

Confidentiality

The fastest way to lose a source is to break a promise of confidentiality. Few sources give reporters sensitive information without a promise of secrecy. Once a reporter gives that promise, it must be respected, regardless of the consequences. A reporter's right to protect sources has often been tested in the courts, and reporters do not always win. On rare occasions, reporters have gone to jail or been fined for refusing to disclose a source.

Before entering into such an agreement with a source, reporters must analyze what they are agreeing to keep secret. Reporters disagree, for example, on whether it's a good idea to offer confidentiality to those who admit that they are actively involved in crime. Some reporters say they agree to such a pact if that's the only way to break the story. Other reporters say they would never enter into such an agreement and warn those sources that if they disclose any information about criminal behavior on their part, the reporters will not guarantee secrecy. Pulitzer Prize-winning columnist and investigative reporter Jack Anderson said, "We will give immunity to a very good source as long as the information he offers us is better than that which we've got on him."

If a reporter promises to keep a source secret and that promise is broken, it can be costly. The U.S. Supreme Court ruled in 1991 that news organizations cannot break promises of confidentiality to news sources. The landmark decision was the result of a suit brought by a public-relations consultant in Minnesota after two newspapers in that state broke their promise of confidentiality. The plaintiff, Dan Cohen, was working for gubernatorial candidate Wheelock Whitney when he agreed to give the *Star Tribune* of Minneapolis and the *St. Paul Pioneer Press Dispatch* information about a shoplifting conviction of Marlene Johnson, a candidate on the opposing ticket. *Pioneer Press Dispatch* reporter Bill Salisbury and *Star Tribune* reporter Lori Sturdevant had promised Cohen confidentiality. Their newspapers decided, however, to withdraw the agreement and identified Cohen in the stories. He was fired from his job with a large advertising agency the next day.

The lawyers for the newspapers argued that the public had the right to know who had disclosed the derogatory information about the candidate and argued it was the newspapers' First Amendment right to publish Cohen's name. The Court voted 5 to 4 that Minnesota law requires "those making promises to keep them," and that the newspapers had no right to break their promise of confidentiality.

Salisbury said the Cohen case "may permanently change the relationship between reporters and anonymous sources. It should discourage editors from breaking reporters' promises, thus making sources feel more confident that their names will be protected." Salisbury said the ruling also "chips away at the press's First Amendment protections, and it invites more lawsuits over broken promises." Cohen was awarded $200,000 for breach of contract.

Accuracy of Sources

A reporter should never use a source as a basis for a story until the information is checked for accuracy. Verifying a story is not always easy, especially when a reporter is working under deadlines. One of the best ways to ensure that a story is accurate is to find several other sources who will disclose exactly the same information. This is known as double- or triple-sourcing. Dan Rather and *CBS News* discovered that the hard way when they based a widely criticized story about President Bush's alleged failure to fulfill his National Guard duties during the Vietnam War to a single source that turned out to be unreliable.

Most station managers have a policy that requires reporters to disclose their sources or documentation to at least one person in authority at the station before they are allowed to broadcast the investigative material. Failure to provide such safeguards invites disaster. The classic reporting example cited in every textbook—and in every newsroom—is the Janet Cooke incident in which editors at *The Washington Post* failed to check a story about a child addicted to drugs. The well-written story won a Pulitzer Prize. Unfortunately, the profiled child was a composite of children the reporter had met, not an actual person, and the newspaper had to return the prize. Janet Cooke was fired, and *The Washington Post* changed its policy on checking its reporters' sources. Surpassing Janet Cooke in deceiving the public and editors by a wide margin was *New York Times* reporter Jayson Blair and *USA Today* foreign correspondent Jack Kelley. The details on their journalistic crimes are described in Chapter 20. Like Cooke, Kelley and Blair made up much of what they reported and pretended they spoke to sources.

In their book *Investigative Reporting*, authors David Anderson and Peter Benjaminson wrote that it is sometimes a good idea for reporters to "talk to other reporters" about a source before investing a lot of time in documenting a story. They note that other reporters might already be familiar with the source, and the story he or she has to tell, and might have already "researched and debunked the information." They also say, "Nothing is quite as discouraging as working for days on a top-notch investigative piece only to discover that another reporter is typing out a final draft while you are still looking for the phone booth your source called from."

Gaining Confidence

Reporters who find good, reliable sources and prove to them that they will protect their confidentiality usually find that those sources will continue to provide information, sometimes for many years. Self-esteem is often one motive for tipsters, and feeling good about being involved in the breaking of a story often encourages them to find new items. Smart reporters tell their sources that they are providing a service to the community. This allows sources to see themselves as part of a team, and they will actively look for new information to provide to their colleague at the radio or TV station.

Making Friends

Other good information comes from "friends" whom reporters cultivate in offices where records and documents are housed and, particularly for crime-beat reporters, at police desks.

Experienced reporters also suggest that "hanging out" at restaurants, coffeehouses, and bars where politicians and city and county employees gather is another good way to develop new sources. These sources begin to accept you as one of them, and if they have any stories to tell or have heard some interesting rumors, they may share them with you.

Leaks

Information from an unidentified source in the government, political, or corporate world is known as a *leak*. As with sources who provide tips, government insiders, for one reason or another, reveal information of a sensitive nature to the press with the promise of confidentiality. Such insiders could be White House staff members, assistants to members of a state assembly, or someone in a mayor's office who wants the media to know something about an individual or about an action that is being planned or debated behind closed doors. Leaks from grand jury deliberations during the White House scandal involving President Clinton and intern Monica Lewinsky were commonplace, and police leaks played an important role in the often unprofessional media coverage of the JonBenét Ramsey murder case. (Both of those cases are discussed further in Chapter 22.)

One of the most celebrated leaks in recent years involved the information from a high government official, perhaps in the White House itself, that may have threatened the life of a CIA agent, Valerie Plame, the wife of former U.S. Ambassador Joseph C. Wilson.

As this is being written, the Justice Department is investigating a CIA complaint that White House officials leaked the name of agent Valerie Plame in an apparent effort to punish her husband and stifle criticism of the Bush Administration's case for going to war in Iraq. The husband, Joseph Wilson, a former ambassador to Iraq, had angered the Bush administration earlier in the year by claiming that the White House knew when Bush made statements about Iraqi efforts to buy uranium in Africa that the evidence was dubious. It was a close friend of the President, CIA Director George Tenet, who charged that White House officials had leaked the name and occupation of Wilson's wife, Valerie Plame. The White House denied knowing anything about the leak and Bush promised to cooperate with the Justice Department in trying to locate the source of the leak. According to an unidentified high-level official, CIA lawyers contacted the Justice Department in July of 2003 after conservative syndicated columnist Robert Novak identified Plame in print. But Novak, of course, has not identified his source and is not likely to.

The CIA's concern about the identification of one of its agents is understandable for a variety of security reasons, not the least of which is that it poses a possible threat to the life of the identified agent. Conviction on a charge of leaking such classified information carries a maximum penalty of 10 years in prison and $50,000 in fines. *The Washington Post* quoted an administration official as saying that two White House officials phoned at least six journalists and disclosed the name and occupation of Wilson's wife. Novak printed the name in a column and said Wilson, a critic of the Bush policy on Iraq, had been sent by the CIA to Africa after his CIA agent wife suggested it, which was denied by the couple. But only a week before the Novak story broke, Wilson had written an op-ed piece in *The New York Times* in which he revealed that he had, indeed, been sent to Niger, Africa, to investigate reports that Saddam's regime had sought to purchase uranium to help it produce nuclear weapons. Wilson concluded that the reports were based on false information and not to be believed. Despite this, President Bush cited the reports in his State of the Union address. White House officials have since admitted that that was a mistake. Wilson has charged that "at a minimum, Karl Rove (Bush's top political adviser) condoned the leak." The FBI, as of this writing, had interviewed Rove and some three dozen other people at the White House, including President Bush, as part of its investigation. But in Congress, there has been a wave of Democratic calls for an independent prosecutor to probe into the affair, because of the obvious conflict of interest that exists in an investigation of possible White House involvement by an Attorney General, John Ashcroft, who is a close ally to both the President and Carl Rove. A poll by *The Washington Post* and *ABC News* shows that 7 out of 10 Americans believe that a special prosecutor should be named to investigate the case. Meanwhile, a grand jury has been investigating the leak and in October 2004, U.S. District Court Judge Thomas F. Hogan found *New York Times* reporter Judith Miller in contempt for refusing to testify in connection with the case. The action came as something of a surprise because although the reporter did reporting on the case, she never wrote an article about it. Other high-profile journalists who received subpoenas in the case, after initially resisting, agreed to meet with the special prosecutor involved in the case. Miller shared a Pulitzer Prize with other *Times* journalists for coverage of al Qaeda. Judge Hogan ordered that the reporter be confined but allowed her to remain out of jail pending appeal. Commenting on the judge's decision, Miller said "this is really not about me," it's about the ability of all journalists to do our job by having people who trust us know that their identities will be protected if they come to us with allegations of wrongdoing or disagreement with policy." The Times is appealing the judge's decision to the U.S. Court of Appeals. There is little doubt that by the time you read this information, the case will most likely have changed, perhaps dramatically, although President Bush has said the source of the leak may never be found. In any case, look on the author's Website for this book for updates on this story and other continuing stories discussed in this book. (Go to www.broadcastnewsbook.com)

The Clarence Thomas Case

The most notorious example of a leak, prior to this case, involved the nomination of Supreme Court Justice Clarence Thomas. Just before the Senate was to vote on Thomas' nomination, the press was leaked a story that Anita Hill, who once worked for Thomas, had told federal investigators that he had sexually harassed her. As a result, the vote was delayed as the Senate Judiciary Committee extended the hearings.

Two reporters, Nina Totenberg of National Public Radio and Timothy Phelps of *Newsday*, reported the information. The leak sparked a national debate within Congress and among Americans, who found themselves divided on the propriety of such information being leaked to the media. There were new calls for the plugging of such leaks and suggestions of penalties for those who were found guilty of perpetrating them.

Phelps and Totenberg were subpoenaed by a special Senate counsel, who attempted to discover the source of the leak. When both reporters refused to identify their source, the counsel attempted to gain support for some action against them, such as a contempt citation, but he failed. Senators apparently

Figure 18-1
Nina Totenberg, legal affairs
correspondent for National Public
Radio, testifies before a congressional
committee during the Clarence
Thomas confirmation hearings. (Photo
by Michael Geissinger)

were not anxious to test First Amendment rights by compelling the reporters
to disclose their sources.

Totenberg said she "simply wasn't going to tell" who gave her the information and that she was "prepared to go to jail" rather than reveal who
leaked the information to her. In an interview with Professor Emeritus Ben
Silver of Arizona State University, Totenberg noted that she did not identify
Anita Hill by name until Hill agreed to be interviewed. Otherwise, Totenberg
said, "I would not have done it. I don't think you can trust an accusation as
long as it remains anonymous."

When asked how she felt about reporting such allegations, Totenberg
said: "It's more than just reporting an allegation; she [Hill] turned out to be
a credible witness, although I can't vouch for the truth of the allegation."

Totenberg said her mail "is full of allegations," but unless she can verify
them, she doesn't broadcast them. "You can't fully corroborate all the time,"
said the NPR correspondent. She said that was true in the Anita Hill case, but
she eliminated the problem by speaking with a person she considered credible, Susan Hoerchner. She said Hoerchner, a judge on the California Workers'
Compensation Appeals Board, told her that Hill had made the same sexual
harassment allegation against Thomas eight years earlier during a conversation she had with Hill. Hoerchner said that she and Hill had met when they
were students at Yale University. Hoerchner later gave the same information
to the Senate Judiciary Committee.

Leaks, of course, have been a way of life in Congress and probably in
every administration since the creation of the U.S. government. Most Washington observers both in and out of government agree that it is impossible to
stop leaks. There is also a common point of view that leaks, for the most part,
provide a service to the American people. A leak from a source believed to
be in the Nixon administration, the so-called Deep Throat, led to the Watergate scandal that resulted in the downfall of President Richard Nixon.

As for the leak involving Clarence Thomas, former *CBS News* correspondent Richard Threlkeld said he may be "getting jaded" as he gets older. He

noted that "one man's leak is another man's essential release of timely information. The Republicans were mad because a Democrat apparently leaked information about Anita Hill. But," Threlkeld pointed out, "some years ago during Abe Fortas' contentious removal from the Court, Senator Strom Thurmond's office leaked information about him, and his misdoing, to the press, and that made him leave the Court." Threlkeld asked, "What's wrong with that? Senator Thurmond, I am sure, would have called that timely release of essential information, so I'm not that concerned about leaks." Threlkeld concluded, "There always have been leaks and there always will be. . . . There are no gaskets in the faucet of public information that would stop them."

Trial Balloons

A different type of leak is the *trial balloon*. In this case, the leak has the endorsement of the White House, the mayor, or some other government official or agency. The trial balloon tips off one or more people in the media about some controversial action the department or official is thinking of taking. The purpose of the trial balloon is to measure reaction in advance not only from the people but also from the media, lobbying groups, and others. If the trial balloon is greeted with strong opposition, then the official or agency could quietly forget the action it had contemplated. On the other hand, if there is no loud protest, or the planned action is received with enthusiasm, the action probably would proceed as planned.

Authoritative or Informed Sources

When sources of information cannot be substantiated by ordinary means, reporters often attribute the information to a spokesperson, or authoritative or informed sources. There are times, for example, when correspondents at the White House, State Department, and Pentagon obtain information from government officials that may only be used with the understanding that the source is not to be named. So reporters who wish to use the information must say, "a spokesman at the Pentagon or a source at the State Department revealed today . . . "

Reporters who do not wish to use such vague attribution would be unable to use the information.

Most people in the radio and TV audience take such attributions for granted, assuming that if the reporter is quoting a spokesperson the story is probably true. Often it is, but there's no guarantee. The use of the term *informed sources* and *unidentified sources* was almost as much of a scandal in the media coverage of the Clinton-Lewinsky scandal as the scandal itself. That topic is discussed in great detail in Chapter 22, "Tabloid Journalism."

Background Briefings

Government officials often give information to reporters but insist that neither the officials nor the agencies they represent be identified. These meetings are called *background briefings*. If reporters wish to use the information revealed at such briefings, they must attribute it, again, by using phrases such as "official sources" or "well-informed sources."

Summary

Developing good sources and keeping them confidential constitute the backbone of effective reporting. This chapter focuses on the importance of maintaining relationships with sources. Most reporters honor confidentiality agreements, and some have even gone to jail rather than disclose their sources. They knew if they had revealed their sources, they would have lost their credibility and effectiveness as journalists.

It is equally important to know whether your sources are reliable. It is essential to check and double-check the information they provide; never use information from only one source as the basis for a story. At the same time, don't dismiss information without thoroughly checking to see if it could be true.

If you agree to keep information off the record, make sure you do; otherwise it will be the last time that person gives you any information. Also remember that when you do agree to keep something off the record, start looking for sources you can quote for the record.

Review Questions

1. What motivates people to give tips to a radio or TV station?
2. Explain why you would or would not broadcast information provided by a tipster.
3. Discuss some ways to develop sources.
4. What is a leak? Give an example.
5. What is a trial balloon?
6. What does "off the record" mean?

Exercises

1. Suppose that you are a TV assignment editor and you receive a call from an individual who claims she saw the mayor meeting with a well-known mobster. Describe in detail how you would handle the situation.
2. Suppose you are a news director for a radio station. You get a call from a student at the local university who says he has been dealing in narcotics but wants to quit. He says he will tell you the whole story about drugs on campus, but you have to keep his identity secret. Do you agree and put a reporter on the story? Explain your decision.
3. An individual has been leaking information to you for several years and has always been reliable; however, she now tells you a story about corruption that could bring down the city administration if it is true. Do you tell anyone else at the station what you have been told? Do you disclose your source? Explain in detail.

19 Specialty Reporting

Investigative Reporting

Some journalists believe that the term *investigative reporting* is redundant—that all reporting is investigative. There is some truth in that statement. Earlier chapters in this book have been devoted to the techniques that all reporters use, such as Chapter 15, "The Interview," Chapter 16, "Collecting Information from Documents," and Chapter 18, "Developing Sources." It is true that reporters ask questions and do some research for just about every story, but little in the way of actual investigation takes place, and, in probably 90 percent of the stories we hear and watch on radio and television, not much investigation is required.

It is not investigative reporting to ask a fire chief if the cause of a fire was arson. Likewise, it is not investigative reporting to ask a police detective if the double homicide he's investigating was drug related. And, for good or bad, aren't those two of the most common questions asked by reporters during the course of a day or week, at least in most large communities? We are not claiming that this is the way it should be—that's another debate—but it is reality; however, there is a great need for investigative reporters to deal with the 10 percent of the stories that most of us are not even aware of.

The best investigative reports reveal information that otherwise might not be revealed to the public and often involve information that some individual or group either in government or industry might be trying to hide. Sometimes the stories produced by such investigations may be contrary to the versions set forth by government or business officials trying to conceal the truth. The very best investigative reports—the kind that often win the coveted Pulitzer Prize—effect some change in the way government or private industry does business.

As mentioned earlier, we have gone into great detail throughout the book about how to prepare for such reporting. The most important things to learn are basic reporting, how to dig out information, how to develop sources, and how to use the sunshine laws.

One of the most celebrated investigative reports was the Watergate investigation by *The Washington Post* in 1972 that began as an apparent routine break-in of Democratic Party offices in the nation's capital. It ended in the resignation of President Richard Nixon and brought fame to the lead reporters on the investigation, Carl Bernstein and Bob Woodward.

In recalling how they uncovered one of the most sensational scandals in political history, Woodward and Bernstein stressed that what they did in

Watergate was the most basic, empirical police reporting of the kind you first learn when you get into the business or even that you learn in journalism school. They said they went about the Watergate story "the same way we would do any other story we were assigned to—we knocked on a lot of doors."

The reporters said they started at the bottom, talking to secretaries, clerks, chauffeurs, and administrative assistants, and gradually worked their way up. Woodward and Bernstein said that part of the post-Watergate myth is that investigative reporting is a "highly refined pseudoscience, different and apart from the rest of journalism."

Bernstein is among those who question the use of the term *investigative reporting*. He said that maybe *saturation reporting* is a better term. He described that as "a commitment of resources that would enable us to gather every fact, conduct hundreds of interviews, if necessary, and really learn our subject before we jump into print or go on the air."

Earlier in the book, two investigative reports were cited that involved the use of freedom of information laws (Chapter 16, "Collecting Information From Documents"), one by investigative reporter Mark Lagerkvist dealing with health maintenance organizations (HMOs) paying doctors bonuses not to refer patients for special medical treatment when they need it; and a second report by Chris Szechenyi concerning medical devices that were supposed to save lives but often didn't because they were defective. A third investigative report, which follows, about an Olympics scandal in Salt Lake City was the product of a tip, a subject that was discussed in detail in Chapter 18.

The Salt Lake City Scandal

In the previous chapter, we referred to tips and how they often can lead reporters to important stories. A tip brought the most important story of his career to Chris Vanocur, a reporter for KTVX-TV in Salt Lake City, according to Alicia C. Shepard's story in the April 1999 issue of the *American Journalism Review*.

Vanocur had worked as a reporter for the Salt Lake City TV station for about eight years. His beat was politics, but it was not politics that brought him fame—it was the Winter Olympics. It all started with a letter that someone sent to him. Just who sent the letter has not been revealed, but it was addressed to a young woman whose father was an influential member of the International Olympic Committee (IOC), which in 1995 chose Salt Lake City as a host city.

The woman identified in the letter, Sonia Essomba, had been receiving money for two years for tuition at American University in Washington, D.C., along with rent and expenses. But the letter that ended up in Vanocur's hands said that assistance was about to end. The author of the letter was David Johnson, the second in command at the Salt Lake City Organizing Committee to bring the Olympics to Salt Lake City.

Johnson was informing Essomba that it was no longer possible to continue the scholarship program because of budget restrictions. The letter made mention of a check that was enclosed for $10,114.99, which was described as a final payment. That letter touched off the biggest corruption scandal in

Figure 19-1   Reporter Chris Vanocur interviewing Olene Walker, Governor of Utah.

the history of the Olympics, and Chris Vanocur, son of Sander Vanocur, the former Washington reporter for ABC and NBC, broke the story.

The airing of the letter on KTVX-TV launched a media frenzy that would dominate the news not only in Salt Lake City but in most of the nation. It also touched off new investigations by a variety of journalists around the world that made it an international news story. As the Vanocur report mushroomed in Salt Lake City, officials disclosed that Essomba had received more than $108,000 from the Salt Lake City Olympic Committee and that the Committee had spent more than $1 million on 24 of the 114 IOC members to ensure that the Utah city would win the Winter Games in 2002.

Salt Lake City Olympic officials gave IOC members free credit cards and spent almost $20,000 to take three couples to the 1995 Super Bowl. The city also loaned $30,000 to one member of the IOC and, incredibly, even paid for plastic surgery to remove the bags under the eyes of another IOC member. Although rumors had been circulating that Salt Lake City was offering incentives to IOC officials to bring the games to the city, none of it was documented until Vanocur's report aired.

Within months of Vanocur's report, journalists in other parts of the world would soon discover that payoffs had been made by many officials in cities trying to attract the Olympic Games. For example, Nagano Olympic officials had spent $22,000 on each of 62 IOC members in order to bring the 1998 Winter Olympics to that Japanese city. But, again, there's no telling when and

if this international scandal would have broken if it had not been for the tip—
the letter someone sent to Vanocur.

After getting the letter, Vanocur got on the Internet and started searching. He said he had no idea who Essomba was or what he was dealing with.
He typed in the name Essomba and got some hits, including one reference
to a doctor in Africa, who was an IOC member. Vanocur said he had
heard stories about scholarships, and he began thinking that the Sonia
referred to in the letter he received probably was a relative of an IOC member.
Vanocur said he then called the Salt Lake City Olympics Committee and
arranged for an on-camera interview for the next day. During that interview,
committee spokesman Frank Zang confirmed that Sonia was the daughter of
the IOC member and that the committee had, indeed, been paying part of
her tuition.

Vanocur returned to KTVX and prepared a story for the 10 o'clock news,
revealing the letter about Essomba. It was the lead story, of course. Vanocur
said that the city's Olympic Committee was paying thousands of dollars to a
close relative of somebody who voted on whether or not Salt Lake City should
get the Olympics.

The city's newspapers picked up Vanocur's story the next day, and then
a host of new revelations was exposed, including a bombshell release from
the president of the Salt Lake City Olympic Committee saying that nearly
$400,000 in financial aid or scholarships had been given to 13 individuals over
a seven-year period. Six of those people were relatives of IOC members. Ultimately, an international scandal that started with a 95-word letter that landed
on Vanocur's desk ballooned into thousands of print and video stories and
four separate investigations.

Within Salt Lake City's Olympic Committee, four board members have
resigned, the president and vice president are gone, and other administrative
officials are on leave. Ten IOC members either resigned or were expelled, and
in Salt Lake City four Olympic Board members resigned.

As for Vanocur, he says, "For me there's a little bit of drama with the
story, how a somewhat small-town reporter gets a hold of a letter that ignites
a scandal. A guy who does modest good work over the years. It's kind of nice
for me," he says, "to semi-step out of my father's (Sandy Vanocur) shadow.
He's kidding me now about being known as Chris Vanocur's father."

Here's the script for the first broadcast that Vanocur prepared on the
Olympics scandal:

On Camera
Anchor Kimberly   Tonight, disturbing new questions
                                             about the financial dealings of the
                                             Salt Lake Olympic Committee, and
                                             that's our top story.

Anchor Randall   News 4 Utah has learned that Salt
                                             Lake Olympic organizers have quietly
                                             been spending thousands of dollars to
                                             pay the college tuition costs of
                                             relatives of International Olympic
                                             bigwigs.

Kimberly	Chris Vanocur is here with a News 4 Utah exclusive investigation. Chris . . .
Vanocur (live on set)	This is a letter Salt Lake Olympic folks probably didn't want us to get. It raises very serious questions about how Olympic money is being spent and even about how Salt Lake got the Olympic bid.
Vanocur package 1:45	This confidential letter was drafted in 1996 by a senior Salt Lake Olympic official. It's written to a Sonia Essomba and reads: "Under the current budget structure, it will be difficult to continue the scholarship program with you. The enclosed check for $10,114.99 will have to be our last payment for tuition.
Sound bite: Frank Zang, Spokesman, Salt Lake City Olympic Committee	"I think this is just an example of a program that we had going to help third world countries and to provide people with education opportunities."
Vanocur	But, in fact, Sonia Essomba, this Salt Lake Olympic official later conceded, is not a needy third world student, but actually the daughter of a prominent surgeon, Rene Essomba, who just happened to be an influential African member of the International Olympic Committee.
Vanocur stand-up	In other words, our Olympic Committee was paying thousands of dollars to a close relative of somebody who voted on whether or not Salt Lake should get the Olympics.
Sound bite: Stephen Pace Utahns/Responsible Public Spending	"This looks like, walks like, and quacks like a bribe being paid out of a publicly guaranteed organization."
Vanocur	But Olympic officials say this was all private money and that there was nothing improper.
Sound bite Frank Zang	"Do you think that raises any red flags? Well, these were activities 2 or 3 years ago, when this organization was known as a bid committee."
Vanocur	But look at the date on this letter, September 1996, more than a year after Salt Lake got the bid. And according to several highly placed

Sound bite: Frank Zang

Vanocur on set

Olympic sources, Sonia Essomba was not the only relative of an I.O.C. member to receive large tuition scholarships.

"There were scholarships from other countries around the world. I do not know what all of their connections were with respect to their national Olympic committees.

So, tonight, two lingering questions are: Exactly how much has been spent on other people's tuition, and is the practice still ongoing. What are the answers? We don't know. The answers are in the Olympic budget, which has been seen by only a handful of Olympic officials. That's why tomorrow, News 4 Utah will officially ask to be given access to all of the Olympic budget.

Environmental Reporting

The growing concern for the environment in the past decade has encouraged broadcast news managers to allocate more news to the subject. In many newsrooms, the environment is still covered by general-assignment reporters, but more and more news managers are hiring broadcast journalists who have become familiar with environmental problems. Knowledge of the subject can be acquired in college, but reporters often gain their expertise simply by taking the time to learn about the complex issues.

Numerous periodicals deal with every aspect of the environment, and reporters intent on learning about environmental issues should spend many hours in the library reading these publications or should subscribe to them. A wide variety of environmental seminars also are offered throughout the country by private and government groups. The Environmental Health Center issues a newsletter; "Greenwire" is a news service offering stories about the environment; and the Society of Environmental Journalists provides help and resources for journalists trying to improve their knowledge of environmental issues. The Radio and Television News Directors' Association (RTNDA) often discusses the environment at national and regional meetings. Helpful computer databases, such as the Toxic Release Inventory, which stores information on 366 toxic chemicals, are also available.

Former CNN correspondent Debra Potter, who covered environmental stories, said that no beat is more important. She added, "Broadcasters owe it to their audiences to cover the subject because it touches viewers and listeners where they live." Potter said communities throughout the nation are wrestling with environmental issues such as waste disposal and water quality. She noted that polls show that Americans believe that the environment is one of the five most important issues facing the nation.

Potter stresses that environmental reporters who know and understand the issues—who know where to look and which questions to ask—get a jump on environmental stories. She also pointed out that environmental issues are difficult to explain and that environmental reporters must act responsibly "by not raising false hopes or unfounded fears."

Bob Engleman of Scripps-Howard newspapers says that covering the environment is like covering any other complicated, important issue. He advises following these steps:

1. Learn the issue.
2. Maintain skepticism.
3. Seek out all viewpoints.
4. Ask probing questions.
5. Report the story as accurately and as fairly as possible.

CNN's Jeff Greenfield says that unless reporters covering the environment completely understand the various aspects of the story, they would be "better off not doing it at all." He believes that if reporters misinform people about politicians, they do not cause too much damage. "But," he adds, "if you falsely report to the community that children are at risk because of something in the schools, or the land, or water, you have done much harm." At the same time, Greenfield notes that reporters who fail to inform the public about a real risk do even greater harm.

The editor of the *Freedom Forum Journal*, Craig Le May, says environmental reporters must "look at what local industries are doing—how they make and transport products, how they do business." He also warns reporters that much of the environmental information available is from press releases, which are not reliable.

Le May says that reporters must search through all the public relations and make sense of the issues. He notes that the rule for cultivating sources is the same as for other types of assignments: "Get the best people and find out what they have at stake in what you are reporting." He warns, for example, that researchers at universities are often funded by organizations with a fixed point of view, so reporters have to be skeptical of their findings. Le May also urges reporters to beware of trade groups that "masquerade as environmental organizations." He notes that the National Wetlands Coalition sounds like an environmental group, but it is actually a lobby group for the largest oil, gas, and utility companies.

Robert Logan, the director of the Science Journalism Center at the University of Missouri, also urges reporters to be "skeptical of everybody. Everyone is selling something," he warns, "even if they are not into making money." Logan says reporters should remember that the investigative rule "Follow the money to get to the bottom of something" is bad advice for environmental reporting. He suggests instead, "Follow the best scientific evidence first, and then look for the money."

In Miami, WTVJ-TV takes the environment very seriously. Reporter-producer Jeff Burnside says the environmental beat is one of the most intriguing of news beats: "It's a constantly changing beat because of scientific advancement, economics, population growth, political shifts and more." He also notes that at its fundamental core, the environment—as an issue—escalates in importance ew person born into the world, putting more pres-

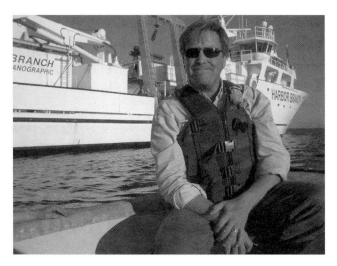

Figure 19-2 WTVJ-TV reporter Jeff Burnside, alongside the oceanographic research vessel Seward Johnson. (Courtesy of WTVJ-TV, Miami)

sure on the environment. Burnside adds that there are myriad stories at the local, state, regional, and national and international levels. The WTVJ reporter says, "It's also a compelling beat because of the potential for blending video with heartfelt stories mixed with a constant flow of new information."

The TV station launched its environmental coverage plan, which it calls "EcoWatch," on Earth Day in 2002, in partnership with the *Miami Herald.* Burnside said it is the only on-going environmental franchise in American television news. He said the goal is to engage the community in a robust debate over environmental issues.

Here now is an environment package done by Burnside called "Cures from the Deep." (Note that this script has all the times and locations of the sound bites and video that the reporter wants to use in the package to help the editor put the story together.)

Nearly one in five of us will be affected by a major disease in our lifetime.

That unsettling news means the job of a team of Florida scientists, with newly announced support from Governor Jeb Bush, takes on greater importance.

(NAT SOUND OCEAN from 10:16:50#1)

(Shot: Sunrise over ship deck 10:12:20 #1 pick best shot)

(track)
    IMAGINE EACH NEW DAY BRINGS THE CHANCE OF DISCOVERING NEW CURES FOR DISEASE.

THAT'S THE LIFE OF SHIRLEY POMPONI.

(SOT Shirley 10:04:50 tape 4)
"It's very fulfilling to know that something I'm working on may one day save somebody's life."

▫**1**]] C1.5 GO [[
Pan to Ship in sunflare 11:31:27 tape 3
(track)

SHE'S ABOARD THE 200-FOOT SHIP FROM FLORIDA'S HARBOR BRANCH OCEANOGRAPHIC

▫**2**]] C1.5 G O [[
Dolphins swimming here

INSTITUTE CRUISING OFF MIAMI IN CRYSTAL BLUE WATERS.

(NAT SOUND Shirley walking fast 7:40 OR 8:00 tape #2)

(track)
DR. POMPONI IS GETTING READY TO SEARCH FOR NEW COMPOUNDS TO FIGHT CANCER AND OTHER MAJOR DISEASES.

▫**3**]] C1.5 GO [[
shot of sub on deck
SHE ANDOTHER DIVERS RIDE IN THIS MULTI-MILLION DOLLAR SUBMERSIBLE.

(SOT Shirley 10:04:59 tape 4)
(covered with sub moving off deck)
"Maybe something that we're collecting today will have a chemical in it that will save my life."

(NAT SOUND SUB HITS WATER 11:30 tape 2)

(track)
THEY'LL DROP TO 1,000, 2,000, EVEN 3,000 FEET DEEP.

(SOT 15:08 tape 2)
"OK. We're on the bottom."

(track)
. . . TO SPOTS ON THE OCEAN FLOOR THAT HUMANS HAVE NEVER LAID EYES ON.
THIS TIME, THEY'RE EXPLORING THE MIAMI TERRACE . . .
20 MILLION YEARS OLD . . . LOOKING FOR RARE SPONGES AND CORALS.

(SOT 17:05 tape 2)
"Ok, this is sample number one."

(track collecting sample 42:24 and 45:00 "Cockpit" tape 57:00 and 59:50)
THEY VIEW THESE SAMPLES AS CHEMICAL FACTORIES BEYOND WHAT HUMANS CAN CREATE.

(andient fish at 36:04 tape 2)
THEY ALSO SEE ALL KINDS OF WEIRD CREATURES . . .
(fish 26:00 tape 2)
. . . AND FISH ENTHRALLED WITH THE BRIGHT LIGHTS.

(SOT audio only 24:44 tape 2)
"Oh! Check it out!"
(Shot is at 25:06 eel-like fish with another fish in it's mouth)

(track)
THE SCIENTISTS KNOW THAT SPONGES ARE THE VERY FIRST ANIMALS. OVER MILLIONS OF YEARS . . . THEY'VE DEVELOPED UNIQUE CHEMICALS TO WARD OFF THREATS BECAUSE THEY'RE ANCHORED AND CANNOT MOVE AWAY. THOSE CHEMICALS MIGHT ALSO WARD OFF HUMAN DISEASE.

(cover with deep sea shots 09:59:47)
"Uh, I love working with sponges."

(9:59:27)
". . . for me it was like sponge heaven there were all kinds of sponges there, it was absolutely glorious."

(STAND UP BURNSIDE LAST TAKE)
"THE GOAL OF THIS VOYAGE IS NOTHING SHORT OF BREATH-TAKING. WITH $10 MILLION IN SEED MONEY FROM THE GOVERNOR AND LEGISLATURE . . . SCIENTISTS ARE GOING FROM JACKSONVILLE TO THE KEYS, PROBING FLORIDA'S RICH WATERS, SEARCHING FOR CURES FROM THE DEEP."

(SOT 10:50:27 tape 1 blast of air hold shot until sun flare disappears)
"Psshhhttt!!"

(SOT Shirley covered at first, then on cam 48:35)
"It was very good. Sponge heaven. We got all four of the sponges we were looking for."

(track)
THE STRANGE CREATURES NOW SUDDENLY FACE A LETHAL PRESSURE CHANGE FROM THE DEEP SEA TO SEA LEVEL.
THEY ARE RUSHED INTO THE SHIP'S WAITING SCIENCE TEAM.

(NAT SOUND HUSTLE AND BUSTLE)

(track)
INCLUDING THIS BIZARRE SPONGE MADE OF GLASS. SPUN GLASS. LIKE FIBERGLASS.

(SOT Shirley covered with coral lab 10:07:56)
   **"The mission that we're on is important to Florida, because what
we're doing is exploring for new resources in Florida waters, new
resources that could be used, you know, for drug development. We're
taking an inventory of what's in Florida waters, that's not been done
before."**

(track over breathtaking sunset shot with Shirley)
   IT TAKES 10–20 YEARS TO CREATE MEDICINE OUT OF THESE
DISCOVERIES.
   AND TOMORROW TAKES THESE SCIENTISTS ANOTHER DAY
CLOSER TO THAT GOAL.

   Live, in Dania Beach, Jeff Burnside, NBC 6.

   Here's a report from environmental reporter Don Wall of WFAA-TV in
Dallas on the possible dangers of electromagnetic fields.

on cam/2-shot	((CHIP)) ARE ELECTROMAGNETIC FIELDS PRODUCED BY POWER LINES . . . DANGEROUS TO YOUR HEALTH?
	((TRACY)) THE PUBLIC UTILITY COMMISSION OF TEXAS HAS RELEASED THE RESULTS OF A 3- YEAR STUDY THAT SAYS PEOPLE WHO LIVE NEAR POWER LINES HAVE NOTHING TO WORRY ABOUT.
turn to box: a current danger	((Tracy turn box)) BUT EVEN T-U ELECTRIC SAYS MORE RESEARCH NEEDS TO BE DONE. CHANNEL 8's ENVIRONMENTAL REPORTER DON WALL EXPLAINS IN THE FIRST OF HIS TWO-PART SERIES, "A CURRENT DANGER."
sot supers on tape runs: 4:14 SCENE FROM FRANKENSTEIN	SOT (THUNDER AND LIGHTNING . . . POWER EXPLODING AS THE CURRENT PASSES INTO THE MONSTER.) IT WAS THE POWER OF ELECTRICITY THAT GAVE LIFE TO FRANKENSTEIN'S MONSTER. (it's alive, it's alive . . .)
(WIDE WITH CHILDREN WALKING IN FRONT OF	IN A LESS SPECTACULAR, BUT NO LESS DRAMATIC WAY,

POWER LINES . . .
GRAPHICALLY FIELD
EMANATES FROM
POWER LINES)

ELECTRICITY GIVES POWER TO OUR
DAILY LIVES. AND EVERYTHING
THAT CARRIES ELECTRICITY EMITS
AN ELECTROMAGNETIC FIELD—AN
EMF—WHICH OUR BODIES ABSORB.

S: DON WALL, WFAA
TV, FORT WORTH
(AT NIGHT, HOLDING
TWO FLUORESCENT
BULBS)

THIS IS WHAT WE MEAN BY AN
ELECTROMAGNETIC FIELD.
I'M STANDING UNDER A
TYPICAL 138,000-VOLT POWER
LINE, LIKE THOSE THAT RUN
THROUGH MANY NEIGHBORHOODS,
AND THE EMF IS STRONG ENOUGH
TO ILLUMINATE THESE
FLUORESCENT LIGHTS.
THERE ARE NO PLUGS, AND NO
CORDS. THE POWER TO LIGHT THESE
BULBS IS IN THE AIR.
AND THERE ARE STUDIES WHICH
CLAIM THAT EMF EXPOSURE IS
DANGEROUS.
SOME STUDIES LINK PROXIMITY
TO POWER LINES WITH CHILDHOOD
LEUKEMIA.
ANOTHER STUDY SAYS
EMF'S MAY CAUSE BRAIN CANCER.
THE FINDINGS ARE
CONTROVERSIAL AND
SCIENTIFICALLY SOMEWHAT
UNCERTAIN. MANY RESEARCHERS
BELIEVE POWER LINES ARE
PERFECTLY SAFE.
BUT THERE IS NO DOUBT THAT
PEOPLE WHO LIVE NEAR POWER
LINES ARE EXPOSED TO GREATER
EMF LEVELS THAN PEOPLE WHO
DON'T.

S: PLANO

THESE THREE WOMEN WALKING
ALONG THE BLUEBONNET TRAIL
THINK EMF'S FROM POWER LINES
MAY HAVE CAUSED THEIR SONS'
BRAIN TUMORS.
("OBVIOUSLY, BY BUILDING THIS
PATH UNDER THE POWER LINE,
SOMEBODY'S ASSUMING THAT IT'S
PERFECTLY SAFE?")

"I'M NOT SURE THAT ANYONE
TOOK IT INTO CONSIDERATION,
FRANKLY."

NINE CHILDREN WITH BRAIN TUMORS HAVE BEEN DIAGNOSED IN THE HIGHPOINT AREA OF PLANO, A CLUSTER OF DISEASE THESE MOTHERS HOPE WILL BE STUDIED.

KRIS ALBERTA'S FAMILY LIVED IN A TOWNHOUSE RIGHT NEXT TO THESE POWER LINES.

("YOU WERE OUT HERE ALL THE TIME?") "QUITE A BIT. I USED TO WALK THE DOG OUT HERE. MY SON WOULD COME OUT HERE AND HE RODE HIS BIKE, JOGGED."

HER 16-YEAR-OLD SON, DUSTIN, WAS HEALTHY, UNTIL THEY MOVED HERE. A YEAR AGO, HE WAS DIAGNOSED WITH BRAIN TUMORS; HE DIED IN MARCH.

S: KRIS ALBTERA

"BEING HERE FOR TWO YEARS, IT'S A POSSIBILITY THAT IT COULD HAVE CONTRIBUTED OR CAUSED HIS BRAIN TUMOR, AND NO, I DON'T FEEL SAFE WALKING UNDER HERE, WHEN I SEE PREGNANT WOMEN OR YOUNG CHILDREN UNDER HERE, I DON'T THINK THEY ARE SAFE."

THAT'S HOW SUE FARROW FEELS TOO. SHE AND HER SON PLAYED IN THIS PARK SEVERAL TIMES A WEEK WHEN HE WAS SMALL.

NINE-YEAR-OLD DUSTY HAS HAD 6 OPERATIONS RELATED TO HIS BRAIN TUMOR. FOR NOW, HE'S DOING WELL.

BUT HIS MOTHER SEARCHES FOR ANSWERS.

S: SUE FARROW

"HE'S A YOUNG KID. HE'S EATING GOOD FOOD, HE'S NOT OUT POISONING HIS BODY IN OTHER WAYS. THERE HAS TO BE SOME TYPE OF AN OUTSIDE INFLUENCE THAT COULD TRIGGER, OR PROMOTE, OR SET OFF A TUMOR." ("AND YOU

THINK IT COULD BE POWER LINES?")
"POSSIBLY, YES."

THESE WOMEN BELIEVE SIGNS
SHOULD BE POSTED, WARNING
PEOPLE OF POTENTIAL EMF
DANGERS FROM POWER LINES.

KRIS

"I DON'T WANT ANY OTHER
CHILD, OR ANY OTHER PARENT, TO
GO THROUGH WHAT WE DID, IF IT
CAN BE AVOIDED. AND THIS IS
SOMETHING THAT COULD BE
AVOIDED."

DR. JOEL GOLDSTEEN AGREES.
HE'S AN URBAN PLANNER AT THE
UNIVERSITY OF TEXAS AT
ARLINGTON.

(SEE AERIAL OF POWER
LINE NEIGHBORHOODS
IN TARRANT COUNTY)

HE'S DONE A STUDY OF
TARRANT COUNTY THAT SAYS
ROUGHLY 70,000 PEOPLE ARE
POTENTIALLY AT RISK FROM
OVERHEAD LINES.

GOLDSTEEN SAYS UNTIL THE
RESEARCH ABOUT POTENTIAL
DANGERS IS CONCLUSIVE, CITIES
SHOULD NOT BUILD JOGGING PATHS
OR SCHOOLS, AND CHILDREN SHOULD
NOT BE ALLOWED TO PLAY UNDER
OR NEAR POWER LINES.

S: DR. JOEL GOLDSTEEN
UNIV. OF TEXAS
ARLINGTON

"YOU CAN'T DO THAT. YOU
CAN'T CONTINUE BUSINESS AS
USUAL. CITIES THAT ARE DOING
THAT ARE DOING A DISSERVICE TO
THEIR RESIDENTS AND THEY ARE
ACTING UNETHICAL AND
UNPRINCIPLED."

AND, FOR NOW, IT REMAINS AN
EMOTIONAL ISSUE—PERHAPS EVEN
MORE THAN A SCIENTIFIC ONE.

SUE FARROW

"YOU TALK ABOUT EMOTIONAL
MOMS. WE MAY BE EMOTIONAL.
MAYBE THAT'S WHAT IT'S GOING
TO TAKE TO GET PEOPLE AWARE
TO COME OUT AND SPEAK ABOUT
IT."

> T.U. ELECTRIC DOES NOT
> BELIEVE POWER LINES ARE
> HARMFUL, BUT THEY AGREE THAT
> MORE RESEARCH NEEDS TO BE
> DONE.
>   AND THEY SAY THERE ARE
> THINGS YOU CAN DO TO MINIMIZE
> YOUR EXPOSURE TO
> ELECTROMAGNETIC FIELDS. MORE
> ON THAT TOMORROW.

Business Reporting

Until a few years ago, business reporting was a fairly routine story for most radio and TV stations. Only the larger stations considered it important enough to assign a reporter full-time to the beat, and for the most part, business news consisted mostly of stories on the stock market. Radio and TV news organizations routinely include reports on the Dow-Jones and Nasdaq averages each evening, and if there is a good local business story, like the move of some major corporation to town, it would be assigned to one of the general assignment reporters. For the most part, people who are interested in finding out more about the world of business are forced to go to cable where they can find financial news on CNBC and CNN. PBS also has some financial programs. But it's somewhat rare to find a business story leading a newscast at either the local level or the networks unless, perhaps, the market had an outstanding or extremely poor day.

But all that changed in 2001 when big business frequently became the lead story. An avalanche of corporate scandals rocked the business world and the rest of nation in an unprecedented fashion. There were so many scandals making headlines, it was difficult to keep track of them. Business news was suddenly requiring lots of work by lots of reporters, and special reports became common. The reason, of course, is that while most Americans are heavily invested in one way or another in the financial markets through private investments, mutual funds, 401ks and pension plans, they don't, for the most part pay, much attention to the ups and downs of the markets unless something really goes wrong, like a crash. But the scandals that started to unfold in 2001 quickly got everyone's attention. It all started in October when it was learned that Enron boosted profits and hid debts of more than one billion dollars by improperly using off-the books partnerships; manipulated the Texas power market and bribed foreign governments to win contracts aboard.

One Enron executive pled guilty to two felony charges, and others in the corporation are facing possible jail time. Ex-Enron CEO Kenneth Lay has been indicted on 11 counts. The corporation filed a Chapter 11 and thousands of company employees and stockholders lost millions, many their life-savings. The firm's auditing company, Arthur Anderson, was convicted of obstruction of justice for its role in the Enron collapse. In March of 2002, the World Com scandal took the spotlight, when it was discovered that the corporation overstated its cash flow by almost $4 billion dollars in operating expenses and that founder Bernard Ebbers had obtained $400 million in off-the-books loans. The company went into bankruptcy. The *Wall Street Journal* called the World Com Scandal "the biggest accounting scam ever." We can not list all of the corporations that found themselves in trouble with the law these past three years, but among the other headline-grabbers was Martha Stewart who, as of this writing is serving a jail sentence as a result of lying to a government investigator about the circumstances in which she sold her stock in Imclone after reveiving a tip that would send the pharmaceutical stock plummeting. Imclone's former CEO, Sam Waksal, was charged with insider trading and pleaded guilty to six counts, including bank and securities fraud. Among the other scandals, Tyco's CEO was indicted for tax evasion. Qwest Communications inflated revenue and used improper accounting practices. Peregrine Systems overstated $100 million in sales. Xerox falsified financial record for five years, boosting income by $1.5 billion dollars, and Bristol Meyers inflated 2001 revenue by $1.5 billion dollars.

So what happened? That consumed much of the conversation on cable talk shows and the traditional networks for many months. The highly-respected Dean of the Harvard Business School said he was appalled at the instances of greed and corporate wrongdoing that was uncovered at firms and organizations once held up as paragons of success. Dean Kim B. Clark said he "was dismayed to see the destructive effect these instances of corruption and ethical misconduct have had on our society and our economy." Dean Clark said a lot of people have attempted to explain what happened and most have suggested two possibilities: one puts the primary responsibility on a few bad apples and sees that solution as catching them, prosecuting them and putting them in jail or fining them. The other suggestion, he said, is that "there really is something wrong with the barrel, it's not just a matter of a few bad apples, and what we really need is a wholesome revamping of the systems of governance and the web of laws and regulations." In other words, "the solution is to remake the barrel with new legislation and new regulation." Clark said he thought there are elements of truth to both these suggestions. But he added that "we need a deeper understanding of what has happened and a broader conception of what must be done."

As indicated, the scandals—as unpleasant as they were—brought new life to business reporting and those in the newsrooms assigned to dealing with the scandals were kept very busy. Their work was often made easier if they had experience covering the complex world of business.

For those who think that world is fascinating and would like a future in reporting such news, we have these suggestions: Take courses in economics, marketing, and other business-related subject and, perhaps, coinsider graduate work in business. An MBA degree carries a lot of weight with many news managers.

As always, research is a necessity. Broadcasters specializing in business reporting should read periodicals such as *Barron's, Business Week,* the *Economist, Forbes,* and *Fortune.* The *Wall Street Journal* is the bible for the business world. Similarly, *The New York Times, The Washington Post,* and their counterparts in other large cities have excellent business columns and reports that business specialists should follow.

Many good trade publications are also devoted to business and industry. Although many of these publications have biases that the reporter must consider, they should by no means be discounted. They are full of information that helps reporters learn about industries and new systems, techniques, and products.

The business reporter uses the same basic techniques as a general-assignment reporter—developing good sources and cross-checking information for reliability. Covering business is a little like covering politics. There's a lot of speculation, and a good reporter soon learns to be skeptical about any predictions concerning the economy, interest rates, and the stock market.

Reporters thinking about specializing in business news should remember that the opportunities are not as great as in some other specialties, such as environmental and medical reporting because, as we mentioned earlier, radio and TV stations do not normally spend as much airtime on business subjects as on these other issues. This lack of coverage results partly because many news directors think that most business news is either too dull or too complicated to explain to the public. At the same time, many stations that do have business reporters say they get good feedback from the public on business news.

Health and Medical Reporting

Health and medical subjects rank high in interest among radio and TV audiences for obvious reasons—we all want to remain healthy. Reporters with a knowledge of health and medical issues are assets to news managers. Most large news staffs have someone assigned to a medical and health beat. Many broadcast news producers regularly include health and medical stories in newscasts. Reporters do not have much trouble selling producers on a good medical story. Likewise, depending on the size of the market, good health and medical stories are usually not difficult to find.

Because they are public-relations conscious, hospitals and research centers often bring stories involving their facilities or research to the attention of radio and TV newsrooms. Listeners and viewers also provide tips on medical-related stories, usually when someone close to them has been involved in something good or bad at a medical facility. Many tips concern malpractice, but some involve lifesaving techniques and appealing human-interest stories about children waiting for organ transplants and the generosity of people who contribute hundreds of thousands of dollars to make the surgery possible.

Objectivity is always an essential part of all reporting, but sometimes medical reporters must be particularly sensitive about their reports because providers often appear to be in the wrong. Doctors are accused of charging too much or refusing to accept Medicaid patients. Hospitals are criticized for turning away some patients and price gouging others. Many of these stories are true, but reporters must examine both sides of any issue. Reporters sometimes discover that hospitals are on the verge of financial collapse because of rising costs and heavy investment in equipment. They find that the government is slow in paying Medicare patients' bills and is often unrealistic when deciding on the amount doctors can charge.

Good medical reporters look for positive stories about doctors and hospitals to balance the negative ones. If and when reporters find they are beginning to dislike the medical profession as a whole, it's probably time for them to start looking for another beat. Health and medical reporters also cannot allow themselves to be duped. They must constantly ask tough questions about the medical establishment and whether it is meeting the needs of the American people.

Science and health-related courses in college help journalism students prepare for medical reporting. These students also should read the many health and medical magazines that are available. Teaching-hospital libraries also have stacks of journals from major research centers. Although these resources are provided primarily for medical students, persuasive reporters usually have no difficulty gaining access to the journals once the staff is convinced the reporters are not malpractice attorneys.

Here's an example of a medical story by former CNN medical reporter Dan Rutz about chronic fatigue syndrome.

O/C	**Anchor**
	The Center for Disease Control has completed a study of chronic fatigue syndrome. As Dan Rutz tells us, this mysterious ailment apparently is more common than experts had believed.
Rutz V/O Doctor is examining patient	**V/O** People with chronic fatigue syndrome fight an illness with no known cause. Many shuffle from doctor to doctor in search of care and understanding.
SOT Font: Dr. Richard Prokesch	**SOT** "For many years, it was thought that these people were crazy and that this really is not a disease . . . and now I think a lot of people are believing that there is something, probably more than one thing, that is causing it."
V/O Gunn at computer Computer screen Over-the-shoulder shot of Gunn at computer	**V/O** Walter Gunn and others from the Centers for Disease Control sampled patients' records and interviewed people diagnosed with chronic fatigue syndrome. The researchers disqualified everyone with a history of any other disorder, such as depression, that might have caused or contributed to their symptoms.

SOT

Font: Walter Gunn
Centers for Disease
Control

SOT
"We were quite surprised that about 26 percent of fatigued people referred to us did in fact meet the case definition. We didn't expect to find it to be more than five percent originally."

V/O
Full Screen Fonts

*Severe Prolonged Fatigue
*Other Diseases Ruled Out
*Chronic Flu-like Symptoms

V/O
To be counted, patients had to have sustained at least six months of fatigue severe enough to have cut their activities at least by half. All other possible causes had to be ruled out by test or examination, and patients had to have had the flu-like symptoms associated with the disorder.

O/C Standup

O/C
The survey in Atlanta and three other cities reveals far fewer cases of chronic fatigue syndrome than activists claim. The CDC admits that the estimate is low but nevertheless considers it valuable in proving to skeptics that the disease is for real.

V/O
Mary Niebling

V/O
Mary Niebling runs a chronic fatigue support group when she feels strong enough to attend.

Niebling sitting
at sink while she
washes dishes

Numbers are important to Niebling, who pushes for more research into a cause and cure for her chronic mystery.

SOT
Font: Mary Niebling

SOT
"I have lost everything that means anything to me, my marriage, my children, my home, my career, my finances, my intellect."

V/O
Neibling entering
doctor's office

Doctor examining Niebling
Nat sound

V/O
Since there is no test for chronic fatigue syndrome, public health officials say it is hard to come up with an accurate count. Doctors are seeing more people like Mary Niebling, and

the CDC receives from one thousand to three thousand calls a month from people who think they have it, too. Dan Rutz, CNN Medical News, Atlanta.

Consumer Reporting

Pollsters tell us that most Americans are more concerned about their economic situation than they are about their health. People without jobs often do not worry about their health until they have no money to pay their medical bills. So, news stories that affect a consumer's pocketbook are popular with audiences and news directors.

Consumer reporters have fertile fields to till—shady business operators, inferior products, overpriced services, undelivered goods and services, and many others. They do not have to look far to find their stories. They hear from listeners and viewers by the hundreds, many who have been victimized or swindled in one way or another.

The consumer reporter often has to try to correct the problem, but those reports can be tacky. We see a reporter talking to a person who has been unable to get a rug that she ordered 90 days ago. The dealer keeps promising that it will arrive any day and keeps breaking the promise. Then the "action reporter" takes over, and the next thing you know the person gets the rug (and a cameraperson is probably there), and the dealer promises it will never happen again.

Consumer reporting works best when the reporter investigates serious problems and scams that affect a lot of people. Reporters provide a real service when they alert the audience to beware of a company that guarantees consumers credit cards for a fee and then doesn't produce; a home-siding company that's tricking retired couples into paying double what they should to repair their homes; or a garage that charges customers for unnecessary repairs.

Consumer reporters also provide other services to the public. They often report on new products that may be useful to the physically disabled, a new low-cost prescription service for senior citizens, or the best way to discover low-cost airfares. They also are at their best when exposing serious "ripoffs," as in this report from consumer reporter Jack Atherton.

KEL/EXCLUSIVE	WHEN YOU BUY A NEW CAR... JUST HOW NEW IS IT? TROUBLE-SHOOTER JACK ATHERTON HAS (2
TWO BOX	BOX) EXCLUSIVE NEW DETAILS... AND ADVICE ON HOW TO BEWARE!
TAKE JACK LIVE...	(TAKE JACK LIVE) KELLY, THE INITIAL COMPLAINT WE GOT WAS ABOUT A FORD TAURUS ...BUT NOW WE'RE HEARING THAT

LOTS OF NEW CARS MAY BE OLDER
THAN YOU THINK.

TAKE ENG INSERT . . .   (TAKE ENG INSERT)
CG/ EXCLUSIVE   THIS HIALEAH DOCTOR SPENT A
WHOLE YEAR HUNTING FOR A NEW
CAR UNTIL HE SAW A MAGAZINE AD
FOR THE TAURUS SHO.

CG/DR. WILLIAM WAGNER   DR. WILLIAM WAGNER, A FORD
FORD CUSTOMER   CUSTOMER, SAYS:
"WHAT FINALLY MADE ME
DECIDE WAS THAT THEY HAD
IMPROVED THEIR 5 SPEED MANUAL
TRANSMISSION."
"THEY ADVERTISED THAT?"
"YES."

CG/HOLLYWOOD   ACCORDING TO DR. WAGNER'S
DEALER, HOLLYWOOD FORD, THAT
CG/LAST WEEK   IMPROVEMENT WAS A NEW WAY OF
CONNECTING THE STICK SHIFT TO
THE TRANSMISSION; WITH STURDY
METAL RODS INSTEAD OF AN OLD-
FASHIONED CABLE. ONLY TROUBLE
WAS . . . DR. WAGNER—AND AN
UNTOLD NUMBER OF OTHER FORD
CUSTOMERS—DID NOT GET THE
RODS.

CG/RICK REICHANADTER   RICK REICHANADTER,
HOLLYWOOD FORD   HOLLYWOOD FORD, SAYS:
"WERE CUSTOMERS, TO YOUR
KNOWLEDGE, NOTIFIED OF THE FACT
THAT SOME OF THE CARS HAD OLD-
STYLE SHIFTERS?"
"NO. UH. UH."
"WOULDN'T YOU WANT TO BE
TOLD?"
"IF I BOUGHT A CAR?"
"WOULDN'T YOU WANT TO BE
TOLD?"
"SURE."

BUT HOLLYWOOD FORD SAYS
EVEN DEALERS DIDN'T KNOW. WELL,
THE HELP CENTER VOLUNTEERS
HELPED GET DR. WAGNER A NEW
CAR—WITH RODS. BUT NOW THE
STATE ATTORNEY GENERAL'S OFFICE
IS ALSO INVESTIGATING.

CC/MARK BARNETT
ASSISTANT STATE
ATTORNEY GENERAL

MARK BARNETT, ASSISTANT
STATE ATTORNEY GENERAL, SAYS:
"WHEN THEY MAKE AN EXPRESS
CLAIM THAT A CERTAIN
IMPROVEMENT HAS BEEN MADE
AND IN FACT IT HASN'T BEEN MADE
IN ALL THEIR CARS, THEN THAT'S
AN UNFAIR AND
DECEPTIVE TRADE PRACTICE. BUT
MORE IMPORTANTLY, I THINK AS A
GENERAL RULE THERE'S AN IMPLIED
STATEMENT MADE THAT WHEN YOU
HAVE A 1991 CAR YOU'RE GETTING
THE 1991 PARTS."

CG/TRACY HOPPE
MASTER MECHANIC

BUT THIS A-S-E MASTER
MECHANIC TOLD US THAT MANY
CAR MANUFACTURERS PUT
OUTMODED PARTS IN WHAT ARE
SUPPOSED TO BE NEW CARS. TRACY
HOPPE, MASTER MECHANIC, SAYS:
"UNTIL THEY RUN OUT OF THOSE
PARTS, THEY USE THEM UP."
"YOU'VE SEEN THIS?"
"YES. I'VE SEEN THIS MANY
TIMES."

Sports Reporting

Many people are attracted to broadcast sports reporting because of their interest in sports and because they think it's more fun than covering city council meetings. The problem is that so many beginners have the same idea that not enough opportunities are available to provide jobs for them all. TV stations that may have six or more general-assignment reporters usually have only one full-time sports reporter-anchor.

Sports reporting also requires some additional skills that general reporting does not. Personality has become important; knowing sports inside out is not enough anymore. Most news managers look for sports people who can attract an audience with their style of delivery.

Good organizational skills also are important. Sports reporters, particularly in small markets, are expected to cover local games and to be able to cut a lot of video quickly from a variety of sports contests that are being recorded throughout the evening. Sports seasons tend to overlap, which means that college and professional football and basketball games are often held at the same times as professional hockey matches, amid a variety of other sports. Many stations also cover high school sports. Collecting all this information and cutting video of all these activities is demanding.

How does a journalism student prepare for a sports reporting job? The best way is probably through an internship. Sports reporters look for sharp college students who know sports and know how to edit videotape. Quick

Figure 19-3   TNT NBA Analyst Kenny Smith.

learners may find that they soon cover high school games and even anchor on the weekends. Because most sports anchors, like news anchors, are looking for opportunities in larger markets, frequent turnovers sometimes occur at the sports desk. The weekend sports person who learns the job well sometimes gets the sports anchoring job during the week.

Sports anchors with a lot of talent and personality can demand good salaries in large markets. Like other anchors, however, they often are subject to the ratings and whims of management. Job security is less certain for sports anchors than it is for most beat and general-assignment reporters.

One of the most successful and popular sports anchors on television is ESPN's Dan Patrick, who started out loving sports as a young man playing basketball in high school and college. But he never achieved the kind of success as an athlete that he has as a sports anchor. As the host of ESPN's *Sports Center*, Patrick has, as stated by Mark Lisheron in the *American Journalism Review* (May 1999), "earned a reputation as one of the nation's premier sports broadcasters."

Patrick says he knows it sounds corny, but "I'm still this kid from Mason, Ohio, who got a chance to be on ESPN. I never want to lose sight of that." Patrick says he's at a place where he always dreamed of being; not only to

Figure 19-4   Dan Patrick of ESPN Radio Network. (Courtesy of Ray Martin, ESPN)

have interviewed the biggest names in sports and to count some of them among his friends; but also to have achieved such respect in his profession that he can call star athletes when he needs to and talk to them.

While attending the University of Dayton, as a broadcast major, Patrick's success on the basketball court was modest (he didn't make the varsity team), but his career as a sports reporter was enhanced when the team allowed him to go courtside for home games, where he would call the play-by-play into a tape recorder to practice his skills. That practice calling the games helped Patrick get his first job as weekend anchor at WDTN-TV in Dayton.

Patrick was unable to get off the weekends at WDTN, so when he graduated from the University of Dayton, he took a job as a morning anchor on that city's WTUE radio. Not satisfied with his situation, Patrick rented video equipment and taped five minutes of sports news he had memorized and sent the tape to ESPN. Patrick says the network was kind but said he wasn't quite ready for ESPN. Patrick did end up at CNN and, he says, they taught me how to be a journalist. After spending almost six years with CNN, Patrick says he asked for a $10,000-a-year raise. When management offered only $5,000 more, Patrick knocked on ESPN's door again, and this time he was ready.

The man who hired Patrick, managing editor John Walsh, called Patrick the quintessence of what the network was trying to accomplish. Walsh says it was obvious that Patrick was a passionate sports fan—that he was really into his job.

Baseball's Mark Grace says Patrick has earned respect among top athletes in a way few broadcasters have. Grace says Patrick is very knowledgeable about sports. But he says players also know he can ask tough questions without trashing them—he does what he does with respect.

Patrick's interviewing skills, and attitude, were demonstrated in an interview he did with hockey great Wayne Gretzky. Patrick says he avoided the cliché question about his retirement because he thought it would be presumptuous to suggest he knew when Gretzky should retire. Patrick added, "I want a person I interview to know they are a person, not a sound bite. I want the people I interview to know that I am not going to attack them, that I care about every answer they give me." He said, "You can be hard on an athlete without carrying a hammer."

A broadcast journalism professor at Syracuse University, Hubert Brown, has nothing but praise for Patrick. Syracuse's Newhouse School of Public Communication is often referred to as "Sportscaster U" for having produced Bob Costas and Marv Albert, among many others. Brown says that Patrick's style and thoroughness make him a good model. Brown notes that it's hard to convey to students how people like Patrick make it look so easy. "They think it is stringing together catch phrases, but what you don't see," says Brown, "is that Patrick is knowledgeable about a lot of different things—things beyond sports; that he writes and delivers his own material; that his delivery is appropriate to the subject matter; and that he makes subtle shifts in the delivery as the show moves along." Brown concluded, "To put Patrick in a class with Al Michaels and Bob Costas is not a stretch."

Mark Lisheron, who wrote an article about Patrick for the *American Journalism Review,* says that athletes are candid with Patrick because he coaxes rather than cudgels them. Lisheron says Patrick's Q and A feature, "Outtakes," in *ESPN, The Magazine,* rarely fails to produce a provocative exchange with a news-making athlete. Lisheron points out that despite ESPN's location, in Bristol, Connecticut, athletes go out of their way to visit Patrick. Lisheron notes that Michael Jordan, "who needs another interview like he needs another product endorsement, enjoys sitting down with Patrick."

Bob Costas says Patrick is a guy who has a style, not a shtick, that is welcome in this time of trying to impress, to get noticed, to come up with a catch phrase. Costas adds, "Patrick manages to inject some personality into his delivery without overwhelming the subject matter. He doesn't grab you by the lapels to speak to you."

Patrick obviously has had such success because he learned many of the skills already stressed in this book—good reporting and interviewing techniques and caring and sensitivity. This same point is made by longtime Cleveland sports anchor Jim Donovan. He says that whether a student eventually wants to cover the White House or the White Sox, he or she needs to learn the same reporting skills. Donovan recalls that he has often led newscasts with sports stories, such as the Indians winning the World Series, but he also has found himself at the top of a newscast covering a spring training boating accident that killed two Indian pitchers. Donovan says such a story takes him back to the basics of news reporting. "You're not dealing with your opinion on why this guy should be traded, you're dealing with some really hard facts, and you have to make sure you have it right."

He also has this advice for those who want a future with ESPN. "When you walk into a locker room, interviewing skills are more important than knowledge of sports trivia." Donovan says, "you'll have to deal with athletes who have won and lost, who want to talk and those who never talk, and if you don't have the reporting skills, I think you'll really fail pretty miserably."

Keith Olbermann, a co-host with Patrick on ESPN before moving over to Fox Sports, says sports reporters need to understand journalistic ethics: "What you can say and what you cannot say, how to develop sources." He adds, "You have to have the same equipment that Dan Rather, Tom Brokaw, and Peter Jennings have. When you have mastered these things," he says, "you can go work on the jokes."

Weather Reporting

Good weathercasters are also well rewarded. In large markets, weathercasters are often paid almost as much as the news anchors and sometimes even more. In medium-sized markets, weathercasters usually do not earn quite as much as the anchors but often earn more than sportscasters. The competition for jobs is not as keen as it is in sports because most people entering the field consider weather reporting rather dull, which means many opportunities are available for those who pick weather reporting as a career. It's not always as dull as it may seem, however. Most stations expect weathercasters to report from the oceanside when a hurricane is on its way or to be knee-deep in flood-filled streets while predicting when the rain is going to stop.

The weather people most in demand are those with degrees in meteorology. Unfortunately, those delivering the weather in many markets are not trained meteorologists. Many viewers do not notice the difference in the weather person's background, particularly when sophisticated-looking radar maps and graphics are employed. But students who are serious about anchoring the weather should study meteorology; the money invested in earning a degree will certainly pay dividends.

If weather reporting is your goal, you also have to learn about computer and chroma-key (special effects) technology. Jerry Brown, a meteorologist for KVVU in Las Vegas says: "The [reporter's] discomfort level in front of the chroma board too often is readily apparent. It's not that the weathercaster

Figure 19-5 Jerry Brown, Meteorologist, KVVU-TV, Las Vegas, NV. (Courtesy of Eric Foerch.)

doesn't know what to say. The problem is how to visually integrate a story-line and chroma-key graphics into a cohesive 'show-and-tell' presentation."

Brown says weathercasters must "maintain continuous eye contact with one of three monitors, ad-lib and synchronize hand and body movement, all the while pirouetting across the screen. Done right," he says, "it looks effortless." But it's not easy.

Brown says that when weather interns ask for help setting up a weathercast audition tape, he tries his best to help, but he warns, "While a novice news anchor may on rare occasion master a teleprompter, I have never seen anyone approach professional level on their first try at chroma-key." Brown adds, however, that "marked improvement does come with practice." He suggests seeking a good professional coach. Coach Jeff Puffer, who is with Frank N. Magid Associates, works with people at the company's offices in Marion, Iowa, but he says he also likes "to work with meteorologists at their own chroma board where they are familiar with the aspect ratio of key wall and graphics." He notes, "You can't be talking about Dallas and looking at Omaha."

Weathercaster Brown makes another important point: "A personable weathercaster is the single most important aspect of a weather presentation." He says, "It constantly dismays me how little attention the average viewer pays to the weather maps I create."

Station managers look for personality along with a knowledge of maps, computers, and chroma-key technology. The auditions for weather anchors are considerably different from auditions for beat reporters. Although the news director looks for good writing and reporting skills, the general manager looks for a great smile and a quick wit.

Weathercaster Brown also notes that "the expansion of internet services has had a major effect on the way TV weathercasters do their job. First, there is more competition! Access to accurate, up to the minute weather data and forecasts is only a few clicks away on a personal computer. To counter that the weathercaster must emphasize the strong points of the medium in which he or she performs. Watching televised news is primarily a visual experience. The crafty on-air meteorologist will make the most of the expensive weather graphics systems that are de rigueur in the competitive TV weather field, and also try to integrate as much raw weather video as possible into the presentation. On the other hand, PC access to weather data makes the weathercaster's job a lot easier. I can formulate the initial outlines of that evening's televised forecast over a morning cup of tea at my home computer. I have a very strong sense of what is going to be the thrust of my presentation before I ever arrive at work. Thank you, World Wide Web-that was never the case in years past."

Ultimately the weathercaster must use journalistic skills in the organization and presentation of his or her product. The immediacy of a "live" newscast gives the forecaster the ability to tell a story about what is happening in the atmosphere; stories with unhappy endings (that is, serious weather events such as tornados or hurricanes) tend to be the most compelling, but the best TV weather people can make the most quotidian days (Partly Cloudy and 70 degrees) interesting.

Credentials have become more important in the weathercasting field-especially in areas where the weather can be life-threatening. Even meteorologists with degrees are pressured into testing for the seals of respected

Figure 19-6   CNN's Bill Hemmer reporting from Florida during 2004's Hurricane Frances.

weather organizations such as the American Meteorological Society (AMS) or the National Weather Association (NWA). To obtain such certification, weathercasters take comprehensive tests in their field and undergo stringent evaluations of their on-air work by peers.

Sometimes the weather is more than just looking at the day's highs and lows and the five-day forecast. Sometimes the weather is the lead story for days, as it was in September of 2004, when four hurricanes devastated the Carribean and parts of Florida.

Here's an example of a cold weather story from reporter Paul Gates of WAFB-TV in Baton Rouge:

```
SLUG: COLD WEATHER
REPORTER: PAUL GATES
NEWSCAST: SIX P.M.
```

OUTDOOR CONSTRUCTION WORKER WITH BOARDS OVER SHOULDER TALKS TO CAMERA AS HE WALKS AND PUFFS WHITE BREATH.	NAT SOT :03 "IT'S ICE COLD OUT THERE THIS MORNING, MAN . . . 28 DEGREES THIS MORNING WHEN I CAME OUT, MAN, BUT I GOTTA DO IT THOUGH."
VO-CONSTRUCTION GUYS STANDING AROUND FIRE	BOB IS LIKE A LOT OF OTHER FOLKS . . . CAUGHT A LITTLE OFF

CLAPPING HANDS AND
STOMPING FEET.
HEATING MAN BOB
WALKS UP TO DOOR OF
HOME AND DOOR
IS OPENED BY
HOMEOWNER.

GUARD BY THIS FIRST EARLY
FREEZE OF THE SEASON.

BATON ROUGE IS ONE OF FOUR
CITIES IN LOUISIANA SETTING A
RECORD LOW OF 27 DEGREES. THE
OLD RECORD WAS 29 DEGREES,
SET BACK IN 1899. HEATING
CONTRACTORS WERE DOING A
BOOMING BUSINESS
TODAY . . .

MAN IN DOORWAY
TALKING TO BOB—THE
HEATING MAN. BOB THEN
WALKS INTO HOME
OUT OF FRAME

NAT SOT:02
"WELL, THE HEATER WON'T COME
ON."
"OK, LET'S HAVE A LOOK AT IT."

BOB—THE HEATING MAN
SOUND BITE.

FONT: BOB LEE
SUPERIOR HEAT

SOT :11
"THIS IS THE MOST CALLS I'VE EVER
TAKEN IN ONE DAY, EVEN DURING
THE SUMMER, SO WE'RE REALLY
BUSY AND WE'RE TRYING TO GET TO
EVERYONE AS QUICK AS WE CAN,
BUT UNFORTUNATELY WE'RE GONNA
HAVE SOME OF THEM SPILL OVER
INTO TOMORROW."

VO-TIGHT SHOT OF BOB'S
HANDS INSIDE HEATING
UNIT . . . WE SEE BOB—IN
THE ATTIC WORKING ON
UNIT, VARIOUS SHOTS.

BOB SAYS 65 PERCENT OF HIS
CALLS ARE TO LIGHT PILOT
LIGHTS . . . AND IF YOU DON'T KNOW
TOO MUCH ABOUT ALL THAT STUFF
IN THE ATTIC, IT'S BEST TO CALL A
HEATING EXPERT.

BOB—THE HEATING
MAN SOUND BITE.

SOT :05
"WHEN WE LIGHT A PILOT LIGHT,
WE ALWAYS CHECK AND SERVICE
THE FURNACE FOR THE WINTER. IT'S
ALWAYS A GOOD IDEA TO HAVE A
PROFESSIONAL DO IT."

FILE VIDEO AND NAT SOT
OF HOUSE BURNING

FLAMES UP . . . NAT SOT
HOLD FOR :02 SECONDS

VO-CONTINUE FILE
VIDEO OF FIRE.

THERE IS DANGER IN THIS COLD
WEATHER. TOO MANY PEOPLE MUST
RELY ON SPACE HEATERS AND TOO
OFTEN THAT CAN BE FATAL

SOT OF FIRE
DEPARTMENT'S PUBLIC
INFORMATION OFFICER.

SOT :11

"YOU'LL HEAR OF A STORY BEFORE
THE WINTER'S OUT THAT SOME
ELDERLY COUPLE OR SOMEONE HAS
PLACED THEIR SPACE HEATER TOO
CLOSE TO THE BED WHILE THEY'RE
SLEEPING, AND IT STARTS A FIRE
AND THEY LOSE THEIR LIFE."

FONT: TERRY KENNEDY
PUBLIC INFORMATION

GRAPHICS
PRODUCTION.

KEEP SPACE HEATERS CLEAR OF
FLAMMABLE OBJECTS. AND GIVE
SPACE HEATERS A SOURCE OF
OXYGEN.

1. KEEP SPACE HEATERS . . .
2. GIVE SPACE HEATERS
A . . . GRAPHICS OVER
BACKGROUND OF FLAMES.
REPORTER STAND-UP

GATES BRIDGE STD

SOT

"ONE GOOD THING ABOUT THIS COLD
SNAP FOR AREA MERCHANTS . . .
SLUGGISH WINTER CLOTHING SALES
. . . WELL, THAT'S REALLY PICKED
UP."

VO-SHOTS OF CLOTHING
SHOPPERS

FOR WEEKS WINTER CLOTHING HAS
HUNG LISTLESSLY ON THE RACKS
. . . BUT NOW, THE WHEELS OF
WINTRY COMMERCE ARE TURNING
AND THE STUFF IS MOVING OUT.

TIGHT SHOT OF SHOPPING
CART WHEELS ROLLING
DOWN AISLE

REPORTER WALKS IN
AND CHATS NAT SOT
WITH A SMALL CLUSTER
OF LADY SHOPPERS.

NAT SOT :03

"WHAT ARE YOU LADIES SHOPPING
FOR?
INSULATED THERMAL UNDERWEAR.
KINDA GOT CAUGHT BY SURPRISE,
UH?
YEAH . . . UMMMMM, IT'S SO COLD."
MEANWHILE, BACK WITH BOB OF
SUPERIOR HEATING . . .

VO-BOB—THE HEATING
MAN WITH A NOTEPAD
AND PHONE JAMMED TO
EAR RAPIDLY
SCRATCHING DOWN
NAMES AND NUMBERS

CUT TO TIGHT SHOT OF
BOB'S NOTEPAD FULL OF
NAMES . . .

NAT SOT :03

"YEAH, I GOT A BIG PIECE OF
PAPER . . . GO WITH THEM."

VO-WIDE SHOT OF BOB—
THE HEATING MAN
TAKING THE INFO OVER
THE PHONE.

HE'S STILL MAKING
APPOINTMENTS, AND THE ONLY
WAY TO GET SERVICE IS TO GET
IN LINE.
PAUL GATES, WAFB NEWS.

Summary

As with just about every other position in this technological era, the better prepared you are, the better chance you have of getting a reporting job. If you have a minor in environmental studies, health studies, economics, or business, for example, you could be more attractive to news directors than people who have only general knowledge. Specialty or beat reporting is one of the most interesting jobs in broadcast news because it provides an opportunity to spend more time developing and working on stories. Many beat reporters also find their work more rewarding because they can develop an expertise that provides an added dimension to their stories; however, one disadvantage is that not as many jobs are available for specialty reporters. There may be 10 general-assignment reporters at a large TV station and only a couple of specialty reporters.

From a practical point of view, however, whatever extra knowledge you have when you apply for work is going to be to your advantage. Even if you do not get a job as, say, an environmental reporter, the news director may be impressed that you took several courses in the subject. If you get a general-assignment job, you will probably find that when an environmental story shows up, you'll be assigned to it. If your work is particularly good, you may wind up with a beat.

Review Questions

1. Why is there a debate over the use of the term *investigative reporting?*
2. What is the difference between investigative reporting and most other types of reporting?
3. Many radio and TV stations are hiring environmental reporters. What's the best way to prepare for such a career?
4. Why do radio and TV stations devote a lot of time to stories about health and medicine?
5. How can students prepare themselves to be health and medical reporters?
6. One of the most popular specialties is consumer reporting. Why are consumer reporters so popular with audiences?
7. Many people want to be sports reporters, but they face tough competition. Why is that so?
8. Do you believe that there are opportunities in weathercasting? Discuss.

Exercises

1. Arrange to accompany a radio or TV reporter who is covering an environmental story. Try to understand the issues involved, and check to see if the reporter covered them fairly. Turn in a report.

2. Ask friends and fellow students if any consumer issues annoy them. Select one that you think has particular merit. After researching it, do some interviews and put together a wraparound or package.

3. If a radio or TV station in your community assigns a reporter to a health and medicine beat, ask the reporter how she gets most of her story ideas. If there are no medical reporters, ask the news directors how they cover that beat and whether they are happy with the results.

4. Ask a TV sportscaster if you can spend an afternoon or evening with him to see if you think you would like the job. Later, do the same thing with a weathercaster.

20 Ethics

This chapter and Chapter 21 focus on the important and complex issue of ethics, one of the cornerstones of good journalism. You have read earlier about some of the other cornerstones of journalism: accuracy, fairness, and objectivity and all of these characteristics are also among the major ethical requirements for those who practice good journalism. Since the last edition of this book was published, there has been a growing debate over whether the media has compromised its objectivity by becoming too liberal.

Objectivity: Does the Media Have a Bias?

The debate heated up when a former *CBS News* correspondent, Bernard Goldberg, wrote a best-selling book titled *Bias: A CBS Insider Exposes How the Media Distort the News*. The title contains two words that are particularly onerous to journalists, *bias* and *distort,* and the suggestion that respected journalists and the colleagues he worked with at *CBS News* for so many years were guilty of bias and distortion angered a lot of people. At the center of Goldberg's charges was that most journalists are liberal and because they are they have difficulty with objectivity, allowing their political bias to cloud what they write and report. Almost without exception, the men and women who bring the news to us every day in print and broadcast denied Goldberg's charges and one of them, Eric Alterman, wrote a book of his own, titled *What Liberal Media? The Truth about Bias and the News*. Altman currently writes the "Stop the Presses" media column for the *Nation* and a Web log for MSNBC.com. He's also a Senior Fellow at the New School University and an affiliated faculty member in the journalism program at New York University. As for Goldberg's contention of bias in the media, Alterman says if there is a bias it's not a liberal one, "It's to the right not the left." Alterman does acknowledge a liberal bias on some social issues like gun control, abortion, and homosexual rights, but when it comes to economic issues, particularly around union rights and trade issues, the media parrots Wall Street, he said, painting workers as "obstructionist dinosaurs." So, those are the battle lines, and here are some of the other arguments offered by the two.

Speaking of the nightly network news anchors, Goldberg, who now reports for the HBO program *Real Sports* said he's convinced that "Dan and Tom and Peter don't even know what liberal bias is." He said the problem is that the anchors "think that liberal bias means just one thing: going hard on

Republicans and easy on Democrats." He added that "real media bias comes not so much from what party they attack. Liberal bias is the result of how they see the world."

Goldberg admits that not all of the big—time media stars "bat from the left side of the plate." And he also acknowledges that a lot of the media is conservative. He noted that talk radio is overwhelmingly right of center and there are plenty of conservative newspaper columnists and right-wing magazines. And he included in that category the Fox Cable News operation.

This author, who worked with Goldberg when he was at CBS, was surprised by the tone of the former CBS newsman's book. His often unpleasantly worded critique of fellow journalists was a considerable change in the attitude he displayed for so many years in the CBS newsroom where he impressed me as a rather gentle, mild-mannered, agreeable individual who did excellent work and, as far as I know or observed, said little at the time that was unfavorable about the *CBS News* product. There certainly were some correspondents and others who worked at the copy editor's and assignment desks who were critical from time-to-time of *CBS News*, and this author was sometimes among them. But I got the idea that in those days Goldberg was happy in his job and more or less content. Goldberg claims that he often complained to the network's management about the bias that he perceived but no one wanted to discuss the subject. Goldberg's views on his fellow journalists are curious, to say the least. In his book he writes, "journalists you see think they're better than 'regular' people, smarter than them, more sophisticated, fairer, and more sensitive." Obviously Goldberg became more jaded as his career progressed but why I have no idea. I was aware that most newspeople at CBS were liberal, as I was, but I observed no intentional bias at CBS, CNN, or any other news organization for which I worked for a couple of decades.

Writing about his beliefs in the conservative *Wall Street Journal*, Goldberg said there are lots of reasons fewer people are watching network news, "and one of them, I'm more convinced than ever is that network viewers simply don't trust the networks, and for good reason." Goldberg added, "The old argument that the networks and other media elites have a liberal bias is so blatantly true that it's hardly worth discussing anymore." But, of course, Goldberg *did* want to discuss it more, and devoted more than two hundred pages to the subject in his book.

Goldberg also noted that journalists don't sit around in dark corners and plan strategies on how they're going to slant the news; it just comes naturally to most reporters.

Goldberg's disdain for his old co-workers was evident in this critique of a story done by *CBS News* Washington correspondent Eric Engberg about presidential candidate Steve Forbes and his flat tax, which was the centerpiece of the Forbes campaign.

Goldberg said he decided to watch the Engberg piece after a friend criticized the story. Goldberg said as he watched the videotape, it became obvious that this was a "hatchet job, an editorial masquerading as real news, a cheap shot designed to make fun of Forbes." Goldberg said the more he watched the story the more he saw that it wasn't simply about a presidential candidate and a tax plan, "It was about something much bigger, something too much of what big-time TV journalists had become: a showcase for smart-ass reporters with attitudes, reporters who don't even pretend to hide their disdain for certain people and certain ideas that they and their sophisticated friends didn't particularly like."

Goldberg was particularly angry with the Engberg story because he interviewed three tax experts who opposed the idea of a flat tax but did not interview anyone who thought the idea had merit. That certainly was a mistake on the part of Engberg and his producers. But, in questioning the fairness of the story, Goldberg offered a more devious motive. He said Engberg didn't try to find someone who favored the flat tax because "putting on a supporter of the flat tax would have defeated the whole purpose of the piece, which was to have a few laughs at Forbes' expense."

Is the Bias to the Left or the Right?

In responding to Goldberg's charge of a liberal media bias, Eric Alterman asks "what constitutes liberal bias anyway?" He notes that the Fox News Channel claims that its programs are "fair and balanced" rather than conservative, and that Fox chairman and CEO, Roger Ailes, says that all his network is trying to do is to provide a little more balance to the news. But Alterman says no one actually believes that and "it's hard to believe that Ailes does." Alterman pointed out that Ailes' Republican Party ties are strong, noting that he even sent memos to Karl Rove, President Bush's strategist, offering him advice after 9/11 and that Ailes was also an advisor to Ronald Reagan and the elder George Bush.

Much of Alterman's criticism that the media is more conservative than liberal is focused on the cable industry. He writes, "across virtually the entire cable television punditocracy, unabashed conservatives dominate, leaving lone liberals to offer themselves up to be beaten up by gangs of marauding right-wingers."

Alterman admits that he does not quarrel with the notion of a liberal media but that no sensible person can dispute the existence of a conservative media. Pointing out that one of his employers is MSNBC, Alterman said, "I work in the middle of it." He said the liberal media is a tiny and profoundly underfunded element compared to its conservative counterpart. He noted not only the success of Fox News but other major conservative news organizations such as the *Wall Street Journal*, the *Washington Times*, *New York Post*, *American Spectator*, *Weekly Standard*, and the *National Review*. Alterman also pointed out that in radio the domination of conservative voices is so extensive as to be undisputed. He says there is a not a single, well-known liberal talk show host in the nation and barely a host who does not at least lean well in the direction of the extreme right. He cited Rush Limbaugh, G. Gordon Liddy, Oliver North, Sean Hannity, and Michael Reagan among the dozen or so top conservative talk show hosts who dominate the airwaves. As for Goldberg's book, Alterman says that during the 220 pages of complaining, Goldberg never bothers to systematically prove the existence of liberal bias in the news or even define what he means by the term.

Alterman warns that what Americans really should fear is the far better organized, more powerful and effective propaganda machine of the right that postulates the presumption of the right through research groups, religious organizations, ideological news organizations and conservative personalities "that skews the entire discourse toward the right."

Alterman adds, "unbeknownst to millions of Americans who continue to believe that the media are genuinely liberal—or that conservatives and liberals are engaged in a fair fight of relative equality, liberals are fighting a near-hopeless battle in which they are enormously outmatched."

Alterman attributes this imbalance and resulting right-wing drift to new media-ownership patterns and to the enthronement of a veritable aristocracy of right-wing talk-show hosts and pundits whose party-line discipline and take-no-prisoners attitude toward liberal guests have kept conservatives on message, thereby giving their collective movement "the appearance of unity and clarity of vision."

Walter Cronkite, one of the most respected broadcast journalists, who often was described as the most trusted man in America, said he is neither Republican nor Democrat, but a registered Independent because "I find I cast my votes not on the basis of party loyalty but on the issues of the moment and on my assessment of the candidates." Cronkite added that he believes most reporters are liberal, but not because they have chosen that particular color in the political spectrum. "Most likely," he said, "it is because most of us served our journalistic apprenticeships as reporters covering the seamier side of our cities, the crimes, the tenement fires, the homeless and the hungry, the underclothed and undereducated." The former *CBS News* anchor added, "We reached our intellectual adulthood with daily close-ups of the inequality in a nation that was founded on the commitment to equality for all. So we tend to side with the powerless rather than the powerful." He concluded, "If that is what makes us liberals, so be it, just as long as in reporting the news we adhere to the first ideals of good journalism—that news reports must be fair, accurate and unbiased." Cronkite also noted that when he looked up the definition of 'liberal' in a dictionary, it listed synonyms for liberal as *progressive, broad-minded, unprejudiced,* and *beneficent.* He said the antonyms for liberal were listed as: *reactionary* and *intolerant.*

The debate over bias, objectivity, and fairness, as important as it is, is only one of the major ethical issues that journalists must consider.

The rest of this chapter and the next chapter will deal with the many other issues.

Gratuities

Reporters are often tempted with gratuities, or gifts. It is impossible for reporters to maintain their credibility if they accept any kind of gift from people or organizations they cover. Many offers come from public-relations people. Some gifts may come at Christmas, whereas others may arrive at the door of a reporter or producer after the broadcast of a story about a product or service. The gifts should be returned.

Some news directors pass out such gifts to non-news staff, but doing so sends the wrong message to the donor. If the gifts are not returned, the senders have no way of knowing that they were not appreciated and might assume that they can expect some favor the next time they're promoting something.

One news director says that when Christmas gifts arrive, he does give them to the people in the mailroom but does not say who sent them. He says he also calls the donor and lets him or her know that he can't accept gifts and has passed them along to the mailroom staff. "That's easier than packing the stuff up and sending it back," he says. "It also lets the PR people know that I can't be bought, and it makes the people in the mailroom a little bit happier."

Conflict of Interest

Sometimes the issue of what is an acceptable practice is not so clearly defined. Is it wrong for a theater or film reviewer to receive free tickets from the show's producers? Some newspapers pay for their reviewers' tickets, but most reviewers do accept free tickets, and there is no reason to believe that this practice influences what they write about a film or play.

Some news organizations, however, fear a *conflict of interest*. For example, hotel owners sometimes offer newspeople a free plane ride and accommodations to promote a new hotel. Is it possible for the reporter to maintain objectivity when the host has provided him or her with a thousand dollars or more for travel and entertainment? Some journalists claim it would take more than that to corrupt them. Some of them may even write negative stories about the trip, but the temptation to be favorable toward the host is great. To avoid such potential conflicts of interest, many news directors forbid such trips.

Accuracy and Responsibility

The need for accuracy in journalism has been stressed throughout this book. Accuracy is also discussed in this chapter because it is an essential part of the discussion of ethics.

Some inaccuracy will always creep into news writing and reporting because people write and report news and people make mistakes. If errors occur, the reaction is to correct the mistakes immediately.

NBC News correspondent Roger O'Neil says, "I'm very concerned about getting the facts straight. I double-check what I say because I know how powerful and frightening my words can be. I can ruin people's lives, and I have. I can ruin businesses, and I have. But fortunately, my facts were right."

Accuracy also means taking the responsibility to write and report the truth in a manner that is as objective and fair as possible, despite—as was discussed earlier—any personal feeling, belief, or attitude on the subject. Taking responsibility means the following: (1) looking at *all* the issues, not just the easy or popular ones; (2) examining controversies and producing special reports throughout the year, not just during the sweeps rating periods; (3) covering important stories that don't always offer good pictures; (4) writing and reporting with care, understanding, and compassion; and (5) dealing with people in a professional and civil manner.

Figure 20-1   An anti-abortion demonstration in Baton Rouge. Reporters must always present both sides of a controversial subject. (Photo by James Terry)

The Jayson Blair Scandal

The world of journalism was shocked in May of 2003 when *The New York Times* revealed to the world that one of its reporters, 27-year-old Jayson Blair, committed frequent acts of journalistic fraud while covering significant news events over an extended period of time. The *Times* stated that the widespread fabrication and plagiarism represented a profound betrayal of trust and a low point in the 152-year history of the newspaper.

The *Times* said that Blair, an African American reporter with the *Times* for four years, had misled readers and his colleagues with dispatches that purported to be from Maryland, Texas, Ohio, and other states while he actually was in New York. He fabricated comments and concocted scenes and, the *Times* added, he stole material from other newspapers and wire services. *Times* officials said Blair also selected details from photographs to create the impression that he had been somewhere or seen someone, when he had not.

In all, the *Times* charged, Blair had deceived the public and his editors in an incredibly large number of stories, 36 of the 73 he wrote for the newspaper.

Blair's ability to concoct so many false stories also pointed up another embarrassing reality for the *Times*—the failure of a variety of middle level and top editors to heed one red flag after another about his reporting, while promoting him to national reporter. One editor who was so alarmed about Blair's performance had warned his superiors in an e-mail that "We have to stop Jayson from writing for the *Times* right now." The advice was ignored.

To compound the problem, even after such warnings from editors, Blair was given sensitive assignments such as the Washington sniper case and interviewing the parents of soldiers wounded or killed in Iraq. Blair repeatedly plagiarized the comments of those involved.

To its credit, the *Times* spared no effort in investigating Blair's transgressions, assigning five staff members to unravel all the lies, misrepresentations, and plagiarisms committed by the reporter. The newspaper devoted numerous pages to reveal all the details of Blair's cheating and lies.

The *Times* management said that in the final months before his deception was discovered, the audacity of his behavior grew by the week, suggesting "the work of a troubled young man veering toward professional self-destruction." But there really was no other published explanation for Blair's behavior.

In one of his stories, Blair described two wounded Marines lying side by side at Bethesda Naval Medical Center, though he was never there. On another occasion, Blair deceived his own freelance photographer when he was supposed to be in Cleveland interviewing the father of a serviceman killed in Iraq. The photographer said he called Blair three times on his cell phone to arrange to meet Blair for the interview but Blair kept giving him excuses for why they could not get together. The reason: Blair was not in Cleveland and never interviewed the man. He lifted a half-dozen passages from other news accounts, including some from *The Washington Post* to produce a fake story.

The *Times* reported that in the two months before his resignation, Blair "was fabricating quotations and scenes, undetected and was lying in his articles and to his editors about being in a court hearing in Virginia, in a police chief's home in Maryland and in front of a soldier's home in West Virginia." The *Times* said Blair's behavior became more erratic after September 11, when he claimed to have lost a relative in the attack on the Trade Center and was unavailable for long stretches. But relatives of a victim named Blair said they were not related to the reporter.

Blair's deceptions finally caught up with him when the *San Antonio Express News* complained that Blair had plagiarized its account of a Texas woman whose son was found dead in Iraq. Blair had never been in San Antonio. He was able to fake the story by using photos of the woman's home and garden from the paper's archives.

Many news organizations have suffered major embarrassments over the last two decades, including *The Washington Post's* return of a Pulitzer Prize in 1981 when one of their reporters, Janet Cook, invented an 8-year-old heroin addict for a story on drug addiction that she made up.

But in scope and sheer human inventiveness for deception, Blair stood above all others.

Blair joined the *Times* in 1999 as an intermediate reporter after supposedly being graduated from the University of Maryland School of Journalism. He had been a student in the program but never obtained a degree.

Blair reportedly charmed many of his colleagues and reportedly was given some extra pushes up the promotion ladder because of the *Times'* strong diversity program that was constantly looking for promising minorities.

There also were reports that some suspicions were aroused at the paper because Blair was running up company expenses at a bar around the corner from the *Times* building and had taken company cars for extended periods in which he collected numerous traffic tickets.

Blair gave no interviews after resigning, citing personal problems for his deceptions.

His actions brought about the resignation of two top managers at the paper, Executive Editor Howell Raines and Managing Editor Gerald Boyd.

The Blair incident was particularly painful to the *Times* Publisher, Arthur Sulzberger Jr. who noted that "We took a gamble on a promising young journalist and may we always have the courage to take a risk." He added, "Blair will not 'poison the well' to attract talented journalists."

USA Today Has a Major Scandal

Only months after the *Times* scandal, a new shock wave hit the journalism community. The nation's largest newspaper, *USA Today,* revealed that its foreign correspondent, Jack Kelley was forced to resign because he repeatedly fabricated stories. His journalistic sins were described as "sweeping and substantial."

As in the case of the *Times, USA Today* did an internal investigation of Kelley and found evidence of fabrications in eight major stories. A review by a team of staffers found that Kelley's explanations of how he reported high-impact stories from around the world "were contradicted by hotel, phone or other records of sources he said would confirm them." The newspaper retracted one of Kelley's page one first-hand accounts of a Jerusalem suicide bombing that helped him become a 2002 Pulitzer Prize Finalist.

Kelley had reported that someone had been decapitated before his eyes, and he claimed to have bumped into the bomber moments before the blast. The investigators said neither of those events occurred. Executive Editor Brian Gallagher said the probe of Kelley began after Gallagher received an anonymous note suggesting that some of Kelley's stories might have been embellished or made up. Kelley had been with the paper since its launch in 1982. He was the paper's star and had traveled the world covering the most important stories. He was nominated for five Pulitzer prizes.

The paper also found that Kelley's account in 2000 of a Cuban woman who fled for the U.S. but drowned "was a lie from start to finish." The paper found the woman living in the Southeast after arriving legally. The paper said files retrieved from Kelley's laptop computer showed he even wrote scripts for at least three people to help them "mislead *USA* reporters trying to verify his works."

As in the case of Jayson Blair, Kelley enjoyed wider latitude from his editors because he had the blessing of some key people at the paper, including the now-retired Gannett chairman, Al Neuharth. Some fellow reporters at the paper said they were suspicious of Kelley's stories because "they seemed to be too good to be true." As in the case of the *Times* staff, there is a lot of resentment because *USA Today* editors did not recognize Kelley's misdeeds earlier. The overriding question in both the Blair case and the Kelley fraud is why? With that in mind, *USA Today* editorial director, John Seigenthaler, said he had asked Kelley to consider the possibility that "he had some sort of emotional block that prevented him from telling the truth," but Kelley rejected the premise. We may have to wait until Kelley, like Jayson Blair, writes a book to find out why Kelley betrayed his newspaper and colleagues.

In reacting to this new betrayal of journalistic standards, the Poynter Institute's Chip Scanlan described how he received an e-mail from a young reporter who was doing a summer reporting fellowship with the Institute, questioning whether "the only way to become a big time reporter these days is to make stuff up?" "Of course not,' replied Scanlan, "but how persuasive, or accurate, is that answer?" he added. "Seems like I've been reading a lot about lying, cheating journalists this year." And of course, the public has been growing more distrustful of the media each year. Although Scanlan noted that he doesn't have all the answers he would like to respond to the young reporter's question, he said "what I can tell him, is that I don't believe the only way to become a big-time reporter is to make things up. I know too many reporters who die a thousand deaths when an error creeps into their copy, who fact-check every word, who double and triple-check and still lie awake at night worrying they screwed up." Scanlan also observed that making it up may look like an easy route to glory, until you consider the career paths of Jack Kelley, Jayson Blair, and the other reporters who have lied and stolen before them. "Their trajectory, from newsroom star to disgraced pariah, is worth consideration by anyone who wonders whether making it up is the only way to make it in journalism." Scanlan concludes, in the age we live in, "the odds of fabrication and plagiarism going undetected are getting slimmer. It seems increasingly unlikely that success born of deceit will be a steady or permanent perch."

Another Poynter faculty member, Gregory E. Favre, observes that despite the Blairs and Kelleys, "good things happen in newsrooms every day. Men and women practice excellent and ethical journalism. They truly care about what they do." But Favre said that what they do is too often lost in the negativity that surrounds the Kelleys and Blairs. The Poynter faculty member said, "I don't know what's going to happen to Kelley now but what I do know," he said, "is that Jack Kelley is losing a precious gift, the gift of being a journalist, a gift no one has the right to mess up."

Libel

Although it should not be the motivating factor for insisting on accuracy, there is always the threat of libel facing those journalists who through carelessness, ignorance, or malice make inaccurate statements in their scripts and reports that reflect on the character or reputation of an individual or group. Libel laws differ from state to state, but essentially writers or reporters can be sued for libel if anything they write or report (1) exposes an individual or group to public scorn, hatred, ridicule, or contempt; (2) causes harm to someone in their occupation or profession; or (3) causes someone to be shunned or avoided.

Reporters must also remember that it is not necessary to have actually used a person's name to be sued for libel. If the audience knows to whom a reporter is referring, even without the name, the reporter could be sued for libel if the comments harm the person's reputation.

Although libel traditionally refers to printed material and slander to spoken words, the distinction between the two terms has little meaning for broadcast reporters. Recognizing that broadcast material is usually scripted, many state laws regard any defamatory statements on radio and television as subject to libel laws.

Attorney and former reporter Bruce Sanford says writers and editors should be wary of using certain words. Here is a partial list of what Sanford refers to as "red flag" words:

adultery	deadbeat	illegitimate
atheist	double-crosser	incompetent
bigamist	drunkard	intimate
blackmail	ex-convict	liar
bribery	fascist	mental disease
cheat	fool	perjurer
corruption	fraud	shyster
coward	gangster	unethical
crook	hypocrite	unprofessional

Remember also that using the word *alleged* before a potentially libelous word does not make it any less libelous.

Defenses

Courts usually recognize only three defenses against libel: truth, privilege, and fair comment.

The *truth* is the best defense, but in some states the courts have ruled that truth is only a defense if the comments were not malicious.

Privilege covers areas such as legislative and judicial hearings and debates and documents that are in the public domain. If a reporter quotes a potentially libelous comment made by a senator during a debate, the reporter could not be sued for libel.

Fair comment also is used as a defense against libel. Public officials, performers, sports figures, and others who attract public attention must expect to be criticized and scrutinized more than most people. If a sports commentator, for example, says that college football coach Joe Brown is a "lousy coach and the team would be better off if this inept, incompetent jerk moved on to a high-school coaching job, which he might just possibly be able to handle," he might get a punch on the nose if he ran into the coach, but he would not end up in court for libel.

There are limits, however, to what reporters can say even about public figures—the facts must be true. If the sports commentator had included the comment that "Brown's real problem is that he is smoking too many joints at night," then Brown would have a libel case unless the sports commentator could prove that Coach Brown actually spends his nights smoking marijuana.

False Light

A complaint similar to libel, called *false light*, involves the improper juxtaposition of video and audio that creates a false impression of someone. This invasion-of-privacy issue has actually caused more suits against TV news organizations than libel has, and it is more difficult to defend.

Karen Frankola, professor, described a case involving a reporter working on a story about genital herpes. The reporter was having difficulty figuring out how to cover the story, so she relied on some walking-down-the-street file video. Frankola said that in the package used on the 6 o'clock news, none of the passersby was identifiable. The story was edited differently for the 11 o'clock news, though, and the audience saw a close-up of a young woman while the anchor was saying, "For the 21 million Americans who have herpes, it's not a cure." The woman in the close-up won damages from the TV station.

Frankola said that false light "may get past a journalist more easily because it's not as obvious that false information is being given." She noted that the reporter in the herpes story did not say "the woman has herpes," which would have been a red flag to the editor. But, Frankola said, "the combination of words and pictures implied that the woman had the disease."

The Reporters' Committee for Freedom of the Press issued a report showing that 47 percent of subpoenas issued to TV stations deal with such invasion-of-privacy actions. The group's executive director, Jane Kirtley, believes the number of suits is growing because "people are developing a much greater sense of privacy, a desire to be let alone."

Most Americans believe that privacy is a cornerstone of their existence. They expect it to be respected. Journalists should invade that privacy with trepidation, particularly at times of grief, as was discussed in the chapters on reporting.

Boundaries

How far should reporters go to get a story? If reporters have a strong suspicion that someone in government is a crook, don't they have the right to do whatever it takes to report the story to the public? Some journalists say they do. Other newspeople believe that if they bend the rules too much, they become suspect and may be viewed no differently than the people they are investigating. Each reporter must decide the ethical merits involved in certain investigative practices.

Controversial Techniques

Some of the controversial information-gathering techniques employed by investigative reporters include impersonation, misrepresentation, and infiltration. Should journalists use such techniques to get a story? Consider the following scenarios:

- Is it right for a reporter to pretend to be a nurse so that she can get inside a nursing home to investigate charges that residents are being mistreated?
- Is it proper for a journalist to tell a college football coach that he wants to do a story about training when he's really checking on reports of drug abuse and gambling?

- Is it permissible for a reporter to pose as a pregnant woman thinking about having an abortion in order to find out what kind of material a right-to-life organization is providing at its information center?
- Is it ethical for journalists to take jobs in a supermarket and then spy on the operations to try to show improper food handling?

All of these incidents actually occurred, and they represent only a few examples of the controversial methods used on a routine basis. Are they ethical?

Investigative reporter Jim Polk, who moved over to CNN after spending many years with NBC, says he never misrepresents himself, impersonates others, or uses any other techniques that he thinks are unethical. "Our business is the truth," he says, "and I do not think you get the truth by practicing deception."

About the reporter who posed as a nurse to get into a nursing home, Polk admits that there are times when an argument for using such tactics is "honest," but he adds, "All too often the argument is simply an excuse for those who prefer a short cut rather than long-term hard work and drudgery to nail down the facts."

Polk says there is one role that he will play—that of citizen. He says he may go into a courthouse and ask for a document without signing in as a reporter because any citizen is entitled to the same information. "If I am going to put somebody on the air, gather information about an individual, I believe in disclosing who I am."

John Spain, the former general manager of WBRZ-TV in Baton Rouge, who won many awards for investigative reporting, says that while he worked in the public's interest, he "never took that as a license to break the law or be immoral or do things that are justified under the glorious heading of the First Amendment." Spain said, "I don't think we have any special rights, and I think we have to be very careful when we start thinking we do in terms of being dishonest or breaking the law."

Spain also said he had great success being "upfront with people and telling them who we are and why we've come to talk to them. I don't think I, or anyone on my staff, has ever misrepresented themselves." He adds, "I think we've done some very serious investigations over the years and have been able to practice our craft without misrepresenting ourselves."

NBC's Robert McKeown admits that he has misrepresented himself at times in order to get the "truth." He believes you can't always accomplish your goal if you admit you are a journalist. He recalled that during the Gulf War, he and a camera crew stole some fatigues, flak jackets, and helmets in order to work their way through roadblocks. "I am not sure we would have been successful getting our story—a story that we should have got—unless we misrepresented ourselves."

McKeown says everyone has a "gut feeling about what is right and wrong" when it comes to ethics. He says reporters also have to bring a sense of mission to what they do and, by definition, have to bring "a kind of anti-establishment attitude" to the job. "You have to be prepared to piss people off and realize that in some stories if you don't, the stories are not going to be successful."

Hidden Cameras and Microphones

Reporters sometimes use hidden cameras and microphones when they're doing an investigative story in an effort to record incriminating material. They also use wireless microphones to eavesdrop on conversations. Such devices are routinely used by teams working for *60 Minutes, 20/20,* and other investigative TV news programs.

There seem to be no laws against using a hidden camera to videotape something that is going on in public. Reporters must know state and federal laws, however, if they plan to use hidden microphones. Federal law forbids their use unless one person involved in the conversation knows of the recording. If a reporter places a hidden microphone in a hotel room to record a conversation between two or more people, that would be a violation of federal law. If a reporter is carrying a hidden microphone, there is no federal violation, but some states do forbid the practice. It's also a violation of some state laws to use so-called wires—microphones that transmit a conversation to another location.

CNN's Jim Polk admits that he has used hidden cameras from the back of a truck with one-way glass, but he says it is really "espionage, spying—a dirty little technique." But, he says, "We have used it on the mob." Polk says that as long as the video that's shot with a hidden camera is of people doing illegal things in public view, he has no problem using the technique. He says, however, that using hidden microphones is "playing with fire. It's a dangerous technique that is easily mishandled, and it should be used with caution and only under certain circumstances."

John Spain agreed, for the most part, but he admitted he did use hidden cameras on some stories when he thought the video was essential. He recalled using a concealed camera in a story about some alcoholic beverage control officers who were getting drunk while they were on duty. "They were supposed to be enforcing the alcohol laws," Spain said, "and we needed the video to show what they actually were doing."

But Spain added that hidden cameras shouldn't be used unless necessary. He cited the example of back-to-back stories that appeared on the now-defunct *Prime Time Live.* The first story was about a meat-inspection facility. The plant had been exempted from having federal inspectors because it was doing its own inspection. *Prime Time Live* had help from someone at the plant and got a camera inside. What they taped and played on the air was video of carcasses being dragged along the floor and intestines being ruptured on top of meat that had been stamped "U.S. Inspected."

Spain said, "I bought into that story big time, because it was providing a public service. Most people eat meat, and they have a right to know how it is processed. The story also brought about change. The day after it was aired," he said, "the Secretary of Agriculture sent inspectors into the plant."

On the other hand, Spain said he had a lot of trouble with the story done by *Prime Time Live* the following week. Hidden cameras were used again, this time to "expose" a man who had moved to another state to avoid paying child support.

Spain said it bothered him that the network picked on one man out of millions to point out a problem that admittedly is a serious one. "The network crossed the country with the man's wife and daughters and then walked into a place of business and cornered the father with a hidden camera." Spain said that what the man had done was wrong, but that he now had a new wife and children and that, in Spain's opinion, the network was not justified in embarrassing the individual to illustrate the problem.

Spain added that the audience never did hear the man's story because, after the ambush interview, he refused to speak with the reporter. Spain said, "I don't know what the public interest was in the life of a father who didn't pay child support."

Case Studies Involving Ethical Issues

CASE STUDY 1: A MERCY KILLING ON TV

Dr. Jack Kevorkian, who played a role in more than 121 deaths since his assisted suicide campaign began in 1990, was finally convicted in a Michigan court and sentenced to 10 to 25 years in jail because of his decision to give *60 Minutes* a videotape of his assisted suicide of 52-year-old Thomas Youk, who had Lou Gehrig's disease. At this writing, Kevorkian is still in prison. A U.S. Court of Appeals turned down his appeal for a new trial in June of 2004. His earliest release date would be 2007.

Kevorkian had given *60 Minutes'* producers the videotape of the killing because he wanted to challenge authorities in Michigan to prosecute him for what he claimed was his first case of actual euthanasia, or mercy killing. In all previous cases, Kevorkian assisted his patients in taking their own lives. Although he had been tried in court several times, juries refused to convict him of the assisted suicides. On the *60 Minutes* program, Kevorkian said of Michigan authorities, "either they go or I go. If I'm convicted, I will starve to death in prison or I will go."

The *60 Minutes* decision to broadcast the Kevorkian tape sparked widespread debate and much criticism about the airing of a person dying on primetime television, particularly because it came during a "sweeps" period when ratings are used to set advertising rates. The rating for the program was the highest *60 Minutes* had all season. CBS denied that the "sweeps" had anything to do with its decision to broadcast the material. One source quoted someone with *60 Minutes* as saying that getting the videotape from Kevorkian was "just too good an opportunity to pass up."

A network spokesman, Kevin Tedesco, said, "We're just letting Dr. Kevorkian tell his story." He added, somewhat defensively, "I really don't think there's a news organization in this country that would pass up this story." That statement was, perhaps, a bit overstated because several CBS affiliates refused to carry the program. The CBS statement said the program performed a public service.

But there was plenty of criticism of the network's decision, not only from journalists but also from those who do not agree with the idea of mercy killing. Even Jerry Lewis, host of a longtime annual Muscular Dystrophy Association telethon, was among those complaining to *60*

Minutes, saying it "amplified the fear" of people who have the disease or who will get a diagnosis of it in the future.

Others criticized the program because they said CBS allowed Kevorkian to "use" the network to present his views. One physician opposed to physician-assisted suicides said that Kevorkian manipulated the legitimate press—that the videotape should not have been shown anywhere except in a court of law. Indeed, what was to prevent CBS from simply turning over the tape to authorities without airing it? In the minds of many, and as acknowledged, in effect, by Tedesco, it was too good a story to ignore.

In a stinging column, *The New York Times* media critic, Caryn James, called the airing of the tape a "stunt death." Marvin Kalb, a former *CBS News* correspondent and director of the Shorenstein Center on the Press, Politics, and Public Policy at Harvard University, was especially critical: "To me, it is sad that death has become a form of news-entertainment."

CASE STUDY 2: FOOD LION SUES ABC

In 1992, two ABC producers for the now-defunct *Prime Time Live* sought undercover jobs as a meat wrapper trainee and a deli clerk in order to investigate allegations of improper food handling by the supermarket chain, Food Lion. It was a misguided idea from the beginning, and it brought ABC and Food Lion into a courtroom battle that lasted seven years.

Although the producers used controversial hidden cameras and microphones and other questionable techniques that were discussed earlier, it was not the techniques themselves that landed the network in court. To obtain the entry-level positions, they concealed their association with the network by lying about their work experience and references on their employment applications. Although the ruse was unethical, it worked and the two producers were hired. But what they did from then on inside the Food Lion store would be tainted. As most investigative reporters were quoted earlier as saying, they don't break the law to get a story. It obviously did not occur to the producers that there was anything illegal about their actions, or they simply did not care in their quest for "good news."

The hidden-camera exposé by the two producers over a two-week period charged that Food Lion stores knowingly sold rotten meat, fish dipped in bleach, cheese that was nibbled on by rats, and produce removed from fly-infested dumpsters. Although officially, *ABC News* has a policy of using hidden cameras only if less-intrusive methods of reporting are unavailable, the decision was made to use them at the Food Lion store anyway. Could the story have been completed without them?

Fortune magazine talked to the key participants in the case and examined thousands of pages of sworn testimony, court documents, and internal memos. It's conclusion: Food Lion may have had a point.

Case Study 2 continued

It wondered, like many investigative reporters, if the story could have been done without deceit and hidden cameras. *Fortune* questioned why ABC did not check state or federal health inspection reports to see whether Food Lion had food safety problems. The magazine suggested that producers also could have tested groceries purchased at Food Lion for contamination. ABC did neither. ABC also failed to report that, in general, Food Lion received favorable reports from state and federal health inspectors. ABC also worked closely with union members, whom the network knew had a grudge against the company.

Food Lion charged that it was victimized by ABC's unethical conduct and one-sided reporting. It claimed that ABC producers told lies and induced others to lie and that it ignored evidence that would have undermined its story.

During the week that the *Prime Time Live* story was broadcast about the supermarket chain, the market value of the company's stock fell by 1.3 billion dollars. The chain also said that its profits were clobbered by the program, from $178 million in 1992 to a mere $3.9 million the following year.

Food Lion sued ABC for $2.47 billion dollars. It took four years to get the two sides into court and another three years for the case to end up in the United States Court of Appeals. After millions of dollars in legal fees, the court reversed an earlier court ruling that had found in favor of Food Lion's damage award. The higher court held that Food Lion could not circumvent the First Amendment by seeking to recover defamation-type damages without first proving that the story was intentionally or recklessly untruthful and inaccurate.

Although ABC's damages were limited to its weighty legal expenses, Food Lion could take satisfaction in the court's ruling that ABC was guilty of trespass and breached a duty of loyalty to Food Lion by bringing hidden cameras into nonpublic areas of their employer. The court also said, "We are convinced that the media can do its important job effectively without resorting to the commission of run-of-the mill torts." Nevertheless, all that Food Lion ultimately received for its costly legal effort was $2 in nominal damages on the trespass complaint.

For journalists, the case is more important for ethics than who won or lost money. One of the producers trying to get a job at Food Lion wrote on her application that "I love meat wrapping. I have heard Food Lion is a great company. I would like to make a career with the company." The producers got phony letters of reference from some union members who had a grudge against Food Lion.

After getting the jobs and gaining access to the Food Lion store by lying, both producers had microphones in their underwear and tiny cameras hidden in their wigs. Most investigative reporters told us that they believed ABC went too far.

CASE STUDY 3: ABC STINGS THE COPS

Another *Prime Time Live* hidden camera story that tried to sting some cops "[raised] as many questions about its own reporting as it did about the police," according to Brill's *Content* (July/August 1999). So-called racial profiling—the practice used by some police authorities of stopping cars when the cars and/or the people driving them meet the profile of suspected criminal activity—has been making headlines lately. Many African Americans have charged that they have been stopped by police just because of their race and often because of the kind of car they are driving, particularly if it is an expensive one.

Some of these complaints were made about police in New Jersey, so *Prime Time Live* decided to launch a sting operation to see if the complaints were true. Producers hired three African American men and sent them to Jamesburg, New Jersey, in a new Mercedes with hidden cameras in the rearview mirror, the sunroof, and at the rear of the car.

A description of the sting operation in Brill's *Content* told how the Mercedes and its three ABC undercover black men cruised around Jamesburg hoping that they would be stopped by police. Patrol officers Louis Hornberger and Robert Tonkery obliged them. The car, by the way, had been seen the previous night circling the town. This night, at one of the town's two traffic lights, the Mercedes made an illegal lane change, prompting the two officers to pull the car over.

Brill's *Content* said the traffic stop seemed routine and it might have been handled quickly, but the backseat passenger made the white officers nervous because when they asked for identification, the young man scowled, poked at his heavy leather jacket, and told officers he left his I.D. at home. One of the policemen said later that he became more suspicious when the men in the front of the car identified their companion by two different names.

The officers ordered the men to get out of the car. The officers frisked each of the men and searched the car. They found nothing and told the men they could go. They would say later that they thought they were doing the men a favor because the men did, technically, commit a driving infraction when they made an illegal lane change.

But Brill's *Content* said that when ABC's *Prime Time Live* producers came to Jamesburg three months later and started asking questions, the police officers learned that the three black men in the Mercedes were working for ABC and that their encounter with the officers was on videotape.

Some carefully edited footage of the sting was included in a *Prime Time Live* segment called "Driving While Black." Jamesburg officials were understandably concerned about the program and demanded an explanation from their police officers. They claimed that the newsmagazine did not tell the whole story. They said that two detectives working undercover with a county-wide drug task force had put them on the lookout for a Mercedes similar to the one used by ABC. The officers also said that ABC had failed to mention several negative and provoking

Case Study 3 continued

statements made by the backseat passenger, whose conduct had caused them to fear for their safety.

Brill's *Content* said that unedited video of the encounter shows indisputably that the officers were polite and that their decision to order the men out of the car was precipitated by the backseat passenger saying he left his I.D. at home. No law requires that passengers identify themselves to police officers, but the three men apparently were advised by an ABC attorney that refusal to produce I.D. would make the officers suspicious and probably bring about some sort of reaction similar to what the ABC producers were looking for. According to Brill's *Content*, the ABC attorney also advised the ABC undercover men that by having all of their credentials in order and by complying with officers' basic requests, there shouldn't be any reason for them to be ordered out of the car. *Prime Time Live* made no mention on the program of the lawyer's advice, and the men either forgot or ignored it.

The *Prime Time Live* report also failed to mention that their sting Mercedes was driving around the town for two nights before the encounter with the police officers, and the car was not stopped. Another ABC sting car was roaming the streets a month earlier, and the taped conversation showed the men's disappointment when police failed to stop them. A police car had followed the ABC car for several blocks and then suddenly turned away. The tape of that incident showed that one of the men in the car was disappointed: "Oh," the man exclaimed, "he turned, son of a bitch we lost them, damn." The tape then heard the men discussing what they could do differently to make the police officers pull them over. The program that aired made no mention of these unsuccessful attempts to sting police.

Also omitted from the program, for obvious reasons, was the taped conversation in the Mercedes after the encounter with police. The men discussed whether the man in the back should have produced some I.D. "Do you have it with you?" asked one of the men in the front. "Yeah, I got it," the man in the backseat said. "Well, then you should have shown it to them," said the driver. The man in the back then said: "Yeah, but then they wouldn't have forced us out of the car." The driver is then heard saying, "Shh, shh," a reminder that the videotape was still rolling.

In the end, the police officers filed suit against ABC for defamation. The mayor of the town said "there is a law that says police officers can't entrap a suspected criminal. What *Prime Time* did was to make every effort to entrap a police officer." The policemen charge that ABC unfairly branded them as racists.

Brill's *Content* said the unedited tapes do not clearly vindicate the police officers and in some cases even contradict their accounts. As a result, the magazine adds, the hidden camera footage, which in theory could have resolved the dispute, has raised as many questions as it has answered.

As for the officers, they said their run-in with *Prime Time Live* has sapped their enthusiasm for the job. "I'm just worried about making stops," said Officer Hornberger. "I see a violation at night, and if I see the

Case Study 3 continued

driver is black, it's like the blood runs out of me, I want to get out of there. I wonder did they see me on TV? Are they going to start calling me a racist?"

Ironically, the Brill's *Content* report said that the three black men in the Mercedes underwent a transformation of their own. The magazine said the three men who decided to test the police for a nationwide TV audience—and then laughed and bantered on tape after the incident—now claim they suffered an invasion of their privacy, humiliation, embarrassment, and emotional distress.

CASE STUDY 4: CNN RETRACTS ITS STORY

One of the most sensational retractions by any news organization in recent years was CNN's admission that its report on the military's alleged use of poison gas was untrue. The CNN "Valley of Death" investigative report was scheduled to launch the network's new magazine show, *News Stand: CNN and Time*. It was a dynamite story about the U.S. military using lethal nerve gas during the Vietnam War. But the story set off a different kind of explosion than was expected in the Atlanta headquarters of CNN. The story wasn't accurate, and several CNN producers lost their jobs in the fallout.

According to the investigative report voiced by one of CNN's top journalists, Peter Arnett, the U.S. conducted a raid into Laos that used nerve gas to kill American defectors. It was a sensational exposé that CNN executives hoped would impress audiences and bring high ratings to its new series that would rival the likes of CBS' *60 Minutes*, NBC's *Dateline*, and ABC's *Prime Time Live*.

The only trouble with the story was that no solid evidence supported that the incident in Laos ever happened. After the program aired, so many questions arose about the story's validity that CNN hired an outside team of investigators to check on its investigators. Less than two weeks later, the team reported: "CNN's conclusion that United States troops used nerve gas during the Vietnamese conflict on a mission in Laos designed to kill American defectors is insupportable."

CNN was forced to retract the story and apologize for a broadcast that had drawn on some of its best talent. In addition to Arnett, the network had involved veteran journalists Jeff Greenfield and Bernard Shaw in the investigative report. The producer of the story, April Oliver, her senior producer Jack Smith, and executive producer Pamela Hill lost their jobs. *Time* magazine, which ran its own version of the story, also had to apologize.

Pulitzer Prize–winning journalist Peter Arnett, who was not fired but no longer reported for CNN, was criticized for insisting he was simply a mouthpiece who bore no responsibility for reporting the story. That statement set off a new debate about just how much involvement celebrity

Case Study 4 continued

broadcast journalists such as Mike Wallace, Ed Bradley, and Diane Sawyer have in the stories they voice.

Although the public no doubt believes the reporters' involvement is significant, the truth is that producers historically have done most of the work on all investigative reports, developing the storyline, digging for facts, and pre-interviewing those individuals involved in the investigation before they appear on camera with the celebrity reporters. The networks have always been guilty of perpetuating the idea that their stars are much more involved in the investigative reports than they really are and of downplaying the role of producers who number in the 30s or more on many of the investigative units at the networks. Peter Arnett may have a point.

But how could a story like "Valley of Death" get on CNN and in *Time* magazine when little evidence corroborated the story? Much of the blame seems to rest with editors and top executives who didn't ask enough questions about the story when it was being developed. Too much reliance was placed on the integrity of the staff that was working on the story. Oliver, Hill, and Smith had good track records. They were good journalists and their editors trusted them. In this case that trust—the failure to pay enough attention to the story in its development and final stages—would burn them.

Ted Gup, a former investigative reporter for *Time*, who now teaches journalism at Georgetown University, said the "Valley of Death" fiasco should not be dismissed as an aberration. He says the controversy "represents most ominously of all, with the media at large, a very disturbing trend of senior editors increasingly becoming more gullible, and a tendency for more and more journalists to work in the realm of possibility rather than truth."

CASE STUDY 5: *CBS NEWS* ALSO RETRACTS A STORY

In the middle of a very contentious presidential election in September of 2004, the most highly regarded investigative news program on television, *60 Minutes*, was forced to apologize for and retract a story which indicated that President Bush had neglected his duties when he was serving in the National Guard during the Vietnam War. The story, which was presented on *60 Minutes* by anchor Dan Rather, included documents which were said to be from the personal files of Lt. Colonel Jerry B. Killian who was President Bush's commander in the Texas Air National Guard. The documents, reportedly written or dictated by the Colonel, who died 20 years ago, said the Colonel complained that Lt. Bush had refused to take a physical exam and that he had felt pressure to "sugarcoat" Mr. Bush's national guard record because a congressman's son was talking to someone upstairs. But soon after the story aired, there were numerous complaints about the authenticity of the documents and charges that the

Case Study 5 continued

type face on the documents indicated they were typed on a computer which was not available when the Colonel allegedly wrote them. After defending the *60 Minutes* report rigorously for several days, *CBS News* admitted that the man who gave the documents to *60 Minutes*, former National Guard officer Bill Burkett, had "deliberately mislead" the network about how he had obtained the documents. A CBS spokesperson said that "based on what we know now, we can not prove that the documents are authentic, which is the only accpetable journalistic standard to justify using the documents in the report." The President of *CBS News*, Andrew Heyward said, "We should not have used them. That was a mistake, which we deeply regret." He added: "nothing is more important to us than our credibility and keeping faith with the millions of people who count on us for fair, accurate, reliable, and independent reporting. Heywood watched the *60 Minutes* report before it was aired and another top deputy, Betsy West closely supervised the production. The *60 Minutes* report unraveled after Guardsman Bill Burkett, who had originally said he obtained the documents from another former Guardsman, retracted that statement, saying he got them from another source. CBS admitted that it had no idea who the real soruce was and that raised a lot of questions in the minds of journalists who generally agree that you need more than one source, particularly on a volatile story of this nature, and that the sources you do use have to be realiably identified to at least one or more top editors or officials in the news organization, a premise pointed out more than once earlier in this book. CBS would no doubt argue that it had identified the source, but it turned out not to be reliable which, of course, is why you don't do such a story wihtout a second source. The story, which was heralded as an exclusive expose by the network when it was broadcast, brought immediate attacks from the Republican Party and White House officials as being a political ploy that was probably set in motion by Mr. Rather who has been a frequent target of the GOP, which views him as a staunch leader of an alleged biased liberal media. President Bush's chief spokesman, Scott McClellan, said that, while the White House appreciated CBS's statement of regret, there are still serious questions that need to be answered and fully investigated." McClellan added, "The one thing that is not in question is the timing of theses recent attacks on the president. He said it is clear that there has been an 'orchestrated effort' by Democrats in the Kerry campaign to try to tear down the president." A few days after the *CBS News* retraction, it announced that a former attorney general, Dick Thornburgh, and a former Associated Press executive, Louis D. Boccardi, would investigate what was described as the "journalistic breakdowns," that led to the flawed *60 Minutes* report. Rather reportedly was upset with the naming of Thornburg to investigate the CBS report becuase he served two Republican presidents, Mr. Bush's father and Richard Nixon, with whom Rather publicly clashed. In a report in *The New York Times*, it was said that one important line of inquiry in the investigation is the role of Mary Mapes, the lead producer of the report who arranged to receive the documents, which were supposed to be from the personal files of Colonel Killian. According to the *Times*, the panel also is expected to pursue what led Ms. Mapes to put Bill Burkett in touch with a top aide to Senator John

Case Study 5 continued

Kerry before the *60 Minutes* report was broadcast. CBS said Mapes violated network policy when she did this. A statement released by the organization said "it is obviously against *CBS News* standards and those of every other reputable news organizations to be associated with any political agenda." *The New York Times* said the rebuke of Mapes underscored the change in her status, noting that the producer was burnished a few months earlier when she produced a report on a Wednesday edition of *60 Minutes* that detailed the abuses at the Abu Ghraib prison in Baghdad. The newspaper said that some colleagues at CBS expressed worry that Mapes would be a scapegoat for the Bush story while Rather and more senior producers would not be held accountable. The independent investigation of the 60 Minutes report resulted in the firing of four people. Mary Mapes, the story's producer; Josh Howard, executive producer of *60 Minutes* Wednesday, Howard's top deputy, Mary Murphy, and CBS News Senior Vice President Betsy West. The report by Boccardi and Thornburgh, was extremely critical of *60 Minutes*, saying the producers demonstrated "myopic zeal" in rushing the report on the air. They added that CBS compounded the damage with a circle-the-wagons mentality once the report came under fire. They added that they found no evidence of political bias by the network against Bush. CBS News President Andrew Heyward and Dan Rather escaped without any disciplinary action. But Rather, who narrated the story, and subsequent follow-ups, was criticized by CBS Chief Executive Leslie Moonves for "errors of credulity and over-enthusiasm." Somewhat ironically, some of the strongest criticism of the firings came from *60 Minutes* veteran Andy Rooney who said "the people on the front lines got fired while the people most instrumental in getting the broadcast on the air escaped.

Other Stories That Backfired

Referring to some of the cases we just discussed and others that raise serious questions about media practices, the *Columbia Journalism Review* (CJR) said the past decade was a humbling time for journalism, particularly inves-tigative television journalism. CJR noted that an *NBC news* magazine had to apologize for its fakery in the investigation of General Motors trucks, and ABC and CBS both backed down under pressure from tobacco corporations, with ABC settling out of court a $10 billion libel suit and apologizing on air.

CJR also referred to a misguided investigative report by WCCO-TV about Northwest Airlines, for which the station won an Emmy award. Northwest charged that WCCO had painted a "distorted, untruthful picture" of the carrier's safety practices. The Minnesota News Council, a private watchdog group, upheld the airline's complaint. No monetary damages were involved, but the TV station was badly bruised, according to CJR.

CJR also writes that many journalists mistakenly assume that the First Amendment protects reporters wherever they choose to go, whatever they may do in pursuit of a story. Courts have never supported these assumptions, says CJR. The journal says one way to react to all the court actions resulting from investigative stories may be to ask whether such journalism on television—whether intended to serve the public or lift ratings—is too often brittle, showy, and mean-spirited, besides dancing along the edge of the law.

One such story involved the *Cincinnati Inquirer* and Chiquita Brands International. In 1998, the *Inquirer* published an investigative report about the company, in which it accused Chiquita of bribing foreign officials, mistreating its Central American workers, and using illegal means to circumvent foreign laws forbidding land ownership.

But in less than two months, the newspaper shocked the journalism world with an unusual front-page apology, renouncing the story and announcing that it would pay Chiquita in excess of $10 million.

And as you read earlier, two of the most embarrassing retractions in the past decade were issued by CNN for its nerve gas story and *CBS News* for its 60 Minute report on President Bush's National Guard service.

Ambush Interviews

The type of interview described by John Spain earlier in this chapter regarding the delinquent father who was hounded—an *ambush interview*—is often used by TV reporters, although the technique has received much criticism. As the name implies, reporters who are unable to schedule an interview with an individual often stake out the person's home or office until they are able to ambush the person as he or she comes into or goes out of the building. We have all seen such interviews. The reporter and cameraperson force themselves on the individual, trying to shoot video and ask questions as the person tries to escape. Is this reporting technique appropriate?

ABC News correspondent Barry Serafin says an ambush interview is justified only when there's "a genuine public accountability involved. Sometimes you cannot allow a person in public office to refuse to talk to you; you really have to get to the person and make him accountable." Serafin recalled that, during Watergate, journalists "would do an ambush or whatever else it took to get some information."

John Spain said he does not like the ambush interview unless, as Serafin notes, it involves the public interest. "If we have made every effort to interview an individual and have been denied access," said Spain, "we would do an ambush. If you raise your hand and take an oath," he added, "you have an obligation to answer to the public."

60 Minutes co-editor Lesley Stahl recalls that when she was covering the White House during the Watergate scandal, she was assigned to numerous stakeouts, a polite phrase for ambush interviews. Or, as Stahl described it in her book, *Reporting Live* (Simon & Schuster, 1999), "an opportunity for reporters to relinquish their dignity by loitering around someone's office or house waiting to ask a question the target wants to avoid." Stahl said the stakeout became a prime tool of newsgathering once Woodward and Bernstein had guided the Watergate story into the Nixon White House.

Stahl said it was difficult to reach anyone close to Nixon, so CBS decided to intercept the principles at their homes before they left for work in the morning. In her book, she writes: "I was one of the instruments through which CBS practiced this degrading form of journalism, chosen because I was too new to say no." She said, "I became a *stakeout queen*."

Stahl said it wasn't unusual for her to catch many of the Watergate suspects in their pajamas as they opened their doors to pick up *The Washington Post*. The assignment desk told Stahl to be at the homes before the sun came up. She said it was dirty work, especially when wives came running after you in their bathrobes, hollering, "get off my lawn." Stahl recalled how one day she was sent to stake out Jeb Magruder, deputy director of the Nixon campaign, and she asked his children as they walked to school if their father was still at home. She said Gail Magruder "tore out of the house and chewed my face off. She was right," said Stahl.

On another occasion, Stahl was told to stake out the home of Justice William O. Douglas for a profile that legal correspondent Fred Graham was doing. The desk said they wanted pictures of the justice jogging. When Stahl protested that Douglas was 75 years old and it was hailing out, the assignment editor said condescendingly, "If you knew more about this town, kid, you'd realize that Douglas is a great outdoorsman and if he doesn't jog, he'll be out there walking his dog, so get there before the sun comes up." Stahl said the crew was just delighted to be sitting in the dark at 5:30 A.M. in front of Douglas' house with hail banging on the car roof. She said the crew blamed her. Nothing happened outside the house until four hours later. "You have to have an iron bladder," she noted, "to be a good staker-outer."

Stahl said Watergate changed journalism forever. She said it introduced an era of reporting through anonymous sources and ushered in a "swarm-around-'em mentality" where reporters and camerapersons hounded people. She called it "undignified and lacking decorum." She added, "It [the practice] reduced our standing with the public."

Stahl said that from Watergate on, nearly every government utterance would be subject to skeptical scrutiny; the assumption was that government officials skirt the truth. Before Watergate, Stahl pointed out that presidents had been protected by newsmen: Franklin D. Roosevelt's wheelchair and John F. Kennedy's women had gone unreported. Hereafter, said Stahl, "presidents would view the press as a squad in a perpetual adversarial crouch, always ready to pounce."

Reenactments

Considerable debate has been generated over the use of reenactments of events to tell a news story. Most news directors frown on the technique, but some see nothing wrong with them as long as they are clearly designated as such with a supertitle plainly stating "This is a reenactment."

The most important ethical consideration in the use of reenactments is that they should not confuse the audience about what they are looking at. Viewers should be able to determine quickly which scenes are actual and which are reenactments.

Some news directors believe reenactments have no place in news. As one news director puts it, "Let the tabloid newspeople do the reenactment."

Crime-Stoppers

The TV program designed to help police catch criminals sometimes uses re-enactments of the very worst kind. In two examples aired in Baton Rouge, the TV station provided the TV cameras as actors provided by the police and the local branch of *Crime-Stoppers* reenacted the actual crimes for the TV audience. As in any major city, some of the crime is carried out by African Americans, including the two crimes depicted in the *Crime-Stoppers* segments. But the reenactments raised serious ethical issues because the actors who were selected for the videotaping were African American and no effort was made to disguise their race.

In one episode, two African American males were videotaped jumping over the counter in a bank, where they grabbed money from teller drawers before escaping. As was discussed in this book earlier, the race of people involved in criminal activity should never be disclosed unless police are looking for the suspects and race can help in identifying them; however, showing two black actors jumping over a railing in a bank can hardly help viewers identify the two men who actually committed the crime.

In a second *Crime-Stoppers* reenactment, an African American couple was engaged to play the roles of two victims of a bedroom shooting. Two additional black people were provided to act as the perpetrators. Although both men wore ski masks, it was obvious they were black. After the shooting, the men were filmed fleeing the room.

When I questioned spokespeople at the TV station and for *Crime-Stoppers*, they were clear that they had no intention of trying to hide the racial identity of the actors in the reenactments; quite the contrary. "We knew they were African-Americans," said the *Crime-Stoppers* spokesperson—who was not a journalist, by the way—"so why would we keep that secret?" he asked. When I pointed out that just showing two black actors in a reenactment of a crime would be of no use in solving a crime, the spokesman said, "Well, we get results."

The TV news spokesperson said basically the same thing, that *Crime-Stoppers* reduces crime and the station believes its reenactments are effective. At the same time, the spokesperson acknowledged that his newsroom normally does not identify the race of a suspect in its copy or voice-over stories about a crime, an inconsistency in this writer's opinion.

Staging

Another serious ethical concern is *staging*, the faking of video or sound or any other aspect of a story. Staging can and should be a cause for dismissal. Ironically, some reporters see little harm in staging if the staging is accurate. "What's wrong," one reporter asks, "if you round up protesters at an abortion clinic who may be out to lunch and get them shouting again? That's what they would be doing after lunch, anyway."

It is not the same, and reporters who think that way pose a serious threat to their news organizations. Many other kinds of staging go on all too often. All of them are unethical. Here are a few examples:

- A reporter misses a news conference, so he asks the newsmaker to repeat a few of the remarks he made and pretends the sound bites actually came from the news conference.
- A news crew goes to a park to film some children playing on swings and seesaws, but there are none there. A cameraperson is sent to find some children.
- A reporter doing a story about drugs on campus needs some video to support the story, so he asks a student he knows to "set up" a group smoking marijuana in a dorm room.
- A documentary unit doing a story on crime asks police officers in a patrol car to make a few passes by the camera with the sirens blasting. Harmless deceptions? Perhaps. But where does staging end? If reporters are willing to set up a marijuana party, is there anything that they would feel uncomfortable about staging?

Dateline Rigs a Truck

A particularly dramatic example of dishonest journalism was *Dateline*'s rigging of a General Motors pickup truck with small rockets to make the gas tank explode. In that case, a few executives at NBC did lose their jobs, including News President Michael Gartner. Some news directors insist that staging is never acceptable; others are more flexible. For example, if a reporter arrives to do a feature story about a pizza parlor that claims to make the largest pizzas in the city and discovers no one in the restaurant has ordered the large size, it would be permissible to have a pizza made to show on camera; however, the reporter also should note in the story that while she was in the restaurant, no one actually ordered one of the big pizzas.

Few news directors would object to a reporter asking a clerk in the IRS office to accompany her to the racks displaying various tax forms so that the cameraperson would have an appropriate background for the interview. This activity is not really considered staging but setting up a shot, and it is viewed as acceptable. The same would be true, of course, if the crew moved the furniture in the office of someone to be interviewed on camera so that the cameraperson could get a better shot.

CBS Also Blows Up a Truck

There was nothing devious about CBS' *48 Hours* decision to blow up a truck. It was just bad journalism.

While the jury was still being picked for the trial of Timothy McVeigh and Terry Nichols for blowing up the federal building in Oklahoma City, CBS decided, as they put it, "to test and investigate a key defense argument that it must have taken more than two people to make and set off the truck bomb. In introducing the *48 Hours* experiment, *CBS News* Anchor Dan Rather stated, "We had explosives experts load a truck with the same ingredients used in the Oklahoma City bomb. Then they ignited it."

There are so many problems with this CBS "experiment" that it is hard to decide where to begin. How about the question: should a news organization be in the business of trying to disprove a defense argument in a criminal trial, especially when that trial hasn't even begun? But even if the trial had started, it could be argued that it is the job of the defense to make its case and to conduct it without the interference of a major news network. By injecting itself into the case, CBS became a part of the story. That's never a good idea. Then, of course, the network's experiment itself was anything but scientific.

It went out and found two men who, by CBS' own admission, were explosive experts to load a truck "with the same amount of the same ingredients used in the Oklahoma City bombing." Although it's not clear exactly what CBS blew up, reporter Jim Stewart used this sentence in his report: "Five hundred gallons of fuel oil, and 25 tons of ammonium nitrate are the same ingredients used in the most common of all terrorist tools: the ANFO bomb." It's assumed that that is what the two experts picked by CBS to put on this stunt loaded into the truck before they ignited it. Anticipating the defense contention that McVeigh and Nichols could not have done all this by themselves, CBS went to a farm and talked to a farmer and a fertilizer salesman who told reporter Stewart, in effect, "Oh sure just about anyone can put one of these bombs together—farmers use the stuff all the time to blow up tree roots, and the like." Of course, the federal building in Oklahoma City was neither a tree nor a root.

Why all the fuss? All CBS was doing was helping the prosecution get those two nasty guys who killed all those innocent people and explain to the American people how simple it all was. Remember, when CBS got into the demolition business, the jury in the trial hadn't even been picked yet.

"Unnatural" Sound

Natural sound is one of the most effective tools used by broadcast journalists. No one wants to see children riding down a hill on sleds without hearing their shouts, and video of a marching band would not be interesting without the music. What does a reporter do, however, when the audio recorder or camera does not pick up the sound? Should the reporter add "unnatural sound," that is, sound effects? Sound-effect tapes and records are available to match just about any activity. Certainly, the sound of laughing children is available. The reporter might not be able to match exactly the music the band in the parade was playing, but how many people would know the difference?

The answer to these questions is that such use of sound effects would be unethical. The same goes for dubbing in any natural sound that the recorder might have missed at the scene of a story. If the sound of fire engines was lost at the scene, that's unfortunate; the answer is not to substitute sound effects. It would be better for the reporter or anchor to admit to the audience that there were sound problems on the story.

Video Deception

Most TV stations maintain a videotape library that includes footage of events going back several years. Most stations pull some of that video, known as *generic footage*, when they need shots of a general nature to cover portions of the script. Some stations routinely superimpose the words *file footage* over such video, but other stations run the video without any such admission unless it's obvious that the video is dated.

Most journalists have no problem using file footage of people walking down the street or shots of cars and trucks rolling down the highway if it works with the script; however, pulling old video from the morgue about disturbances in the Little Haiti section of Miami for a story about a new outbreak of violence in that neighborhood would be deceptive unless the audience knew the difference between the old and new footage they were watching. Instead of the font "file footage," many news directors insist that the file footage have the original date superimposed over the old video.

TV stations usually do not plan to deceive the audience when they use old footage; they are just careless. There have been examples of deliberate deception over the years, however; instances when old war footage was used, for example, to cover new fighting. In some cases, stations have used footage of a completely different war to go along with a story on fighting in another country. Such deception, if discovered (and it often is), could cause the station to lose its license.

Improper Editing

Video and audio recordings are rarely accepted in court cases because they can easily be doctored. As one audio engineer puts it: "With enough time, I can make people say anything I want." Most of the time, the distortion of people's comments on radio and television is not intentional; the tape is just poorly edited. There have been many cases in which people who have been interviewed by radio and TV reporters complained that the editing changed the meaning of their comments. By clipping or editing a statement, they charged, the editing distorted the point they were trying to make. A reporter or producer intent on showing someone in a certain light can accomplish that goal rather easily. The error of omission is a serious concern. The individual's remarks could certainly be distorted by picking up one part of a person's statement and ignoring an equally important part of it.

When tape must be edited for time purposes (which is almost always the case), the reporter or producer must ensure that the sound bite is representative of what the person said. If it is not, it is essential that in narration following the bite, the reporter accurately sum up the part of the sound bite that was eliminated.

Avoiding Jump Cuts

Some of the tricks employed in the editing process also raise ethical questions. In order to avoid *jump cuts*—the jerking of the head that occurs when video cuts are juxtaposed—film editors (it started long before the advent of video) came up with cutaways, reversals, and reverse questions.

These techniques are designed to cover up video edits. Editors, producers, and everyone else in the newsroom defend the use of most of these techniques because they make the finished product much smoother to watch. "Who wants to watch a head jumping across the screen?" is the answer editors give for using a cutaway, or a reverse shot. It is hard to argue with that response. Such techniques are not completely honest because the audience usually does not realize what the editors are doing. In an effort to avoid jump cuts, editors also distract the audience's attention from what the editors are doing by inserting other video between the edited material.

In a *cutaway*, it appears that the cameraperson just decided in the middle of an interview or speech to show the TV audience that the room was crowded with spectators and reporters. This cutaway shot may show another cameraperson shooting the scene, or a reporter scribbling in a notepad, or just a row of the audience. That shot makes it possible for the editor to take part of the video comment and marry it to any other video comment made by an individual while he or she was speaking. The first part might have been at the beginning of the speech, while the second comment might have been made 10 or 21 minutes later.

"So what? There's nothing dishonest about that," is the response from many editors. In general there probably isn't anything dishonest about this technique if one accepts that it is not necessary for the audience to know that the tape was edited. The real harm comes when the video is badly edited and does not accurately represent what the individual said during the interview or speech and the audience has no way of knowing this.

Another editing technique used to avoid jump cuts is the *reversal*, also referred to as a *reverse shot* or *listening shot*. After completing an interview, the reporter pretends to be listening to the interviewee while the cameraperson takes some shots of the reporter. The worst examples show the reporters smiling and nodding their heads in agreement. These shots then are sandwiched between two bites of the interview and, again, the audience usually believes that the cameraperson simply decided to take a picture of the reporter at that point in the interview or believes there were two cameras in the room.

One key scene in the Hollywood film *Broadcast News* pointed out the unethical use of the reverse shot. In the film, an ethically minded TV news producer breaks off a relationship with an anchor-reporter because he used a reverse shot of himself crying in the middle of an interview when he actually had not cried during the interview itself. A cameraperson took the crying shot later—that was outright deception.

Fortunately, such examples are not typical of the reverse shots that appear in TV news stories. Most objections to the reverse shot are not about deception but about concern over the audience's inability to discern that the video has been edited.

The most dangerous technique, which is not as popular as it once was, is the *reverse question*. A reverse question is one the reporter asks a second time after the interview has been completed. The camera is facing the reporter this time. The technique allows the editor to avoid a jump cut by inserting video and audio of the reporter asking the question. The problem occurs when the reporter does not ask the question exactly the same way the second time.

Newsmakers themselves have sometimes complained about reverse questions when they realized that the questions they heard on their televisions were not exactly the same as those they were asked when they were in front of the camera. If any change at all is made in the second version of the question, it could be a serious ethical issue. Most newsrooms have stopped using reverse questions.

Producers and news directors who routinely allow the use of such techniques sometimes draw the line when the president or some other top official is making an important policy statement. In such cases, many producers allow the jump cut—particularly if it is not jarring—so that the audience knows that the remarks by the chief executive or other official have been edited. Instead of using a jump cut, some producers prefer to use a wipe between bites.

Inflating the News

Reporters must attempt to keep a news story in perspective. Otherwise, it is easy to give the audience the wrong impression about what is actually happening. As mentioned earlier, a reporter should never stage video by rounding up demonstrators who were on a lunch break; however, let's assume that when the reporter showed up, the protest was in full swing. Did the presence of the camera have an effect on the demonstration? Did the shouting suddenly get louder? If the camera did have an effect on the crowd, which would not be unusual, the audience might get the wrong impression. In such a case, it might be appropriate for the reporter to make a statement like the following:

Actually, the turnout for the demonstration was smaller than was predicted . . . and our camera seemed to encourage some in the crowd to whip it up just a bit more than when we first arrived.

It is also important for the cameraperson to show accurately what was going on at the scene. If there were only a half-dozen demonstrators, the audience might, again, get the wrong impression if the camera shot used was a close-up, when a wide shot would have revealed that the group was small.

Will the Real Reporter Please Stand Up?

There always has been a certain amount of glorification of anchors in broadcasting, and there's a growing tendency to give more credit to anchors and less to those who actually do the work. It's common practice for producers and writers to write copy for anchors. Everyone knows about this practice, and there's no ethical issue involved, even though a portion of the audience probably thinks anchors write their own copy. Many do write part of it; however, some journalists are concerned about the growing practice of using writers and producers to prepare packages that make use of the anchor's voice; packages that, some would argue, would best be prepared by reporters. Part of the problem, of course, is that some stations are cutting back on their reporting staffs and are compensating for the loss by having writers and producers handle some of the work reporters once did, without leaving the newsroom. Is this deception?

Bill Small, former senior vice president of *CBS News*, said it's "always improper if you leave the impression that you covered a story when you didn't." Small noted, however, that at CBS and other networks it isn't "uncommon" for producers to do most of the work on some stories. It's routine for producers to conduct an interview in advance of a correspondent's arrival on the scene to "tie it all together."

Small is also concerned about the proliferation of material available to broadcast stations via satellite and the increasing use of the same syndication video by all the networks. "I'm a firm believer that there shouldn't be one story for all the networks," he said. "Each one should do its own." Small is even more annoyed by video news releases, which he calls "handout journalism." He said that if any of this material is picked up, its source should be properly identified.

Professor Robert Mulholland, former president of NBC, shares some of Small's concerns, particularly on the question of anchors and reporters voicing-over syndicated video. Mulholland asked, "How do you know that the video was honestly gathered or edited?" "Things get up on a satellite," he said, "and everybody brings it down. The days when you only broadcast news that your own employees gathered is pretty much gone. . . . The gathering of news has become a pool process, and that disturbs me."

The late Rob Sunde, former news director of the ABC Information Network, also was concerned about these issues. Regarding the question of writers and producers doing packages that the audience thinks are the product of anchors, Sunde said, "Everyone involved is cheated; those involved in the production and those at home receiving it." He added, "When we see reporters at the scene, we expect that they covered the story, giving us what they saw, heard, felt, smelled. That's reporting. When someone else takes credit for that or pretends that he or she did the work, that's unethical."

Sunde said one of the worst examples of unethical conduct that he could recall was when a radio reporter for a network used two different names so that he could report for another news group.

Summary

Accuracy is an ethical journalistic concern, but when information in a story is inaccurate because of bias or carelessness, it can also become a legal issue—libel.

Likewise, the use of certain undercover devices by reporters, such as hidden microphones and cameras, raises ethical questions that must be resolved by each newsperson or news manager. Their use also has legal implications because, in some states, it is forbidden. Certainly, the argument used by many journalists that you "do what you have to do" to catch someone breaking the law or deceiving the public seems reasonable on the surface; however, many reporters believe that they must stay within the law or they are not acting much better than those they are investigating.

Many reporters admit that they "bend" the rules. For example, when NBC's Robert McKeown was still with CBS, he misrepresented himself as a soldier in order to get at what he called the "truth" during the Gulf War. A strong argument could be made that the American people had a right to know what was going on during the conflict when the military was less than honest in dealing with the media. Was it wrong for McKeown to circumvent military rules to get his story on the air? Perhaps McKeown expresses it best when he says, "Everyone has a gut feeling about what is right and wrong" when it comes to ethics.

Review Questions

1. Should reporters ever accept gifts? Discuss this issue.
2. When does accuracy become an ethical issue?
3. What are the defenses against libel? Do they always work?
4. Explain the term *false light*.
5. Name some of the controversial techniques employed by investigative reporters.
6. All ethical journalists are opposed to staging the news. Give some examples of such unethical behavior.
7. For what purpose are reversals used by most TV stations? Is there anything unethical about them?

Exercises

1. Ask two or more reporters from radio and TV stations to take part in a discussion of controversial techniques used by some investigative reporters. It might be a good idea to record the session so that it can be played for other classes to get their reactions.
2. Which of the following statements do you think could be considered libelous, and why? Would the defense have any arguments acceptable to the courts? Explain.

   The governor drinks so much it's a wonder that he gets any work done.
   Part of the governor's problem is that his wife is a drunk.
   The governor is a lazy, good-for-nothing fake.
   If the governor would stay at home more instead of running around with women, he wouldn't be in such hot water with the voters.

3. Suppose you are a TV reporter assigned to a demonstration. When the assignment editor sent you out, the demonstrators were shouting and waving fists. When you arrived, however, they had stopped for lunch, except for one person who continued to picket. How would you and your cameraperson handle the situation?

21 More Ethical Issues

Cameras in the Courtroom

The use of cameras in courtrooms has raised serious questions about journalistic ethics and the responsibility of the broadcast media, particularly television. The issue of whether to allow camera coverage of trials has been a continuing debate. TV news representatives generally argue that cameras should be allowed in courtrooms. Those opposed to the idea argue that the cameras compromise the rights and privacy of everyone involved in a trial and could have an impact on the outcome of the trial itself. Even in states where cameras are allowed to record the proceedings, the cameras are operated on a pool basis to minimize the intrusion. The jury is not shown.

There also are a variety of restrictions in most of the states where cameras are allowed. In some states, the judge decides; in others, everyone involved in the case must agree to allow the cameras; in still other states, the decision depends on the nature of the case. And in some states, cameras are permitted only in certain courts. Sound confusing? It is.

As of this writing, in the early part of 2004, the camera issue was having an impact on a number of high-profile criminal cases. Judges banned cameras from two of the most sensational murder cases in the country—Scott Peterson, who was convicted of killing his wife and unborn child and actor Robert Blake, also accused of killing his wife.

Judges in both cases cited the chilling effect they said cameras could have on witnesses who might alter their testimony if they knew their face were to be on the nightly news. One of the judges also said he wanted to protect the privacy of family members and maintain proper order in the courtroom. When one of the lawyers representing the media in the Peterson case tried to compare the importance of cameras in the courtroom to watching the Super Bowl on TV instead of reading about it in the newspapers, the judge replied "This isn't the Super Bowl."

The judge in the Blake case said that she would allow cameras for the opening statements, closing arguments, and the verdict but nothing else. In the past two years, judges in numerous other high-profile cases—including D.C. sniper John Muhammed—banned cameras in the courtroom. In Muhammed's Virginia trial, the judge did allow still photography, but said video cameras could compromise the sniper suspect's right to a fair trial. All cameras were banned by another Virginia judge in the case of Muhammed's fellow sniper suspect, Lee Boyd Malvo.

In still another high-profile case in which NBA basketball star Kobe Bryant was accused of rape, most court observers had expected that Colorado State District Judge Terry Ruckriegle, would probably ban cameras because of his reputation as a no-nonsense judge who likes to keep the circuses outside his courtroom. But we will never know because, suddenly and dramatically, the prosecution decided to drop the case against Bryant, in the middle of jury selection. More on that in the next chapter.

Although the camera issue reached its peak during the O.J. Simpson trial, there has been absolutely no consensus on the role of cameras in courtrooms since that trial. But those advocating their presence have made significant progress in the past few years. With the exception of the nation's capital, cameras are allowed, with some restrictions, in all of the states. Court Justice Lance Ito agreed to permit cameras in the Los Angeles courtroom for the Simpson trial, but even before the jury was selected, he started to have second thoughts about *all* the media coverage. Ito threatened to ban all broadcast coverage of the trial after KNBC-TV reported erroneously that DNA tests showed that Nicole Brown's blood was found on one of Simpson's socks. He said the story was "detrimental to Mr. Simpson's right to a fair trial and it is fundamentally unfair." Judge Ito decided to allow the cameras to remain in the courtroom, but only after threatening to bar them completely.

Few people believed that Judge Ito had the power to terminate media coverage of the trial, which is protected by the First Amendment, but he certainly had the right to forbid cameras in the courtroom. Like the rules in 12 other states, California statutes give judges the power to permit or bar cameras in court.

In South Carolina, the judge in the murder trial of Susan Smith—charged in the drowning deaths of her two children—barred cameras from the court. Judge William Howard also said the cameras would have a "chilling effect" on the trial.

Pros and Cons

What are the advantages and disadvantages of allowing cameras in court? The most obvious reason for cameras, in the opinion of most of the media, is the "public's right to know," which is guaranteed by the First Amendment. Others argued that camera coverage would educate the American people on how the jurisprudence system works.

Cynthia Tucker, writing in the *Cleveland Plain Dealer*, said the only problem with that theory is that "it is not true." She said, "You will learn precious little about the average criminal case from watching the Simpson trial." She added, "You will learn, instead, about the particular justice that is dispensed when a wealthy celebrity is charged with a horrendous crime." Tucker said, "If you want to learn about the average murder trial, you'd be better off spending a month or two in your local county courthouse."

The most important argument against allowing cameras in the courtroom is that the coverage may impact the trial itself and the defendant's right to a fair trial. It is not easy to determine the effects of the live camera in the courtroom, but the acquittal of Simpson of all murder charges made it plain that it did not impact on his right to a fair trial.

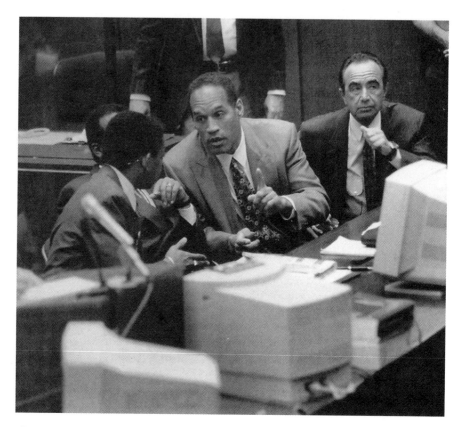

Figure 21-1   O.J. Simpson confers with one of his attorneys during his murder trial in Los Angeles. (AP/World Wide Photo)

Do Cameras Influence Witnesses?

Elizabeth Semel, a prominent San Diego defense attorney, said she believes cameras change the performances of witnesses. "Who is the audience for the witness?" asked Semel. She said, "*Audience* is a troubling word, but if there is an audience, it should be the jury and not the camera."

That view is shared by Professor Norman Karlin of Southwest Law School. "Lawyers," he said, "tend to 'play' to a camera"; however, a three-year experiment regarding television coverage in selected cities completed by the federal court system showed that cameras had little effect on trial participants, courtroom decorum, or any other aspects of the trials. Regardless of that survey, the federal court system decided to resume its total ban on TV cameras in federal courts. A spokesperson said federal judges remain concerned about the impact that cameras would have on trials. However, a bill is presently working its way through Congress for the second consecutive year that would allow federal judges to decide whether they wanted cameras in their courtrooms.

Although CNN was the only network to carry the Simpsan trial from beginning to end, all of the networks devoted substantial amounts of time to the story, situating correspondents and cameras at strategic locations outside

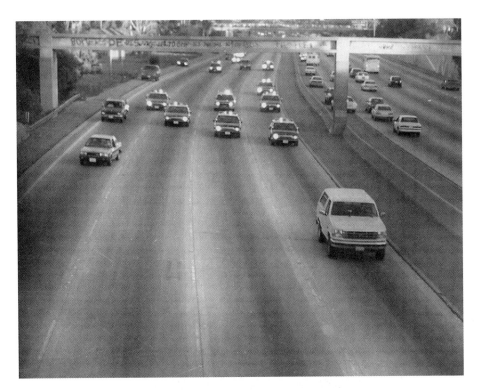

Figure 21-2 Police follow the infamous white Bronco in the so-called nonchase of O.J. Simpson in Los Angeles. (AP World Wide Photo)

the courthouse. Writing in *Esquire,* John Tyler said the Simpson trial became a "modern pagan spectacle." He noted that to get an unimpeded view of the courthouse and a sweeping cutaway shot of the glass-towered banking district, every network had to construct a skybox on the parking lot adjacent to the courthouse that was higher than the ones in front. "They were staggered, taller and taller, toward the rear of the lot," observed Tyler, "until those at the very back soared some five stories into the air."

The skyboxes were made of construction scaffolding with white canvas awnings and the "spindly, swaying edifices resembled primitive burial towers," said Tyler.

Jeff Greenfield, then a reporter for *ABC News,* described the scene outside the Los Angeles courthouse as the "media's Chernobyl." He suggested that if Judge Ito had thrown out the cameras there may have been a "less hysterical approach to the story by the schlock end of our business."

The Fourth Amendment

In an article in *Playboy,* former Los Angeles Deputy District Attorney Vincent Bugliosi agreed that the Simpson trial had a "faintly festive atmosphere . . . and the TV coverage contributed to this tawdry atmosphere." He said it "cheapens and devalues the whole (trial) process." But Bugliosi said he had "much more substantive reasons why I oppose cameras in the courtroom."

Figure 21-3   Skyboxes used in O.J. Simpson trial.

He said a trial is a serious and solemn proceeding that determines whether a person's liberty, and sometimes his life, should be taken away from him. "Anything that interferes, or even has the slightest potential of interfering, with the resolution of this determination should be automatically prohibited," said Bugliosi.

As the famed prosecutor who convicted the Charles Manson clan, Bugliosi noted that most people are intensely self-conscious about speaking in public, and with cameras in the courtroom some are not going to be as natural. He said they are either going to "be more shy and hesitant, or perhaps they will put on an act, not just in their demeanor but, much worse, in the words they use in their testimony." Bugliosi said when that happens, the "fact-finding process and the very purpose of the trial have been compromised."

As for the argument that televising the trial educates people, Bugliosi described that as "transparent sophistry. Their only motivation, though not an improper one, is commercial . . . it's a form of entertainment for them, pure and simple." Bugliosi repeated that "the sole purpose of a criminal trial is to determine whether or not the defendant is guilty of the crime. It is not to educate the public."

Many media observers agreed that the trouble was not so much the TV inside the courtroom but the TV coverage outside. Judge Burton Roberts, who chaired a New York State panel that looked into the camera-in-court issue, said he believes that "the more public scrutiny there is of a defendant on trial ensures that defendant greater fairness." The judge said the camera also prevents the government "institutions such as the prosecutors and the judiciary from comporting themselves in a fashion which results in a defendant being treated unfairly."

Paul Thaler, author of *The Watchful Eye* (Greenwood Publishing Group, 1994), which deals extensively with media coverage of trials and TV cameras in court, had this assessment: "The media are not just a benign observer. They interfere with the system. And television is driving the other media." Thaler, a former reporter and director of journalism and media at Mercy College in New York, also questioned the premise that TV cameras in court are producing objective reality. Is it "reality . . . or the imagination of the producer or editor?" asked Thaler. He stressed that: "At stake . . . is the very linchpin of our democracy: the right to a fair trial, and to equal justice under the law." Thaler added, "Since it is the defendant who stands uniquely to suffer from excessive, intrusive, or skewed publicity, surely it should be the defendant's interests that are uppermost in any consideration of audiovisual coverage." While the debate continues, it's important to note again that the cameras were not a factor in the O.J. Simpson case, at least for the defense.

Don Hewitt Has Second Thoughts

The former executive producer of *60 Minutes,* Don Hewitt, said he's no longer sure that cameras in court are a good idea. He noted that "Although for years I favored cameras in courtrooms . . . the issue needs a lot more thought than people in my profession were willing to give it."

The veteran CBS newsman noted that "*Open to the public* doesn't have to mean *open to cameras.*" Hewitt said that broadcast journalists obviously have to be in courtrooms to "observe and report . . . we're reporters and that's what we do. But," he added, "letting cameras in court can turn a courtroom into a movie set."

In his strong criticism of the cameras at the O.J. Simpson trial, Hewitt asked, "Would freedom of the press suffer if there were no cameras? Would TV journalists again be second-class citizens if they had to go back to pad and pencil to cover this trial? No."

Hewitt said, "Even if TV does have the right to go anywhere it pleases . . . it doesn't have to stick its nose into every nook and cranny. An occasional door closed in our face," said Hewitt, "would be good for our souls and might even get some of us off our backsides and back to reporting instead of watching."

Hewitt observed that many reporters "will call me a turncoat," but in discussions with broadcast newspeople and educators during the past several years, I discovered that many of them agree with Hewitt, as does *this* author.

Supreme Court Eases Rules—A Bit

The U.S. Supreme Court made broadcast history during the aftermath of Presidential Election 2000. For the first time, it released an audiotape of the legal arguments concerning the presidential election. The tape, recorded by the court, was broadcast to the nation almost immediately after the arguments ended. Although they released an audiotape, the justices turned down a request to permit live television and radio coverage of the proceeding.

Barbara Cochran, President of the Radio and Television News Directors' Association (RTNDA), who made the request on behalf of the broadcast media, called the release of the audiotape, "a great first step for electronic journalism, and, most important, for the public."

Arguments before the Florida Supreme Court, concerning Election 2000, were broadcast live on television and radio.

Checkbook Journalism

Critics of the media coverage of the Simpson trial also strongly criticized checkbook journalism—the purchase of witnesses' statements. Admittedly, most purchases were made by the tabloid papers and TV programs at the time that posed as news broadcasts—*The Enquirer*, *Current Affair*, and *Hard Copy*. Did those tabloids have any impact on the trial? Did they influence the jury decision in any way? Did it taint the witnesses in the trial?

New Yorker writer Jeffrey Toobin condemned the practice as a "disgrace to law." He said there was no good purpose to the tabloids' purchase of witness statements and "it does seriously damage cases . . . taints witnesses . . . and really makes their testimony less credible."

During a televised debate on the subject on *The Charlie Rose Show* (WNET—Educational Broadcasting Company), former prosecutor Toobin said that paying witnesses to publish their stories "undermines what prosecutors are able to do in court." Toobin says that repeated questioning of witnesses by the prosecution and defense is going to "generate inconsistencies," but paying for witnesses' statements is going to make the situation "infinitely worse because jurors aren't stupid. They know what the tabloid shows want out of people. They want scandal . . . sensation . . . and they'll jazz up a story to get that."

Attorney Raoul Felder, who also took part in the WNET debate, said he was not sure that media payments were always bad. He cited the incident in which people who worked in a store selling knives were paid to tell how they sold a knife to Simpson. The owner was paid $3,000 for his story and it was corroborated by three other people, who also got paid. But Felder said he didn't think "anybody thought he was not telling the truth."

Felder admitted that there seemed to be a question about whether another witness, Rosa Lopez, was telling the truth when she sold a story to a tabloid claiming that she saw Simpson's white Bronco parked on the street outside his home at the time of the murders. Toobin's argument was that a witness might tell a story one way and then change it after realizing that the tabloids would only pay for a story if it was told in a way that appealed to the public.

There was a lot of criticism about the media, particularly the tabloids, for paying for information in the JonBenét Ramsey murder case.

The Fairness Doctrine

Like many of the issues discussed in this chapter and Chapter 20, fairness is both a legal and an ethical consideration. Until now we have concentrated on the ethical importance of fairness. Now let's consider the legal aspects. Do broadcast stations have a legal responsibility to be fair? Broadcast managers, the FCC, Congress, and numerous special interest groups have been fighting over that issue for decades.

In 1949, the FCC established the Fairness Doctrine, which said, in part, that broadcasters had an obligation to serve the public interest by "not refusing to broadcast opposing views where a demand is made of the station for broadcast time." It also said that licensees have a duty "to encourage and implement the broadcast of all sides of controversial issues."

Over the following years, the broadcast industry and the RTNDA applied extreme pressure on the FCC to eliminate the doctrine, arguing that because newspapers are not forced to present all sides of an issue, broadcasters should not be required to do so either. According to supporters of the Fairness Doctrine, the major distinction between newspapers and broadcasters is that the government, in selecting only one licensee for a frequency, is in effect limiting access to the airwaves, which have traditionally been considered the property of the public.

The Fairness Doctrine was challenged on occasion but was upheld in the courts. In 1964, the Supreme Court upheld the doctrine. But over the intervening years, even the FCC itself questioned the Fairness Doctrine. In 1984 it acknowledged that the doctrine was not serving the public and was probably unconstitutional. It ceased trying to enforce the doctrine. But there has always been strong support in Congress for the doctrine and, in 1987, it passed a bill making the Fairness Doctrine law. But the bill was vetoed by President Reagan.

The Fairness Doctrine got a new look in Congress and elsewhere, in 1995, because of the bombing of the federal building in Oklahoma City. President Clinton started a controversy when he accused certain broadcasters (not by name) of spreading hate on the airwaves. He appeared to be speaking of Oliver North, J. Gordon Liddy, Rush Limbaugh, and other right-wing commentators and talk-show hosts who criticize the government, often suggesting that strong action by President Clinton could increase antigovernment violence and spread hate that divides Americans.

Should these commentators go unchallenged? Should they be allowed to use the airwaves, which supposedly belong to all Americans, to urge radical and often violent behavior? The ultra-conservative broadcasters claim their First Amendment rights, and they have a legitimate point. But some people ask: Shouldn't those who oppose such views have a right to use the airwaves to express their opinions as well?

Pollsters tell us that about 20 percent of Americans strongly oppose any sort of government. How many of those people are capable of violence is, of course, unknown. But should those who feed that hatred of the government be allowed to espouse their views on radio and TV without allowing equal time for opposing views? The constitution and the First Amendment do *not* refer to fairness in speech, just to its protection.

Many people believe the Fairness Doctrine, when it was in force, was unconstitutional, and it may very well have been; however, one cannot help but wonder if our founding fathers were sitting around the table in Philadelphia today, would they add a line or two to the First Amendment after watching the coverage of the bomb attack on the federal building in Oklahoma City, and listening to convicted criminal J. Gordon Liddy speaking about "shooting federal agents in the head or groin," if they invaded one's domain.

Invasion of Privacy

Privacy is defined generally as "the right to be let alone," and that concept has become increasingly more difficult with the *explosion* of the Information Age. The explosion was mainly the result of the development of a variety of electronic devices, particularly the computer. For broadcast journalists, microphones, tape recorders, cameras, and telephoto lenses have been wonderful additions to the practice of collecting news. But they also have caused their share of troubles when it comes to privacy.

The Constitution does not say anything about the right of privacy, at least by name; however, several amendments to the Constitution and the Declaration of Independence's demand for the right to "life, liberty, and the pursuit of happiness" make it clear that the founding fathers were concerned with privacy. Also, the Supreme Court for more than 40 years has recognized privacy as a constitutional right.

From a media perspective, the right to privacy often conflicts (as was pointed out in other parts of the book) with the First Amendment, freedom of the press, or the people's right to know. For example, the courts have found that it is not an invasion of privacy in most cases to take photographs or to use film and video cameras in a public place; however, the use of these same devices to get pictures in private places can, and often does, get broadcast journalists in trouble.

CBS was among those charged with such violations when a reporter and camera crew for the now-defunct *Street Stories* accompanied the Secret Service on a raid on a Brooklyn, New York apartment, which was supposed to be the site for a credit card scheme. The Secret Service, apparently anxious to get a little publicity for its activities, invited the camera crew and reporter to follow agents as they crashed into the home of Babutunde Ayeni. He was not at home at the time, but his wife and four-year-old son were.

The agents had a search warrant, but Mrs. Ayeni was puzzled about the camera crew. She thought, quite naturally, that the camerapeople also were agents. She wanted to know why the raid was being taped. As it turned out, the agents found no evidence of any credit card scheme and said so on camera.

Writing about the incident, Cessna Catherine Winslow, a freelance writer, said that *CBS News* argued that because the reporter and crew had permission of federal agents to accompany them on the raid, they should be entitled to qualified immunity enjoyed by government officials. After that argument was dismissed, CBS settled out of court with the Ayeni family, who claimed that their rights were violated during the raid.

In explaining his refusal to dismiss the case, Federal District Court Judge Jack B. Weinstein chastised CBS and the federal agents, saying that "CBS had no greater right than that of a thief to be in the (Ayeni) home." The judge further said, "The images, though created by the camera, are part of the household . . . and cannot be removed without permission or official right." He added, "The television tape was a seizure of information for non-governmental purposes," and "the case raises grave issues of the right to privacy in the home from the intruding eye and ear of a private broadcaster's camera."

One lawyer for the Ayeni family, Harry Batchelder Jr., criticized programs in which TV crews "just blow in with agents and take everybody's photographs and say they have consent." The attorney for RTNDA agreed. Larry Scharff said the incident "calls into question many assumptions newspeople have about their legal right to accompany police and public officials onto private property." He warned journalists to be more sensitive about shooting stories on private property.

Videotaping in a public place also can be a problem for broadcast journalists. A CBS-owned station, WCBS-TV in New York, was sued after a camera crew and reporter entered a famous restaurant, Le Mistral, unannounced and began filming the interior of the restaurant and its customers. The film was for a series the reporter was doing on restaurant health code violations. The restaurant won its suit against CBS for invasion of privacy and trespass.

In summary, broadcast journalists can photograph in public places, but if their behavior becomes overly intrusive, they also can find themselves in court.

Civic Journalism

In various parts of the book, including the two chapters on ethics and the chapter on tabloid journalism, we indicate that journalism is in trouble. The American people do not have the same high regard for the media that they once did. The line between news and entertainment has narrowed. There has been an alarming increase in tabloid journalism and irresponsible reporting. In the minds of many serious newspeople, journalism is *broke* and needs some fixing. Many people believe that the media is no longer adequately serving the needs of the people.

One of those people who share this view is Ed Fouhy, a former network news executive and founder of the Pew Center for Civic Journalism. Fouhy said one way to serve viewers is to provide what some people refer to as "civic journalism" or "public journalism." Fouhy said many stations are attempting to secure their future by getting more involved with their audiences, or what he calls "digging roots into the community, deeper than ever before." Fouhy said: "It's time for a fundamental change in the way we do our business, including how we define what news is and how we serve our viewers."

The former network executive cited as a positive example of change the news operation at WISC-TV in Madison, Wisconsin. He said one of the ways Station Manager Tom Bier has dug roots into the community is by getting involved in the "we the people" project. Fouhy says the project is a "model of civic journalism."

Bier is a member of a journalistic roundtable that meets and picks an issue facing the state, such as financing the public schools or the choices in health care. The topic is then discussed at a televised town meeting on WISC-TV and the public radio and in the *Washington State Journal.* Most of the group's focus recently has been on political campaigns. In 2004, most of the attention was on the U.S. Senate race in Wisconsin. Bier says, we asked all the candidates (Russ Feingold and the four GOP) challengers to meet with the media and the people in various locations to discuss the issues and also included a couple of debates, one before the primary and another during the election campaign itself. Bier said all four media did major stories on these events as a way to introduce citizens to the candidates.

Similar experiments have been going on in various parts of the nation: At WSOC-TV in Charlotte, North Carolina; WCTV in Tallahassee, Florida; WHAS-TV in Louisville, Kentucky; and KRON-TV in San Francisco.

In San Francisco, thousands of people engaged in an online conversation about race relations. KRON-TV launched "About Race," its year-long exploration of how race and ethnicity shape the Bay Area, with an unprecedented five-part series on the 6 P.M. newscast during a sweeps period. Coverage explored the genetics of race, diversity in the workplace and in schools, talking about race, and a look at efforts to bridge the racial divide. The TV station scheduled 18 other stories over the year, including a one-hour special. Collaborating with KRON-TV were the *San Francisco Chronicle,* KQED-FM public radio, and the Bay-TV cable affiliate.

Fouhy stressed that this sort of alliance among TV and radio stations and newspapers in the market is essential because the "alienation of citizens is so deep that early efforts to re-engage them through the media are dismissed as just more cynical attempts to manipulate viewers or readers—to build circulation or ratings."

But, Fouhy said, when all the media cooperates—and is seen to be doing so—"there is a mutual validation effect." He said that when the community understands that if the traditional rivals for advertising dollars are cooperating, then the topic they are organizing around is important.

Fouhy said that this kind of cooperative effort shows a respect for the wisdom and intelligence of ordinary people. "What you won't find," he says, "is the journalistic model that encourages what one critic calls 'learned helplessness.'" Fouhy said the traditional way of telling a story that spotlights a problem encourages the feeling that it is so big and complicated that the viewer or reader is left with a sense that solving it is beyond the capacity of ordinary men and women.

"Does this mean that civic journalists pander to the desire for neat and simple solutions to complex policy questions?" asked Fouhy. "Of course not," he said. "The people who are practicing civic journalism are thoughtful men and women with a deep devotion to enduring journalistic values."

So, if Fouhy is right and civic journalism is a solution to the often-voiced criticism that journalism is not the force it used to be, why aren't more news organizations getting involved in civic journalism? Probably because many news managers still think that journalists must keep themselves separate from the rest of society and shouldn't be joining forces with any other constituencies or it will conflict with their traditional position of maintaining complete objectivity.

A newspaper executive from Colorado tried to defuse some of these concerns during a symposium honoring media organizations for their accomplishments in civic journalism. Steve Smith, editor of the *Colorado Springs Gazette*, says part of the misunderstanding about civic journalism is that some news managers think in terms of it being different from the traditional practices of journalism.

He said one of the reasons some journalists react negatively to civic journalism is that they believe that the values that brought them into journalism are in conflict with the civic journalism concept of serving the whole community. But Smith stressed that civic journalism is not meant to replace traditional journalism practices, routines, and reflexes—but is "the combination of a set of overarching values, a combination with our best practices, values, and ethics, that I think constitutes civic journalism." He said this is a powerful combination and is what begins to separate civic journalism from traditional practice.

Smith said the core values of journalists are pursuit of truth, fairness, and balance. He said these values drive our "Fourth Estate" watchdog responsibility. But he asked, "What about the value we share with citizens—that we want our communities to be good places in which to live? I would argue that 'community' is a core value." He said that we should not think of communities in terms of their segments or their separate elements, but as a whole, an aggregation of citizens who have a collective responsibility to their community. He said community value is the core civic value behind the experiments in civic journalism.

Reviewing the strides made by the civic journalism movement, which he founded a decade ago, Fouhy said, "I think we stirred a journalistic pot that badly needed stirring.

I believe we prodded some editors and news directors to examine the arms-length relationship they had with their communities in the name of objectivity and to realize that they were too removed, too far from the everyday concerns of their readers and viewers. That was certainly our purpose." Fouhy cited some specific accomplishments. He said he was proud to see a big city newspaper like the *Boston Globe* using the classic techniques of civic journalism to help stakeholders think through the implications for the city of setting aside 20 odd acres of downtown for parkland to be named the Rose Kennedy Greenway. Fouhy also said he was delighted when *The Washington Post* ombudsman told him that he gets an average of 500 e-mails a day from readers questioning news judgments, praising and criticizing the newspaper—a paper they consider their newspaper. Fouhy added, "The fact is that we were successful in persuading editors to listen more closely to their readers/viewers; to get down from their lofty disdain for the concerns of ordinary people and to look at issues like education, not as an 'issue' with all the implications of that word, but as a concern to parents, teachers and students who deserve to have a voice in news stories, not to be relegated to the sidelines while experts dominate the conversation." Fouhy said, "I think we started an important process of re-examination which subsequent advances in technology and other factors have continued to stimulate." He cited the "amazing editor's note" in *The New York Times* in May of 2004, in which the newspaper admitted that it had been wrong in its coverage in the run-up to the war in Iraq, when it did not sufficiently challenge the Bush Administration's poorly documented claims of a dire threat that received prominent, uncritical coverage, while there was a considerable amount of evidence to the contrary that was ignored or played down by the newspaper. The *Times* admitted that its coverage of whether Saddam Hussein had weapons of mass destruction "was not as rigorous as it should have been" and that "we wish we had been more aggressive in re-examining the claims as new evidence emerged—or failed to emerge."

A few months after the *Times* admitted its mistakes, another of the nation's most prestigious newspapers, *The Washington Post,* also acknowledged that it didn't do enough to challenge the White House on its reasons for going to war. Writing in the *Post,* staff writer Howard Kurtz pointed out that only days before the Iraq war began, veteran post reporter Walter Pincus wrote a story questioning whether the Bush Administration had proof that Saddam Hussein was hiding weapons of mass destruction, but he ran into resistance from the paper's editors and the story ran only after assistant managing editor Bob Woodward helped sell the story. But even so, the story ended up on the paper's page 17. Woodward said "We did our job but we didn't do enough, and I blame myself for not pushing harder." Woodward, who wrote a best-selling book (*Plan of Attack*) about Bush's decision to go to war said, "We should have warned readers we had information that the basis for this was shakier" than widely believed. He said, "Those are exactly the kind of statements that should be published on the front page."

The *Post* published a number of stories challenging the White House, but rarely on the front page. According to Kurtz, some reporters who were lobbying for greater prominence for such stories complained to senior editors who were unenthusiastic about such pieces. The *Post*'s Pentagon correspondent, Thomas Ricks, noted that the administration assertions about the need to invade Iraq were on the front page while stories challenging that position were on page 18 or 24. He said there was an attitude among editors of "Look, we're going to war, why do we even worry about this contrary stuff?"

In acknowledging the paper's shortcomings, Executive Editor Leonard Downie Jr., said, "We were so focused on trying to figure out what the administration was doing that we were not giving the same play to people who said it wouldn't be a good idea to go to war and were questioning the administration's rationale", Downie admitted that was a mistake. "Not enough of those stories were put on the front page," he said "and that was a mistake on my part."

Michael Massing, a *New York Review of Books* contributor and author of the forthcoming book, "Now They Tell Us," on the press and Iraq, said the *Post* actually did better than most news organizations, featuring a number of solid articles about the administration's decision to go to war, but on the key issue of Iraq's weapons of mass destruction, he said, the paper was "generally napping along with everyone else."

As reported in the previous chapter in great detail, the admission by the *Times* that the reasons for going to war were not investigated sufficiently was the second major embarrassment that the newspaper suffered within a year's time, acknowledging earlier that one of its highly regarded young reporters, Jayson Blair, had plagiarized, lied, and made up details about scores of stories. Coincidentally, the newspaper used some identical words in explaining how these two calamities were allowed to happen. In re-examining its pre-Iraqi war coverage it acknowledged that "editors at several levels who should have been challenging reporters and pressing for more skepticism were perhaps too intent on rushing scoops into the paper." Editors also were blamed for not challenging Jayson Blair enough about his writing and reporting. But the positive aspect of both these embarrassments was that the management at the *Times* had the courage and wisdom to re-examine, in complete frankness and great detail, the things they did wrong and how to do better in the future. That's the kind of self-examination that supporters of civic journalism suggest has to be an ongoing process within the media if it's going to restore the public's faith and confidence in its integrity.

Summary

This chapter discusses the responsibilities that accompany the new technology available to broadcast journalists. Radio and television stations, for example, are broadcasting more trials but most states have restrictions. Judges seem divided on the propriety of having cameras in the courtroom, particularly when they are used to report on so-called sensitive issues.

Almost all broadcasters support cameras in the courtroom, maintaining that they have a First Amendment right to bring their gear into court because it is just a much heavier version of a print journalist's pen and pencil. A slight exaggeration, perhaps, because pens and pencils have no "live" capability.

Even if you accept that cameras have a right to feed trials, regardless of their nature, into living rooms, the question of responsibility remains, and that is an ethical issue in the minds of many newspeople. Does a network have a responsibility to feed out "everything" from a courtroom, as did CNN during the Simpson trial? If they do not broadcast everything, some executives claim, they would be censoring the news. Others argue that journalists always have censored news because of time and space constraints and to eliminate bad taste.

Review Questions

1. Are cameras still banned in some courtrooms?
2. What types of restrictions do some states have on cameras?
3. What is the media's argument for using cameras in courtrooms?
4. Did the camera in the Simpson courtroom impact on the fairness of his trial?

5. What was the Fairness Doctrine? How do you feel about the issues?
6. What was the *Red Lion* decision?

Exercises

1. Attend a trial where cameras are being used, and discuss whether you believe they were beneficial for the public or detrimental to those involved in the trial. If a judge bans cameras in a trial in your city for some reason, interview the judge about the issue.
2. Assemble a group of journalists, lawyers, professors, and other appropriate people to discuss all aspects of journalistic ethics.
3. Watch each of the TV stations in your market, and report on their selection of stories and if you believe they presented those stories fairly.

22 Tabloid Journalism

As alluded to in Chapter 21, one of the most serious concerns of the past decade for journalists has been the increase of tabloid journalism. The explosion of the Internet and the emergence of a host of new magazine and talk shows on cable and the traditional networks brought about a new wave of sleaze journalism. But even more alarming than the expansion of such so-called news was the narrowing of the line between tabloid practices and those appearing in the so-called mainstream media. In recent years, it has become increasingly more difficult to distinguish between the two.

We will look at a number of such examples, including the sex scandal involving President Clinton and Monica Lewinsky; the Washington, D.C. area sniper shootings; the murder of six-year-old JonBenét Ramsey in Boulder, Colorado; two other murders involving a young Congressional intern, Chandra Levy, and a young pregnant woman, Lacy Peterson, in California; and the alleged rape of a young woman by NBA basketball star Kobe Bryant. All these stories were marked by irresponsible reporting. Although in many cases, the tabloids were out front in such reporting, the mainstream media often picked up the stories, ran with them, and even developed sleaze of their own. Sometimes the so-called legitimate media even outdid the tabloids. Both the print and broadcast media were guilty of exploiting the subjects, resorting to rumor, and using unidentified and uninformed sources and unsubstantiated leaks.

The coverage has concerned serious journalists who fear that the spread of tabloid news and practices would further alienate a public that has become increasingly more suspicious and untrusting of the media.

The Clinton-Lewinsky Scandal

The reputation of President Bill Clinton was not the only thing to suffer in his affair at the White House with intern Monica Lewinsky. The news media also lost prestige through its coverage of the sexual encounter. As the *Columbia Journalism Review* put it, the American news media's reputation as truthteller to the country was besmirched by perceptions, in and out of the news business, about how the story was reported.

Although many news outlets acted with considerable responsibility, especially after the first few frantic days of the scandal, the *Review* said the story also triggered "a piranha-like frenzy in pursuit of the relatively few tidbits tossed into the journalistic waters."

Figure 22-1   Former White House intern Monica Lewinsky meeting former President Bill Clinton at a White House function. (Courtesy Getty Images)

The writer of the *Journalism Review* story, Jules Witcover, said that "while it was evident there were wholesale leaks from lawyers and investigators, either legal restraints or reportorial pledges of anonymity kept the public from knowing with any certainty the sources of key elements in the saga."

The veteran journalist, now with the *Baltimore Sun,* said that into the vacuum created by a scarcity of clear and credible attribution "raced all manner of rumor, gossip, and especially, hollow sourcing, making the reports of some mainstream outlets scarcely distinguishable from supermarket tabloids." He added that the rush to be first or to be more sensational created a picture of irresponsibility seldom seen in the reporting of presidential affairs.

Among the speculative reports was *ABC News'* White House correspondent Sam Donaldson's claim shortly after the scandal broke that Clinton could resign before the next week was out. "If he's not telling the truth," Donaldson said, "I think his presidency is numbered in days. This isn't going to drag out." Really?

Almost from the beginning, and throughout the scandal, the president had most of the American people's support, and much of the president's troubles were rubbing off on the press. A *Washington Post* poll taken 10 days after the story broke found that 56 percent of those surveyed believed that the news media were treating Clinton unfairly, and 74 percent said the media were giving the story too much attention.

The combination of all-news TV channels, the Internet, and the traditional networks assured nonstop coverage. But that coverage came under fire almost immediately for its rumor-mongering, unattributed sources, and speculation. Commenting on the lack of credible sources, Witcover said, "As leaks flew wildly from these unspecified sources, the American public was left as seldom before in a major news event to guess where stories came from and why."

Witcover noted that it was sadly appropriate that the first hint of the Paula Jones story, in which she accused Clinton of making sexual advances to her when he was governor of Arkansas, really broke not in the mainstream media but in the "wildly irresponsible Internet site of Matt Drudge, a reckless trader in rumor and gossip who makes no pretense of checking on the accuracy of what he reports."

After *Newsweek* magazine, which had been cautiously holding the same story, published it, the scandal spread quickly. A few days later, *The New York Times* reported that President Clinton had denied accusations of having had a sexual affair with a 21-year-old White House intern. After that, the media jumped on the story and ran with it, quoting questionable sources in an effort to beat the competition.

The usually responsible *Washington Post* cited "sources familiar with the investigation" as saying that the FBI had secretly taped Lewinsky by placing a wire on Linda Tripp, a friend of Lewinsky's, and had gotten information that helped persuade Attorney General Janet Reno to get authorization from a three-judge panel overseeing the independent counsel to expand the Clinton investigation.

The next day, Witcover said, "taste went out the window" when ABC correspondent Jackie Judd reported that a source with direct knowledge of Lewinsky's allegations said she admitted going to the White House for sex with Clinton in the early evening or early mornings on the weekends when certain aides, who would have been alarmed by her visits, were not in the office. Judd said that according to the source, which was not identified, Lewinsky said she saved a dress with the president's semen stain on it. Judd said, "if true," this information could provide physical evidence of what really happened between Clinton and Lewinsky. Witcover said this use of the phrase "if true" became a gate-opener for any rumor to make its way into the mainstream.

Unconfirmed Reports Abound

The story of the stained dress spread through the media like a brushfire, with all sorts of additional unconfirmed elaborations about searches for the dress and DNA tests on it. All of these reports were printed and broadcast despite disavowals from Lewinsky's attorney.

The *New York Post* added its own twist to the story, saying that Monica kept the dress as a souvenir and didn't send it to the cleaners. The *Village Voice*, in a strong attack on the Judd story, called it hearsay and noted that it was picked up by other news organizations as though the dress really existed. Shortly after the ABC story ran, *CBS News* reported that no DNA evidence or stains had been found on a dress that belonged to Lewinsky and that was tested by the FBI.

Witcover said a close competitor for the sleaziest report award was the one regarding the president's alleged sexual preference. *The Scripts Howard News Service* reported that one person who had listened to the Lewinsky-

Tripp tapes said Lewinsky described how Clinton allegedly first urged her to have oral sex, telling her that such acts were not technically adultery.

Many Ways of Saying the Source Is Unreliable

Here are some other phrases used by the media to attribute information when they had no real sources on the sex scandal:

The *Los Angeles Times:* "People familiar with the investigation" say . . .

The Washington Post: "Sources familiar with the probe" say . . .

The *Wall Street Journal:* "A law enforcement official and unsubstantiated reports" say . . .

The Chicago Tribune quoted *ABC news* on the dress story, and even used the same ABC disclaimer, "if true."

The *Dallas Morning News* quoted "sources" for its story, saying that a secret service agent was prepared to testify that he saw President Clinton and Monica Lewinsky in a compromising situation at the White House.

Of course, every time these "mainstream" publications and broadcasts carried such stories, the late-night tabloid talk shows had a feast and moved the already unconfirmed reports to a new level of speculation.

For example, Larry King referred to a *New York Times* story about a message allegedly left on Lewinsky's answering machine when there was, in fact, no such story. Before the broadcast was over, King had to apologize, admitting the *Times* was not actually going to print such a story. The use of terms like *unconfirmed* and *usually reliable* sources snowballed so much that it was impossible to determine whose unconfirmed or usually reliable source belonged to which newspaper or broadcast.

CNBC gave much of its broadcast time to reckless talk and speculation, and one of the worst was a comment by conservative columnist Arianna Huffington, offering a report on "Equal Time" that Clinton had an affair with Shelia Lawrence, the widow of the late ambassador whose body was exhumed from Arlington National Cemetery after it was revealed he had lied about his military record. Huffington tried to cover her tracks a bit when she confessed "we're not there yet in terms of proving it."

White House Scolds the *Wall Street Journal*

The *Wall Street Journal*'s recklessness in reporting this case shocked many of its most loyal supporters. Not wishing to wait for its paper to come out the next morning, the *Journal* put on its Website and wire service that a White House steward had told a grand jury that he had seen Clinton and Lewinsky alone in a study next to the Oval Office. The *Journal* was in such a rush it didn't bother to check the story out with the White House, which brought a response from White House deputy press secretary Joe Lockhart that the "normal rules of checking and getting a response to a story seem to have given way to the technology of the Internet and the competitive pressure of getting it first."

The *Journal* story, by the way, used as its source "two individuals familiar with" the steward's testimony. The steward's attorney denied the story, but it did not stop a rash of other media outlets from giving the public the same story, sometimes with a different set of sources.

White House press secretary Michael McCurry called the *Journal*'s performance "one of the sorriest episodes of journalism I have ever witnessed." The *Journal*, by the way, apologized for the story a few days later, saying it was not true.

Even the usually responsible *60 Minutes* got caught up in the trash, opting to give air time to Kathleen Willey, a former White House volunteer, who had claimed that when she was visiting the president at the White House, he took her hand and placed it on his genitals. Her claim received a wave of media attention, as might be expected, but no one had actually interviewed Willey on television before she sat opposite Ed Bradley.

During the interview, Bradley asked the woman if the President had been "aroused" when he allegedly placed her hand on his genitals. Many journalists believe the question was in bad taste and should not have been asked. There also was some criticism of *60 Minutes* for scheduling the interview in the first place because of Ms. Willey's questionable credibility. Shortly after her appearance on the program, the White House released several letters of a friendly nature that Ms. Willey sent to the President after she allegedly was groped by Clinton. When Bradley was asked if the question about Clinton being "aroused" was his idea or a producer's, he refused comment.

When questioned about why he decided to put Willey on *60 Minutes*, executive producer Don Hewitt was defensive. He said he did so because he was convinced that there was a lot more to the Clinton scandal than just sex and that the American people were entitled to know about the other issues. Just how Willey's fondling claim against the President on national TV could play a role in uncovering such evidence of other wrongdoings was not made plain by the producer.

According to *60 Minutes*, at the time Willey was scheduled to appear on the program, producers did not know that she had written those friendly letters to the President *after* the alleged sexual encounter with him. Whether that information might have influenced the producers' decision to have her on the program is not known. As of this writing, there still is no evidence that Willey's accusations are true.

Commenting on the Lewinsky-Clinton-Starr coverage, the veteran journalist and best-selling author, David Halberstam, said the year of the scandal was "the worst year for American journalism since I entered the profession forty-four years ago." He added, "What is disturbing about the bad odor of journalism today is that, I think, many of the critics are right, and the people who have been performing as journalists have in fact seriously trivialized the profession, often doing what is fashionable than what is right."

Media Gripped By Sniper Obsession

That was the headline of a BBC *News World Edition* story on the media coverage of the serial sniper killings in the Washington, D.C. area in 2002. The British Broadcasting Corporation noted that at the height of the search for the sniper killer, the U.S. was getting ready to hold a presidential election, the debate on what to do about Iraq was in full swing, and there were new nuclear revelations about North Korea, but the media was "covering every major, minor, insignificant and sometimes irrelevant development" in the sniper case. The BBC added, all those major stories were buried under a mountain of coverage of the serial sniper. It cited this example of excess coverage: A Fox News anchor opens a new hour of sniper coverage with the words, "You are looking live at the sniper task force headquarters," and while he's speaking the camera cuts to a podium and a bank of microphones. The BBC report noted that there were no officials at the microphones, no people at all, just a podium and a bank of microphones.

Many news managers defended the coverage, pointing out that 13 people were shot and 10 of them died. They also argued that the exhaustive search and the tension and sometimes panic that existed in the Washington, D.C. area before the arrest and conviction of Lee Boyd Malvo and John Allen Muhammad was to be expected, and should have been no surprise.

But the sniper story wasn't just about excessive media coverage, which was common in the rest of the high-profile cases discussed in this chapter. It also shared some other problems with these other cases: too much speculation, which sometimes reached to the level of absurdity; the reporting of inaccurate and unfounded information; frequent arguments between authorities and the media about how the case was being handled; and a frustrated police chief who accused the media of meddling in, and complicating his investigation.

Washington Post columnist, Howard Kurtz wrote about all the speculation from so-called experts who were flat wrong about who the killer might be. He wasn't for example, a loner with no family as some of the experts claimed. Many of the "experts" suggested that the killer was a white male. An NYU psychiatrist described the shooter not only as white, but single, in his 20s or 30s with a long-time fascination with hunting and shooting. A former FBI agent told NBC's Katie Couric that statistically, the sniper is going to be a white male, and is going to be a young person, young 20s emotionally, but also because that's the age most likely, statistically, that somebody's going to commit a crime like this. Another so-called expert predicted confidently that the killer is "kind of a wallpaper white male, a disenfranchised, disrespected man who's getting back at society." The "angry white male theory" was quickly embraced by most of the media. *Washington Post* columnist Marc Fisher referred to the coverage as "breaking speculation." Cal Thomas of the Tribune Media Services noted that when the few facts available were reported, television "swarmed like bees, or more precisely like the pack of rats that overwhelmed the Gary Condit story" in the summer of 2001. Thomas said one effect the profilers may have had was to help the snipers with their killing agenda. For example, a former FBI profiler suggested to CNN's Larry King that the sniper "might travel as far south as Richmond, Virginia, perhaps down to Ashland." The next day, a man was shot leaving a restaurant in Ashland. Thomas also noted that the day after a former New York detective told a CNN audience that the sniper is a coward, there were more shootings.

Thomas also pointed out that an anchor at the Fox News Channel, where he also works, demonstrated bad taste and good marksmanship. She let viewers see how easy it is to blow someone's head off with a rifle and scope. She repeatedly fired into the head and torso of a target shaped like a human.

A Fox opinion poll, by the way, found that 52 percent of the public believed the coverage of the sniper story was "sensationalized" and 36 percent said it wasn't. But a whopping 67 percent believed the extensive coverage "encouraged the sniper." Cal Thomas's conclusion: "In these days of 24-hour news coverage and local news cut-ins, this blanket and often sensationalized coverage probably won't change as long as people watch. The problem," he added, is that "it encourages the crazies and American-haters who are watching." But *The Washington Post's* Howard Kurtz said that despite the embarrassing excesses during the shooting spree, the media did one very important thing near the end: The TV networks reported that the cops were looking for the two suspects in a blue 1990 Chevy Caprice and gave the New Jersey license plate—details that Kurtz noted, the police somehow failed to announce—and that's what led to the tip that produced the arrests.

Kurtz also pointed out that the arrests of Malvo and Muhammad marked the start of new relentless around-the-clock coverage of the story. He noted that while Phil Donahue and Connie Chung were interviewing Muhammad's cousin, Ed Holiday, at the same time, and getting the predictable comment from Holiday that "it doesn't sound like the John I knew," Larry King decided to interview the sister of Muhammad's first ex-wife. Of course the trials themselves were classic media overkill with the convergence of dozens of TV trucks and hundreds of reporters with video and still cameras wrestling for advantage locations around the courthouses.

As for the running battle between the media and Montgomery County Police Chief Charles Moose, PBS's Terrence Smith said police needed to communicate with a jittery public and the press needed to inform the public and remain independent from law enforcement. In a *News Hour* discussion on the sniper shootings, Smith noted that, although the police relied on the media, the chief lashed out at the news coverage on several occasions. He blasted the CBS affiliate WUSA and *The Washington Post* for reporting on a tarot card message left near the scene of one shooting.

The angry chief said sarcastically that "I have not received any message that the citizens of Montgomery County want Channel 9 or *The Washington Post* or any other media to solve this case. If they do, then let me know."

The media itself had different views on its performance. Andrea McCarren, an anchor at WJLA-TV said local station news was a daily balancing act. She said we have an obligation to our communities, and we also have an obligation to report the news. McCarren cited several examples in which her station did not divulge information at the request of police. By contrast, she said, the 24-hour cable stations reported for hours that a shooting had occurred at an elementary school, a report that was completely false and, she said, "fanned hysteria." She criticized the cable networks again for reporting that a shooting had occurred at a motel when, in reality, it was a domestic incident. A Fox News correspondent, Rita Cosby, defended her network saying that she knew personally that during at least seven or eight of the sniper shootings, the network had details but withheld them until they were verified. She added, the 24-hour networks did have a lot of time to fill, but we did a very good job of putting it in perspective, trying to understand the story and understand the context.

Figure 22-2   Jersey walls block the entrance to the street in the back of the Circuit Courthouse for the Joha Allen Muhammad sniper trial case. (Courtesy Jeff Caplan/Getty Images)

There will be a variety of appeals, of course, but as of this writing, Malvo faces life in prison without parole, and Muhammad faces death by injection.

The JonBenét Ramsey Murder Case

When six-year-old JonBenét Ramsey was found murdered in her home in Boulder, Colorado, it launched a media frenzy that had not been equaled since the O.J. Simpson murder case and the Clinton-Lewinsky sex scandal.

Like the O.J. case, Boulder police bungled the case from the start. They did not secure the crime scene or protect forensic evidence. Police also had a running battle with the DA's office on how to handle the investigation and leaked information to the press on a regular basis.

At first, the story looked like a routine kidnapping. On Christmas Eve 1992, Mrs. Ramsey discovered a ransom note allegedly written by someone representing a foreign power. The note threatened that JonBenét would be beheaded if the family called police. But they did. Later, during a routine search of the house by a detective and Mr. Ramsey, the father discovered the body of the child in a room in the cellar of the home. Her skull had been fractured and she was strangled.

The police quickly centered on the parents as the perpetrators of the crime, and the media fully embraced that conclusion, although there never was any hard evidence that John and Patsy Ramsey were guilty. After a year-long investigation, a grand jury refused to indict them or anyone else.

Approximately 800 children ages 12 and under were murdered in the United States in the year JonBenét was killed, and the murder should have been no more than a Denver-area story, but according to Brill's *Content* magazine, the media was hungry for a sensational story to follow the void left by the end of the Clinton-Lewinsky affair. The magazine said the fact that the child beauty queen was murdered during the slowest news week of the year—between Christmas and the new year—also contributed to the extraordinary media interest in the story. Several hundred representatives from the tabloids and the mainstream media would flood Boulder shortly after the murder. The strong interest in the little girl was fueled by the widely publicized videos and photographs of JonBenét performing at various child beauty pageants.

Brill's *Content* said the murder case had nothing to it except the alluring pictures and video of a little girl dolled up for a beauty contest. The magazine said there never was any real news in the story, but that didn't stop the media. In the two years between the time the story broke and the failure of the grand jury to indict the Ramseys, the tabloids and mainstream media printed and broadcast almost 1,000 stories about the murder case.

Among other TV shows, *20/20, 48 Hours, Hard Copy, American Journal, Dateline NBC,* and *Entertainment Tonight* aired more than 400 segments about the case. The scandal-loving Geraldo Rivera did 195 shows on the Ramseys on both CNBC's *Rivera Live* and the now-defunct *Geraldo Rivera Show*. CNN's Larry King had at least 44 segments about JonBenét. Even the usually more conservative print magazines *Newsweek* and *Time* carried 55 stories on the murder case and, of course, the tabloids feasted on it. The *Globe,* the *National Enquirer,* the *National Examiner,* and the *Star* published more than 500 stories on the subject.

NBC News' legal correspondent, Dan Abrams, defended the media's coverage of the story, saying that unsolved murders always fascinate the public and that this case had much more, including a mishandled police investigation. But Patricia Calhoun, the editor of Denver's weekly alternative paper, the *Westword,* disagrees. She noted that the murder case was a national springboard for a lot of people. It was a career-builder for many journalists, all of whom had a strong motive for keeping the story alive.

Brill's *Content* said "a cadre of journalists who made it their business to keep the business of JonBenét alive relied on sensationalism, untraditional tactics, and rule-bending to keep this nonstory in the headlines." In the process, the magazine added, they and their nonstory became "the quintessential symbol of a new age in which journalists, faced with the job of finding the next Big Story to feed the insatiable news machine, will reach down for material that by any standard is not news and rely on the work of bottom feeders to fill their pages and airwaves."

One of those bottom feeders was Jeff Shapiro, who worked as a stringer for the *Globe*. He said that there wasn't anything he would not do to get a story except break the law and pay sources. He quit after a year when he said he began to question the *Globe*'s fairness, particularly their interest only in stories that "fingered the Ramseys as the killers."

Shapiro, who would later string for *Time* magazine, cited one example of the *Globe*'s duplicity when an editor called Shapiro and claimed he had a new lead for him. The so-called new lead was that a *Globe* source had discovered that John Ramsey had given his pilot a box of evidence to hide for him. The *Globe* editor said the box contained the rope used to kill JonBenét and the duct tape used to cover her mouth.

Shapiro then told police about the *Globe* "scoop," and when the cops arrived at the pilot's house to talk to him, Shapiro was there to observe the incident and report it back to the *Globe*. The *Globe* had gone full circle with the story, making it up, suckering the cops into it, and then reporting that the cops were investigating the pilot.

This tabloid determination to "get the Ramseys" and the mainstream media's frequent willingness to go along brought about a special *Investigative Reports* program on the Arts and Entertainment (A&E) network. It was titled "The story of JonBenét Ramsey—the Ramseys vs. the Media."

Veteran journalist Bill Curtis anchored the program and set the tone by declaring that "almost all Americans now believe that the Ramseys committed the murder of their child because that has been the verdict of the American media." Curtis said that from the very beginning, police were leaking stories to the media indicating they were suspicious of John and Patsy Ramsey and that only the parents could have killed the child. The police leaks to the media also said that only someone who knew the Ramsey home could have killed the child.

Even Boulder City police chief Tom Koby became concerned with the leaks and the media reporting of them. Koby said that in his 28 years in the business he had never seen such media focus on an event and that it was making it more difficult for him to do his job. Curtis said the media-fed leaks reported one alleged fact after another, which taken together could only implicate the Ramseys.

Two of those leaks dealt with police concerns about finding no footprints outside the house and no signs of a break-in. Actually, there was a broken window and even some open windows in the house, a fact that police didn't tell the media for a year. It also was confirmed by experts not working for police that there was not enough snow on the ground around the Ramsey house on Christmas for there to be any footprints, if there had been an intruder. This finding was virtually ignored by the media.

Curtis noted that just four days after the murder, the media were reporting another leak, that police were suspicious of the Ramseys because of their behavior—that they thought the couple was faking their grief. *Vanity Fair* had reported that a policeman told them that he observed Mrs. Ramsey supposedly weeping, but instead she was really peering at him through her fingers.

Another false leak published by *Vanity Fair* that was not corrected by police was that they, the police, were concerned because John Ramsey had allegedly left the house for an hour, supposedly to get mail, shortly after JonBenét's body was found. The *Vanity Fair* article said police did not know where Ramsey had gone. Police later confirmed that this story was false.

There also was a wave of irresponsible media stories that the Ramseys had sexually abused JonBenét. There was absolutely no evidence of sexual molestation during the investigation.

The media also reported that the Ramseys were not cooperating with the police investigation, but Curtis pointed out that they had given police samples of their blood and hair and their fingerprints and writing samples.

The nation also watched District Attorney Alex Hunter's news conference, in which he claimed that the list of suspects in the JonBenét case was narrowing. He said the killer or killers of the child should know that the list would

Figure 22-3 Boulder District Attorney Alex Hunter arriving with prosecutors to make a statement to the press about the JonBenét Ramsey murder case, Colorado, October 13, 1999. Hunter said that the grand jury had finished its work without finding enough evidence to warrant an indictment. (Courtesy Reuters/NBC TV/Archive Photos)

soon have just one name on it. This was generally interpreted to be a reference to the Ramseys.

Some media reported that the police had sought a search warrant to look for pornography in the Ramsey house, which also was not true. The *Star* tabloid carried a headline: DAD LINKED TO KIDDIE PORN SCANDAL. Another head read: DADDY CHOKED BEAUTY WITH BARE HANDS. There also were media stories that John Ramsey had visited a porn store in Denver, a claim that was never substantiated. Even the *Sunday Times* in London carried a headline about "KIDDIE PORN" being involved in the child's death.

The media also tried to make something out of the fact that Mrs. Ramsey had taken JonBenét to a pediatrician 27 times in the four years before her death. The child's physician was interviewed on *Investigative Reports* and said there was nothing unusual about such visits, that there were absolutely no signs of abuse, and that many of the visits—some 21 of them—were for colds, hay fever, and routine medical examinations.

Vanity Fair's irresponsible coverage of the story included a report that the Boulder Police were so sure of the Ramseys' guilt that they had been holding a murder warrant for them since May following the murder. The magazine also carried a story saying that police were investigating whether JonBenét's nine-year-old brother could have killed his sister. There was no foundation for either story.

Fox in Depth featured on one of its programs an interview with Kim Ballard, a woman who alleged that she had been Ramsey's mistress. Ballard said she didn't know whether Ramsey had killed the child, but that she thought he was involved in some way. There has been no evidence that Ramsey even knows Ballard.

Geraldo Rivera even held a mock trial for the Ramseys on one of his shows. There was a make-believe judge and jury, and when the verdicts convicting both Mr. and Mrs. Ramsey of the wrongful death of their child were read, the studio audience broke out into wild cheers. It's difficult to remember that Rivera was a legitimate journalist for many years until he realized he could make a lot more money in tabloid journalism.

On another Rivera show, author Cyril Wecht told the audience that Boulder police "just need to do what they should do—arrest the people," an obvious reference to the Ramseys. The audience cheered wildly.

When questioned about the mainstream media's behavior, Barrie Hartman, the editor of Boulder's largest paper, the *Daily Camera*, said that when the tabloids print a story the rest of the media think they have to report it too. What happens then, he said, "is that a lot of those tabloid stories become fact when the legitimate media picks them up."

Bill Curtis summed up the media coverage of the JonBenét killing this way: "Journalists are worried about a profession driven by intense competition, a lack of regulation, and corporate ownership that increasingly views news as a profit-making rather than a journalistic activity. The result," concluded Curtis, "is that news has become entertainment and tragedy, public spectacle."

The media accusations against the Ramseys continued relentlessly for several years while no progress was made whatsoever in trying to solve the child's murder.

Finally, in April of 2003, it appeared that a judge's ruling might at least end the speculation about the Ramseys' involvement in their daughter's death. In an order dismissing a defamation lawsuit against the Ramseys, U.S. District Judge Julie Cames offered a thorough defense of the Ramseys, criticized the Boulder police investigation, and censured the lawyer whose civil suit sought to prove the couple killed their daughter. The judge said there was virtually no evidence to support the theory that they murdered the child, but abundant evidence to support their belief that an intruder entered their home and killed their daughter.

A Young Congressional Intern Dies and a Congressman Loses His Job

The skeletal remains of a former Washington, D.C. intern, Chandra Levy, were found in a park in Washington almost 13 months after she disappeared without a trace.

The medical examiner's office offered no conclusions about the manner and cause of death. The 24-year-old woman was last seen in Washington in April of 2001. The discovery of Ms. Levy's remains closed one chapter to the case, but the mystery of what happened to her continues. The case had generated tremendous publicity because of her relationship with Congressman Gary Condit of California. As in the cases of the Clinton-

Lewinsky scandal and the murder of JonBenét Ramsey, the media had a field day with the Chandra Levy story. Although Congressman Condit denied any involvement with Levy's disappearance, the fallout of their affair destroyed his political career and he was defeated in the Democratic primary. Condit, a 53-year-old married grandfather, had said little publicly about his relationship with Levy but police sources say he admitted to an affair with her during one interview with investigators.

Almost from the beginning, when Levy disappeared, Condit became a suspect in the minds of the police and in the media and the belief that he was in some way involved in Levy's disappearance never really ended. The talk shows on cable did endless programs on the mystery with hours of speculation about the involvement between Levy and Condit and all sorts of unconfirmed reports about the state of mind of Levy before she disappeared and why she vanished.

One rumor that made the evening cable show rounds was that Ms. Levy was pregnant and the assumption, never supported in any way, was that Condit was the father.

Condit sued CNN political commentator Dominick Dunne for $11 million dollars for implying that Condit was somehow connected with Levy's disappearance and murder. And Condit's wife Carolyn filed a libel suit against the *Star* tabloid for $15 million dollars because the paper claimed she had threatened to kill herself over her husband's relationship with Levy.

Strangely, Levy's Modesto California home would be the scene of another major tragedy, the disappearance and murder of a pregnant 27-year-old mother, Laci Peterson.

The woman's husband, Scott, was charged with her murder and the unborn child's. Their bodies were found about a mile apart along the eastern shore of San Francisco Bay. That location was within miles of the spot where Scott Peterson said he launched his boat for a fishing trip. At Peterson's initial arraignment, there were 28 TV cameras outside the small courthouse in Modesto, an indication that the trial itself would challenge the media coverage of the O.J. Simpson murder trial in Los Angeles. And as in that case, the Peterson story has the talk show hosts, tabloids, and the national news media hanging on every development. "The media shows all the symptoms of an addict, all the way down to denial," said Matthew Felling of the Center for Media and Public Affairs, a nonprofit research group. "Despite their protestations," he said, "they are and remain scandal-story junkies, waiting for the next fix."

On the days when Peterson was in court, the street outside the courthouse was fenced off to traffic and reporters and photographers jockeyed for position to see and take pictures of the defendant as TV trucks beam video from the scene on satellite dishes. Included in the mob outside the courthouse were such well-known media celebrities as Greta Van Susteren and Geraldo Rivera. As in other such high-profile cases, the coverage raised legal concerns about Peterson's ability to get a fair trial. The judge in the case sealed search and arrest warrant information and muzzled lawyers, investigators, and witnesses with a gag order. Still the feeding frenzy carried on. The local newspaper, the *Modesto Bee*, had published 102 articles and columns on the story in the first two months of the case and, of course, the coverage on cable television has was intense. Anyone with the slightest connection to the story was featured on the *Larry King* show, along with an assortment of lawyers and former prosecutors who always seemed eager to voice their views. The traditional evening network news programs have devoted some but not a particularly large proportion of their shows to the story, but the case consumed considerable time on the network morning shows targeting a largely female audience. For the six months after the Peterson story surfaced, it was the third-biggest story on *Today* and the other morning shows. Only the Iraq war and its aftermath rated more attention than the 415 minutes, nearly seven hours of talking, that the three shows devoted to the case. That's more time than the space shuttle *Columbia* disaster and homeland security received. Fox's Van Susteren discussed the story with panelists 42 times during the first two months after the story broke. Although NBC's *Nightly News* spent very little time on the Peterson story, the executive producer for *Today*, Tom Touchet, defended his decision to give *Today* anchors so much time for the case. "It just has so much," he said. "It's an unfathomable tragedy. She was the girl next door, she was full of hope and enthusiasm, she was thrilled to be pregnant and she goes missing on Christmas Eve. There's just so much our audience can relate to." He failed to mention that Scott Peterson also was having an affair when his wife disappeared. By the way, the Chandra Levy story which we discussed earlier, was allotted 603 minutes on the morning network talk shows.

Earlier we pointed out that the media, both tabloid and mainstream, were in virtual agreement that the Ramseys had played some role in the death of their daughter despite all the evidence to the contrary. There was growing concern that the media was already decided that Scott Peterson is guilty of

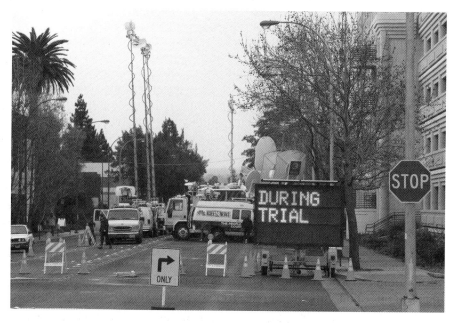

Figure 22-4   Television trucks set up outside of the San Mateo, Superior Court of California for pre-trial hearings of the Laci Peterson murder trial. (Courtesy Jed Jacobsohn/Getty Images)

the death of his wife and unborn child. Writing in *The New York Times*, Jim Ruttenberg noted that "one does not have to listen too carefully to surmise where Geraldo Rivera, the Fox News Channel correspondent and anchor, stands on Scott Peterson's alleged role in the killing of his wife and unborn child." He cited this quote from Rivera, "Fertilizer salesman Scott Peterson's alibi stunk as badly as the stuff he sells." Rivera made the comment one night to his TV audience, referring to Peterson as "the rat now caught in the trap."

Nancy Grace, a court TV anchor and a regular guest on CNN, did not seem to have much doubt about Peterson's culpability, either. Asked on *Larry King Live* whether Mr. Peterson could have accidentally killed his wife during an argument, Grace asked, "Why would you attach her feet to a concrete block and throw her into the bay?" King pointed out that there is no proof that Peterson did any such thing.

The *Times* reporter also noted that some news media critics are saying that there were elements of the media, particularly some commentators and anchors on the cable news networks, who reprised the worst journalistic habits exhibited during the coverage of the disappearance of Chandra Levy, all but convicting Peterson while repeating damning rumors.

Tom Rosenthal, director of the Project for Excellence in Journalism, said that "there's a profound journalistic question at play here. Is any speculation or assertion fair game? Or do we have a responsibility to weigh the rights of the accused along with the right of fair trial?"

Rutenberg noted that supposition of guilt was not confined to television news. He pointed out that on the day after Peterson's arraignment, the *New York Post*'s front page showed a photograph of Peterson in shackles with the headline "Monster in Chains."

It also should be noted that while the Peterson case was getting headlines there are a number of similar crimes in California's Bay Area that have gone virtually unnoticed. Four other young women have disappeared, and the remains of one of the women, a young Salvadoran immigrant, were washed up in San Francisco Bay just months before the Peterson case made headlines.

Criminologist Steve Schoenthaler of Cal State Stanislaus, who did a study on why some missing person cases get more attention than others, says "The stars lined up perfectly for the Laci Peterson case to become an instantaneous success in the media." He added, "In the newsrooms they're interested in covering that which sells newspapers and increases ratings and attractive women sell ratings more than anything else."

A university professor, Jeffrey McCall of De Pauw University, says the coverage of the Laci Peterson story demonstrates broadcast news at its worst. He says a story with no national significance and minimum relevance has taken on a larger-than-life perspective simply because viewers seem enamored with all the seedy behaviors of Scott Peterson and camera-ready attorneys. Professor McCall noted that, although the story was tragic, it affected only a handful of lives in a relatively small town, but the story was prominently featured in news programs on Fox News Channel, CNN, and MSNBC.

McCall said, "One must question news executives whether Laci's story would have been as important to them had she not been pregnant, attractive, young," and in California. He added, "Would they have been as interested in the story of a missing woman whose body later showed up if she was middle aged, not attractive, and living in Nebraska? And would that story have made the national news radar screen?" McCall concludes that every minute spent on the trial of Scott Peterson was one minute that news executives did not tell us about state budget problems, education needs, national security, and any number of newsworthy matters.

Peterson was convicted in November of 2004, of murdering his pregnant wife and dumping her body in San Francisco Bay. Shortly after the conviction the jury sentenced Peterson to death. One might think that the end of the trial would bring closure to the endless discussion of this case on the cable networks, but it didn't and no one really expects it to go away soon, because of the lengthy appeal process.

As we indicated earlier, the story was irresistible to the cable networks which almost every night brought in experts to pick apart the defense and prosecution cases, and debate the soap opera aspects of the case.

A Star Pro Basketball Player Is Accused of Sexual Assault

Still another story that received too much attention in the media, particularly on cable, was the rape accusation made against the Los Angeles Lakers star forward Kobe Bryant. The athelete was awaiting trial for allegedly sexually assaulting a 19-year-old hotel clerk when he was a guest at a mountain lodge where she worked in Eagle, Colorado.

The 25-year-old Bryant, who is married, admitted having had sex with the woman, but insisted that it was consensual and that he did not assault her. Suddenly, during the middle of jury selection, the woman decided to drop the charges against Bryant and that decision launched a whole new round of discussions on cable about why she dropped the charges and whether this was part of a deal that would end the threat of jail-time for Bryant in return for a financial settlement. There was endless new speculation on whether the woman would or would not pursue a civil case against Bryant, which she filed shortly before the criminal trial was to have begun. Bryant's comments after the woman dropped the case were strange, to say the least, and added fuel to the new discussions on cable. After pleading his innocence for months, Bryant suddenly gave us a new look, which the cable talk shows devoured. Bryant issued a written statement apologizing for the pain suffered by the woman. Still pending is a civil suit against Bryant. If the criminal case had gone to trial there is no doubt it would have turned into a circus. There already had been reports of threats against the woman from supporters of Bryant, including one from a man who allegedly offered to kill the woman for money. Kicking off the media frenzy was a quickly assembled TV production by the usually professional Arts and Entertainment network's Bill Curtis. Not content with outlining all the details of the case itself, the report detailed all of the accomplishments of Bryant in pro basketball; how he got started playing and a history of his family and their travels overseas where Bryant spent a good deal of his youth. Then the program speculated on what might happen to Bryant if he was convicted of the charges and placed on probation, including a very unnecessary and graphic description of different sexual tests he would have to undergo that would, for example, measure his erections to certain stimulations. I have no idea what purpose Curtis was trying to achieve by speculating on what treatment Bryant could expect if convicted and placed on probation when it had not even been decided if he would go to trial. The program certainly was not typical of the very professional work usually done by Curtis and neither he nor his producers would comment on the show.

The other cable networks also ran with the Kobe Bryant story, most notably Larry King on CNN who devoted scores of programs to the subject.

Newspapers were equally guilty of overplaying the Bryant story, but one paper, a relatively small one, the *Aspen Daily News*, ended its coverage of the case, saying, "it was opting out of the media mob." The paper said it would no longer have any daily coverage of the story unless there was a settlement or verdict. An editorial in the *Aspen Daily News* said "We're not going to add to the over-amplification of the Bryant story and perhaps the readers who feel the same way will enjoy reading a Kobe-less newspaper."

However, one journalism expert questioned the newspaper's decision. Kelly McBride, a member of the ethics faculty at the Poynter Institute, said that she agreed that the coverage of the Bryant case was salacious and sensational, but thought it would be better to "acknowledge the celebrity case in a minimal way and then use it to delve into the phenomenon of rape in our society."

One of the most contentious issues of the case was the alleged victim's identity. The debate over identifying a rape victim's identity was discussed earlier in the book (Chapter 11). The majority of the news media covering the Bryant case had kept the woman's identity secret, but a radio talk show host and several Web operators published the 19-year-old woman's name and photograph, with more than a dozen sites identifying the wrong person. During a court hearing, Bryant's defense attorney mentioned the name of the alleged victim three times.

When the judge rebuked her, the attorney claimed it was an accident. The judge warned reporters that she might bar any of them from her courtroom if they or their news organizations revealed the woman's identity.

Meanwhile, there were numerous newspaper and Internet stories about the young woman, some suggesting she was sexually promiscuous and may have had sex with other men shortly before the alleged rape.

Once again, this story will be updated as needed on our home page.

Are News Standards Dwindling?

Are respectable news organizations lowering standards and is the public turning against "trash TV" or is TV giving the public what it wants to know? Both questions were asked at a DuPont Forum at Columbia University. Joan Konner, the dean of the Columbia University Graduate School of Journalism at the time, set the tone for the forum, saying that the "very definition of news seems to have changed radically in the last decade. Sleaze and titillation from all news sources mirror the content of the sensational supermarket tabloids."

The keynote speaker, Hedrick Smith, a former *New York Times* correspondent and PBS documentary producer, shared Konner's disappointment in the media, complaining that TV offers so much opportunity "for mischief and slanting the news."

NBC News President Andrew Lack noted that news is a business and social mayhem has never been more marketable. He said, "We can pretend that each and every scandal has real news value, and they do because they are serious subjects after all, but," Lack added, "that's not why they top the news morning, noon, and night. My guess," he said, "is that the audience laps them up because in some ways they are pure entertainment." In other words, the public wants entertainment more than it wants news, and that is what the media is giving it. A frightening but rational explanation for what, in the minds of many journalists, is seriously handicapping the news industry.

In their excellent book on the media coverage of the Clinton-Lewinsky scandal, *Warp Speed*, Bill Kovach and Tom Rosenstiel say that the ordeal with Kenneth Starr and the impeachment trial that the ordeal precipitated "were part of a kind of cultural civil war in America in which the press plays a peculiarly important role."

The authors say that the Clinton scandal represented for the press the moment when the new *post-O.J. media culture* turned its camera lens to a major political event for the first time. They describe the *post-O.J. media culture* as a "newly diversified mass media in which the culture of entertainment, infotainment, argument, analysis, tabloid, and mainstream press not only work side by side but intermingle and merge." It is a culture, they add, "in which Matt Drudge sits alongside William Safire on *Meet the Press*, and Ted Koppel talks about the nuances of oral sex, in which *Hard Copy* and *CBS News* jostle for camera position outside the federal grand jury to hear from a special prosecutor."

Kovach and Rosenstiel say that many of the new media outlets are engaged in commenting on information rather than gathering it. They say the rise of 24-hour news stations and Internet news and information sites has placed demands on the press to have something to fill the time. "Whole new news organizations such as MSNBC are being built around such chatter," the authors say, "creating a new medium of talk radio TV."

23 Producing

The Producers

Most TV news producers will tell you that they are the creative force that makes the difference between a good newscast and a poor one. It's hard to argue with them. Producers are responsible for laying out the newscast, deciding what stories will lead the newscast, and determining the flow of the rest of the stories so that they best hold the attention of the viewers. The producers also play an important role in deciding how to use the video and sound bites that are available to them and their reporters and how to best work them into the newscast to maintain a maximum of interest. Each producer brings his or her own particular skills and abilities to the process and at the end of the day each newscast has a different look. After explaining the roles of different producers, we will take a close look at some of these different approaches to news producing in a market that boasts no fewer than five English and two Spanish stations—Phoenix, Arizona. The battle for viewers is intense. Because of the strong competition in the city, it's a great place to look for changes, trends, and innovation in news, particularly as it applies to producing.

The success of television news programs—regardless of whether they are at the network or local level—depends not only on the quality of the news gatherers, reporters, and camerapeople, but also on the ability of the producer, the executive producer, and the line producer. The producers determine not only what goes into the nightly news, but also how much time is devoted to each story, and as we said, in what order the stories will appear. The producers determine how many packages and how many voiceovers and readers will be used. In other words, they shape the news broadcast.

No two producers would create exactly the same newscast, just as no two writers or reporters would write or report a story the same way. However, there are certain rules and philosophies about the production of a newscast. You have read about the differences and similarities in style and philosophy in writing and reporting in various parts of this book. This chapter discusses the thinking of producers on news and how they put their newscasts together. We also illustrate how producers are used differently in various stations.

The Executive Producer

The executive producer is in charge of show producers and is responsible for the long-term look of the newscasts. He or she determines, in consultation with the news director and the station's general manager, the set, the style of the opening and close, the choice of anchors, the philosophy, and other details. The executive producer reports directly to the news director. If there are problems with the newscast, the executive producer will have to do some explaining after the show. Of course, the executive producer will go over the problem, whatever it might be, with the line producer before the news director calls.

If the ratings slip, the executive producer must explain why and try to fix the problem. Otherwise, he or she may be looking for another job. Because ratings are a serious concern for all producers, they constantly *work on the edge*.

The Line Producer (Show Producer)

On a day-to-day basis, the line (or show) producer is mostly responsible for deciding what goes into the news broadcast and makes sure it's ready to go on the air. The executive producer and news director will be watching in the wings, but most of the responsibility for preparing the newscasts is given to the line producer. He or she prepares the *rundown (lineup)*, which outlines which packages, voiceovers, and readers will appear in the show, and in what order, and how much time will be devoted to each story. If there is any doubt about which story should lead the newscast, the line producer consults with the executive producer and often includes the news director in that conversation. That also applies, of course, to any problem that may arise concerning the newscast that cannot be resolved simply.

The line producer works closely with the assignment editor and reporters. They talk about the rundown, reporter assignments, the angle the producer wishes the stories to take, story times, and whether the story is used as a package or a voiceover. As the day progresses, the line producer usually updates the rundown to reflect any breaking stories. If the producer has a special liking for a story, he or she tells the assignment editor and a reporter is assigned to the story. Sometimes the producer, in consultation with the assignment editor, decides which reporter covers a particular story. But a good producer doesn't micromanage and allows the assignment editor to determine most staffing decisions. As you can see, it takes a lot of people, working as a team, to put a newscast on the air. They're like links in a chain.

Associate Producers

In large cities and network newsrooms, the line producer sometimes has assistants to help carry the load. These assistant or associate producers help reporters put together packages when they are in a rush or have been assigned to a second story. They cut sound bites and pick video for the packages. When a package is reduced to a voiceover, the associate producer usually handles all the details, including writing the script. They also produce the vo-sots.

The associate producer also takes in the microwave or satellite feed from reporters in the field. Working closely with the line producer, the associate producer informs him or her if the feed has any problems. The associate producer often selects and edits parts of the feed to be used as voiceovers. Again, depending on the size of the news operation, there may not be any associate producers—writers are assigned the same duties. In many smaller markets, reporters are always responsible for cutting their own tape and putting the package together—with little or no help.

Not all stations in large markets use associate producers. "We don't use them anymore," said one executive producer. "Instead, he said, we hire more show producers. It's more expensive since producers are paid more than associate producers. But since they have more experience, it gives us more flexibility. If a show producer calls in sick," he adds, "any of the other producers can step into her shoes, whereas associate producers aren't qualified to handle newscasts."

Field Producers

Usually found in larger markets and at the networks, field producers help reporters with research, plus the detail work, setting up interviews, locating people at the scene of the story (often in advance), directing the cameraperson, and making travel arrangements. The field producer is often described as the "advance" person—the "facilitator." He or she often speaks with the newsmakers in advance of the reporter's arrival, briefs the reporter on what the interviewees know about the story, and suggests questions to ask in interviews.

The Staff Meetings

The producers can be found in various parts of the newsroom, speaking to each other, with reporters, the assignment editor, and the news director. Most of them hold staff meetings as many as three times a day—in the morning, the late afternoon, and after the early evening newscast—to discuss that day's news coverage. That's where initial newscast decisions are made: What will the lead story be? Which stories will be covered? Which reporter and cameraperson will cover them? Keep in mind these decisions are subject to change, depending on the day's events. The last meeting of the day is a debriefing to discuss what went right and wrong with the early evening newscasts and to plan coverage for the late evening news.

The meeting is a place to discuss story ideas—it's not unlike a *war room* where the battle plan is set for that day's action. All staff members are expected to contribute and share information. A good producer is a good listener who realizes that ideas are not limited to the assignment editor.

During the meeting, the staff goes over each story available for the day's newscasts. Decisions are made, and the line (show) producers of the early evening newscasts create a rundown (lineup), which is a list of stories planned for those newscasts. Reporters and camerapeople are then assigned to stories.

As stated above, the early rundown is subject to change as the day's news events unfold. Sometimes the pre- and final rundowns look alike. On other days, there are so many new developments and breaking news stories that the final rundown lineup barely resembles the pre-rundown.

A Busy News City

In Phoenix, Arizona, as mentioned, there are five war rooms—seven, when you consider the two Spanish-speaking stations. It is one of the most crowded

TV news markets in the nation. Until the fall of 2004, all the stations had head-to-head 6 o'clock newscasts, but KPHO-TV, the CBS affiliate, decided to break out of the pack "after research showed a large number of viewers would welcome a later newscast," said News Director Tom Bell. Viewers told of having trouble getting home in time to watch the news because of work demands and heavy traffic.

Listening to viewers, KPHO moved the *CBS Evening News* to 6:00 PM and the local news to 6:30 PM. They also added a half hour to their early news block. Bell said that since TV ratings drive the marketplace, there was an urgent need to get around the competition. He said, by switching to a later time slot, "we found ourselves with an island of viewers and no news competition."

He added, "The results are great so far with our audience up 80–90%."

"KPHO emphasizes hard news, not features," said Bell. "People want to know what's going on," he said. "Hard news drives the bus, but that does not mean we're only interested in accidents." In the past, TV news has "alienated viewers with blood and guts."

"Our goal is to generate a quality, interesting, 'need to know' product. That's the future," he added. "Everybody will cover the car accident, but quality will stick." he said. "Quality does not have to be boring. Quality does sell."

Bell emphasized that adding a half-hour to the early news time slot was inexpensive. The added cost involved two new positions, an editor and writer.

Who's the Real Boss?

Sometimes, it's not easy to spot who is in charge. For example, at KTVK-TV in Phoenix, the executive producer is "the real hands-on, day-to-day manager of the newsroom." According to news director Dennis O'Neill, the executive producer oversees all content and has the final word on what goes into the shows. O'Neill said, "The executive producer supervises all reporters and producers, making sure the style is consistent from day to day."

"Executive producers are more like what news directors used to be," said O'Neill. They make sure all detail work is performed daily. "She's responsible for both coverage and content," O'Neill added, "and if there's a breakdown in coverage, or a problem with the broadcast, we go to the executive producer." The executive producer works closely with and supervises show producers, who are responsible for individual shows. O'Neill said the assignment editor used to decide what stories to cover, but now the executive producer makes those decisions. The assignment editor makes the logistical decisions, by assigning reporters and photographers to stories.

The individual show producers (line producers) put together the rundowns and determine the form of the stories—whether they should be packages or V/Os, and so forth. The show producers also write part of the script. KTVK-TV broadcasts 6.5 hours of news daily and has a staff of 125. It's an independent station, which means that it often covers national stories in addition to state and local news.

The executive producer, in addition to overseeing the other producers, checks all scripts before they get on the air for accuracy and libel and makes certain that quotes are properly attributed.

The Golden People

O'Neill says that "good producers are worth their weight in gold. We have 11 producers," he said, "and they're hard to keep." Producers are in such demand, according to O'Neill, that Don Fitzpatrick Associates—a broadcast news headhunter—has one person assigned full-time to searching for show and executive producers.

Most producers advise those considering a broadcast journalism career to give serious consideration to becoming a producer. "The future is unbelievable. One producer in Phoenix said it used to take five years to get a producing job in Phoenix, the 17th largest market. Now it takes only three years." She said, "We get four or five reporter resume tapes a day. By contrast, I may get one good tape a month from a producer." O'Neill also discussed a growing trend in the industry—the use of field producers who don't get on TV. KTVK-TV has four or five such producers who do most of the research and legwork for the reporters. They are paid a lot less than the reporters.

Philosophy

One important change is that producers seem to have cut back on some of the small talk on the set. One thing is certain: Phoenix viewers have an incredible number of choices, as was mentioned earlier, with seven TV stations doing early evening newscasts. O'Neill says you will not see a lot of Washington stuff on his station, although the station does cover national news now that it's independent and no longer gets any help from a network.

Ethics

One major concern at KPNX-TV is ethics. The news department is very serious about the issue—and has seminars on ethics for the whole staff. A spokesperson for the station said the news department did a lot of soul searching after three members of the staff "became the news." The spokesperson said the staff began to notice how callous some journalists act and decided to change their ways, to "put ourselves in the shoes of the newsmaker."

The events that resulted in the attitude change at the station occurred when a KPNX-TV sports reporter was killed in an auto accident in Washington, D.C., and became a front-page story, as did a photographer who lost part of his leg, and an anchor who suffered a heart attack. "For the first time we realized what it was like to be on the other side of the camera," the station official said, "and we didn't like what we saw." She added: "We had forgotten why we got into this business in the first place." A producer agreed. "We've changed. We have discovered that we can be successful without being flashy."

Everyone involved in news coverage should learn what it's like to be on the other side of the camera as the subject of a news story. And they should periodically take a refresher course.

Another member of the KPNX-TV news team, executive producer Mark Phillips had this to say about producing strategy: "Viewers attention span is getting shorter. They don't have the patience to watch long stories. With few exceptions, the viewer won't sit still for a story that runs longer than one minute and 20 seconds." Phillips cites as an example Phoenix station, ABC-15. He says the station uses the long form and is doing very good work, but not getting the audience. He says viewers want to be informed, but they are not looking for depth. Commenting specifically on the 10 o'clock news program, Phillips said the viewer is looking for fresh news, not a rehash of the 6:00 pm news, although they want a summary of it. Phillips added that viewers want news they can use. He said newscasts should present information clearly and interestingly, using "great" pictures. He pointed out that TV news is "technology driven, hence the producer needs to understand the technology in order to appreciate the medium so she can use it wisely." Phillips also has this advice; "Don't go the first break until you're at least nine or ten minutes into the newscast. At that point, you've hooked the audience."

The news director of KNXV-TV, the station alluded to by Phillips earlier, also has some good advice on producing. Joe Hengemuehler provided his "Golden Rules of Producing" First, he says, make certain that the newscast you put on the air every night is a true reflection of your community. "Listen to the viewers when they call you on the phone or send you an email, he says, "they are your customers, you work for them."

His second rule, "Come to work with ideas borne from your life experience. Take a different route to work so you can experience different parts of your community. His rule on writing: "Be very clear about your copy. Simple, declarative sentences are better than long, jargon–filled run-on sentences that can confuse viewers. He added, if you are a producer, you and no one else should write your lead story and, as the producer, he says, you also should write your internal teases. He also noted that words on graphics should always be supported by words in the copy." Another rule, for the producer, from Hengemuehler, "Review every reporter package you can, time permitting."

The Rundown (Lineup)

The rundown, or lineup, as mentioned earlier, is what comes out of the staff meetings. The decisions reached at the morning meeting determine what goes into the rundown for the evening news, and the discussions at the afternoon meeting establish what the late-night news looks like. But all this, as noted, is subject to change depending on breaking news stories, because the rundown is a living document. At times, the rundown looks exactly like the newscast, but at other times it looks nothing like it because of unpredictable developments.

An example is the 2001 earthquake in Seattle that occurred on the morning of February 28. Typically, when a major story like that occurs, the station's entire effort is devoted to that story and the planned coverage is shoved aside. The day of the earthquake, Seattle's major stations were continuously on the air live. CNN and other stations around the nation were picking up the Seattle station's coverage. Of course, the final rundown was nothing like the original. The uncertainty of television news can make life difficult, but at the same time it makes it interesting and sometimes exciting.

Some nights, producers wish they could just toss everything in the air and put it in the show the way it falls down. Unfortunately, it doesn't work that way. A lot of thought must go into the arrangement of stories in the newscast to make it clear and interesting. As mentioned earlier, no two producers are likely to agree on the exact order of the stories in a newscast. If you examined the newscasts produced at stations in the same market on the same night, even the lead stories are often different unless some story completely dominates the news.

So, the news judgment of each producer comes into play, along with individual biases and the ability of assignment editors, reporters, and others to come up with good material.

Peaks and Valleys

One popular approach to producing a newscast is known as the *peak-and-valley* format. Although the phrase has been around for decades, many producers use the format without using that name. This format treats every segment, or block, in the newscast as a sort of mini-newscast that can stand on its own. That doesn't mean that each section has weather, sports, and financial news; but there is a good, strong story at the top of each segment, along with some less important stories and, in some segments, perhaps a feature or special report. Each segment ends with a strong story before the commercial.

The concept behind peaks and valleys is that if you sprinkle your most interesting and important stories throughout the newscast, you'll hold your audience. If you place all your top stories in the early part of the newscast, you'll lose the audience because the newscast—and your audience—will fizz out by the middle. Worse yet, the audience will switch to your competition. Instead, you should spread your most interesting and important stories throughout the newscast.

It's also important to remember that weather is the most promotable element in a newscast. Many viewers say that weather is the main reason they watch local news, and that's why producers tease it throughout the newscast.

For those producers who make use of the "peak-and-valley" theory, it is extremely important before going to a commercial to tease not only with the weather, unless it's a major news story, but with a strong story and one or two other stories that have special appeal. The idea is that if you do not hook listeners on the first tease, you may get them on the second or third. If you do, it will help keep the audience around through the commercial, which is the valley of the newscast. After the commercial, the audience expects another good story at the top of the next segment, and the process begins all over again: A peak and then a valley and another peak and another valley, throughout each section of the newscast.

This theory of producing is different from the traditional approach (which started in radio), which gives the audience the best stories at the top of the newscast and follows them with stories of less and less interest until it's time to say goodbye. This format made sense for radio and for the early TV newscasts, which did not run more than 15 minutes. The same so-called *inverted pyramid* system also was used by many TV producers even when newscasts expanded to 30 minutes. (Actually they only had about 20 minutes of news to offer because of commercials and opens and closes.)

The inverted pyramid approach continues in many small markets because it often is difficult even to find just one strong story each night. Too many producers still try to hold an audience by teasing sports and weather. In many communities, of course, sports and the weather are important news, as are college and high school sports scores. In farming communities, the weather may be the best story of the day, night, and week; however, creative producers, even in small markets, should try to use the peak-and-valley theory that teases other important stories or good features.

Rhythm and Flow

Commenting on the peak-and-valley theory, former CNN executive vice president Ted Kavanau said packages, voiceovers, and copy stories (anchor readers) should be used to create a rhythm and flow in each section. He suggested using a good tape story at the top of the segment, then some anchor copy and maybe a voiceover, and some more copy until "you build to a package," a story with some emotion in it. If you have more time in the segment, Kavanau says, start the process again: good tape-copy-tape-copy-package-copy-tape-copy-package-copy.

Although packages appeal most to the audience, producers shouldn't play one off another. You should place them effectively throughout the newscast, limiting one to each section. The package also serves another important purpose: It gives the anchors a breather and a chance for them, the producers, and the director to get organized for the rest of the show.

The line producer, who sits near the director in the control room, often needs time to reshuffle parts of the rundown and script because of late-breaking news and because packages often are not ready on time to be aired. Problems also develop when videotapes, or the decks that play them, malfunction.

Diane Doctor, news director for WCBS-TV in New York City, also stresses the importance of including hard news throughout the newscast and not placing all your feature or soft stories near the end of the program. She says that could send the message to viewers that they have heard all the important news of the day and they might decide that it wasn't necessary to watch any longer. Doctor added that each block of the newscast should be like a piece of music, with a beginning, middle, and end. "Even if it's a short block," she said, " it has to feel that way. Viewers should feel like they've been on a little journey." The news director also criticized programs that concentrate too much on crime, which is easy to do in a city like New York. Doctor said viewers get weary of newscasts that place too much emphasis on crime. She also emphasized that while it's important to promote important stories, like the funeral of President Reagan, she tries to make sure that her station's viewers get something that goes beyond routine coverage, perhaps including interviews with people in New York who were close to the late President or may have some special anecdotes to share about him. "You have to try to find something that everybody else doesn't have," she said, "We have to set the bar higher, by finding stories that differentiate us from the competition—stories that are more unique."

Doctor paid her dues, working in a variety of small, medium, and large markets. Before moving over to the CBS flagship station, she worked for WNBC-TV in New York, and was a news director and assistant news director for major stations and also was a line producer which, she says, allows her to share her experiences and expertise with younger producers. But Doctor says she keeps a low profile with her producers, engaging them with suggestions and ideas when appropriate, and going over the rundowns, but without exerting undue influence or pressure.

A Difference of Opinion

As we stated earlier, no two producers are likely to decide the exact same order of the stories in a newscast. If you examine the newscasts at different stations in the same market on the same night, you'd see that even the lead stories are often different unless some story completely dominates the news.

"Producers should always consider the who-cares and so-what factors," says Denise Clodjeaux, a former producer and now news director of KEZI-TV, Eugene, Oregon. "If your reaction to a story is who cares or so what, then it doesn't belong in a newscast," she said.

At Phoenix's KTVK-TV, an executive producer recalls leading a newscast with an interview with the mother of a Phoenix man who committed suicide with the help of Dr. Kevorkian. She admitted that the mother had already been interviewed by a Phoenix newspaper but said "It's different on TV. You

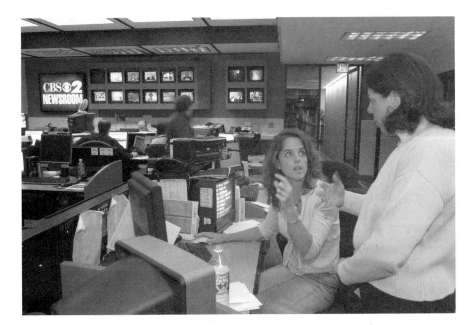

Figure 23-1 WCBS-TV Senior Vice President and News Director Diane Doctor (right) reviews news copy with Executive Producer Maura McHugh (left). (Courtesy of WCBS-TV, New York, NY)

see and hear the mother. The emotion and facial expressions that don't come through in a newspaper story come through on TV." The producer also noted that her news runs 90 minutes and that her audience changes. When the show starts at 5 P.M., the audience is older. As the newscast continues, the makeup of the audience becomes younger. She said she treats each block like a different newscast, designing it for the changing audience.

The producer also said that at 5:30 P.M. she goes head-to-head with the network newscasts, so she packs that segment with a lot of national stories, leading with the big national story of the day.

More Producing Tips

TV news consultant and former producer Mary Cox provides her "baker's dozen" suggestions for news producers:

1. Ask: What's the viewers' benefit?
2. Win the lead.
3. Put news in every section.
4. Make the show video-driven—go from video to video to video. (Most producers disagree on this one.)
5. Write tight, to the point.
6. Look for live opportunities without going live for the sake of going live.
7. Give stories the time they need.
8. Don't "force" a package, even if a reporter worked all day on it. If it doesn't work, dump it.
9. Tease news at the end of every section.
10. Include some of the newscast's best writing and video in the teases.
11. Go out strong, with a big finish (generally a package) to keep the audience with you.
12. Create a "magic moment" consisting of something memorable, such as great photography.
13. Avoid getting locked into local, local, local, national, national, national. People don't think that way and they don't tell stories that way.

The rundown, shown in Figure 23-2, was prepared by the executive producer at WHAS-TV in Louisville, Kentucky. This particular rundown was for the evening news on the day after the Oklahoma bomb blast, so it was top heavy with news of the bombing. WHAS-TV dumped the regular newscast and went live with the network feed from the scene.

Producers Need Good Writing Skills

The Executive Producer for Fox 5, in New York, Luke Funk, is concerned that producers do not get enough writing training before they start producing and then get too little help in that area when they get a producer's job. He said he had to learn to write on his own. Funk noted that the emphasis in training producers is on formatting a show, placement of stories, and timing—all of which is important—but that there's not enough help in writing. He said

PAGE	ANC	SLUG	FORM		PB	TAPE#	WTR	?	TTIME	TRT		BKTIME
S-38	GARY	VA BOMB SCARE	ENG# VO OS	--	------	---	R	:30	0:51	JE	1:58
*****	****	B:OOPM***********	************	XX	******	***	R	0:00	0:00	-	1:07
*****	****	DATE: 04/20/95	P: BUNTON				R		0:00	-	1:07
		HEADLINES					R		0:00	DB-	1:07
		§§	↑↑				R		0:00	-	1:07
		§§	↑↑				R		0:00	-	1:07
		§§	↑↑				R		0:00	-	1:07
							R		0:00	-	1:07
00000	----		OPEN CART				R	:20	0:20	-	1:07
S-1	G/S	VIDEO OPEN	ENG# SOT		X		R	00:05	0:25	DB-	0:47
			W/BANNER	B2	------	---	R	0:00	0:00	-	0:22
			2SHOT				R		0:00	-	0:22
S-1A	SGC	WEATHER UPDATE	WX STUFF		X		R	0:30	0:39	DB-	0:22
							R		0:00		0:17
							R		0:00		0:17
S-2	S/G	OKC TODAY	INTRO/ESS/OS		X		R	0:00	0:35	DB	0:17
00	----	ROEDEMEIER CART	ENG# PKG	B3	95-54	---	R	0:31	1:11	KD	0:52
			ESS BANNER				R		0:00		2:03
NEW2A	GARY	OKC TAG	COPY		X		R	0:00	0:13	KD	2:03
							R		0:00		2:16
S-3	SWAN	GENERAL SECURITY	ENG# VO OS	B4	------	X--	R	0:00	0:25	SC	2:16
			WIPE TO				R		0:00		2:41
S-3A	SWAN	SECURITY SOUND	ENG# SOT/VO	B2	------	X--	R	0:11	0:17	SC	2:41
							R		0:00		2:58
S-38	GARY	MISSING WOMAN	ENG# VO	B3	------	X--	R	0:00	0:26	AJ	2:58
							R		0:00		3:24
S-4	SWAN	TOSS TO JTURNER	IN/OS/DBLBOX		X		R	0:00	0:21	JE	3:24
S-5	JTUR	BOMB FACTS	CAM 7		X		R	0:00	0:15	JE	3:45
00	----	JTURNER CART	ENG# PKG	B4	------	---	R	0:48	1:30	JE	4:00
			ESS BANNER				R		0:00		5:30
S-5A	S/J	BOMB TAG	DOUBLE BOX		X		R	0:00	0:17	JE	5:30
							R		0:00		5:47
S-6	GARY	PEOPLE REACTION	INTRO/OS		X		R	0:00	0:08	PC	5:47
00	----	CTURNER CART	ENG# PKG	B2	------	---	R	1:15	1:38	PC	5:55
			ESS BANNER				R		0:00		7:33
S-7	SWAN	CHURCH SERVICE	ENG# VO	B3	------	X--	R	:05	0:21	DB	7:33
							R		0:00		7:54
S-9	G/S	TEASE#1(CRIME	ENG#	B4	_____	X	R	0:08	0:22	AD	7:54
		WEATHER RADAR					R		0:00		8:16
*****	****	===== BREAK #1 ***	************	XX	******	***	R	02:20	2:20		8:16
S-10	SWAN	THUNDER PREPS	INTRO/OS		X		R	0:00	0:13	LS	10:36
00	----	LASMITH CART	ENG# PKG	B2	------	---	R	0:32	1:30		10:49
S-10A	SWAN	THUNDER TAG	COPY		X		R	0:00	0:12	LS	12:19
							R		0:00		12:31
S-12	GARY	TOSS TO DOYLE	INTRO		X		R	0:00	0:00	AD	12:31
S-13	DOYL	KIDS & CRIME	INTRO/OSONSET		X		R	0:00	0:13	AD	12:44
00	----	DOYLE CART	ENG# PKG	B3	------	---	R	0:49	1:28	AD	12:57
S-13A	DOYL	CRIME TAG	ESS		X		R	0:00	0:24	AD	14:25
	GSD	WRAP UP	THREE SHOT				R		0:00		14:49
							R		0:00		14:49
S-14	S/G	TEASE#2(WEATHER)	S RADAR		X		R	0:00	0:15	DB	14:49
*****	****	===== BREAK #2 ***	************	XX	******	***	R	02:10	2:10		15:04
		WX OPEN/TAYLOR					R	00:10	0:10		17:14
S-15	TAYL	WEATHER	ENG# VO&KEY	B4	_____	X	R	02:15	2:15	KD	17:24
							R		0:00		19:39
S-16	WXR	WRAP	2SHOT		X		R	:10	0:10	KD	19:39
							R		0:00		19:49
S-17	S/G	TEASE#3(SPORTS)	COPY		X		R	0:00	0:15	DB	19:49

DEARING   THU APR 20 17:37   PAGE   2

		RADAR	RADAR				R	0:00	0:00		20:04
*****	****	===== BREAK #3 ***	************	XX	******	***	R	02:10	2:10		20:04
		SPORTSOPEN/GUPTON					R	00:10	0:10		22:14
S-18		1ST SPORTS	ENG # /VO	B3	_____		R	00:03	0:05		22:24
							R		0:00		22:29
SP-1	GUPR	ROYAL DONATION	ENG # /VO	B4	_____		R	0:00	0:21	DB	22:29
			WIPE TO				R		0:00		22:50
SP-2	GUPR	ROYAL BITE	ENG# SOT	B2	_____		R		0:10		22:50
SP-5	GUPR	ELTISH	COPY				R		0:15		23:00
SP-6	GUPR	HUBBARD LEWIS	ENG# VO	B2	_____		R		0:20		23:15
			WIPE TO				R		0:00		23:35
SP-7	GUPR	RYDER REAX	ENG# SOT	B3	_____		R		0:15		23:35
SP-8	GUPR	HOLE IN ONE	ENG VO		S-___		R		0:00		23:50
							R		0:00		23:50
S-19	GSD	SPORTS WRAP	3SHOT		X		R	:10	0:10	KD	23:50
							R		0:00		24:00
S-20	G/S	TEASE #4(BOMB)	ESS FULL	___	_____	X	R	0:00	0:15	DB	24:00
*****	****	===== BREAK #4 ***	************	XX	******	***	R	02:55	2:55		24:15
S-21	SWAN	NIGHTTEAM TEASE	ENG# VO OS	B4	_____	___	R	00:20	0:20		27:10
							R		0:00		27:30
S-22	GSC	WXR WRAP	3SHOT/GRAPHX		X		R	:20	0:20	KD	27:30
							R		0:00		27:50
S-23	G/S	BOMB ESSAY	INTRO		X		R	0:00	0:22	DB	27:50
00	----	SAMLER CART	ENG# PKG	B2	------	---	R	1:46	1:46		28:12
							R		0:00		29:58
			AUDIO CART				R	:02	0:02		29:58
*****	****	**** END BREAK ***	************	XX	******	***	R	0:00	0:00		30:00

Figure 23-2 It's a good idea to avoid leaving viewers with a sense that "there's nothing good in the news tonight" by working some "uplifting" stories into the show.

young producers are "left to fake their way through some vos and vo/sots and copy stories."

Here's some other advice from Funk: "Don't be afraid to let an anchor change your copy if it doesn't change the facts. We all like to think we are the best writers out there," he said, "but anchors have to read the copy and may want to change it to suit their style of delivery."

Funk also suggested that producers learn to respect and work with field crews. He said producers should try to work out a schedule with the news director to get out into the field with a crew once in awhile to see news gathering from their perspective. Here are some other tips that Funk says he's passed along to young producers over the years:

- Check your facts, AP wire copy is not "the truth"; you need to independently confirm information.
- Think simple thoughts, simply expressed. If your writing is confusing, complicated, poorly written, or misunderstood, the viewer has an excuse to leave.
- Have another person read your copy. If you don't have an executive producer or copy editor, make sure your anchor reads copy before it hits air, which should be a must in any case, even if you do have a copy editor.

Finally, Funk recommended that producers "read, read, read—not only the local paper every day, but a variety of periodicals, most of which are available on the Internet, free of charge."

Enthusiasm

Al Tompkins, who has 24 years of professional experience in major markets, says good producers manage things and lead people; they learn the skills of communication; they remember to use active listening. Tompkins—now with the Poynter Institute in St. Petersburg—says successful producers come to work with "first-day enthusiasm." Tompkins offers the following list of things that news directors want from producers:

- *Be an adviser to your boss.* Be strong enough to give him or her the good news as well as the bad. Help your boss know what is really happening out in the trenches.
- *Value the judgments and contributions of others.* Listen to reporters, directors, and photojournalists; respect their ideas and expertise; allow them to help you discover that there is not one truth, but many truths.
- *Discover all you can about your audience and seek to serve them.* Draw from personal experience, research, and a wide network of diverse contacts; recognize that viewers are usually not all like journalists in the way they live, think, or view the content and execution of newscasts.
- *Be a writing example.* Teach, delegate, coach, and resist the tendency "to do it all yourself." Help to develop associate producers. Ask open-ended questions. Listen more than you speak.
- *Anticipate major events.* Tompkins says effective producers know what graphics are needed to cover the big story and what special decisions about spending or staffing or equipment need to be made in advance.
- *Recognize that lead-in programming is important.* Tompkins advises producers to know their lead-in programming because it will help them to step back from the show, consider the lead-in, and write preshow teases to

the ear of the audience. He says the best place to capture the viewers is the show before your own program.

- *Step back from the show.* Tompkins says producers should take a good look at the broadcast they are about to present and ask if it truly reflects what happened in the community that day. Does it portray the community as it really is, or as the producer narrowly defined it?
- *Producing is the glue that holds the newsroom together.* Producers set the tone; they regulate style; they shape content. Effective producers nurture, value, and defend the principle of an individual's right to express ideas even if they are unpopular.

Energy

Veteran producer, Ted Kavanau, says energy is the key to success for a TV producer. He says a casual person rarely makes a good producer. "An energetic producer always does a more exciting program . . . a fast-moving and interesting-looking newscast," said Kavanau. He also stressed that flow is important. Kavanau added that producers should find the most important reason a story should follow the previous one. Here is some other advice from Kavanau:

- Bridge your stories by using those that help bring you from one category to another.
- Write short leads to tape. Don't punish people with talk when you have good video.
- If you have good pictures, make them last by writing enough copy.
- End segments with strength. Never use a weak story at the top of a segment.
- Like packages, never put features back-to-back.

Still Pictures

Many producers tend to avoid still pictures, but when used correctly, especially in a sequence, they can be effective—almost as much as video.

Maps and other graphics also should be used to support copy. If a plane has crashed in some relatively unknown area, it helps the viewer if you show a map and indicate with a star where the plane went down. The map should include at least one town familiar to your audience.

Live Shots

Ever since the technology allowed TV stations to go live from the scene on a daily basis, there has been a debate about whether the technique is being overused.

If there is a major traffic snarl in New York City because of road construction during the rush hour, does it make any sense to send a reporter back to the scene for the 11 P.M. news—as one station did—when the highway is virtually abandoned? Even the reporter at the scene was annoyed by this decision, because it was cold and she was shivering. "What the hell am I doing here?" she asked on the two-way radio, before the anchor tossed the broadcast to her.

The need to use the live shot as much as possible seems to have diminished somewhat as the novelty wore off and station managers have complained less to news directors. In the past, the managers often said, "We paid a bunch for this stuff . . . make it pay for itself."

In the Phoenix market, by the way, most of the stations that we discussed in detail are heavy "live" stations. Why live? One executive producer said it demonstrates to the audience that "you're out there, in their community, covering a story important to them. Our research shows that the viewer's perception of a reporter, who appears live, has more facts than the reporter doing a story from the station even though both use the same facts."

Most news managers also say the public tends to believe that a reporter at the scene is more on top of a story than a reporter getting his or her information over the phone. Finally, they say, newsmakers are more likely to talk to a reporter in person than on the phone. "It's easy to say no to a strange voice on the phone," said a producer, "but it's difficult to say no to a reporter while looking him in the eye."

Back Timing

One major task for the line producer is to ensure that the newscast gets off the air on time. This is particularly important when computers are in charge of establishing when programs and commercials start and end. We all have witnessed situations when one program is cut off abruptly by a new program. That situation happens because a computer has established the time when the new program or commercial is supposed to start, and start it will, on time.

The timing is particularly critical when local news is followed by a network program. The network computer will take over regardless. If the local news anchors are still saying goodbye, or the station's final commercial or logo is still playing, something is going to get cut off if the newscast timing is not accurate. If your commercial is cut, that revenue goes down the drain.

To defend against such problems, the show producer must always know whether the newscast is "running on time." It is virtually impossible for the producer to keep the newscast flowing exactly on time for 30 minutes or an hour because sometimes anchors stumble on some lines or make an unscheduled remark coming out of a tape, or a package sticks in the tape deck and has to be re-cued. That's why producing is so difficult; the unexpected often happens.

The producer must always know if the newscast is ahead or behind schedule. If the newscast is short because a tape gets caught in the playback, the producer must find something else to take its place. The same is true if the show is running long—something must be cut. So, producers use a technique called *back timing* to make sure the program ends on time. In most newsrooms, the computer system back times a show for you, but a producer always needs to be able to do the math on her own.

The computer automatically tells you where you stand on time at each point in the newscast. A "minus" sign means the show is running long. Figuring the time works like this: Take the total amount of time for the show (i.e., 30 minutes). Subtract time for commercials (usually 8:00), time for weather (usually 2:30), and time for sports (usually 3:00). The number left is your news hole—the time you have for news. In most cases, it's between 10 and 13 minutes. Add up the time each story takes—from the anchor introduction, the tape time, and the anchor time, then see how it works!

Throughout the show, the producer must keep track of the time—whether the show is "short" or "long." At times, you make split-second decisions to drop a story if the show is running long. If the show is running short, you may ask your anchors to chat a little more or read pad copy (extra news stories that the anchor can read if the show is running short). Sports and weather often lose time if there's a lot of news happening. With experience, a producer can often sense if the show is running on time.

The bottom line—whether you use a computer or your own math—is to get off on time. Network news waits for no one, especially a producer who mistimes a show.

Bright Future

There seems little doubt that the future is bright for those who decide to go into producing. The expansion of local news and the spread of all-news channels to more cities have created a need for producers of all kinds.

There is a high demand for producers because so many young people want to be on the air. What they do not understand is that producer jobs also require lots of talent. Terry Likes and Barry Gresham of Western Kentucky University say "the general perception is that, until recently, the producer was the unseen, underpaid, unheralded coordinator of the newsroom . . . that captures little limelight compared to on-air talent." But the authors of an article in the *RTNDA Communicator* say that, to the news director, "the producer position requires loads of talent." The authors quote a variety of news managers on the subject:

- Michael Castengera, TV news consultant and former news director, notes that good producers need a lot of skills not required in the past, such as knowledge of ESS, microwave, satellite, and computer technologies. He says that, at his former station, producers were on a faster career track and were paid more than reporters. He adds that the lack of good producers has reached a crisis point.
- Producers also have to be good writers and reporters. Former WSMV-TV news director Allan Griggs reminds us that producing is a "tough, demanding, physically and emotionally draining job." He adds that good producers are "unique" because they are not bothered "by long hours and the tough demands of the job."

Authors Likes and Gresham say the good news for those who decide on a future in producing is that salaries are probably going to keep climbing as the demand for good producers increases. It's also important to remember that producers have a much better chance of getting into management than anchors.

Summary

The best opportunities for young people entering broadcast news are in producing. The expansion of local news and the spread of all-news channels to more cities have created a need for producers of all kinds. There is a high demand for producers because so many young people want to go on the air because of the perceived "glamour" and higher salaries usually associated with such jobs; however, the competition for anchor and reporter positions is much greater.

There also are substantial rewards in producing news programs. Certainly, salaries are going to continue to improve as the demand increases for people to produce news. Although producers work behind the scenes, their jobs are exciting and occasionally also glamorous. The excitement comes in the realization that as a producer you are "in control." What you do in the newsroom determines what goes on the air. You are limited only by your own imagination and creativity. As was pointed out, in many newsrooms, the producers are in complete charge of the news.

Along with that power, however, comes a lot of responsibility and risk. You will need good news judgment and other skills in many areas. Good writing is essential. Some experience in reporting is also desirable. You will also need to have an excellent knowledge of production techniques—microwave and satellite feeds, computer technologies, video editing, electronic still storage, and emerging technologies.

Another important consideration is stress. It's a tough, emotionally and physically draining position with long hours. But the potential rewards are great if you have any interest in management. Producers are on the best track to the management offices. You must learn how to do just about everything in the newsroom, and how to work with and manage a variety of co-workers. Who could be better qualified for the "boss's" job?

Review Questions

1. List the various duties of the executive producer.
2. What are the responsibilities of the line producer?
3. Describe what the field producer does.
4. What is a rundown and why is it so important?
5. Explain the "peak-and-valley" theory of producing.
6. What is the meaning of the term *inverted pyramid* in producing?
7. What is a live shot and when should it be used?
8. What's the purpose of the staff meetings?
9. Explain the term *back time*. Why is it so important?
10. Why are the meters so important?

Exercises

1. Try to arrange with one of your local TV stations to "hang out" with a producer. Weekends are the best time because the pace is usually slower.
2. Arrange to accompany a field producer on a photo shoot. If there are none in your market, go along with the reporter who, in this case, is the field producer.
3. Take notes as you watch a local newscast, and try to determine what kind of a format the producer is using. See if you can spot "peaks and valleys."

24 Using the Hardware

Although we emphasize the need for journalists to develop writing and reporting skills, students also need to acquire some basic technical and production skills, such as how to use video cameras and editing machines. These skills are necessary in the increasingly competitive world of broadcast journalism.

Some stations have always required reporters to shoot their own stories, interviews, and even standup reports and then bring that material back to the station, where they edit it for that evening's newscast. At some of these stations, the reporters sometimes even anchor the news and introduce the packages they have shot and edited. The advantage of working at small stations is that you get to do everything and, therefore, have an opportunity to learn *how* to do everything.

This chapter introduces some of the technological tools used in broadcast news and the skills necessary to operate them.

Checking the Equipment

Camera and editing equipment keeps getting lighter, better, and easier to operate. Most people with even minimal technical skills can learn how to work a camera and edit with a few lessons. This chapter does not attempt to provide those lessons, but it does offer some advice on how to shoot the kind of video necessary to put together a good package. Before discussing shooting techniques, let's look at some basic procedures that reporters must follow when using video equipment.

Make sure all the equipment is operating properly before leaving to do a story. Shoot some video and play it back to be sure that the camera and recorder are functioning. Also, test the microphone and the lights. Don't wait until you arrive at the scene to discover that something is not working.

Batteries and AC Power

Be sure to have plenty of battery power, and carry an extension cord and an AC adaptor. Some new batteries will power equipment for up to eight hours. One good battery and a backup should be all you need to complete your story. Batteries are often the weak link in your equipment chain. It's hard to tell

Figure 24-1   Microwave dishes outside CNN headquarters in Atlanta. (© 1992. All rights reserved.)

exactly how long batteries will last, especially under different temperature conditions.

A word of caution: Keep all types of batteries away from extreme temperatures. Always keep them as close to room temperature as possible. Batteries can quickly lose their power in below-freezing temperature. Many photographers keep their batteries in inside jacket pockets in winter. Never leave batteries in the trunk of a car or in direct sunlight when it's hot outside.

If you are working indoors and doing interviews, using an AC power source helps conserve your batteries for shooting outdoors. It's also a good idea to carry a three-to-two-prong adaptor because many older buildings do not have three-prong outlets. A four- or six-outlet power strip also comes in handy. If a backup microphone and light are available, bring them along in case a problem develops.

Tripods

Most camerapeople who have been in the business for a while have little trouble shooting video with the camera on their shoulders. But even the pros use a tripod for an interview if they have the time to set it up. For beginners, it is best to use a tripod as much as possible, particularly for interviews, because weaving and bobbing heads are not acceptable in professional newscasts. Try shooting some of your cover footage (discussed later in this chapter) without a tripod when the video is not critical, so that you can start to feel comfortable with the camera on your shoulder. Unfortunately, many of the cameras used in colleges are difficult to use on the shoulder because they are lightweight models. It is easier to shoot from the shoulder with the heavier, more expensive professional cameras because the weight adds stability.

Earphones

A common problem for young people just starting to work with equipment is recording good sound. A particular problem is the set of switches on the camcorder that directs the signal from the two microphone inputs to the two (or four) audio channels on the tape. A set of earphones is critical in ensuring that you are getting the signal from the handheld microphone to the tape. If you aren't listening, you could end up with both audio tracks containing a signal from the shotgun microphone mounted on the camera. If you are responsible for recording good sound, wear earphones during the interview. You cannot depend on the camera's sound-meter reading or the tiny monitor speaker because they just tell you that sound is being picked up. They do not guarantee that the sound quality is good. The only way to pick up radio interference or microphone problems is to listen to the sound through earphones.

Filters

Every camera has a built-in filter system to accommodate different lighting situations. If you are shooting indoors with artificial light, you should use a different filter than you would outdoors in natural light. If you use the wrong filters, the colors on the tape will be badly distorted. Professional video photographer Lennie Tierney says there are two essential numbers to remember when thinking about filters: 3,200 degrees K (Kelvin) and 5,600 degrees K.

Indoor light or artificial light is 3,200 K light, and outdoor or sunlight is 5,600 K light. Cameras may also have additional filters for shooting outdoors in bright situations, such as after a snowfall or on the beach. The initials ND that appear on some 5,600 K filters stand for "neutral density." These filters produce the same colored video as the 5,600 K filter but reduce the amount of light entering the camera.

White Balancing

Along with filters, a white balancing system is also built into video cameras to provide accurate color. Tierney explains how the system works: "Anyone who has ever looked at a sunset knows that sunlight varies quite a bit in color. Indoor lighting also varies, but our eyes naturally adjust to different lights to make things look normal. To a video camera, fluorescent lights look green, incandescent lights look red, and sunlight looks blue. If you don't use the right filter and white balance your camera, the video will be off color."

To white balance the camera, you must aim it at something white—such as a white wall or piece of white paper—while you push the white balance switch or button on the camera. You must repeat this process each time you shoot at a different location.

All modern ENG video cameras have preset and automatic white balance settings. In the preset mode, the video will look good if the color temperature of the light in which you're shooting is near 3,200 K indoors or 5,600 K

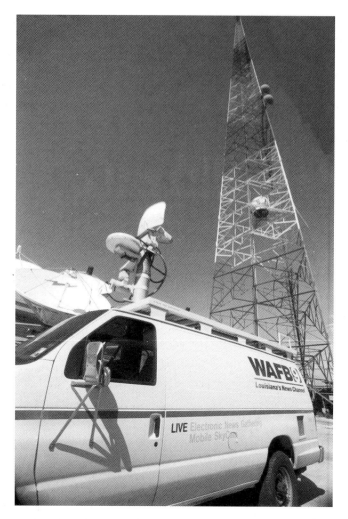

Figure 24-2   A WAFB-TV microwave truck prepares to send a live signal to the Baton Bouge station's tower, seen in the distance. (Courtesy James Terry)

outdoors. Many photographers use the preset white balance for most of their shooting.

The automatic white balance setting is for use when the light in which you're shooting is not near 3,200 K or 5,600 K. Fluorescent lights, for example, are not close to 3,200 K, so to make the video look right, flip the white balance selector to automatic, fill the screen of your viewfinder with a white object, and then hit the white balance switch on the camera. This process prevents the video from having a sickly green fluorescent look.

Mixed Light

Any light entering a room through a window can cause problems for news photographers. The best practice is to avoid shooting with windows anywhere in your background. Even a window with the blinds closed can create a distracting blue highlight in the background of an interview shot. For a beginner, it is best to shoot the interview either with all artificial light or outside with natural light. If there is enough light coming through windows, the interview can sometimes be shot nicely with the natural sunlight if the outdoor camera filter (5,600 K) is used or if the camera will take a white balance while set to the indoor filter (3,200 K). Just remember to keep windows out of your background. As you gain experience, you'll learn the various filter and white balancing combinations to use in mixed lighting.

Most professional news photographers use what are called *dichroic* or "dicro" filters that clip onto the front of their lights. Dicro filters simulate sunlight and allow you to use your artificial light during the day to augment the natural sunlight already present. Dicro filters on a light can be used to illuminate a head when shooting in a room already filled with natural sunlight from windows. Dicro filters also are commonly used during the day to brighten the face of your subject when you have a bright background, to light a reporter doing a daytime shot, or to brighten a head when shooting during the day in deep shade.

Meanwhile, Lennie Tierney provides these tips to help you avoid mistakes:

1. Always check your filter first. It must be on 3,200 K for artificial light or 5,600 K for sunlight.
2. When in doubt about lighting color (temperature), check that you are using the appropriate filter, then switch to automatic setting and white balance your camera on a white object.
3. When in a hurry, use the preset setting and the appropriate filter.

Focusing

Poor focus can destroy a story. Tierney advises beginning photographers to focus every shot. "I zoom in to every subject, focus on it, and then pull out to set the composition I want. When shooting a large subject, such as a stadium," Tierney says, "I'd zoom in to the farthest part of the subject, like the backfield fence, focus on it, and then pull out to reveal the entire subject."

Tierney says shooting moving subjects is more difficult, especially in low-light situations such as at some high school basketball games. "It is second nature to an experienced photographer to roll the focus barrel on the camera lens in the right direction in order to keep the subject in focus as it gets closer or farther away," says Tierney. He suggests that beginning photographers practice this technique by shooting people as they walk around the newsroom. When you are shooting a head, zoom in and focus on the eye. Most lenses have a "macro" function that allows you to shoot small things at close range. However, the macro function can cause problems. If your lens is in "macro" function when you are trying to shoot normally, everything will be out of focus no matter if zoomed in or out. In most cases, the macro function is a ring on the barrel of the lens near the aperture (iris) ring. You can feel it click into place when it is secured in the disabled mode.

Time Coding

Most ENG camcorders record not only pictures and sound but also a numbered index called a *time code* which advances by hours, minutes, seconds, and frames. This time code can be set for "R-Run" which means "Record Run" or "F-Run" which means "Free Run." When the time code is set on "Record Run" the time code on the tape will advance only while the tape is being recorded. When the time code is set to "Free Run" the time code advances regardless of whether the tape is being recorded or not. The "Free-Run" setting is often used when shooting sports highlights. The photographer is often on the sidelines shooting in "Free-Run" with the time code set to the time of day. Meanwhile the reporter is in the press box with his or her watch synchronized to the camera. When an exciting play is made, the reporter simply notes the time. During the editing process, the editor then finds the time of day on the tape specified by the reporter, and the desired play is easily located. "Free Run" should be used only when the camera is left recording for long periods such as when shooting a sports event. In the "Free Run" mode, when recording is stopped then started again, a change or "break" in the time code occurs on the recorded tape. Breaks in the time code can cause problems while editing.

Shooting Techniques

Let's look now at a few fundamental shooting techniques that beginners should learn immediately. First, avoid zooms and pans. Unless there is some important reason to zoom in or pan on to something, avoid those movements. It is better to cut from one shot to another. Consider composition carefully. Shoot heads slightly off center, not right in the middle. Shoot the head over the reporter's shoulder or at a slight angle. Profiles do not work well because they lose the viewer's attention. The head should be looking at the reporter and, if the camera is positioned correctly—just behind or slightly to the side of the reporter—the audience at home will see the whole face of the interviewee. It is sometimes effective to shoot the head tightly at a slight angle. The head should be in the corner with little or no open space. These shots are common on *Sunday Morning, 60 Minutes,* and other investigative and magazine programs. Some of the best photographers in the business are assigned to these programs, so students should routinely watch these shows for both their editorial content and their camera work.

Keep in mind, however, that these programs normally do not superimpose titles over heads. Camerapeople working for a regular newscast must get some medium shots that will leave enough room for "supers." Some news directors discourage tight head shots because most sound bites are short, and it is difficult to super them. Tight shots are sometimes effective, however, if the interview is dramatic or emotional or the head is interesting because of age, beauty, or some other reason.

Some camerapeople like to get a variety of headshots, but it is important to remember not to change shots while someone is speaking unless there is a good reason. If, for example, the person on camera begins to cry, you would probably want to slowly zoom in for a close-up.

Remember that the reporter will not appear on camera most of the time, so all of the shots should concentrate on the head. The reporter is brought into the picture after the interview is completed, when the cameraperson shoots the cutaways and reversals that are used as a part of the editing process to avoid jump cuts. As discussed earlier, editing interviews presents a problem because sound bites cannot be juxtaposed without creating a jump cut. Without something in between the two sound bites, the head appears to jerk when the sound bites are edited together.

Although Chapter 20, "Ethics and the Law," details the ethical aspects of using reversals, we have included examples of how to shoot this popular method of avoiding the jump cut because reporters and camerapeople are routinely expected to shoot them.

In Figure 24-3, the cameraperson is shooting the newsmaker. In Figure 24-4, the camera is reversed, and the reporter is being photographed as though he were listening to the newsmaker. The reverse shot works best when part of the interviewee's shoulder and cheek is in the picture. It is important, however, to remember that the camera must shoot over the correct shoulder. One way is to imagine that a line is running between the reporter and the newsmaker. The cameraperson should not cross that line

Figure 24-3 LPB Anchor, Public Affairs Director, Jeff Duhé interviews Louisiana State Senator Allen Bares.

Figure 24-4   Reversal shot of Reporter Jeff Duhé, anchor, Public Affairs Director, LPB, Baton Rouge, LA interviewing Louisiana State Senator Allen Bares.

when shooting the reversal or the reporter will appear to be looking in the wrong direction.

Cover Footage

The best way to avoid jump cuts is to use appropriate *cover footage*—video illustrating what the newsmaker is discussing. Good pictures usually are more interesting than heads, anyway, and cover footage allows editors to connect as many sound bites as they like without jump cuts.

Establishing Shots

Some of the first pictures a cameraperson takes at the scene are establishing shots. These are wide shots of the activity at the scene of a fire or an accident, of floodwaters pounding against seawalls, or of baseball fans lined up outside the stadium before a World Series game. Establishing shots set the stage for what is to follow, and they often provide the opening video for the story.

Sequential Shooting

Good videographers shoot their cover footage in a sequential manner to make the story visually interesting and to greatly reduce editing time. Sequential shooting is a way to tell a story with pictures and lead the audience along. Here's an example of a feature story on a police cadet at a practice range shooting a pistol at targets:

Shot 1: Tight on the trunk lock as the key is inserted. Pull out as trunk lid opens to reveal gun case.

Shot 2: Tight shot looking up at cadet's face as he works in trunk.

Shot 3: Over the shoulder of cadet's hands lifting gun from case.

Shot 4: Tight shot of box of bullets in case as cadet's hand grabs them and moves them out of the shot.

Shot 5: Shot from behind as the cadet walks with gun toward range.

Shot 6: Medium shot of table at range. Cadet's hands place gun and bullets in shot.

Shot 7: Tight face shot.

Shot 8 Over-the-shoulder shot of bullets being loaded in gun.

Shot 9: Empty shot with out-of-focus background, then gun is raised into shot creating closeup of gun filling screen. Bang, Bang.

Shot 10: Closeup downrange of holes being made in target.

When things are shot in this manner, there is no question about what shot comes next when you get in the editing booth to cut your story. Of course, discretion must be used. This type of shooting requires you to direct your subjects a bit—something that can be inappropriate and even unethical in some circumstances. As you get better at using this technique, however, you'll find ways to shoot sequentially on most assignments.

Shooting Enough Footage

Reporters, especially inexperienced ones, often wonder whether they've asked enough questions. Camerapeople often feel the same way. With experience, they learn when they've shot enough pictures, but initially they all tend to overshoot, fearing, like reporters, that they might miss something. Eventually, a cameraperson and a reporter who work together come to know when they have enough video. Until that time, shooting too much video is better than returning to the newsroom with too little.

Recording Natural Sound

The importance of natural sound was discussed earlier; however, we will end this chapter with a reminder. Good pictures are essential for good television, but pictures are not nearly as effective without their natural sound. As for radio, natural sound is crucial because the sound provides many of the "pictures" for the radio audience.

Figure 24-5   Ed Elkins, Control Board Operator at WAFB, Baton Rouge, LA.

Videophone Technology

Like consumer electronics, electronic news gathering equipment is quickly becoming lighter, more capable, and less costly. Perhaps nowhere is this more evident than in the equipment used for war coverage.

The Gulf War in 1991 was the first major conflict fought in the era of 24-hour news. CNN and Sky News reporters and camera crews used portable, although not exactly lightweight, satellite dishes and satellite phones to keep a 24-hour on-air presence never before seen in war coverage.

By the Iraqi conflict of 2003, broadcast-ready packages could be shot on amazingly small camcorders, edited on a laptop, and sent via a satellite phone to the news room. Using digital compression technology a 270-megabyte two-minute video package could now be compressed to 8 megabytes and transmitted to the newsroom in about 30 minutes.

By far the most significant development in news gathering since the introduction of satellite and microwave equipment and video recorders in the 1970s has been the advent of portable satellite equipment.

To help us understand this sometimes complex technology, we asked an expert in the field, John Stoltz, GCS, to explain how it began and matured.

A Brief History of Portable Satellite-News-Gathering (SNG)

By John Stoltz (GCS)

The First Gulf War—the Genesis of Truly Portable SNG

After the conflict in the Persian Gulf in 1991, news networks realized the need for a portable system that would allow a small team of field reporters to transmit video back to the studio without the use of an extremely expensive VSAT satellite uplink or fully equipped satellite truck or driving tape to transmission sites. Obviously the large satellite equipment was too heavy and cumbersome to hand-carry or even too big of a target to transport through the desert or a rugged terrain wherever the story may be.

With the use of the Inmarsat's global satellite network and its "B" satellite-phones, SNG (satellite-news-gathering) crews were already using such satphones for voice communications back to the studio. Inmarsat, a UK-based company, was created over 20 years ago to develop an international maritime satellite network for communications for vessels at sea.

Later, using its four geo-stationary satellites with global coverage, it developed satellite equipment for the land/mobile markets. Government, military, energy, and then shortly thereafter media customers started using the now portable satellite-phones for communications in non-maritime remote areas. However, this data transmission was used without accompanying video. Then, in the mid-1990s, per the request of major news networks, a components-manufacturing company called TOKO America developed a portable field box designed to transmit MPEG video clips back via the Inmarsat B-satphone. This unit was called the "VAST-p," an acronym for Video-Audio-Storage-&-Transmission portable type. However, it became affectionately known in the SNG world as the "Toko box".

To use an Inmarsat & Toko system, cameramen would simply plug an analog camera into the Toko box, then digitize and compress (or encode) the video package into typically a one-minute MPEG clip, which could be sent by the Inmarsat phone back to another Toko box connected to an ISDN telephone line back in the studio. This video transmission process is called "store-&-forward," where one 'stores' the recorded video into an encoder box or laptop and then 'forwards' it back to the studio, in this case, via satellite-phone. The studio producers would then play out the transmitted video from the Toko box to further edit or air the program. Typically, one minute of MPEG1 video, encoded at a picture-quality rate of 1 Mbps, would take approximately 15 to 20 minutes to send via one Inmarsat-phone channel. If a user increased the picture-quality (to a higher encoding rate) or duration (to more than one minute), the transmission time would also increase respectively. At the time, the Toko boxes cost approximately $20 K each and the Inmarsat B-satphones cost approx-

Figure 24-6   Inmarsat "B" satellite-phone. (Courtesy Global Communications)

Figure 24-7   Toko VAST-p. (Courtesy Global Communications)

imately $30 K. So, a complete, end-to-end system would cost approximately $70 K, which only the major news networks could afford. Furthermore, the suitcase-sized Inmarsat B-satphone weighed approximately 50 pounds and the shoebox-sized Toko box was approximately 15 pounds. This first Inmarsat & Toko system was transportable but not necessarily portable enough to be hand-carried by one person when one included the camera, accessories, and editing system.

Hainan Island & Afghanistan (2001)—Satellite-Phone Video Goes LIVE!

In the late 1990s, the need for "live" video for remote field reporting pressed manufacturers to develop a truly portable system that could deliver live video via the next generation satellite-phone, called the Inmarsat "M4". The briefcase-sized "M4," sometimes also referred to as "GAN," satellite-phone weighs only 15 pounds and costs around $8 K. Toko, then later the U.S.-based company GCS and the UK company 7E, developed the next generation Inmarsat video boxes called the "videophone." Based on standard video-tele-conferencing (VTC) compression, the videophone now allowed for two-way video and audio transmission via the M4-satphone to terrestrial data (ISDN) telephone lines connected to the studio. With this H.263 VTC compression, one could achieve 5–10 frames-per-second (FPS) for live video. If one bonded two M4-satphone and channels together to get double the bandwidth, one could receive approximately 10–15 FPS. With video satphone technology, one's bandwidth would determine not only how fast one could send a video clip, but also the picture quality for live shots. Along with store-&-forward video, now done with digital video (DV) cameras and laptops with editing and compression software instead of Toko boxes, reporters could give live "talking head" field interviews with the studio, which had its own video-tele-conferencing system in place. Low-end videophones cost anywhere from $2 K with more rugged and robust systems (i.e. 7E's "Talking Head") costing approximately $10 K. Using the M4-satphone, SNG reporters could send a video package back to the studio's server as well as give a field report "live via videophone."

Probably the most famous videophone report was given in April 2001 when an American spy plane was downed by China near Hainan Island. CNN first reported its crew's return using the videophone technology. Earlier "live via videophone" reports had been given via Toko videophones from Mount Everest in 2000, but none were as famously reported as the Hainan Island story. That story made videophone and satellite-phone reporting apparent to even everyday broadcasters as well as to ordinary news channel viewers. Since then, field reporters could also use the M4-satphone for voice, Internet and e-mail access, and other video/data communications.

The need for these types of "satphone," or satellite-modem if you will, communications became even more relevant after the September 11th attacks in the U.S. and the corresponding conflicts in Afghanistan and Iraq. Now, with a system costing approximately $10–15 K, even local affiliates could use and afford the technology.

As seen during the Iraq conflict in 2003, videophones were used most commonly to show the progress of U.S. troops with "embedded reporters." The portable-type M4-satphone and even tracking-antenna systems were used to provide live video reports from the field or even from moving vehicles or aircraft carriers in the Persian Gulf. Almost all the major networks used the "vehicular" antenna with the M4-satellite-phone/modem to transmit live and store-&-forward video from moving trucks. U.S. viewers witnessed the networks following U.S. armed forces into Baghdad using their "vehicular videophone" systems. It was quite revolutionary to be able to transmit live video while moving almost 50 mph down a highway toward Baghdad. So now Inmarsat satellite-phone technology went from maritime to portable to mobile with the implementation of the vehicular M4-satphone.

Figure 24-8   Inmarsat "M4" satellite-phone/modem. (Courtesy Global Communications)

Figure 24-9   "Talking Head" Videophone. (Courtesy Global Communications)

Figure 24-10 Live via videophone. (CNBC, Mt. Everest, 2000)

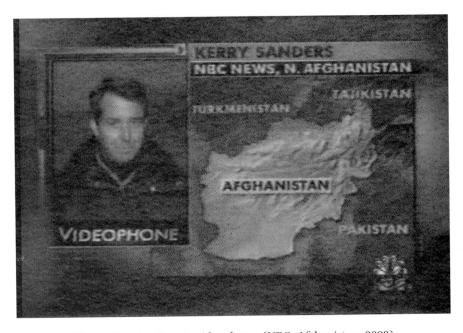

Figure 24-11 Live via videophone. (NBC, Afghanistan, 2002)

Figure 24-12   "Vehicular" videophone system. (CNN, Iraq, 2003)

Figure 24-13   M4-satphone with "Vehicular" tracking antenna. (Courtesy Global Communications)

Digital Laptop News Gathering—The Next Generation of Satellite News Gathering

With the use of the hardware compression, first with Toko and later with videophones, the need for lighter and also less equipment in the field grew even stronger. Software compression can now be used, instead of hardware boxes, on laptop computers to generate video clips for store-&-forward applications as well as for live feeds. With compression technologies constantly improving, and now based on software, all a SNG reporter would require is a DV camera, a laptop with editing software (such as Avid© or Final Cut Pro©), and some compression/encoding software, plus a satellite-modem. No longer is a videophone or Toko box required to generate video in the field. Of course, satellite phone and modem technologies have improved as well. In the early 1990s, suitcase-sized terminals weighed 50 pounds and cost $30K. By the late 1990s, briefcase-sized satphones dropped to 15 pounds and cost $8K. By the middle of this decade, satellite-phones will be more like a laptop-sized modem weighing less than 5 pounds and costing around $2–3K. Bandwidth will also improve. Inmarsat "B" and "M4" systems could only deliver data rates of 64 Kbps or two units and channels bonded together to achieve 128 Kbps (i.e. ISDN speeds). The next generation terminals from Inmarsat, called "BGAN" (acronym for Broadband-Global-Area-Network), will deliver speeds up to 432 Kbps. These DSL-like speeds will enable a laptop news gatherer to deliver package stories quicker than ever before as well as go "live" with better picture quality at nearly 30 frames-per-second (FPS), which is nearly broadcast quality.

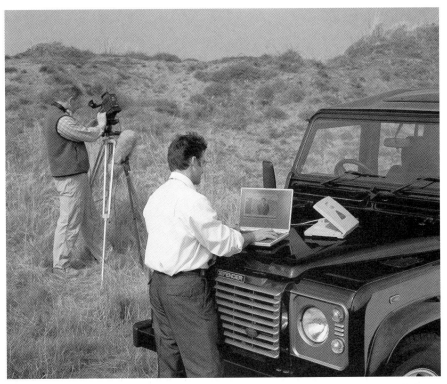

Figure 24-14 Laptop satellite news gathering via the Inmarsat regional "BGAN." (Courtesy Global Communications)

Figure 24-15   Inmarsat regional "BGAN" satellite modem. (Courtesy Global Communications)

Figure 24-16   Al Franken—the NVC original "One-Man-Mobile-Uplink." (Courtesy Global Communications)

In the late 1980s, the NBC *Saturday Night Live* spoof of a "One-Man-Mobile-Uplink" by Al Franken seemed laughably impossible. Now, just more than ten years later, it is not that far away—camera, laptop, and satellite-phone/modem.

25 The Job Search in a Changing Industry

It is difficult to predict where broadcast news is heading, but the Internet already has had a major impact on news and all other programming. The Internet and broadcasters' use of Websites, which allow viewers to punch up news and ask for more details about certain stories that they are interested in, has been a major factor. The growing use of databases and the ability of people throughout the world to communicate with each other through their computers on the Internet also have presented a major distraction from TV.

Think of it this way: All those who loved shortwave radio over the decades have a new way to talk to one another instantly. Following the Oklahoma City bombing and the terrorist attacks on 9/11, thousands of Europeans, Asians, and others worldwide discussed the crime and tragedy and offered condolences to Americans via their computers.

The communications expansion has meant new jobs for young people and new opportunities for those already in communications, as many workers leave traditional jobs in news to accept employment in allied areas, like the Internet. Some broadcast managers report losing workers to the new opportunities on the Internet.

So these are exciting times for young people going into communications. There are lots of new opportunities, but many of them may be different from the traditional ones. For example, "news-on-demand" is requiring a lot of people to gather additional information on stories and to work on the "out-takes" of stories that are normally gathered for the traditional two-minute packages. The only thing certain about the new technologies is that they are moving fast—almost too fast to keep up with. By the time you read this book, many of the things we say are likely to happen may well have already come about.

Another trend is that some television newspeople are now required to file their television stories not only over the air but also on the Internet and other media owned by their employers. This process is called *convergence*. Additionally, increasingly more television reporters are expected to be "one-person bands," doing their own camera work and editing in addition to reporting.

In 2003, as the economy began to slow, the exodus of traditional broadcasters to the Internet had slowed, and CBS, NBC, News Corp, *The New York Times*, and Knight Ridder had cut back their online staffs. Is this situation a temporary aberration reflecting a soft economy? Perhaps.

The Future of Broadcast News

The debate about the future of the traditional news networks has been going on for a number of years. There continues to be a serious question about whether the networks will continue to provide the kind of news that we have come to expect, but that conjecture itself is wearing thin. Because they have surrendered most of their coverage of breaking news to the all-news cable channels, the traditional networks are spending more time on soft news, features that might not get that much attention elsewhere.

The all-news cable networks and even some local stations doing all news have taken away much of the clout that ABC, CBS, and NBC once had. CNN, Fox, and MSNBC have virtually taken over breaking news at all times from the networks. The traditional networks have found it difficult to compete with news operations that *never sleep*.

The days when Americans turned to CBS and the other networks for breaking news have disappeared for all but those who do not have cable, and that number is few. Even the number of households that have the Internet is growing at an explosive rate. The challenge of CNN and the rest of the cable news networks and all-news local stations has caused serious financial problems for the networks, which have cut back their news staffs drastically. The days when CBS, ABC, and NBC had almost unlimited funds for covering the news have long disappeared because of shrinking advertising dollars and a shrinking audience. Advertisers now have more places to spend their money, and they are spending much of it on cable channels that allow them to target specific audiences. The catch-all approach to reaching consumers—which is what the networks offer—has become much less attractive.

Does this mean that anchors of network evening newscasts will disappear? That suggestion has been around for some time now, and the trio is still on the air. But there is some reason to believe that what they will be anchoring may be different in the coming years. The financial resources the networks have to work with for news will no doubt continue to be limited. The networks have closed down some of their national and international bureaus, and the extensive cutbacks in news personnel that have been going on for several years may not be over.

ABC News correspondent Ted Koppel predicted in *Modern Maturity* magazine that one network evening newscast will eventually disappear, one will take the high road, and one will take the low road.

The three network news anchors discussed the state of their newscasts on PBS's *News Hour with Jim Lehrer* in a segment hosted by media correspondent Terrance Smith. He noted that the network evening news broadcasts of today are a far cry from what they once were and that collectively, their share of television sets in use at that hour, a key industry barometer, has declined precipitously from an average of 75 percent 30 years ago, to 44 percent today. "Where," Smith asked, "has the audience gone?"

Peter Jennings responded, "Everywhere. Absolutely everywhere. It's gone to the cable channels, which deliver news, it's gone to all of the 75 or 275 channels that you can get on an average home set today." Tom Brokaw, who retired as NBC anchor at the end of 2004 recalled, "In 1970, when it got dark in America, there were only two planets in the universe: CBS and NBC. ABC wasn't even a player then. Now when it gets dark in the television universe, it's filled with planets out there and people have that many more choices."

Dan Rather, who also retired his anchor job early in 2005, said that he thinks it's inevitable that the traditional network audience share will go even lower. Smith offered this explanation, "Many Americans get their news from all-news radio, the Internet, local news, and cable news—long before network anchors say 'good evening.' Critics sometimes assail the evening broadcasts as 'news you already know.'"

Smith also observed that three white male anchors still deliver the half-hour broadcast at essentially the same time and in the same format since Cronkite began the tradition.

Rather replied, "I think it's valid criticism to say that our networks haven't been thoughtful enough, nor have we acted quickly enough . . . to the changing needs of the audience and new ways of coverage and new ways of broadcasting." Brokaw said, "We have reduced the number of stories, we've spent more time on them, and what we try to do is say we think these are the biggest stories and the most important stories in your life. And by the way, here are some stories as well that are not in the day's news that are going to affect your lives as well in a variety of ways." Smith concluded with this observation, "Reports of the death of these broadcasts are premature. Taken together," he said, "the big three command a huge audience, some 30 million viewers a night. No other news media—print, broadcast, or Internet—approaches that collective reach." However, he added, "The network evening news broadcasts have lost the primacy they once had within their news divisions to the more profitable primetime magazine shows. And, worse yet," said Smith, "although the network news audience has always had a large number of older viewers, the collective audience is even older than it used to be. And there is the unknown variable of the Internet, especially among younger viewers." On the plus side, Smith added, the evening news broadcasts still do make money—a lot of it. The ratings leader, *NBC's Nightly News,* for example, reportedly generates $200 million a year in revenue and tens of millions in profits.

The networks themselves appear to be accepting their limitations in news, as indicated by some networks' decisions to ignore live coverage of some events that would have been routine in the past.

Actually, media-watchers were quite surprised when the networks carried live coverage of U.S. Senate and House hearings in May of 2004, into

Figure 25-1 *NBC News* anchor Tom Brokaw, who retired in 2004.

Figure 25-2   Brian Williams at Democratic Nomination Debate, September 2003. Williams replaced Tom Brokaw as NBC anchor in 2004.

the shocking abuse of Iraqi prisoners by American soldiers at the infamous Abu Ghraib prison, the scene of widespread torture and death by the regime of Saddam Hussein. Media analysts had difficulty remembering when the big three networks cancelled their regular programming to bring the nation live coverage of such hearings. As one observer put it, the story was just so important the networks had to *bite the bullet* and return to a practice they had mostly forgotten—preempting soaps for important breaking news.

The networks returned briefly to breaking news big time in 2004 when the Asian tsunami struck eleven nations, dispatching Rather and other journalists to Asia. The networks saw a surge in ratings and even found time for special reports which were once so popular, and had virtually disappeared.

The networks' philosophy seems to be that those who want such in-depth material can find it on CNN and the other all-news outlets and public broadcasting—their attitude, apparently, is why lose revenue from profitable sit-coms and other programming for special reports that, by comparison, would have much fewer viewers?

It also seems clear that the increasing influence in broadcasting of profit-minded corporations, such as General Electric (which owns NBC and WNBC), and Disney which owns ABC, and Viacom which owns CBS, means that network news will be expected to do more to pay its own way than it has in the past. *CBS News* correspondent Ed Bradley and former CBS *Evening News* anchor Walter Cronkite both criticized the personnel cuts at the traditional networks in recent years. Cronkite acknowledges that the networks have economic problems, but claims that they have "cut more than the fat of the [news] budget, they've cut right down to the bone, to the point of amputation."

Bradley uses a similar analogy, saying the personnel cuts took not only the fat but "the muscle, bone, and the sinew of the news organizations. . . .

We lost a lot of good people." (Some of those people moved to CNN.) Bradley adds, "There's more concern about news being profitable . . . and justifying expenditures, and I think it's going to dictate the kind of news we see on the air." All three Network anchors, by the way, lamented the fact that they were unable to expand their newscasts to one hour.

Peter Herford, a veteran journalist and former *CBS News* vice president, said the three New York–based networks "are trying to maintain an image of national and international coverage while simultaneously making the transition to a different kind of network evening news."

He says stories that report on lifestyles and trends and background reports on the news are "becoming a staple of the network diet . . . because it is easier to control the costs of stories planned in advance than for the kind of crash-and-burn coverage which characterized network news in the past."

There are some bright spots. ABC's *Nightline* takes the high road, covering the major story of the day, in depth, without talking down to its audience. It does it five nights a week during a half-hour program that sometimes runs longer. Also taking the high road weekdays is PBS's *News Hour with Jim Lehrer*, the only one-hour noncommercial news program. While the traditional networks have cut back on their worldwide coverage, the network news magazine shows, such as *60 Minutes* and *60 Minutes II*, *20/20*, and *Dateline* have proliferated, and have good audiences.

The New Players

Although many jobs are disappearing along with the networks' viewers, Herford said he is optimistic. "From the standpoint of broadcast journalism as a craft," he says, "there is a great deal of hope." He said that instead of only three broadcast networks, there are now several new nationally distributed sources of information.

What impact does the reduction of jobs at the networks have on the future of people who hope for careers in broadcasting? Actually, not too much because the entry-level jobs available to college graduates are rarely found at the networks, with the exception of CNN.

Because of its nonunion status, CNN still offers opportunities for newcomers, although not as many as it did in the 1980s when the network was just getting started. Many of the people who began with CNN in Atlanta started in entry-level video journalist (VJ) jobs and moved on to become anchors, writers, reporters, editors, and producers. There should continue to be good opportunities for achievers as more local all-news operations expand, but by far most of the positions for people entering the field are still likely to be at local stations, which have shown good profits for years. Many of those stations are expanding their news programs, which means more jobs for you.

One of the most distressing developments for young people is a problem we mentioned earlier in the book, the demise of local radio news jobs. The change in FCC regulations allowed broadcast corporations to gobble up more and more stations and turn them into computer-programmed juke boxes with little or no local personnel even in the building, let alone doing any news. As mentioned earlier in the book, the FCC bears the burden for much of that deterioration in local news by eliminating the public service requirements that were once required of stations for keeping their licenses. With few exceptions, the profit-minded Clear-Channel and Cumulus operations are providing no news staffs and no training grounds for young people trying to break into the field. More and more, students are doing their internships at local television stations which, happily, are prospering.

Getting Started

Before you send out résumés and audition tapes, ask yourself some questions: Do I want to stay in my hometown? If I'm willing to move, do I want to head for a big city, a small town, or anyplace where there's an opening?

The best answer to all of your questions should probably be "I'll go any-place I can find a job and I'll do whatever they want me to as long as it's in broadcasting." If that is your answer, you have the best shot at finding work. A lot of young people will not go to Alaska, for example, so finding work there is much easier than in California, New York, or Florida.

The best approach is to complete an internship while you are still in college. Try to get one at a local station in the town where you wish to work. If the news director gets to know you and likes your work, there may be a job waiting for you when you graduate. News directors like to hire people who want to stay around for a while because there is usually a high turnover at local stations. So if you let the boss know you plan to stay in the area, it could work to your benefit.

All things being equal, an intern has an advantage on others in the job market because when a job becomes available, that person is a known quantity. The news director knows his or her work. For those who want to go to large-market stations right away, it usually means starting as a researcher or desk assistant. Large metropolitan-area radio and TV stations do hire college graduates without experience for entry-level positions that sometimes lead to writer, reporter, and producer jobs; but there is no guarantee they will, and it sometimes takes a year or more to climb out of those entry-level situations.

Which is the best approach—the large or small market? Most professionals would probably say the small market because it gives you an opportunity to learn how to do everything. Former network correspondent Betsy Aaron says the small stations are the best route to go because "you get a chance to do things, to make mistakes. Starting at the networks leaves a big hole in your education and experience." Aaron started out as a secretary-researcher for a network radio commentator in Washington in 1959. "In those days," she says, "very few women were being hired as reporters."

Aaron recalls that while she was working in Washington, she got an offer from ABC. "It had a fancy job title," she says, "but it was basically another secretary job." She stayed at that job for two years and finally decided to send out a résumé tape to approximately 80 stations.

She was hired by a Philadelphia station. "I was hired as a token," she acknowledges, "but I ended up being the first woman to cover city hall after

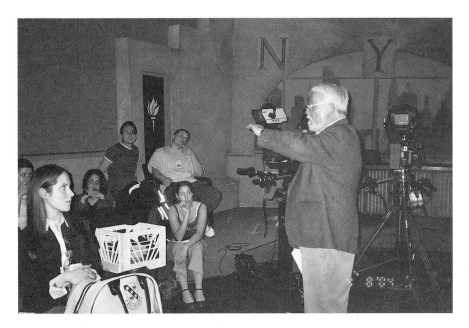

Figure 25-3 Professor Mike Ludlum teaching a broadcast news class at New York University.

I warned them that I would not do very well on the cooking and social beat. I'm sure that's what they hired me for." But she quickly adds that it was a great place to learn because "they let you do everything, even edit your own film."

Aaron says that when she started with CBS in 1976 the only women she can recall being in TV news at the time were Lisa Howard at ABC and Pauline Frederick at NBC. Aaron says, somewhat bitterly, "For a time, I thought I was 'one of the boys' and was being treated equally. It wasn't until much later that I realized that I had never been treated equally."

Aaron says that what saddens her the most is that "the young men who are making the decisions about which women go on the air today are making those decisions the same way the older men used to make them. Women in their fifties don't fit anyplace."

Lesley Stahl, co-editor of *60 Minutes*, is among the top women to have achieved success in television news, but she admits the road was not always easy. In her memoir *Reporting Live*, she writes: "I knew my colleagues saw me as a lightweight unqualified to join the Super Bowl champs of TV news." She added, "I had to find ways to convey my seriousness, to send out signals that I was resolute and earnest, not what the wrapping said I was." She said to improve her image she "wore glasses and worked around the clock." Stahl said she kept telling herself that if she worked hard and was good, they'd have to use her.

Stahl says that by the time she was 30, she knew two things for sure: one was that "I wanted to be a journalist, which would mean, in the environment of the early 1970s, surmounting my femaleness and my blondness."

Stahl started her career in broadcasting in 1972 as an on-air reporter at Channel 5 in Boston. During that same year, the Equal Employment Opportunity Act had just passed and the FCC had recently included women in its affirmative action program for television broadcasting.

Because of the Act, the networks were scouring the country for women, and a friend of Stahl's in New York called her to say that CBS had issued a memo mandating that the next reporter hired had to be a woman. Stahl said she applied to all three networks and got the attention of the *CBS news* bureau chief in Washington. He gave her two days to get rid of her apartment in Boston and be at work in Washington, and she did it.

After several weeks of doing reports for CBS Radio, she started doing stories for *The CBS Evening News* with Walter Cronkite. Stahl continued as a reporter for *CBS News* for more than 25 years, including assignments as White House correspondent during three administrations. She has been with *60 Minutes* since 1991.

Although Stahl admits that her career has been all she could have asked for, she said it was far from easy and she was often insecure. One reason was that her very presence at CBS, in her early years especially, seemed to inspire resentment among several of the camera crews. Most of the CBS cameramen were veterans in their 50s and 60s, she said, and their attitude toward the new hires was not exactly welcoming. "They acted as though we had cut in line," Stahl said, "like we hadn't paid our dues, didn't belong in the precious orbit of the CBS Washington Bureau."

Stahl recalled that on one occasion when she was covering a political rally, she asked a cameraman to shoot some video of the buses that had carried the people to the scene and the cameraman yelled at her, "What kind of stupid idea is that?" Stahl said the urge to weep became a recurring problem, but she would hold it until she got to a stall in a ladies' room, where she would sob out of sight of her crew. Stahl said that often in the crew cars she would be locked up "with her tormentors" for hours. She recalled one time when one of the cameramen argued into his walkie-talkie, "Do I have to work with her," making sure that she heard the comment.

In *Now This: Radio, Television . . . and the Real World*, ABC News correspondent Judy Muller recalls how she began in broadcasting. Her career started after she quit teaching in New Jersey to be home with her two baby daughters. Muller had been writing for a weekly newspaper, which she said had its limitations—namely, no money and no hope of any to come, so she decided to try her hand, and voice, at radio news. She applied for a job at a little station, WHTG in Eatontown, New Jersey, which was so little, she said, that you were expected to unlock the door in the morning, read all the dials and gauges, and note them in a log that got that station actually operational. After that, she says, you literally sat down, switched on the microphone, and started talking.

Although Muller learned what she was supposed to do, she never got to do it. Two days before she was to start, the news director (who also was program manager, general manager, and sales manager) called her to say that the owners had changed their minds because they thought a woman with two small children might be unreliable. "Today," Muller said, "such comments would be fighting words—litigious, even. For me," continued Muller, "WHTG was the first ambush along the trail, the first pounce of the cougar, albeit a minor skirmish."

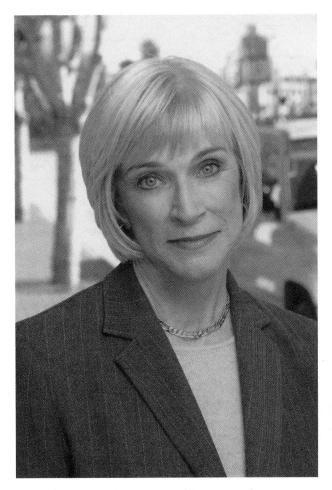

Figure 25-4 *ABC News* correspondent Judy Muller.

Muller had better luck at WHWH in Princeton. She said she wandered into the station at a time when broadcasters were under growing pressure to add women to the mix. So, despite never having worked at a radio station before, Muller said the fact that she could write coherently and speak clearly pretty much guaranteed her the job, particularly because her voice sounded like a guy's.

Muller says that initial job in broadcasting slanted her thinking on affirmative action ever since, noting that she probably would never have had an opportunity to demonstrate her own abilities had those men in the radio station not felt the pressure to add "diversity" long before that term became a buzzword.

Muller notes that the training she got as a reporter was terrific because "you learn to ask good questions and to write fast and succinctly, and it teaches you to ad-lib."

When Muller's husband was transferred to Denver, she made the rounds of top radio stations there and landed a job at KHOW as a morning news anchor. She says that station also was a great place to hone her skills. She also learned how to stand up for her rights.

When she learned that the news director had hired a man from another station and was paying him more money, she stormed into the boss's office to demand to know why. She said he told her because the man had a family to support and that she, Muller, had a husband who was making a good living. Muller said she threatened to get a lawyer and the news director recanted, bringing her salary up to the level of the man's almost immediately.

Muller said she was anxious to move up and applied to WCBS Radio in New York. The station did not need a reporter but sent Muller's résumé and audition tape to the network and, to her surprise, she was hired.

After several years with the CBS Radio network as a reporter and commentator, ABC offered her a TV reporting job. Muller said the offer was flattering but a little frightening. "I had never expected to start a new career at the age of 43 in a whole new medium, especially one that so clearly favored youth and beauty. But Muller sold her house and moved with her children to Los Angeles to begin a new world in TV news.

Countless other women struggled throughout their careers to break the "glass ceiling." Speaking at the Radio and Television News Directors Association (RTNDA) annual banquet in 1980, when she received the Paul White Award, Pauline Frederick said she never knew Paul White, but "it probably was just as well because he probably would not have hired me." Frederick said she had what was considered taboo at the time—a woman's voice. Nan Siemer, a former editor for WTOP-Radio in Washington, D.C., says that when she started out in the 1970s, she probably got her first job because she had a deep voice.

Thankfully the situation for women and minorities has greatly changed from those days. Now, let's examine just how much they've changed.

Figure 25-5   Gwen Ifill, senior correspondent for PBS's *The News Hour*. (Courtesy MacNeil/Lehrer Production)

Figure 25-6 Jim Lehrer, news anchor for PBS's *The News Hour*. (Courtesy MacNeil/Lehrer Production)

In a national survey, most news directors who responded indicated they are interested in getting applications from minorities, particularly African Americans, who have strong writing, reporting, and anchoring skills.

Will Wright, an African American journalist who has held a number of management positions, including news director at WWOR-TV in metropolitan New York and former vice president and news director of KRIV-TV in Houston, says African Americans are at a disadvantage because they do not complete enough internships that lead to many jobs in broadcast news.

Wright, one of only a few African Americans to be hired as news directors in major markets, recalls that he broke into broadcast news as a desk assistant for *CBS News* in New York some 30 years ago. Wright notes that he paid his dues at CBS, going for coffee, running copy, and stripping wires. He believes minorities must be prepared to do the same hard work through internships and entry-level jobs.

Wright adds, however, that those "who are determined to win in a business that is set up to discourage them have to be quick learners. Don't let anyone have to tell you twice what to do," he advises. "Do it right the first time and you will succeed."

CBS News correspondent Ed Bradley agrees that "menial tasks come with the territory . . . and when I got into broadcasting, I was a gofer." He says that's the way entry-level positions work "whether you are black, white, brown or red." Bradley added that he knows young African American men and women "who are eager to take entry-level jobs to get their foot in the door."

When asked if being African American had had any effect on his career, Bradley said, "I think it has helped and hurt. It helped because I came along at a time when there was an effort to find more minorities who could do a job and I always showed that I could do a job no matter what they put me into." He added that being African American may have hurt him in some instances because there were people who wondered whether they should take a chance on hiring an African American person for a given job because they had never done it before.

Asked how he thinks African Americans are treated in broadcast journalism, Bradley said, "Better than we used to be, but not as well as I would like to see." He adds, "I'd like to see more opportunity (for blacks) on the air and off the air."

For women—black and white—advancement to management positions isn't always about race and gender. "The demands of the job are harder for women" says Penny Parrish, former news director at KMSP in Minneapolis. "It's hard to run a newsroom without that being the top priority in your life. Going into television didn't help my marriage and probably led to my divorce," she notes.

Susan Stamberg, a correspondent for National Public Radio (NPR) and the first woman to host a national news show, says that women have done well at NPR, but "it was never easy. A handful of us worked hard and had to be very, very good," says Stamberg. "We punched a hole through the wall, which allowed a lot of other talented women to walk through." Now many women hold top jobs with NPR—as vice presidents, executive producers, as well as producers, editors, and reporters; however, Stamberg also notes, "Women are paid less at NPR than they are at commercial stations. But then, so are the men!"

As for the absence of female anchors on the traditional commercial network news programs, Stamberg calls it "ridiculous." She thinks commercial TV is still living in "the dark ages." Top policy decisions are still being made by men. Women can be accepted as anchors in the morning, but not in the evening. But the cable channels—CNN, CNBC, MSNBC, and others—understand that women can be talented news anchors at any time of day. "That's a welcome relief," says Stamberg, "to those of us who have been doing this work for many years."

Veteran broadcast news expert Lou Prato agrees that "more women are running and staffing newsrooms than ever before, but they still have to deal with sexism, especially when it comes to pay." Female news directors, on average, make about 30 percent less than their male counterparts, but Prato says this difference may not be the result of sexism alone. He says many women are unwilling to argue for more money because "subconsciously or not, women do not want to be perceived as overly aggressive."

"The Corn Fields"

Like Betsy Aaron, Nan Siemer thinks people entering the broadcast field should start in small markets or, as Siemer puts it, "the corn fields." She began at a radio station in Danville, Illinois, after graduating from Lindenwood College, a small school in St. Louis. She worked for several other small stations over a seven-year period, getting fired a couple of times when new owners took over the stations. She took some time off to complete her master's degree. Then she returned to work but lost that job in another ownership change. At that point, she says, "I decided to set my sights on Washington, D.C. I spent six months interviewing with every station in the city."

When she was about to give up, Siemer heard of an opening at WTOP-Radio. "Because I had made some good contacts at RTNDA meetings," she says, "I got the job." She admits, "Sometimes it's not what you know but who you know." Her advice to college students: "Get involved in RTNDA as soon as you can."

The late Rob Sunde, former news director of the ABC Information Network and past chairperson of RTNDA, agreed that the place to start a career is at smaller stations. "Work long hours, do as much as you can, and perfect your skills as much as possible," was Sunde's advice to those starting out in broadcast journalism.

Sunde started out in the 1950s at age 15, working weekends for a station in his hometown in Connecticut. He worked at five different radio stations over a three-year period, and, after a break for military service, he spent another six years with local stations before ending up at CBS and later at ABC. Was it a good way to get started? "It was at the time," Sunde said, "but times have changed."

Education Is Essential

Sunde said that today the most important thing for young people is a college education. He dropped out of Brown University when he found that juggling his studies and full-time employment at radio stations was too much to handle. "In those days," he said, "things were still experimental, and there was a lot of 'flying by the seat of your pants,' but things are different now and young people must be better educated."

Walter Cronkite, who also did not finish his college education, agrees that people didn't need a degree to break into journalism in those days. But now, he notes, a college degree is necessary to get a good newspaper or broadcast news job, and many successful people in journalism have advanced degrees in specialty areas, such as economics.

The Job Search

You should start your job search by reading the help-wanted advertisements in *Broadcasting and Cable* magazine and in flyers available from the RTNDA and other broadcast and professional associations, such as the Society of Professional Journalists (SPJ).

As you look for such leads, prepare a good résumé and résumé tape so they will be ready to send if you find any interesting openings. Undoubtedly, the most important factor in getting a reporting job is a résumé tape.

If you want a job in television, the tape should include an assortment of your very best packages and, if possible, a sample of some anchoring. If you want to work in radio, put together a sample of some good wraparounds and any anchoring you may have done.

The most important thing to remember in preparing a résumé tape is that you will not have much time to sell yourself. News directors get numerous tapes every week; they do not have the time or the desire to look at tapes unless they are hooked immediately. Most news directors admit that they rarely watch or listen to a tape for more than 20 seconds unless they hear or see something that impresses them. If something does, you have a good chance that they will continue to watch or listen to the rest of the tape. So, put your best package or wraparound up front, use strong video and sound at the top, and make sure the story itself is a grabber.

Don't make compromises. News directors may take into consideration that you are not using top-of-the-line equipment in your college journalism courses, but don't count on it. You will be competing with students who do have access to professional equipment. If your video is poorly shot and out of focus, you will be at a great disadvantage, even if your story is a good one. The same applies to sound. If it is distorted or hard to understand, news directors will be turned off, so use high-quality video and sound.

Should you use gimmicks on your videotape? Some news directors say they don't mind these techniques, provided they are done well. If you have a strong on-camera presence, a standup open on your tape may be effective. A montage of such standups, if kept to 5 or 10 seconds each, might also impress news directors. If you do not have a strong personality, you are better off starting your tape with strong video and sound. Most news directors will be evaluating your ability to package or wrap a story in a professional manner. If they are looking for a combination reporter-weekend anchor, they will be looking for samples of anchoring as well.

Also remember that most news managers will not return your tapes unless you include an envelope with postage. Sometimes it's possible to find

Figure 25-7   Senior Lecturer Marea Mannion works with students in the control room at Renn State University. Photo by Manoe.

short tapes that are being discarded by advertising agencies and TV stations to use for your audition tapes. Otherwise, the cost of buying tapes can be high, so you may wish to send along envelopes and postage in the hope that you will get your tapes back.

The Résumé

Although the audition tape is the most important job-search material you send to radio and TV stations, you also should include a printed résumé. Make it brief. If you are applying for your first job, news directors will know that you do not have much experience, so don't try to embellish your résumé. If your only experience is working with the university radio or TV station, list it first. If you have completed an internship with a commercial station, you certainly should list it first, with details about what you did. Do not start off the résumé, as so many students do, with your career goals. News directors want to know what you have done, not what you want to do.

List your education after your experience. If you have taken a minor in business, political science, economics, or some other area that might make you more attractive to news directors, you should include that information as well. Be sure to list any foreign languages that you can speak fluently.

If you have won any awards from RTNDA, SPJ, or any other organization for your broadcast work, you should mention those citations. Also list any involvement that you might have with student chapters of RTNDA or SPJ, particularly if you headed up one of those chapters or served on any committees that might have taken part in regional or national conferences. Attendance at those conferences, by the way, is a valuable experience and a great way to make contacts with working broadcast journalists and news directors.

If you have computer skills, say so. Also list any cameras, editing systems, or other radio or TV control room equipment that you know how to use.

References

If you have developed relationships with people in the field who are willing to give references, such as the general manager or news director of a radio or TV station where you did an internship, you should list these people. Ask references if it's okay to use their names before listing them, however.

Most news directors are not likely to call your journalism professor to ask about you unless they are really impressed with your résumé tape. But sometimes your professor can be helpful. He or she may be active in RTNDA or SPJ and may have served on panels with news directors at national or regional meetings. The news director you're contacting may even be a graduate of your university.

Unless your hobbies have some practical application, such as flying or photography, don't list them. News directors are not likely to be interested in your stamp or coin collections.

Put some effort into the way you lay out and design your résumé. If it shows creativity, the news director is likely to think that you are creative. Consider a professional résumé preparation service, but only one with a good reputation. Some less professional services have been known to make grammatical errors.

Be sure to list your name, address, and telephone number at the top of your résumé. Figure 25-5 shows how a student who did an internship at a local TV station might organize her résumé.

KAREN DRAKE
110 E. Main St.
Baton Rouge, LA 70810
(504) 555-1234

WORK EXPERIENCE

Summer 1992—Summer intern as assistant at assignment desk, WBRZ-TV, Baton Rouge, LA. Monitored and logged satellite feeds, prepared, read stories for anchors and helped sports anchor select game footage for broadcast. Accompanied reporters on shoots and worked Teleprompter.

1993-95 Reporter and producer, "Impact," the Southern University weekly TV news and features program on Channel 22 in Baton Rouge. Responsibilities included reporting and producing a package each week, anchoring the program twice a month, working the studio camera and shooting ENG.

EDUCATION

1996 B.S., Mass Communications, Southern University
Major: Broadcast News sequence
Minor: Political Science
GPA. 3.4/4.0 On dean's list five of eight semesters

SPECIAL SKILLS
.
Proficient with Macwrite, Macintosh computer system.
Experience with Panasonic ENG cameras F-250 and AG460, Panasonic 300CLE and WV-F300 studio cameras and panasonic AG-7750 and AG-7700 editing systems.

MEMBERSHIPS

National Association of Black Journalists

REFERENCES

John Spain, Station Manager
WBRZ-TV
Baton Rouge, LA 70832
(504) 555-5678

Professor Ted White
Chair, Department of Mass Communications
Southern University
Baton Rouge, LA 70821
(504) 555-9112

Professor Mike Kabel
Executive Producer, "Impact"
Southern University
Baton Rouge, LA 70821
(504) 555-3456

Figure 25-8   A sample résumé.

Cover Letters

A brief cover letter addressed personally to each news director you contact should be included along with your résumé tape and printed résumé. Be sure to use the news director's name—never write "Dear News Director." And spell the news director's name correctly; also be certain there are no misspellings or grammatical errors in the letter. If there are, the news director will never get to your résumé or your videotape. As stressed throughout this book, accuracy is the most important aspect of journalism, and if you cannot be accurate in your job-search materials, you are not likely to find a job.

Your letter should be straightforward and honest. If you do not have much experience, say so, but stress the skills you do have. Make it clear that you are eager to learn and are prepared to work hard. Figure 25-9 is an example of a cover letter.

The cover letter accomplishes several things. It introduces you to the news director and lets him or her know where you heard about the job opening. It also tells the news director a little about you before he or she looks at the résumé, but it does not summarize the résumé. In this case, Karen Drake indicates what skills she would bring to the job and makes clear that she is enthusiastic and expects to work hard. The tone of her letter shows a modest confidence. The letter also mentions the name of her strongest reference, a TV station general manager with a national reputation. Note that the letter also expresses Drake's desire to hear from the news director. The letter is only four paragraphs, which is as much as any news director will probably read from someone applying for a job.

Writing Tests

Some news organizations, such as CNN in Atlanta, which encourages graduating students to apply for entry-level positions, require applicants to take writing tests. The best way to prepare for a writing test is to practice rewriting newspaper wire copy into broadcast style. Do several such rewrites before you take the test, and ask one of your professors or someone you are working with at a radio or TV station to review the copy.

The Job Interview

If he or she is impressed with your videotape, the news director may contact your references. If he or she gets a positive response, you will be asked to visit the station for a personal interview. The materials you sent got you an interview; now the interview will decide whether you get the job.

As soon as you hear about the interview, talk to your professors about the station that has invited you. They may know someone at the station or something about the station's reputation for news. Check out the station's Website. This enables you to find out about the station and look at a newscast. Another important way to prepare for the interview is to learn as much as possible about the city or town in which the station is located. Find out the name of the major newspaper in the city, and if you have time, have a Sunday

110 E. Main Street
Baton Rouge, LA 70810
June 27, 1993

Mr. Frank Walsh
News Director
KTHU-TV
Centerville, CT 06880

Dear Mr. Walsh:

I would like to be considered for the opening you listed in *Broadcast* magazine. I recently received my degree in mass communications from Southern University, where I reported, produced and anchored many stories for "Impact," the university's weekly television program on Channel 22 in Baton Rouge, Louisiana. The enclosed videotape displays some of my "Impact" stories.

As the enclosed résumé describes in detail, last summer I worked as an intern at WBRZ-TV in Baton Rouge, where I performed various tasks at the assignment desk. I am sure that Station Manager John Spain would tell you that I carried out my duties with enthusiasm and diligence.

I believe that my experience with "Impact" and at WBRZ-TV makes me an ideal candidate for the position at WZZZ-TV.

I hope for a chance to meet with you after you view my videotape. I can be reached at (504) 555-1234.

Sincerely,

Karen Drake

Figure 25-9 Sample cover letter.

edition sent to you. If there isn't enough time to do that, try to arrive in the city as early as possible before the interview and read through the papers. The chamber of commerce is also a good source of information.

If you can, arrive a day early. If you are interviewing for a radio job, listen to the station in your motel room; if you are interviewing for a TV station job, watch as many of the station's newscasts as possible. Appearing knowledgeable about the station and the city during the interview will let the news director know that you are interested enough in the job to have done your homework. For example, tell the news director that you arrived in town the night before and that you were impressed with the station's news coverage of a breaking story. But be honest. If the story really was good, then the news director will be impressed that you knew it; however, if it was a dull news day and the show was not that exciting, you will lose points by saying that you thought it was. The news director will know better.

Once the interview shifts to what you can do for the station, the pressure will build. This is when you must be at your best. During the interview, don't stress your feelings about pay, benefits, work shifts, and vacations. You will impress the news director if you ask intelligent questions about the news operation, story coverage, and station philosophy in covering the news. But unless asked, don't offer your own philosophy because you may come across as a "know-it-all." The questions about pay and benefits are legitimate, but they should be asked at the end of the interview if the interviewer brings them up first and should not be your emphasis.

Minority Opportunities

In the year 2004, there were noticeable gains for minorities in both television and radio. According to the latest figures from the RTNDA/Ball State University annual survey, the minority workforce rose 18.1 percent in 2003 to 21.8 percent in 2004, with about half the growth among African Americans and half among Hispanics. The percentage of Asian Americans fell and Native Americans remained the same.

The survey also found that at non-Hispanic stations, the minority workforce rose to 19.8 percent in 2004 from 17 percent in 2003 and 19 percent in 2002. According to the report, the minority workforce in radio went up for the first time since the stringent EEO rules were eliminated in 1998. The minority radio workforce rose from 6.5 percent in 2003 to 11.88 percent in 2004. Again, the report said, about half the increase came from African Americans and half from Hispanics. The RTNDA/Ball State survey also found that there were sizable gains for minority news directors in both radio and TV, with the percentage of minority TV news directors doubling, from 6.6 percent in 2003 to 12.5 percent in 2004. In radio, the percentage of minority radio news directors rose from 5 percent in 2003 to 8 percent in 2004 the drop.

In the same study, few of the numbers for women in TV news have changed meaningfully from 2003 to 2004. The percentage of women in the workforce remained essentially the same, 39.1 percent in 2004, vs. 39.3 percent in 2003. The report said the percentage of women news directors edged lower from the record 26.5 percent in 2003 to 25.2 percent in 2004.

In radio, the percentage of women employed dipped from 24 percent in 2003 to 22.4 percent in 2004. But the report noted that the percentage of women radio news directors soared (14.4 to 25.9 percent) to a little more than the figure two years earlier (22.3 percent).

In a national survey, most news directors who responded indicated they are interested in getting applications from minorities, particularly African Americans, who have strong writing, reporting, and anchoring skills.

Will Wright, a former African-American news director at WWOR-TV in metropolitan New York, and former vice president and news director of KRIV-TV in Houston, says African Americans are at a disadvantage because they do not complete enough internships that lead to many jobs in broadcast news.

Wright recalls that he broke into broadcast news as a desk assistant for *CBS News* York some 30 years ago. Wright notes that he paid his dues at CBS, going for coffee, running copy, and stripping wires. He believes minorities must be prepared to do the same hard work through internships and entry-level jobs.

Wright adds, however, that those "who are determined to win in a business that is set up to discourage them have to be quick learners. Don't let anyone have to tell you twice what to do," he advises. "Do it right the first time and you will succeed."

CBS News correspondent Ed Bradley agrees that "menial tasks come with the territory . . . and when I got into broadcasting, I was a gofer." He says that's the way entry-level positions work "whether you are black, white, yellow, brown, or red." Bradley says he knows young African-American men and women "who are eager to take entry-level positions to get their foot in the door."

When asked if being African American has had any effect on his career, Bradley said, "I think it has helped and hurt. It helped because I came along at a time when there was an effort to find more minorities who could do a job and I always showed that I could do a job no matter what they put me into." He added that being African-American may have hurt in some instances because there were people who wondered whether they should take a chance on hiring an African-American person for a given job because they had never done it before.

Asked how he thinks African Americans are treated in broadcast journalism, Bradley said, "Better than we used to be, but not as well as I'd like to see." He adds, "I'd like to see more opportunity [for blacks] on the air and off the air."

For women—black and white—advancement to management positions isn't always about race and gender. "The demands of the job are harder for women," says Penny Parrish, news director at KMSP in Minneapolis. "It's hard to run a newsroom without that being the top priority in your life. Going into television didn't help my marriage and probably led to my divorce," she notes.

Susan Stamberg, a correspondent for National Public Radio (NPR) and the first woman to host a national news show, says that women have done well at NPR, but "it was never easy. A handful of us worked hard and had to be very, very good," says Stamberg. "We punched a hole through the wall, which allowed a lot of other talented women to walk through." Now many women hold top jobs with NPR—as vice presidents, executive producers, as well as producers, editors, and reporters; however, Stamberg also notes,

"Women are paid less at NPR than they are at commercial stations. But then, so are the men!"

Consultant Nan Siemer agrees with Prato. She says most women think that "they are lucky to have a job in broadcasting and aren't supposed to negotiate for wages." Because of this attitude, Siemer began a consulting service called Breakers, which, she says, teaches women how to break the "glass ceiling."

Some Final Words

The supply of entry-level job seekers greatly exceeds the demand. Entry-level applicants outnumber hiring by 10 to 1 in TV news. As a result, the average TV news director gets about 60 applications for every entry-level hire. Most of these applications are, as might be expected, for jobs as reporters and anchors. Why such an interest in broadcast news?

As many people have stated in this book, broadcast news is exciting. It is a fascinating business—one that pays you to read newspapers and magazines; to interview politicians, celebrities, and other exciting people; and to know what's going on in every part of the world before most other people. Unfortunately, because the work appeals to many people, the pay is not very good unless you have outstanding abilities that permit you to work in a large market. For many journalists, money is not the most important consideration, but rather the challenges that await reporters every day.

Trust me—you'll tell yourself how nice it is to be in a business that excites you so much that you don't look at the clock except when a deadline is involved. Although you may be exhausted at the end of the day, you often will look for colleagues to join you for coffee or drinks so that you can recreate what transpired that day, to analyze what you and the news team accomplished, and, of course, to commiserate about some of the things that went wrong. If you have trouble sleeping, it probably will not be because you're not tired but because you have trouble relaxing your mind.

You can join this exciting field, but remember: You'll need a dedication to develop your skills and a determination to pursue a career that is going to demand responsibility, accuracy, and fairness in whatever you do.

Glossary

Actuality Voices of people involved in a news story. Also called a sound bite.

ADDA A system that electronically stores graphics and other information in a computer for random recall.

Affiliates Radio and TV stations that are serviced by networks.

Ambush interview Forcing someone to speak with you on camera against their will.

Anchor Someone who reads news on the TV set.

AP Associated Press, one of the major wire services.

Assignment editor Newsperson who assigns stories to reporters and camera crews.

Attribution The source of a news story.

Audio Sound used in a radio or TV newscast.

Back timing The timing of the final part of a broadcast to assist the newscaster or producer to get off the air on time.

Beat An assignment given to a reporter on a continuing basis.

Black Control track on a videotape. Also, a complete fade from a picture.

Blind lead-in A general lead-in to a report from the field, used when you do not know what the reporter will say at the top of the report.

Box Used primarily with ADDA or ESS to indicate that picture, freeze-frame video, or graphic will appear in a box next to the anchor's head. Some newsrooms use BSS, which stands for box, still store.

Bridge Words that connect one piece of narration or sound bite to another.

B-roll A film term still often used to describe the use of video to cover an interview or narration.

Bulletin Important late-breaking news item.

Bump tease A short audio headline covered by video, used before commercials in a TV newscast, to hold the audience's attention.

Character generator Electronic device used to produce supers (fonts).

Chroma-key The electronic placement of pictures behind the newscaster.

Close The ending of a reporter's news story. Also referred to as a sig-out.

Copy Material written for broadcast. Also, wire copy distributed by wire services.

Cover footage Video shot at the scene of a news story; used to replace the newsmaker and/or reporter while their voices are heard.

Crash Colloquialism for serious problems in a newscast.

CU Close-up camera shot.

Cue words The words at the start and end of audiotape or videotape to identify how a sound bite begins and ends.

Cutaway A video shot used to avoid a jump cut.

Cutoff time The time when a reporter must leave the scene of a story in order to make broadcast.

Delayed lead Keeping the most important information in a story until the middle or end to create suspense.

Dissolve Special video effect that slowly replaces one image on the screen with another.

Drive-time Indicates the time of day when people are going to or coming from work. Usually the highest rated time periods for radio stations.

ESS Abbreviation for electronic still storage. See *ADDA*.

Establishing shot A wide shot of a scene, usually used at the beginning of a news story.

Evergreen A story, usually a feature, that can be used anytime.

Fade A dissolve from a picture to black.

Feeds Material distributed by networks and others to affiliates and other stations for use on local newscasts. Also known as syndication feeds.

Freedom of Information Act Passed by Congress to permit anyone who wishes to have access to all but the most sensitive government documents. Similar acts, called "Sunshine laws," have been established in all 50 states.

Fill copy (Also called *pad copy*.) Relatively unimportant news copy for use near the end of the newscast if needed to fill time.

Flash Headline used by wire services to describe news of an extreme nature, like the death of a president.

Font See *Super*.

Freeze frame A still video image seen next to or behind the anchor while he or she is reading copy. Mostly used in a box next to the anchor's head.

Future file Folder or computer file used by the assignment desk to keep track of stories that may be covered in the future.

Graphics Graphs, photos, maps, and other visuals used in a TV news story or newscast.

Hard lead A lead that places the most important information in the first sentence.

Headlines A series of one-line sentences describing news events. Used at the top of a newscast.

Hold for release Wire service story or press release that cannot be used until the time specified.

Information overload Putting too much information in a lead sentence or paragraph.

Investigative reporting Developing news reports in depth, usually about something that someone is trying to hide.

Jump cut An erratic movement of a head that occurs when video is edited to eliminate some of a speaker's words.

Kicker A light story used at the end of a newscast.

Lead The first line or two of a news story or the first story in a newscast.

Leading question Asking a question during an interview that tries to elicit information the reporter wants to hear.

Lineup The arrangement of stories in a newscast. Also called the rundown.

Live Reporting from the scene of a story as it is happening.

Local angle Details of a news story that are of special interest to the audience in your community.

Local news Stories dealing with your community.

Long shot (LS) Wide view of the scene. See *Establishing shot*.

Medium shot (MS) Between a close-up and long shot.

Microwave Beaming a TV signal between two points using microwave antennas.

Minicam A lightweight video camera.

Negative lead A lead sentence that contains the word "not". To be avoided.

News director The person in charge of the news operation at a radio or TV station.

News judgment Ability to recognize the relative importance of news.

O/C Abbreviation for on camera.

Out cue Last words in a sound bite.

Package A story put together by a reporter that includes interviews, narration, and cover footage.

Pad copy See *Fill copy*.

Peaks and valleys   A TV production technique that spreads important stories throughout a newscast, not only at the top.

Primetime   The time when radio and TV have their largest audiences.

Privacy Act   A law that is designed to prevent unwarranted invasion of a person's privacy.

Producer   The newsperson who decides which material will go into a newscast and in which order. Also, in larger markets, someone who helps reporters put together packages.

Prompter   Electronic device that projects news scripts on monitors so they can be read by anchors. Also known as teleprompters.

Reader   A story without video read by an anchor on camera.

Reuters   British news agency.

Reversal   A shot of the reporter looking at the person being interviewed; an editing device.

Reverse question   Shot of the reporter repeating questions asked during the interview; an editing technique considered by some newspeople as somewhat unethical.

Rip and read   The broadcasting of radio wire copy without any rewrite.

RTNDA   Radio and Television News Directors' Association.

Running story   A news story in which there are new developments, usually for more than one day.

Shotgun lead   A news story lead that includes information about more than one related story.

SIL   Abbreviation for silent; used on the video side of split page to indicate the use of videotape that has no sound.

Slug   Word or two written in the upper left corner of script to identify the story.

Soft lead   A lead in which the most important fact is not given immediately.

SOT   Abbreviation for sound-on-tape; used on the video side of the split page to indicate the tape has sound.

Sound bite   Portion of statement or interview that is in news broadcast or package.

Sound under   Keeping the natural sound low when used under the voice of a reporter or newscaster.

Source   Someone who provides information used in a news story.

Split page   The standard TV news script. The left side of the page is used for video directions, and the right side is for the script and audio cues.

Staging   Unethical practice in which a reporter asks people to behave in a certain way—one that is not natural—when they are on camera.

Stand-up   A report on camera at the scene.

Super   (Also called a *font*.) Short for superimposing lettering, graphics, or videotape. Used mostly for the names, addresses, and titles of people being identified in a news package or newscast.

Suspense lead   A lead that keeps the most important part of the story until the very end.

Syndication   The sale and distribution of news material to stations by independent companies and the networks.

Tag   A sentence or two used by a reporter or anchor at the end of a story or newscast. Sometimes referred to as an on-camera tag.

Talking head   Colloquial for person being interviewed on camera.

Tease   A short headline that describes a story to follow a commercial. In TV, usually accompanied by a few seconds of the upcoming video story. Commonly referred to as a bump tease.

Time coding   The recording of the time of day on the edge of videotape as it is being shot.

Two-shot   Camera shot of two people.

Upcut   The loss of words at the beginning of audio- or videotape.

Update New details in a news story that require a rewrite.

UPI United Press International, one of the major wire services.

Urgent A wire service term indicating an important story, but not as important as a bulletin or flash story.

Video phone A device that allows reporters in the field to send sound and video to a receiving station without technical support.

V/O Abbreviation for voice-over. Used on the left-hand side of the split page to indicate that the anchor is speaking over video. Also to indicate a reporter doing narration over cover footage.

Voicer A story read by a radio reporter that has no sound bites.

VTR Videotape recording.

Wire News services provided by AP, UPI, Reuters, and other organizations.

Word processing The use of computers to write and store information.

Wrap To complete work on a story. Also short for "wraparound," in which a reporter's voice is heard at the beginning and end of a sound bite.

WS Wide camera shot.

Index

NOTE: The Italicized *f* following a page number indicates a figure on that page. Italicized *ff* indicates multiple figures on that respective page.